IN QUEST OF THE 'MIRACLE STAG':
THE POETRY OF HUNGARY

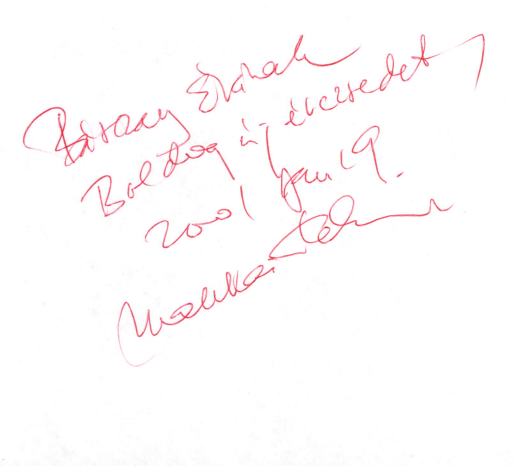

IN QUEST OF THE 'MIRACLE STAG': THE POETRY OF HUNGARY

An Anthology of Hungarian Poetry in English
Translation from the 13th Century to the Present
in Commemoration of the 1100th Anniversary of the Foundation
of Hungary and the 40th Anniversary of the
Hungarian Uprising of 1956

Edited by

Adam Makkai

with the co-operation of
†George Buday and Louis I. Szathmáry II
and the special assistance of
Agnes Arany-Makkai, Earl M. Herrick, and
Valerie Becker Makkai

Foreword by

Dr. Árpád Göncz

PRESIDENT OF THE REPUBLIC OF HUNGARY

Co-published by
ATLANTIS-CENTAUR (Chicago), M. SZIVÁRVÁNY (Budapest)
and CORVINA (Budapest):
International Distribution by UNIVERSITY OF ILLINOIS PRESS
(Urbana, Chicago & London)

IN QUEST OF THE 'MIRACLE STAG': THE POETRY OF HUNGARY

An Anthology of Hungarian Poetry
in English Translation
from the Thirteenth Century
to the Present

Edited by
Adam Makkai

Woodcut Illustrations by
George Buday

Cover Design by
Andrew Kner

LIBRARY OF CONGRESS CATALOG NUMBER: 96-86073

ATLANTIS-CENTAUR, Inc., Chicago, c.: (ISBN 0-9642094-0-3)
p.: (ISBN 0-9642094-1-1)
M. SZIVÁRVÁNY, Budapest, c.: (ISBN 0-936398-86-8)
p.: (ISBN 0-936398-87-6), and
CORVINA PUBLISHERS, Budapest, Hungary (ISBN 963-13-4282-4)
International distribution by
UNIVERSITY OF ILLINOIS PRESS, Urbana, Chicago & London

In memoriam

Ladislas Gara (1907-1966)
Watson Kirkconnell (1895-1977)
Paul Tabori (1909-1975)

Pioneers
in the Field
of the Translation
of Minority Literatures
into French and English

FOREWORD
BY THE PRESIDENT
OF HUNGARY

Foreword

To write poetry is an act of daring. Obeying an inner imperative, poets set out toward the unknown, toward many, or maybe one single stranger who — so poets believe — is or will be capable of sharing the message of that inner command with them.

To translate poetry is sheer audacity. Translators of poetry write poems under the inspiration of the poetry of another, attempting to cross the inter-language ocean toward someone who — so translators believe — will be able to share with them that particular message which carries the underlying intention that occasioned the original poem.

To edit an anthology of translated poetry invites the fury of the gods. The world of poetry has as many viewpoints as there are readers of poetry and an anthology takes aim at all of those readers at once, while remaining fully aware that it is impossible to reach all of them.

Honor and respect, then, to all of those who, in full knowledge of the consequences of this temptation, nonetheless set out on the voyage. Columbus's enterprise is dwarfed by theirs. But they, too, like Columbus, are led by faith — faith in the fact that there are human beings on the other side as well, and that the human spirit is one, even as it manifests in many languages. They are all of this, those who gathered and launched the poetic messages of a small linguistic island, Hungarian, toward the distant shores of The World Language, because they believe that there will be a few people capable of picking individual flowers out of this bouquet of messages, and delight in them either as a whole, or just stem by stem. And this in order that the recipients themselves may be enriched.

I trust that their faith will become reality. It is in this hope that I launch this volume, whose roots sprouted in the very depths of our souls.

Árpád Göncz
PRESIDENT OF THE REPUBLIC OF HUNGARY

Előszó

Verset írni merészség; aki verset ír, belső parancsra, az ismeretlennek vág neki valaki — valakik felé — akik hite szerint képesek megosztani vele e belső parancs üzenetét.

Verset fordítani vakmerőség; aki verset fordít, az verset ír egy más vers ihletében, s nekivág a nyelvek közti óceánnak valaki — valakik — felé, akik a túlparton hite szerint képesek megosztani vele azt az üzenetet, amit az eredeti verset létrehozó belső parancs üzenete hordoz.

Antológiát szerkeszteni istenkísértés; a költészet világának annyi közepe van ahányan verset olvasnak, s egy versantológia egyszerre célozza meg valamennyit. Bár tudván-tudjuk, hogy mindet eltalálni lehetetlen.

Tisztelet-becsület mindazoknak, akik erre — a kísértés természetének ismeretében — vállalkoznak. Columbus vállalkozása eltörpül az övékéhez képest. De őket is, mint Columbust, a hit vezérli. A hit, hogy a túlparton is emberek élnek, s az emberi lélek egy, ha sok nyelven nyilvánul is meg.

Mindazoknak, akik egy kis nyelvsziget — a magyar — belső parancsra kelt vers-üzeneteit összegyűjtötték s útnak indították egy távoli világnyelv partjai felé, mert hitük szerint lesz, aki ott képes ezt az üzenetcsokrot szálaira szedni, s szálanként is, egészében is gyönyörködni benne. Hogy ezzel maga is gazdagodjék.

Hiszem, hogy hitük valóraválik.

Ebben a reményben indítom útjára ezt a lelkünkből lelkedzett kötetet.

Göncz Árpád
A MAGYAR KÖZTÁRSASÁG ELNÖKE

THE LEGEND
OF
THE 'MIRACLE STAG'

The Legend of the 'Miracle Stag'

The great Oriental King, Nimrod, had two sons, Hunor and Magor. They went hunting one day and saw a creature that was snow white and had golden antlers — it was both female and male, "hind" and "stag." It lured them farther and farther to the West, where the hunting grounds were richer and the land more fertile. The sons of Hunor became the Huns, and the sons of Magor became the Magyars, the Hungarians.

Some people could see the miraculous creature flying in the air. They saw the stag with the huge golden antlers between which it carried the Sun and Moon.

The "Miracle Stag" thus led the Magyars to present-day Hungary where they arrived in the year 896. They were shamanists and warriors who terrorized Europe for over a century. In the year 1000 Saint Stephen, who ruled until 1038, converted the Hungarians to Christianity.

Then once again the "Miracle Stag" appeared. It had burning candles on the tips of its antlers — it was, in fact, a living cathedral and the very messenger of the Virgin Mary and of Jesus Christ Himself.

Hungary's poets have been pursuing the "Miracle Stag" for over seven centuries, each according to his or her vision. In all its incarnations, the image of the "Miracle Stag" is a perennial symbol of an Oriental people whose destiny it was to become European and to act as the guardians of the West — against the Tartar invasion of the 13th century, the Turkish invasion of the 16th and the 17th, and the Soviet Communist invasion of the 20th century. In Hungary's poetry, ancient Oriental Shamanism blended with the Christianity of Europe.

The "Miracle Stag" prances ever westward. It has appeared in Germany, France, and England, giving voice to the poetry of Hungary. And now, on the 1,100th birthday of Hungary, the "Miracle Stag" has reaches the shores of America.

Chicago, 1996   *ADAM MAKKAI*

THE LEGEND OF THE "MIRACULOUS HIND"[1]
by **János Arany (q.v.)**

The lark's aloft from bough to bough,
the song is passed from lip to lip.
Green grass grows o'er old heroes now
but song revives their fellowship....
       Forth to the hunt they ride again
       two brave sons that fair Enéh[2] *bore,*
       Hunor *and* Magyar, *champions twain,*
       Ménrót's[3] *twin sons in days of yore.*
Each chooses fifty doughty knights
to go in escort at his side;
armed as for bloody war's delights,
they seek out game in youthful pride.
       Wild beasts in pools of blood they drag;
       they slaughter all the elk they find;
       they have already killed the stag,
       and now they all pursue the hind.
They chase the hind continually
along the Salt Sea's[4] barren shore,

---

[1] 'Miraculous Hind' or 'Wonder Hind' in Hungarian is *csodaszarvas,* literally 'the miracle-antlered-one,' as *szarvas* is a generic term covering both sexes. Arany's epic seems to concretize the hunt; the English translation separates 'stag' from 'hind.' The mythological creature the title of this volume designates was androgynous, as expressed by the fact that it carried both the Sun, the ancient masculine symbol, and the moon, the symbol of femininity.

[2] In Hungarian mythology, the wife of King Ménrót (Nimrod) about whom see footnote 3. The name *Enéh* is cognate with both *anya* 'mother' and *ünő* 'doe' or 'hind.'

[3] Known in the West from the Bible as *Nimrod* the founder of cities in Sumer and Assyria as well as a great hunter. His figure is similar to that of *Gilgamesh,* but cannot be precisely identified with any one personage. He became a part of Hungarian mythology in the 13th century because of the zeal of the Chronicle writers in the reign of King Béla III.

[4] The migration route of the early Hungarians, as reconstructed by archeologists and linguists, most probably took them past the Caspian Sea and Black Sea. Old Ossetic and Turkish loanwords indicate extended contact with Indo-Iranian and Altaic tribes. Arany's place names, which were based on oral tradition, are partly borne out by this newer research.

where neither wolf nor bear may be
lest it be lost forevermore.
>   *But 'cross those wastes of prairie earth*
>   *the panther and the lion yelp;*
>   *the tawny tiger there gives birth*
>   *and in her hunger eats her whelp.*
>   *On flies the bird, the song flies on*
>   *of* Enéh's *sons' fair fellowship:*
>   *the lark's aloft from bough to bough,*
>   *The song is passed from lip to lip.*
> *The sun is passing from their view,*
> *piercing the clouds with fiery spears,*
> *but still the hind they all pursue...*
> *at sunset, lo, it disappears.*

They found themselves as daylight sank
where Kúr's[5] broad waters sweep and swell.
on meadows by the river-bank
their weary steeds may pasture well.
>   *Says* Hunor: *"Let us bivouac,*
>   *water our steeds, and turn to rest."*
>   *Says* Magyar: *"When the dawn comes back,*
>   *let us go homeward from our quest."*

But: "ho, ho my heroes, knights of mine,
what mystifying land is this?
To eastward see the sunset shine.
it looks to human eyes amiss!"
>   *"It seems to me," a warrior said*
>   *"the light from down south issues forth."*
>   *Another vowed: "I swear, instead*
>   *that it is glowing in the north..."*

Dismounting all, their steeds they tend
and slumber by the river's foam,
and purposed, when the night should end,
to journey with their escort home.
>   *The dawn was cool; a breeze arose;*
>   *the broad horizon brimmed with blue;*
>   *the hind across the river goes*

---

[5] The *Kura* river which has its origin on the Armenian Plateau and flows into the Caspian Sea.

and bravely leaps before their view.
      On flies the bird, the song flies now
      of Enéh's *sons' fair fellowship:*
      the lark's aloft from bough to bough,
      the song is passed from lip to lip.
"Now, my quick lads! Speed on the chase,
let's catch this apparition hind!"
Blithe or reluctant, forth they race
and press on, to their task resigned.
They then forded the river Kúr,
and found the waste-land still more wild;
no drop of water dewed the moor
no blade of grass in verdure smiled.
      The crumbling surface of the land
      sweats soda from its sterile brow,
      springs ooze with poison from the sand
      and sulphur stinks in many a slough.
With bubbling oils the springs are bright;
they burn untended here and there;
like watch-fires in a gloomy night
their fulgor flickers everywhere.
      Each night they bitterly repent
      their longing for this game they traced
      with such unwearying intent
      into the mazes of the waste.
But when the dust of morning thinned,
to chase the hind their hearts were stirred
as thistledown obeys the wind
or shadow-wings pursue the bird.
      On flies the bird, the song flies now
      of Enéh' *sons' fair fellowship:*
      the lark's aloft from bough to bough,
      the song is passed from lip to lip.
They search the waste: they track the Don[6]

---

[6] The Don river flows into the Sea of Azov, the northeastern arm of the Black Sea, cut off by the Crimean Peninsula.

as far as Meót's *lesser sea;*[7]
through boggy marshes they press on
to isles of fenny greenery.

> *And there the hind, like fleeting mist*
> *of fog about her in the skies,*
> *— again? But how could they have missed? —*
> *now disappears before their eyes.*

"*Halloo!*" *they cry,* "*where is the game?*"
"*Yonder she dashes!*" *one does call.*
Another shouts: "*this way she came!*"
A third: "*she is not here at all...*"

> *Through every nook and copse they search;*
> *through every bush they track the hind,*
> *by lizard-lair and partridge-perch,*
> *but what they seek they cannot find.*

Then Magyar *spoke with many a sigh:*
"*Who knows the way that leads us back?*
on every side there's boundless sky —
we'll perish on this far-off track."

> *Said* Hunor: "*Let us not retreat!*
> *But build a camp and call it home —*
> *the grass here's soft, the water's sweet —*
> *and trees with sap are all afoam.*

Bright fishes are the river's gift,
and tawny game makes tasty food.
The bows are taut, the arrows swift,
and booty — our adventure's gift..."

> *On flies the bird, the song flies now*
> *of* Enéh's *son's fair fellowship:*
> *the lark's aloft from bough to bough*
> *the song is passed from lip to lip.*

But soon they wished to venture out,
they yearned for newer, different game —
as they got bored with fish and trout,

---

[7] *Meót* or *Meotis* was the name of the Black Sea in antiquity, along with other names such as *Pontus Euxinus*. "Meót's lesser sea" refers to the Sea of Azov on whose northern banks was *'Levedia,'* historically attested as the penultimate station of the Hungarians on their westward march; they left there ca. A.D. 840-850.

and so descended on the plain.
> *And there across the level prairie*
> *at dead of night, strange music streams,*
> *out in the wasteland, wide and airy,*
> *as if from heaven or in dreams.*

There fairy maidens did subsist
and danced with joy in elfin measure;
housed in a tent of woven mist,
they passed their nights in tuneful pleasure.
> *No man may spy the elfin school;*
> *for mortal maids surpassing fair —*
> *daughters of Kings, Belár and Dúl,[8]*
> *are learning elfin magic there.*

Fairest are Dúl's two girls to view,
old Belár's twelve are sweet and warm;
their company, five-score and two,
are poised to take on fairy form.
> *To win it, each must kill a man,*
> *bewitch nine youths with magic lure,*
> *tease them along to love's hot plan*
> *yet keep their own white bodies pure.*

Thus are they taught the fatal art
the fearful knowledge of the fairy;
each night their progress they impart,
each night in dancing they make merry.
> > *On flies the bird, the song flies now*
> > *of Enéh's sons' fair fellowship —*
> > *the lark's aloft from bough to bough,*
> > *the song is passed from lip to lip.*

The men follow the fairy-sound
they stalk a-tiptoe on the sly;
the flickering lights they spy and hound,
as if chasing a butterfly.
> *Said Magyar: "Brother, that sweet fife*
> *tickles my marrow through and through!"*
> *Said Hunor: "Nothing in my life*

---

[8] Legendary figures of the Hungarian Chronicles whom history has not been able to identify.

has stirred me as those maidens do!" —
"*Up, knights, and at them! Join the chase!*
Let each one bear a woman back,
holding her tight in his embrace!
The wind will cover up our track!"

> *They spur their horses on and fling,*
> *the reins aside that they may seize*
> *the maidens dancing in a ring*
> *all unprepared for deeds like these.*

The girls run wild with piercing cries,
but fire and stream hem in their charms;
whichever way a virgin flies,
she falls into a rider's arms.

> *Away their fairy teachers flew,*
> *on frightened wings they fluttered free...*
> *But what can mortal maidens do*
> *to save their sweet virginity?*

Now, in that place, no maid remains;
the horsemen gallop with a will,
exultant; and upon those plains
the empty night is dark and still.

> *On flies the bird, the song flies now*
> *of Enéh's sons' fair fellowship —*
> *the lark's aloft from bough to bough,*
> *the song is passed from lip to lip.*

King Dúl's two daughters, the most fair,
to Hunor and to Magyar fell.
The hundred knights in rapture share
the hundred girls, and love them well.

> *Proud maids in time grew reconciled,*
> *though thwarted in their virgin plan.*
> *They sought their homes no more, but smiled*
> *atonement, bearing sons to man.*

Their isle became a country sweet;
their tents became a treasured home;
their beds became a blest retreat,
from which they did not wish to roam.

> *They brought forth boys, brave clans to please,*
> *fair girls they bore for love's warm hour —*
> *the handsome slips of youthful trees*

in place of their lost virgin flower.
Heroic children, two by two,
became the heads of every clan;
five-score and eight their branches grew,
and fertile marriage spread their span.
        Brave Hunor's branch became the Huns,
        and Magyar's was the Magyar nation;
        beyond all number were the sons
        that overran their island station.
On Scythia[9] then they swept in spate,
King Dúl's rich empire in the south —
since when, O pair of heroes great,
your glory flies from mouth to mouth!

Watson Kirkconnell, Anton N. Nyerges [& A.M.]

***

The reader is asked to turn
to the following poems
in order to see
the development of the 'Miracle Stag' theme:

(1) *I Chant of the Miracle Stag* (Shamanistic version) p. 22
(2) *I Chant of the Miracle Stag* (Christian version) p. 23
(3) *The Stag of Irisora* p. 520
(4) *The Sons Changed Into Stags* p. 556
(5) *The Splendid Stags* p. 557
(6) *The Young Miracle Stag* p. 833
(7) *The Boy Changed Into a Stag Clamours at the Gate
of Secrets* p. 854

***

---

[9] An ancient region extending over a large part of European and Asiatic Russia, inhabited by the Scythians.

The Coming of Age of a National Anthology of Poetry and Editor's Acknowledgments

This book originated as a private conversation between two Hungarian émigré writers in London, shortly after the French publisher Les Éditions du Seuil produced the collection entitled *Anthologie de la poésie hongroise*.[10]

The French anthology's editor, Ladislas Gara, had realized several years earlier that the French practice of translating foreign poetry always into prose could only be changed to result in actual French poetry if the French translators could somehow be made to hear and appreciate what poetry in a foreign tongue sounded like. He thus invented what came to be known as the "Gara Method of Translation," which, at least theoretically, works as follows.

The Editor, helped by a team of volunteer co-editors, prepares a word-for-word, indeed morpheme-for-morpheme 'Pidgin-French' (or in our case, 'Pidgin-English') translation to help the native poet-translators appreciate the grammatical structure of the text at hand. This is accompanied by a free prose translation in idiomatic Target Language diction without any regard for the rhyme and meter of the original piece. Then, in order to help the translators appreciate the sound of the original, the editors create a series of mock stanzas in the Target Language — this time without regard for the meaning of the original — solely in order to suggest a rhythmic and rhyming pattern that may be followed.

In order to make the package complete, the editor and his colleagues should also add a tape-recorded reading of the poem in the original Source Language (Hungarian in our case) in educated and clear poetic diction.

The French became intrigued.

Gara's *Anthologie de la poésie hongroise* opened a new chapter in the history of French literary translation. The poets collaborating with Gara and his team included Guillevic, Alain Bosquet, Éluard, Aragon, Lucien Feuillade, Anne-Marie Backer, and many more — all known and respected French poets with voices of their own.

---

[10] The book appeared in Paris in 1962; Gara tragically took his own life in 1966.

The results were of exceptionally high quality. The *Anthologie* received some of the highest critical acclaim ever accorded a foreign anthology in France. Some of the translators took their job so seriously that they wound up giving themselves crash courses in Hungarian; some even travelled to Hungary.

Even so, Gara did not include every possible translation in his book. In fact, he sometimes asked the various poets to translate a certain piece more than once; additionally, he often gave the same piece to several poets, sometimes to ten or more. He then judiciously compared all the possible versions harvested in this manner and only included what he and his team thought were of the highest quality. Gara actually concludes his famous *Anthologie* with an essay in which he shows how four particularly difficult lines by Hungary's greatest poet of the 19th century, János Arany (q.v.), sound in a dozen different versions.

Les Éditions du Seuil became known as the publisher of innovatively translated foreign literatures, mostly poetry. Other anthologies followed. They all used the by now famous "Gara Method" with considerable success.

Shortly before his death, Ladislas Gara spoke to Paul Tabori,[11] the London-based Hungarian expatriate writer of over one hundred books, three dozen feature films and hundreds of essays and articles (including some early Hungarian poetry), and suggested that Tabori do in English for the poetry of Hungary what Gara had done in French. Tabori recalled that Gara's voice was unusually heavy, sounding foreboding and prophetic. Tabori felt mesmerised by it and agreed on the spot.[12] In the ensuing conversation Gara explained his method to Tabori and urged him to follow it to the letter.

Tabori contacted his friend, the young Hungarian writer and librarian, Thomas Kabdebo, a 1956 emigré, who had studied at University College London and was, *inter alia,* in charge of the linguistics section of the Library, working with Professor Michael A.K. Halliday. A gifted poet, novelist, and essayist in both Hungarian and English, Kabdebo undertook the Herculean task of preparing the word-for-word 'Pidgin English translations' of some of the oldest texts and began to distribute these to the then best known available poets and translators in Britain including René Bonnerjea, Neville Masterman, Dermot

---

[11] Born in Budapest in 1910; died in London in 1975.

[12] Personal communication from the late Paul Tabori in 1972.

Spence, John Wain, Roy Fuller, Watson Kirkconnell, Vernon Watkins, Alan Dixon, Ted Hughes, and W.H. Auden.[13] Excellent progress had thus been achieved by Tabori and Kabdebo and the roughly one hundred contributing editors and translators scattered over Europe, North America, Australia, South America, and even India, when the present editor, at Tabori's and Kabdebo's joint invitation, joined the team in late 1966.

After several years of concentrated labor, the volume was accepted for publication by Mouton in the Hague, but the publisher's subsequent financial problems, long delays in production, and eventual removal to Berlin persuaded the editors to cancel the contract.

At this point, Tabori suddenly died in London of a heart attack in 1975. This, in turn, led Kabdebo and me to various reconsiderations of the book. Was it too long as it stood? Were all the authors originally included truly representative of the poetry of Hungary? Should we perhaps judiciously prune it? And if so, on whose advice? Our own?

One problem was that the manuscript was physically enormous.[14] With a generous financial contribution from Louis Szathmáry[15] and with additional financial contribution from the Hungarian Cultural Foundation, directed by the late Dr. Joseph Értavy-Baráth and his wife, Katalin Értavy-Baráth, M.D.[16], the editors succeeded in obtaining the co-operation of the eminent linguist-anthropologist and American poet Roger W. Wescott[17] and of Paul Carroll of the University of Illinois

---

[13] For a full list of the contributing translators please see the Table of Contents in the present volume.

[14] 1,300 pages in typescript.

[15] He also generously sponsored the artist, George Buday, who prepared the 25 original woodcuts for this anthology. A restaurateur, painter, sculptor, essayist, poet, and philosopher, Szathmáry has made innumerable contributions to Hungarian culture in America, his involvement in this book being only one of many.

[16] Formerly residents of Buffalo, N.Y., now of Stone Mountain, Georgia, Prof. and Mrs. Értavy-Baráth were the Founders of the Hungarian Studies Foundation. They published English translations of Sándor Petőfi, János Arany, Endre Ady, and Attila József (qq.v) by Anton N. Nyerges.

[17] Roger W. Wescott taught at Michigan State University, then at Drew University. He is the author of hundreds of articles and numerous books on language and is a poet and translator featured in numerous anthologies.

at Chicago, the poet, critic, and Professor of creative writing,[18] who agreed to read the entire manuscript and to provide guidelines as to which poems should be retired and which should be included. Wescott and Carroll never met, but their recommendations were so strikingly similar as to be nearly identical.

Thomas Kabdebo, who bore the brunt of this project for decades, withdrew in 1993 to my immense personal regret. His invaluable work remains present throughout the entire volume, though I alone am responsible for any mistakes or inaccuracies that remain.

When the political situation drastically changed in the wake of the collapse of Communism in Eastern Europe and the former USSR, ideological problems, such as allusions to 1956 in the Introduction as originally written in 1971-1972 by the late László Cs. Szabó, ceased to exist. Cs. Szabó, the leading Hungarian essayist, was Section Chief of the Hungarian Program of the BBC in London. Shortly before his death, he asked me to update, amend, and annotate his preface as I might deem necessary.

Hungary celebrates its 1,100th anniversary in 1996, on which unique occasion an International World Fair was planned jointly to be organized in Vienna and Budapest, but was subsequently abandoned as economically unfeasible. Although an isolated and modest event in itself, the appearance of this anthology may be an appropriate tribute.

We live in an age of a general decline of interest in literature in the West, with television and its familiar topics holding the public attention. The post-Cold War economy of East-Central Europe is dismal and the publishing of serious literature has sustained one blow after another.

We are extremely grateful to the Hungarian Ministry of Culture and Education without whose generous grant this book could never have been published. Thanks are due also to Minister Dr. Bálint Magyar, Under-secretary Péter Inkei, former Minister Gábor Fodor, former Under-secretary András Török, and Mr. Pál Perlik, Executive Secretary of the Hungarian National Cultural Foundation. Two past Presidents of the Hungarian Writers' Association, novelist Anna Jókai and József Tornai, a leading poet, have given the National Cultural Foundation and the Ministry their endorsements on behalf of this

---

[18] Paul Carroll, the noted American poet, has been poetry editor of *Chicago Review* and *Big Table*. He taught poetry in the Creative Writing Program at UIC, whence he retired in 1993.

volume. Miklós Hubay, novelist and playwright, and Éva Tóth, poet, translator and editor, President and Vice President of the Hungarian P.E.N., respectively, have given their endorsement to the project and helped organize public discussions on the translation of Hungarian poetry in the spring of 1995. A large number of excellent poets I wanted to include in Volume I will instead appear in Volume II, due to severe space limitations. The poem by Ferenc Juhász 'The Boy Turned Into a Stag Clamours at the Gate of Secrets' appears nevertheless in this volume, because the stag theme brings our millicentennial theme to a modern conclusion. We intend to make the forthcoming Volume II as comprehensive as possible.

My special thanks go to the following who, jointly and severally, helped me with all aspects of the production of the present version of this book including bibliographical and reference work, wording, typography, alternative rhyming, etc.: Kate Barlay, István Bart, Bruce Berlind, David Cohen, Elisabeth Cserenyey Cserép, István Csicsery-Rónay, Joseph Értavy-Baráth, George Faludy, István Gál, George Gömöri, Clara Györgyei, Ferenc Györgyei, József Jankovics, Agnes W. Kabdebo, Thomas Kabdebo, Alajos Kannás, Albert Kner, Rebecca Rose Makkai, Kenneth McRobbie, Ferenc Mózsi, Krisztina Passuth, András Sándor, Mátyás Sárközi, Béla Szász, George Szirtes, and Peter Zollman. Whatever inflicities remain, are my sole responsibility.

I am most grateful to the late Watson Kirkconnell and the late Anton N. Nyerges for their verbal permissions over the phone to carry out a few minor touch-ups. My initials in brackets indicate all such editings. My special thanks go to Mr. Peter Tabori, executor of the literary estate of the late Paul Tabori, who gave us the full rights to all materials included in this anthology.

We are collectively most grateful both to the authors, to their heirs, and to the translators, who have unselfishly donated their labor in agreement with the late Paul Tabori, the originator of this project, and agreed to accept one copy of the book in lieu of honorarium. Their generosity is fully in keeping with the nature of this commemorative volume and the time of its publication: "an act of faith and love."

ADAM MAKKAI,
Chicago and Budapest, October 23, 1996.

A Note on the Hungarian Language:
Provenance, Spelling, and Pronunciation

Hungarian is spoken by fifteen million people, with ten million living inside the borders of today's Hungary and five million outside. Most of these, possibly up to 2.8 million, live in Romania; the rest are in Slovakia, Serbia, Austria, and Ukraine, with one million in Canada, the USA, Latin America, Australia, New Zealand, and Western Europe. Recently even South Africa acquired pockets of Hungarian speakers variously acculturated to their new surroundings.

The majority of Hungary's leading poets were born outside of today's Hungary. This is the result of the tragedy of the Versailles-Trianon peace treaty of 1920 in which Hungary lost two thirds of her territories.

The Hungarian language belongs to the Ugric subgroup of the Uralic family of languages. It is an "agglutinating" language, i.e., a language that uses large numbers of suffixes and post-positions. Typical constructions in this sytem are the one-word phrases *kezemben* 'in my hand', which breaks down into *kéz-* 'hand', *-em* 'my', and *-ben* 'in'; and *házamban* 'in my house', which can be analyzed into *ház* 'house', *-am* 'my', and *-ban* 'in'. In Indo-European languages these relationships are shown by separate words; Hungarian piles them up as suffixes. Yet Hungarian is easier to learn than Greek, Sanskrit, or Russian, because it lacks obligatory gender and the usual Indo-European agreement rules between adjectives and nouns.

The Hungarian alphabet consists of 44 Roman letters and combinations as follows: **A, Á, B, C, CS, D, DZ, DZS, E, É, F, G, GY, H, I, Í, J, K, L, LY, M, N, NY, O, Ó, Ö, Ő, P, Q, R, S, SZ, T, TY, U, Ú, Ü, Ű, V, W, X, Y, Z, ZS.** The acute accent does not mean stress—stress is always on the first syllable of each word, no matter how long—but means a difference in vowel quality; the double acute accent—unique to Hungarian—similarly indicates length of the umlauted vowels. An impressionistic English example (using both British and American pronunciations) follows after each letter:

A as in *Bob, lot, got* (British); or *saw, moth* (US).
Á as in *father (most dialects)* or *Bob, got* (US).

B as in *Bob, bean, better*.

C like English *ts* in *cats;* word initially as in *tse-tse*.

CS like *ch* in *Charlie, chicken, choose*.

D as in *do, did, Douglas*.

DZ like *ds* in English plurals such as *lads, lids, needs*.

DZS like English *j in June, Jill,* or *dg* in *judge*.

E as in 'open *e*' pronunciations of *let's get set,* noticeably
    different from Australian and New Zealand 'closed *e*' pro-
    nunciation.

É as in French *été*, Australian *leg, Meg, keg;* does not have a
    glide at the end like the Anglo-American 'long a' in *Able,*
    came, bay.

F as in *Frank, fist, foot, fight*.

G is always 'hard' as in *goose, go, get*.

GY is a 'palatalized d', as in the British pronunciation of *due,*
    dew, adieu.

H as in *Howard, hill*.

I is as 'high' and 'tense' as *ee* in English, but shorter; it
    has no real English equivalent.

Í has the same quality as Hungarian **I** but is long; it therefore
    approximates English *ee* as in f*eet, sheep, heel,* but it lacks
    the diphthongal glide at the end of those English sounds.

J like English *y* in *yes, you, Yankee* and German *j* in *ja,*
    Jugend, jemand.

K as in *skill, school, skate*; it does not have the extra puff of
    air after it that occurs in *kill, cool, Kate*.

L as in *look, like, love*.

LY is a historical digraph always pronounced with a silent **L**,
    like English *y* in *buyer, by-and-by, you*.

M as in *mom, Mike, limb*.

N as in *no, enemy, bend*.

NY is a digraph for the 'palatalized n' sound spelled *ñ* in
    Spanish in *español, otoño* and spelled *gn* in French in
    espagnol, agneau; a similar sound, divided between two
    syllables, occurs in English in *canyon, onion, opinion*.

O as in Northern British and some quasi-Scottish pronun-
    ciations of *lots, hot, boy, mob*; distinct from the
    pronunciations of **A** discussed above.

Ó has a similar quality to Hungarian **O** but is long;
    comparable to the Scottish pronunciation of *go, so, no,*

woe; does not have a glide at the end like either the British or the American pronunciations of these words.

Ö as in German *ö* or *oe* in *Götter, Goetz* and French *e* in *meurt*; it has no real English equivalent.

Ő has the same quality as Hungarian **Ö** but is long; comparable to the long French *eux* in *deux* and to German *öh* in *ohl;* it has no real English equivalent.

P as in *spill, spoil, lisp;* it does not have the extra puff of air that occurs after it in *pill, Peter, pull.*

Q is mostly used in foreign words and is pronounced like **K.**

R is a trilled sound as in Scottish English; it is never pronounced as in American *hear, her, murmur;* most British dialects pronounce a similar but shorter trill in the words *very American.*

S like *sh* in most English words, *shoe, she;* and like English *s* in *sugar, sure.*

SZ like English *s in Sam, Sit, sew, this*.

T as in *still, stole, empty;* it does not have the extra puff of air that occurs in *Tom, till, tidy.*

TY is a 'palatalized *t*' as in the British pronunciation of *student, stew, Tudor;* American *get you, meet you, met you,* come close unless turned into the *ch* sound in faster, more informal speech.

U lies between English *oo* as in *soot, foot* and *u* as in *tube.*

Ú has the same quality as Hungarian **U but is long,** resembling North English and Scottish English versions of *who, knew, woo,* unlike the diphthongized Anglo-American forms which have a glide at the end.

Ü like French *u* in *tu,* and German *ü* in *zünden, Sünde;* English has no real equivalent.

Ű has the same quality as Hungarian **Ü,** but is long. It is like German *spüren, fühlen, Mühe.*

V as in *victory, nave, live.*

W is pronounced the same way as Hungarian **V.**

X occurs only in foreign words and is pronounced like **KS.**

Y forms digraphs with preceding **N, G, T**; after any other letter it is pronounced like **I.**

Z as in *zoo, zany, amaze.*

ZS like English *s* in *pleasure, leisure, measure;* and like French *g* in *garage, mirage, dommage.*

Most Hungarian given names have Western equivalents, thus *András*= 'Andrew'; *Dezső*= 'Desider' or 'Desiré'; *Endre*= 'Andrew'; *Ferenc*= 'Frank' or 'Francis'; *Frigyes*= 'Frederick'; *György*= 'George'; *Gyula*= 'Julius'; *Imre*= 'Emery'; *István*= 'Stephen'; *János*= 'John'; *József*= 'Joseph'; *Károly*= 'Charles'; *Lajos*= 'Louis'; *László*= 'Leslie' or 'Ladislas'; *Lőrinc*= 'Lawrence'; *Margit*= 'Margaret'; *Mátyás*= 'Matthias' or 'Matthew'; *Mihály*= 'Michael'; *Miklós*= 'Nicholas'; *Sándor*= 'Alexander'; *Sebestyén*= 'Sebastian', etc.

Some names are, of course, international: *Ádám, Ágnes, Anna, Dániel, Dávid,* etc.

Balassi's name *Bálint* is related to *Valentine,* but *Béla, Géza, Levente, Zoltán,* etc. have no English equivalents. Several family names have obvious meanings, too; e.g. *Arany*='gold'. *János Arany*'s whole name could therefore be rendered as 'John Gold'. The surname *Szabó* designates the occupation 'taylor'; hence the name of *Lőrinc Szabó* could be Anglicized as 'Lawrence Taylor.'

Petőfi's name, which was originally the Slovak *Petrovics,* means 'Peterson' both in Slovak and in Hungarian; *Sándor Petőfi,* is therefore, "translatable" as 'Alexander Peterson'. Even *Vörösmarty*'s family name has an etymology; the first part means 'crimson,' and its second part means 'bank' or 'grave'; his entire name rendered into English could therefore be the same as that of the famous actor, (Sir) 'Michael Redgrave.' These possibilities are merely mentioned as curiosities. Other family names are derivatives of toponyms or are of obscure etymology.

Adam Makkai and *Earl M. Herrick*

Table of Contents

Sándor Petőfi (1823-1849)

INDEX OF TRANSLATORS

I. FOLK POETRY

Folk Poetry

At the beginning of every literature, folklore is present in some shape or form. It is thus appropriate that the present volume should also start with characteristic examples of Hungarian folk literature. The oldest samples of these are shamanistic chants, whereas the youngest ones are folk ballads. Between the shamanistic song and the folk ballad stretches the area of the folk song, which is generally the most popular kind of folk poetry. Hungarian folk literature was discovered only in the 19th century — a situation parallelled in Finland, where the Kalevala was only discovered at the same time. The most diligent researchers in the 19th century were János Arany (q.v.), Antal Reguly (1819-1858), and János Kriza (1811-1875); in the 20th century the work was continued by Gyula Ortutay (1910-1986), Lajos Vargyas (1914-), and Zsigmond Kallós (1876-1955). Béla Bartók (1881-1945) and Zoltán Kodály (1882-1967) have proven what others had only been guessing before: the fact that the folk song is like a "migratory bird" meaning that not only the tune can travel from one country to the next, but textual motifs travel as well. This is not to disclaim the historicity of certain songs or ballads that are known to be closely associated with particular historic events. The Kossuth songs, for example, or several ballads of Transylvanian origin can be tied to specific events at specific dates. Even so these historically originated pieces are also firmly rooted in a long oral folk-tradition and the elements are traceable in many cases right back to the pre-Christian era and are thus comparable to the folk poetry of other Finno-Ugric peoples.

In the first centuries of Hungarian Christianity, folk poetry had to move "underground" because of its associations with paganism. A cruder and less established order than the German "Minnesänger" or the "troubadours" of Southern France, the Hungarian "regős" and "igric" chanters, singers and poets succeeded in keeping alive the ancient shamanistic tradition of chanting tales and incantations in semi-secrecy. All forms of Hungarian folk poetry continue to be produced even in our days, though the numbers of its practitioners have greatly diminished. Of particular interest in this volume celebrating Hungary's 1,100th birthday are the chants collected by Dr. Irén Lovász, an ethnographer-anthropologist and vocalist. Her work took her to remote areas in Romania, the Slovak Republic, Slavonia, an area in Slovenia now independent from the former Yugoslavia, and several isolated villages in the Hungarian Great Plain. The versions of the folk ballads presented here were originally composed in the 17th and 18th centuries, but written down and collected considerably later. Locations wherever known, are given.

SHAMAN'S SONG

Where a great road has its start,
and of which a fish-pond's part,
  hey, I spoke a mighty spell,
  yea, a mighty spell!
      But the pond was stemmed by mud
      closing in on the stag-boy stud
      who just shrugged it off in dance —
        hey, I fell into a trance,
        yea, a mighty trance!

Saint King Stephen, don't you brag
that you put game in your bag,
while you're hunting, dear King Stephen
you won't catch no game, not even
hares — you'll see the stag at dance!
  hey, I fell into a trance —
  yea, a mighty trance!
      Saintly King, please do not hurry
      me, thy serf, in mud to bury,
      I ain't no wild deer to shoot —
      but a messenger of God, to boot!
        hey, I fell into a trance,
        yea, a mighty trance!

On my forehead bright sun glows
on my side the fair moon grows,
stars on my right kidney prance —
  Hey, I fell into a trance,
  yea, a mighty trance!
      Thousand horns my head holds high
      on the horns loom thistles, thorn,
      which, unlit, shine and adorn,
      and without a dimming, die.
        Hey, I fell into a high,
        a very high trance!

Adam Makkai

DEAR CHILD, MY DARLING DAUGHTER

"My dear child, my darling daughter,
my garden's only rose!
Would you wed a nobleman,
a carefully bred nobleman?"
>"He can keep his nobility,
>and his early senility!
>Gout visits on a weak body;
>like the law it divorces me
>from your nobleman..."

"My dear child, my darling daughter,
my garden's only rose!
Would you wed a hooded friar,
a monk with a tonsure?"
>"Lord defend me from such an ape,
>ugly, uncouth — people would gape!
>Until death a bedecked virgin
>two times thirty would I remain
>rather than to wed one...!"

"My dear child, my darling daughter,
my garden's only rose!
Would you wed a man in a skirt
and a large hat — would you wed a priest?"
>"And why should I marry a priest?
>Of all menfolk they know the least
>about wives; they know more about books
>than a woman's good looks,
>do your priests..."

"My dear child, my darling daughter,
my garden's only rose!
Would you wed a shopkeeper,
a wealthy shopkeeper?"
>"A shopkeeper would keep me
>in gold and silk finery
>well housed in luxury

> but he'd bed me rarely,
> your shopkeeper!"

"My child, my darling daughter,
my garden's only rose!
Would you wed a soldier,
a rascally soldier?"
> "A soldier would be all right
> except that a soldier likes to fight
> and often he does dance with whores —
> it could be I'd feel the spurs
> of your soldier..."

"My child, my darling daughter,
my garden's only rose!
Would you marry a student,
a nimble-footed student?"
> "Oh, yes, I'll marry — I was meant
> to marry my dove-sweet student!
> My eyes have seen nothing
> more graceful or more charming
> than a student!"

Anthony Edkins

I LEFT MY HOME

I left my home in a fair land —
Hungary the little, Hungary the grand.
Halfway to somewhere, I turned and scanned
till the tears came fast 'neath my shading hand.

Over my meals hover gloom, misery, sadness
misfortune dogs my hours, gone from me's all gladness.
Each night I look up to the vast starry steep,
each night I weep more than a man should weep.

God, give me leave to stop and stand,
Who knows I am weary of wandering and

of the stranger's roof I alone command
while my tears flow with the hourglass's sand.

Dermot Spence

FISHERMEN, HEY!

"Fishermen, hey! Fishermen, hey!
What did you catch in the net today?"
"We toiled all day in deep mid-stream —
and all our catch was a red-wing bream."

"Hey, for the bream! Tell us what it ate
aboard the boat when it left the net!
"Only the one thing seemed to suit —
all it could chew was a parsley root."

"Followed the current, did our bream,
to Törökkanizsa,[1] way down-stream,
with never a hope of turning back —
why, this was clearly a one-way track!"

"Fishermen wait! Fishermen wait!
your clothes are in a terrible state!
You haven't a doxy, perhaps, to rate
as washerwoman and put you straight?"

"Fisherboy, harken to what was said —
why won't you pull out to shore and wed?
Get you a girl — it is easily done —
go, pick on me, or another one!"

Dermot Spence

---

[1] 'Turkish Kanizsa' was the name of a town south of the city of Szeged,
in today's Serbian Republic. Its name in Serbian is *Novi Kneževac*.

THE FIRE IS LAID

However heaped the fire,
it still dies in the grate
and all love has one ending —
black ashes, soon or late.

Love, universal thief,
damned specialist in grief,
why were you not a flavor
in every forest leaf,

in every common leaf,
but the lemon most of all —
so that each passing, poor boy
might have his bait at call,

as I did? (I, who aimed
and missed the prize I claimed —
trying for the stock-dove
I caught the hawk untamed!)

Dermot Spence

BLESSED PENTECOST

Blessed Pentecost is here again that comes up new each year:
the fields surround the leafing woods with roses in their hair
and from each branch of every tree sweet birdsong fills the air.

Can you hear and will you hear the words that swallows sing?
Each day brings its sufficiency of joy in everything,
and sadness in the wounded heart finds true relief from wrong.

Why and again why should a lad be sore if violets blue
and roses in their many kinds be there for him to view?
He stoops to bend the bloom with care: it will not fade nor curl,
that posy which a lover picks for giving to his girl.
'Tis time for roses' blossoming, spring's season clear and plain

when buds break out in flowers, the woods put out fresh sheen.
The young horseman is ready when the clouds of war are seen
to couch his lance and shatter it when charging o'er the green.

But what's your reason, sweetheart, to bid me go from here?
My heart is brimming over with love that's full and rare,
and my ring is on your finger, dear. Tell me you find it fair!

Find it fair, my sweetheart, and put an end to grieving.
So be it that I please your eye, let bitter words go hang.
The worm is eating out my heart, and all the pain you bring
has stolen the savour from the rose and left the thorn to sting.

Down meadows mild meander myriad streams that go
to make a mighty river where the ships take on their crew.
The cattle in lush pastures have a merry cud to chew,
and over greenest gardens 'twas but happy birds that flew.

Dermot Spence

THE KING'S COURTYARD

I will go and plough in the Palace Yard
and scatter the wrinkled pods real hard —
of the Magyar's bitter sheaf of days
and let them grow in the royal gaze:

the sorrel of sorrow, the tare of tears,
the ragged robin of suffering years.
May the King above whip the King below
for treating his Magyar subjects so!

Dermot Spence

THE WIFE OF MASTER MASON CLEMENT

When that Master Masons twelve gathered presently
that they might erect High Déva Castle rightly,
that they might be paid a half bushel of silver,
and that they might earn a half bushel of gold coins,
they made their appearance at the town of Déva
building its High Castle they set out with favor.
What they built by noontime, did collapse by evening —
what they built by evening, did collapse by morning.

Then the Master Masons sat in one more meeting
how they might succeed at keeping those walls standing,
finally they came up with this smart conception,
swearing to each other faith in their transgression:
"Whosoever's wife should come hitherward firstly,
must be gently seized and burnt at the stake firmly...
Let us mix her ashes right in with the mortar
so the walls of Déva's High Castle won't falter..."

"Hey thou, there, my coachman, thou, my elder driver,
for to see my husband do I pine and hanker,
'tis the wife of Master Mason Clement bids thee,
go, harness the horses, tie them to the carriage,
go, harness the horses and get thee ready quickly!
Let us drive, let us drive to the town of Déva...!"
When they reached the mid place between home and castle,
storm-clouds burst, it did rain, winds began to whistle.

"My Lady, my bright star, let's end this adventure,
I have seen a dream, it bodes ill, I conjecture,
I did dream I was in Master Clement's courtyard,
lo and behold, his courtyard was all dressed in black drapes
in the middle courtyard bottomless a well gapes.
Master Clement's small son fell in it and drowned there.
This, my dream of last night, brings no happy message —
let's go home, My Lady, let's turn 'round the carriage!"

"My coachman, my driver, we shall do no such thing,
I own horse and carriage, thou hast not a farthing!
keep whipping up the horses to make better mileage!"
They went on a-driving towards the town of Déva,
Master Clement caught sight of his wife approaching,
fell in fearful fright and thus he prayed for favor:
    "Lord, Heavenly Father, Make them lose direction,
may my horses break four legs, though they be perfection,
may my splendid carriage break in every section,
may the lightning strike right before my horses,
let them stagger rampant, homewards turn their noses!"
But they calmly rolled on towards the town of Déva,
neither horse nor carriage was harmed by God's favor.

    "Greetings, Master Masons, all of ye twelve, good day!
and thou Master Clement, may thine be a good day!"
Thus his wife did greet him, to which Clement answered:
    "Sweetest spouse, we wish thee, too, a very good day!
Why hast thou decided to come here in danger?
We shall seize thee gently, and throw thee in the fire.
We twelve Master Masons made this resolution
that a burnt wife's ashes must bring our solution.
No matter whose wife should come hitherward firstly,
must be seized gently and burnt at the stake firmly —
we must mix her ashes right in with the mortar
so that, for our wages, Déva's walls won't falter"

When that Mistress Clement understood quite clearly
what fate her awaited, her heart answered sorely:
    "Wait a while, wait a while, murderers a dozen,
till I bid farewell to neighbor, child, and cousin,
till I bid farewell to women-friends and my son —
lo, even the poorest dead hear church-bells ringing
thrice, but I, an orphan, get no bells, no singing."
Having spoken thusly she turned 'round and sped home
to say all her farewells to the neighbors back home,
to the women back home, to sister and to cousin,
and to her little son, whom she loved so dearly
to do what was ordered by the murderous dozen.

Having said her farewells, Mistress Clement crying
starts now back for Déva to rescue its ceiling —
gently she is seized and burnt, fiercely the fire rages —
mixed in right her ashes are with all of the mortar
so that Déva's ramparts should no longer falter —
it's the only way the Masons earn their wages.

When that Master Clement reached his home, the work done,
he was thusly greeted by his own little son:
    "Hearty welcome to you, God has brought you, father,
but, pray tell, what happened to my dearest mother?"
Whereupon his father gave this muffled answer:
"Fear thou not, fear thou not, she'll be home for dinner."

"Oh my God, oh my God, past are dinner, evening,
but my dearest mother can't seem to be nearing!
Father, dearest father, please do tell me truly
where's my dearest mother, tell me where's she hiding?"
    "Go my good son and wander all the way to Déva,
there you'll find your mother — the wall's her enslaver."

Sobbing, the boy sets out, small but all the braver,
he would find his mother in the wall of Déva —
thrice he yells out loudly conjuring her essence:
"Mother, dearest mother! Speak to me thy presence!"
"Sorry, child, I cannot, for the stone walls squeeze me,
between hefty stones the Masons did enslave me."

Whereupon her heart broke and the shattered Earth gave
mighty quakes that swallowed boy, mother, and stone grave.

(From Udvarhely in Transylvania, now Romania)
Adam Makkai

THE DEAD BROTHER

Once a woman who had nine sons,
nine sons and a single daughter,
when she had wives for her nine sons
wished to have a wedded daughter.
 When the time for that had ripened,
 strangers came from distant kingdoms
 and they sought her hand in marriage
 those strangers from distant places.
To her eldest son she ventured
telling him about the suitors —
"they all came from faraway lands
faraway lands, distant countries...
 If we let one take your sister
 we'll probably never see her —
 should we let her wed a stranger
 we'll probably never see her!"
Thus the eldest son did answer:
"She must not marry a stranger —
for we'd surely never see her,
never — not sooner, nor later."
 To her middle son she next turned
 telling him about the suitors:
 "Strangers came from distant kingdoms
 distant countries, faraway lands —
shall we let her wed a stranger?
What do you think, my middle son,
they came from faraway places,
shall we give her to a stranger?"
 Thus the middle son did answer:
 "She must not marry a stranger —
 for we'd surely never see her —
 never — not sooner, nor later!"
To her youngest son she next turned
telling him about the suitors:
"They came asking for your sister,
but they're all from distant kingdoms.

Should we let her wed a stranger?
If we do, we'll surely lose her —
if she should marry a stranger
we won't see her now, nor later!"
But her youngest son said: "Mother,
there's nothing wrong with a stranger —
you can see her now, or later,
let her go and marry that stranger."
No sooner did this son say so
when an Evil Shadow grabbed her,
only sister of nine brothers,
and to regions unseen dragged her.
In her mindless grief the mother
cursed her youngest son a-swearing:
"When you die, may God avenging
grant you no place down, in under,
in the Earth's grave find no cover!"
When the time for that had ripened
and the youngest son was coffined,
folks had tried to do their duty,
but the Earth spit out his body.
Whereupon the dead starts walking
unburied, in ghastly pallor —
unburied, in ghastly pallor
lo and behold, the dead starts walking!
Over hill and dale the brother
— unburied in ghastly pallor —
over hill and dale the brother
dead, unburied, starts a-walking.
Soon he finds a locked-up mansion,
it has neither doors nor windows,
though it has no doors nor windows
yet it moves, the locked-up mansion.
In astonishment he sees it,
doorless, windowless the mansion —
in astonishment he watches
that on wheels does roll this mansion.
Then the sister sees the brother
and to him in great fright she speaks:

"What seek you here, oh, my brother?
They'll behead you, if you enter!"
   "Let's go home, you, come on with me!"
   and he puts her high on his back —
   "Let's go home, you come on with me"
   and he packs her right on his back.
Homewards now they start a-walking
over hill and dale, the twosome,
backwards, homewards, ghastly twosome,
lo and behold, they start a-walking.
   Dense the woods and vast the meadows
   they traverse in such arrangement —
   dense the woods and vast the meadows
   they must cross in strange agreement,
while the birds look on a-chirping:
 "Lo and behold, the dead one carries
  on his back the one that's living —
   lo and behold, the dead one carries
    on his back the one that's living —
Look, the dead carries the living!
  Look, the dead carries the living!
    Look, the dead carries the living!
      Look, the dead carries the living!"
"What is that those birds are chirping?"
"Don't you mind them, sister, nothing!"
"What is that those birds are chirping?"
"Never mind — don't listen — nothing!
   Don't you listen to those birdies
   for what they chirp cannot be true —
   don't you listen to their chirping
   what they chatter cannot be so!"
Thus they reach their erstwhile homestead
where the brother left his sister —
there the brother left his sister
at their very erstwhile homestead.
   Just as soon as she was back there
   he rushed to the cemetery —
   he rushed to the cemetery
   just as soon as she was inside.

And in his grave, down in under,
Earth embraced him with her cover —
Earth embraced him with her cover —
Earth embraced him with her cover —

(From Magyarfalu in Moldavia, inside Romania,
populated by numerous Hungarian-speaking villages)
Adam Makkai

ILONA BUDAI, THE CRUEL MOTHER

Ilona Budai leaned out through her window —
learning that some bandits were looting the region.
Then her box of jewels quickly she remembered,
picked it up carefully, fast under her arm-pit,
leading her fair daughter forwards by the right hand,
leading her playful boy forwards by the left hand.
On she walks, on she goes, through the dense fir-forest,
all along an untrod path, in the darkness fiercest.
Then she thinks that she hears galloping of horses —
quickly her fair daughter Ilona releases:
Then her fair daughter cries, pleading with her thusly:
"Mother, Dearest Mother, on this path don't leave me!
Do take pity on me! Please do not forsake me!"
"Indeed, my fair daughter — I shall right here leave thee!
Because for a daughter, God will give another,
but for my treasure-chest, God won't give another!"
On she walks, on she goes, through the dense fir-forest,
all along an untrod path, in the darkness fiercest.
Then she thinks that she hears galloping of horses —
quickly her playful son Ilona releases.
Then her little, playful son begged Ilona thusly:
"Mother, Dearest Mother, on this path don't leave me!
Do take pity on me! Please do not forsake me!"
"Indeed, my little son — I shall right here leave thee!
Because for a small son, God will give another,
but for my treasure-chest, God won't give another!"
On she walks, on she goes, through the dense fir-forest
all along an untrod path, in the darkness fiercest,
until she should reach and see an open meadow —

lo and behold there ambles down a buffalo-cow,
carrying her young calf braced upon her horned head,
calling to her yearling that behind her she led.
This, in great amazement, Ilona sees sighing,
she falls to the ground and then she starts out crying,
bitterly she sobs, herself bitterly blaming:
    "Lo the mindless creature doesn't leave her yearling!
    God, Heavenly Father, I, who am animate,
    how could I have done so? I'll die inconsolate!"
Back she turns, back she goes through the dense fir-forest,
all along the untrod path, in the darkness fiercest —
soon she finds her little boy, sticks her hand out calling:
    "Come to me, my dearest son, come to me, my darling!"
    "No, I will not, I won't go, for you weren't maternal —
    if you had been, I'd be yours, your loss is eternal!"
Back she turns, back she goes through the dense fir-forest,
all along the untrod path, in the darkness fiercest —
soon she finds her daughter, sticks her hand out calling:
    "Come to me, my daughter dear, come to me, my darling!"
    "No, I will not, I won't go, for you weren't maternal —
    if you had been, I'd be yours, your loss is eternal!"
  When Ilona heard these words, thus she sobbed out ceaseless:
"Cursèd I must live my life, purposeless and useless —
like a dying roadside tree, whose dead branches rattle
when passers-by do tear at them like the roaming cattle."

(From Udvarhely in Transylvania, Romania today)   *Adam Makkai*

THERE WAS A PRINCE

There was a Prince, in days of yore,
who took it into his head — no less:
    "I must put on the clothes my coachman wears..."
    And out he went in his coachman's dress.
"And now I must go to Szoda Town
the Sheriff's daughter to woo..."
    "Good evening, Sheriff's daughter," he said to her;
    "good evening young coachman to you."

"Come in, sit down on this painted couch,
sit down there" — to him she said.
  "I haven't come to sit down, my dear,
  what I want is for you and me to wed."
"Oh no! Oh no! You can't marry me...
Not a poor, young coachman" — said she.
  "The cobbler has a daughter, and they do live quite near."
  "Cobbler's daughter, may I speak to you my dear?"
"Come in, young coachman, take this snow-white seat,
I was looking forward, hoping we should meet..."
  "I didn't come here to sit so neighbourly!
  What I came for is to ask, will you marry me?"
"Oh yes! Oh yes! I will marry you,
poor, young coachman, I will marry you!"
  There was a Prince, in days of yore,
  who took it into his head — no less:
"I must put on the royal robes
and go to Szoda Town in royal dress,
  to ask the Sheriff's daughter, if she
  will now agree to marry me..."
"Please sit down in this painted seat!
It's such a pleasure a Prince to meet!"
  "I haven't come to sit down," said he,
  "I've come to ask you to marry me."
"I'll marry you!" she cried happily —
"I'm only too glad your wife to be!"
  "Then the devil take you!" — he cried,
  "may the father of all devils make you his bride!
There is another maid who'll marry me —
the cobbler's daughter my bride will be!"
  "Good evening, cobbler's daughter, greetings to you!"
  "Good evening, Your Highness, greetings to you, too!
Please sit down on this snow-white seat —
it's such a pleasure a Prince to meet!"
  "I haven't come to sit down," he said,
  "What I want is for us to wed!"
"Oh no! No! I can't marry you...!
I gave a young coachman my promise true!"
  "I'm the young coachman you promised to wed —
  so give me a kiss, my dearest!" — he said. *Joseph Leftwich*

KATIE KÁDÁR

"Mother, Mother, my Dear Mother,
Lady Gyulai, my Mother!
I shall marry Katie Kádár,
the fair daughter of our yeoman."
          "You'll do no such thing, I tell you,
          Martin Gyula, I forbid you,
          go and get yourself a richer,
          marry a Lord's wealthy daughter!"
"I don't want a Lord's rich daughter,
do you hear me, dearest Mother?
I only want Katie Kádár,
the fair daughter of our yeoman."
          "Then away with you, you stupid
          son, go, get lost, Martin Gyula!
          I disown you, dispossess you,
          you're not my son, now or ever!"
"Hey my coachman, my dear coachman,
favorite of all my servants,
go bring out my speedy carriage,
harness two good, speedy horses!"
          When the horses thus were harnessed
          they took to the road in earnest.
          Katie had given him a scarf
          saying: "When its color turns red,
          you may feel great sadness and dread;
          when you see its color changing
          then my life, too, will be waning."
Martin Gyula goes a-driving
over hill and dale he's riding —
suddenly he sees the color
in the scarf's complection changing.
          "Hey my coachman, my dear coachman
          favourite of all my servants,
          let the Almighty own the land here,
          let the wolves the horses' flesh tear,
          let's go back: The scarf has turned red,
          Katie must have died, I now dread!"

At the entrance to the village
stood the swineherd, looking worried.
"Hey, good swineherd, what's the news here?"
"Ours — good, yours — pretty horrid,
      Katie Kádár — she was done in,
      your own mother had her kidnapped;
      in a lake she had her thrown in."
"Show me that lake, swineherd, kindly" —
Martin Gyula pleaded thusly,
"all my gold, horses, and carriage
will be yours if you will lead me!"
      Thus they moved on to the lake-shore:
      "Katie, my love, speak just one word!"
      When she answered from the water
      Martin jumped in deep to meet her.
Lady Gyulai sent in divers —
fished them both up, his arms in hers,
buried the one before the altar
buried the other behind the altar.
      Two pale chapel-flowers sprang up
      from their graves and touched each other —
      Lady Gyulai in anger
      tore them off. The flowers spoke up:
"May you be cursed, cursed forever,
Lady Gyulai, my mother!
Live, you were my sore tormentor —
dead, you commit a double murder!"

Adam Makkai

HEY THERE, PEACOCK

Hey there, peacock, peacock — peacock of the Empress!
I started as a poor boy, but married up to money,
try as I would, couldn't please my golden honey —
bought some red boots at the Fair for a pretty penny — —
brought them home and slapped them down at the table bonny:
"Honey" — I cried — "Oh! My sweet! Yield in matrimony!"

"No, Sir! Never, Sir! while the breath is in me!
Better men than you by far thronged my father's tower.
...and they never made me bow — nor have you the power!"

Hey there, peacock, peacock — peacock of the Empress!
I started as a poor boy, but married up to money,
try as I would, couldn't please my golden honey —
bought a fringed suit at the Fair for a minted guinea —
brought it home and slapped it down on the table bonny:
"Honey" — I cried — "Oh! My sweet! Yield in matrimony!"

"No, Sir! Never, Sir! while the breath is in me!
Better men than you by far thronged my mother's bower.
And they never made me bow — nor have you the power!"

Hey there, peacock, peacock — peacock of the Empress!
I started as a poor boy, but married up to money,
try as I would, couldn't please my golden bunny —
so to the wild wood I went — cut a dogwood dandy;
brought it home and laid it down where the bench stood handy.
"Honey" — I cried — "Oh! My sweet! Yield in matrimony!"

"No, Sir! Never, Sir! while the breath is in me!"
I took the stick and walloped her for a quarter hour.
"You're my dearest husband, dear, yours my life and dower."

Dermot Spence

THE MALLARD NESTS

The mallard nests among the reeds,
In rich black earth the millet breeds,
But where a faithful maiden grows —
That is a soil that no one knows,
        Anywhere.
My eyes are wet with many a tear:
Another's arms possess my dear.
And yet she told me long ago
She could not love another so,

Anywhere.
Ah, if you knew you would forget,
Why did you catch me in your net?
You would have granted peace to me;
Another would have heard my plea,
    Somewhere else.
Since poverty was my disgrace,
Choose another in my place:
Yet I shall know a brighter day,
The sun will drive my clouds away,
    And bless me!   *Watson Kirkconnell*

I CHANT OF THE "MIRACLE STAG"

I. *(Shamanistic version)*

Lo, my good son, lo, my dear son, hey,
    Yea I chant tales, I chant tales,
I have seen the sun a-rising, hey,
    I chant tales, I chant tales.
I saw the li'l Moon descending, hey,
    I chant tales, I chant tales,
Twixt them I spied a stag's antlers, hey,
    I chant tales, I chant tales,
One o' them antlers held up the sun, hey,
    I chant tales, I chant tales,
The other held up the li'l Moon, hey,
    I chant tales, I chant tales.
One pair of feet touched the forest, hey,
    I chant tales, I chant tales,
Another pair touched the ocean, hey,
    I chant tales, I chant tales.
On its right side a huge bonfire, hey,
    I chant tales, I chant tales,
On its left side blue fogged mire, hey,
    I chant tales, I chant tales.
Before its eyes the dawn was cracking, hey,
    I chant tales, I chant tales,
Behind its back the night was falling, hey,
    I chant tales, I chant tales.

Should you ever stray in those woods, hey,
     I chant tales, I chant tales,
You'd stay awake till the sun rose, hey,
     I chant tales, I chant tales.
You'd shoot at the stag with arrows, hey,
     I chant tales, I chant tales,
On your way you'd find new meadows, hey,
     ...till I live, I'll chant my tales.

(Slavonia, Chroatia)
Adam Makkai

II. *(Christian version)*

And lo, there is descending, yea, a narrow footpath,
On it comes descending, yea, a fine white lambkin.
On its right it carries blessèd light of sunshine,
On its left it carries blessèd light of moonlight.
Sixty High-Mass candles ride upon its fine fur,
Twixt its horns it carries the heavenly church-bell.
Don't you take fright, don't you take fright, fair Ilona Márton,
That we've come hitherward, God Himself has ordered.
For the door of Heaven opens, though it stays unopened,
And the bells of Heaven will ring, even if they're unrung.

(Moldavia)
Adam Makkai

BY THREE KINDS OF FLOWERS
I'M CHALLENGED

By three kinds of flowers I'm challenged —
  With thee, my flower, I'll depart,
  From thee, my flower, I shall never stray.
Don't you dare challenge me, you pretty wheat-flower,
For you're being used up by this very wide world!
  With thee, my flower, I'll depart,
  From thee, my flower, I shall never stray.
Don't you dare challenge me, you pretty grape-flower,
For you're being used by priests to serve the High Mass.
  With thee, my flower, I'll depart,

From thee, my flower, I shall never stray.
Don't you dare challenge me, you pretty rose-flower,
For you're being bragged with by the pretty maidens!
  With thee, my flower, I'll depart,
  From thee, my flower, I shall never stray.   *(Zobor, Slovakia)*
                                                      Adam Makkai

RARE IS THE WHEAT-FIELD
IN WHICH THERE'S NO BLEMISH

Land here, little birdie, come across the green woods!
Look in on my mother, she's the one who's lonesome.
If she asks you how I feel, tell her I am sickly,
For my poor heart aches so much, I feel I will soon die.
  Don't you cry, my mother sweet, that's the way one's life runs,
  For in every family, one must be the black sheep.
For my dearest mother, if only you'd been sterner,
If you'd only beaten me with a narrow reed cane!
For if you had beaten me, I'd have gone the right way,
Such a wanton, sinful girl I would not have turned out!
  For rare is the wheat-field in which there's no bad weed,
  For rare are the maidens, who don't bear a blemish.
  But my wheat's all fresh and pure, not a single bad weed,
  I did love but one young man, may God grant him Godspeed.

                                                      (Hungary)
                                                      Adam Makkai

II. MEDIEVAL POETRY

Medieval Poetry

The medieval poetry of Hungary bears most of the signs of a common heritage with the rest of Western and Central Europe. In its motivation and content it is Christian; according to its style and origin it is Latin — not, however, without a certain admixture of the elements of Hungarian folklore.

Hungarian medieval poetry can be found usually in hand-written codices. A tune usually accompanies the text, which contains religious material such as hymns, homilies, prayers of legends, some of which have been preserved up to the present day. The poems or songs are, at best, artistic translations of the Latin originals. The earliest example of a coherent literary text in Hungarian is the Funeral Oration [Halotti beszéd], which can be dated back to approximately 1200. The original text is in Old Hungarian, which differs from the modern literary language—mutatis mutandis—almost as much as Chaucer's English differs from today's English. The twenty-six rhythmic lines of the oration, whose Latin model can be found in the same codex, are accompanied by a six-line commendatory prayer, probably an actual translation from Latin.

The first known poem in Hungarian, The Lament of Mary [Ómagyar Mária siralom], dates from around 1300. The hundred-year gap between these two dates does not imply a great difference in their language, because the grammatical structure of the Funeral Oration suggests that there were earlier, similar texts in the language, while the composition, vocabulary, and style of the Lament of Mary suggest that the anonymous poet-translator must have had an earlier, continuous poetic tradition to rely on. The earliest relics of Hungarian literature were discovered abroad—in Vienna and in Louvain, Belgium, as war-torn Hungary was no ideal preserver of the literary records of ages past. Yet the spreading of literacy among monks, nuns, and noblemen of the 14th and 15th centuries increased these records substantially. Legends of saints were written, some of them being composed in song form; "historical accounts" (that is, verse chronicles) of heroic exploits and battles fought by saintly sovereigns were recorded and are now extant in more generous quantities. The songs to the Virgin Mary and the accounts of the lives of Saint Stephen, Saint Ladislas, and Saint Catherine are good examples of Hungarian poetic development in the later Middle Ages. From the humble imitations of Latin originals at the hands of scribes to the translations of migratory motifs and the adaptation of the octosyllabic lines of Hungarian songs, the connoisseur of early poetry will find a rich, beautiful variety of medieval poems copied or composed mainly by anonymous Hungarian authors.

FUNERAL ORATION

My brethren, you see with your own eyes what we are —
surely we are but dust and ashes.
God in his divine grace made Adam our ancestor,
and gave him Eden for his dwelling place.
He bade him live on all of the fruits of Eden,
forbidding the fruit of one tree only:
"If you eat of this fruit,
on that day you shall surely die the death of deaths."
And Adam heard God, his creator, speak of his death;
yet he forgot. He yielded to the Devil's tempting,
and ate of the forbidden fruit.
In that fruit, he partook of death.
So bitter was its juice, it burnt his throat.
He ate death, not only for himself,
but for all his children's children.

In anger, God cast Adam out of Eden,
into this world of toil and pain,
and he became the nest of death and damnation,
he himself, and all his children's children.
Who are those children? We are they,
as you can see with your own eyes.
None of us can escape that pit of doom,
that grave towards which we surely go.

Therefore, we beg God's grace
for this poor soul, His pity,
His mercy, and the forgiveness of sins.

We ask the Blessèd Virgin and the Blessèd Archangel Michael
and all the Angels to pray for him.
We ask Saint Peter, to whom God gave the power
to bind and unbind,
to deliver this man from his sins.
And we beg all the Saints to speak on his behalf
before Our Lord, that hearing their prayers
he may forgive his sins,

set him free from the Devil and the tortures of Hell,
lead him back to Eden's rest, show him the way to Heaven,
and let him share in Heaven's blessings.
Let us cry out to the Lord three times:
Kyrie eleison!

    Dearly belovèd brethren,
let us pray for the soul of this poor man,
whom the Lord has this day freed
from the prison of this false world,
whose body we bury today
that God in His grace may gather him
to the bosom of Abraham, Isaac, and Jacob,
among the chosen ones,
His saints who sit upon His right hand;
and that this man's soul may ascend
when the Day of Judgment comes.
So be it for you all.
Clamate ter: Kyrie eleison!

                                                  Alan Jenkins

THE LAMENT OF MARY
(Non-rhyming version)

I knew not grief
But now I faint with grief
I languish and am dried up with sorrow.
The Jew hath parted me from my light
from my Son, my sweet joy.

O my dear Lord,
My only Son,
Look upon thy weeping mother,
Deliver her out of her sorrow.
My eyes flow with tears,
My heart fainteth
From the spilling of Thy blood.
Light of the world
Flower of flowers

Cruelly art Thou tortured
And pierced with iron nails.

Alas for me, my Son,
Sweet as honey,
Thy beauty is dishonoured,
Thy blood flows like water.

My grief, my earnest prayer,
Burst forth from me,
And the inner sorrow of my heart
Which can never be assuaged.
Take me, Oh Death,
And let my only One live.

Let my Lord remain
That the world may fear Him.
The true words of righteous Simeon
Have come to pass;
I feel the dart of grief
He once foretold.

I must be parted from Thee,
But not with such a parting
That Thou art given up, my Son,
To torture and Death.
What doest thou, Jew, unlawfully?
Why dieth my Son, though innocent?

Arrested, dragged away,
Beaten and bound,
Thou puttest Him to Death.
Have mercy upon my Son,
Let there be no mercy for me
Or with Death's pang
Kill ye the mother
With her belovèd Son.

[ca. 1300 A.D.]

Michael Beevor

(Rhyming version I)

I was innocent of grief,
now I faint because of grief —
languishing I waste away.

I was parted from my Son
by the Jew, torn from my world,
from my sweet pleasure and joy.
Oh, my only little Son,

Oh, my only dearest Lord!
Look upon Thy mother weep,
rescue her from grief so deep!
Lo, with tears mine eyes do well,
in mine heart Thy torments swell —
yea, the spilling of Thy blood
makes my heart sink in the Flood.

Light of all Lights,
Flower of all Flowers!
Crude and cruel Thy torture's Cross,
raging rivets ram Thy flesh.

Woe unto me, dearest child,
sweet art Thou like honey mild —
while Thy beauty ebbs away
Thy blood carves a water-way —
on these waters spread and ride
grief and prayers from inside
till my heart with grief will burst:
naught can quench my spirit's thirst!

Take me, Oh Death, for Him —
let my only Son live,
let my only Lord live
that the world may fear Him!
Words of righteous Simeon
lo, came to pass truly —
sorrow's daggers egg me on:

He foretold all surely.

I must be parted from Thee
but why must it be this way —
that Thou art tortured to death
oh, my Son, from Nazareth!

Jew, thou art unlawful, senseless,
for my Son was always sinless.
Arrested, and dragged away,
beaten, bound is Whom ye slay.

Upon my Son, please, take mercy,
let there be for me no mercy,
or with all the pains of Death
kill the mother with the Son —
kill us both from Nazaret*h*

Adam Makkai

(Rhyming version II)

Witless of my grief was I;
Now with sorrowing I sigh,
How in sadness I must cry!

Foes my happiness destroy —
Tear me from my little Boy,
Take me from my sweetest Joy.

Ah, my Lord, my dearest One,
Ah, my only little Son,
Look upon Your mother's grief,
Grant her sorrow true relief!

Flooded are my eyes with weeping;
Deep in pain my breast is steeping;
For Your blood is being shed
By my heart, so nearly dead.

Light of all the world's dark hours,
Flower of all mortal flowers!

Bitter pain Your flesh assails,
You are nailed with iron nails.

Woe is me, my dearest Son,
Honey-sweet to heal man's sins,
How Your beauty fades away
As Your blood to water thins!

My laments and woeful prayers
Issue forth in bitter spate;
In my heart are sorrow's wells,
Springs that never can abate.

Take me, Death! I'd gladly die,
Could my dearest One but live!
Let that Lord remain on earth
Shrinking man's Restorative.

Ah, fulfilled are Simeon's words;
Grievous truth his words did hold;
For I feel the sword of grief
That his prophecy foretold.

I must part from you, my Son,
I must part, but not forever,
Though in agony He dies,
Though this death our lives may sever.

Jews, not laws, these deeds invent,
For my Son is innocent!
Lo, you capture, drag, betray Him,
Bind Him, buffet Him, and slay Him.

Ah, have pity on my Son,
But on me let death be done!
Else with mortal agony
Son and mother you destroy,
Slay at once both Him and me!

Watson Kirkconnell

THE LAY OF KING SAINT LADISLAS

Hail to thee, merciful King, Saint Ladislas!
The sweet protection of Hungary,
Of all the sainted kings, most precious pearl,
Of all the stars, the star that shineth brightest.

Faithful servant of the Holy Trinity,
Follower in the steps of Jesus Christ,
Unsullied vessel of the Holy Ghost,
Thou art the Chosen Knight of the Blessèd Virgin.

Thou art, of the royal seed of Hungary,
The radiant mirror of holy kings;
Bred by thy father, pious King Béla
To be a pious monarch in his image.

Sent from Heaven to perform a miracle,
Thou wert born for our causes in Poland
And, born again in Holy Baptism,
Christened Ladislas, after thy ancestor.

King Béla brought thee here for fair Hungary
When thou wert still in thy minority,
Brought thee to gain glory in two domains,
Hungary, the one, and the other, Heaven.

Bihar-Várad thou didst make thy resting-place,
And sweet protector of that city wert;
And there thou restest yet, within a church,
That thou didst raise in honour of the Virgin.

Thy body hath been in fine true gold encased,
And oil from thy sacred coffin seepeth;
To keep thee company, around thee lie
Three emperors, bishops, kings, and lords of fiefs.

Thou art praised in sacred psalms and psalmody,
By priests, by students, and by townsfolk praised;

Around the great globe thou art well praised
For, in truth, by God's own Angels art thou praised.

Thou didst give glory to the royal throne,
Thy image hath been placed upon a rock,
Upon which height it shineth like the sun
And gloweth like gold, and none can sated be.

Full of face, handsome and rubicund wert thou,
Thy gaze kinder than that of other men,
Thy speech was eloquent, strong was thy arm —
Behold, all who strove with thee thou didst bring low.

Thy limbs were lithe, noble of stature wert thou,
By thy shoulders, taller than other men;
Thy beauty alone claimed emperorship,
Naught but the Holy Crown was thy just desert.

Thy body pure, glorious of soul wert thou,
Thy heart was brave as a wild lion's heart,
Wherefore they called thee Ladislas the Brave
Even when thou wert still in thy bloom of youth.

Because the blessèd Virgin Mary did choose thee
To be endowed with many goodly gifts,
Into her keeping didst thou recommend
Fair Hungary's protection and support.

Upon thy head did the Sacred Crown descend,
Thou wert encouraged by the Holy Ghost,
Thou didst then follow thy father's footsteps,
Didst roses pluck and entwine them in thy crown.

Thou wert the scourge and destroyer of Tartars,
Didst dismember them in the snow-mountains;
Thou wert the dread and terror of pagans,
The Turks entitled thee The Fear of the Earth.

Thou hast extirpated all the heretics,
Thou didst tear them to pieces, weed them out;

During thy lifetime was no evil done
Because all men on earth greatly feared thy fame.

And therefore wert thou truly the judge of truth,
Thou wert the crown of beautiful virgins,
The pure protector of all purity,
The perfect upholder of mercy wert thou.

Let Hungarians praise King Saint Ladislas
For, verily, he deserveth our praise!
Let us praise him, all ye Angels, saying:
Hail to thee, merciful King, Saint Ladislas!

Anthony Edkins

THE BETROTHAL OF SAINT CATHERINE
(Extracts)

...And when thus the night availed,
she did as that by sleep travailed;
then did she rise out from her bed,
nor did she leave her own homestead.
She knelt before the saint's image
and prayed to Him with much courage,
and praying fast she soon forewatched,
and fell asleep upon that spot.
Again, the selfsame dream she dreamed,
in which a wondrous meadow there seemed,
with on that meadow a maiden fair,
who in her lap an infant bore.
And both of these were so comely,
that they outshone the sun brightly.
So Catherine, who was amazed,
went nearer them and at them gazed
for to see them right better near
and share with them their gladsome cheer.
When she saw her, The Holy Virgin Mother cried
unto Holy Jesus, her child:
"My sweet belovèd Son, Jesus,

who art in Heaven full glorious,
behold Catherine before Thee,
obedient to Thy word is she."
Our Lord Jesus thus replied
words of wisdom and great weight:
"I know full well this maiden fair,
of her virtues I am aware.
Yea, I see that she, beautified,
would be worthy to me be tied."
And Holy Mary has right begun
addressing her most Holy Son:
"My dearest Son, I Thee beseech,
place this one boon within my reach:
take Catherine into Thy troth
and give her, as token, Thy oath."
Quoth Jesus to his mother pure:
"Of Catherine Thou be well sure!
For Thee, dear woman, sweet mother,
I do this with pleasure and cheer,
take her as my betrothèd fair.
In token of this and as pledge
of our most holy marriage
I do give unto her this ring."
Having thus spoken, Christ drew forth a ring
placing it onto the finger of the virgin bride,
and said to her, standing at her side:
"My loving, beautiful, betrothèd, Catherine,
my bride select and well-be-seen,
look at my glory eternal
thus accepting thy betrothal.
    Have faith, fear not, good Catherine,
I know that in this world of sin
no one lives in virginity,
but in the haven of Heaven
all retain their virginity.
For thee, today thou shouldst rejoice
to be the sweet bride of my choice —
since thy bridegroom is not mortal,
he lives always and eternal.
He was not of this world begot,

He is from Heaven, He is thy God.
So thus today be of good cheer,
because the time is now so near
when thou wilt die in thy belief
and be a martyr for thy life —
for His Name thou wilt suffer woe
but, dead, be happy ever more."

René Bonnerjea

LAMENT FOR THE TARTAR DESTRUCTION
(Planctus destructionis regni Hungariae per Tartaros)

God of all the universe
thou who judgest error's curse,
bounty issues from they grace,
evil sees thy frowning face.
       The truth is now at stake.

Though our fathers lived in sin,
though we too have evil been,
when in sins we had been soiled,
guilt upon our heads recoiled,
       in times of misery.

Soon to death we sank in pain,
famous warriors now were slain,
slavery's yoke our people knew —
why born, alas, if only due
       for grief and sorrow here?

Now in blood our women perish,
murdered children cease to flourish,
rape and shame our girls appal,
old folk by the sword's edge fall,
       the age is drowned in blood.

Vile men slew the house of Saul,
Jacob's flights in death forestall,
flocks of Job by force were taken,

God's own stainless Lamb forsaken
        dies as we are dying.

Spouse and mother meet their fate,
virgin maids fiends violate,
priests are slain by devils bold,
none has mercy on the old,
        the infant also dies.

From what land and sex begot
come these tribes so fierce and hot,
ruthless, ever grim to slay,
terror's sons in every way,
        a horde in iron clad?

Cold are you, O mother nature,
to produce so wild a creature:
how could you breed this tribe abhorred,
this devastating Tartar horde,
        a scourge to every land?

Watson Kirkconnell

[ca. 1280-90 A.D.]

ON THE DEATH OF KING MATTHIAS

Good King Matthias, whom we mourn,
possessor of many a land,
praised by so many for so much!
No foe could against you stand.

Your strength you demonstrated
when you took Vienna into your realm.
You held your court in that proud city —
it trembled before your soldiers' helm.

When you wanted the land of the Germans
you took it for the Holy Crown.
You divided it into many parts,
and your Magyar lords held it down.

The nations wanted you as their ruler.
Prague sought you as its King.
Its royal line was failing,
and you took it under your wing.

The Turks gave you ransoms
not to devastate their land,
not to hunt down their pashas,
to let their Sultan stand.

You raided many countries
and made many cities yours,
you ruled Venice on its waters,
the Italians bowed to your force.

Bright light of Hungary,
hero of our story,
protector of all misery,
founder of our glory!

You are our proudest ornament.
Our history round you rolls,
protector of the Hungarian people,
the Terror of the Poles!

Among the Kings you were mighty.
In the affairs of the world you were great.
Your people loved and revered you —
rest with God, Illuminate!

Joseph Leftwich

Janus Pannonius
(1434-1472)

Born as János Csezmiczei of a Croatian father and a Hungarian mother, Janus Pannonius is the first significant Hungarian poet. He wrote in Latin which had to be translated into Hungarian by poet-translators. His maternal uncle, János Vitéz, Bishop of Várad, sent him to Ferrara, Italy, where he came under the tutelage of Guarino, the famous Humanist. Besides rhetoric, Greek, Latin, philosophy, and poetics, he was also trained as a diplomat. His sharp-witted Latin poetry made him famous well beyond Ferrara. In 1454 he was created Canon at Várad; this was an occasion for a brief visit to his homeland. He was sent to Padua where he became a friend of Galeotto Marzio. Mantegna painted a portrait of the two which was later lost. Pannonius became a doctor in 1458 and returned to Hungary to assume the role of personal secretary to King Matthias Corvinus, Hungary's Renaissance Monarch. In 1459 he became Bishop of Pécs, southwest Hungary's most important city. He delegated his ecclesiastical duties to substitutes and devoted most of his time to political writing. He was appointed Head Chamberlain to the Queen. Shortly afterwards his poetic output dwindled, probably due to his being ill with tuberculosis. The King sent him to Rome to consult with the Pope about the Turkish threat. He brought Galeotto with him on his return, together with valuable books. He read Plutarch, Plotinus, and Homer, and became interested in astrology. In 1468 he accompanied the King on his expeditionary war in Moravia. Around 1470 he was Palatine in charge of southern Hungary and Slavonia. The King, however, distanced himself from Janus, probably due to the intrigues of Lando, the Prelate of Crete. Subsequently, Janos joined a conspiracy against the King, and when it was quashed he was forced to flee. He died in the castle of his friends the Brothers Thuz near Zagreb. His poems were collected after his death for the King's library, the famous Corvinae.

Janus's career came in three phases: first in Ferrara, then in Padua, and then finally back in Hungary. Although the influence of Martial is evident in his early poems, his own personal wit predominated from the very start and gave rise to a realistic lyricism, describing the Hungarian countryside and towns with their particular culture. His later poems show the lyricism of Ovid, particularly his poem written to an almond tree that is destined to freeze in a hostile, cold climate. Janus Pannonius is, by any standard, a major neo-Latin, European poet whose Hungarianness is not suppressed by the Latin, but made to surface in a uniquely striking way.

ONE FOR POPE PAUL
(De Paulo Summo Pontifice)

Rome, do not ask for the Pontiff Paul to be testicle-tested!
    Isn't his daughter herself *manly enough,* like her Dad?

George Burrough and *Adam Makkai*

A DIFFICULT AND WEIGHTY QUESTION
(Questio ardura et difficilis)

Why do boys' dicksies for a soft cunny yearn and the girls *vice versa?*
    Folklore tells us why this gravitation occurs:
Back in the ancient days, when Prometheus shaped our elders
    From soft clay, his hands skipped variation in art;
He made no body-parts that could separate us into sexes
    And so our human kind could not regenerate.
Later on — since as he wanted to use Mother Nature —
    He did divide us in two opposite sexes, alas.
So he removed some flesh from between girls' legs, and placed it
    Right in between the thighs of all the innocent boys.
Lo, the ravine keeps chasing after its erstwhile appendage
    While the appendage, in turn, yearns to fill in the ravine.

Adam Makkai

ABOUT THE SHIPWRECKED FRANDUS
(De Frando Naufrago)

Frandus fell in the Po and, struggling, cried to Olympus:
    "Oh, what an ill-turned fate! What with an ocean of wine,
Since my destiny rules, and I must drown in a liquid,
    Bacchus, oh why must I swill in a *watery* grave?"

Iain MacLeod

(The same in modern idiom)

When Frank was drowning in the River Po,
He made a last indignant gurgle: "O,
In a world awash with wine from every quarter,
What a dismal fate to drink this filthy *water!*"

Iain MacLeod

ABOUT A TRANSDANUBIAN ALMOND TREE
(De amygdalo in Pannonia nata)

Not even Hercules saw in the yard of the Hesperides' land
    your like — nor Ulysses, on Alkinoos' isle —
"miracle" you'd be perceived in the balmier isles' lusher clearings,
    miracle more, in the cold soil of Pannonia, you!
Boldly the almond tree in the frost of the winter is blooming —
    although its buds very soon under the hoarfrost will freeze!
My Phyllis, little almond tree, not a stork has returned yet —
    ...or has it been so hard for you to wait for the spring?

Adam Makkai

FAREWELL TO VÁRAD[1]
(Abiens valere iubet sanctos reges, Waradini)

The endless fields sit under snowy blankets
and all the verdant glens where foliage bloomed,
are all embraced by wintry sheets of hoarfrost.
It matters not how fair the river Kőrös
we'd better go if we're to reach the Ister[2] —
    Well, then, my friends, let us be gone with Godspeed!

---

[1] The city's full name in Hungarian is Nagyvárad. It is in Romania today
and is called Oradea.
[2] The Roman name of the river Danube used in Latin writings.

Rivers and swamps they can't delay us either —
even the deepest lakes with ice are laden,
and where the cautious owner steered his row-boat
he gallivants around carelessly bragging
and may be kicking at the edge of dead waves —
        Well, then, my friends, let us be gone with Godspeed!

No wind can drive so speedily a lean skiff
(even if oars should help propel it forward
when on the ruffled surface of the waters
Zephyr runs back and forth giving it gooseflesh),
as my sled runs if pulled by crafty horses —
        Well, then, my friends, let us be gone with Godspeed!

Farewell to you, too, tepid, lazy fountains
on top of which no sulphur clouds pursue us —
your salts were splendid for the eye — above you
the purer steam our noses never bothered,
while all your waters poured in great abundance —
        Well, then, my friends, let us be gone with Godspeed!

Farewell to you, library, rare and famous,
in which I found the ancient masterpieces —
this was the place where Phoebus, too, alighted
and whence the virgin Muses never hurry
back in the woodlands of distant Iberia —
        Well, then, my friends, let us be gone with Godspeed!

Farewell to you, too, Statues of the Monarchs,
no fire did manage to consume you, even
under the heavy ruins you never faded,
when savage flames burnt up the Royal Palace
and clouds of smoke have darkened skies above —
        Well, then, my friends, let us be gone with Godspeed!

And you, too, King Equestrian, in armor
holding a dreadful sword, ready for battle,
whose marble-framed sepulchral monument

was once with ghostly beads of sweat surrounded,[3]
Saint Ladislas! Protect us — be our leader!
    Well, then, my friends, let us be gone with Godspeed!

Adam Makkai

TO MARS, A PRAYER FOR PEACE
(Ad Martem precatio pro pace)

Mars, brilliant lord of the sky's fifth sphere,
launcher of glittering beams of blood-red light,
son of mighty Juno, grandson of Saturn,
guardian of the sky, utter terror of the Titans,
rejoicer in trophies, arbiter of war and peace,
glorifier of men, consecrator of gods,
Mars, ever protected by gleaming iron,
destroyer of fields, sacker of towns,
despoiler of the world, supplier to savage Hell,
drinker of blood, devourer of bodies,
destroyer of warriors, execration of women,
enricher of the poor, impoverisher of the rich,
hater of peace, begetter of foul hunger,
creator of fear, inciter of dread,
spare now the weary Pannonians, I beg you, Father.

Anthony A. Barrett

---

[3] Allusion to the famous legend, according to which the 13th-century Hungarian king Ladislas [László], who was later made a saint, periodically returned from the dead to lead the Hungarians in battle against the Tartars.

ON THE BIRD WHICH STILL FLEW, THOUGH ITS HEAD WAS SEVERED

(De ave quae capite licet absciso, adhuc volabat)

Who could believe it? A twin-bladed arrow
severed the head of a bird as it flew,
but the bird continued to fly, though missing its head.
What sort of power makes a thing fly though dead,
what sort of death is it, when the dead thing still moves?
Or was part of it dead, part still alive,
and though the brain was scattered afar,
did the heart retain its vigour?
Or did some simple chance trick us of a sudden,
while the momentum it had in life
stayed with the limbs now chill.
Or while death, summoned late, tarried,
did the bird retain its motion,
and for a brief moment, as it lingered,
did sensation retain its hold?
Or can we assume a middle phase,
between life and final death
where the two are blended in equal shares,
so that each must be deemed the other's match,
as boundaries of the night and day
are not called light or dark
but take a name that covers both?
Find out the likely cause, you who ponder
creation's depths and nature's mighty works —
I have done my share just to tell of it.
Greece, land of fables, tell us if your games,
the Pythian, Nemean, Isthmian, Olympian,
can match this feat.
Tell us, Rome, honoured by a hundred games,
have your theatres seen the like —
a headless body living, a lifeless body moving?

Anthony A. Barrett

III. POETRY OF THE HUNGARIAN REFORMATION AND THE SIXTEENTH AND SEVENTEENTH CENTURIES

The Hungarian Reformation

A time of extreme turmoil, uncertainty, violence, and death, the Hungarian Reformation coincided with the Turkish occupation and the resultant tripartition of the country. László Cs. Szabó in his concluding essay characterizes this as the "time when Hungarian literature was born." **Albert Szenci Molnár** *(1574-1634), an oft-cited poet of the time, is omitted here, as much of his work was a translation of Psalms. Some of the poets of this era were Catholics.*

András Vásárhelyi
(?-1526)

Born in Palotabozsok before the turn of the century, Vásárhelyi died at the hands of the Turks near Mohács in 1526. He was a Franciscan friar and a writer of religious songs. His Cantilena to the Virgin Mary *was written in Pest in 1508 and was preserved in the Peer and Thewrewk codices. His name was often hidden in the first letters of each line, in accordance with medieval custom.*

SONG TO THE VIRGIN MARY

Madonna of the Angels in the skies,
Mother of our Lord Jesus good and wise,
Beautiful door of Heaven otherwise —
Thou art the broad, wide gate of Paradise!

To Thee I raise my voice, Virgins' Flower,
Of all the Saints consolation's bower,
Of all the Angels' purity's firm tower,
Of the Patriarchs the strength and power.
Glory to Thee on Thy Angel's throne,

In saintly affection of the Seraphim,
In the great wisdom of the Cherubim,
In the wise judgment of those who love Him.

To thee the Saints turn their beatific eyes,
And old folk turn their bitter hearts likewise,
And the orphans, too, their heart-rending cries,
And the singing souls, their repentant sighs.

For our own great cause, Oh Mary, pray,
So that our hearts great courage should display,
Thy Holy Son we do respect, obey —
Our hope in the life after death alway.

We bless Thee, Jesus's nurse, at leisure,
Holder of God the Father's great Treasure,
The Holy Ghost's quietude and pleasure,
And the Truth's brightness, the supreme measure.

Help those who place in Thee their confidence,
Pray for the Apostles' benevolence,
That Martyrs help us with their innocence,
And the Confessors give us full indulgence.

Thou, the glorious Saints' holy utterance,
The Trinity's great secret Conference,
The saintly Apostles homilies' sense,
The Martyrs' most terrible sufferance.

Remember the Angels' fall, the beginning,
Remember the first sin, Eve's sinning,
Remember the flood destruction bringing,
Beg for the Lord's merciful forgiving.

All full of tears is this our earthly life,
With our many, many sins it is rife,
Dreadful were the fruits of our sinful life
If Thou didst not help us in our sore strife.

Of the orphans Thou art the provider,

Of the widows Thou art the supporter,
Of the needy Thou art the rich giver,
And of those in exile, the good helper.

Miserable were we from our very birth,
Unbearable were life's sorrows and dearth,
And terrible the evils of this earth,
If with Thy fortitude we were not girt.

Of women the beautiful reflection,
Of men the most abiding affection,
Of the dead, faith in the Resurrection,
And against the Devils, great protection —

Thou art the glorious Saints' holy utterance,
The Trinity's great secret Conference,
The Saintly Apostles' homilies' sense,
The Martyrs' victorious deliverance.

Of the dead, Thou art the deliverer,
Against the Turks, Thou art the great leader,
Of the Kings, Thou art the Good Counsellor,
And of us, Hungarians, the Protector!

In the Town of Pest this poem was made,
In Saint Peter's Street and this estate,
After Christ's birth and bearing this date:
The year one thousand five hundred and eight.

So let us give thanks to the Trinity,
To Lord Jesus and his Divinity,
And to the Holy Virgin similarly —
Bless me, and all this vicinity!

AMEN.

René Bonnerjea

András Batizi
(ca. 1510-1550)

Born in the village of Batiz, he was active between 1522 and 1546 in the years immediately following the Disaster of Mohács. A preacher and composer of religious songs, he worked as a teacher in towns of northern Hungary: Kassa, (Košice today in Slovakia), Sátoraljaújhely, and Szikszó. In 1540 he studied at the University of Wittenberg and became a Lutheran minister in Tokaj. His surviving fifteen songs were composed between 1530 and 1546 to be sung in church. Author of biblical stories, he is regarded as a pioneer among the psalm writers of the Hungarian Reformation.

REMEMBRANCE OF DEATH

Remember, Man, Death's grief and sorrow,
Consider the short time you may borrow —
Remember, Earthling, you must die, that you, too, soon must die!
    Man changes like a meadow flower,
    Blooms in the morning, then fades in his power —
    Remember, Earthling, you must die, that you, too, soon must die!
You came out naked from the womb;
Dust gave you birth, dust you'll be soon —
Remember Earthling, you must die, that you, too, soon must die!
    No one can tell when Death will hold its sway,
    No one knows when, in what mysterious way —
    Remember, Earthling, you must die, that you, too, soon must die!
Be, therefore, duly warned, for Christ did say,
You do not know if it comes night or day —
Remember, Earthling, you must die, that you, too, soon must die.
    Christ is the Resurrection and the Life,
    He who has Faith can overcome all strife —
    Remember, Earthling, you must die, that you, too, soon must die!
Remember all these things that I relayed,
Meet Christ in Death and do not be afraid —
Remember, Earthling, you must die, that you, too, soon must die!

Adam Makkai

Ferenc Apáti

(early 16th century)

Probably born in the village of Apáti in Zala County (in western Hungary), Apáti's exact dates are unknown. In 1518 he attended the University of Vienna. His Cantilena, which was preserved in the Peer Codex, written down around 1526, is a series of reproaches to his faithless friends and complaints against those who flatter the rulers. He attacks in bitter and sarcastic words the wealthy nobles, who collect fortunes in this world but refuse to fight against the Turks. He also chides women who prefer dancing to being good housekeepers; he lashes out at greedy priests and peasants whose ambitions he judges to be too high. His style is lucid, his rhyming lively — a typical example of the so-called 'Hungarian Sapphic stanza' which consists of three 12-syllable alexandrines followed by a half alexandrine of 6 syllables.

SONG OF REPROACH

You, who thought that my heart would be full of anguish
You, who'd been my cherished, trusted friends — you brandish
Frequently many a noble word before me —
You have sore deceived me!
     He who trusts a liar gets plenty of trouble,
     Gently spoken, smooth words his misfortune double;
     His polite double-talk snares you like some wild game —
     So you're steeped in deep shame!
There are folks who sell out and tell lies that flatter,
They never feel scruples during their cheap chatter;
They disguise their meanness by their gentle speeches —
Their tongues suck, like leaches.
     Great and mighty Lordships! Please don't mind my saying
     Your great silver sabres in their jobs are failing —
     Of the pagan folks, please, stop the mindless slaying
     For what are you gaining?
Students, stop your bawdy, lewd, and dirty verses,
Quit combing your hair, quit chasing after nurses,
You chase girls in vain, for you — indeed overtly —
Screw your own poverty.
     Don't have any dealings with the ordained clergy,

> For they will abduct your daughter to an orgy,
> Having gained your trust, they'll even spurn your money;
> Honest — this ain't funny!

Your hard dancing daughter — she will surely flounder,
Though we think her virtues couldn't have been sounder;
Should her whirling motions get a little wilder —
They will have defiled her!

> Don't fly, like butterflies, too far from your houses —
> See to your brooding hens, be virtuous spouses,
> It is good to garden! Rock your babies' cradles —
> Spin, and thread your needles!

Peasants though they were as strong as mighty Samson,
In their angry madness held their lords at ransom.
Grab their grubby beards and confiscate their holdings,
Quell their lowly loathings!

> In the olden days priests were respected duly,
> For they kept their vows and served religion fully;
> When they weren't enamored by their cloak-like garments
> Or red-capped ornaments.

Now their dress is fancy, money's made them crazy,
Though their speech may please you, all their deeds are lazy;
They collect their gold coins, save them in their hiding —
They shun work and building.

> In the old days, our kings governed with a fair hand
> As long as they lived did justice rule this poor land,
> They faithfully worshipped Hungary's Holy Crown —
> To it they prayed, knelt down.

So should the great lords act now, watching with much care,
When the cunning fox hides deeply in his woods lair;
Greyhounds have no way to catch the foxes out there —
Death awaits the poor hare.

> They are thin on hair, but their treasure it is ample,
> Though they're rich on rites, they won't sing in the temple;
> All their fancy servants walk in velvet habits —
> They're the Master Abbots!

Adam Makkai

János Erdősi Sylvester

(ca. 1504-1555)

One of the most important poet-scholars of the sixteenth century, János Erdősi Sylvester is known as the author of the first distich of Greco-Latin type written in the Hungarian language. Dating from 1541, his poem 'To the Hungarian People,' herein featured, was actually a Preface *to his translation of the New Testament. His thought was greatly influenced by the teachings of Erasmus, whose works he encountered while he was a student in Poland at the University of Cracow. In the summer of 1529 he went to Wittemberg, the birth-place of the Reformation, but he was less attracted by Martin Luther [1453-1546] than by Luther's somewhat independent collaborator, the humanist Philipp [Schwarzerd] Melanchthon [1497-1560], who published the* Augsburg Confession *in 1530.*

Erasmus's ideas can be seen to be present throughout Erdősi Sylvester's Bible translation, for instead of having accepted the Vulgate *as the ultimate authority, he returned to the Greek original. He was the first Hungarian Bible translator to do so.*

In 1539 he published his Grammatica Hungaro-Latina, *an important classical document of 16th-century Hungarian linguistic scholarship. His Grammar was considered important enough to be reissued in 1808 by Ferenc Kazinczy (q.v.).*

He also wrote a number of epics in Latin, such as De bello Turcis inferendo; Querela domini Jesu resurgentis; and Querela fidei in *1551.*

TO THE HUNGARIAN PEOPLE

God has, of old, been speaking to you through his Seers,
   Lo, Whom he thus foretold, his Son he finally sent.
Through Him, with fervent soul, He now preaches to you here,
   Through Him that you have heard, Him He now bids you to heed.
Rescuer thus he became, indeed he's your Doctor and Healer,
   He is your Master now — gift from the Father himself.
He is the one you must heed; otherwise the Creator
   Casts you without one trace into destruction anon!
Here, through the lines of His book, did He choose to engage you,
   So that those swollen with pride might be made humble again.
He, who before, touched you in Hebrew, Greek, and lastly in Latin,
   Speaks to you in this book in the Hungarian tongue.
Nations on Earth should hear their Lord in their natural language,
   So that they all may see; so that they all can obey.
Here is the Old Treasure hid — here starts the Perennial Fountain,
   Immortality's key — here is the Science of Life.
Bread for the soul will you find in here! If you eat, you will earn your
   Immortality, through Christ's crucifixion and death.
He who created you, saved you, bids you life everlasting
   Through this Bible here — trust you in no other source!
Serve it, your Scripture true, with the purest heart and a constant
   Bearing of sacrifice onto its worthiest cause.
Here is a bridge that leads to God; He won't lie when He calls you:
   "Come to Me all you who pray, and perish all you who sin."

Adam Makkai

Sebestyén Tinódi "Lantos"
(1505 or 1510-1556)

Sebestyén Tinódi, nicknamed "Lantos" (see below) was the son of a wealthy peasant family who were able to afford to send him to the Latin school in Pécs in southwestern Hungary. He was hired as the personal secretary to the warlord aristocrat Bálint Török, whom he met in Dombóvár in 1538. He then moved to Török's castle, Szigetvár, where he lived until 1542 when Török, one of Hungary's most important political and military figures of the 16th century, feared by the Turks, was captured by the Sultan and dragged off to captivity near Istanbul. After the loss of his master, Tinódi was employed by two more influential politicians, Werbőczi and Nádasdy, and later by the Báthory family.

He settled in Kassa (today's Košice in the Slovak Republic) where he had a house and a large family. He used this as his headquarters to visit the sites of famous battles, e.g., the siege of Eger in 1552, where the Turks were repelled by Captain I. Dobó. (This siege became the source of The Stars of Eger *by Géza Gárdonyi, a popular historical novel.)*

King Ferdinand ennobled Tinódi in 1553 for his poetic achievements. His is a uniquely Hungarian 16th-century career: he became a rhyming war correspondent. As a result he paid less attention to form than to content. His Chronicle *appeared in Kolozsvár in 1554, printed by the famous Heltai press. He died in Sárvár (in western Hungary) on the Nádasdy estate. Tinódi practiced all genres of 16th-century epic literature. He wrote up the story of* Jason and Medea *(ca. 1537); he took themes from the Bible as in* The Story of Judith, *in 1540, and in 1549 the story of* King David as He Fought the Great Goliath.

His war chronicles—which are numerous—were detailed and quite accurate. Hungarian historians regard them as invaluable eye-witness accounts. Although he was a protegé of the aristocracy, he frequently criticized both them and the clergy, always emphasizing the anti-Turkish war from the point of view of the people and the simple soldiers.

Tinódi composed his poems to lute accompaniment, hence his nick- name, 'Lantos' — the lute-player.

THE FALL OF ZOLNOK[1]

Bernald, who the rural affairs was placed o'er,
Aldanai Bernald, a warrior of power,
on hearing of Temesvár's[2] downfall so sore,
has Lippa abandoned and Solymos's[3] tower.

Great Ahmet, the Pasha, could scarce understand
how great forts like these could fall into his hand,
with food all provided and cannons so grand,
and plenty of florins from King Ferdinand.

Then Ali of Buda and great Ahmet were
encouraged to say: "We will push on our war
to Zolnok and Eger, less trouble by far —
they'll cost us to take them than did Temesvár."

So Ahmet, the Pasha, to Zolnok has ta'en
he took with him troops twenty thousand amain
Ali Pasha preceeded, and with cannons atrain
the city was battered a week, but in vain!

Bold Lorentz Nyári was Governor there,
with seven hundred soldiers all proper men fair,
but alas! They of different languages were,
so that all was dissension and trouble and care.

---

[1] Spelled today as Szolnok, located about 60 miles east of Budapest, near the confluence of the Tisza and Zagyva rivers. The city held strategic importance, as it provided an obstacle to attacks on the fortress of Eger.

[2] In Transylvania, under Romanian rule today, called *Timişoara,* where the Romanian Uprising of 1989 was started, actually by the Hungarians.

[3] Both Lippa and Solymos are in Romania today.

Of cannons and mortars there were twenty-four
in Zolnok, of sakers[4] a thousand and more,
fifteen muskets from Biscay brought o'er,
nine hundred pood[5] weight of good powder in store;

there were firearms a-plenty, much iron and tin
and gold, which had late in the royal chest been;
but, alack! ...all well-guarded the city within.
So how could a foeman hope Zolnok to win?

Oh, mighty was Zolnok and beauteous, I trow,
on one side the Tisza its current did show,
on the other side Zagyva did murmuring flow,
uniting together the city below.

On the side of the north was a trench deep and wide,
three bastions stood up at three corners in pride;
huge ramparts the place of high walls supplied,
the house-tops behind them could scarce be descried.

Now Ahmet, the Pasha, so stern and so dread,
before Zolnok Town his appearance has made;
upon the green plain he his army has stayed,
his camp he has pitched and his banner displayed.

What tumult and noise from the campment arise!
The bells ring, cymbals clang 'midst a thousand wild cries;
fifes squeal and drums speak, trumpets shriek to the skies —
the ends of the great host aren't seen by the eyes.

The sight and the sounds to the townsmen recall
Losontzi's destruction and Temesvár's fall;
there's whisp'ring and murm'ring amongst great and small —
the power of the Sultan their minds does appal.

---

[4] An old form of cannon, smaller than a demi-culverin, used on ships and in sieges.

[5] A 16th century weight, from the Russian *pud;* one pood equals 16 kg. or roughly 35 lb.

At length they resolve from the city to fly,
they think if they stay, by the Turks they will die;
on the fourth of September when midnight is nigh,
they depart, without bidding their leader good-bye.

Full quickly Laurentius Nyári he knew
that Zolnok was left by his soldiers untrue;
all alone he remained — what alone could he do?
They closed not the gate when from Zolnok they flew.

Long doubtful he stood in unspeakable woe —
Should he follow the fugitive traitors? Ah, no!
Far better be slain by the hands of the foe,
than to live in disgrace and become a vile show.

Around thus he sped to the city's wide gate,
determined on death, for his courage was great;
'twas dawn and the drum of the Turks loudly beat,
they knew not that Zolnok was left to its fate.

But as they came onward in order to fight,
a huge burst of smoke from the town met their sight.
They guessed that its soldiers had left it outright,
and they pushed for the entrance as fast as they might...

In the gate of the city bold Lorentz[6] did stand —
alone he withstood them with terrible brand.
Many Turks he dispatched ere they mastered his hand —
oh, woe to his dastardly runaway band!

How glad were the Pashas I scarcely need tell,
nor the joy of the Sultan when fair Zolnok fell;
to the clouds the glad Turks "Allah akhbar!" they yell —
in the town they found stores of all things they liked well.

---

 [6] Spelled *Lőrinc(z)* in modern Hungarian. The name equals English Lawrence/Laurence. The original Latin form is *Laurentius*.

In Colosvar[7] city these lines composed I,
Sebastian Tinódy in great misery,
I blow on my nails in a cold chamber high,
for want of a penny some fuel to buy.   *George Borrow*

THE CHRONICLE OF SIGISMUND[8]
(Extract)

I've heard it sung — it may be true or no —
that Lőrincz Tar into Hell once did go.
And there he saw prepared a fiery bed,
four fiery men stood at the foot and head.

There they gave a message to Lőrincz Tar and said
that for King Sigismund they kept his bed;
an Archbishop, Bishop, and two nobles they were —
all four false and knavish Lords they were.

The Archbishop for levying false tithes was damned,
the Chancellor for selling title deeds was damned,
two noble Lords for ravaging the land were damned;
one of them for imposing wrongful dues was damned.

Many and great marvels saw Lőrincz Tar there,
a great and fiery bath-house he saw there;
and Sigismund, the Emperor, was stewing there
and with Princess Maria was writhing there.

Many a maid without her maidenhead,
sweet young wives and ladies finely clad;
King Sigismund the measurements of all had read,
their lovely paps, their navels, and their heights he'd read.

---

[7] Spelled today *Kolozsvár,* the Romanians call it *Cluj-Napoca;* the Saxon-German name of the city is *Klausenburg.*

[8] Tinódi who was concentrating on the contents of his "rhymed war reports" was a notoriously careless poet. He used the same rhyme line after line, and the present translation intends to render the same effect in English.

Lőrincz Tar told the Emperor what he had learned,
who answered that it now would be his great concern
right speedily to have his bed from Hell ejected
and upon true road to Heaven directed.

He broke a point off his imperial crown,
he severed thirteen towns from his domain.
Those did he for eighty thousand forints pawn
and built therewith St. Sigismund's in Buda town.

Priests he installed and much wealth he gave to it,[9]
many great estates did he assign to it;
to St. Sigismund he dedicated it —
and so, perchance, his bed was saved by it.

Michael Beevor

CALL TO LIEUTENANTS
(Condensed extract)

You, who are lieutenants in the army,
those of you who profess our Christian creed,
if you have the wish that your cause should triumph,
this is a lesson you all ought to heed!

. . . .

Put your trust in God, and all your courage,
line up your soldiers as it should be done,
and when you go out to fight the pagans
address them in loud and ringing tone!

---

[9] The translator was specifically asked by the editors to use *it* four times as the end rhyme in order to indicate the monotony of the Hungarian *vala* 'was,' Tinódi's favorite excuse for a rhyme. The English translation could have embellished the poem, but the present anthology is also a historical record showing the evolution of Hungarian poetry. See the essay on Hungarian prosody at the front of this book.

Listen to me now, all of you, listen!
You kinsmen of mine in God, hear my word!
Put your trust in God alone, brave soldiers,
and he will be your buckler[10] and your sword.

Confess to God — all make your confessions! —
say you repent, that you will sin no more.
Forgive your enemies, and encourage
your comrades to fight bravely in the war.

If one of us should fall in this battle,
Angels to Paradise will bear his soul.
His name in this world will be honoured.
The saints in Heaven his courage will extol.

Those of you who will survive the battle
will receive rich booty and much drink and food.
You will see the defeat of the pagan,
and you will offer gratitude to God.

No one is to turn tail, to run away,
or other good men may do so as well —
if being deserters you should perish,
you will be buried down in deepest Hell.

So all of you now, with me together,
call on the name of Jesus Christ, our Lord;
call and appeal to the Holy Spirit,
say it with me, repeat it word for word:

"We are waiting for you, Lord and Saviour,
be with us in this cause for which we fight!
Let us not faint or fall in battle...!"
— Fight to your last breath with all your might.

. . . .

---

[10] Historically, a small, round shield held by the hand. Figuratively, any means of defense. The word derives from Old French, like its relative, *buckle.*

Then, Son of God, be with us in the battle!
And God the Father, too, will with you be.
Let us not fall before the pagans,
nor in this cause to perish cruelly.

. . . .

You raised up the young lad David
when he was grazing his father's sheep.
You guided his hand to slay Goliath,
to make the cruel Philistines mourn and weep.

Therefore, O God, remove us from your anger!
Pity us, and make our arms grow strong!
Let the pagan warriors fall before us,
destroy them, destroy their wicked throng!

Our limbs are free and unfettered.
You have listened, Lord, to our prayer!
Now you are with us; our lances are uplifted,
cry: 'With Jesus leading us, we dare!'

He who wrote this, conceived it at Kassa,
where the lords have gathered with their host.
Now, each of them, in fighting the pagan,
build under Zolnok a castle post.

Joseph Leftwich

András Szkhárosi Horvát

(early 16th century)

Undoubtedly the most significant song writer of the early Reformation, Szkhárosi Horvát was originally a Franciscan friar. He was active first in Nagyvárad (today Oradea in Romania); later he worked in Tállya as a militant propagandist for the Reformation. His ten extant songs show a highly talented and eloquent fighter thoroughly committed to speaking up with great poetic force for the downtrodden, poor Hungarian peasantry who were exploited by the feudal aristocracy and the Catholic clergy and decimated by the Turks. Most of his writings—with the exception of one lyrical prayer—are sermons and theological argumentations in verse form. His main goal was to get his message across, a fact which led him to neglect artistic detail. There is a great deal of beauty to be found in many a detail, but these are often immediately followed by drier didactic pieces.

The main source of his inspiration was the Bible, more specifically the Old Testament and the poetically powerful language of the ancient Hebrew prophets. Outstanding among these is his piece entitled 'About Two Kinds of Faith,' *dating from 1544, his denunciation of the cruelty of the powerful landed aristocracy called* 'About the Princes,' *dating from 1545, and his sermon lashing out at avarice, also from 1545, called* 'About Stinginess.'

He was a master of sarcasm and irony in parodying certain scenes from the life style of the lazy priests and friars. In expressing his hatred, he personified the vices of the enemy criticized and addressed them in the second person singular — thus he treated 'avarice' *as a person full of criminal intent. He lined up his stanzas in a way that shows a graduated intensification of the threats and curses he heaped on his targets. The outstanding example of this is his poem* 'On Cursing,' *written in 1547, which clearly breaks through the mould of a rhyming sermon and rises into the realm of real artistic creativity. The piece was influenced by the 5th Book of Moses* (Deuteronomy), *which Szkhárosi actually amplified in his own way. In his poetic vision inspired by Moses, the entire Earth became a huge prison for sinning humanity.*

Szkhárosi's songs are additionally valuable because they provide insight into the everyday life of the peasants and the poor hired hands of his day.

His versification is flawless. His ten extant songs were preserved in Péter Bornemisza's (q.v.) Book of Songs.

ABOUT TWO KINDS OF FAITH:
THAT OF CHRIST AND THAT OF THE POPE'S
RAGGED PATCHWORK

(Excerpts)

[1544]

Hurry up, Christendom, think about salvation,
Carefully recall the danger of damnation,
For you have forgotten God's one true religion,
Nor can the Last Judgment waken your cognition.

> Christendom has suffered shame and major damage,
> Since the Papacy turned treacherous and savage;
> Wholesome truth can't light the smallest light of pleasure,
> For they mock the Lord brazenly, without measure.

How come we deserve this, all you Christian brethren?
How come we are mocked by foes, the Turkish heathen?
I can tell you why: our loss of faith's the reason:
God keeps punishing us for our lowly treason.

> Great heaps of foolishness can appear as goodness,
> God's own truth can look like sore demented madness;
> Such is the delusion we must bear: It's blindness
> For having misheard God's speech bereft of kindness.

Dreadful are the times that are visited on us,
All our views of truth have gone quite rotten on us;
We are led in circles, curse upon curse rakes us —
Into raging madmen our great blindness makes us.

> Our allegiances are randomly divided;
> Some opted for Germans, some for Turks decided;
> Similarly, some have Jesus Christ derided,
> Cheering for the Pope; others the True Faith minded.

Let us, therefore, enter into dissertation
First, about the True Faith — Christ's — and His Salvation;
Then let us discuss the Papal machination,
Its tremendous lies and ultimate damnation.

. . . .

Let me tell you plainly what the Pope is doing,
No calumny, this, but facts, truly ongoing;
His faith is a patchwork, quite ragged and motley,
What it's all about — why, I must tell you boldly:
What the Lord Jesus said can be stated simply,
Even in Isaiah it is written clearly,
That the Lord Creator doesn't like when people
To his Revelation man-made patches needle.
Now, here is, my Brethren, how the Pope has acted:
Human patchwork has he foolishly contracted;
He saw fit to tamper with God's Revelation
Which is why I tell you he goes to damnation!
What's the good of Christ's death for him, if he uses
It as means to safeguard his own tricks and ruses?
"Deeds of Saints will save me!" Eyes rolling, he chants it —
He sells pardon-coupons, quite willing to chance it.
Christ has surely died in vain, all one needs is coupons,
Money comes in handy, but so do geese and capons;
Thirty Masses get you off; pay for psalms and candles —
It's gold coins that Saint Peter most willingly handles.
Murmuring of priests and friars in furtive collusion
Ready your departure — you need no absolution;
Boldly you can do without spiritual function,
Just have salt-water and oil for the extreme unction.
What's the use of Christ, then, his grave cross a-bearing,
Blood, spit on his face, his hushed disciples staring?
If the Pope redeemed you with his stinky ointment,
Not by Christ—you were to heaven by your coins sent!

. . . .

Save us, God Almighty, from patchwork-religion,
Liberate us from the Devil's own perdition;
That we may be rid of greed and hypocrisy,
Save us from the Turks — save us from the Papacy!

Adam Makkai

ABOUT THE PRINCES
(Condensed Excerpts)
[1544]

You live in dishonor grave, Dukes and Mighty Princes,
"Killers of the country: you!" — public cry evinces;
You're said to be robber-knights, thieves and looters greedy,
But you hide in silence deep, for such news sounds seedy.
     You treat other people's serfs quite as if you owned them,
     You treat their possessions, too, as if you had loaned them;
     Your own proper income's wealth doesn't satisfy you —
     God's Commandments and His Wrath cannot mollify you.
Great Saint John the Baptist urged workers to be thrifty,
And to live within their means, lest their ways be shifty;
"Quarrelsome" he calls all, who grab things helter-skelter,
It is wrong to hide in false tax-collectors' shelter.
     Also Jeremiah says that the Dukes and Princes
     Turned out greedy bastards (as history evinces);
     They're all cheats and cruel knaves (words He never minces!)
     Scavengers and vultures are all the heartless Princes!
Isaiah, Ezekiel, and the other Prophets
All decry the lawlessness of the Princes' profits;
Micah, Zephaniah, Solomon, and Moses,
All would like to rub in dirt mighty Princes' noses.
     It's in vain you gather clothes, unused things get dusty;
     It's in vain you trust in coins; money can get rusty —
     Cursed be he who trusts his own strength—the Ancient Crier
     Definitely testified, wise old Jeremiah.

. . . .

Year one thousand five hundred fifty-four in *A.D.*,
All the dealings of the Lords have been cruel and shady;
Citizens of Tállya lived midst a huge upheaval,
All poor peasants suffered from inequity's Evil.

Adam Makkai

THE CURSE
(Condensed Excerpts)
[1547]

Dreadful are the happenings of our evil ages,
Nothing helps — God's punishments; mercy; nor His sages;
Dreadful is the blindness and lawlessness that rages —
So watch out! This curse secures all your rightful wages!

. . . .

    If you won't listen to God's sacred, holy message,
    May you meet with pestilence; may you wreck your carriage;
    Cursèd be your silo's grain, may Turks rape your daughter —
    May she suddenly forget everything you taught her.
May the sky above your head turn into a steel-pan,
May the ground under your feet kick up like no heel can;
May your flocks and herds come down with the plague and rabies —
May your women give birth to dwarfs and headless babies.
    If you don't believe in God, may you writhe with twitches,
    May your skin go wrinkled with pestilence that itches;
    May there never come a leach or country physician
    Who could cure your malady; may you lie there stricken!
Should your thatched roof burst aflame, may you find no succour;
Should you take a wench to wife, let another f... her —
Should you once a shelter seek, may you find no hospice,
Should your vineyard yield some grapes, let them taste like horse-piss!
    From afar God, in his wrath, brings the foreign armies,
    Savagely they beat your child, but the greater harm, is
    In what they to women do, and the older generation —
    They will kill your sheep and cows; scorch your vegetation.

. . . .

Do protect, Almighty God, this Thy Christian country,
Here in Tállya where the ills are various and sundry.
Fifteen forty-seven, I penned these angry verses
In hopes my drift the deafness of Hungary reverses.   *Adam Makkai*

Péter Bornemisza

(1535-1584)

Descendant of a wealthy, noble family related to the Balassis, Bornemisza[1] was an influential literary figure in 16th century Hungary. He studied in Italy and at the University of Vienna.

In 1564 he entered the service of the Balassi family as a Lutheran minister and as tutor to young Bálint, who would become the most significant Hungarian poet of his age.

Bornemisza's prose writings, such as his sermon Temptations of the Devil [Ördögi kísírtetekről], *published mostly at his own expense, are bitter attacks and tirades against the faithless aristocracy of his age. He went so far as to accuse the higher Austrian nobles of consorting with the Devil. He was arrested on several occasions and was hounded both by the Catholic Church and the Austrian imperial authorities. An accomplished classicist, Bornemisza translated Sophocles'* Electra *into Hungarian.*

As a poet, his best remembered pieces are 'Upon Seeing St. John' ['Szent János látására'] *and* 'Cantio Optima.' *His* Book of Songs *appeared in 1582. Two of his wives and five of his children became victims of the plague.*

---

[1] The name literally means 'wine-he-drinks-it-not' and refers to an ancestor who was abstinent. The equivalent of the name is found in Italian as *Bevilaqua*, literally 'drinks-the-water.' Not all Hungarian names are built on recognizable words or morphemes, and we only translate the more memorable ones.

HOW WOEFUL IT IS FOR ME

How woeful it is for me from thee to be parted,
Blessèd land of Hungary — I leave broken-hearted.
When, pray, shall fair Buda be, once again, my dwelling?

Our highlands[2] are possessed by the boastful Germans,
Our province of Szerém[3] held by Turkish pagans.
When, pray, shall fair Buda be, once again, my dwelling?

I'm being hunted and chased by those boastful Germans,
I have been near trapped and snared by those Turkish pagans.
When, pray, shall fair Buda be, once again, my dwelling?

I have been so wearied by those Hungarian nobles,
They have rendered our homeland forsaken and godless.
When, pray, shall fair Buda be, once again, my dwelling?

Fare thou well forever more, my blessèd Hungary,
For there is no greatness left any more within thee.
When, pray, shall fair Buda be, once again, my dwelling?

In the stout Castle of Huszt[4] this song was composèd,
By Péter Bornemisza, to merry mood disposèd.
When, pray, shall fair Buda be, once again, my dwelling?

Paul Tabori [& A.M.]

---

[2] Refers to today's Slovakia.

[3] Formerly a part of southern Hungary belonging to Croatia today.

[4] Located in the Eastern Carpathians, Huszt, whose name recurs in the poetry of Ferenc Kölcsey (q.v.) is in the Republic of the Ukraine today, since the Soviet Union forced its way to a common border with Hungary after the Second World War.

Mátyás Nyéki Vörös
(1575-1654)

He studied at the Catholic Seminary of Nagyszombat (today Trnava in the Slovak Republic). In 1611 he became Roman Catholic Canon of Győr in western Hungary and in 1642 he became Deputy Bishop of the same city.

Opposed to the Reformation, he collaborated with Péter Pázmány, the leader of the Catholics. His poems deal with death, the last judgment, hell, and heaven. He is considered a pioneer of Hungarian Baroque poetry.

HELL
(Excerpt)

Of what avail are palaces in hell,
Or old Darius' chains of perfect gold?
Salome's dancing there can cast no spell;
Her kingdom-charming cheek turns brown and old.
> Can skill in dancing help you here at all,
> Or chess, in which you battled all night long,
> Or tankards that you downed at carnival,
> If flames about you crackle fierce and strong?
That in immortal fame has been your wage,
And pleasure in your work, beyond desire,
And you survive to venerable age —
What will it matter, when you fry in fire?
> What use is eloquence? That sweet of tongue
> You preached from your high pulpit with your arts,
> And every ear upon your utterance hung
> As your wise knowledge nourished many hearts?
And what avails your skill in martial power
That shed the blood of countless infidels
And often devastated town and tower,
If in eternal fire your spirit dwells?
> Does it avail you that you own a realm,
> O king and kaiser, count and gentleman,
> And your proud wars their millions overwhelm,
> If an eternal bonfire ends your span.

Watson Kirkconnell

Bálint Balassi
1554-1594

Bálint Balassi
(1554-1594)

Born in the fortress of Zólyom (today Zvolen in Slovakia), the scion of a noble family, Bálint Balassi (he also spelled his name 'Balassa') is, by universal agreement, the first major Hungarian poet, comparable to Sir Philip Sidney in England and to Ronsard and Du Bellay in France.

His poetry (including a verse form he invented, of which more below) signals the maturity of the Hungarian language as a full-fledged medium of literary expression, on a par with the other languages of 16th-century Europe.

Balassi was sent to Nuremberg at the age of twelve to learn German and was later educated by Péter Bornemisza (q.v), another writer in the vernacular, who instilled a deep religiosity in him. In the early 1570s, on the basis of false allegations, his father was accused of high treason and had to flee with his family to Poland. Bálint himself later took part in a campaign against Prince István Báthory of Transylvania and was taken prisoner. However, Báthory, who was elected king of Poland in 1576, refused to extradite Balassi to the Turks, freed him, and took him to Poland. The poet spoke fluent Turkish, Italian, German, and Polish.

In 1577 he accompanied Báthory to Danzig [Gdańsk] to put down the city's rebellion, but upon hearing the news of his father's unexpected death he returned home. Then he became a professional soldier in Eger, defending the border-lands against the Turks. In 1578 he won the heart of Anna Losonczy, the wife of the Palatine of Croatia. She became the eponymous heroine of Balassi's "Julia Poems."

He declared his loyalty to the King of Hungary, but because of his Polish connections and family relations with the Transylvanian Prince, he remained under suspicion. In 1585 he married his cousin, Krisztina Dobó, the daughter of a famous military commander. He was tied up in a lot of fruitless litigation about his various possessions, some of them large fortresses. Both he and his wife became Roman Catholics. Despite this, he was granted a divorce when it became known that his wife had been unfaithful to him. He started courting the wealthy Anna Losonczy again, who had been widowed in the meantime, but she scorned him and married someone else. After this point his life became one calamity after another.

In 1594 he fought in the battle of Esztergom and was mortally wounded on May 19th; he died of blood poisoning a few days later. His orphaned son was cared for by his sister, who later sent the boy to Transylvania where he died at age sixteen.

This tormented, adventurous, and typically Renaissance character, whose fate resembles that of the Italian Benvenuto Cellini, wrote some of the most sublime poetry, frequently sung to lute accompaniment. Although his religious poems were published in 1632, it was not until two hundred years later that his martial and erotic poetry reached print. His work is a deeply focused mirror of his own troubled life and contains elements of contemporary Turkish, Polish, and Hungarian folk poetry. He was also influenced by the Psalms and by neo-Latin Western European poets such as Michele Marullus (1453-1500) and Hieronymus Angerianus, (ca. 1520).

Balassi was the first Hungarian poet who wrote entire cycles of poems dedicated to given subjects, such as his cycle of poems dedicated to "Júlia" and another cycle which he dedicated to "Célia."

Additionally, Balassi wrote a five-act play entitled Szép magyar komédia [A Beautiful Hungarian Comedy] *in 1589, patterned on the Italian Castelletti's pastoral play* Amarilli, *dealing with the love of 'Credulus' and 'Júlia.' This play is prefaced by a statement in which Balassi indicates that he intends to create love poetry in the Hungarian language. He points out that love poetry is respectable all over the world and should therefore be accepted in Hungary also.*

Balassi made a unique contribution to Hungarian poetry: he invented the 'Balassi stanza.' Its basic structure, which he occasionally varies, is 6-6-7 syllables with an aab/ccb/ddb[/eeb] rhyming scheme. The most typical Balassi stanza can be seen in the first poem featured herein 'Soldiers' Song.' In the original it goes as follows:

Vitézek, mi lehet	Soldiers, what finer worth
ez széles föld felett	is there upon this earth
szebb dolog az végeknél?	than the borderlands can show?
Holott kikeletkor	Where in the time of Spring
az sok szép madár szól	beautiful birds all sing
kivel ember ugyan él;	setting our hearts all aglow —
Mező jó illatot,	the fields have a fresh smell
az ég szép harmatot	where dew from heaven fell,
ád, ki kedves mindennél.	delighting us through and through.

He performed numerous variations on this pattern both in his religious poetry and in his martial and erotic poems, using far better and more original rhymes in Hungarian than any other poet before him. This verse form became highly popular and was imitated for a long time by lesser poets as well as by unknown writers. Echoes of Balassi's lyrics return in the work of Hungary's greatest Rococo poet, Mihály Csokonai Vitéz (q.v.), and that of some 20th-century poets.

SOLDIERS' SONG

Soldiers, what finer worth
is there upon this earth
than the borderlands can show?
Where in the time of Spring
beautiful birds all sing
setting our hearts all aglow —
the fields have a fresh smell
where dew from heaven fell,
delighting us through and through!

Let the foe but appear —
brave soldiers have no fear,
their hearts are roused by battle.
High-spirited they rise,
and shouting their war-cries
quickly they prove their mettle.
Some fall, wounded or slain,
but the foe flees again —
our lads have suffered little.

Banners and gory spears
each one of our men bears
riding in the army's van.
They dash like the sharp wind,
footmen follow their lead,
for such is the battle plan.
Pommels of leopard-hide,
gleaming shields at their side
hang beside each crested man.

Arabian steeds — dash, fly,
heeding the trumpet-cry,
then, those standing sentinel
dismount, and with swords drawn,

wait until the new dawn.
When night on the battle fell,
the soldiers, tired and spent,
go to sleep in their tent
for a brief refreshing spell.

For honour and good name,
for manhood and for fame,
they leave everything behind —
they give up all they own
nobly, and quite alone,
staunch models of humankind —
like hunting hawks they fly
across the smoke-stained sky,
of the wind they one remind!

So when the Turks they spy,
joyous, give battle cry,
wielding lances gallantly.
Should the odds prove too great,
sharply they turn and wait,
though blood-drenched, unflinchingly
fall on the chasing foe
and strike them, blow for blow,
routing them victoriously.

Open fields and grottoes
are the spots where each goes,
to lay ambush on the road —
fighting hard night and day
is their work and their play,
they crave battlefields and blood;
thirst and hunger's their treat,
they do not dread the heat,
this, their life, they find is good!

Loving their soldier's trade,
they wield their trusty blade,
to roll heads down on the ground!
Many men met their doom,

eaten by wild beasts, soon
after they were slain. And 'round
now come hungry vultures,
carnivorous creatures —
such reward their bravery found!

Braves of the borderland,
noble and glorious band!
Warriors of grand repute!
Through the whole world your name
has won honour and fame,
like rich orchards ripe with fruit.
With good luck and riches
may God fill your britches —
may God's boon be absolute!

Joseph Leftwich [& A.M.]

HAVING TO PART FROM HIS MISTRESS AT DAWN

The dew is aflame on the flowers and trees,
The bush looks greener at dawn;
There is singing of birds, and rejoicing of beasts
When night and darkness are gone —
Yet for me there's trouble and danger and grief,
Because of all I have done.

Yakov Hornstein

FOR WINE DRINKERS

Blessèd sweet Pentecost's weather brightly glowing,
Beautiful sky on all healthiness bestowing,
 Wind that brings relief onto tired wayfarers blowing!
  It is thou who givest perfume to the roses,
   The once mute nightingale now its song composes,
    And trees, too, thou dressest in many-coloured clothes.

It's through thee that hedges bloom, violets appear;
Flowing waters and wells through thee turn crystal clear,

And our speedy stallions, too, prance along with good cheer.
  For after their long run, the tender grass bedews
  Their exhausted bodies, while their vigour renews,
   Infusing new energy in their nerves and sinews.

And even the good, brave frontier soldiers alight
And through the scented fields roam about with delight,
 Now they, too, are overjoyed that the weather's so bright!
  In the soft grass leaving their horses to run free,
  With their brothers-in-arms they go off on a spree
   While with their blood-stained weapons their pages are busy.

The whole earth is renewed, thanks to thee everywhere.
Thanks to thee, the blue sky breaks through the misty air,
 And every living creature emerges from its lair.
  Enjoying, as we do, this weather through God's grace,
  From our hearts let us all His holy name praise,
   Let us drink, and to true friendship our glasses raise!

René Bonnarjea

WHEN HE MET JULIA, HE GREETED HER THUS

None of this world do I care for
Without you, my fair belovèd,
To stand by me were you made for,
You, my soul's health, whom I covet!

Of my sad heart — you're the pleasure,
You're my soul's fondest desire —
You're my good cheer without measure
You're the Godsend I require...

You are like a palace to me,
Like a rosebud, red and fragrant,
Like a violet you draw me
Life eternal may God you grant!

My sun's light is resurrected,
Through your eyebrows black as charcoal —

Light to mine eyes is directed
Live on, live — you are my life's goal!

Scorched with love, my heart's a-fading
You alone I've been awaiting —
Oh my heart, my soul, my darling
Hail to thee, my Queen, my Lady!

Overjoyed, I hailed her thusly,
When I found my Julia lastly,
I bent head and knee, politely,
...She? — She smiled, though somewhat crossly.   *Adam Makkai*

IN WHICH HE REJOICES
OVER HAVING DISCARDED LOVE

At last here is freedom for my poor, bedazzled head,
No more pain and thraldom for my soul from love, hot-red,
   I am calm and peaceful,
    My mind, too, is cheerful,
      My heart's pain hath vanishèd.

I am like an inmate who's managed to make his run,
Prisoner-like, I, too, never had a bit of fun,
   While love in me did move,
    I sat in a deep groove
      Worried under moon or sun.

Freely I rejoice in every kind of happy game,
Nobody sees sadness, when they call my merry name,
   Reason is I have quit —
    Now I live by my wit
      don't shine up to ladies' fame.

Happily I soar now, like a falcon who's been freed
From his yellow harness, feet and wings can try to speed,
   I'm no longer in pain,
    Since I've broken love's chain
      Love I did forsake indeed.

Only things I need now are a good horse and a hound;
Good company; sharp sword; falcon from my wrist unbound —
    Drink with soldiers dashing
    I wouldn't mind smashing
        Empty goblets to the ground.

All the maidens, virgins, may now come and ogle me,
But what all they'll get now is whatever it may be —
    Their coy love, or good will,
    Schemes supreme or evil
        Just won't cast me out to sea.

Let the young and old folk understand and learn from me,
How tormented lovers can in hellish sickness be;
    Sometimes I would be glad,
    Mostly they drove me mad,
        I was worried constantly!

Let this counsel save you from love's cruel misery
If you're smart enough to live your life out quietly,
    Those who follow love's way
    They will very soon pray
        For riddance from usury.

I've composed these lines with tune alert and easy drone.
I'm off now to meet some brave chaps of my very own.
    Good young men, such as I,
    Hungry looks in their eye,
        Not old wrecks who cough and moan.

Joseph Leftwich [& A.M.]

HE PLEADS FOR FORGIVENESS
BEFORE HIS INTENDED MARRIAGE

Bless me with forgiveness, Lord, for all my sins of youth,
all my doubts, my misdeeds, my betrayals of Thy truth,
    wipe out my transgressions, ugliness and falsehood,
        ease from my soul its grave load!

As a bird is drifting, tossed and pummelled by the storm,
thus my restless spirit wanders through my earthly form,
    so greatly fearing Thee, dreading to look at Thee,
            prone to perish in alarm.

Listing the many boons Thou hast bestowed upon me,
for which, Lord, I have not given equal quittancy,
    seeing my selfishness, falsehood, and foolishness,
            I loathe myself bitterly.

No matter how often I would wish to pray to Thee,
because of my sins I fear to make approach to Thee,
    heavily my sins weigh, thus I lost my true way,
            Lord, I fear Thy face to see.

So, quite like a beggar, I have naught to offer Thee,
nothing in return for all Thy good deeds done for me,
    naught this poor sinner hath to soften Thy great wrath
            to arouse Thy great mercy.

So many temptations terrify my very thought,
forcing me through fear into impiety and doubt.
    Unless Thou shouldst save me, I shall perish gravely,
            I shall drop into the pit.

Tortured, I keep calling often on Thy Holy name.
I say "if God only would have pity on my shame,
    I would sin no longer but follow Him yonder
            who, to save me, man became."

Do encourage, therefore, Lord, Thy servant, shield his side,
for how wouldst Thou profit if, condemned to hell, I died?
    Let me praise Thee, rather while alive, and gather
            grateful thanks — be glorified!

As soon as I hear Thy answering word, I do know
I shall cry Thy Great Name in a great and loud 'hallo!'
    with my arms spread cross-like, eyes with tears filled, pond-like,
            on my knees myself I throw.

Cascading, my tears flow, as I plead my case with Thee,
surely, Thou hast pity, and wilt my repentance see —
    as in great convulsion I conduct repulsion
        of my sins, and beg mercy.

The more Thou forgivest, the more pleasing Thy great peace.
The more Thou forgettest, the more freeing is Thy space.
    How couldst Thou be gracious if we weren't so vicious?
        In our sins lieth Thy grace![1]

Thou wilt not persist in — I know now — Thy righteous wrath.
Stretched out is Thy right hand, sign of peace its gesture hath.
    Thou seest those mostly, who seek Thee devoutly,
        for Thou art the Primal Word.

Therefore, my soul, do turn to God merciful today,
Answer to His calling — He loveth us all, alway!
    Listen to His wording, answer thou His calling —
        submit thyself to His way!

Let us, therefore, all put all our trust in Him alone!
Let us conquer sin, and from Him be no longer gone!
    let His Name be blessèd, in the Heavens sacred,
        for He doth let us atone.

I have sung these verses with my sore heart, bittermost,
awaiting God's mercy, to come with the Holy Ghost —
    languishing and hiding, guilty-sore, a-pining,
        wrestling with the Devil's host.

Joseph Leftwich [& A.M.]

---

[1] It is noteworthy that Balassi's rather long and sincere confession of his "sins and inadequacies" has a markedly Renaissance twist to it. The logic of their argumentation: man's sins serve a purpose, because it is God's pleasure to forgive us. This is the voice of Benvenuto Cellini.

Count Miklós Zrinyi
1620-1664

A. Borsa
'72

Miklós Zrínyi
(1620-1664)

The great-grandson of Count Miklós Zrínyi the First, who died a hero's death while defending a fortress against the Turks in the 16th century, and the scion of a great Hungarian-Croatian noble family, Miklós, the younger, was educated by Péter Pázmány, Roman Catholic Archbishop and leader of the Hungarian Counter-Reformation.

After his early education in Vienna, he visited Italy where he became familiar with Machiavelli's work; then he returned to Hungary to pursue a military career. Constantly engaged in fighting the Turks, he rose to the rank of general and built his own fortress, Új-Zerinvár [New Zerin Castle] in 1661. Besides his lyric poetry and his long narrative epic, Zrínyi also wrote prose treatises such as The Antidote to Turkish Opium [A török áfium ellen való orvosság] *in which he advocated self-reliance for the Hungarian nation in their struggle against the expansion of Turkish imperialism. In a sharp essay he criticized General Raimondo Montecuccoli, the Imperial commander, who was not a great soldier, because Montecuccoli would not attack but kept on marching in "parallel columns".[1] Zrínyi's own biography, an anonymous compilation, was published in English in London in the spring of 1664.*

Zrínyi composed his poetic epic The Siege of Sziget *or* Obsidio Szigetiana, *also known as the Zrínyiad of Sziget, in which he erected an enduring poetic monument to his great ancestor. In early 1664 he conducted a long and successful campaign, but later that same year he was accidentally killed during a boar-hunt. His lyric poetry was gathered in a cycle entitled* The Siren of the Adriatic [Az Adriai tengernek Syrenaia]. *In it he became the first Hungarian poet to publish his love poetry. Zrínyi's significance is twofold: he was a multicultural and bilingual politician and general whose career presaged a United Europe; his political and military treatises had an obvious pan-European significance. As a poet he joins the ranks of Balassi and Petőfi (qq.v.) who were, like Zrínyi, 'poet warriors' fighting for Hungary's survival.*

---

[1] Raimondo Montecuccoli (1609-1680) was an Austrian general of Italian descent. Zrínyi blamed him for the loss of Transylvania. This gave rise to a Hungarian saying characterizing hesitancy and the inability or unwillingness to act: "He is marching in parallel columns like Montecuccoli."

ELEGY

The outworn year has altered his apparel,
Winter has turned to spring, serene and warm.
The earth grows fresh, the forest sings its carol
As lovely song-birds in the branches swarm.

The nightingale, in outbursts of lamenting,
Mourns her bereavement in the ancient days —
No self-absorbing grief is she presenting
But thanks to God, to whom she looks and prays.

Alas, her song has touched my spring with sorrow,
Hanging good fortune into winter's chills;
My eyes are flooded with a rainy morrow,
with icy floes of grief my spirit fills.

Oh, little nightingale, my matchless chanter,
Why does your form so suddenly depart?
My own song, having laughed in pleasant banter,
Now flies and leaves a shadow in my heart.

It once had framed a future for my longing
And many times redeemed my erring hand,
Repulsing all the tempests that were wronging
My efforts for my failing fatherland.

I sought to trumpet forth Hungarian valour,
To sing our land's invincible right arm,
To check forever any hint of pallor,
And by my verse to exorcise all harm.

Oh, fairest nightingale, Death's envious power
With ruthless scythe has reaped from out my breast
My little Izsák, who was a flower.
He goes, alas, too early to his rest.

Watson Kirkconnell

IDYLL
(Extract)

Early in the spring-time a huntsman full of sorrow
once did equip himself with a light bow and arrow,
and a swift-footed hart through paths trackless and narrow
in Drava's deep forest for long in vain did follow.

At last from this vain chase exhausted he did see
not far away from a large uprooted poplar tree,
and sitting down believed that he surely could be
at rest with his body, peaceful and sorrow-free.

But he couldn't find any rest because of Cupid's bow,
who sat down next to him and said: "To India I go,
or, if you will, fly to wild Libya — and lo!
in all climes you will see the force of my dart-blow,

beyond Iceland, or where Tanais' waters glide,
or if Atlas fling wide Earth's bowels, there inside
just as the hart you shoot, its bleeding wounds does hide,
you shall feel everywhere my arrow in your side."

Thus spoke Cupid, and what he said was, alas, right,
for at all times the coals of Love in him burnt bright —
when the New Year was young, when it passed out of sight,
in every season Love in his poor heart did fight.

René Bonnerjea

THE ZRINYIAD
(Extract)

INVOCATION

I, who in times before, with youthful mind
my pleasure in the poems of sweet love would find,
and battled with Viola's depriving cruelty
would sing this time a louder, martial poetry

of weapons and men, the might of the Turks I sing,
of him, who bravely faced the Sultan, expecting
the wrath of the arms of the great ruler Suliman,
who all over Europe held in terror the hearts of men.

Muse of mine! You won't wear a laurel on your brow
made of withering green, or out of a tree's bough:
but one that was made out of the stars of heaven
of moonlight and sunrays a beautiful crown;

you, who are a virgin yet gave birth to the Lord
He, who had existed, is, and shall be adored
by you as your own God and your powerful King —
Saintly Queen! Your mercy I am now invoking!

Give strength to my pen to describe what took place,
to relate his story who has died in God's grace,
having discarded all his earthly possessions
kept his soul alive, though his body became ashes.

Wherever the sun rises, may his name
exalted be! And let them see, the heathen dogs,
that he who fears the Lord can never die,
but shall eternal heav'nly life achieve.

Thomas Kabdebo [& A.M.]

THE SORTIE[2]

Zrínyi, who knew well that his life's end was nearing,
surrounded himself with five hundred brave soldiers
cannons overwhelmed them, the great fort was burning,
but by breaking siege-lock they took the offensive.

Though he left the castle he built one in his heart,
Turkish army ranks where he turned did fall apart,
he stopped in the market, destruction in his eyes
measuring up the foe as quietly he tries.

Like a savage lion emerging from its den
or a terrifying comet up in heaven,
bringing down destruction local and country-wide
carrying a horrible future like the tide.

Just like a wildfire biting at the rushes
in the form of swift death on the Turks he rushes,
like a flooded river pouring down the mountain
Zrínyi, from top to toe, is clad in destruction.

Thomas Kabdebo [& A.M.]

EPILOGUE

My monument is done, my task is ended,
that steel nor covetious Time shall overthrow;
fire shall not spoil, nor Heaven's wrath offend it,
nor Envy, the great enemy, bring it low.

---

[2] Known as 'Zrínyi kirohanása' ['Zrínyi's Dashing Escape'], the phrase
is quoted to this day when someone suddenly gets up and leaves.

The day that dawns to claim my mortal heart
shall spend its might upon my flesh, and die.
Then, as it fades away, my nobler part
shall sweep upon the wind towards the sky.

As long as time endures, my name shall sound
in distant Scythia, whence the Magyars came,
in all lands where their exploits still resound,
to men who know their honour and their fame.

I have earned fame not only with my song
but also with this warrior's sword men dread —
I battled with the Turk my whole life long,
and joyed to strew my homeland with their dead.

Michael Hatwell

István Gyöngyösi
(1629-1704)

One of the best known epic poets of the seventeenth century, Gyöngyösi was born into the a family of the lesser gentry. He studied in the famous college of Sárospatak, under the guidance of the Moravian Protestant pedagogue and humanist, Johannes Amos Comenius (1592-1670). Gyöngyösi served during his long life a number of wealthy Hungarian aristocrats, among them the famous Miklós Wesselényi and his second wife, Mária Széchy, as their personal secretary and legal adviser. Though a lesser talent than Miklós Zrínyi (q.v.), his popularity overshadowed the warrior-poet during his life-time and for many decades afterwards. His rich baroque language is full of classical allusions, not always properly integrated into the story.

His main work was a narrative poem describing the Wesselényi-Széchy romance with elaborate allegories, entitled A Márssal Társalkodó Murányi Vénus [Venus of Murány Conversing with Mars]. *It is the story of an adventurous marriage and the occupation of the Castle of Murány in 1644, and at the time it served a definite political purpose.*

He had great skill in handling the heavy Hungarian four-line stanza with its single rhyme.

THE BEAUTY OF ILONA ZRÍNYI

It may be true that she has passed her spring,
But summer decks her with rich colouring,
Such as with Dido claims comparison
When she the favour of Aeneas won.
      Her cheek's a rose, her throat is alabaster,
      Her charming presence makes the heart beat faster,
      Her gentle speech is like a cordial,
      Her godly life would grace a convent-hall.
Her brow's a lily, and her choral lip
The grace of Spartan Helen's might outstrip.
Such flowers should not droop in loneliness —
'Twere meet your dewy kiss made haste to bless.

A cedar is her waist, her glance a hawk's;
Her foot in hunting like Diana's stalks;
Grave in their tasks her patient days await
No common noble but a royal mate.
A swan in body, in deport a dove,
Mild as a turtle to its mate in love;
Sharp as a heron should the case require,
Yet no proud thoughts her quiet ways inspire.
It seems as if where'er her feet may stray,
Sweet flowers in her footprints blossom straightway;
And one might swear such in her speech's worth,
That all her words breathed honey's sweetness forth.
So rare her lips, when they glad words are making,
It seems as if the rosy down were breaking;
While her bright self, to the enraptured eye,
Moves the risen sun that mounts the sky.

Watson Kirkconnell

JÁNOS KEMÉNY
(Extract)

The day is done; the twilight grows more dark;
across the heavy sky the eye can mark
wild fantasies of fire as if the stark
great smiths of Etna smote an anvil-spark.
Their every stroke strikes out a comet's tail,
the sparks from off the anvil leap like hail,
or dance like gnomes of flame that numbly flail
a fire with the frenzy of a gale.
The glowing iron glistens in its place,
the smitten anvil trembles to its base
as ponderous sledges clang upon its face
and massive welded patterns grow apace.
At last the knot of iron has been tied,
and deep in hissing water certified;
the task is done, the sledge is laid aside,
and sweating brows and necks are wiped and dried.

Watson Kirkconnell

Kata Szidónia Petrőczy

(1662-1708)

The daughter of Baron István Petrőczy, an influential Lutheran aristocrat who was involved in the Hungarian Independence Movement of Count Ferenc Wesselényi (1605-1667) against Austria, Kata had to live with her father in exile in Poland until she became eighteen years of age. There she married the Hungarian land owner Lőrinc Pekry with whom she returned to Hungary and settled in Ózd, Transylvania.

In 1680 Lőrinc Pekry left Kata, joined Emperor Leopold of Austria, and embraced Catholicism. This won him the rank of a baron and later even a counthood. Meanwhile the unhappy couple had eleven children, of which six died. Lamenting over her husband's political, religious, and marital infidelity as well as mourning for her dead children, Kata secretly wrote sorrowful melancholy poems. In 1690 she published the Hungarian translation of a German book dealing with religious polemic entitled Pápista vallásra hajlott Lutheránusok lelkek isméretének kinnya [The Misery of the Conscience of Lutherans Gone Catholic]; *she financed the entire operation by herself.*

At this point her fickle husband returned from Austria and became the Bailiff of Udvarhely. He was then captured by the anti-Austrian freedom fighters of Prince Ferenc Rákóczi II, and, reneging on his pro-Austrian stance, swiftly joined up with them. The French mercenary general J.L. Rabutin de Bussy, however, who fought on the Austrian side, captured the treasonous Pekry. Further saddened, Kata wrote more lamenting poetry grieving for her husband in 1705; she also translated poetry from German and Latin.

In 1708 she translated from German a book entitled Jó illattal füstölgő igaz szív [The True Heart Emanating Good Frankincense], *dealing with religion. She was proud of her work as a translator and commented on her own work in the prefaces to these works. Her own poems, however, which were a well kept secret, were not found until 1864; there were forty-five of them in her handwriting. They deal with her miserable marriage and her search for religious comfort; she had never intended to publish them.*

Her knowledge of theology was as amazingly comprehensive as the purity and expressive power of her language. She is acknowledged as the first significant Hungarian poetess. The first complete edition of her poetry appeared in 1915 entitled Petrőczy Kata Szidónia Versei [The Poetry of Kata Szidónia Petrőczy].

LIGHT OF OUR SOULS

Light of our souls, to you we call,
Good Shepherd of your sheep —
Look down on us with kindly eye,
Our lives are in your keep.
    We turn to you with heavy hearts,
    For help from you, we plead;
    Come, intercede in our defense,
    Most urgent is our need.
Your wrath has fallen on our sins,
Our attitudes displease;
A foreign nation, ruling us,
Has brought us to our knees.
    For like the Jews once had to bear
    The dread Egyptian yoke,
    So now we are enslaved, because
    Your anger we evoke.
They devastate our country sweet,
They rob us like a thief;
They mock our sorrows at our loss,
And ridicule our grief.
    They persecute our very souls,
    Our worship they upset;
    Pursuing us from place to place —
    Oh, we are sore beset.
In secrecy we gather here,
On worship we are bent;
Oh, let your hand protect us now,
And let your heart relent.
    They will continue to harass,
    Our faith they will destroy;
    And to compel us to obey,
    Armed force they will employ.
Resistance is of no avail —
To exile we are sent;
Like beggars we are driven off —
Oh death is our torment.

You know the evil in their hearts,
How loathsome is their aim —
They are upon destruction bent,
Our land they would defame.
Destroy their vicious councils, Lord,
Annihilate their power;
So black are their intentions, that
In misery we cower.
Restore us in your Holy Name,
For merits of Your Son!
And let the goodness of your heart
Cause justice to be done.
We pray Your Gospel will be preached
Among us evermore;
Our hearts be purified by faith,
That God we may adore.
Permit our children to behold
The true and holy light;
That they may nurture in their hearts
The knowledge that is right.
That they may worship holiness,
And ever understand
To follow it with a pure heart —
Protect them with your hand!
One day, in Heaven's Great Beyond,
Among your faithful crew —
Together we will sing your praise,
And worship you anew.

Marie B. Jaffe

RAPID FLOODS

Of rapid floods and cruel winds,
I hear the constant roar;
The anguish in my aching heart,
The eyes that ever pour
Their tears, at grief that now prevails,
And that which is in store.

For ceaselessly, from day to day,
Increase the winds of sorrow;
They wound the heart, and teach the mind
More misery to borrow;
Devouring with persistency
Each vainly-dawning morrow.

Already drained of every hope,
Acquainted with much pain,
The sorrow-laden days and nights
Arrive for me in vain;
There is no remedy in store,
It's useless to complain.

And all this pining of the heart,
This overwhelming grief,
Discourages the few who might
Bring pity and relief;
Of no avail their sympathy,
And mercifully brief.

Therefore, with prayers fortified,
Resigned to meet my fate,
I wish to leave this wretched life,
My miseries abate;
I am prepared to meet my God —
No longer need I wait.

To ease my sorrow, death would be
A blessing and a boon;
It would alleviate my grief,
With peace my heart attune;
And dry the ever-flowing tears —
With love I would commune.

Marie B. Jaffe

IV. ANONYMOUS 'KURUC' AND PATRIOTIC POETRY OF THE EIGHTEENTH CENTURY

Kuruc Poetry
(18th century)

The so-called "kuruc" *[pronounceable as KOO-roots] were a class of rugged freedom-fighters between 1670 and 1710 and after, supporters of Prince Ferenc Rákóczi II in Transylvania's Freedom War against the Habsburg Dynasty. Those who fought on the opposite side were called the* labanc, *[pronounceable as LAW-bonts]. It was believed for a while that the word* kuruc *originated from the word for 'crusader,' but etymological research proved this wrong. The word remains of unknown origin; the Czech language in which it also occurs borrowed it from Hungarian.*

Broadly speaking, the term "kuruc poetry" includes poems of local and national resistance, from all walks of life, in the period mentioned. Soldiers' songs, exhortations, laments, and recruiting songs are the forerunners of the proper "kuruc poems," while the era closes with verses of resistance and pro-test songs by nameless members of the Hungarian nobility.

When the Turks departed, the Austrians took over, and this change is reflected in the poetry of this age: its central theme, the love of independence remains, and so does the misery of fighting for it, alone, abandoned, in need of good weapons and bright hopes, although the enemy's identity has changed. Real "kuruc poetry" started at the time of General Thököly, stepfather of Ferenc Rákóczi. In the early kuruc poems, the ember of optimism barely glimmered, but when Rákóczi's sun was at its zenith and his troops were victorious against those of the Emperor's generals, the poems burst with life. Accompanied by the trumpet, the drum and the tárogató *[an oboe-like musical instrument], the kuruc poems inspired, teased, and lamented in turn. When Rákóczi was finally defeated and betrayed, the poems became full of lament and sorrow, keeping alive just a ray of hope that the prince might return from exile. In the heyday of the kuruc era, the poems circulated in hand-written, single copies or in song-books. In the 19th century most of them were printed and became so popular that fakes were produced by minor poets. The style lends itself to imitation: Kálmán Thaly successfully mislead the public until qualified linguists unmasked and exposed his "discoveries." The notion of this kind of poetry was so deeply ingrained in public consciousness in Hungary that one of the greatest poets of the Hungarian language, Endre Ady (q.v.), deliberately wrote kuruc poems.*

Many of the original kuruc poems have become folk songs and are still sung by partying Hungarians the world over, accompanied by demijohns of wine.

MILITARIS CANTIO

All hazards of the field
I dared to face for fame
— not mine but Hungary's —
fought fiercely in her name.

Untarnished honour, arms
bright, and unbroken will,
my fame and fine renown
are at her service still.

Courageous at the head
of my courageous men,
against the pagan Turk
I led my army then.

Now I am left alone,
and left alone, I weep.
My constant prayers arise
out of a dungeon deep.

And Fortune, having set
a price upon my head,
delights that I now stand
in peril of my head.

This endless war goes on
and sorrow eats me up —
poor and a stranger now
I drink from danger's cup.

Where shall I see again
all those who hold me dear?
Who knows where we shall meet
and who can tell the year?

Had I the magic art
I'd vanish from this place

and fly to greet my love
and kiss her flower-like face.

My jealous enemies,
exultant in their rage,
rejoice that I am caught
in this accursed cage.

Well, let them so rejoice
if only God will guide
and bless me on the road
that I again would ride.

In Castle Fogaras[1]
beside the river Olt
a young man wrote this song
confined by lock and bolt.

And setting down his name
he called to God in prayer
asking that God's good grace
protect him everywhere.

Matthew Mead

WITH TEARS A-FLOWING

With tears a-flowing I sign
This sad letter of mine;
At home will you still find
Sorrow for my decline?

If you asked how am I,
If I live or die?
Tell them in reply
That every day I cry.

In stables' dust I've lain
Impatient, torn in twain
Clothing ragged, frayed,
Hunger was my fate.

Thus grows my misery,
Tears are my destiny,
Grief is consuming me
Daily, unceasingly.

---

[1] Today *Făgăraş* in Romania, this castle used to be the favorite residence of the Princes of Transylvania.

I long for my home and
For my mother's hand,
For my sweet homeland
And many a true friend.

The anger of a foe
Exiled me from my home
So many years ago —
To live a life of woe.

In places far and strange
To unknown lands I came,
With ill-luck on the way
A pauper I became.

Oh, dear God Almighty
Behold! My own country
Shows no trace of pity;
I pray Thou standest by me.

A mortal enemy
Threatens, surrounds me,
All are against me —
My last hope is in Thee.

The hilltops and valleys,
The towns and villages,
The woods and green fields,
Are full of enemies.

John P. Sadler

THE VERSES OF A TRUE HUNGARIAN PATRIOT

Awake, O Magyar nation, and open wide your eyes,
long you have been asleep, your interests now apprise!
The star of your good fortune has risen from the night —
the day of your past freedom has come again in sight.
Now the time's at hand when you must needs endeavour
today and for the future your German bonds to sever.
If this time again the Germans keep you under,
if you should fall victim to their lies and plunder,
never will you stand up free and independent,
but will stay forever crushed down and repentent.
Have no faith in Germans — they'll forever hate you
for your fame and glory, they can but berate you.

They will promise honey, but put poison in it.
if they could, they'd strangle you this very minute.
It is not without cause Germans are called tricky,
deceitful in their ways, trying to be sneaky.
They flatter you today, fawn, and wag their tail,
but will bite in you in the back tomorrow, without fail.

And so if you today a German ruler crown,
the heavy German yoke on you he'll soon press down.

Call me, then, a dog if what I say's not true —
he who believes a German, at leisure it shall rue!
If you feel, however, that you still wish to stay
in the Germans' hands, and under Germans' sway,
here's your chance to take a tight hold of their bit,
and, of crushing our land, to break their old habit!
I fervently implore you, hear you my entreaty —
you can keep them down with the following treaty:

(1)   Andrew the Second's law[2] establish and restore,
    and you will retain all your rights of yore —
    if the King enacts a law repugnant to our land,
    any Magyar may rise up with sword in his hand.
    This law of King Andrew's was a most useful thing,
    the Covenant of Faith 'tween country and the king.
    When it was abolished, your country lost its might,
    and your brightest liberty fell into darkest night.
    So many patriots have died for our liberty
    slain at vicious German hands, like Zrínyi and Nádasdi.[3]

(2)   The wealth of Hungary must be in your deposit,
    and without your knowledge the King must not take of it.
    All the money the king spends should come from his treasure,
    out of which he can live well and spend at his pleasure.

(3)   Our military forces should your command obey,
    and only after you decide, should it march or stay.
    All the army Generals should be Magyars only;
    in their number foreigners should be denied entry.

---

[2] Reference to King András II's Golden Bull of 1222, a royal charter which allowed the Hungarians to resist with arms any illegal acts of their king, and which formed part of Hungary's constitution until 1848.

[3] The names of members of the nobility who were executed in 1671 for conspiracy against the Habsburgs.

(4)   All the functions, offices, and posts of Magyarland
       at all times, and forever, should be in Magyar hands.

(5)   From the land of Hungary the Germans should clear out,
       we want no *ober, unter,* or *hinter* here about!

(6)   Let the King of Hungary in Hungary settle down;
       in Buda, not Wien, he'll get the Holy Crown.

(7)   He should speak Magyar well, not need interpretation,
       to Hungarians he should speak the language of our nation.

(8)   In the land of Hungary, the law should only be
       written in the Magyar tongue, throughout Hungary.

(9)   What the King has promised, we can from him demand;
       let him pledge you his word and give to you his hand.

(10)   Let the King be first to proffer you his troth,
       and the Magyars then, in turn, will pledge oath for oath.[4]

There are so many other abuses which have crept
into the rule of Hungary while most of you have slept!
To those, to, very soon, my words I will apply
and give you many reasons those evils to decry.
I'll put them down on paper as with these I have done,
and then before your eyes I'll place them, one by one.
And seeing them will make you open up your eyes
and then you'll be inspired to fight these German lies.

René Bonnerjea and *Earl M. Herrick*

---

[4] While not one of the 'kuruc' poems per se, this poem, which was also written by an anonymous 18th century author, offers a fine example of the literature of the movement known as THE RESISTANCE OF THE NOBILITY AGAINST THE HABSBURGS. The resistance had its historical justification in the ancient law of King András II, hence the reference to him above.

THE EXILE OF RÁKÓCZI

Upon the walls of Munkács[4]
Stood Rákóczi in pain,
And leaning on his hilted sword,
Yes, leaning on his hilted sword,
He cried to his kettle-drummer
And spoke in grief profane:
    "My drummer, O my drummer,
    Young drummer of my court,
    Harken to what I have to say:
    Don't beat your drum for 'March' today!
    Attack's the right retort!
    The devil skin your mother!
    The devil damn you black!
    Don't beat your drum that foolish way,
    Nor as you did before today,
    But beat it thus and let it say:
    'Attack! Attack! Attack!'
"Beat, that the earth may tremble
And skies may echo back,
That he who lives may hear it,
And every slumbering spirit
Wake from the dead to cheer it:
Attack! Attack! Attack!
O Bercsényi[5] and Bottyán,
Bold chiefs in bivouac,
Bezerédi and Pekry,
Whoever are my soldiers,
Come to the last great battle —
Attack! Attack! Attack!"
    A deathlike fog and heavy
    Screens everything from sight.

---

[4] An old Hungarian city, today in the Republic of the Ukraine, called Munkačevo.

[5] Bercsényi, Bezerédy, Bóné, Bottyán, Esze, Károlyi, Kemény, Majthényi, Ocskai, and Pekry, mentioned by name in these poems, were the better known noble officers and common soldiers in Prince Rákóczi's army.

Better he cannot see it,
His great heart could not dream it, —
Perchance 'twould break outright.
The drummer now may beat Attack
The great Chief urged them fast;
That Kuruc camp he calls to aid,
In meadows of Majthényi laid —
Poor Kuruc camp, so ill betrayed —
Has struck its flag at last...
"Ho, Alexander Károlyi!
Speak, Károlyi, you scamp!
What fate has overtaken
My splendid Kuruc camp?
Tell me what has become of it:
The truth I must be told.
Give me your answer without sloth
Upon your seven times sworn oath!
Confess your treason, nothing loath:
Your master you have sold!
But things will surely go with you
As they with Judas went:
My loyal knights' posterity
Revenge on you will vent;
Great Bóné's sons, and Esze's too,
Towards you will not relent!
            "I ask not for my homeland.
            Forth in the world I'll stray.
            I know too well the bitter truth
            That I must go away.
            My smith! My court smith! Come and turn
            My brown steed's shoes for me,
            Changing the front shoes for the back,
            That he seek not the homeward track,
            And I, in truth, shall not come back
            To lovely Hungary!
"Hungarians and Széklers,
Folk of my countries twain,
Heroic souls that love me,
God bless you once again!
Patak, may God be with you!

The German rules you know,
God save you, Munkács, ne'er I'll see
Thy fort I love so tenderly
In this sweet land, my Hungary,
For ever more, I vow!
       "The time some day is coming,
       Poor land that knaves devour,
       When you will curse the bitterness
       Of this unhappy hour!
       The alien yoke is heavy,
       You'll feel it through the years —
       And grieve for chiefs misunderstood,
       Your leaders born of Magyar blood,
       And mourn us with your tears.
"But Hungary now loves me,
And Transylvania, too,
Pities and grieves for me till death;
Even their children's faithful breath
Will wish for me anew!
When I have long departed,
You'll sigh me back once more;
When I have long been dead, I trust,
You'll mourn me, and bring home my dust.
And gather up my crumbling bones
To bear them to this shore!
       "But where the ocean bellows,
       And where the far winds blow,
       And where the stars go falling —
       An exile now I go."
The kettle-drum sounds sadly.
The Leader turns his back.
No more it throbs in ardour:
"Attack! Attack! Attack!"
Far off its beat comes faintly
With sobs that slowly die:
"O Hungary that gave me birth,
Most hapless land in all the earth
Good-bye! Good-bye! Good-bye!"

Watson Kirkconnell

AUTUMN 1710

Autumn winds descend and sweep
From the frozen mountain-steep
Down to dewy hollows, down to dewy hollows:
My red boot its track has made
In the forests' dewy glade,
Where the winter follows,
Where the winter follows.
       Vanished now are joy's old days,
       Changed, how changed are all my ways!
       Now my lot is sorrow,
       Now my lot is sorrow.
       As a wanderer must I plod
       Far from home; my gracious God
       Guide my steps tomorrow,
       Guide my steps tomorrow!
Stars above me march on high,
Winds are wailing, cloud-wraiths fly —
Upwards still I'm pressing.
Upwards still I'm pressing.
If all men forsake or hurt me,
God Himself will not desert me!
I invoke His blessing,
I invoke His blessing!

Watson Kirkconnell

O, MAGYAR

O, Magyar, think no German true;
No matter how he flatters you:
For though his promises invoke
A letter bigger than your cloak,

And though he add (the big poltroon!)
A seal to match the harvest moon,
You may be sure he means not well —
May Heaven blast his soul to hell!

Watson Kirkconnell

V. POETS
OF THE
HUNGARIAN
ENLIGHTENMENT

Ferenc Faludi
(1704-1779)

Born into a family of country squires, Faludi, who became a Jesuit priest and a brilliant teacher, presided over various educational institutions both in Hungary and in Austria. He spoke native-like German. After the dissolution of his order, he became the director of a poorhouse. He was an accomplished translator and also a pioneer collector of folk poetry. He made frequent trips to various villages to observe the local dialect; he kept detailed notes on how the peasants spoke. He was the first to transcribe the Funeral Oration *(q.v.), considered the first Old Hungarian text. Among other translations, he also published a narrated story-version of Shakespeare's* The Tempest.

His own poems have a happy, musical quality, with a touch of the Italian Rococo. He experimented with various metric forms and holds the distinction of having written the first Hungarian sonnet.

SPRING

Regal is the pleasure, afoot, threading the trees
and ambling down the shadow-dashed alleys at your ease;
    in singing of the nightingale
    and sighings of a gentle gale
        to find joy, and to live
        in pleasures it can give;
to rouse up from the bush the hare scarce waked from rest
and unawares to start the fledglings from their nest;
    to go about by dale and hill
    to watch the freshet's basin fill;
        then home at noon to feed
        as much as one could need;
to hang dark cares high up, on a high nail under the slates,
with glad and careful relish eating the furnished cates
    but not to surfeit, nor to scant
    light-hearted talk as condiment;
        to take wine, and protest
        that clear spring-water's best;

to lean upon your elbow, after meat and drink,
and into thirty minutes dreamless slumber sink;
     and then, the freshened body freed
     from wanting sleep, and other need,
          to make the large ball bound
          and vie the clock around;
than at Diana's court anew to make your bow
and find the tented shade of it as pleasing now;
     to try the cuckoo's lucky throw
     upon her future, and to go
          with echo to exchange
          jests with a mountain-range.
The pigeons making moan, the finch's cry from the bush,
the penetrating whistle of the sportive thrush;
     the calling stock-doves' need to pair,
     a seeking sorrow in the air;
          to see, to hear no less,
          your only busy-ness!
From forest shadows on open fallows to debouch
and mark the sun's wain sinking as he seeks his couch;
     to loiter on the shepherd's way
     harkening to his artless lay,
          Corydon's pipe to heed
          and Mopsus' various reed;
to have the curved horn call you, from the porch of home,
post-prandially rejoicing then till bedtime come —
     friend, you have made th' experiment,
          regal the pleasure is,
          harmless the revelries.

Donald Davie

FICKLE FORTUNE

Ride Fortune's chariot with care and doubt.
Watch well her axle, lest you tumble out.
Ride Fortune's chariot with care devout:
     Should she sometimes be kind,
     With courses fair inclined,
          Let joy not shout! —

Ride Fortune's chariot with care and doubt!
Her favours and her wheels revolve together;
Both fast and loose. Today she brings you treasure;
      Tomorrow brings you pain;
      Then makes you whole again.
         Trust me, it's plain:

Her favours and her wheel revolve together.
Most impudently blind to human worth;
One day she showers gold, the next day dearth.
      They know her wanton sports
      Who in her camps and courts
         Endure her mirth,

Most impudently blind to human worth.
Now like a mother, now a vicious bitch,
Whom nobody's permitted to reproach,
      She lauds, puts to the blush,
      Praises, drags you through slush,
         Makes you a wretch:

Now like a mother,
now a vicious bitch.

J.G. Nichols, Watson Kirkconnell [& A.M.]

UNSPEAKABLE

A spinster near Gyöngyös displays
an ugly wart upon her face;
her skin is shrivelled and criss-crossed;
and all her hair a mass of frost:
      ugly, terrifying thing!

Inside her mouth three teeth stand guard —
her watery mush is barely chewed;
foul mouth and belly run together;
her lungs are rotten with her liver:
      every part is perishing.

Since her old tongue is always prattling,
her rusty throat is always rattling;
she's always twitching at the waist;
her rheumy eye can never rest;
        and her hands are quivering.

While she was still fed at the breast
she cried out for a taste of sex;
while dad was still a stranger to her
Venus's little bastard knew her
        stricken with love's burning sting.

She grew to be so lickerish
her tongue would lick round any dish;
yes, anyone her wandering eyes
fastened upon she clung to, as
        honeycombs round honey cling.

Much fondling's worn her neck away,
much kissing caused her lips to fray,
and yet the ashes of her heart
are still transfixed by Cupid's dart;
        the old pot's still simmering.

Pandering to her own desire,
she hoists her breasts a little higher
and, having done her best to draw in
her ugly bottom, wriggles, pawing
        at the ground and whinnying.

She simply can't leave it alone;
but still the old grey ashes burn.
Oh, when your master comes, he'll beat
you, too-much married, milkless goat,
        beat you hard until you sing!

                                        J.G. Nichols

József Gvadányi
(1725-1801)

Born into a noble family of Italian origin (the family name was Guadagni), József Gvadányi was educated in Eger and later studied philosophy at the University of Nagyszombat (today Trnava in the Slovak Republic). He early showed a talent for classical Latin forms. He served in the War of the Austrian Succession (1740-1748) in the Austrian army, first in Moravia and later in Italy where he was seriously wounded and captured by the French. After his release, during the brief interval of peace, he married and, in 1756, was drafted again into the army and fought throughout the Seven Years' War.

Gvadányi's military exploits were so audacious that the Prussian Commander-in-Chief, anxious to capture him, set a reward of a hundred gold pieces on his head. He retired in 1783 with the rank of Major General.

Gvadányi was in close contact with the writers of his age, and embarked on a literary career with occasional verses. A long narrative poem, A Village Notary's Journey to Buda *[Egy falusi nótáriusnak budai utazása], which appeared anonymously in 1790, contrasted a naive provincial hero and the urban sophistication of the Hungarian capital. His hero sets out for Buda in order to study the public policies of Emperor Joseph II. Part one depicts the vicissitudes of the notary on his trip. It is always the simple people who rescue him from trouble. In part two, however, he becomes the mouth-piece of Gvadányi himself and passes judgment on contemporary morality. He finds the chief source of trouble not in the political oppression of the day but in the people's tendency to ape foreign customs. Both János Arany and Sándor Petőfi (qq.v.) praised Gvadányi's attempts at purifying the language and his ability to strike a chord of popular sentiment. Gvadányi's language is simple and expressive, and his earthy humor won him many devoted readers. In the 19th century this story was adapted for the stage by József Gaál (1811-1866).*

Although Gvadányi lived during the age of the Enlightenment, he remained fearful of its main ideas, especially because he thought that it would usher in atheism. In 1791 he wrote a satirical poem about the Hungarian Diet in Pozsony (today Bratislava in the Slovak Republic). He also translated Voltaire's biography of Charles XII of Sweden.

ON THE DRESS OF THE HUNGARIANS
(Excerpt from A Village Notary's Journey to Buda)

I thought to view the comeliness
of freely chosen Magyar dress,
of scarlet velvets without flaw
and sables from Siberia.

I looked for capes, for cloaks of fur,
for trousers fine from belt to spur,
new girdles gay with golden threads
and sable calpacks on their heads.

Red riding-boots should grace their shins,
their backs be hung with leopard skins,
their caps be plumed, while greet the ears
their jingling jewelled bandoliers.

I thought: their long hair graceful flies,
while sabre-scabbards smite their thighs:
with battle-axe or mace they play
or dress in armour for the fray.

Watson Kirkconnell

Dávid Baróti Szabó
(1739-1819)

A poet and translator, he was the most important member of a triumvirate which also included Miklós Révai (1750-1807) and József Rajnis (1741-1812), who were of lesser importance.

A descendant of an old Transylvanian Székely [Szekler] family of the lower nobility, Baróti Szabó became a member of the Jesuit order at the age of eighteen. Like many of his fellow Transylvanians, he was firmly opposed to the Habsburg Dynasty's rule over Hungary, although he also disliked revolutionary views, especially Jacobinism, because he considered them to be harmful to Hungary.

He translated Virgil's Aeneid, *and Milton's* Paradise Lost—*the latter, however, not from the English original, he knew no English, but from a Latin version.*

He reintroduced classical meters into Hungarian poetry after János Erdősi Sylvester's (q.v.) early 16th-century attempt to replace the then overly popular and rather monotonous twelve-syllable alexandrine, and he thus paved the way for the future success and greater achievements of Dániel Berzsenyi and Mihály Vörösmarty (qq.v.).

As a poet he was not overly interested in the aesthetic value of a given piece of literature; rather he was anxious to see the Hungarian language become richer in its means of expression.

In his own writings he often daringly used unusual folk expressions and turns of phrase. His poetic inspiration was one of tenacious patriotism and love for the Hungarian language.

After his retirement in 1799 he retired to the country estate of one of his former students in Vitre (today in the Slovak Republic), where he died.

TO HUNGARIAN YOUTH

Awaken Hungarian youth! See how your national language
— of a nation's value the seal — falls to disuse and the Devil.
Take up the pen and start writing, seek out the lutist Apollo
and talk with him in the tongue you learnt at your mother's knee;
that is the proven method the sensible Englishman uses,
and the Frenchman, Italian, and German, none of these yet found a
     better,
and you know what fine volumes of poems pour from their presses
     daily
for greedily you devour these alien works when they reach you
and make your country a storehouse of dazzling foreign treasure
while Árpád's speech and your fathers' withers away in silence!
Wake from your dream and take pity upon your national language,
for I tell you if that should perish you too will die with it forever.

Matthew Mead

TO A FALLEN WALNUT TREE

You, whose head once gazed at a sky so lofty,
standing kinglike, regal among your comrades:
do I see you, beautiful walnut-monarch
          down on the earth now?

Stout's your waist, but clear from its trunk 'twas shattered:
only bark, thin tendons were left to link you;
boughs are wilting; leaves, as the moisture fails them,
          wilt in the dryness.

So your breast, its offspring in vain begotten,
lets them go; they fall from your wilted main bole,
all unconscious, witless of brief existence,
          dying in order.

Must this tree, brave victor o'er sundry tempests,
great in honour, lie in the dust unseemly?

Must it be, that you, the august, the stately,
      take to such outrage?

Kind you were, rejoicing, at no one's losses!
Cool your shade, that gave all its leaves to thousands!
Gracious tree that pleased with your fruit men's fancy —
      tell us who hurt you!

Need I ask? When here in my eyes are staring
those who killed you? 'Twas no external tempest!
Deep within, deep hid in your heart 'twas traitors
      slew you in secret.

See there, gnawed right through, to your roots' tough marrow,
evil maggots; these to their cave invited
swarming ant-tribes; seething, they crawl beneath you
      this very moment.

Cursèd guests! Ill offspring of evil vipers!
Hapless tree! May Heaven serene and strong-armed,
hold erect our nation in virgin flower,
      guard it forever!

Watson Kirkconnell

TO THE MOON

Fair Moon! You shining lady of the sombre night,
      whene'er I turn my eyes to you,
admiring of the virgin snow your lovely face
      and silver cart reveal to us,
I seem to take to wings and hardly note the time
      but even if I were aware
of it, I'd like to stay under the cooling sky
      just so that I can stare at you.
But you, rushing, follow the sun that sets too soon
      and quickly leave the lovely skies
studded with stars; you run. But why is all this haste?
      Your face for quite some time has not

been shining with such clarity, your court so bright.
       The leaving of your brother is
noticeable but barely; look, the hunter still
       walks back and forth; with loaded gun
ready to aim, hides in the foliage and waits,
       hoping for hunter's luck: Behold!
From ponds arising here the lovely Nereids
       alight on banks with flowers decked;
they dance and frolic in the valleys of the woods;
       hark to the flute of Titirus
and to the songs Dametas wrought for tender love
       to woo his Phyllis. All the woods
resound with Phyllis; but the greater part of praise
       is aimed at you, Full Moon, you dear,
they praise you with ardent constancy, they believe
       that all their joys sweeter than mead
are due to you. Do hark to them, and stop your cart
       accept their chants and harmonies.
I bid you stay in vain! You leave me; furthermore,
       your side turns darker; starts to sag —
your horns stretched thin begin to face each other now;
       in shades you start to disappear.
Behold, you vanish altogether; not part
       of you is left. Is it my fate
I see in such celestial signs? Is it my end
       approaching? Do I see in you
my rest being exchanged with troubles and travail?
       O Moon, you will recover soon,
but what can I be hoping for? When autumn comes
       you may be shining on my grave.

Adam Makkai

Ábrahám Barcsay
(1742-1806)

The first significant poet of the Hungarian Enlightenment, Barcsay was a descendant of a noble Transylvanian family, of which Ákos Barcsay, Prince of Transylvania, (1610-1661) was the most prominent member.

The poet Ábrahám Barcsay was an important member of the circle of György Bessenyei (q.v.), which was formed among the Hungarians who served in the Guard of the Empress Maria Theresa. It was at the Imperial Court in Vienna that the poet became acquainted with French culture and civilization.

He recognized that in order to change society the natural sciences, too, must be further developed. He was sharply critical of the colonizing efforts of the powerful European nations, as one can see from his short poem 'On Sweet Coffee,' two versions of which are included in this anthology.

He was the first Hungarian writer to have described folk customs without distortion or sentimental exaggeration.

Towards the end of his life he withdrew to his small estate in Transylvania. While his thought was bold and progressive, he stuck to traditional verse forms such as the alexandrine in most of his poetry.

ON SWEET COFFEE

(1)

Blood-stained fruit of labor, sweated out of Black slaves,
Which the greedy English ship abroad for fat sales,
They fill up their coffers with delightful profit
Melted from sugar cane — England gets rich from it.
Coffee bean, which of yore, grew around far Mocca,
You're now in the West, too, slave-labor's crude mocker,
The sage feels disgusted, seeing how a thin cup
Makes him an accomplice, sipping British guilt up.

Thomas Kabdebo [& A.M.]

ON SWEET COFFEE
(2)

Crop of sweat and blood, of African slave labour,
Sold around the world by the grasping English trader,
Sugar cane produced a sweeter taste to offer,
And to line with gold a wealthy English coffer.
And you, tiny bean, in Mocca cultivated,
By the slaves who pick you, so bitterly hated —
Thinking men are shamed to sip you in their parlour
And to share the guilt that the greedy English harbour.

Peter Zollman

TO THE POETS

If you plow foul furrows filling up fine paper,
you can't teach your nation, your verse's just a caper,
so long as you hurt our ears with faulty scansion,
you will destroying poetry's new mansion.

What about your feelings? Where's the heart in limping?
Broken lines galore can constitute no singing.
If you cannot use imagination's mirror
and, to boot, you're not blessed with euphonic vigor,

in vain will you praise the choir of Apollo,
reaching Mount Parnassus sure will never follow;
clumsy tampering with nature's gentle flavor
cannot ever gain the human judges' favor.

Adam Makkai

WINTER'S APPROACH

Whistling fury of the frozen northern tempests
falling of the leaves in pale and sombre forests

indicate that autumn's now ready to vanish
and that winter's here the last sun-rays to banish.

Frosty fog descends on tops of mountain ridges,
dew and snow descends on all the fields and hedges,
Pan hurries away to rest inside his warm cave,
shamelessly he hides and hibernates, the old knave.

Hordes of groaning Dryads everywhere keep lurking,
crystal clear rivulets desperately searching,
but in vain for warmer quarters are they hunting,
so they quit their quest and scramble into hiding.

Autumn takes its leave of our vineyards and gardens,
gathering the flowers it weaves its last garlands;
having picked up all there was in fields and meadows,
to the barren valley for a last spell he goes.

Mounted on frosty clouds the winter wins the race,
conquering the mountains it occupies the place;
it blows dreaded frost down on the open prairie,
it brings death to nature desolate and dreary.

But this transformation's nothing but a mirror
of the human cycle, ending in death's horror,
when our hair turns white, it's like the snows of nature,
our old frozen corpses' final discomfiture.

Roses of the spring we tend not to remember,
nor the blissful harvests of the last September;
day-dreams point the way to where the secret door is
where we plucked our kisses from the lips of Chloris.

Get thee gone, foul weakness, what's this painful shadow?
Why should my mind in the past and future wallow?
Once I look in my heart, with the pining lessened,
my true self is living right here, in the present.

Thomas Kabdebo [& A.M.]

TO PÁL ÁNYOS[1]

Relent at last, you, lightnings wrought of steel,
you, toys of kings, invented for destruction;
let gentle farmers go back to their fields
let them plow in manure — forget the guns;
you've chased them out from all their tiny huts
and turned their silos into armories;
one son is taken by the infantry,
the mother sees the other tied on horse back.
His daughters, if they're virgins, it's a wonder,
for they've grown old — there are no men for husbands.
Their kerchiefs cover hair that's turned to grey
barren they lie in cold and empty beds.
The whole of Europe writhes in misery
increasing ruination to the fullest.
There are more soldiers than those who plow the land
there are more priests and knights than honest merchants.
Such is the business of the mighty kings
who spare no effort to indulge their pleasures,
they capture simple folk two-fold; this is
how they fetter the hands in every land:
poverty is one; the other's slavery;
this way your strength and freedom ebb away.
Tyranny's dreaded stick they promenade
and grinningly display their sabers' blades.
But Jupiter will surely look upon
the groaning nations, tortured little people,
when Nature claims the truth back as her own
returning freedom to the world of men.
The tyrants then will run like hunted wolves
and seek refuge with wild beasts of the forests.

Adam Makkai

---

[1] A fellow poet of the Hungarian Enlightenment (1756-1784).

György Bessenyei
(1747?-1811)

The son of a half-ruined noble family, a writer, philosopher, and politician deeply involved with cultural matters, Bessenyei was the leading figure of the first phase of the Hungarian Enlightenment. His grandfather, Zsigmond Bessenyei, served as a colonel in the army of Ferenc Rákóczi II, Prince of Transylvania, who led the War of Independence of 1711 against Austria.

He studied in the famous Calvinist College of Sárospatak for five years, and he finished the "poetic class", that is the humanities, but he never actually graduated. His father took him home to their estate to become involved with agriculture.

At age twenty Bessenyei joined Empress Maria Theresa's Hungarian Guard. In Vienna, he gained access to the works of Locke, Pope, Rousseau, Voltaire, Holbach, and Montesquieu, which opened new, wide vistas to him. Simultaneously he was able to witness the awakening cultural movement of the German bourgeois middle classes. In the Imperial Library he found many a product of old Hungarian literature. He gained the confidence of the powerful Empress.

He started to write in 1769 — in addition to his native Hungarian he also wrote in German and French. Toward the end of 1773 he quit the Imperial Guard and started to act as a lobbyist for the Protestant Churches in Hungary. He published political flyers aimed at arousing and uplifting Hungarian national culture in 1778 and 1779. His financial situation did not permit him to stay in Vienna at the very time when his literary plans seemed to succeed. As a result, following the instigation of the Empress, he converted to Catholicism, upon which he was given the title of Honorary Guard of the Library. The Empress' son, Joseph II, cancelled his annual pension, and this forced him to return to his estates in Hungary.

While still in Vienna he founded a literary circle with other like-minded young officers. Widely eclectic in his choice of subjects, he tried his hand at writing tragedy, comedy, epistolary novel, historical essays, epic and philosophical poetry, and the popular eighteenth century genre of imaginary voyages. He brought into Hungarian literature the genres and intellectual achievements of the Enlightenment. He was a passionate thinker to whom philosophy was no idle pastime but an existential necessity. His use of the Hungarian language was of a pioneering nature, because Hungarian was still too undeveloped to be used for philosophy. His style was rich and powerful, and he contributed to Hungary's language reform with Kazinczy (q.v.).

THE MORNING SPLENDOUR OF THE TISZA

Again I'm on the Tisza's banks as the sun climbs,
where in my younger days I stood a thousand times,
where I have seen the sky-blue vault of a good day
grow fiery from that sun's same penetrating ray.
Dawn is beginning to smile on our world of cold,
lighting the sleep that still numbs us, now as of old,
as the mists begin to disperse over the hill,
and lurk like dogs in the valleys, sending a chill
into the lap of the morning. Quiet Nature wakes,
wrestling with sleep, to her tasks, as the day breaks.

The forests and the mountains rest still in the old dark,
in silence, blank till the probing light sets its mark
on their outlines; the waiting world begins to stir
and Nature's living sons wake to their work, with her.
Our sun, which drives into the sea the moon and stars,
in spreading her with nets of gold and golden bars,
the woods and hill-tops are all golden with his fire,
the dew glitters, a plaything bright with his desire.

Night with her leaden staff is sinking slowly away
as the sun takes on brilliance and sends a bright ray
from the round earth's edge out into the naked sky,
banishing the dark with one edict from on high.
Nature bursts into laughter, everything rejoices,
waking so gladly, with a hundred thousand voices.

The forests echo with the hunt and singing bird,
axed trees grow on, afar the hound and horn are heard.
The waters ripple under the fisherman's boat
as through the early mists he seeks his prey afloat.

The lowing herds are driven towards the reedy shore,
their mouths range through the meadows, always seeking more.
Among the shepherds' pipes I stand by the Tisza's banks,
quietly I stand, and gratefully I give thanks.

By the water giant poplars seem to prop the sky,
deeply rooted, rough-barked. As the river hurries by
they bend their spreading branches down as if to drink,
green and white wind-rustled leaves by the Tisza's brink.
Tranquilly the river flows, as though moved by thought,
twigs and leaves amidst the foam on its surface caught.

Small eddies mill and circle, crowd the banks, foam-flecked
while in the listening forests the noise of life is checked.
Turtle-doves in pairs above, linked like a true rhyme,
flutter gently through the air, joying in their time.

The Tisza from their amorous murmur takes new heart —
but the unmusical cry of cranes from another part
over the broad meadows raspingly fills the air,
such discords, that none willingly would ever hear.
The calling swans fly over and are gone, with sounds
from agitated wings like the baying of hounds.
The birds are happy, singing under the bright sun —
but many will drop to the harsh staccato gun.

Gazing on the Tisza, both now and long ago
I often strolled along beside its whirling flow,
by the willow groves and by the long sandy plain,
as it worked its strange enchantment in my brain.
I smelled the wind-borne Spring scents, here where I began,
and it was here that Nature claimed me as a man.

Gavin Ewart

GYÖRGY BESSENYEI TO HIMSELF

Who and what am I then? Whence do I come?
Where have I been? How is this world my home?
I feel, I think, I struggle, and I tire,
and so I live while I ever expire.
To build my soul, my body I abuse;
I strive to live, and thus my life I lose.

My heart with pangs rejoices in the pit,
for pain and pleasure co-exist in it.
With doom of death inherent in my mind,
my freedom bound to slavery I find.
How often must I feel what I shall be?

In crossing history's precarious sea,
a small fire guides me as I wander free,
by whose illumination in the gloom
I shun the rocks where others met their doom.
I love, I think, hope, and skulk a fugitive,
I walk, sit, move, and do not know I live.

Some sorts of essence in my body fight —
soul, mind, fire, intellect, how keen a light!
Its hue and shape I cannot understand
or how my human person has been planned.
But though I feel its conflicts of desire,
I cannot pause its battles to admire.

It keeps on pledging immortality,
though in a pain-racked body it must be.
Thus ever tossed between the earth and sky,
I moan and laugh, and all my life I sigh.
Above my head, the sky's expanse is blue;
the earth's deep fissures at my feet I view.

Eternity may summon forth my breath;
my body lies beneath the shades of death.
In bondage to my senses I decay,
and ever in their clutching hands I stay.
All things of earth turn to nothing, alas,
and I myself, I know, must also pass.
Eternal truth God can alone dispense;
all else is shadow, pain and transience.

Watson Kirkconnell

Benedek Virág
(1754-1830)

A descendant of a poor family of serfs from Transdanubia, Virág won a scholarship with the Piarist Fathers and later entered the Catholic Theological Seminary in Pest. He became a monk of the Paulist Order, but when Joseph II dissolved most of the religious orders in his empire, Virág continued his educational work as an ordinary priest.

In 1794 he resigned his post and, after a short period as a private tutor with the rich and aristocratic Batthyány family, he spent the remaining thirty years of his life subsisting on a very modest pension, and by the aid of his friends, in a small house in the hills of Buda. Here he was often visited by the leading poets of his age, many of whom were his admirers.

His ardent patriotism and his mastery of the classical verse-forms earned him the name of "The Hungarian Horace."

Virág is generally considered as the greatest master of the classical ode until Dániel Berzsenyi (q.v.).

THE SPARTAN MOTHER

Our people spread the news each day —
A great army is on its way
Against Sparta, a hurricane —
A fury nothing can restrain.

But everywhere one word is said —
By all whose blood is warm and red,
Whose soul is open and is free —
The path of glory calls to me!

I bore you, son, for our land's good.
I raised you up for this great day
and you have listened to what I say.

I told you tales of hardihood.
I begged you with this holy shield,
To go forth to the battlefield.

Joseph Leftwich

INVOCATION

O holy Justice! Hiding your puissance,
Yea, masking all your radiant majesty
    In this deceitful world we wander
        Numberless foes that would oft profane you —

Come, come and cloak your heavenly effigy,
Close veiled from rebels, they who assailing you,
    Still fierce against your crown and sceptre,
        Thrust at your throne with weapons insensate.

Before your face, in impotent bitterness,
All shaken, shamed, bewailing their blasphemies,
    These vile shall envy shining virtue
        Versed as they are in malignant rancour.

But born to greatness, bold, though in thunderings,
Sad skies be rent and tumble tumultuous,
    You, born to greatness, shall revering
        Worship the glory of God Almighty.

Those ivy-branches, woven so worthily,
Assailed in vain by envious sorcery,
    In grace shall deck your living lyre,
        Green shall remain on your brows forever.

Watson Kirkconnell

Ferenc Kazinczy
(1759-1831)

Poet, essayist, and organizer of literary activities, Kazinczy was the leading figure of Hungary's Language Reform Movement which also involved him in reforming the literary style and the aesthetics of his age. He was born in Ér-semlyén in south-eastern Hungary in a well-to-do noble family. He studied law in Kassa and Eperjes (today Kosice and Prešov, both in the Slovak Republic) and finally in Pest, where he obtained a thorough knowledge of French and German literature.

In 1784 he became sub-notary of the county of Abaúj and in 1786 he was appointed Inspector of Schools in Kassa. In 1788, together with Baróti Szabó (q.v.) and Batsányi (q.v.), he started the Magyar Múzeum [Hungarian Museum], *the first Hungarian literary magazine; two years later he launched, by himself, the review* Orpheus. *When Leopold II acceded to the throne, Kazinczy was forced to resign his post because he was not a Catholic. Implicated in the Martinovics conspiracy against the Habsburgs, he was arrested in December of 1794 and condemned to death, but his sentence was commuted to imprisonment. After his release seven years later, he married Sophie Török, daughter of his former patron, and retired to his small estate at Széphalom.*

In 1828 he was active in the establishment in a Hungarian Academy of Sciences of which he became the first corresponding member. Kazinczy was the most tireless and persistent worker in the cause of the regeneration of the Hungarian language; his translations of Hamlet, La Rochefoucauld, Klopstock, Anacreon, Molière, Sterne, *and many others, introduced these writers to the Hungarian public. His style had great beauty and flexibility although his thought was rarely original. His collected works, including his translations, were published in Pest between 1814 and 1816 in nine volumes; editions of his poems appeared in 1858 and 1863.*

His philosophy was influenced by the fact that he was a Free Mason; as such he was a pioneer of educating the citizenry in the spirit of the Enlightenment. The Language Reform Movement, which had a lasting effect on Hungarian, became a matter of public concern. Without it Hungarian could not have handled philosophy or the natural sciences. Those against it wrote a pamphlet in 1813, Mondolat [The Think-talk]; *Kazinczy and his group replied in 1815 in* Felelet [The Answer] *and were from then on considered the winners of the debate between the "neologues," the reformers, and the "orthologues," the conservative reactionaries.*

OUR TONGUE

Grace of old Greece the divine and the greatness of Rome
    the majestic,
strength of the German and charm of the French and the passion
    of Spaniards,
softness of Polish — all hail! My language has envied your beauties.
Yet do you envy us nothing? O, ocean-deep speech of old Homer,
tongue of the Mantuan, too, as you turn from the past to our Europe,
where but in Magyar indeed is your holy lute faithfully cherished?
Full of rich resonant thunder, it rolls out its music sublimely;
swift as a man to his mark, it can leap with the vigor of lightning;
heart-searing sorrows will find it is full of the sighs of affliction;
warm as Italian or Polish, it whispers the fervors of passion,
hail, O ye tongues of the past, for our tongue as a peer stands among
    you!

Watson Kirkconnell

THE BOAT

Past eddies dangerous and rock-reefs wild
my boat darts onward in a merry race,
laughing at spiteful winds and foam's embrace
and cliffs where spuming breakers are up-piled.
      I turn to calm my wife and little child;
      I kiss away the worry from each face;
      and hanging from the mast 'mid flowers' grace,
      my wind-blown harp resounds in murmurs mild.
The mist and night close o'er my way again,
yet still one star shines radiant and plain
to fill with sacred trust the hearts below it.
      Forward! No matter what the terrors be! —
      The gods desert not in extremity
      the worshipper, the lover, and the poet.

Watson Kirkconnell

MERITS OF WRITERS

Speak! And I'll say what you are. 'Tis enough! Altogether I know you.
    Chatter that's empty denotes empty chatterers indeed.
Color and fire and taste are in wine, if 'tis *Hegyalja*[1] vintage.
    Taste, colour, fire are in verse, if it be masterly work.

Watson Kirkconnell

HARD AND EASY

Difficult verse I dislike that comes hard, and the easy writ easy:
    these things together are fair; separate, each a mistake.
Ever let verse that is difficult come when I feel that it's simple;
    verse that is simple is best, when it is wrought by the file.

Watson Kirkconnell

VAJDAHUNYAD[2]

Fortress of stone, as unmoved as the arm and the breast of our
    builder!
Great as your builder was great, great as his comrades and sons!
Where is your master? O where is your Mátyás? What fate had your
    László?
Where is your glory of old? Where is your din of the past?
"They are no more" comes the voice of your silence, of walls dark
    and tomb-like.
Are they no more? — What is this? Do I see opening gates?

---

[1] The word means 'Foot of the Mountain'; it is a region to the south-east
of a mountain range which is famous for its wines because of the richness of
its volcanic soil; the best known localities are Tokaj, Tolcsva, and Olaszliszka.

[2] The castle of Vajdahunyad was built in the 13th and 15th centuries in
Transylvania, today under Romanian rule; the Romanians call it *Hunedoara*.

Capistran[3] yonder. I see, is already unfurling his banner.
Lo, he is issuing forth, leading his army to win.
Loud the Hungarian horn and the pipe and the trumpet are calling:
mute and heroic in wrath, now he strides forward himself.
László[4] to left and to right is deploying the steeds of the host,
taking his father's commands, passing them faithfully on.
Fortress, what are you? What were you of old time? I shudder. The
    faithful
knowing the holiest sign, starts from his visions of sleep.

Watson Kirkconnell

THE SOUL OF A MAN

Flee trouble, as you desire: it will catch you and hold you in bondage,
    should you cower on your knees, sure it will trample you down.
Fight like a man, never fear, and refrain from the lowly complaining,
    hardships will be afraid, falling in front of the brave.

Adam Makkai

---

[3] János Kapisztrán, an Italian Franciscan monk and itinerant preacher (his name was originally Giovanni di Capistrano; he lived from 1386 till 1456), who acted as a papal ambassador. He went to Hungary in 1455 to recruit volunteers for the Crusades. Kapisztrán succeeded in assembling an army that defeated the Turks at Nándorfehérvár (today's Belgrade) in 1456. He was canonized as a saint in 1724.

[4] László and Mátyás Hunyadi were brothers; their parents were János Hunyadi and Erzsébet Szilágyi. László was beheaded, whereas Mátyás became Hungary's Renaissance king.

Ádám Pálóczi Horváth
(1760-1820)

Son of a clerical family, Pálóczi Horváth studied for the ministry, but as a free-thinker soon found himself in conflict with the professors at the Calvinist Theological Seminary of Debrecen. Later he practiced law for a while and then took up engineering.

He succeeded through his various labors in saving enough money to buy a small estate where, although the last ten years of his life were overshadowed by grave illness, he was able to devote the second half of his life to literature.

His first poems were published in 1792. Emulating Voltaire's Henriade, *which appeared in 1786 and in which Voltaire criticized his own age by comparing it to the greatness of Henry IV, Pálóczi Horváth wrote an epic entitled* Hunniade [Hunnias], *published in 1787, and a* Rudolphiade [Rudolfias] *in 1817. This latter piece includes interesting passages of Rosicrucian philosophy. His light comedy* The Girl from Tétény Visiting King Matthias [A tétényi lány Mátyás királynál látogatóban] *was published in 1816.*

He also experimented with novels and was an avid collector of proverbs and folksongs.

LOVER UNDER SUSPICION

Sarah, my rose, where are you off? Please stop a minute.
    My lingering look last Wednesday had such sadness in it
    because I came before you when the day was over
    and had the door slammed in my face by your mad mother.

She notices all right, I think she keeps a file on
    the honey of your lips, more sweet for being stolen.
    If I half say your name, or look as if I'm thinking
    I might, she peers across to see if we are winking.

The Devil brought her to our room — and may he take her!
    We were, it's true, about to start love's secret labour;
    but, had we been divided by a stretch of ocean,
    she would have been suspicious still of my last motion.

Could I be sure the hag herself desired the apple,
> I would, my Sarah, for the love of your so supple
> lips, kiss her wrinkled mouthpiece! I would be love's martyr,
> to stop her stopping me from turning to her daughter!

Sarah, my rose, love me! I want to have you lying
> now on my shepherd's coat, now while there's no one spying.
> Let's love each other now. Even suppose we are followed,
> what use to kick the kittens once the cream's been swallowed?

J.G. Nichols

THE DANCE OF THE MAGYARS

Magyars, they say, are not fit for the art of dancing.
True — when they are badly shodd or, in their breeches prancing.
But in their spurs and pearls and egret-plumed head-dresses
and Magyar headscarves — where is dancing as fine as this?

French dance is pretty-pretty; German dance is slattern;
neither varies enough, though, to break the deadly pattern.
English dance is a bore, too fancy. But the prancing
dance of the Magyars is Saint David's style of dancing!

J.G. Nichols

János Batsányi
(1763-1845)

The creator of political poetry in the Hungarian language, Batsányi can be seen as the direct intellectual ancestor of Sándor Petőfi (q.v.).

He was born in Tapolca, near Lake Balaton, into a bourgeois family. He was educated in various towns in western Hungary. He studied philosophy at the University of Pest, obtained a law degree, and became a civil servant.

After the death of Joseph II who, though no friend of the Hungarians, was nevertheless an enlightened reformer, revolutionary ideas crystallized in various segments of Hungarian society during the repressive reign of Leopold II, which lead to further repression. Batsányi, as one of the Hungarian Jacobins, was tried and sentenced to a four-year prison term in the fortress-prison of Kufstein in Austria. After his release he settled in Vienna; obtained a modest position, and married a famous Austrian poetess, Gabriele Baumberg. During the Napoleonic invasion of Austria, Batsányi helped to compose Napoleon's appeal to the Hungarians to rise up against the Habsburg Dynasty. As the French troops withdrew, Batsányi followed them and settled in Paris where Napoleon granted him an annual pension of two thousand francs.

In 1815, when Paris was occupied by the Holy Alliance, Batsányi was seized and extradited to Austria, where he spent one more year in jail. He was eventually released with the help of his influential wife. Upon his release he was sent into forced residence in Linz.

He was elected to the Hungarian Academy in 1843. He died two years later in Austria without being permitted to return to his native country.

His collected poems were first published in 1827, but his complete works did not appear until 1853-1861.

As a poet he initially expected Providence to improve the lot of Hungary, but his famous poem On the Changes in France *[A franciaországi változá-sokra], featured herein, was written in 1789 directly under the influence of the French Revolution. Before Batsányi such a strong revolutionary voice had never been heard in Hungarian literature, and it was not heard again until Sándor Petőfi (q.v.). It was this poem that was used against him during the trials that led to his two imprisonments. He was first and foremost a political poet. Historic events and ideas were important to him only in direct proportion to their usefulness as examples for action or as intellectual stimuli. His poem* On the Changes in France *is now a part of the Hungarian school curriculum.*

THE SEER

You in despair, take heart! Life shall renew
itself before the century is through.
All mourning cease! Now let the harp sound clear
so every patriot may lend an ear
who underneath the changing Magyar sky
still looks to manhood and to liberty.

You who have cultivated your despair
against the unexpected moment, there
look, it has arrived, and the truth shines
beneficent upon those crawling shrines
of superstition which for centuries
have laved with gore their god of miseries

and fall now as a mighty nations rears
herself, a saviour of the hemispheres,
snapping the chains that bind Necessity,
raising the arm that shows the Will is free!
Across the Alps she trades man's natural rights
for now disvalued relics; where she fights

thrusts our enemies into damnation,
turning to us in friendly exhortation:
"Let us endow schools of morality
for studious nations, where philosophy
shall teach no harm or falsehood to slip past us,
Justice and Liberty our only masters."

The world is stilled and trembling at her voice,
awed by the long-awaited hour of choice
when, monuments of exploitation, thrones
must totter on their edifice of bones
and crowned assassins, connoisseurs in crime,
with pale horror view the approaching time;

when hints no more turn murders as they planned
or thousands die by gestures of a hand
that with an equal pity could contrive
the firing of a throne, or for a hive.
You in despair, take heart! Life shall renew
itself before the century is through!

[1791]   *John Fuller*

RHYTHM IS ONLY A SERVANT

Rhythm is only a servant.
To serve is its affair.
This is the secret of making poetry.
He who knows it is rare.

Joseph Leftwich

ENCOURAGEMENT

To suffer for this land, to live for it and aid
its cause with open heart, its claims with ready blade,
careless of ill or harm, of dungeons unafraid,
prepared to give up all, by no demand dismayed —

these are the things, my friend, that after life is spent
raise on the field of fame for men a monument,
these virtues while you live the many will resent
but to your grave they'll bring a blessing and lament.

Matthew Mead

ON THE CHANGES IN FRANCE

Countries still trapped within the snare of servitude,
Nations that groan in pain, by iron bonds subdued,
Who have not shaken off the collar of the slave,
The yoke that drags you down into your wretched grave,

And you, too, sacred kings, who, consecrated, kill
— Since Earth cries out for blood — the subjects of your will,
To Paris turn your eyes!!! Let France elucidate
For king and shackled slave your future and your fate.

[1791]   *Matthew Mead*

THE HUNGARIAN WRITER

"Like a burning torch which flames on in the darkness
creating light for all consuming but itself..."

Whereas he's bravely judged by the illiterate
and those with souls enslaved think they can mock him;
behold the sage: he watches in glad delight
the dissolution of the mental fog;
he — though there are few who truly praise him
and recognize that he had good intentions —
finds his reward in his own inner merit,
and casts all hope on the merit of his people
and hopes against hope that the seed of Árpád
will pay a "thank you" for his efforts spent.

Adam Makkai

Sándor Kisfaludy
(1772-1844)

The elder brother of Károly Kisfaludy (q.v.), Sándor Kisfaludy was born into a wealthy, noble family of landowners in Transdanubia. He chose a military career and served in Maria Theresa's Imperial Guard, like so many of his contemporaries. Falling in love with an Italian dancer, he learned Italian for her sake and thus became familiar with the poetry of Petrarch (Francesco Petrarca, 1304-1374).

During the War of the Austrian Succession (1740-1748), which tried to deny the right of a female to inherit the Hapsburg throne but which Maria Theresa won, he was captured by the French in Milan and was a prisoner of war near Draguign in Provence. After his release he was in a garrison in Klagenfurt, Austria, where he wrote a series of plaintive love poems Unhappy Love [Kesergő szerelem], *even though his bachelors' life was far from sad and uneventful. The lady to whom the poems were addressed actually responded most kindly; Kisfaludy married her and settled down on his family estate in Transdanubia.*

His cycle of poems entitled The Loves of Himfy [Himfy szerelmei] *and his equally popular poem* Happy Love [Boldog szerelem] *celebrated conjugal bliss and feminine beauty. Unlike his brother Károly (q.v.), Sándor Kisfaludy avoided sad and heavy political themes. Jointly, the brothers Kisfaludy became enormously popular and proceeded to give their name to one of the most prestigious Hungarian literary societies of all times, the* Kisfaludy társaság [Kisfaludy Society], *which survived until the War of Independence in 1849.*

UNHAPPY LOVE
(*Extract*)

As the suffering hart confounded
    by the lance that tears his veins;
flies — in vain — for he is wounded,
    vainly flies to woods or plains:
since thy piercing eye looked through me,
    so I flee — and vainly flee;

still thy magic barbs pursue me —
       I am wounded, maid! by thee.
And the wound but seems the stronger,
       as my flight is further — longer —
smitten heart! Alas! Thy pain
seeks relief or rest in vain.

Watson Kirkconnell

SONG

(From the 'Happy Love' cycle)

I have heard the silvery note
of her lovely spoken word
and the nightingale's plaintive throat
was not so divinely heard.
Nature listened attentively,
was seen to soften and relent;
the brook's waters flowed more slowly
and the trees' crowns were silent.
The singing of the birds ended,
Zephyrs waited hushed the while,
every gentle breeze abated
suffering began to smile.

Of the fair family of flowers
the rose is the most excellent;
of the multiplicity of stars
the sun's the most magnificent.
And, blossoming in life's garden,
love is such a flower as this,
it is a reigning prince, a sun
in a paradise of bliss.
Happy is he for whom this sun sheds
light, and whose gardens roses bring;
without one the earth is only weeds,
without the other there's no spring.

Anthony Edkins

Mihály Csokonai Vitéz
1773-1805

Mihály Csokonai Vitéz
(1773-1805)

Born in Debrecen, the son of a barber, Mihály Csokonai Vitéz proved to be something of a child prodigy. At the age of eleven he was admitted to the famous local college run by the Hungarian Reformed Church, showing remarkable talent for languages and for poetry. Unfortunately his passion for wine and women was equal to his thirst for learning and so the stern Protestant school masters expelled him.

He spent the rest of his life wandering restlessly all over Hungary, staying as a guest at various schools and at the mansions of wealthy patrons. Thus he managed to eke out a meager living as a tutor while trying in vain to make a living on his poetry. In his social and political orientation he was a follower of the European Enlightenment, and felt particularly drawn to the ideas of Jean-Jacques Rousseau, whom he mentioned by name in his writings. A near contemporary of Mozart, he resembled the Austrian composer in more than one way — his frail health, his love of beauty, his sympathy for progress, his bitterness against the ecclesiastical establishment. Above all, musicality was a major element in Csokonai's poetry. He was a gentle masochist, who seemed to thrive on rejection. The love of his life was Julia Vajda, the daughter of a well-to-do merchant, whom, he called 'Lilla,' and to whom he wrote some of the most charming (and, also some of the bawdiest) verses in Hungarian literature.

He died of tuberculosis at the age of thirty-two. His collected poems were published posthumously in Vienna in 1813. It was not until 1956 that a complete collection of his poems was published in Budapest. Reminiscent of Robert Herrick (1591-1674) in his erotic verse, he also resembles the great Scottish poet Robert Burns, but the strongest influence on Csokonai was Alexander Pope, whose Rape of the Lock *reverberates throughout Csokonai's comic epic* Dorothy [Dorottya], *written in 1804.*

Csokonai was somewhat neglected throughout the revolutionary days of the 19th century because of the splendor of the Vörösmarty-Petőfi-Arany (qq.v.) triumvirate, and in the 20th century under the political impact of Endre Ady and Attila József (qq.v.), but during the second half of the 20th century, the greatest poet of this era, Sándor Weöres (q.v.), claimed Csokonai as his master, and so did many other modern poets including Dezső Kosztolányi, Árpád Tóth, and Mihály Babits (qq.v.).

There is a view among Hungarian literary historians that Csokonai is, along with his near contemporary, Dániel Berzsenyi (q.v.), one of the main influences on modern Hungarian poetry.

SUSIE'S LAMENT FOR JOHNNY

In the evening came the order,
The pink-sealed order to go;
On a fine night in the springtime
They rapped on Johnny's window.

He'd only that instant left me,
He lay sleeping on his bed;
He'd started to dream about me,
He dreamt that he stroked my head.

But soon, as the trumpets sounded,
A man and his horse together
Must straghtway leave to fight Turkey,
And, alas, perhaps forever.

Weeping, I walked to his billet
And in the gardens near my love
I gave voice to a joyless song,
Just like a widowed turtle-dove.

On his horse I scattered roses,
On his shako[1] I cried and cried;
I gave him a thousand kisses
And crepe to his shako I tied.

Even my soul dissolved in tears
When he bade farewell to me —
He flung his arms around my neck:
"God be with you" — no more said he.

Anthony Edkins

---

[1] A military cap in the shape of a truncated cone with a peak and either a plume or a ball or a pompom. [From the Hungarian *csákó*.]

TO HOPE

To mortal eyes, you, Hope, do seem
a form divinely sweet;
but eyes of gods can pierce the dream
and see your blind deceit.
Unhappy men in times of ill
create you for their easing;
and as their Guardian Angel still
they worship without ceasing.
Why do you flatter me with praise?
Why do you then deride me?
Why in my bosom do you raise
a dubious heart to chide me?
Stay far and fair beyond my reach,
as first my soul you greeted!
I had depended on your speech,
but you have ever cheated.

With jonquil and with daffodil
you planted all my garden,
and introduced a chattering rill
to be my orchard's warden;
you did bestrew my laughing spring
with many a thousand flowers,
the scents of Heaven did you fling
to perfume all its hours;
my thoughts, like bees, found morning sweet
'mid garden plots and closes,
and hovered 'round in fragrant heat
above my heavy roses.
One hope possessed my soul apart,
one radiant prospect joyed me,
my garden lay in Lilla's heart
its wonders never cloyed me.

But, ah, the roses of my ease
Have withered quite away;
my sparkling brook and shady trees

are dead and dry today.
The springtime of my happiness
is winter now instead;
my dreams are gone beyond redress,
my fairy world has fled.
Ah, would you leave me but my lass,
the Lilla of my passion,
I'd let all sad complaining pass
nor mourn in any fashion.
Within her arms I could forget
misfortune, grief, and pain;
no wreath of pearl could match my girl
were she with me again!

Depart from me, O cruel Hope!
Depart and come no more;
for blinded by your power I grope
along a bitter shore.
My strength has failed, for I am riven
by all my doubt and dearth;
my tired spirit longs for Heaven
my body yearns for earth.
I see the meadows overcome
with dark consuming blight;
the vocal grove today is dumb;
the sun gives place to night.
I cannot tune this trill of mine!
My thoughts are all askew!
Ah, heart! Ah, hope! Ah, Lilla mine!
May God remember you!

Watson Kirkconnell

LOVE SONG TO THE FOAL-HIDE FLASK

Darling, dearest foal-hide flask,
I am yours for life — just ask!
You're a treasure beyond value,
Hoards of girls cannot replace you.

Eager more is my embrace
For your cheering little face
Than for Susie's mouth to kiss:
Sucking *yours* I cannot miss!

Ah, what throb is in your bosom
Whose great passion I can't fathom,
And how beautiful your mouth
Ripe to hold pearls from the South.

Shoulders round; your neck's erect;
Who needs fishbones? — Their effect
Quite destroying — unlike Lulu's;
Oh, hell, no, I won't tell you whose...

Your hair's very beautiful
Even though a dutiful
Little foal once wore those furs
— Prettier than Trixie's curls!

And how lovely is your singing!
Just like laying chicken's clucking;
All your chuckling: festive songs
For my sad heart merry dongs.

When I tell you all my sorrows
And you answer, all the furrows
On my brow fast disappear;
All my woes you turn to cheer.

When the winter winds blow outside
You diffuse their fury outright:
When the scorching summer flays me,
You will come along to raise me.

But when you're beyond my sight,
My heart's full of cries and fright;
Once I've come across your face,
I shed tears of joy and grace.

You I always carried with me,
Night on night, in bed beside me,
And as often as I'd get up,
Songs of love for you I'd set up.

Often we two lay together
Never married — does it matter?
Which reminds me, dear, tonight
Let's do it again — all right?

If this complex love affair
Could produce a living heir,
We'd have kids both yours and mine,
Row on row and full of wine!

Could you be swapped for a wife
Greatly it would help my life;
I would put you to the task
To give birth to flask, flask, flask...

Horses, too, should be a tavern
Holding wine within their cavern,
Aren't they made of good foal's hide?
They'd be filled up neat and tight.

Woe to me though, I'm so old,
I'll be laid out in the cold,
This great love will soon consume me
And a widow sad you'll soon be.

Dreadful fate! What misery!
Bring the Feast! More wine to me!
Quickly now, let's have it brought,
Best to gulp it down the throat.

My last coins will do me proud,
They'll pay fully for the shroud.
I'll be blind? Don't mind at all.
Why, then, should I need a pall?

Let us kiss and let us hug
True to death, dear army-jug.
When I'm buried, I shall ask
Next to me must lie my flask,

And my grave-post they'll inscribe:
"Wanderer, drink and do imbibe,
For this most devoted couple,
Man, and his good foal-hide bottle!"

Thomas Kabdebo and *Valerie Becker Makkai*

HAPPINESS

Now in the jasmine arbour
on this cool summer evening
I sit close to my Lilla
while Lilla joins me humming
and plays the game of kisses
While her brown, pretty tresses
Zephyr's whisper caresses.

I placed upon the meadow
a demijohn of good wine,
and with a tender rosebud
I closed its mouth *comme il faut*.
Inside my basket waited
Anacreon's good verses
with strawberries I'd just picked.

Whoever has in one place
seen so much delight gathered?
Whose bliss can ever match mine?

Paul Tabori

CONSTANTINOPLE

The Bosporus laps on Europe's shores
over 'gainst Asia its thunder roars;
here beneath the walls of high Istanbul
its billows surge proudly and foaming full,
while the crumbling grandeur of this 'other Rome'
casts over the waters a terrible gloom.

But come with me, Muse,[2] inside the town
you, to whom fear is a thing unknown,
what heaps of treasure piled on every hand!
What crowds swept along as at one command!
Those Turks there, decked in red silken splendour,
how they strut on the boulevard, how they swagger,
arrogantly mounted on superb Arab steeds
they smoke their pipes filled with sweet Asian weeds;
the finely-cut diamonds of each glittering blade
putting all cheaper gold in the shade.

Here's a lady at a window, but her jealous veil
makes all our gazing of no avail.
But, Muse, there are hundreds of greater beauty
that in the curtained harem perform their duty;
there's a depot for you, or a bird-cage, rather,
where the Emperor's innermost secrets twitter;
it's an antechamber where his courtiers all
come crowding to wish the Sultan well
and whenever it's announced that Selim is coming
countless females for one single male start cooing.

---

[2] There is no record of Csokonai ever having been outside of Hungary, let alone having visited Turkey. His information on Istanbul came from his readings.

When by study he wishes to relieve his boredom,
he enters this library of lovely whoredom,
where folios of choice Asiatic membrane
lie open for the skillful touch of his pen.

But watch, Muse, take heed of my warning words,
or you'll find yourself joining the imperial birds,
the wide-awake eunuchs are already at your heel,
so let's move to other parts of glittering Istanbul.
Look at those temples bragging of their fame
swollen with Mahomet's heavenly name.
There a lot of holy bellowing is heard
to Allah, who delights in every blessed word
and likes to hear his own name praised to the heavens
by his Moslems from under their green-silk turbans,
taking on the throng such compassion that truly
their glorious Koran becomes all the more holy.

Here, too, stand the mosques with their lofty spires
soaring to the clouds with their sacred desires;
each golden dome as it glitters on high
adding to the number of moons in the sky.
Oh, what a thick cloud's descended on this race
by superstition daubed with the varnish of grace!
You old bat, Superstition! You screech-owl, Bigotry!
How long will you nestle on human history?
How long will you roost on all the royal crowns,
on the swords of warriors, on people's chins and brows?

When in far-off times the human creature
lived in the lap of simple nature
you had not yet raised your moaning cries
to benefit all those devils in disguise.
The world was happy and that empty word: *holy*
was no mere excuse for the direst folly;
the eternal frame of nature stood fast;
only one law — *humanity* — from first to last,
but since then, Black Fowl, you've built your nest
in humanity's side — so it's crumbled to dust.

Since then the mind in fetters has raised
those churches wherein you are constantly praised;
since then, even mothers, at the pitch of madness,
will relinquish the very bread from their houses,
even snatch it from the mouth of their starving offspring,
so your devilish jaws will never stop munching.
Many fools will spend their very last penny
paying — as they think — a kind of heaven's rent-money
so that when the altar's built at last,
they too, can turn up with a goatskin and be blessed.

While you sleep in the day you dream up visions
which at night you wail into people's decisions.
Step out in the daylight! Let yourself be seen
if your face is adorable and not, in fact, obscene!
You keep building churches in the darkest night
and from their depths promise heavenly light
so people will worship you, obeying your laws,
while you keep courage and intellect under your claws.
But, tell me, to fast one day in the week,
to trudge to holy places all worn out and weak,
to mumble over prayer till you start to nod,
is that the way a man becomes a son of God?

In order to sit on the heavenly thrones,
must we turn ourselves into wandering bags of bones?
For a Turk to be saved, are these the only ways,
even though he's been an honest man all his days?[3]
By practices like this, every single nation
builds itself a private heaven — or is it damnation?
Nature! Let the standard of your own law unfold,
and the world will listen to your true words of gold.
Chastised by this darkness as black as soot,
the ghoulish night-bird will cease to hoot;
a benevolent world will burst from the skies,
and all false heavens will drown in their lies.

---

[3] It was obvious to Csokonai's readers, influenced by the Enlightenment, that the 'Turks' and 'Allah' were in fact a thin disguise for the poet's ardent anti-clericalism engulfing all religions.

Ah! Sweetest emotions born of this glad vision,
fill full my tongue's forces with glad inspiration!
Rise up, my soul, for at fairest Reason's true voice,
men's hearts, disencumbered, will awake and rejoice!
Curtains of the darkness shall be ripped asunder —
Oh rise, my soul, sing your gladness and wonder!
Humanity opens all her hidden stores
and heals her beloved ones' festering sores;
the spirit of love will fly over all lands,
people will embrace — all will be shaking hands.
All holy lamentings will fade away swiftly
even church-bells ring forth new sounds that are sprightly,

with the cash that goes now to a gaudy steeple,
great things will be done for the good of the people.
Old century, vanish! Come, the happy new day
(although when this happens I'll be mute as dead clay)
So I sing in gladness this, my heartfelt welcome,
and if only, just once, my name you might mention
      I'd look on this owl of a world without fear,
      and fade nobly out of it, shedding no tear.

Kenneth White [& A.M.]

EVENING

   The resplendent chariot of the sun goes down inside
the gates of death that open beautifully, thrown wide.
Where the horizon flushes, the sunbeams fade away,
above the gold-strewn clouds evening smiles back at day,
lets delicate droplets fall from her cool wings anew
to lay on the open hearts of roses a balm of dew.
The small birds doff their array of late songs and rest,
sleepily balanced on the cool edges of a nest.
And now the woeful nightingale has cried her fill,
and the lark that warbled sadly in the nest is still.
The wolves, wild creatures in the wood, all slumber there,
from within his den come the grim roars of the bear.

Ah, gently breathe into my ears, breeze,
your sweet concerts, with your quiet airs ease
my soul, immerse it in the soft flow of gladness,
let your affable music drown my every sadness;
float around me, zephyrs, lingering about,
pour life into my soul that droops in doubt.
What do I feel? The air, even as I speak,
wafts tender fragrances upon my waiting cheek,
in the shade of trees creates with a flash of whirring wing
an aromatic center of joy where the Graces will sing,
perched on the soft arms of delight for them outspread
under the vibrant Moon, and because of that light overhead
the brown outline of the grove will begin to shimmer and sway —
in a word, the pleasant abodes of joy have opened their day.

Tarry still with your somber hours, stay on, night,
do not let your cold wings cover me, blight
my blithe mood, for in truth of that world I have no part
which would shed its peace on my unwilling mind and heart,
I, who object to it in all its blatancy,
to the jostling hordes that bustle around me noisily,
to the hollow rattle of the pompous miser in his pride,
to the drunken desires bumping each other at my side.

You crazy human race! Why abandon your state
of freedom? This earth was wholly yours, yet you create
your own fetters, allow the hoarder and the proud
to take from you their tithe, your kingdom disavowed.
Wherefore these frontiers to shut out your son?
See, you are separated, each from the other one.
The *"mine,"* the *"yours,"* once created, how loud the outcry,
now that the good old word for *"ours"* has passed us by.[4]
Farmland, before it became private property,
fed many, without lawsuits and angry talk of legality.
More, even, than now were fed, for in those early days
the generations had not died in the poisonous blaze
of war; law had no beggars then, no one was born

---

[4] These two lines have become proverbial in Hungarian. *[Az 'enyim' s a 'tied' mennyi lármát szüle / Miolta a 'miénk' nevezet elüle.]* Here is the poem's semantic fulcrum — his earlier worship of nature gives way to Rousseauian ideals.

rich or poor — all inherited plenty's horn.
The legal rights of hills and boundaries, the obsession
to prohibit that anyone touch what was another's possession
had not yet given rise to mutual belligerency,
for to possess enough was considered a man's sufficiency.

The arrogant lord had not yet come forth with his proclamation
of laws that vassals must heed under pain of condemnation.
Even on Christmas to have only a dry crust for feast,
that the lord might have cakes and kidney pies as his very least.
Not yet did the king own multiple millions of souls,
from whom to extort tithes as he levied his heavy tolls.
He might have procured the means of making them happy and blest,
instead of acquiring his own luxurious Tonkin nest.
The miser had not yet hidden away from the human fold,
scared of his fellow men, of brigands after his gold.
And the brigand himself was made by a brigand world, no doubt,
for none is born evil; the good in man is put to rout.
And small wonder, for around the fields are dug forbidding trenches,
and every man-made ditch that encircles a meadow wrenches
land from the poor; about the forests barriers rear
their prohibitions: the lord's game dwell in here.
As for the waters, the poor of these may not have any;
trees they themselves have hewn, to fence out the thirsting many.

You are the only one, Oh golden light of the Moon,
that the world has not yet leased, earth's sole remaining boon.
And you remain safe still, Oh vivifying air,
from the ducts of engineers that move in everywhere.
And you, choirs of loveliest voices, can still be heard
by every mortal who listens free to the song of a bird.
You, sweet sounds of woodlands not heard in any town,
on the shepherd and laborer filter softly down,
while in the world of fashion at high society's call
they dance the artificial strains of a tiresome ball.

Oh, blessed Nature, my estate and community,
I, the proud landowner in perpetuity:
Grant that was made to me by you alone, seeing
that through you only, I was created a human being.

Madeline Mason

TO SOLITUDE

Blest solitude, be with me; even now, take me
  into your dream, receive me there.
  Let others quit me, do not you forsake me;
  embosom me, without a care.
  Thus to have lingered where you still are haunting
  at Kisasszond, is to feel nothing wanting,
  delight in such a place to roam,
  and for a poet to feel at home.

Here in the dell and dingle seldom footed
  reviving shadows shelter me;
  among the deep-grown hornbeams mossy-rooted,
  the stream sings in its purity.
  From hill to hill naiads of pool and runnel
  find homes in bulrush tents, and none will
  catch sight of them swimming along
  but such as live for thought, or song.

The sylphid Moon arising with soft splendour
  brightens the pale-gold beech-tree boles;
  still night's good angel, by that beauty tender
  cool-clad, the evening's veil unrolls.[5]
  My gentle solitude, in such scenes joying,
  such time and space as these so well employing,
  I pray you, often bear
  my soul to comfort there.

---

[5] These four lines have been cited literary historians, including by Ágnes Nemes Nagy (q.v.), in her university lectures in Budapest, as the most beautiful ones written in 18th century Hungarian. In the original they are: '*A lenge hold halkkal világosítja/ A szőke bikkfák oldalát,/ Estvéli hűs álommal elborítja / A csendes éjnek angyalát.*' Literally: 'The sylphid moon illuminates with quiet / The sides of the blond beech-trees, / [and] Covers with [the] cool dream of the evening / The angel of the quiet night.'

Kings' places you do not greatly care for,
    castles with all their grand old power,
    when you chance into them, are your horror; therefore,
    you bring forth troubles that devour.
    Then you are lost to life while round you wrangle
    fearsome disputes, which all peace would strangle.
    What you would give, the great world rates
    as nothing worth; yourself, it hates.

Misers would have your company; but coldly
    you punish those for their dull thought.
    Ambition's sons with all their vaunts you boldly
    fling to the tumult they had sought.
    From battle's bugle-calls amazed a-flying,
    from crowded cities' walls and multiplying,
    only there pleased, sweet, to live,
    meadowy, cottaged, sensitive.

The safety of the lonely ones and grieving
    only in your sacred forests dwells,
    where those whose sadness may at times achieving
    Heaven's voice respond to miracles.
    You, solitude, befriend the child of sorrows
    who has rejected all the world's tomorrows,
    or whom the world has cheated —
    and whom you have well treated.

You, spirit, were and are the one creator
    of such as made some ascend
    (in body small) to wisdom, ever greater,
    and these as characters have without end
    into eternal greatness brought. Your touch
    brings out the poet lightening-like in the dark,
    when he imagines such so much
    that lay beyond your farthest mark.

Divinest, among all the rest, I longing
    at many moments sigh — a shade,
    wishing his friend, among his trials thronging
    to listen and be well repaid —
    innocently indeed you call me,
    and utterly, profoundly your words thrall me,
    for faith is what you have, and are,
    from the false modern world so far.

Consider in what discord, in what crashing
    the days of arrogant mortals swirl,
    from crag to crag like the fierce waters flashing
    where the Rhine's currents hurl.
    When the immortal veils of solitude are shielding
    our quiet hours, like night's dews they are yielding
    to time, serenely, with deep peace,
    and we may live so, and so cease.

Then even when my eyes their latest
    glimpse through the death-veil, then
    some way assure me in the dusk thou, thou awaitest,
    when my eyes close, look even then!
    Yet come with me into my burial, lead me
    where only loneliness and ignorance precede me;
    there also, in that quiet space,
    be my good angel, to my grace.

Blest solitude, upon thy breast so gathered,
    I have my last of tears to shed;
    with you in dreams past ending, later fathered,
    my painful world will all be dead.
    Blest solitude, I hail thee, my true treasure,
    when the grave otherwise is all my measure.
    And when shall that become my fate?
    Blest solitude, be yet my mate!

Edmund Blunden

TO THE ECHO OF TIHANY[6]

Rise up, Oh, Tihany's clamorous daughter,
  fly forth from your sacred hills!
He, whom fate has tossed on stormy waters,
  sits facing your bank and wilts...
Here by the moon's faded lighting
crying over hopes lost in the fighting
    beats an orphan's lonely heart,
        beats an orphan's lonely heart.

While those, who won't suffer pain and sorrow
  in the arms of happiness,
bathe and drink at Füred through tomorrow
  knowing naught of loneliness,
I must sob here, sob a-crying,
and what I can't, Nymph, help! I've been a-trying —
    make it ring out on your peaks,
        make it ring out on your peaks!

Fierce forests, rough rocks, loath lethal ledges!
  You should sing my mute complaint!
You may have hearts, though hid by hedges,
  that in fellow-humans aren't;
from their midst they've exorcized me,
called me names so they could ostracize me,
    one who's hapless, lonely, poor,
        one who's hapless, lonely, poor.

Those who, in the old days, once were true friends
  turned their backs and turned their heel,
they've joined ranks with all my evil portents
  what discomfiture I feel!
When in the end they treat me so

---

[6] A strikingly beautiful peninsula on the northern shores of the Balaton, Europe's biggest lake (6 km. wide, 80 km. long), home of the country's first Christian abbey, founded in the year 1011. It is famous for its echo.

rushing at me as though I were their foe,
   although I stayed true to them,
      although I stayed true to them!

There's no one to comfort now my spirit
   I have surely lost all friends,
   he who hears my name, wants naught to do with it,
   no one consoles, none defends.
   There's no heart inside you, humans —
   let me pour in hollows of the mountains
      all the sorrows of my heart,
         all the sorrows of my heart!

Lilla too, who was the only ransom
   of a spark of hope in me,
   caved in to the tyranny of custom,
   and social hypocrisy.
   Blessèd soul, how are you doing?
   I'm alone, I live forlorn and brooding
      midst a sea of misery,
         midst a sea of misery.

Is there still somewhere a hermit's lodging
   one old cave, one holy roof,
   where a sage in silence could be watching,
   mountain-safe and mingle-proof?
   Give me just one rock for cushion!
   No human, no bird shall find my prison,
      none, who could disturb my peace,
         none, who could disturb my peace!

I don't think I'd be expropriating
   anybody's ancient right,
   if I made this rock my place of dwelling
   with a scorned virtue beside,
   on this isle beneath a foothill

and, like Rousseau in his Ermenonville,
 I'd be man and citizen,
  I'd be man and citizen.[7]

Here, with secret wit, then I would study
 how to rouse my sleeping soul,
 nature with intelligence would feed me
 making me all wise and whole.
 Far away here, in a distant
 unknown world, that's holy, lonely, instant —
  I'd live out my days in tears,
   I'd live out my days in tears.

This is where I'll die. A peasant neighbor
 in the woods will dig my grave,
 future happy tourists will then wager
 they might find my place he gave.
 And the tree in whose shady tent
 my lonely grave will slumber in content
  they'll hold sacred for my bones,
   they'll hold sacred for my bones!   *Adam Makkai*

SHY REQUEST[8]

Mighty love's consuming fire
Has most deeply scorched my soul,
Cooling balm for hot desire,
Gracious tulip, make me whole.

Lively morning fires glitter
In the sparkle of your eyes,
many thousand worries flitter
From your dewy lips' sunrise.

---

[7] These two lines are some of the most often quoted ones from the poetry
of the Hungarian Enlightenment 'to be man and citizen like Rousseau.'

[8] Perhaps the most quoted poem of the 18th century, in Hungarian it has
a unique feature — RHYTHMICAL DUALITY, untranslatable into English. On the
one hand, it can be scanned trochaically, on the other, anapaestically.

Save me, Angel, speak, be willing,
Mend my heart so sorely rent —
And with ardent Grecian kissing
Will I pay for your consent.

Ena Roberts and *Adam Makkai*

ONCE MORE TO LILLA

Surely, I suffer on your account
ever since you have stolen my heart,
        my sweet and cruel one!
I die again and again without
any relief from memory's smart
        for good I am undone.

The spring of my life broods over you
for there's no sunshine to drive away
        the fog that sits on me.
Morning or night, without much ado,
I cry, because I cannot display
        what fed my ecstasy.

Your admirer weeps in despair
ever since he was separated
        from you; hopes gone like steam—
a dream that has died weighs down my lair
often I cry, feel decimated,
        "Lily, Lily!" — I scream.

My arms reach out when I sound this word
but all they touch is skeletal dusk:
        Lilla, there's no joy left!
Nights bring no rest for I thought I heard
your lovely name, so sleepless, I must
        day-dream, of you bereft.

O, bitter is the life of him, who
has lost all reason to be hoping
        and yet is forced to live!

Although he may live, his soul withdrew;
behold my lungs lifelessly breathing
       life's breath they cannot give.

And what of you, my radiant flower?
Does your life's flare the darkness banish
       while languishing I die?
Could but the Lord grant you the power
to thrive — my tears would dry and vanish —
       through Angels from the sky.

But p'rhaps you too are sad and anguished
a captive dove, by an eagle caught,
       calling for me to come —
It's too late... With all hope extinguished
in Death's ice-hut shall we two be brought
       to hug in final sum.

Adam Makkai

ON MY PNEUMONIA

Moon in the sky, floating overhead,
see how I toss in agony!
Say, am I lying in my bed?
Or is this a coffin holding me?
No, it's a boat on the dark sea
of doubtful hope and certain fear.
And the waves of life and death are here
floating along with me.
The scorching heat of siroccos
dries up the membranes of my lungs.
An icy wind from the graveyard blows,
freezing each limb that to me belongs.
An arrow sticks in the heart of me,
shot by a hand.
And on the bone-frame of my chest there stand
two deaths that kick me mercilessly.
Where are these waves carrying me,
tossing me wildly up and down?

Now this shore, against a cypress tree,
where silent horror reigns alone,
then to the opposite slope
where friendly greetings bring some hope.
And from yonder woodland mound
joyfully the trumpets sound.
On this side, with sour nitrogen
I am choked in icy caves, and then
from over there, from flower and tree,
scented breezes blow across me.
I choke, I breathe — I freeze, I am on fire.
This will kill me, or the other will!
I swoon and recover. I am still
tossed on the waves, tossed ever higher!
Who are you, with veils like snow
approaching with a welcoming smile?
You lift me from the bleak shore below,
and bear me inward in this pleasant isle.
Oh, earthly messenger from Heaven, you
brought me recovery — daughter true
of the Great Creative Power, the wise —
you, with blessèd healing eyes.
You, who with rosy fingers lain
on the broken pillars of my breast,
make it pulse with life again;
like a new phoenix, from its burning nest,
my soul rises living from the fire,
my weakened fingers strike again the lyre.
But you fled! You fled from me, you ran!
Doctor Sándorffy's sitting by my bed.
Thanks to him I'm still a living man!
Songs of gratitude ring through my head.
My heart is full of praises that I send
to this, my doctor, who's also my friend.

Joseph Leftwich

Mihály Fazekas
(1776-1828)

Mihály Fazekas was born in the eastern stronghold of Calvinism, the city of Debrecen, where his father was a veterinary surgeon. He left college in order to enlist in the Hussars, who took him into combat in Galicia and Moldavia and along the river Rhine.

After his return to Debrecen in 1796, he took up gardening and astronomy; accompanied by a number of close friends he produced the first scientific study of botany in Hungary. He was also the editor of a popular calendar.

His literary style is akin to that of his close friend Csokonai (q.v.), both Fazekas and Csokonai having been exposed to student humor in Debrecen that was circulated in manuscript form.

His most important work was a long humorous epic entitled Matt the Gooseherd [Lúdas Matyi], *in which a poor peasant lad pits his wits against a rich and cruel landowner, Mr. Döbrögi, who once had the boy beaten up badly. Matt repays the landowner for the beating not once, but threefold.*

This story was immensely popular, went into many editions, and was also later dramatized. A popular humorous weekly by the title Lúdas Matyi *was started soon after World War II by Andor Gábor.*

TO SPRING

See now, tender anemones are lifting up
their heads, out from under watery wolds of heath,
    slowly opening up for us
        downy chaplets of feathered green.

Come hither, gentle breeze, come to embrace and kiss
this child, thus newly roused, lest, with bewitching eye
    ardent suns of noonday
        smite, yea blast, with excessive heat.

Lo, still many the birds moving about afar
fly through mistiest air, here where mankind survived
    in these parts, in the cold days,
        still less brave than the wintering birds.

Against freedom from these, man with his guileful ways
scatters fodder abroad, hiding beneath with craft
    birdlime, seeking to snare them;
        such are the wiles of sons of men.

Watson Kirkconnell

MATT THE GOOSEHERD
(Extract)

        "...but good Sir, look here" — said he
"I'm no nurse, but the Gooseherd, Matt, the fellow whose
geese you'd taken away and had him trounced; not a word more
must be wasted, enough! This is it: I've come to repay you!
Do not shake, let's go and get down to it, this very instant.
I will surely return if God will grant me a third time."
   While so speaking, Matt beat up Sir Döbrögi badly.
Then the key to the old money-box was found at a bedstead:
"I will now repossess my price for the geese and the lease, too!"
and mounting his horse he departed the Döbrögi mansion.
   Soon thereupon there came all hands of the Döbrögi household;
they'd been gone to the woods to pick herbs and nice, juicy
    mushrooms.
First then a maid, who saw in dreadful amazement Döbrögi lie there
ran to the courtyard crying "Help! Help!" — every one clamoured:
"What happened? Say, what's wrong? Run fast, say, where is the
    doctor?"
They all rang their hands, cogitated, talked, argued about who
might have done what appeared such a great and amazing
deed of success shutting up that loquacious bore, dear Döbrögi squire.
Döbrögi — why, he himself was knocked out cold, half dead, to be
    heard meant
major work; what a groan! "He says what?" — "That Matt... He, the
    gooseherd..."

Thomas Kabdebo [& A.M.]

Dániel Berzsenyi
1776-1836

Dániel Berzsenyi
(1776-1836)

Berzsenyi was born, educated, and married in the village of Egyházashetye in Transdanubia, Hungary's Western wine-growing region, dominated by picturesque Lake Balaton and the Bakony mountain range. *He died in Nikla in the southern county of Somogy, which he considered his "place of exile" but, in fact, where his considerable estates lay.*

Seldom did he leave Western Hungary, making only brief visits to Vienna and Pest. Having visited friends, men of letters, and politicians involved in Hungary's Reform Movement, he quickly returned from each trip to his agricultural studies, his Latin classics, his quest for a perfect aesthetics, but above all to his poetry. This shy, introverted Hungarian nobleman, endowed with a philosophical turn of mind yet also turbulent passions and great physical strength, was persuaded by Ferenc Kazinczy (q.v.) in 1812 to publish his first Book of Poems [Versei].

Within a few years he found himself in the midst of controversy. A small circle of Transdanubian devotees praised him as the "Hungarian Horace," but a vicious anonymous pamphlet called the Speak-Think [Mondolat] *attacked his use of modern words in classical verse forms. In 1817 he was strongly criticized by a rival poet, Ferenc Kölcsey (q.v.) for his alleged pathos and provincialism. Berzsenyi devoted long years to defending his style and "Horatian" philosophy, especially in an essay entitled* Harmony in Poetry [Poetai harmonistika], *to such effect that he finally won general respect, membership in the Hungarian Academy of Sciences, and, in a funeral oration, apology from Kölcsey. Berzsenyi is viewed today as the unsurpassed master of classical verse forms (the hexameter, distich, and Sapphic and Alcaeic stanzas, along with the lesser known ones) in Hungarian, and as the creative genius of the concise poetic idiom.*

His poetic diction is very hard to translate—the medium of English has proved particularly challenging because of the lack in English of consistent practice in metrical versification. His passionate plea for a return to forgotten old moral and national standards inspired the 20th-century composer Zoltán Kodály *to set to music his second poem,* To the Hungarians II, *which is included in this volume. Berzsenyi's* Collected Works [Berzsenyi Dániel összes művei] *were first published in 1864, but his influence is felt even in 20th-century poetry, and it is hard to overestimate his significance in the development of Hungarian poetry.*

PRAYER

Oh God, beyond the wit of the genius,
Though felt and wanted secretly by his soul,
  Your light is like the blazing Sun, but
    Mortals are not to behold its splendour.

The ordered planets of the Empyrean
In sempiternal orbit around your feet,
  Are even as the lowest insects:
    Wonders Your masterly hands created.

You wrought the countless forms of the Universe
From emptiness. By raising Your lofty brow
  You bring about, or end Creations,
    Order the endless advance of aeons.

By Zenith and by Nadir be glorified.
The raging tempest, fulgurant stormy sky,
  The humble dew drop, dainty flower
    Faithfully witness Your mighty handprint.

Oh, Holy One, behold! I am on my knees.
The day my bounden soul will be free to rise
  And enter in Your sacred circles,
    It will have reached then its true desire.

But now I wipe my tears as I go my way
Along the path my destiny has defined,
  The path of righteous, noble souls, while
    Sinews and stamina stand the journey.

I face my deep sepulchral night reassured.
It may be bleak but evil it cannot be,
  For it's Your work. Your hands will hold my
    Earthly remains in eternal shelter.

Peter Zollman

TO THE HUNGARIANS
(The First)

Oh you, once mighty Hungary, gone to seed,
can you not see the blood of Árpád go foul,
      can you not see the mighty lashes
            heaven has slapped on your dreary country?

Amidst the storms of eight hundred centuries
the battered towers of Buda still stand aloft,
      although a thousand times, in anger,
            you trod upon your own self, your own kin.

Your beastly morals scatter it all to dust —
a brood of vipers, venomous, hideous,
      lay waste the castle which beheld the
            hundreds of sieges it used to smile at.

You stood defiant even against the wild
Xerxes-like hordes of Outer Mongolia;
      you could resist world-conquering Turkey's
            mighty assault on the East and yonder;

you did survive the murderous century
of Zápolya[1] — the secret assassins' hands —
      while you stood firm amidst the flames of
            family blood-feuds in retribution,

for you were led by virtues of yesteryear —
with Spartan arms you conquered throughout your wars;
      wrestling you won, and Hercules-like
            war-hammers shook in your steely fist-hold.

---

[1] János Zápolya (or Szapolyai, 1487-1540), was the Palatine (Voivode) of Transylvania from 1511 onwards. Although he did not participate in the tragic Battle of Mohács in 1526, he was elected king of Hungary by the lower nobility, suffering defeat by Ferdinand I of Habsburg, who was the choice of the upper nobility. He asked for help from the Sultan, thereby preparing Hungary's 150-year-long Turkish occupation.

But now — you're gnawed by venomous, stealthy death.
Behold: the oak that proudly withstands the storm
  that cannot break it from the North, but
    vermin can chew up its mighty root-work

and then it's felled by only a flimsy breeze!
That's why the firm foundation of every land
  must be morality untarnished
    which, if destroyed, Rome will fall and founder.

What are Hungarians now?! Sybaritic wrecks —
they've ripped their splendid native insignia off
  while, from their homeland's ravaged bulwarks,
    building a palace as lair of leisure —

they shed their ancient mantle of champions;
forget their tongue; they're aping the strangers' talk;
  they stomp the nation's Guardian Soul, and
    foolishly worship a childish idol.

How diff'rent rang the thunder of Hungary
amidst the blood-soaked battles of Attila,[2]
  who boldly faced half of the world in
    punitive anger against the foul West!

Árpád,[3] our Chief, the founder of Hungary,
had braver troops to fight the Danubian shores,

---

[2] Unlike his appearance in Hollywood movies and other Western records of a more serious kind, the legendary and fearsome 'Attila the Hun' was, and still is, regarded by Hungarians as their noble Asiatic relative whose mission it was to scourge the decadent West for its atheism and sins. Attila, whose name means 'little father' in Gothic, spoke Greek, Latin, and Gothic beside Hunnish, and when asked by the Pope not to take Rome by siege, he left. Also see the book by Anthony Howarth, *Attila the Hun,* London 1994.

[3] Son of Álmos (?819-?895), Árpád was the Chief of the Hungarians from 889 to 907. The Christian kings of Hungary descended from Árpád's line which lasted till 1311 when the Anjou Dynasty inherited the throne through dynastic marriage.

how diff'rent were the swords of Hungary
Hunyadi[4] used to repel the Sultan!

But woe — this is how everything perishes.
We bear the yoke of fickle vicissitudes;
the fairy mood of Luck has tossed us
playfully upward and down, while smiling.

The iron fist of centuries finishes
but all that man has built: gone is noble Troy;
gone are the might and pride of Carthage,
Babylon, Rome — they have all gone under.

Adam Makkai

TO NAPOLEON

Victor alone you were not — 'twas the Age's Soul, that of Freedom,
she, whose banners streamed over your glorious troops.
Nations worshipped you, having fallen to shiny delusions,
Holy Humanity's cause into your hands did evolve.
But you abased your good fortune with the throw of a gambler:
haughty Olympian wreaths yield to the Crown of Thorns.
God's hand raised you aloft and the same will cast you to hell now,
in you, Humanity's fate had to be truly avenged.

Adam Makkai

---

[4] János Hunyadi (?1407-1456), father of King Matthias Corvinus, became Hungary's most successful military leader against the Turks. He was Hungary's Governor from 1446 to 1452. At the Battle of Belgrade on July 21-22, 1456, he defeated the Turkish army, thereby delaying Europe's occupation by half a century. It was in memory of this victory that the Pope ordered the church bells rung at noon all over Christendom.

TO THE HUNGARIANS
(The Second)

The Seas of Sorrow boil with a rage, Magyar,
the cursèd soul of wrathful Erynnis[5] rules,
      behold his blood-soaked dagger urging
        peoples of Earth into mindless combat!

One day took down the throne of old Prussia,[6] proud;
the Adriatic Coast and the Baltic Sea
      are dyed with blood — the Cordilleras[7]
        and the Haemi[8] are consumed by tempests.

The lands of Baktra[9] holler and scream of arms,
the Dardanelles give thunder above their banks;

---

[5] Treated by Berzsenyi as a single entity and spelled with the *y* preceding the *i* in Greek mythology the Erinnys were Allecto, Tisiphone, and Megaira, the three daughters borne of the blood of Ouranos, the sky-god. They were the Goddesses of revenge and consuming feelings of guilt. The Romans identified them with the 'Furies.' What makes this poem most remarkable is that nearly two hundred years ago Berzsenyi identified the future 'trouble spots' of the 20th century and maybe beyond.

The 20th-century composer Zoltán Kodály set the first stanza to music, bringing out both the native Hungarian rhythm and the Alcaeic stanza's dactyls of the first stanza's last line.

[6] Most likely an allusion to the Treaty of Tilsit (1807) in which the victorious French dictated the terms, by which Prussia's territory was reduced to half its former size. Prussia existed as a state until 1934 when Hitler amalgamated it into the Third Reich.

[7] The name of the largest mountain range on Earth stretching along the West Coast of North America and South America; the South American portion is better known as the Andes. Berzsenyi was probably alluding to the violent weather conditions about which Europeans of his age had heard inexact stories, but probably also to Simón Bolívar, his contemporary, (1783-1830) whose wars of independence led to new states in the New World.

[8] The mountain range stretching across the Balkans, *Haemus* in Latin.

[9] A kingdom until the 6th century B.C.; the ancient name of today's Uzbekistan, Tadzhikistan, Turkmenistan and part of Afghanistan.

the iron railings of the nations
     tumble and fall, ropes and reins a-breaking.

You with your Titus[10] into the castle fort
of your great elders wisely assembly sought —
     to guide our boat adrift to safety,
         over the breakers, by law and counsel.

Arouse your sleeping national genius!
Should hurricanes howl, dangers galore await:
     I shan't be scared. The screeching trumpets
         and the wild leap of the rampant horses

I'll oversee with courage. Not multitudes,
but souls and people free conjure miracles — —
     this is how Rome the whole world conquered,
         Buda and Marathon wound up famous!

Adam Makkai

HORACE

Over Mount Kemenes howls Boreas in rage,
Biting blustery winds intimidate the sun,
Snow drifts up to the Ság, right to the distant peak,
     All succumb to the winter's gloom.

Hear now Flaccus's song, hark to the golden lute,
Stoke your brazier high, empty the noble cup,
Dress your hair with a balm boiled with a scented spice,
     Bengal's gift to the barber's art.

Savour every delight while it is yours to taste,
Greet each day as a friend, shy not away from love's
Tender ecstasy while your lucky star of youth
     Shines in splendour upon your sky.

---

[10] Allusion to Roman Emperor Titus (39-81 A.D.), son of Vespasian, whose rule was usually characterized by rational decisions. Berzsenyi recommends restraint against jumping headlong into the Napoleonic wars.

Leave sly future alone, trust not in idle dreams,
Be wise, be debonair, celebrate while you can,
Time flies swiftly away, faster than words could speak,
    Like swift darts and the racing streams.

Peter Zollman

MY PORTION

Haul the mainsail down. I have reached the harbour
Weathering wild seas in a noble contest.
    I have steeled my heart to defy Charybdis
        In sweaty fighting.

Peaceful is my heart as I dock my good ship,
She cannot sail forth anymore to dreamlands.
    Sheltered home, oh greet with a warm embrace this
        Fiery young man!

My estates are small, not as fine and fruitful
As Tarentum was, or divine Larissa,
    And you will not find in the shaded parkland
        Tiburtine fountains,

But my nectared hills and my golden plainlands
Grow me all I need. My abode is blessed with
    Freedom. Is there more that a man can ask for
        From the immortals?

Cast me, tyrant Fates, anywhere you fancy,
Only abject want should avoid my doorstep.
    With contented heart I obey the rulings
        Sent from Olympus.

You abide by me, you alone, Camœna,
Lay your hand on me in an act of kindness,
    With your gentle song you create a garden
        From rocky wasteland.

Come the constant cold of the Greenland snowfields,
Come the burning blaze of Saharan sunshine,
    Your hot breast or cool parasol, Camœna,
        Brings me protection.

Peter Zollman

THE APPROACHING WINTER

See, our languishing park's finery fades and falls.
Rustling ochreous leaves drift in the naked shrubs.
Where's the briery maze? Zephyrus' perfumed breeze
        Wafts no longer among your paths.

No dawn chorus attends, amorous turtle doves
Do not coo in the trees, violet-margined banks
Breeze no scent any more under the willow's veil,
        Rough weeds strangle the peaceful stream.

Twilight hangs heavily over the brooding hill,
Not one grape berry shines on the denuded vine.
Once joy sang merry tunes there in a cheerful key,
        Now it's all desolation, gloom.

Time flies swiftly away on never-tired wings
And so will disappear everything man has made,
All things are but a dream; all the created world
        Fades like tiny forget-me-nots.

Soon my flowery crown fades to shapeless bunch,
Spring will leave me behind: scarcely could I partake
Of her nectarous juice, scarcely could I enjoy
        One or two of her tender blooms.

Farewell wonderful years, my happy youth is gone,
Springtime will come again, but never brings you back.
Nor will Lolli again charm my reclusive eyes
        With her beautiful auburn brows.

Peter Zollman

HUNGARY[11]

Here, where the Danube pours its tawny waters
by Árpád's golden meadows, O my country,
the wreathèd brow of Ceres gives you fragrance,
the gleaming horn of plenty smiles upon you!
The dews of fertile heaven bathe your fields;
Europe is jealous of your granaries.
Here, on the Eden-slopes of mountain-ranges,
God Bacchus fills his glass, and dips you draughts
out of the noblest vessel of the gods.
Here bloom Arcadia's green hills again,
where Pan makes music for his famous flocks,
such beasts as never Araby the best
nor any other nation e'er beheld.
The golden loins of your Carpathians,
surpassing all the gifts of proud Peru,
bring forth for you their everlasting treasures.
All that Olympus' lord e'er planned for good,
all that for human nourishment fair Tellus[12]
creates below, the gods' most generous measure,
is poured on your estates in ample store.
The guardians of your folk are Tituses,
so many fathers and indulgent gods,
above whose thrones float Thracia's martial spirit.
Stern cherubim protect your laws and crown,
these no rude tyrant's hand can desecrate;
law, and not violence, above you rules
and all the glory of your ancient honour.
Ah, if among your lovely wreaths of pearl
one more sweet rose could bud and blossom forth,
the gods of Hellas would alight on you,

---

[11] This poem records the contentment of the Hungarian with his patrimony in the early 19th century, just as "To the Hungarians" records his alarm over its doubtful destiny. The golden mean probably lies somewhere between the two poems. [W.K.]

[12] In Roman mythology, the goddess of the earth; the earth personified; the terrestrial globe.

they who once brought to Attica's fair land
the mighty masters and their sage sciences!
Then would your proud head smite the lofty stars,
the Zenith and the Nadir stare in wonder.   *Watson Kirkconnell*

SOLITUDE

Holy Solitude, in the skies above you
Cloaking mists of Heavenly quiet hover!
Now your wand would beckon my heart with magic
          Into your bosom.

From the world's tumultuous place of revels,
Like a weary traveller, worn and panting,
I approach your shelter, and press my forehead
          Soft on your mosses.

Here the heart is sure of a gallant refuge;
Here find freedom, sentiments pure and lofty:
Here are hung no fetters to please the rabble,
          Fools in their folly.

Laurel-wreaths of every sage here blossom,
Themes of ever-loftier songs are chanted;
Here grows freely innocent love's and rapture's
          Amaranth[13] verdant.

Solitude! Be ever my friend and teacher;
To your quiet shelter I haste for respite.
Here are Plato, Xenophon, cool Ilissus'
          Copses of myrtle.

You I yearn for, if in my eyes there trembles
My sad soul's outbursting complaint of sorrow!
You I yearn for, if with my fair young darling
          Gladly I wander.

                                    Watson Kirkconnell

---

[13] An imaginary flower that never fades.

PHILOSOPHY OF LIFE

I, too, was born for happiness
  In Arcady's cool bowers;
I've slept in Aphrodite's lap
  Soft-pillowed upon flowers;
And Saturn, in his Age of Gold,
Made me a shepherd, bright and bold.

But fleeting as the golden world
  Is that of rosy wonder!
Another god Olympus treads;
  Dodona's[14] groves now thunder.
Gone are spring's leaves, they fall in droves,
And with them the Hesperian[15] groves.

My spring has likewise bloomed and gone,
  With all its buds and kisses;
Infinity drawn near to drown
  My life in its abysses, —
One drop within the raging main,
One sigh across the hurricane.

Let gentle dreams or judgment come,
  I'll bravely face death's welter,
Brave as a weary traveller
  That seeks a desert shelter:
For if 'tis judgment, I've no crime;
If dreams, their place must be sublime.

I've been a man; my only fault
  Is honour that convulses;
If virtue be not vanity,
  'Tis warmth within my pulses;
And if my heart more boldly beat,
Its guerdon in itself is meet.

---

[14] Zeus' ancient oracle in Epirus, situated in a grove of oaks.

[15] From *Hesperus,* 'the western star'; lands lying to the west.

And shall I weep because I failed
     To use life's clearest vision,
Because I followed pleasant ways
     In dreaming indecision?
Could I begin my life once more,
I'd take the path I took before!

I clasped the ardent joys of youth
     And all its ardour has meant,
But better instincts of my heart
     Have never reached fulfilment:
The shores of Ithaca I've scanned,
And did not know my native land.

I have so lived my life that now
     I gladly would repeat it;
I have so lived it that with joy
     I'd end it and delete it.
I've kissed its roses, sweet and tart;
I've sweated as they tore my heart.

I've seen the smiling days of spring,
     I've seen the summer burning,
I've seen all seasons of the year
     To all horizons turning.
If I could live forever here
Life could offer no further cheer.

My fleeting, mortal brevity
     I therefore do not mourn for;
The doubtful scenes that lie ahead
     I have no fear nor scorn for.
Each age has its Olympian god;
I shall not grumble at his nod:
     Obedience I'm born for.

Watson Kirkconnell

UNFINISHED LETTER TO MY LADY

Do not ask me, dear friend, how I spend my leisure,
      What are my diversions that fill the lonely day...
I have lost, you know, my sweet-natured refresher,
      I am all on my own, because you are away.

I depict the vintage, the moon is awaking,
      It is time to leave my servants to retire.
I can faintly hear their noisy merrymaking;
      Under my old nut tree I tend to the fire.

I lean on my elbow, rapped up in my mantle,
      Seeing noble dreams in my ivory tower,
Meditating over a flickering candle
      On the inward beauty of this sacred hour.

As the autumn insects drone their lamentations
      Untold feelings echo in my heart's recesses,
And on airy wings my memory awakens
      Bringing back to me my long lost happinesses.

This is how I live now. — My days are on the wane,
      Darkness dulls a lifetime's merry masquerading.
Keeping vigil with me two good fellows remain:
      The glow of gentle love gradually fading
      And my melancholy softly serenading.

Peter Zollman

Károly Kisfaludy
(1788-1830)

The leader of the first generation of Hungarian romanticism, Károly Kisfaludy was born in Tét in Transdanubia into a famous family of the landed nobility. He was the younger brother of Sándor Kisfaludy (q.v.). The famous Kisfaludy Society, frequently mentioned in this book, was founded in 1836 in memory of the literary oeuvre of Károly Kisfaludy by poets such as József Bajza and Mihály Vörösmarty (qq.v.).

He was the eighth child of the family, and his birth took his mother's life. Presumably because of this fact, Károly's father could not warm up to him throughout his entire life. He joined the army at the age of 16, serving with distinction in various battles in Italy, Serbia, and Bavaria.

Meanwhile he also became a talented painter in Vienna — he produced oil canvases depicting scenes of nature and the perils faced by humans exposed to the elements. As such he was one of the forerunners of Hungarian national painting. During his Viennese days he frequented the theater and gained mastery of the genre of the comedy, but he returned to Hungary in 1817. His plays include The Tartars in Hungary [A tatárok Magyarországon], *1809; but it was not until his drama* Ilka *(a woman's name) in 1819-20 that he became a literary celebrity with no less than seven theatrical premiers.*

Together with his older brother Sándor (q.v.), he founded the periodical Aurora, *which he continued to edit until his death.*

As a poet he rose to national prominence through the epic poem in elegiac couplets entitled Mohács, *which commemorated the famous battle lost to the Turks in 1526. Through it he managed to achieve a sense of national unity with the goal of cultural and political renewal.*

After 1826 he started writing folk-songs which represented an innovation in Hungarian poetry at this time; most of these poems appeared in Aurora. *As folk-songs, his poems were highly popular; the style spread far and wide, preparing the way for the century's greatest poet, Sándor Petőfi (q.v.).*

His funeral was an occasion of a public demonstration. The city of Pest, which he had transformed into a literary center, was anxious to show its gratitude and appreciation to the poet who set an example for the gradual transformation of a rural society into an incipient urban intelligentsia.

MOHÁCS
(Excerpts)

Sighing, O greet you and mourn you, O meadow of burial, Mohács —
  grave of our national life, reddened with blood of the brave!
Over you hovered destruction, it hovered on raven-dark pinions,
  wreaking its ravaging strength, wrathfully, madly on you,
branding with thunderous lightening the marks of infatuate triumph
  fierce on the flesh of the slain, hot on our warriors dead.
Tomori,[1] proudest of leaders! Ah, why did you flee from your palace?
  Surely the best of our land, fighting by you, had not died!
Kindled with zeal for the fray, in a rapture you rode out to battle,
  many illustrious men fell for your sake before night.
Narrow one kingdom had been for your pride! Now your dwelling is
    narrow,
  silent your trumpet has grown, rusty your battle-axe lies.
Peace to your dust! For unkindly has treacherous fortune betrayed you;
  soft lie the sod o'er your bones, cover your ashes with sleep!
Many a gallant young spirit, exultant with life and its promise,
  merciless blows of defeat crushed into palsies of death!
Many a lad in life's spring, whom pleasure had lulled in its bosom,
  suddenly turned to the night, finding a tomb at Mohács!
Foully disfigured he lies, with his radiant manhood all mangled,
  trodden by iron-shod hoofs, trampled to naught by their nails.
Graceful were once his curls, but no more shall the hands of his sweet-
    heart
  play with their chestnut sheen, sticky with blood and with mire.
Vainly she stands on the highway and waits with a garland to greet
    him,
  hoping her hero will come, fearing he lingers too long.
Let but a leaf make a stir, and she thinks that it heralds her lover;
  panting and burning she seems, tightly her bosom is wrung.
Ah, but in vain her watching, her gaze in the mists of the distance;
  never returns her betrothed, slowly she sinks in her grief.

---

[1] Pál Tomori (1475-1526), Commander-in-Chief of the Hungarian
Army and Archbishop of Kalocsa. He was against confronting the Turks at
Mohács, but at the king's orders, took the lead in the battle in which he died.

News comes at last from the field, black news, and she wilts like a
   flower,
silently fading away, dying of bitter despair.
Over her grave in the twighlight the winds sadly linger and whisper,
   quiet Fidelity's self sits in the dusk by her tomb.
Many a noble retainer deserving long ages of glory
   sleeps on this field unnamed, marked by no honoring stone!
Armed in the weapons of manhood, he fought for his age-hallowed
   freedom,
   hewing with riotous zeal, slaking his sabre in blood.
....

Yonder fought Louis, ill-fated, a monarch of ghastly ill-fortune,
   yonder his battle-horse plunged, stumbling all armed in the marsh.
Vainly he stretches his arms, for no friend is at hand to relieve him,
   all of his knights are no more, none is at hand in his need,
wide gapes the slough where he lies in the stained royal gold of his
   armour,
   slowly the foam and mud cover the wreck of his corpse.
Grievous the death that he died there! The pitiful loss that he suffered!
   There where you came to your doom, surely our sun did go down!
Wounded by treacherous sons, not by the sword of the foe.
   Region of sorrowful memories, source of despairs without number:
mist from your darkening field rises in pillars of grief,
   under Suleiman's anger now murmur the peaks of Old Buda;
led by the pathways of strife, see us in deserts most foul.
   Many a virgin died slowly in lustful embraces of tyrants,
many a prisoner sank, deep in the Danube's dark stream!
   Nothing was ours any more, with our home in the hands of the
   stranger,
only the crescent was flown, flaunting from tower and wall —
   hence, you dark pictures, go hence, you demoniac spectres of
   darkness!
After such dangers gone by, suns have arisen once more.
   Magyars yet live; Buda stands; the pangs of the past are a lesson;
burning with patriot zeal, forward our vision is turned.
   Yet may you bloom, field of sorrow! May peace brood at last on
   your bosom,
grave of our national life, Mohács, the tomb of our past!

Watson Kirkconnell

PLOWMAN OF RÁKOS[2] UNDER THE TURKS

My father with great sadness used to say,
life here was better in a far-off day.
I feel it in my heart, and heave a sigh,
as here in Rákos fields my plow I ply.
Where now is Mátyás, the all-righteous king?
You saw him, happy Rákos, in your spring!
Perhaps he rode here once upon a time,
where I plow nowadays in dust and grime.
Here, so they tell us, noble lords would come
and would confer in projects venturesome;
and if the trumpet summoned them to fight,
they flew to battle with an eagle's flight.
They all have vanished, Rákos. You remain.
How many men you nourish on your plain!
Ah, but I hardly see a Magyar now,
and with a heavy heart I plow and plow.
The people come from Buda by the score;
they scarcely know our language any more;
one of these days, a Magyar word, I know,
will come as seldom as a snow-white crow.
From yonder eminence a cool wind springs;
a dark fog sits upon its murmuring wings;
perhaps the dust, across these meadows spread,
comes from the ashes of the noble dead.
O dark-haired maiden from the village square,
drink not the waves of Rákos unaware!
Above Hungarian bones its waters flow;
a salty taste Hungarian tears bestow.
O Rákos, in what sorry state
do you from glorious fame lie desolate!
My heart aches at the sights my vision yields;
and weeping deep, I plow my country's fields.

Watson Kirkconnell

---

[2] A brook flowing through Pest; its name means 'crabby.' It was the scene of numerous battles during the Turkish occupation of Hungary.

Ferenc Kölcsey
1790-1835

GJ Berky
'72

Ferenc Kölcsey
(1790-1838)

Ferenc Kölcsey, son of an old noble family in Transylvania, completed his studies in the Protestant College of Debrecen and became a lawyer. His parents died early and an illness destroyed the sight in his left eye — these blows of fate contributed to his becoming a life-long melancholic.

As a major literary figure in the early 19th century, he exerted a lasting effect on Hungarian literature. Together with his friend Ferenc Kazinczy (q.v.) he led the fight for the renewal of Hungarian literature and indeed of the Hungarian language itself. The last decade of his life turned out to be the most active—he launched the magazine Life and Literature [Élet és irodalom], *and contributed to Kisfaludy's (q.v.)* Aurora. *Meanwhile he lectured widely all over the country and acted as representative of his home county in the Hungarian Diet.*

His poetry combines the elements of Classicism, the French Enlightenment, and German Romanticism in a harmonious whole. He was equally outstanding as a critic and political writer. He demanded perfection from poets in scansion and meter, cultivating the classical forms of Horace; he therefore sharply criticized Dániel Berzsenyi (q.v.) who became greatly upset by Kölcsey's adverse reaction. When Berzsenyi died, it was, nevertheless, Kölcsey who delivered the eulogy at the dead colleague's grave-side, apologizing to him and characterizing him as one of the greatest.

Kölcsey was an ardent patriot, greatly concerned with the decline of his native land. His poems 'Zrínyi's Song' and 'Zrínyi's Second Song,' which refer to Miklós Zrínyi (q.v.) of the 17th century, both featured herein in their entirety, predict the end of Hungary as a homogeneous national entity. In Kölcsey's pessimistic vision, the country would be overrun by foreigners, and visitors will no longer be able to recognize the place.

His sardonic poem Vanitatum Vanitas *describes world history as a series of vain, irrational cock-fights. Kölcsey's complete works were first published in 1840-1848 and an enlarged, revised edition appeared in 1886-1887. His poem 'Himnusz' [Anthem] became the Hungarian National Anthem (the first stanza of which is sung on official occasions). It was set to music by the composer Ferenc Erkel (1810-1893). We present it in the Appendix.*

NATIONAL ANTHEM

Lord, bless us Hungarians
with good cheer and harvest;
Shield and save us when we are
pressed by foes the hardest!
After storms of bygone days
favor our endeavor;
sins of future, sins of past
are atoned forever.

Peaks of high Carpathian[1] hills
once you gave our elders,
sons of Bendeguz[2] received
thus their lands and shelters.
Where the waves of Tisza[3] glide,
where the Danube rages,
valiant seeds of Árpád grew,
prospering through the ages.

With Your winds on Kúnság's[4] plains
You waved wheat a-plenty,
in the vineyards of Tokaj[5]
You poured Your nectars amply.

---

[1] The Carpathian mountain range was the natural border of Hungary for one thousand years until the country was mutilated in the Versailles Peace Treaties of 1920.

[2] Name of one of the ancient noblemen, a member of the Árpád Dynasty, who played a major role in the original occupation of the homeland.

[3] Hungary's second biggest river (977 kms. long), running from the Carpathians near Máramaros (today in Romania) and joining the Danube in the south (in the former Yugoslavia).

[4] The flat prairie-like lowlands between the Danube and Tisza rivers settled by the Cumanians in 1239 at King Béla IV's invitation. They were a Turkic people who originated in northern China and have been fully integrated into Hungary since the 16th century.

[5] Hungary's most famous wine growing region in the northeast, usually spelled Tokay in English.

Often You have raised our flags
on the wild Turks' towers;
proud Vienna prostrate lay
under Matthias' powers.[6]

But our sins Your wrath provoked
as our deeds You pondered;
flashes through the Heavens burst
as in rage You thundered.
Soon the Mongols'[7] arrows rained
down upon your people;
then the Turkish yoke was set
on every house and steeple.[8]

Often from wild Turkish lips
chants of joy were shouted,
raised in triumph as they saw
all our armies routed!
Often 'gainst you, Hungary,
did your very sons rave:
thus the fairest Mother Earth
did become her sons' grave!

Chased, we ran and hid. The foe
probed our caves with armed hand.
We looked 'round, but could not find
homes within our homeland...[9]
O'er the plains and through the hills
grief and pain still drove us;
seas of blood flowed at our feet,
seas of flame around us.

---

[6] Matthias Corvinus (1443-1490), Hungary's renaissance king, defeated the Austrians at the Battle of Vienna in 1483.

[7] Allusion to the Tartar Invasion of 1241.

[8] Allusion to the catastrophe of Mohács in 1526.

[9] These are the lines quoted by László Cs. Szabó in his essay that appears later in this volume.

Once a castle — now but stones —
rang with fife and laughter;
now laments and death-rattles
groan in anguish after.
But, alas, no freedom thrives
where our dead lie sleeping;
tears of tortured slavery fall
from our orphans weeping.

Pity then, our people, Lord,
shaken by disaster!
From our sea of woes we cry:
Save Hungary, Master!
After storms of bygone days
favor our endeavor;
sins of future, sins of past
are atoned forever.

Watson Kirkconnell, Adam Makkai and
Earl M. Herrick

ZRÍNYI'S SONG

Where is that homeland, on which Árpád's blood
poured consecration in victorious flood
that stirs up true affection by her name;
at whose sweet image exiles will return
and even in Calypso's bosom, mourn
with yearning arms that land from which they came?

Here is that homeland, but her grace is gone:
in ruined wastes her regions linger on;
here dwells no Victory in Paradise.
Fidelity's burned out; its heats have fled;
the passions that should soar aloft are dead,
locked in her faded heart and breasts of ice.

Where is the hill, the citadel and fort
to whose bold moats brave Szondi gave support,
pouring his life-blood out with fervent ease —
that hill whence fame arises, from whose face

the flame of honor streams in burning rays,
casting its light to distant centuries?

Here is the hill, but ruins on its crest
have buried deep the hero and his quest;
a mound of mute oblivion hides his dust;
low in a valley sits the craven age
and glances giddy at that heritage
that eagle's nest of old, from days august.

And where's that nation that had learned to sweat
on high, heroic paths without regret,
and reaped reward like her brave sires of old?
That, though it suffered on from war to war,
bloomed, never fading, scorning wound and scar,
the present, past, and future to behold?

Wanderer, stop! Its mother's blood was base,
and now another nation takes its place,
weak-headed, heartless, selfish, full of fear,
the glorious nation that once learned to toil
and reap heroic laurels as its spoil
lives but in name — it is no longer here!

Watson Kirkconnell [& A.M.]

ZRÍNYI'S SECOND SONG

"Oh fate, take pity on my suffering country
bleeding, in tears of blood, she moans to Thee,
for hawks, snakes, vermin various and sundry,
chew at her breast, torn up by usury.
The poison's hot and spreads over the wounded
alone, defenseless, as the country fights —
Almighty, be her Guardian anointed,
or else she'll face the final of her nights!"

"I gave you blessings and plenty of offspring
who suckled long on Hungary's nurturing breast —
don't wait for others, go, do your own fighting,

why can't *you* rise at your own folk's behest?
With hearts and souls you were all richly gifted
your road stood open for the victory fight —
but you built no defenses, merely drifted,
race of coward grave-diggers, born to spite..."

"But Fate! Take pity on my suffering country!
Once you had ordained wondrous bliss for her —
behold, the wild hordes now attacking Hungary
are her own children, once all nursed by her.
Punish the scum! Squash my own kind, the basest,
damnation dwell on all their cursèd graves!
But keep alive the faithful Mother dearest,
that she may bear new sons instead of slaves...!"

"My Law's in force...Your country's constellation
must sunset for her prodigal sons' guilt —
its starlight sheds no more illumination
upon the grey-haired fathers tombs begilt.
The Four Rivers[10] shall greet another nation,
another tongue, new customs by their banks —
and strangers will erupt in jubilation
as will the grinning mobs who join their ranks."

Adam Makkai

VANITATUM VANITAS

Here is the Scripture, for your mind
in sober age to ponder on,
an apologue in which you find
the sapience of Solomon —
the universal frame we see
is founded but on vanity:
> summer and winter, snow and rain,
> all is irrevocably vain!

---

[10] The Danube, Tisza, Drava, and Sava, which were the principal rivers
of the erstwhile Hungarian kingdom.

Our earth is but an ant-hill's form,
a thing of fleeting fantasies,
the lightning and the thunderstorm
are will-o'-the-wisps and murmuring bees —
proud history is but a breath,
the brief vibration of a sigh;
       all glory is a mist of death,
       and armies, like a bubble, die.

Great Alexander's meteor-life
is but a hunt for hares and cats,
wild Attila's raging hordes and strife
are swarms of wasps and droves of rats —
the fields Matthias[11] fought and won,
the conquests of Napoleon,
       proud Waterloo's victorious shocks,
       these are but jousts of barnyard cocks.

And virtue is but a vain pretence
of vapors out of fever wrought,
the bosom's ardent sentiments
from thick, congested blood are caught.
The martyrdom of Socrates,
stern Cato's earnest loyalties,
       the sacred dust of Zrínyi[12] great —
       these are but wanton jests of fate.

Ye sages, what, with all your pains
have you achieved of fair and bright?
Sure, drunkenness possessed the brains
of Plato and the Stagirite![13]
Philosophy that so enchants
is only ordered ignorance —
       and science with its vain regards
       is but a castle built of cards.

---

[11] See Footnote #6.

[12] Count Miklós Zrínyi, the same to whom the two patriotic songs above are addressed.

[13] A name for Aristotle, from the city of Stagira in which he was born.

Demosthenes' loud eloquence
is but the cursing of a churl,
and Xenophon, with honeyed sense
a tale amid the spinner's whirl.
Exalted Pindar's eagle wing
is but an ague's stammering —
       the grace that Phidias has shown
       is but a chiselled chunk of stone.

Then when is life's great flood of fire?
A falling spark's illusive heat.
What are the tempests of desire?
The air that insect pinions beat.
In endless alternation flow
effect and cause; our guides below
       on life's straight path are hope and faith,
       deceptions of a rainbow wraith.

Mere moonshine is our joy, I claim,
Ill fortune, smoke that drifts about,
the world is but a candle-flame
and death the draught that blows it out.
You seek fame's immortality
that lure of perfume for the bee?
       Remember, when the roses fall
       their scent is lost beyond recall!

Then think not on the world's estate!
That man is wise, whose mind disdains
the greatness of the fame or fate,
stern virtue's good, or learning's gains.
Be like a never-shaken cliff,
inert, unfeeling, stark and stiff...
       Let hopes arise or fortunes die —
       to filth or beauty close your eye!

For let this little planet move
or stand in space, its motion sped,
let light or darkness brood above,
let sun or moon be o'er your head,

no matter what the hue or guise
of all our fickle destinies
    be sure that good and ill but feign...
    For all the Universe is vain!

Watson Kirkconnell

LIBATIONS

Onto the twin and contrasting altars I pour my libations:
  For you, love of mine, my tears; for you, my country, my blood!

Adam Makkai

ONE FOR BALASSI[14]

Full of fear in my doubt, never at rest my pain;
Often I am weeping, my tears spilling in vain —
Wandering homeless, forever by wood, hill, or plain,
Never succor or refuge may the griever gain!

Furious storms, hope, claw at your billowing sail!
Cast anchor, trusty one, to save me, over the rail!
Stay and steady your skiff now! Foam slaps in the gale...
And smile once more on me, Hope! Again bid me Hail!

G. S. Fraser

---

[14] The 16th-century poet Bálint Balassi (q.v.) who was tossed about by ill fortune.

ONE FOR A KEEPSAKE ALBUM

Four little words I send, indeed, mark them well. To your own son
  Leave them as writ in your will: Country before all else!

Adam Makkai

HUSZT[15]

Once, on a lone sorry night, your ruins, Fort Huszt, did I enter,
  Silent, from under the clouds, rose an ethereal Moon.

As from a grave, a breeze then arose — from amidst ruined pillars
  there in the moon-flooded hall beckoned a wavering ghost:

"Patriot, why are you yearning," it asked, "on the peak of these ruins?
  What is the worth of your thought, back on the shades of the past?

Ponder anew why the time is *now,* compare it well to the future,
  toil, be effective, increase — Thus will your land be reborn!"[16]

Watson Kirkconnell [& A.M.]

SZONDI[17]

Longingly homeward the crane out of regions afar is returning,
feeling the warmth of the breath of the days that are born in the
  springtime;

---

[15] A Hungarian fort in the Eastern Carpathians, today in Ukraine. This poem represents Kölcsey's forward looking, progressive thinking.

[16] This last line has become proverbial in Hungarian *'Hass, alkoss, gyarapíts, s a haza fényre derül!'*. This forward-looking attitude foreshadowed the Age of Reform with Count István Széchenyi its leader. See László Cs. Szabó's essay that appears later in this volume.

[17] The name of the captain who defended the fortress of Drégely in the 16th century. See János Arany's poem "The Two Pages of Szondi."

high through the clouds it swims, until, with its journey completed,
down it alights on familiar turf in the lowlands and meadows.

So to your lawns I return, oh holiest home of my bosom,
poetry, heavenly-fair! The storms of a night all-ferocious,

swept through my life, and beneath them the tenderest passions were
frozen,
down fell the star-wreath that fancy had woven of light in the zenith;

scared by its phantoms, the songs in the depths of my heart became
silent.
Now like the twilight when storms have departed, subdued in his
sadness,

rises the poet again, not upheld by the whimsies of childhood,
neither by visions all-golden of youth in divine contemplation,

dark is his visage and restful; his lyre has deep animation,
fired with power, and ripened with pain and dejection of spirit.

Deeds of a knight he extols, who once shed his brave blood for our
country,
fame of the passing of Szondi, who died on the ruins of Drégely...[18]

Watson Kirkconnell

KÖLCSEY

Proud is my Magyar descent, far to eastward my lineage sprouted;
chills of the westerly skies have not cooled off my fiery bosom:
springs of my ardour are beautiful, filling my heart with affection,
customs and lands are my heirlooms, the sword and traditions of glory.
There does it rest 'midst the verdant boughs of the peace of the
nation:

---

[18] A recurring theme in Hungarian poetry, the Battle of Drégely was
written up most memorably by János Arany (q.v.).

this is what shimmers anew as its brilliance is flooding my song's
    inspiration,
ever recalling again all the past in its magic and colour,
shades of my ancestors old, who have lived out their lives in the
    autumn —
it is this: Kölcsey's clan, all the faithful descendants of Ete, whom
    erstwhile
Ond the heroic, by Donside, who was one one of the Seven Great
    Magyars,[19]
took from his spouse's arms as a pledge of their flamelike embracings.
Gladly they lived out their days by the shores of tumultuous Tisza,
yonder where under wild shadows the Túr in its rage pours its waters;
lived till the arrow of death clanged down in its last devastation,
stirring up tear-brooks of grief in their halls at a final departure.
Victims in blood were received in the shade of the sinister archway;
those whom that passing bereaved were received in the cloisters of
    Cégény...

Watson Kirkconnell

---

[19] There are two lists of the "Seven Chieftains" who led the Hungarians
into their present habitat. According to a later, popularized medieval version,
these were   Árpád, Szabolcs, Gyula, Örs, Künd, Lél, and Vérbulcsu.
According to the more authentic *Gesta Hungarorum* written in the 12th and
13th centuries, the Seven Chieftains were Árpád, son of Álmos, Szabolcs, son
of Előd, Kündü (or Kund) son of Kurszán, Ete son of Ond, Lél (Lehel) son
of Tas, Huba and Tétény (or Tühütüm or Töhötöm), sons of Harka. They
headed up the Seven Tribes that constituted the Hungarian nation when they
entered the Carpathian Basin in 896 A.D. Just before then, they elected Árpád
as the Chief of the entire nation during a famous ceremony known as the
"Blood Covenant" [Vérszerződés], during which each of the seven chieftains
cut his arm to create a communal cup of blood from which each drank while
swearing allegiance to Árpád. The statues of these seven chieftains can be
seen in Heroes' Square in Budapest. Kölcsey's point is that his family can be
traced back to one of these chieftains, namely to Ond, son of Ete. Ond lived
in the latter part of the 9th and the early part of the 10th century.

József Katona
(1791-1830)

Born in Kecskemét, a city south of Budapest on the Great Hungarian Plain, Katona studied law in Pest and, although he was strongly attracted to the theater, he became a municipal attorney in his native town. However, he also worked with a few early theatrical companies both as a stage hand and as an actor. He later translated some popular German melodramas.

His famous historical play, Bánk the Palatine [Bánk Bán], *published in 1821, was the first the major Hungarian drama, a passionate outburst against foreign oppression and corruption, set in the 13th century. Although it did not achieve any real success during Katona's lifetime, it has since played the same part in Hungarian dramatic literature as the works of Mickiewicz in Poland, Victor Hugo in France, and Friedrich Schiller in Germany. The extract presented here presents the Palatine, who has been interested only in serving the interests of the foreign queen Gertrude and her retinue, and the peasant Tiborc, who states his complaints in order to open the Palatine's eyes to the condition of the oppressed Hungarian peasantry.*

On March 15, 1848, on the eve of the anti-Habsburg National Uprising that led to the Hungarian War of Independence, Bank the Palatine *was performed in the Pest National Theater at public demand. It was not performed for a long time afterwards — actually until 1858, in a shortened and censored version. A full performance of the original was not possible until 1868 — the year after the Compromise between Austria and Hungary. The play's real value was not properly identified until János Arany (q.v.) pointed out the profound appropriateness of its language to the dramatic action, a dramatic trait that Katona is known to have learned during his extensive studies of Shakespearean drama.*

Although Katona did write a few other plays such as Stephen, First King of Hungary [István a magyarok első királlya] *in 1813 and* The Destruction of Jerusalem [Jeruzsálem pusztulása] *in 1814, most of these other works have been largely forgotten and his place in Hungarian literature is due to* Bánk the Palatine *which, like* The Tragedy of Man *by Imre Madách, is written mostly in iambic pentameter.*

BÁNK THE PALATINE
(Extract)

BÁNK: ...Speak out, speak, well
I do hear your complaint, but now my own
grievance does also speak.

TIBORC: Oh, Lord and Master,
even the great nobleman has such? — Well then,
it's no crime for poor Tiborc to express
his faith and trust in a secret alliance.

BÁNK: How could I have forgotten it? — My God!

TIBORC: Is there another way out? — Don't expect
empty heroics from me; but, behold,
in war some looting is always permitted.
This sad idea seemed to be the best.

BÁNK: *[Looks sadly through the window]*
My Magyar fatherland!

TIBORC: The good Meranians
do this without having to go to war, too;
for Jews pay them enough — we really ought
therefore not call them wild "skinners of men" —
for to be flayed you need to have a skin, but
the Meranians have already torn the skin
from our bare bones; so they're forced, you see,
to cut into the flesh. Victims can scream,
but our oppressors won't listen to them
if there's a chance of profit to be made.
And the Queen...!
[he makes a gesture of contempt]

BÁNK: *[Pressing his head to the window]*
Oh!

TIBORC: She has ornamental, marbled
palaces built; while we — we almost freeze
between the hedge-walls of our huts.

BÁNK: Accursed!

TIBORC: She keeps to the hordes of her scummy palace guards,
just as if each stem of her fancy hairdo
needed a servant; all Meranians.

At times you'd think they're taken to the gallows,
they're so surrounded by those good-for-nothings;
while we can barely hire one measly field-guard
the seven of us peasants put together.
She constantly gives gaudy balls, as though
there were always a wedding or a christening;
our hearts start racing if we meet the clerk
of an inn-keeper in the street, because
he right away reminds us that we owe him.
Meranians cavort on fancy horses;
one day a chestnut, next a grey or white one,
while we must hitch our wives and kids to plows
if we don't want to suffer death by hunger.
They gambol and constantly guzzle wine
as if each small organ within their bodies
were blessed with more than just a single stomach;
with us, the storks vanish from our chimneys
because we ate the straw from all their nests.
They've turned our fields to hunting grounds which we
are not allowed to enter. If a sick
wife or child longs for it and we dare trap
a miserable little pigeon, they
immediately tie us to a tree;
and they who steal by hundreds and the thousands
become the judge of them whom misery forced
to steal a penny...

BÁNK: Oh, how true it is!

TIBORC: They build monasteries and fancy churches
where they play flute-music and bellow psalms
so loud that pilgrims in the muddy street
are coaxed to dance, while we have not a garment
in which to show our faces in a church
in honour of a treasured patron saint.

BÁNK: Oh! Boil, blood, keep on boiling!

TIBORC: If we want
to lodge complaints, first we must learn to write;
for poor peasant folk can no longer enter
the presence of their lord — thus our King Béla
decreed — now the Meranians enjoy this —
for our iron-shod feet — our shoes are such —

would scratch the polished stone-floors of the rich!
And maybe if for our last single penny
some learnèd lawman writes down our grievance,
who will write down the flow of our bitter tears,
so that our good king should be able to see them?

BÁNK: Oh, God!

TIBORC: They ought to blush when belts of silver
and floor-length golden threads cover their legs,
for this is the fruit of our blood and sweat.
They might as well tie shrouds around their bellies;
at least they would show on the outside some
concern for those downtrodden, whom they send
to an early grave through their crude exploitation.

BÁNK: Endure it in peace...!

TIBORC: Endure it in peace... That's what our
abbot preached so often; "bless the meek,
for they shall be called 'sons of God...'" But
meanwhile his own belly was full... God! What's the
  use?
We're not afraid of hell, since we're so poor;
nor does heaven appear in such fine colours
to our eyes.

BÁNK: We shall break all the barriers!
Just wait, dear friend, and then, if we should reach
our goal, there will be no more weeping. I
pity your miseries, my human fellows!

TIBORC: You pity us, great Lord? Even Magyars
do not think not much of us, with pockets filled.
Nature herself has destined that the poor
should live, to toil, to starve, suffer, and die.
Oh, yes indeed! You must well know the fate
of those condemned to life ere you pity them.

Gavin Ewart, Paul Tabori [& A.M.]

VI. POETS OF THE HUNGARIAN ROMANTIC ERA

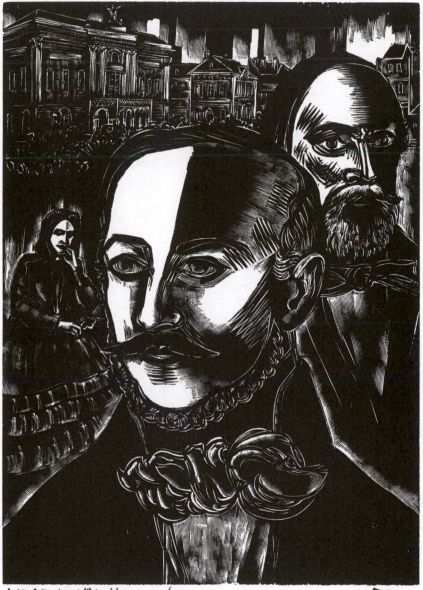

Mihály Vörösmarty
1800-1853

Mihály Vörösmarty
(1800-1855)

Mihály Vörösmarty was born at Pusztanyék into a Roman Catholic family of impoverished gentry. His father worked as steward for the powerful Nádasdy family. He was educated in the city of Székesfehérvár by the Cistercian fathers and in Pest by the Piarists, but when he was eleven years old, his father's death left the family very poor. He nevertheless managed to complete his education by working as a tutor, meanwhile falling in love with the daughter of the family that employed him—Etelka Perczel. This was a hopeless passion for a penniless student.

He was only twenty-four when, in 1824, he finished his great heroic epic, The Flight of Zalán [Zalán futása], one of the mile-stone achievements of Hungarian narrative poetry. In it Vörösmarty used the classical Graeco-Latin hexameter like no one else before him.

Although he was hailed by his fellow poets, he had to live hand-to-mouth, for his contributions to newspapers and periodicals were miserably paid. Between 1823 and 1831 he composed four dramas and eight smaller epics, of which A két szomszédvár [Two Neighboring Castles] and Cserhalom (the name of a castle where an 11th-century battle was fought in Transylvania) are the best.

When the Hungarian Academy of Sciences was established in 1830, he was elected a member and later succeeded Károly Kisfaludy (q.v.) as president, receiving a modest salary. He became one of the founders of the influential Kisfaludy Society and in 1837 he started two periodicals, Athenaeum, and Observer [Figyelmező]. The former grew into the chief belletristic periodical of the country; the latter became the flagship of Hungarian literary criticism.

Beside these major epic works and his brooding poems dealing with the fate of the nation, Vörösmarty could also write charming, playful poetry, such as Young Pete [Petike], which is included here.

Between 1830 and 1843 he devoted himself primarily to dramatic works; Blood Wedding [Vérnász], which won the Academy's prize, belongs to this period. In 1833 he married Laura Csajághy, who was a great deal younger than he was, hence his wistful distich to her, herein presented, along with a number of exquisite love songs. In 1848, together with János Arany and Sándor Petőfi (qq.v.) he initiated a translation of the complete works of Shakespeare into Hungarian; he translated Julius Caesar and King Lear. More modern translations have appeared since, but Vörösmarty's contributions endure nonetheless. In the same year he was elected to the National Diet, and one year later he became one of the judges of the Supreme Court.

The defeat of the Hungarian War of Independence affected him more severely than his contemporaries. He became an alcoholic and, although in 1854 he could still compose what was perhaps his greatest poem, The Ancient Gypsy [A vén cigány], *featured herein, it was to be his swan-song. Grief had driven him into insanity. His funeral was a day of national mourning.*

In his fairy-tale play Csongor és Tünde *(translated by Peter Zollman in 1996), he created the Hungarian equivalent of Shakespeare's* Midsummer Night's Dream. *It is thought to be the equal of* The Tragedy of Man *by Imre Madách (q.v.). Numerous essays deal with the philosophical parallels that can be found between these two dramatic works.*

A philosopher and a great poet, he was the senior member of the great classical triumvirate Vörösmarty-Petőfi-Arany. Vörösmarty lived to be fifty-four. While Petőfi, although only twenty-six when killed in battle, died in a blaze of glory, and Arany died at the age of sixty-seven as poet laureate, Vörösmarty died an agonizing death after a long physical and mental decline. His brooding yet serene statue, surrounded by characters from his plays, dominates a central square in Budapest named after him.

Vörörsmarty was a master of most metrical and rhymed poetic forms, both in the Western style and with the eight-syllable Hungarian dactylic line. Translating him has proved to be a major challenge, as overtones of Blake, Burns, Lovelace, Shelley, and Milton had to blend harmoniously into an original voice calling from the 19th-century.

His completed works were edited by Pál Gyulai and first appeared in 1884.

THE FLIGHT OF ZALÁN

Where are you, glory of old? Lost deep in the night of the shadows?
Eons have passed, and beneath you, the ominous depths of the
  darkness
loom as you wander. Above, dense clouds and Oblivion's mournful
shape float by in ungarlanded sadness, the image of prowess forgotten.
Where is the one who, with lips all bold, could thunder a war-song
rousing the gloom of the deep and unsightly abysses,
lifting to view, once more, brave Árpád, the noble commander,
wearing the skin of a leopard and potent to shatter the nations?
Where are you now? Oh, thousands turn, muted, again to the darkness;
day-dreams extinguish their hearts, and the glory of old turns to
  slumber.

Impotent passes our Age, inefficient from softness of purpose,
children are born, all submissive, less bold than their valorous
    fathers.

Watson Kirkconnell [& A.M.]

YOUNG PETE

Look at Peter: sad and glum,
grim, grim, grim...
Grief and Peter? Hey, by gum
what's wrong with him?
     Tearful are his mother's eyes
     looking on:
     "Are you ill, perhaps?" she sighs
     "Pete, my son?"
"Have some dumplings, darling Pete,
from this tray."
"Nothing, nothing will I eat,
go away!"
     "Then you'd like some wine, I think,
     red and sweet?"
     "Nothing, nothing will I drink,"
     answers Pete.
"For your collar, fox's fur,
feathers for your hat?
For your boots, new shiny spurs,
how is that?"
     "No, no spurs, no fancy frocks,
     nothing smart!
     Sorrow, like a stealthy fox,
     chews my heart."
"Here, this Bible is for you,
don't be sore!"
"Books are empty and untrue,
nothing more!
     Death alone remains my own
     faithful friend —
     he will come to mow me down
     in the end."

"God have mercy! Dearest Pete
do not die!
How a mother's heart does bleed
when you sigh!
      How'd be Jill for company?
      Shall I ask her o'er?"
      "What," demands Pete sullenly,
      "are we waiting for?"
"Ah, so *this* was eating him
just imagine that!
Coats and furs are not his whim
nor a feathered hat!
      He hates the music of the spurs
      he won't eat his fill,
      the neighbour's Bible, too, he spurns,
      all he wants is Jill!
Jill is roguish and demure,
the merry pretty Miss!
Pete's desire for food is poor,
but he wants a kiss!
      Well, my Peter, is that all,
      is it, son?
      I will see that you grow tall
      and live on.
Stop behaving like a dunce,
stop that sniff and bleat,
and be off to school at once,
naughty Pete!
      Wait ten years, and banish Jill
      from your head;
      then, please God, if all goes well,
      you may wed!"

Yakov Hornstein

ONE FOR MISS PARDO'S TRAVEL DIARY

What can we, a small nation adrift, beg of mighty Britannia?
      Glory in spoils of war? How to get wealthy in peace?

Your duty calls: Be a leader of men, be just! Yes, you can afford it;
  Hungary's way to the fold: Strive as we learn to survive.

Adam Makkai

ANOTHER FOR MISS PARDO'S ALBUM

With darkest thoughts my mind is overcast
Within my heart dwells blackest blasphemy.
I long for the doom of the Universe,
and the extinction of all of humanity.

Without a homeland what's the world to me?
Like a damned soul I keep crying in vain
throughout the endless, empty Universe —
this ravaged land can life no more sustain.

From such a man, Dear Lady, what could you
gain for your album? It's for you to give
a ray of hope, some new faith, just a hint
that Hungary still has a chance to live...!

I would turn beggar for such hope and faith —
I'll buy it with my blood, yea, if I can.
Pray — I am sure your prayer will be heard —
and perhaps help such a defeated man.

Paul Tabori

GUTENBERG INSCRIPTION

When night finally fades, when false dreams cease to be worshipped
  And the triumphant day brooks no charlatan art;
When heavy handed tyrants lay their swords to surrender
  And everlasting peace springs from a murderous age;
When from a life of beast and satan, unhappy paupers
  And the exploiting rich rise to be human again;
When a reviving light will spread from west to the eastward
  And dedicated hearts teach great deeds to the mind;
When one day all people assemble into a council
  And with a thundery roar blast their vote to the sky,

And the commotion booms one word in harmony: "Justice!"
  And Providence at last grants this gift to the earth,
Then will victory truly be years: a new generation,
  Their spirit is your most worthy memorial arch.   *Peter Zollman*

FOR LAURA

Won't you become too tired, and quit smiling at me when I languish,
  will you be able still my woes and quirks to endure?
Great is the sacrifice you must make — turn your innocent virtue
  into the sun to erase shades over ruins of my life.

                                                          Adam Makkai

TO THE DAY-DREAMER

Where has the lustre of your eyes descended?
What do they seek in murky depths of space?
Shedding tears for an ecstasy that ended,
or the dark rose that fled without a trace?

Do apparitions on the future's veil
draw nigh with fearful pictures of dismay?
Do you distrust your fate, all wan and pale,
because you once were lost upon the way?

Look at the world and see how very few
among its millions do not weep and sigh —
daydreaming ruins life with lying view
it gazes, cross-eyed, at a painted sky.[1]

For what can give a man true happiness?
Fame? Treasure? Beauty? Pour these out in flood,
and greedy men will drown in their excess
with joy of spirit never understood.

---

[1] These two lines have become proverbial in Hungarian.

He who needs roses does not wear a bower;
to stare into the sun means not to see:[2]
he who seeks pleasure only, finds it sour;
for only temperance brings no agony.

They who are good and noble in their soul
who do not hunger in mouth-watering dearth,
whom pride and greedy fancy can't control,
Only they find a home upon this earth.

Don't look, then, to the distance dreams have shown
for the whole earth is never our estate;
only as much as we can call our own
will the wise heart accept and cultivate.

The past and future are a sea too wide
for the small farmstead of single breast;
fog-forts and dead lights flicker o'er its tide;
the lonely heart grows pale at its unrest.

If faithful gifts your present hour bestrew
with feeling, thought and love your true existence,
remain with life and what it offers you
and do not seek the fair but doubtful distance!

Don't sell serenity for coin of dreams
that will lie useless in your cozened hand —
regret will be the sum of all your schemes
if you frequent that day-dream wonderland.

Bring back, bring back your eyes' most lovely light!
Let it return now like a homing bird
that seeks its own olive branch in its flight
that branch to all sorrowful sighs preferred.

---

[2] Perhaps reminiscent of Lovelace's famous *"Stone walls do not a prison make, nor iron bars a cage"* these two lines have also become proverbial in Hungarian, usually without the users' knowledge of their origin.

Remain among us with your youthful eyes!
Shine forth in brightness on your friend's true face!
Become his sun, high noon in all his skies,
untouched by tears in radiance and grace!

Watson Kirkconnell and *H.H. Hart*

FAIR ILONKA

I.
The huntsman waits with watchful eye
in ambush, holding shaft on string,
as ever upward through the sky
the ardent sun is journeying.
He waits in vain — in coverts cool
the stag still rests by some distant pool.

Long, long he sits in ambush yet
and hopes for game at close of day;
then, as he prays the sun to set,
behold good fortune comes his way —
it is no stag, but a butterfly,
with a girl pursuing, flutters by.
"Merry flyer, fair golden moth,
rest on my finger, do not flee!
Or I will follow, by my troth,
where red sunset gilds bush and thee!"
She speaks, and nimble as a roe,
she hastens on with heart aglow.

"Gad!" says the huntsman, "is this not
most royal game?" — and up he leaps,
pursuing, all things else forgot,
the path the flying maiden keeps.
Thus man and maid, in eager flight,
each seek a vision of delight.

"I have you!" — cries the happy miss,
and pauses, butterfly in hand.
"I have you!" — cries the man with bliss,
and so the graceful couple stand.

Caught in his eye's admiring glow,
the maiden lets the insect go.

II.
Stands yet the house of old Peterdi?
Lives that old son of battle still?
That house, though in decay, I see;
the old man sits and drinks his fill.
By him the girl; their huntsman-guest
looks on with eyes of warm unrest.

For Hunyadi,[3] their chief who died,
the men have drained their glasses deep.
For that great hero, Hungary's pride,
the veteran is forced to weep.
His blood flowed free in days of yore,
his tears in equal measure pour.

"Drink to my old chief's royal son!" —
the patriarch cries, "Long live the King!"
The blushing huntsman seems undone,
he lets his glass stand, faltering.
"Why won't you drink? What seems amiss?
Accept a father's will in this!

I could, in years, be twice your sire;
I drink, believe me, without blame —
the King's a man of faith and fire,
who will not put his blood to shame!"
Stirred by the greybeard's earnest plea,
the youth stands up in fealty.

"Long live the son of that old chief!
As long as Hungary may he live!
Yet may his days be black and brief
if e'er his best he fails to give!

---

[3] János Hunyadi was the father of King Mátyás [Matthias], Hungary's renaissance king. Mátyás was fond of travelling in disguise.

Better no King than one disloyal,
who plagues the land unsound, unroyal."

In deepening ardour and applause
the fleeting hours swiftly soar;
and still the maid's affection draws
more closely to the visitor.
"Ah, that I knew his name and home!"
Her warm heart speaks, her lips are dumb.

"Fair flower of the forest, you,
I also praise the pledge in wine!
And should God e'er direct you two
to Buda, you with me must dine.
In Buda's lofty tower I dwell,
At Mátyás' court they know me well..."

The huntsman speaks, and takes his leave.
A far-off slug-horn bids him go.
Although his hosts entreat and grieve
and seek fresh kindnesses to show.
"Come back to see your friends once more,
in case we do not come before!"

Reluctant on the threshold now
she speaks in modesty polite.
He prints a kiss upon her brow,
then marches through the moonlit night.
The house is still, but not her breast,
where love won't grant a moment's rest.

III.
Peterdi and his grandchild sweet
go up to visit Buda-town.
The old man's wonder is complete
to see new mansions of renown.
The maiden waits in anxious pain
to meet her handsome youth again.

Glad crowds are thronging Buda's streets;
they watch to see their monarch ride
in triumph from the warlike feats
that humbled vile Vienna's pride.
Real subjects long to see their King —
no smiles on the maid's features cling.

"Where is our gentle friend today?
What fortunes has he followed here?
Is he at home, or far away
in shady coverts of the deer?"
She speaks to herself silently,
with cheeks now blushed, now blanched to see.

And now with warlike shouts ride by
Ujlaki and the Magyar lords;
the king himself with noble eye
surveys the escort of their swords.
Old Peterdi in wonder peers,
perceives his guest, and joins the cheers.

"God save the King! God bless his fame!"
Ten thousand throats around him shout;
ten thousand echoes greet his name,
hill, vale, and rampart ring it out.
But whiter than white marble there
Ilonka stands in mute despair.

"Shall we go on to Mátyás' hall
to see our friend once more, my lass?
Methinks our forest mansion small
will give us greater peace, alas!"
The greybeard speaks in pained dismay,
and back they plod their weary way.

As droops a radiant summer flower
that withers from an inner blight,
so drooped Ilonka from that hour
and sickened towards eternal night.

Within her heart a cancer fed
on passion's hopes forever dead.

The brief but anguished life is o'er,
a girl has faded to her death,
a tender lily suffering sore
in innocence and anxious breath.
And when at last their royal guest
came back once more, she lay at rest.

Watson Kirkconnell

TO FERENCZ LISZT[4]

Renowned musician, freeman of the world,
and yet our kinsman everywhere you go,
have you a cadence for the ailing land
to set to strings that play in the marrow?
Have you a cadence, shaker of great hearts?
Have you a cadence that no grief defeats?

Centuries old, life-loads of fate and sin
have paralyzed and overborne us;
dispirited, the race lived on the chain,
saving itself by acting spineless.
And if sometimes it boiled to a release
it was the struggle of a fever case.

Then came a finer age and the return
of hope, a dawn lit by our longing,
recovery, sweet torments in the brain,
new life for dead desires, sick yearning.
We are aflame again to claim the land;
we are once more prepared to shed our blood.

---

[4] The Hungarian romantic composer (1811-1886), Richard Wagner's
father-in-law, known for his *Hungarian Rhapsodies, Les preludes, Les fune-
railles, Piano Concerto in E-flat major,* among others.

Each pulse-beat we can feel within our hearts;
at its sacred name our blood surges;
we suffer all its torments, all its smarts;
at each disgrace a new flame urges;
upon its throne we bid it to be great,
happy and strong within its simple hut.

Great scholar of the land where grievance grows,
where the heart of a world is beating,
where now at last the sun dares to arise
with the purple and red blood mingling,
where, as the people's ocean reached full tide,
the domineering furies disappeared;

and in their stead, walking in whitest robes
of purity, step peace and diligence,
and in resplendent mansions art unfolds
new-found and sacred immanence;
and as a thousand brains are sanctified
the nation toils with one tremendous hand;

Great Universal Master, make for us
another song about days gone by,
destiny in the keyboard of our voice
through battle's thunder forcing its cry,
and on the flood of the earth-shattering sound
let trumpet-blasts triumphantly resound.

Sing out a song so in their deepest graves
our ancestors are compelled to stir,
so each immortal soul awaking proves
new life to descendants, made aware
of blessings in their Magyar fatherland.
They know that traitor sons are shamed and banned.

And if grim times and twilight overtake,
let a faint murmur on muted strings
be by your utmost art made to invoke
soughing breezes over autumn leaves,

suggesting to our hearts with lulling sound
those ancient sites where sorrow packs the ground.

Reflected on the manly arms we take
shall rise that pale lady, pensive Grief,
and the full tragedy of Mohács make
its repetition for our belief,
and when the internecine scourge has drawn our tears
that sorrow shall do much for present fears.

And if you waken love of Fatherland,
which holds the present in its embrace,
and at the same time takes the time at hand
and in the past a fine remembrance,
sing to us with your full concerted strings
so that into our hearts your fine sound sings;

and in awakened passion's purity
trials of daring should be meted,
and our great sons should diligently see
that weak and strong must move united,
and like one man the enduring nation stand
with arms of bronze to hold the strife-torn land.
And if they were our bones, even the stones
should shake into a sacred gladness;
and as the fretting wave on Danube runs
our blood shall make its heated progress;
and where both great and sorry days have passed
this soil shall throb, irascible at last;

and if you hear through your resounding strain
the Fatherland awaken to your theme,
which all the people with their teeming tongues
sing with you when their courage grows extreme,
join with us all and let us say: Thank God
this nation keeps the soul of great Árpád.

Alan Dixon

APPEAL[5]

Oh, Magyar, keep immovably
your native country's trust,
for it has borne you, and at death
will consecrate your dust!
No other spot in all the world
can touch your heart as home —
let fortune bless or fortune curse,
from hence you shall not roam!
      This is the country that your sires
      have shed their blood to claim;
      throughout a thousand years not one
      but adds a sacred name.
      'Twas here brave Árpád's mighty sword
      ordained your land to be,
      and here the arms of Hunyad[6] broke
      the chains of slavery.
Here Freedom's blood-stained flag has waved
above the Magyar head;
and here in age-long struggles fell
our best and noblest, dead.
In spite of long calamity
and centuries of strife,
our strength, though weakened, is not spent;
our country still has life.
      To you, O nations of the world,
      we call with passioned breath:
      "Should not a thousand years of pain
      bring liberty — or death?"
      It cannot be that all in vain
      so many hearts have bled,

---

[5] Written in 1836 and set to music by Béni Egressy, the 'Appeal' has become Hungary's second National Anthem. It is the sign-off signal of the Hungarian State Television at midnight while Saint Stephen's crown is shown. The slightly archaic tone of this English translation is, therefore, deliberate.

[6] János Hunyadi (1407-1456), father of King Matthias Corvinus, who defeated the Turks at the Battle of Belgrade in the year of his death.

       that haggard from heroic breasts
       so many souls have fled!
It cannot be that mind and strength
and consecrated will
are wasted in a hopeless cause
beneath a curse of ill!
There yet shall come, if come there must,
that better, fairer day
for which a myriad thousand lips
in fervent yearning pray.
        Or there shall come, if come there must,
        a death of fortitude;
        and round about our graves shall stand
        a nation washed in blood.
        Around the graves where we shall die
        a weeping world will come,
        and millions will in pity gaze
        upon the martyrs' tomb.
Then, Magyar, keep unshakeably
your native country's trust,
for it has borne you and at death
will consecrate your dust!
No other spot in all the world
can touch your heart as home;
let fortune bless or fortune curse,
from hence you shall not roam!
                          Watson Kirkconnell

THE SOLILOQUY OF THE NIGHT

(From the romantic mystery play *Csongor and Tünde*)

   Darkness and Void was all: myself alone
seclusive, silent, all-forsaken Night,
then light was born to me, my only child.
As blazing light erupted from my womb
the boundless power of the radiation
perturbed the empty space, and from the Void
an all-pervading thousand-headed monster,
the Universe appeared. The moon, the stars,

great wonders of the firmament, became
lone pilgrims of immense trajectories.
The former passive peace has passed away
as matter moved and action came to power.
Then barren space and time were populated,
alive with action, movement everywhere.
Ocean and earth fought desperately, claiming
their heritance where Void had reigned before,
until the oceans calmed their angry waves
and as the fight let up, the waters brightened
with sunny smiles reflected from the sky.
Now, like a bride, in grace and gaiety
young Earth put on her finery of flowers.
The dust began to move, then came the beasts
and lastly man, the animated clay,
in kingly style, to multiply his kind,
the true, the false, the sinner, and the saint.
Darkness and Void remain: I'm here alone,
a fugitive from daylight, gloomy Night. —
An insect is the bubble of a moment,
that's all the time allowed for its existence.
Its wings won't save a bird, nor claws a beast,
and noble, sturdy trees must all decay
under the weight of passing centuries.
As man arrives, his spirit radiates,
the Universe is mirrored in his person.
He looks around with infinite delight,
reviewing raptly earth and firmament,
but youth will soon desert him to decline
to drowsy dotage till his term is up,
and then he's gone, mere fly-speck, whence he came.
Unquenchable desires drive him on
to delve, to dream, discern and deeds to do,
he hopes to launch immortal enterprises
with mortal hands, and even in the grave
memorials of vainness guard his dust,
resplendent marble mountains mark the place
with countless lurid, ostentatious signs,
where intellect has paid homage to power.
But what are homage, signs, memorials,

when earth and oceans vanish into air?
The tired suns desert their stable orbits
collapsing into one vast cataclysm,
the Universe decays and its ruins
the melancholy twilight fades away.
And it will end, as once it all began:
Darkness and Void will be: myself alone,
seclusive, silent, all-forsaken Night.   *Peter Zollman*

THOUGHTS IN THE LIBRARY

   Consider, scholar, when you enter here,
on cast-off rags,[7] man's stigma freshly marked,
with words as stark as the dark winter night,
there looms, written blood-black, the awesome lesson:
"while into misery millions are born
a few thousand might find in life salvation
could they but make use of the days of their lives,
had they the mind divine, the Seraph's temper."
   Why all this rubbish? So, like sheep on grass
we may graze on it? Sated with fodder
and idle hours synthesized by science amoral
to waste God's day, a nation's energy?
Why this rubbish? From its stench I recall
all the sins of the animal man — they reek!
Virtue is written on this page, which once
as rag has garbed an outlaw. This other page?
perhaps — oh happy days of innocence —
the frail dress ripped from a ravished virgin,
perhaps a lust-enraged whore's negligee.
And here on these leaves, the law whitewashed from
remnants of bloody rebels and false judges,
from masks of sanguine tyrants washed white;
the secrets of machines and of numbers laid bare,

---

[7] In the 19th century, paper was ordinarily made from rags. Vörösmarty plays up the contradiction between the material from which the pages of books are made and the contents which those pages may possibly contain.

but those who tore garments, stripped man naked,
flayed dignity that bindings might be vellum,
these, unaccounted for, must render account —
they spin on Ixion's[8] tempest-driven wheel
within the vortex, misery without end
and, gnashing their teeth, wail in the dark outside.

On the madman's sheets ponders a sage's head;
the astronomer, on eyeless beggar's rags
measures bursting universes piled on end —
light and blindness, all on a flimsy page!

The coward and the captive, both hapless roles
are bound forever in one book that sings
of freedom and heroes hewing history...
Stainless sheets, pulped from traitor's rags, now
reward the friend and thus honor the faithful;
yet over all, all-polluting, the Big Lie!
The Word, cursed by the pallid winding sheet
its black image adorns, suffers damnation,
rag-lure of countries, your name is library![9]

Where, then, is the volume that answers all?
The greater part of Man — where is his joy?
Is the world no better for any book?

Yes! The more gloriously man's societies arise
the greater the human refuse at the bottom.
The bursting breast of rags stuffed with man
must breathe contagion into the empire's heart.

Should we, after all, topple what countless brains
have wrought in the linked sunbursts of their minds?
Void the golden knowledge rare brains have
chopped and torn away from the mines of time?

---

[8] The king of Laphites of Thessaly in ancient Greek mythology, the
ancestor of the centaurs. He killed his father-in-law and then went insane.
Zeus took pity on him and accepted him into Heaven, where he made a pass
at Hera. To test his intentions, Zeus formed Hera into a cloud, which Ixion
made love to, thereby producing the centaur (half horse, half man). As a
punishment, Zeus tied Ixion to a flaming, winged wheel perennially rotating,
while Ixion had to repeat the words "you owe gratitude to your benefactor."

[9] This line has become proverbial in Hungarian (Országok rongya,
könyvtár a neved!).

How many bright souls immolated themselves
in vigil at the burning ruins of the heart
to give purpose, strength and comfort
to erring humans humbled by destiny?
Those heroes of unrecognized merit
whom the contemptible public mocked
were praised after death, when praise cost but words:
their thoughts beatified by the martyring mob!
Should the great burn to ashes at the same stake
with rag peddlers, numbskulls, and mildewed hearts?
Glow in embers with dark passion-panders
indiscriminate? Good on account of bad, with them?
    Never! That which I said was pain.
The travail of many a bold spirit,
even those luminous minds could not save
the sons of dust from sinking in the mud.
There is barely a corner of the world,
one little oasis on the barren sand
where the most sought-after name is not that of Man,
where the ancient rites of generation
yield as heritage the name of Man!
Except for those who have been born to blackness,
labeled cattle by the glorious elite
who caress the dark image of God with whips.[10]
    Despite all, despite all, one must travail —
a new spirit is fighting its way up,
through the soul of man bursts a new approach —
to nurture fruitful ideals in races
primitive, to culture finer sentiments
that they may embrace, at last, each other,
and within their hearts reign love and justice.
So the lowest peasant may, in his hut,
say with assurance "I am not alone,
my brothers and sisters number millions,
I protect them, and me they defend;
fate, I fear thee not, despite thy dread will!"

---

[10] The Hungarian intelligentsia of the 19th century, while admiring the
Declaration of Independence, were appalled by slavery in America.

That is why one must not succumb to despair.
Let us, steadfast as ants, set down that which
our brains, in the rare inspired hours, create,
and when we have assembled every stone,
we'll erect the Babel of a newer age,
build it until it towers among the stars,
and when we have looked through the gates of Heaven,
having heard from without the Angels' song,
with every drop of our earthly blood
aglow from elevated flames of delights,
let us then scatter like the ancient peoples
and begin anew, to endure and to learn.
    Is this then our fate, and nothing our goal?
It is not — nor will be while the earth yields life,
and its mortal sons are not turned to stone;
what, in this world, is our task? To struggle,
and to nourish the needs of the spirit;
we are Man, son to both the earth and sky,
our soul is the wing beating toward heaven,
but we, instead of striving up to soar,
would rather, dully, like some bird beneath contempt,
eke out existence sucking mud from swamps.
    What, in this world, is our task? To struggle,
according to our strength, for noble goals.
Before us stands the fate of a nation —
when we, from the irrevocable fall
have preserved it and restored it to its heights,
fighting under the clear beam of the spirit,
we can say, returning to our ancestors
in the dust: "Thank you, life, for thy blessings —
this has been great joy, yea, the Work of Men!"

H.H. Hart [& A.M.]

PROLOGUE
(Fragment)

I wrote this when the sky was still serene.
When blossoming boughs beautified the earth.
When mankind laboured like the humble ants,

When spirit soared, and hands were hard at work,
The thoughtful mind alive, the heart in hopes,
When peace could dry her tired brow at last,
Presenting that most glorious reward,
The happiness of man, her noble aim.
All nature celebrated, everything
Benign or beautiful, came out to feast.

Delight and hope were trembling in the air,
Expectant of the grand inauguration,
Addressing all the world in lofty phrases
In tones to suit a better, new creation.
We heard the word. Its sound reverberated
On high and in the deep. For but a moment
The mighty universe had ceased rotating.
Then all fell silent, lull before the storm.
The tempest broke, its blood-congealing hands
Were lobbing human skulls into the sky,
Its feet were wading deep in human hearts,
And life was wilting in its baneful breath.
The torchlight of the spirit died away,
And on the fading forehead of the sky
A lightning etched the otherworldly lines
Of hostile gods in black, bloodthirsty temper.
The tempest blasted, bellowed like a madman,
A rabid monster raging at the world,
And where it went, along the bloody way
The curses of a butchered populace
Are rising from the steaming hecatombs
And devastation rests her weary head
On grey incinerated city ruins.
It's winter now and death and snow and stillness,
The earth turned white;
Not hair by hair as happy people do,
It lost its colour all at once, like God,
Who on the sixth day, crowning his creation,
Gave life to man, the godly-beastly mongrel,
And shattered by the grim monstrosity
His sorrow turned Him white and very old.

When spring, the makeup-mistress comes again,
The agèd earth may take a periwig
And find a frilly frock of daffodils.
The ice may thaw out on her glassy eyes,
Her perfume-scented, painted-on complexion
Pretending youth and faking happiness;
Ask then the aging, wrinkled prostitute
What has she done to her unhappy sons?

Peter Zollman

A BITTER CUP

If you upon a woman
should wager all your heart,
and she your dream of rapture
should lightly rend apart;
if in her treacherous eyes
are smiles and cursed tears,
and in your breast she plants unrest
and pain that burns and sears —
      Just drink, my friend, just drink, I say!
      The Earth itself must pass away,
      must like a bubble effervesce
      and burst to empty nothingness!
If you, as to your spirit,
have trusted to a friend
your confidence and honour,
your country to defend,
and his smooth hand of murder
prepares for you a knife,
until in cold betrayal
he sells your very life —
      Just drink, my friend, just drink, I say!
      The Earth itself must pass away,
      must like a bubble effervesce
      and burst to empty nothingness!
If you in thought exalted
for fatherland have toiled,
or in its hapless battles

have with your blood been soiled,
and it, misled, now scorns you
with low and crass demands,
and mars your loyal sacrifice
with stupid, craven hands —
> Just drink, my friend, just drink, I say!
> The Earth itself must pass away,
> must like a bubble effervesce
> and burst to empty nothingness!

If in your aching bosom
a worm of doubting gnaws
that leaves you unbelieving
in fortune, men, and laws,
and joy in longed-for honour
is poisoned at the source,
and it is late or useless
to seek some better course —
> Just drink, my friend, just drink, I say!
> The Earth itself must pass away,
> must like a bubble effervesce
> and burst to empty nothingness!

And if both wine and sorrow
within your brain unite,
and its dull, barren pictures
revive to life and light,
think thoughts both great and daring!
On these be all intent!
He is not lost, whate'er his fate,
whose heart is confident!
> Just drink my friend, just drink, I say!
> The Earth itself must pass away!
> But while it stands, whether well or ill
> it keeps on moving — can't stay still.

Watson Kirkconnell

THE ANCIENT GYPSY[11]

Strike up, Gypsy, you have quaffed your wages,
Don't just dangle those feet, brighten up!
Life is boring on mere bread and water,
Pour some wine into that dreary cup!
Mortal life is always playing games,
Shivering or bursting into flames;
> Strike up, play the stately and the quick,[12]
> While your bow is more than just a stick.
> Cup and soul, so full of wine and woe —
> Strike up, Gypsy, let your troubles go!

Let your blood boil like the raging ocean,
Let your brain burst in between your temples,
Let your eyes glow with a comet's fire,
Boom your strings the way the bedrock trembles,
Bellow like a hailstorm at its hardest —
The wretched folk were cheated of their harvest...
> Strike up, play the stately and the quick,
> While your bow is more than just a stick.
> Cup and soul, so full of wine and woe —
> Strike up, Gypsy, let your troubles go!

Learn your music from the blowing tempest,
From its frenzied, shrill apocalypse,
Slaughtering men, devastating homesteads,
Twisting trees and wrecking mighty ships.
The holiest Sepulchre of the Lord
Shivers with the raging war abroad.[13]

---

[11] This poem by Vörösmarty is perhaps one of the best loved by the public. It is in the repertory of major Hungarian actors, all of whom, at some point in their careers, specialize in the reciting of classical poetry. 'The Ancient Gypsy' thus has a history of theatrical recital in Hungary as well as its literary one — with the poet himself being the 'Ancient Gypsy.'

[12] The most popular Hungarian country dance, the *csárdás,* alternates between two *tempi:* the stately *lassú* and the quick *friss.*

[13] Reference to the Crimean War and to the Holy Sepulchre in Jerusalem which was the subject of a dispute between Russia and France over the privileges of monks in the holy places in Palestine.

> Strike up, play the stately and the quick,
> While your bow is more than just a stick.
> Cup and soul, so full of wine and woe,
> Strike up, Gypsy, let your troubles go!

Who has sighed this stifled lamentation,
What roars in this savage storm, forsaken,
Who pounds on the columns of creation,
What cries sobbing like the mills of satan?
Tortured spirit, damned soul, fallen angel,
Daring hopes, or withering betrayal?

> Strike up, play the stately and the quick,
> While your bow is more than just a stick.
> Cup and soul, so full of wine and woe,
> Play on, Gypsy, let your troubles go!

Do we hear again the savage curses
Rebel men so desperately hurled,
Bludgeon blows that caused the brother's murder,
Dirge of the first orphans in the world,
The beat of the cruel vulture's wing,
Prometheus's endless suffering?

> Strike up, play the stately and the quick,
> While your bow is more than just a stick!
> Cup and soul, so full of wine and woe,
> Play on Gypsy, let your troubles go!

Let this blind star, miserable molehill
Go on churning in its bitter juices,
Till the raging fever will have cleansed it
Of illusions, squalor, vile abuses,
Then let Noah's Ark sail into sight
With a reborn humankind inside.

> Strike up, play the stately and the quick,
> While your bow is more than just a stick.
> Cup and soul, so full of wine and woe,
> Strike up, Gypsy, let your troubles go!

Strike up! No! — Allow the strings a rest!
One day we shall celebrate again,
When the evil nightmare fades away,
When all dissension is solidly slain.

Then: play passionately, from the heart —
Let the Gods enjoy your noble art!
>   That's the time to set your bow to string,
>   Cheer up from your gloomy slumbering,
>   Joy shall fill your soul like heady wine,
>   Strike up, leave the troubled world behind!

Peter Zollman

ON MANKIND

Fall silent! Cease to sing your tale:
the world reveals its past —
of frozen winds and scalding flail
that humans' hearts have cast —
showers of tears men's sorrows cause to fly,
winds from the hearts of those who sigh.
Worthless are all things: virtue, sin, and brain:
>   All hope is vain.
>   You've often heard the tale: "The nation
>   had Founding Fathers brave,
>   but as they sinned, their own creation
>   went sinning to their grave..."
>   Those left alive with fear were filled:
>   "Give us the Law!" — But the Law had killed...
>   The virtuous fell, murderers ruled again:
>   All hope is vain.
And then the powerful heroes placed
the Law beneath their feet.
Man bent the iron, toiled and faced
it all — there's no defeat.
The mighty soon to die began;
man, in frustration, turned on man...
And fame? A lightning flash in want's dark reign:
>   All hope is vain.
>   Then a long age of peace arose,
>   men mightily increased;
>   perhaps for a plague the number grows
>   to make a larger feast:
>   man looks to Heaven with longing eyes,

but Earth his ownership denies...
Even for graves too hard is its domain:
   All hope is vain.
How plentifully lush the Earth!
Made even richer by Man's stroke;
yet everywhere there is still dearth,
slaves groan beneath the yoke.
Must it always be thus? If no,
why, for so long, has it been so?
Is it virtue or strength, we can't obtain?
   All hope is vain.

     An ungodly contract there's aglow
     'twixt reason and Evil will:
     therefore your raging follies grow
     in feverish wars to kill.
     Satan and Reason the strife began:
     whichever wins, the loser's Man,
     this God-faced beast, this lump of mud insane:
        All hope is vain!
Man pains the Earth.[14] Beyond the spate
of years of war and peace,
the curses of fraternal hate
upon her brow increase.
And should we think he'll learn in time,
he plots an even viler crime:
from dragon's teeth will spring his budding grain:
   All hope is vain! All hope is vain!

Valerie Becker Makkai,
Neville Masterman [& A.M.]

---

[14] The last stanza of this poem represents the height of 19th-century Romantic pessimism in Hungarian literature. The thought that the Earth is an organism which the human race is hurtfully exploiting has resurfaced in the late 20th century's environmental movements. The refrain 'all hope is vain' has become proverbial in Hungarian *(Nincsen remény...nincsen remény!)*. As a remarkable trouvaille of phonological similarity in translation, the English syllable *vain* and the second syllable of Hungarian *remény* 'hope' are similar.

József Bajza
(1804-1858)

József Bajza was a poet, a critic, an editor, and a journalist — one of the leading figures of the Age of Reform. A descendant of a noble family of modest means, he was born in the village of Szücsi, and he studied law at the University of Pest. His earliest writings were contributed to Kisfaludy's (q.v.), Aurora [The Dawn], *which Bajza edited from 1830 to 1837.*

He also wrote many pieces for Athenaeum, *and he was a member of the ruling intellectual triumvirate of Hungarian letters, the two others being Ferenc Toldy and Mihály Vörösmarty (q.v.). He also contributed to the German* Kritische Blätter [Critical Pages] *and to* Figyelmező [The Guardian]. *He was particularly noted for his theatrical criticism. In 1830 he published a collection of translations of foreign dramas and in 1835 a collection of his own poems.*

The Hungarian Academy of Sciences elected him a corresponding member in 1831, and a regular member in 1832.

In 1837 he became the first director of the newly established National Theater. During the following years he also did a good deal of historical writing, editing and publishing several series, such as The Modern Plutarch [Új Plutarchosz], *and* Universal History [Világtörténet], *which appeared in 1847. Just one year before the outbreak of the Hungarian War of Independence against Austria, Lajos Kossuth, Hungary's future Governor, chose Bajza to be the editor of his daily newspaper* Hírlap [Daily News].

After the defeat of Hungary in 1849 by the Russian armies which came to Austria's aid, he hid in various regions of the country in the company of Vörösmarty. He only returned to Pest toward the end of 1849. His nervous system collapsed under the hardships he had endured, and he spent the last eight years of his life as a helpless mental patient.

His poetry had a moving sentimentality and great sensitivity which were further deepened by the tragic collapse of Hungary's struggle for independence in 1849. His significance as a Hungarian intellectual was enhanced by the fact that he was the first essayist to write about the problems of the novel.

Also noteworthy is his essay 'The Theory of the Epigram' [Az epigramma teóriája], which appeared in 1828. His thought was influenced by the German G.E. Lessing (1729-1781) and the Austrian J. G. Herder (1744-1803), both of whom were writers of the Englightenment.

SIGHING

Your past was bereft of pleasure;
your future knows but need;
my country, sick past measure —
alas, for you I bleed!

For you resound complaining,
eternal grief my song;
from clouds of darkness raining
descend cold grief and wrong.

Disaster hovered near us,
'mid maelstrom, wind, and wave;
no star has shone to cheer us,
no shore appeared to save.

O You who have created
the soul with all its love
to country dedicated,
to home, and You above.

From your celestial station,
let fall, where here we grope,
O God of every nation,
one healing ray of hope!   *Watson Kirkconnell*

AUTUMN SONG

The mists are brooding on the fields;
        the crane flaps from the fen;
it seeks the distant south to find
        its tropic home again
among the Nubian daffodils
where there's no winter on the hills.

The yellowing shrubs are sere and wan,
        the leaves are falling fast;

morality grown ashen-cold
      and withers towards the past;
and stricken souls of human kind
now yearn a better land to find.

Ah heart, sick heart, your autumn's here,
      your frost-killed leaves now fall,
your branches on this wintry earth
      will grow no more at all.
Yet give not way to grief, but roam
to seek another, fairer home!

Watson Kirkconnell

THE PROPHECY

What does the cloudy future hold,
and why does it seem so dark?
Are the many anguished spirits
waiting for a storm to start?
Does doomsday's dreadful trumpet call
to the living and the dead?
Do the fiery wings of Angels
clamour at the tombs ahead?

Ah, no! Now the people rise up,
all the world's a giant sea
torn by the unleashed powers of
minds grown sick of tyranny.
Nations now erupt in fury
half of the world is in flames,
because peaceful life that's sacred
has been crushed by tyrants' games.

All justice has fled from the earth,
leaving its rule to pure force;
freedom is subject to laughter —
O, God! — and prison, or worse.
Possessions are naught but plunder,
nothing is rightly one's own;

and the prize for love of country is
gallows, chains, or loss of home.

Lawlessness has become law here,
fierce oppression acts as order;
living merely from day-to-day
has turned into loathsome labor.
But the day of vengeance will come,
authors of each crime will soon
be punished as they deserve it:
to oppressors — death and doom!

Rebellions are rearing their heads
fierce battles are being planned;
armies of millions will face
those few who their blood demand.
And the tempest of war will rage
'round the palaces so proud,
and the battlements will crumble,
as blood drowns the human crowd.

God will come to render judgement
over commoners and kings,
and will turn to dust with one glance
all thrones where tyranny clings;
he will restore the multitudes'
holy covenant of birth,
and joyful songs proclaiming peace
shall ring on Heaven and earth.

And slaves will again form nations,
under law and liberty;
and man will be a man again
such as he was meant to be.
In the Cathedral of Freedom
the throne of justice we shall raise,
and each insect upon this earth
each blade of grass, will give praise.

Judith Kroll [& A.M.]

János Garay
(1812-1853)

János Garay was born into a bourgeois family with roots in the middle nobility. He was educated at the Universities of Pécs and Pest; he started out as a medical student but later changed to arts and letters.

He was twenty-two when he published his first heroic poem, entitled Warrior [Csatár]. *It was written in classical hexameters, and showed the influence of Mihály Vörösmarty's (q.v.)* The Flight of Zalán. *It was followed by a number of historical dramas, of which* Ilona Országh *in 1837 and* Elizabeth Báthory *in 1840 were the most successful. He was an accomplished journalist; he wrote reports, essays, and criticism and translated German and French short stories for the journals he worked for.*

In order to develop Hungarian theatrical culture, he founded the Dramatic Association of Pest in 1835, and in 1839 he was elected to the Academy of Sciences. He studied the works of Shakespeare in detail and wrote an essay on the dramatic arts in connection with Shakespeare. He urged Hungarian writers to study the form of French romantic tragedies, while pointing out that Hungarian authors should use Hungarian subjects for their writings.

In 1842 he started his own periodical Regélő Pesti Divatlap [The Narrative Pages of Pest]. *In 1848 he was appointed Professor of Hungarian literature at the University of Pest. After the loss of the Hungarian War of Independence he was arraigned before a military court because of his poems favoring the Revolution. He was not jailed, but he lost his university post.*

The last four years of his life were overshadowed by poverty and illness; he had to dictate his last works to members of his family. His funeral was attended by a very large crowd — it turned into a veritable demonstration against Austrian oppression.

His best remembered work, The Veteran [Az obsitos], *which appeared in 1843, is a humorous presentation of a braggart ex-soldier of the Napoleonic wars. It provided the basis for Zoltán Kodály's well known opera,* János Háry. *His last and most famous work was a historical poem in twelve cantos entitled* Saint Ladislas [Szent László], *which appeared in 1852. While still at the University of Pest, he undertook the writing of the first textbook on the history of Hungarian literature and linguistics, but he was unable to finish it and only fragments of it survive.*

THE OLD VETERAN AND NAPOLEON

There were three at one table: the pot-bellied judge —
the hero on half-pay — the journalist drudge;
and scattered about, from their tables a-gape,
were peasant lads drinking the juice of the grape.
  From vespers already they'd sat at their swilling,
  in health after health all their glasses refilling;
  and toasts to King Mátyás brought less off the shelf
  than Háry, the veteran, drank to himself.
There was reason for all the big noise and hurrah,
for the peer of that hero six towns never saw.
All eyes and ears gaped at his utterance bold;
the world was agog at the tales that he told.
  So now, lifting up the quart stein in his hand,
  he tells new adventures by sea and by land,
  recounts where and what he accomplished and heard —
  and silently everyone hangs on his word.
He'd smashed whole armadas asunder alone;
had gone, with a comrade, to oceans unknown;
had hung his tent round with French heads in his mirth,
and dangled his legs off the edge of the earth.
  "But you've heard nothing yet!" he would gravely protest;
  and all would crowd closer to hear out the rest.
  "What! Nought?" — says the judge. "Why, what more could
   remain?
  Drink, comrade!" And everyone drinks like a drain.
"'Tis true," cries a student, on mischief now bent,
"the best is to come!" and they listen intent.
"You lads will know nothing, unless he relate
how 'Uncle' once captured Napoleon the Great..."
  "Ahem!" — said the hero. "Napoleon's a joke.
  He's 'Great' with the French and the likes of such folk.
  But with Magyars, God knows, it is different by far —
  and he's nothing at all to a Magyar hussar!"
By this, 'twas himself he referred to, of course,
although he had never once ridden a horse;
so often, however, he'd mentioned his steed,
he'd become, in his thinking, a trooper indeed.

"Well, once — the exact time and place I forget —
with 'Nap' and full two hundred thousand we met;
against them, just one or two hundred we came,
all fine trim hussars, made of fire and flame!"
The mischievous student here sneezed a great sneeze,[1]
but Háry continued his tale quite at ease:
"Two hundred against those vast thousands and more!
Judge, what is your verdict? Who settled the score?"
"Who settled the score?" said the judge. "If I'm right,
your captain had sense, and avoided a fight!"
"He'd sense," cried the other, "but courage as well!
you bet that we fought them, and how those French fell!
The foremost I struck at those foemen so fickle,
and the French toppled down, like the grass at the sickle.
The sun stopped to gaze at a marvel so mad:
two hundred beat two hundred thousand, by Gad!"
A terrible sneeze sneezed the student once more,
but Háry continued his tale as before:
"The French fled already, like weeds in the wind;
we Magyars rode after in haste unchagrined.
And lo, their Great Leader I saw, if you please,
on a horse with gold stirrups, outracing the breeze!
Then after, I spurred on my stallion so good,
and gallantly caught him beside a great wood.
'By Heaven!' I cried, as I grabbed his fat throat,
'Confess you're Napoleon, and don't play the goat' —
'What's true, Sir, is true,' he replied. 'I am Nap.
But spare me... I'll pay right well, my good chap.
Yes, ask what you will, my brave Magyar, I swear
the French King has treasures enough and to spare!'
'By Gad, Sire,' cried I. 'Not so hasty away!
Come along, you damned Frenchman, you're captured to stay!'"
The student once more sneezed a terrible sneeze,
but Háry continued, as bold as you please:
"Well, onward we went, and arrived on the plain,
where a fine coach-and-six just before us drew rein.

---

[1] It is a traditional Hungarian belief that whatever is said immediately before someone sneezes must be true, so the "mischievous" student has the opportunity to be sarcastic.

A most noble lady that carriage did hold;
her dress was all heavy with diamonds and gold.
At the sight of us two, 'Jesus, save us!' she cried;
for 'twas Marie Louise, the Great Emperor's bride.
    'O mighty Napoleon, what sight do I see!
    Alas, Royal Husband in fetters!' — says she.
    'Who are you, my good Sir, who've captured my lad?' —
    'I'm Trooper John Háry,' I answered, 'by Gad!'
'Now hark what I say, my good Sir,' she replies,
and with that the fair lady looks deep in my eyes,
'your deed most heroic was never outsoared
by Magyar on earth, and deserves a reward.
    Set free your great captive, and you may reply
    that I will be yours till the day that I die!' —
    'By Gad, Royal Madam,' I cried. 'Trust to me!
    I understand honour. My prisoner goes free!
For a beautiful woman true knights will endure
both fire and water, and Hell, to be sure.
I'm Trooper John Háry, a Magyar of zeal.
Step up, Mr. Emperor! Shake on the deal!'"
    The student's loud sneeze was more terrible still,
    but Háry concluded his tale with a will:
    "I spoke, and the king rushed away like a sheep,
    but he pressed in my hands two gold watches to keep.
My captain got one — him I loved like a brother —
and later my subaltern asked for the other.
By Gad, if I'd kept one, 'twould prove every jot —
but that is my tale, friends, believe or not!"
    Believe it they did, though, the pot-bellied judge,
    the bright peasant lads, and the journalist drudge;
    while the mischievous student drank deep, and in mirth
    cried: "Our Uncle Háry's the best on the earth!"

Watson Kirkconnell

KING MATTHIAS IN GÖMÖR

Every one loved King Matthias, when his charger he rode
To victory in all our battles and our enemies bestrode:
In peace his strength made him the velvet couch despise,
He came and went, for his people's good, listening to our cries,

Through Transdanubia, through all our mighty land,
Through the counties of Tisza he waved his judge's wand,
And none who fell before his knees and cried their grief
Went from his court with less than justice and relief.

And last he came to Gömör and held a royal feast,
As is the Magyar custom, from ancient times at least.
Ten thousand toasts were drunk both serious and gay,
The golden wine of Tokay flowed as night was turned to day.

"God damn the bloody Turk, bring Germans to defeat,
May Christ our Saviour lay all Czechs beneath our Champion's feet!"
The warrior toasts were drunk. At last the country's wealth
Was coupled with the cries, "Our good King Matthias' health!"

Alas, when at the end the nobles could drink no more
And when, in silly drunkenness, they fell upon the floor,
One toast they had forgot, "To those who press the wine,
The toiling peasant daylong bending o'er the vine."

"Gentlemen," King Matthias smiled, liking the idea of a joke,
"The workers have toiled all day beneath a heavy yoke
That we might royally feast. 'Tis time we gave them rest,
They shall sit down in our places and drink of the very best."

The king rose from the table, like the sun in midday sky,
"Up, follow me," he cried, "or I'll know the reason why."
The besotted nobles staggered up to fall in with his command,
"Come," he roared laughing, "we go to conquer the land!"

The sun stood still in wonder, wide-eyed the peasants stare
As their mighty king, their Champion, combed out his golden hair,
And wonder more than wonder, no longer the sword and shield
His conquering arm began the humble spade to wield.

But their wonder changed to laughter, when the courtiers they saw,
Full of soft living, the spade making their hands raw.
And while the weak nobles sweated, with anguish filled,
Their Champion, Matthias, more than an acre had tilled.

Oh, the cries that rose from the little men, the sky was rent,
"Release us, O Majesty, from this hard punishment.
None of us fear the sword but, alas, O King, we're afraid
Of this mighty instrument we cannot wield — the peasant's spade."

In the end Kind Matthias relented. Using his spade,
Which he drew from the shining furrow his work had made,
As a royal sceptre, his words and his mien severe,
"Listen, O you fat courtlings, listen to me and hear

This lesson: You now have learned half dead with toil,
That your soft living is founded on this clumpish soil,
That they, who till it and make it yield its crop,
Work till their muscles scream and until they drop.

So, back in your banqueting halls, by riches beset,
Remember my words. When you toast you will not forget
To lift your glasses to lift your hearts and minds
To the vine-dressers, cowherds, the shepherds, and hinds."

In Gömör, thus did King Matthias enhance his noble joke,
Laying upon his people the lightest of heavy yokes,
And so increased their love for him, no sweat was too severe,
That even today they love him, and his mighty name revere.

James Turner

János Arany
1817-1852

János Arany
(1817-1882)

Hungary's greatest epic poet and undoubtedly most influential literary figure in the 19th century, János Arany was born in Nagyszalonta (today Salonta in Romania) of a family of Calvinist yeomen whose property consisted of a thatched cottage and a small plot of land. He was so much younger than his brothers and sisters that he had to be nursed by his older sister, who had just had a baby—his own mother was too old to be able to feed him. He entered school at the age of six, where he read everything he could lay his hands on, both in Hungarian and in Latin. From 1832 to 1836 he was a preceptor at Kisújszállás and Debrecen and by that time had taught himself French and German. For a while he was a member of a company of travelling actors, but he soon became tired of this roaming existence. He therefore borrowed a few pennies and, with all of his property wrapped in a kerchief, returned home. Soon after his return, his mother died and his father went blind. Arany decided never to leave home again. He managed to obtain a job as associate headmaster which provided him with a modest living. In 1840 he also became a notary, and in that year he got married.

A few years of happiness followed, during which he learned enough English to be able to read Shakespeare in the original. His first major poetic work, The Lost Constitution [Az elveszett alkotmány], *a biting satire completed in 1846, won the prize of the Kisfaludy Society. When soon thereafter he published the first part of his* Toldi *trilogy, he instantly became famous. Petőfi (q.v.) was the first poet to embrace him, and the two men became close friends.*

In 1848 Arany was elected to the National Assembly, but he refused to accept any political office—he also refused to do so on subsequent occasions. During the Hungarian War of Independence he worked in the civil service; then he returned to Nagyszalonta where he lived on his meagre savings until, in 1850, Count Lajos Tisza invited him to his mansion in Geszt to be his son's tutor. The next year Arany got a teaching position in the high school in Nagykőrös, where he spent nine years. Many of his great, enduring ballads and his mordant satire, Stevie the Village Idiot [Bolond Istók] *were written there between 1850 and 1853. In 1854 and 1856 he also wrote two brilliant essays on the technique of the ballad and on prosody in general.*

In 1860 he assumed the directorship of the Kisfaludy Society, moved to Pest, and launched his Belletristic Observer [Szépirodalmi Figyelő], *which later became* The Wreath [Koszorú], *an important organ of Hungarian literature and criticism.*

Arany also edited the Kisfaludy Society's Shakespeare series to which he contributed masterly and enduring translations of Hamlet, King John, *and* A Midsummer Night's Dream. *Several of Shakespeare's lines have become Hungarian proverbs in Arany's translation. His impact on the Hungarian language may   be compared to Dante's on Standard Italian and Martin Luther's on High German.*

In 1867 Arany won the Nádasdy Prize of the Hungarian Academy of Sciences for his Death of Buda [Buda halála], *a moving epic poem based on the fraternal rivalry between Attila and Buda, the legendary Hunnish chieftains. Arany is the only Hungarian poet to have served as Secretary General of the Hungarian Academy of Sciences—his appointment took effect in 1865 and lasted until 1879. Three years before his death, Arany published the two final parts of his* Toldi *trilogy,* Toldi's Love [Toldi szerelme] *and* Toldi's Eve [Toldi estéje]. *His final years were saddened by the death of his daughter, but his poetry showed a bitter-sweet, very attractive stoicism expressed in the title of the collection,* Little Autumn Flowers [Őszikék].

Arany was a man of immense probity and intellectual integrity. It is no exaggeration to rank him with the two great Germans, Goethe and Schiller, the Russian Pushkin, and the Englishman John Milton. He became, in the truest sense, a teacher of his nation and a major, determining shaper of its literary standards for the next century and beyond. Dezső Kosztolányi (q.v.), in one of his essays on Hungarian literature, remarked: "Whereas Sándor Petőfi is the greatest poet of Hungary, János Arany is the greatest Magyar poet." What Kosztolányi meant was that whereas Petőfi, who was of Slavic descent, reached world fame as a revolutionary and as a victim of the Hungarian War of Independence, while also being a poetic genius, Arany's contribution sprang from within the depths of the nation's inner vocabulary and diction. Arany's use of Hungarian has left a century's worth of work for Hungarian linguists. His heritage is still strongly and inspiringly alive in his native country.

The narrative poem Toldi *of which we present extracts below, has a quotation heading each canto by a Hungarian poet who lived in the second half of the 16th century, Péter Ilosvai Selymes. Ilosvai wrote a narrative poem about Toldi in 1574. Arany's quotes are from this work.*

The first collected edition of his works was published in eight volumes in 1884-1885.

TOLDI
(Extracts)

CANTO ONE   "I now remember times long passed away,
                             When the good Nicholas Toldi had his day..."
                                                    — *Ilosvai*

As on an autumn night a herdsman's fire
across the sea-like prairie flashes higher,
so Nicholas Toldi to my gaze is cast,
out of his time, ten generations past.
I seem to see his stateliness of height,
and his stout lance in devastating fight —
I seem to hear the thunders of his voice,
like the loud tongue that God's deep wrath employs.
            That was a man, a hero of the best;
            his match cannot be found from east to west —
            if from his grave he rose to you and me,
            you'd think his deeds were wrought by sorcery.
            Three men today could not lift up his mace
            or set his sling-stones or his lance in place;
            you would turn pale to see his massive shield
            and his gigantic jack-boots, spurry-heeled.

                             "He lifted, with one hand, a massive pole,
                             To point the way to Buda, then their goal."
                                                    — *Ilosvai*

Sun-scorched, the spare heat-grass is brown indeed;
grasshoppers there with languid cohorts feed;
among the bulrush-rootstocks nothing's seen
of sprouting grass, nor is the prairie green.
A dozen farm-hands in the hay-stacks' shade
are snoring, as if all were well arrayed,
yet, empty or half-filled, big hay-carts stand
in idleness amid that summer land.
            The lean fork of a draw-well, long and bleak,
            looks deep into the well, its draughts to seek.
            You'd think it an enormous gnat, which dearth

had sent to suck the blood of Mother Earth.
Beside the trough, a herd of oxen lies,
parched, and molested by a host of flies;
but with the noon-day heat the men are spent,
and none draws water for their discontent.
As far as glance can scan the earth and the sky,
only one walking person can you spy:
a mighty pole on his broad shoulder swings,
although upon his chin no down yet clings.

....

Ah, is it not the whirlwind that he sees,
spanning the long, dun road with mummeries,
for there, beyond the grey dust, with its drums
and glittering arms, a brilliant army comes.
And as it penetrates the fog of dust,
a sigh from the lad's mouth breaks in a gust.

....

"Oh, gallant Magyar soldiers, fine and true,
how fain, how longingly I gaze at you!

....

Meanwhile the troops drew near with martial tread,
great Endre Laczfi riding at their head.

....

"Hey, peasant! Which road leads to Buda town?" —
asked Laczfi, looking arrogantly down.
Straight to the heart of Toldi goes that word,
it forthwith gives a thump that can be heard.
        "A peasant am I?" Nicholas mused in hate,
        "who should be squire of this whole estate?
        Perhaps my brother George, that fox unstable,
        busy changing the plates at King Louis' table?"
"A peasant am I?" And his rising gorge
was full of horrid curses against George.
Then whirling his vast pole, without a strain,
by one huge end he seized it, like a cane,
and held it horizontal with one hand

to point them towards Buda across the land.
Bands of wrought steel his arm's stout thews resemble,
the out-stretched tree-trunk does not even tremble.

> The Palatine and all his army bent
> their gaze on him in sheer astonishment.
> Says Laczfi: "That's a man, whoe'er he be!
> Come lads, who'll wrestle now with such as he?
> Or who among you all can hold straight out
> that shabby sign-pole of this dusty lout?"
> They murmur discontented — 'twould annoy
> a knight to wrestle with a peasant boy.

But who would fight a duel with the thunder
when wind and sultry murk are rent asunder?
....

The troops in thronging pageant, pass him by,
and all pay tribute to his potency;
all speak frank words of kindliness and grace;
all beam upon him with a friendly face.
And one said: "Hey, Mate, won't you come to war?
that's what a lad like you is valued for!"
Another says: "My good lad, what a shame,
sired by a peasant, you will be the same!"

> The host has gone; its murmurs are now mute,
> borne down by wind, and dust obscures its route.
> Home wanders Toldi, full of grieving pride,
> the fallow rocks beneath his mighty stride;
> like some insensate bullock's is his gait;
> the glooms of midnight in his eyes dilate;
> like some mad, wounded boar's, his wrath persists,
> the pole is almost crushed in his great fists.

[In Cantos 2, 3, and 4, Nicholas is confronted by his brother George who wants to send him away. George's soldiers irritate him beyond endurance and he hurls a huge millstone across the yard and accidentally kills one of George's men. Having become a 'murderer', he takes refuge in the wilderness where he is found by the old family servant Ben, who brings him food and begs him not to leave the country as his mother would die of a broken heart. In Canto 5 he kills two wolves with his bare hands.]

CANTO FIVE   Nicholas went wandering about the marsh
                              Along the brook, amid the reed-fields harsh.
                                                          — *Ilosvai*

Day to the reedy marsh had closed her eye,
but left her mantle lying in the sky;
then Night prevailed and stopped the crimson mirth,
drawing a funeral cloth o'er sky and earth.
Setting it neatly off with coffin-nails,
a million-million stars in glittering trails;
then laid the crescent moon, in silent walk,
a wreath of silver on the catafalque.
....

          But as he turned backward in slow retreat,
          the marshy soil gave way beneath his feet;
          a wild wolf's lair below was manifest —
          two little whelps were whining in their nest.
          Nicholas was sorry to have trod upon them,
          and, bending down, he set caresses on them,
          as when a shepherd boy, who trains his pup,
          pats his small, hairy head to cheer him up.
But here, kind pats were wholly out of place,
for suddenly reeds rustle; fierce of pace,
the she-wolf, entering with a fiendish howl,
attacked him, and at once the fight grew foul.
....

          All might be well, but now to help his kind
          a howling he-wolf dashed in from behind.
          How now, bold Nicholas? Does not terror fill you?
          Had you a thousand lives, they would still kill you!
          Not in the least! One must rather suppose
          that as the danger grew, so his courage rose.
          He will win out. Don't doubt the lad a winner.
          He was not born to be the grey wolves' dinner.
          ....

Toldi then raised her; with a mighty swing
he flailed her at her mate, about to spring.

Twice beaten back, the male, with a tail-twitch
in utter fury bit at his own bitch.
It was quite clear that he would rise again
unless young Toldi slew him there and then.
He therefore pounded him: from such a fray
he would not wake until the Judgment Day.
....

      If with the wolves he made comparison,
      his brother was far worse to think upon.
      Wild beasts are warlike to defend their lair;
      do not provoke them, and they will not care.
      When the starved belly urges them to kill,
      they slay no more than will their needs fulfil.
      From farmers' herds, only a tithe they win,
      and never prey on their own kith and kin.[1]
But see his brother, see that man of strife,
why did he have designs on Nicholas' life?

*In Canto 6 Toldi goes home to say good-bye to his mother, carrying the two
dead wolves on his shoulder. He throws them at the feet of his brother who is
asleep. The dogs are awakened by the smell and bark, waking up the entire
household:*

As if a nest of hornets rose to sting —
such was that house's furious murmuring.
Colliding down the gallery they go;
on foot or horse, they eddy to and fro.
Whither? No person knew their quarry's tracks.
All of them jumped around like maniacs.
At last George scolded them, in fury bellowed,
then took the lead and all the others followed.
      But did the widow hear the hunt's wild sounds,
      the horns, the shouting, and the howling hounds?
      Did she hear them bawling "Hold him! Boldy snatch!",
      knowing well whom they meant to hold or catch?
      She did not hear it. As her son departed,

---

[1] These two lines have become proverbial in Hungarian: *'Akkor is
barmoknak tizedelve nyáját / Megkíméli mindig a maga fajtáját.'*

her feeble feet gave way; and broken-hearted
she slowly fell unconscious on her bed —
God only knows how long she lay as dead.

*In Canto 7 Toldi encounters a grieving widow in a cemetery who had lost
her sons in single combat with a fearsome Czech warrior who is challenging
anyone who cares to fight him. Toldi assures her that this foreign champion
will soon be defeated. In Canto 8, George, the evil elder brother, is trying to
explain to King Louis why Nicholas must be disinherited:*

"My brother's done for, by all human law;
I am his rightful heir, without a flaw.
I could take over with presumptive claim,
if I were minded to pursue that aim.
But some, perhaps, might afterwards declare
I had been hankering for Nicholas' share,
that having chased him out with harsh command,
I came back home and took away his land.
  But God forbid that I should be his heir
  and add the people's slander to my share.
  And who could guarantee he might not come
  and kill me for the estate I barred him from?
  I don't want that; the title I disown,
  and lay at the footstool of your throne.
  You'll know some worthy man of gentle station
  to whom to give it as royal donation."
  ....

The King caught George Toldi with a chilly smile
by his own words, in colloquy of guile:
"Well, I accept your brother's property,
since you most worthy of the grant must be,
I'll make it yours, if you in single fight
tomorrow kill the Czech, that fearful knight,
and pin his head upon this battlement —
that action wins my seal and royal assent!"
  Red as a parboiled shrimp turned George's face;
  the day was bright, but shadows filled the place,
  the statues danced about him for a spell,
  giddiness seized him, and he almost fell.
  He sweated, yet his body felt a chill,

his face turned pale, as if surpassing ill;
his blood-stream would not service, most and least,
one sole mosquito for a single feast.
At last he started speaking for the nonce
and sadly to the King's words made response:
"My brother's lot, I said, is not my goal.
I turn it down, lest it oppress my soul."
He spoke, and bowing to the King with care,
went home, and started in to tear his hair
and beat his brows — his servants stood behind him
and darkly wondered if they ought to bind him.

In Canto 10 Toldi, now in the capital, stops a raging bull, and then becomes despondent because he has no money for armor to take on the Czech champion. The old family servant, Ben, shows up again and hands Miklós a loaf of bread inside which there is hidden a box containing gold coins, obviously a gift from Miklós' mother. He now has the means to buy a knight's fighting gear. They go to an inn where Miklós dances and drinks more than ten others could. In Canto 11, Toldi rows a boat to the island in the Danube where the fierce Czech warrior is waiting for challengers.

The river seemed a broad stream, fenced with folk;
in mid-stream stretched the island, no mere joke
but murderous: for a week its thirsty beach
had lived on blood like some blood-sucking leech.
        Then down from Buda's castle came the Czech,
        making his big horse dance and toss its neck;
        the tide of his abuse in torrents swept,
        since none was there his challenge to accept.
        But suddenly, upon the bank at Pest,
        a throb of hope is pulsing in each breast:
        an unknown champion on a coal-black steed
        announces he is ready for the deed.
His helmet's front was lowered altogether,
above it fluttered high a snow-white feather.
Toldi (he was the knight) the feather took
and gave it to the heralds. All men look
while they, as was their duty, sought the bank
where the mighty Czech in all his insults, stank.
His plume was red — this he for Toldi's changed —
a sign that single combat was arranged.

Nicholas had hardly landed, when he gave
his boat a push upon the Danube's wave;
as if it skated on the river's crest
it bore its prow into the bank at Pest.
The Czech knight asked the reason for the act.
Said Nicholas: "I have done it, since in fact
a single boat is all that one man needs
and one of us must die in this day's deeds.
A dead man in a boat takes no delight."

*When they shake hands, Toldi squeezes the Czech knight's hand so hard that
all of his fingers bleed.*

Then Toldi with his bare hands seized the Czech
and shook him by the ankle and the neck.
He cracked in Toldi's hands, he seemed to melt,
and presently for Toldi's grace he knelt:
"I beg you, my dear son, don't seek my death!
I offer you with this, my failing breath
all I possess, twelve vassal knights to boot,
a nobleman, your fortunes I'll recruit!"
The heart of Toldi softened at the plea:
"Let all be as you offer it," said he.
"I'll take your wealth, but take it for another,
you've killed two knights, I'll give it to their mother.
For charity, I give you back your life,
but you must promise, without doubt or strife,
that though the sea engulfed your fatherland,
again on Magyar soil you'll never stand."
The champion, in his terror, gave assent,
and so together to the boat they went.
But suddenly the big Czech, base of mind,
sought falsely to stab Nicholas from behind.
Toldi perceived it, mirrored in the stream,
and caught the fellow's hand with strength supreme.
The Czech knelt down again: "Have mercy, pray!" —
"Go, ask it now from God! I'll show the way!"
Then with the sword, wrenched from the treacherous Czech,
he gave him mercy cutting through his neck.
The mighty sword turned scarlet with the gore;
then on the sword-point high the head he bore.

Tumult arose on both the river's banks;
men roared, waved flags, applauded in their thanks;
the Magyars yelled as though their lungs would crack,
and the high hills of Buda echoed back.

*In the final Canto 12, Toldi is taken to meet the King. He confesses that he is
an outlaw. There is a final confrontation with George, his brother. The King
offers Nicholas a large fortune, but he turns it down and asks to be made a
simple soldier in the King's army.*

Then Nicholas spoke: "My King, most kind to me,
I do not crave my brother's property,
nor yet my own. Brother, I give it to you!
So let your stingy heart's desire come true!
Rather, my King, this thing I covet most —
accept me as a private in your host!
God is most merciful, a gracious Lord:
He'll let me make my living with my sword."

Nicholas' mother shows up — it turns out she hadn't died, only fainted.

Said Nicholas: "Had you not my prophecy
that, soon or late, a soldier I would be?
Not by my strength have I this pathway trod
but through the gracious clemency of God.
We'll interchange with George my life's career;
He'll go to Nagyfalu, while we live here.
Perhaps he will grow friendlier, as time flies,
if not, let him be jealous till he dies."
       Great was the love the hero bore his mother,
       the shafts of Cupid drove him to no other —
       no love of women touched him anyhow,
       and never did he voice a marriage vow.
       A god of wars was he, through battles borne,
       foes fell before him like ripe ears of corn.
       King, country, and the weak all praised his prime —
       his exploits stud the annals of his time.
No warrior with his anger could contend,
he'd gladly give his shirt to help a friend;
and when the country had no foes to fight,
with jolly fellows he would find delight.

No cattle, land, or gold he left, perchance,
no children fought o'er his inheritance;
but as a finer crown of his endeavour,
his fame has lasted and will last forever.

Watson Kirkconnell

CIVILISATION

In the past the warring nations
Did not follow any precept:
The strong plundered what he could, and
Everything he looted, *he* kept.

That has changed now, as the world has
A more legalistic flavour:
When the strong now do some mischief
They confer and — vote in favor.

Peter Zollman

THE SCHOLAR'S CAT

Famous might have been this scholar
great his erudition,
If he'd had an ounce of horse sense
in his composition;
oh, dear me!
once upon a time befell him
this mad catastrophe.
      Our scholar felt affection for
      naught to man God's given,
      if it walked on two or four legs,
      lived on earth, in heaven,
      but his cat, a tortoise-shell one,
      oh, dear me!
      as if he would devour the beast
      he loved her dotingly.
The scholar had a servant, too,
for whom it was a duty
to see the house was not burnt down

or thieves made off with booty.
As servants go, she was not bad.
Oh, dear me!
but fasting was her sole reward
daily, even nightly.
> Things were different for the cat. Here
> love guided the scholar;
> the master's breakfast was shared with her
> divided in equal measure.
> His servant gazed sadly on this,
> oh, dear me!
> but she would not, no, she would not
> reveal this outwardly.

"Eh! Hum! What is wrong with pussy,
oh, my much loved creature;
fur's gone mangy, hark! bones rattle;
legs collapse beneath her."
"My master, she is hungry still,
oh, dear me!
with twice the food she'll soon again
be on her feet, you'll see.
> With all the roll, a pint of milk,
> her hunger will be sated."
> To see his pussy put on weight
> the expectant scholar waited.
> But the cat grew lighter still
> oh, dear me!
> and wasted like the waning moon,
> till like a sickle, she.

His puss, his lovely tortoise-shell, gave
no hope of survival,
one autumn she acquired 'the late'
as prefix adjectival.
His cat became etherealised
oh, dear me!
"I always shared my bread with her
yet she deserted me."
> "Do not put the blame on her, since
> I 'twas ate her dinner,"
> the servant said, "at morn and eve

I ate, whilst she grew thinner...
I sent her to go hunting mice,
oh, dear me!
but mice aren't found in pantries where
the room is always empty."
Famous might have been this scholar,
great his erudition,
if he'd had an ounce of horse sense
in his composition;
though he wrote a book on wisdom
oh, dear me!
such mad things to him as this one
happened quite frequently.

Neville Masterman

THE NIGHTINGALE

In bygone days, you surely know,
The Magyars loved going to Court,
Addicted to this native sport;
(And was that quite so long ago?) —
Take *Peter* and *Paul,* neighbours twain
Upon the Great Hungarian Plain
And inseparable like twins;
With them the parable begins.

Though *Peter* and *Paul* get on fine
When it's June and twenty-nine,
To have a shared calendar spot
Just once a year, is not a lot.
But here are Peter and our Paul
Cannot get on, no, not at all:
A single innocent remark
Will set them blasphemies to bark,
And then to squabble, brawl and quarrel,
(Except to kill: that seems immoral!)

When smoke billows from Peter's chimney
Paul will sneeze, and rather grimly;

But now, if Paul's hen lands perhaps
On Peter's roof, that's Peter's proof
The fowl will make the house collapse;
Such a trifling cause can trigger
Quite a big row which grows bigger
As the kinfolk take to arms,
Grandfathers and babes-in-arms;
Curses mix with plucky pledge
As they fight along the hedge
Joined by their respective dogs
Who will bark the epilogues.

I shouldn't stray, I beg your pardon. —
The centre of our scenery,
A handsome, ancient walnut tree
Is pride and joy of Peter's garden.
A branch reaching across the border
Is wisely kept by neighbour Paul
As are the walnuts when they fall
In accordance with Nature's order.
And it passed, one Sunday morning
That the songster of our title
Settled on that branch, so vital
To our story, without warning.
He whistled from that common branch
A philharmonic avalanche:
Thanking God this lovely morn,
Life, the great joy to be born,
And to give His daily due
Praised the scented breeze, the dew,
Thanked Him for the radiant sun,
For the new day just begun,
Thankfully his tiny breast
For his mate guarding the nest,
All that's outside in the world
And inside the little bird,
Thankful that this grace and light,
So glorious
— It's obvious —
Is his own,

His alone,
Made for him for his delight!
As farmer Peter heard the hymn
And happy feeling stirred in him
He uttered this almighty yell:
"Upon my word,
How very well
You sing to *me,* my little bird!"

"Your what? Your bird? That's rather much!
Watch out, or I shall give you such..."
This comes across the garden fence
With other terms of wild offence
"It's mine!" says Peter raising bristles,
"He sits on my tree when he whistles!"
"It may have been your whopper tree,
But he *sang* on my property!"
And Paul bellows like whooping cough
while Peter shouts his own head off,
And so it went from bad to worse,
To fisticuffs from spoken curse,
They jumped the hedge,
Churned up the veg,
They boxed and kicked, they wreaked and wrecked,
— To pay the Lord's Day due respect —
With bruise and blood, with wrench and rip,
But each still claiming *ownership.*

Our farmer Paul without repose,
Just as he was, with bleeding nose,
At once he lodged a long complaint
(The evidence? He's still blood-stained),
Relating to the magistrate
The gory story clear and straight.
He knew his rights and had the will,
And added that he would appeal
To court, to king, he'd crawl and kneel:
Till death he'd fight to own the trill!
Then into Justice' even scales
A gold coin fell, (this never fails).

His worship slipped this with a sleight
Deep in the pocket on his *right*.

Our Peter, after these events,
Is also eager to be heard
And tickled by his innocence
Submits his case about the bird.
The facts were these, the claims are those,
The trill belongs to him, he knows —
"The Court, the Crown
Can't let me down,
By earthly justice and divine
The trill in question must be mine!"
And aiming at a truer truth
He clean forgets a broken tooth,
Deducts some bloodshed from the bill
And adds a coin to gild the pill,
Which enters, rather dignified,
The ample pocket near the heart
Upon his worship's *left* hand side.

The day of truth is due to start
With the long-awaited session.
Each party came to savour it,
Having gained the firm impression
Of being fancied favourite.
The hours pass but neither lawyer
Can turn the scale,
And as they fail,
Resort to rage and paranoia.
They search the Law for *nightingale*,
A fine tooth comb
Through every tome,
More time to waste without avail.
But now his worship wants his dinner,
So more delay is not allowed —
Slaps both his pockets, canny, proud
And then proceeds to name the winner
To the interested crowd.
Here is the gist:

"Claims *one* and *two* are both absurd
The little bird trilled for a *third:*
(Slap on the right) he trilled for *me,*
(slap on the left) he trilled for *me:*
Case dismissed!"

***

It's good to know that such a case
Is quite unheard of nowadays,
For close personal litigation
Is truly junked
And quite defunct,
Detested by the Magyar nation.
Deals are made by word of honor,
Legal jargon is a goner,
Sister, brother,
Love each other,
Be friend to friend
Is now the trend.
And who would murder with a rifle,
Or file a lawsuit for a trifle?
And if his case concerned a *trill,*
Today's honest sollicito-o-or
Would rather not discuss it, or...
But someone always pays the bill!   *Peter Zollman*

FAMILY CIRCLE

The evening comes and everything is hushed,
while darkly nods the leafy mulberry tree;
a buzzing insect strikes against the wall,
a loud crash follows, there is heard no more.
As if the very clods of earth had legs
the clumsy frogs to rolling everywhere
while round the eves there wheels a wandering bat,
an old owl's hooting in a ruined tower.

> Recently milked by the woman of the house
> the white form of a cow is faintly seen
> chewing the cud in silence in the yard:
> a placid beast, though bothered by her calf.

A cat, to lazy to go chasing flies,
her body stretched, moves slow with cautious steps,
she pauses, looks around and is gone —
she's fled into the hall with sudden speed.
The door stands open; on the courtyard hedge
the hearth's reflected light is welcoming.
Before the door, his feet upon the steps,
a faithful dog lies stretched to guard the home.
Within, the woman of the house skims milk;
her small boy asks and has from her a sip.
She then goes mingling with the other ones
just like the gentle moon among the stars.

    A young girl's throwing twigs upon the fire —
    the eldest and most fair, a morning star;
    she warms her iron for her new-made dress
    — and ironing's all it needs — for next day's feast.
    She tells a story to the younger ones,
    sitting around at work, all shelling peas,
    or shredding beans, their little chubby cheeks
    lit by the fire, a flame with crackling pods.
The youngest asks for bread, then munches it
and weaves a circle with a burning brand.
The older boy ignores the rest and reads
(this lad will be a pastor, that is sure) —
such is at least his father's fondest wish,
although as yet he doesn't care for prayers
and much prefers to study songs and rhymes
he's even tried his hand at writing verse.

    But now they hear their father's hoe put down,
    his well-worn satchel's hung upon a nail.
    The children search in it and hope to find
    some bits of bread he left after the day.
    They thrust their hands in; there's a sudden shriek —
    "some devil's in there.... No, a little rabbit!"
    cries of delight... They will not sleep all night
    they go and fetch it cabbage leaves to eat.
The father says "Good Evening" to them all,
sits down to stretch his tired and aching limbs;
with dusty shirt-sleeve wipes a wearied brow
that has been deeply furrowed by life's cares.

But when he sees his little ones around,
delightfully his wrinkles disappear;
he knocks his soothing pipe upon the hearth
and smiles at kind words from his gentle wife.
       The house-wife hurries then to fetch his food.
       It's proper that he should not have to wait.
       Soon she has pushed the small round table out
       and brought the simple dishes she's prepared.
       She and the children have already fed.
       "Come dear," he says, they must all eat again,
       the food tastes better if all feed together:
       then gives the little ones a leg or wing.
"But who's that knocking? Sarah, go and see..."
A poor man's asking shelter for the night.
Don't turn him out if he has got no home;
how many suffer driven from shut doors.
The eldest girl gets up and asks him in,
a crippled soldier bids them a good evening:
"May God bless what you eat," he says to them,
"and those, too, who partake of it," he adds.
       The father thanks him. "Come, and have your share;
       mother, put on his plate a little more."
       Then he invites him to sit down with them
       the man says 'no,' then readily agrees,
       enjoys a simple but a tasty meal,
       a jug of water then quenches his thirst.
       No words are uttered while they have their food
       this is the Magyars' custom when they eat.
But when the meal is done all do their best
to make it easy for their guest to speak.
At first his words come like a little stream,
but like a swelling river they soon flow.
The elder boy, too, lays his book aside;
he leans towards him with attentive eyes;
no sooner does the soldier come to pausing
the boy entreats him: "Tell another tale!"
       "They are not 'tales'" — the father chides the boy,
       the soldier understands and carries on.
       And they are hanging on his every word,
       but it's the eldest girl who's most intent.

When no one's listening, or no one sees,
she asks about 'her brother' with a blush:
for three years she's been asking after him,
she'll wait one more before she weds another.
The evening ends; the warm fire shines no more.
The glowing cinders now begin to wink.
The children, too, are tired, there's one asleep.
His head is resting on his mother's lap.
The guest speaks less, the silences increase;
only the purring of the cat is heard.
Then rustling straw is heaped upon the ground
the crickets reign now in this silent realm.

Neville Masterman

REPLY TO PETŐFI

My soul is clanging like a cimbalom gone mad;
my heart indeed is joyful, but by its pangs unnerved.
Tossed on waves of music: How was this prize had?
Petőfi as my friend I've surely not deserved.
      This was no mere prize won in competition.
      More than good fortune, it is my divine destiny!
      To be the winner — how could such be my ambition?
      I nearly threw in the fire my humble poetry.
The prize itself dazed me: How much I had won!
And, then, what extra treasure came along to shine!
It reaches to the soul of my soul, I the one
to be the holder of your dear right hand in mine.
      You asked me: "What am I?" "A son of the people," I said.
      "Rooted in it, I live by them and for them, belong
      to them only — by their fate my own is bred.
      And if I burst into song, my lips give home to their songs."
I longed to migrate once from the circle of its embrace,
but the wheel of destiny only tossed me aside.
And as I inched back stealthily, I had the grace
to pick a few blossoms from the thorns where flowers hide.
      The worries came — they were companions along the way —
      I wove a garland, but soon I was by these betrayed,
      and as we made friends, grew used to each other, I and
      they, who stole my wreath when I had it only half made.

At last a treasure was gained — domestic happiness —
all the richer as its guarding will be no task —
and on the banks of the Iza a friend's faithfulness:
for what else could I hope, what greater blessing ask?
      As if a comet landed within my narrow walls,
      your letter burns, lighting up my inmost soul.
      Oh, tell him in my name, if Tompa ever calls,
      how fond I am of you, and of him with you — one whole.

Madeline Mason

COSMOPOLITAN POETRY

I have no shame, no regret
that, born Hungarian, I write
as one, that I can never let
my words beyond this soil take flight.
No "Wonder of Two Worlds," my song
if charm it has, is due to them,
my people; I am theirs, belong
to one land wholly, root and stem.
      Let tongues of the mighty propagate
      their own language, sovereignty
      their god, a roaring flood in spate
      that washes all, destructively.
      But let the poet of a small nation
      placed in destruction's very path,
      find at home his true station,
      death, else, the aftermath.
Or is our glory here so small
it needs must sink into the grave
along with the nation? Do you call
us inferior, that neighbors gave
no heed to us? Is there no test
worthy of our strength at home,
subject for song, no native quest?
Must we crave Albion's loam?
      Be a "world poet," if you can,
      stir up the whole crazy West.

The cradle that rocked me Hungarian
is one that I must still call blessed.
A thousand threads bind me — I deal
with motherland, with this one spot.
I sing of no abstract ideal,
voice such, I'd rather not.

Madeline Mason

THE MOTHER OF KING MATTHIAS

Elizabeth
Szilágyi
swiftly wrote a letter;
it was moist
with loving tears
many, too, and bitter.
  For her son,
  held in Prague,
  were those fair words she wrote,
  harshly kept
  in prison cell;
  good news to him it brought.
"Do not move
my sweet boy
from Prague's famous city;
I'll pay the ransom
to get you out
from your captivity.
  Gold coins,
  silver, too,
  will save you from your doom;
  in my heart
  there is the thought
  you must come back home.
Do not start,
do not move,
my only orphaned son;
who shall I
have, if you're
enticed by evil men?

This note must
be handed to
Matthias Hunyadi;
what I've writ
with my own hand
no other soul must see!"
On wax of black
she pressed down
her signet ring for seal;
faithful servants
of her court
lounge, leaning at a rail.
        "Who will here
        quickest take
        to Prague this note for him?
        Sacks of gold
        horses, too,
        I'll pay for weary limb."
"I'll take the note
I'll take the note
seven days the distance clears."
"That will seem
to my heart
seven whole long years."
        "I'll take the note
        In three days
        the answer you will see."
        "In this heart
        so full of love
        three whole months 'twill be."
"Oh my God,
oh my God,
wings a man requires,
that he may
attain the speed
a mother's heart desires."
        What comes here?
        What comes here?
        Look, a pitch black raven;
        one like it

on the shield
of Hunyad is engraven.
He swoops down
he swoops down,
within a tempest bleak;
from her hand
he has snatched
the letter in his beak.
    "Quick, rush quick,
    catch the bird,
    it must from him be taken."
    on its track
    a crowd sets forth,
    that they may shoot the raven.
Not a sign
of that bird,
though they a hundred shoot;
not a word
not a trace
of the bird that seized the note.
    Morn' to eve
    woods are searched,
    the route they saw it go;
    when, night comes,
    hark! a knock
    at the widow's window.
"Who knocks here?
Who knocks here?"
It is the raven black:
in its beak
is the note,
or one like it, brought back.
    Red the seal
    is this time,
    and perfect the folding.
    What great joy!
    What delight!
    His fine hand beholding.

Neville Masterman

THE BARDS OF WALES[2]

King Edward scales the hills of Wales
Upon his stallion.
"Hear my decree! I want to see
My new dominion.

     "Show me the yield of every field,
     The grain, the grass, the wood!
     Is all the land now moist and rich
     With red rebellious blood?

"And are the Welsh, God's gift, the Welsh,
A peaceful, happy folk?
I want them pleased, just like the beast
They harness in the yoke."

     "Sire, this jewel in your crown,
     Your Wales, is fair and good:
     Rich is the yield of every field
     The grassland and the wood.

"And, Sire, the Welsh, God's gift, the Welsh,
So pleased they all behave!
Dark every hut, fearfully shut
And silent as the grave."

     King Edward scales the hills of Wales
     Upon his stallion.
     And where he rides dead silence hides
     In his dominion.

He calls at high Montgomery
To banquet and to rest;

---

[2] Although doubted by scholars, it is strongly held in the oral tradition that King Edward I of England had five hundred bards executed after his conquest of Wales in 1227, lest they incite the Welsh youth to rebellion by reminding them in their songs of their nation's glorious past. — *János Arany*

Arany wrote this poem when the Austrian Emperor Franz Joseph first visited Hungary after he had defeated it in its 1848-1849 War of Independence. The entire nation greeted this poem as the voice of political defiance. Since at various times in Hungarian history powers of the right and of the left have expected poets to praise them, *The Bards of Wales* has never lost its relevance. [A.M.]

It falls on Lord Montgomery
To entertain the guest:
> With fish, the meat, and fruit so sweet,
> To tease the tongue, the eyes,
> A splendid spread for a king to be fed
> A lordly enterprise.

The waiters file with the best this Isle
Can grow in drink and food,
And serve the fine Bordeaux and Rhine
In gracious plentitude.
> "Now drink my health, you gentle sirs,
> And you, my noble host! You Sirs...
> Welsh Sirs... you filthy curs,
> I want the loyal toast!

"The fish, the meat you served to eat
Was fine and ably done.
But deep inside it's hate you hide:
You loathe me, every one!
> "Well, then, you sirs, you filthy curs,
> Who will now toast your king?
> I want a bard to praise my deeds,
> A bard of Wales to sing!"

They look askance with a furtive glance,
The noblemen of Wales;
Their cheeks turn white in deadly fright,
As crimson anger pales.
> Deep silence falls upon the halls,
> And lo, before their eyes
> They see an old man, white as snow,
> An ancient bard to rise:

"I shall recite your glorious deeds
Just as you bid me, Sire."
And death rattles in grim battles
As he touches the lyre.
> "Grim death rattles, the brave battles,
> And blood bestains the sun,
> Your deeds reek high, up to the sky:
> You are the guilty one!

"Our dead are plenty as the corn
When harvest is begun,

And as we reap and glean, we weep:
You did this, guilty one!"
    "Off to the stake!" the king commands,
    "This was churlishly hard.
    Sing us, you there, a softer air,
    You, young and courtly bard!"
"A breeze so soft, does sweetly waft
Where Milford Haven lies,
With wailing woes of doomed widows
And mournful maidens' cries.
    "Maiden, don't bear a slave! Mother,
    Your babe must not be nursed!" ...
    A royal nod. He reached the stake
    Together with the first.
But boldly and without a call
A third one takes the floor;
Without salute he strikes the lute,
His song begins to soar:
    "Our brave were killed, just as you willed,
    Or languish in our gaols:
    To hail your name or sing your fame
    You find no bard in Wales!
"He may gone,[3] *but his* songs live on —
The toast is 'King beware!'
You bear the curse — and even worse —
Of Welsh bards everywhere."
    "I'll see to that!" thunders the King,
    "You spiteful Welsh peasants!
    The stake will toast your every bard
    Who spurns my ordinance!"
His men went forth to search the North,
The West, the South, the East,
And so befell, the truth to tell,
In Wales the famous feast. —
    King Edward fled, headlong he sped
    Upon his stallion,

---

[3] An obvious allusion to Sándor Petőfi (q.v.) Arany's best friend, who was killed in battle against the combined Austrian and Russian armies at age twenty-six near Segesvár in July of 1949.

And in his wake a blazing stake:
The Welsh dominion.
Five hundred went singing to die,
Five hundred in the blaze,
But none would sing to cheer the king
The loyal toast to raise.

> "My chamberlain, what is the din
> In London's streets so late?
> The Lord Mayor answers with his head
> If it does not abate!"

Gone is the din; without, within
They all silently creep:
"Who breaks the spell, goes straight to hell!
The King can't fall asleep."

> "Let drum and fife now come to life
> And let the trumpets roar,
> To rise above that fatal curse
> That haunts me evermore!"

But over drums and piercing fifes,
Beyond the soldiers' hails,
They swell the song, five hundred strong,
Those martyred bards of Wales.

Peter Zollman

THE TWO PAGES OF SZONDI[4]

The ruins of Drégel have sunk in the clouds
The setting sun peers back, fight-worn is its red gaze,
opposite, a gentle green-grassed hill of mounds
with a spear and a flag that the wind frays.

> Two youths are kneeling with lutes in their hands

---

[4] Captain György Szondi became the captain of the fortress of Drégel (also spelled Drégely) in 1545. In 1552 Ali, the Pasha of Buda, decided to take the fortress in one of the major sieges of the Turkish wars in Hungary. Szondi defended it unto death. He wanted to spare the life of his two pages, a pair of orphaned boys, by sending them to become the minstrels of the conquering Pasha. The poem, which is related in spirit to "The Bards of Wales" (q.v.) tells of the young minstrels' resistance. Drégel is today in the Slovak Republic close to the northern Hungarian border.

— looks as if there were a cross struck to the spear's stem —
with victory shouts proud Ali cheers his bands
and he dances and praises and feasts them.
"Szondi's two pages, why do they not come?
Rose-bushes with angels' voice — they rhyme no fury —
let them weave a wreath of songs here to become
the bejewelled neck of a Houri."[5]

"See there, on the hill-top, next to the green mound
the infidel captain's spear and flag they're guarding —
there kneels your precious pair — and sweet is the sound
of their lutes which they pluck with eyes smarting."
"Then Márton, the priest of Nagyorosz[6] climbed up,
sent by Ali's haughty message as befriender:
'Look, good Captain Szondi, you might as well give up;
woman-born, you all die or surrender.'"

"Handsome troubadours, on this sad, barren mound
by this cross and spear you've lost reason for chanting —
come with me, where's dancing, honey, merry sound;
you'll be dined there with sherbet and dancing."
" 'Go good father Márton, this is my response:
Szondi never wanted mercy from your master —
from the hands of Jesus flow true mercy's fonts;
it's to Him I commend the disaster!' "

"Palm-buds, figs and sherbet, all the south's rich fruit
all that grows and ripens in lands of the Sultan —
sweetly scented spices, balm, fragrance acute,
come on! Join Ali's feast, quit the sulking!"
" 'Let the canons roar, then!' heathen Ali speaks;
bombs shower on Drégel, hailstorming grenades fall —
hell's fiery legions rise to scale the peaks
hammering at the fortress' stone wall."

"Gentlemen handsome, the sun's gone to sleep,
over its shoulders are red robes of a kaftan;
wind strikes up the wood-stems, moon spies through the deep,
chilly night swishes o'er the dead captain."

---

[5] A nymph inhabiting the Moslem Heavens, looking like harem favorites.

[6] A village south of Drégely, an hour and a half on foot, called Orosz and Nagyorosz in various times, today in the Slovak Republic. The priest, a Roman Catholic, was pressed into the messengership by the Turks.

"On the fortress' square all the silver and gold
Szondi has them build a treasure-pyre mighty;
with dagger in hand he must, fearless and bold,
put to death every whinnying palfrey."

  "Well then, what of it now, so good Szondi fell.
  ...Ali *acted nobly*... Gave him a hero's rest.
  He rests on the hilltop — this is what befell —
  Start singing of Ali! Give *him* your songs' very best!"
"Well... he had two minstrels, a pair of orphaned boys,
clad them in the best clothes, velvety and soft-hued,
he would not allow them to die in garments soiled
so they mourn...feeling sad, over-valued."

  "He sent us to Ali...'Ali's lavish, Ali's good,
  harsh sun will not darken your fair faces with him —
  you'll sleep in his tent — there's no wind, but good food,
  come on boys, pay your accolades *to him!*'"
"Szondi fought with thousands! Alone, he, and in vain!
Holding off the ruin with his own back merely —
armies fell in droves by his mighty sword slain
in his left hand his hauberk shone fiercely..."

  "True... He fought like Rustem[7] — it can't be denied —
  though his knees and sinews by our guns were broken,
  true... *I* saw the fight... But stop! Ali will chide,
  and his wrath must not vainly be woken!"
"Like crops fell the corpses, the Turks fell or fled,
littering the valley like landfill all gory.
He stood on the blood-soakèd peak of his death
and awaited his own end with glory."

  "Well, when will you stop? Won't you come to an end
  whimpering the praises of your clumsy leader?
  To hell with you bastards! To our whip you will bend
  and you'll languish in Lord Ali's slammer!"

Let his eyes run dry that butchered such a lord
wither, O God, the arms that halted Szondi's darting,
spare mercy, O God, on none who could afford
be the cause of his early departing.
               Adam Makkai

---

[7] One of the legendary heroes of Turkey. The Turkish speaker is
acknowledging Szondis' greatness by comparing him to one of their own.

MISTRESS AGNES

Mistress Agnes in the streamlet
comes to wash her linen sheet;
downward is the blood-stained cover
carried by the current fleet —
Lord, Father of Mercy, protect us!
    "Mistress Agnes, what's that laundry?"
    urchins goad her from the street,
    "Children, go away, keep quiet;
    chicken's blood has stained my sheet."
    Lord, Father of Mercy, protect us!
Neighbors' wives then come, keep asking:
"Where's your husband, Agnes, say?"
"Why, my dears, at home he's sleeping,
do not go and wake him, pray!"
Lord, Father of Mercy, protect us!
    "Mistress Agnes," says the sheriff,
    "come to prison now with me."
    "Oh, my dove, I cannot go till
    from all stains this sheet is free."
    Lord, Father of Mercy, protect us!
Deep the prison, one ray only
brings to its shades feeble light;
this one gleam is all that shines there,
ghosts and visions crowd the night.
Lord, Father of Mercy, protect us!
    All day long poor Mistress Agnes
    facing this faint glimmer sits;
    looks and glares at it unceasing
    as before her eyes it flits.
    Lord, Father of Mercy, protect us!
For whenever she looks elsewhere
ghosts appear before her eyes;
did this one ray not console her?
Sure, she thinks, her reason flies.
Lord, Father of Mercy, protect us!
    In the course of time, her prison
    opens, and she is now led

to the court; before the judges
stands she, without fear or dread.
Lord, Father of Mercy, protect us!
She is dressed with such precision
one might almost think her vain;
even her hair's smooth and plaited
lest they think she's gone insane.
Lord, Father of Mercy, protect us!
In the hall around the table
sit the judges in concern;
full of pity they regard her,
none is angry, none too stern.
Lord, Father of Mercy, protect us!
"Child, what have you done? Come, tell us,
grave's the charge against you pressed;
he, your lover, who committed
this foul crime has just confessed!"
Lord, Father of Mercy, protect us!
"He shall hang at noon tomorrow,
since your husband he has killed;
as for you, a life-long captive
you must be, the court has willed."
Lord, Father of Mercy, Protect us!
Mistress Agnes, seeking clearness,
strives to smooth her troubled mind;
hears the voice and knows the sentence,
clear of brain herself must find.
Lord, Father of Mercy, protect us!
What they say about her husband
she can't even comprehend;
only understands that homeward
more her way she may not wend.
Lord, Father of Mercy, protect us!
"Oh, dear Sirs and Excellencies,
look to God, I pray of you;
I cannot remain in prison,
for I've work at home to do."
Lord, Father of Mercy, protect us!
Forthwith she commences weeping,
freely flow her tears as showers;

like the wet from swans' down rolling,
dew-drops from the lilac flowers.
Lord, Father of Mercy, protect us!
"For a stain is on my linen,
blood that I must wash away —
God! If I should fail to cleanse it,
dread things might come our way."
Lord, Father of Mercy, protect us!
Then, at this appeal, the judges
glance at each other aghast;
all are silent, mute their voices,
by their eyes the vote is cast.
Lord, Father of Mercy, protect us!
"You are free! Go home, poor woman;
go and wash your linen sheet;
wash it clean and may God strengthen
and with mercy you entreat!"
Lord, Father of Mercy, protect us!
And poor Agnes in the streamlet
goes to wash her linen sheet;
downward is her now clean cover
carried by the current fleet —
Lord, Father of Mercy, protect us!
Snow-white long has been her linen,
there's no trace of red-blood stain;
yet poor Agnes can't but see it,
blood-red still she sees it plain.
Lord, Father of Mercy, protect us!
From the early dawn till evening,
sitting there, she scrubs the sheet;
water sways her trembling shadow,
winds her grizzled tressed greet.
Lord, Father of Mercy, protect us!
When the streamlet in the moonlight
shimmers, and her mallet gleams,
by the streamlet's bank she washes,
slowly beating, as in dreams.
Lord, Father of Mercy, protect us!
Thus from year's end unto year's end
winter, summer, all year through,

heat withers her dew-soft cheek, and
frosts her feeble knees make blue.
Lord, Father of Mercy, protect us!
And her grizzled hair turns snowy,
raven, ebon 'tis no more;
while her fair, soft face of wrinkles
—sorry sight—augments its store.
Lord, Father of Mercy, protect us!
    Mistress Agnes in the streamlet
    keeps washing her ragged sheet;
    downward are the cover's remnants
    carried by the current fleet.
    Lord, Father of Mercy, protect us!

William N. Loew [& A.M.]

IMPRISONED SOULS

Is this, then, the star of freedom?
This fiery, blinding sun
through our gloomy prison windows
couldn't shine on anyone.
Now the eyes are dazzled by its
searing incandescent glare:
    Come, our prison cell is calling,
    gentle twilight lingers there.

Here the teeming, roaring chaos
like a savage, stormy wave
sweeps away our sinking bodies
till we meet our early grave.
Leave this feverish commotion,
stop the never-ending blare:
    Come, our prison cell is calling,
    endless solitude is there.

Here the open air is sharper
and the winds are violent,
clouds are gathering in combat,

lightning splits the firmament,
sky attacks the earth in anger,
devastation fill the air:
        Come, our prison cell is calling,
        calmer weather greets us there.

Struggling here in ceaseless labor
day and night we stay awake
between Scylla and Charybdis:
little hope and daunting stake.
In the jail fatigue or danger
never drove us to despair:
        Come, our prison cell is calling,
        restful peace resides in there.

What is this: a flashing sabre,
cannon fires, gory swill,
flaming torches, bloodstained banners,
armies killed and poised to kill!
Fading slowly on our straw-beds
we could end the whole affair:
        Come, our prison cell is calling,
        quiet death awaits us there.

                                        Peter Zollman

Mihály Tompa
(1817-1868)

The son of a village cobbler, Mihály Tompa was born in Rimaszombat in northeastern Hungary (today in the Slovak Republic). He studied law and theology in Sárospatak and Pest and, after many vicissitudes in his personal fortunes, settled down in Beje, a small village. He was later invited to be the Protestant pastor of Hanva, where he spent the rest of his life.

A personal friend of both Petőfi and Arany (qq.v.), he first appeared as a poet in 1841 on the pages of Athenaeum *with a poem entitled* At Sundown [Alkonyatkor]. *He was also the acclaimed compiler and publisher of a collection called* Folk Legends and Folk Tales [Népregék és népmondák], *which appeared in 1846.*

He participated in the Hungarian War of Independence as an army chaplain. After the defeat, he wrote some of his finest allegorical poems during the Austrian oppression. He was twice arrested by the Habsburg police. Also highly appreciated were his Flower Tales [Virágregék], *and his published sermons have been favorably compared to those of major western contemporaries such as Robertson, Monod, and Parker. His collected works were first published posthumously in 1870.*

For a long time he was considered the equal of Petőfi and Arany, but 20th-century critics have relegated him to the lesser place of a significant forerunner of the great Age of Romanticism.

THE BIRD, TO ITS YOUNG

How long, despondent birds, with silent throats
will you sit grieving on the withered bough?
Have you, perchance, forgotten all the notes
that you were taught in happier times than now?
If the old lively songs and ecstasy
have passed away and will not come again,
then sad and pensive let your warblings be,
but sing, my children, even in your pain!

There was a great storm. In our ravaged grove
the soft and shaded haunts accept us not.
And are you silent? Do you seek to rove
and leave your sorrowing mother in this spot?
In other groves, the song sounds different.
They would not know your tongue, your sweet refrain.
Here, to your homeland in its ravishment,
sing, O my children, even in your pain!

Bring forth your fairest songs of recollection
of foliage and blossoming of yore!
Sing of the future, and in resurrection
this wasted soil may blossom forth once more.
The sunshine dawns more swiftly at your singing,
the saplings in the grove shoot forth amain;
to bless the present, it's sweetness you're bringing;
sing, O my children, even in your pain!

Here in the thicket is the ancient nest
where your frail wings were given strength to fly.
Surely you will return to it to rest,
no matter how you wander through the sky!
Alas, like human exiles would you roam,
now that the wind has rent your nest in twain?
Would you depart to seek an alien home?
Sing, O my children, even in your pain!

Watson Kirkconnell

TO THE STORK

The air is mild and winter at an end,
and are you here again, good stork, old friend;
cleaning the place where last your homestead stood
to make it ready for your downy brood?

Go back, go back, good stork, get up and fly —
the sun, the singing streams, are all a lie;
go back — no spring is here, no summer's warmth,
and life itself is frozen, chilled to death.

Avoid the fields, avoid the lake in flood —
meadows are graves, the lake is filled with blood.
You must not seek a tower when you tire —
it may conceal the remnants of a fire.

It is not safe for you to stay. But where
is there a house unravished by despair?
And if you moved your nest and placed it high,
a thunderbolt might strike you from the sky.

Fly to your southern isle — so warm, so free.
Good stork, you are far happier than we:
the Fates gave you two lands to call your own;
we have — we had — but one... and that too's gone.

If you encounter on a southern shore
the fugitives who have a home no more,
tell them we perish and decay with grief,
our nation's scattered like an untied sheaf.

Many in prison meet their final doom;
those living walk in silence and in gloom;
while others rise still weeping from their knees,
and go to find a home beyond the seas.

Here for a barren marriage prays the bride,
no parent grieves over the child that's died;
the old alone feel comforted at heart,
because they know that soon they will depart.

And tell them, too... Oh, what a shame to tell!
We were cut down — the oak not only fell —
the death-worm grinds it now and makes it rot,
as patriot betrays his fellow patriot.

Brother sells brother; father sold by son...
Yet do keep quiet, do not pass this on,
lest those who mourn us — far away, at ease —
despise and hate us like a foul disease!

Yakov Hornstein

HAVEN OF REST

Roaming life's ocean, if your damaged vessel
is prey to whirlpool and to hurricane;
and the wild foam mounts the wheel with a tussle,
rears ever up to fall on you again,

while storms will lour, turn shorewards your wrecked sail,
where fog won't haunt you with its spectral image;
and there rest, being weary now and pale,
who weathered all the stresses of the voyage.

Thus leave behind the dark rocks of the sea,
its pearl for which souls perish recklessly.
A purer joy awaits you upon reaching
the peaceful bay; for borne there by the wind
and waves, your ardent piety will find
the haven you have all your life been seeking.

Doreen Bell

AUTUMN

Now wither all earth's gallantries!
From autumn branches softly sown
the yellow leaves drift dumbly down
in eddies of the evening breeze.
Is not the falling of the leaf
fit season for the forest's grief?
No dew nor song nor heat of sun
can hold it when its day is done.

While I am in my leafy prime
and branches bloom with fragrant breath,
roar not, O boreal blast of death,
roar not on me before your time!
Too soon will autumn come with frost:
then love, delight, and hope are lost.

And if no chance of power reprieves,
a sleep shall on my eyes be laid;
in painless peace my life shall fade
and perish like the woodland leaves.

Watson Kirkconnell

LAST POEM

The ivy on my window sill
loses its warmth, life wanes, grows chill:
faded and wilted, the poor little leaf
yellow now, no longer greens;
half dead, half living, it sadly leans
toward its brothers in mutual grief.

Soon will come the great night.
The winter sunset pours its light
through the glass of the window pane.
On the bloomless stem the quivering ray
brightens gaily, and in its play
what fades below freshens again.

The creeper fights for its very life,
and where in springtime breezes are rife,
and the sky dazzles, it's so clear,
it turns upward those shoots bereft,
longing to pass through the narrow cleft
up to the heights that it would draw near.

The evening rays are playful, alive,
the disappointed roots revive
at the sudden touch of their embrace,
kisses that fall in flame and spark
only to pale, to the quick dark
yield unwillingly their place.

Silent I lie on my sick bed,
by evening's shade through the ivy led
to ponder this, until I see
that I myself am just the same,
and brooding this the fancy came
that this sad image in truth fits me.

Our course is not for long, see how
day changes into night, and now
summer throws winter in our teeth.
Though we strove upward, stoutly running,
we only made for all our cunning
an ever-growing funeral wreath.

The fronds, the aspiring sprouts cannot
grow again in a shattered pot,
the thirsting soil does not inspire
new strength. What seek you, O my soul,
lingering in these ruins? Your goal
must be only to rise up, up like fire.

Madeline Mason

Sándor Petőfi
1823-1849

Sándor Petőfi
(1823-1849)

Born in Kiskőrös on New Year's Day, Hungary's most famous and most influential poet was the son of a village butcher and innkeeper whose name was István Petrovics; his mother's name was Mária Hrúz. The young poet changed his name to Petőfi. ('Sándor Petőfi' is translatable as 'Alexander Peterson.') His fate became interwoven with the fate of Hungary and the country's numerous attempts to gain freedom and self-determination.

Petőfi's childhood was spent in the heartland of the Great Hungarian Plain where he received most of his education, including a thorough grounding in Latin. Later he learned German in Pest and in Graz as a soldier, and taught himself French and English. He became one of the first translators of the French Revolutionary poet Pierre Jean de Béranger [1780-1857].

He began to write poetry at the age of twelve while a student at the high school in Aszód, but he also showed an early passion for the stage, which caused his disapproving father formally to disown him. In the following year, his father suffered financial ruin, and it was not until four years later that father and son became reconciled; the poet supported his parents for the rest of their short lives. Prophetically conscious that his own life would be a short one, he crammed an amazing amount of experience and work into his twenty-six years. From 1839 to 1842 he became a student at the Calvinist college of Pápa where he met and formed a close friendship with Mór Jókai, Hungary's most prolific and finest 19th-century novelist, but in November of the same year he left Pápa and joined a theatrical troop, playing, among other roles, the Fool in Shakespeare's King Lear. *At last he settled in Pest.*

In 1844 his first volume of poetry was published with the help of Vörösmarty (q.v.). From then on his works followed in swift sequence, including his satire The Village Hammer [A helység kalapácsa] *and the fairy tale Sir* John the Hero [János vitéz] *in 1845, which became the basis of a delightful musical comedy, several films and a puppet theater production that is played all over the world. He wrote* Cypress Leaves [Cipruslombok Etelka sírjáról] *in 1845; a collection of elegies about a lost love of his,* Etelka Csapó; *there followed* Travel Notes [Úti jegyzetek] *inspired by Heine's* Reisebilder *in 1845, and many other volumes. At the age of twenty-four he was fully accepted as the leader of the younger Hungarian poets. A fiery patriot, a republican, and a revolutionary, on March 15, 1848 he became the voice of the Hungarian National Uprising against the Habsburgs when he recited his rousing*

National Song [Talpra, Magyar!], *which is included in this volume. Seven months earler he had married Júlia Szendrey, daughter of a country squire, who bore him one son. During the 1848-1849 War of Independence, he continued to write inspiring and revolutionary poems. In 1848 he was attached to the staff of the Polish-born leader General Joseph Bem, who held a special affection for the young poet. He rose to the rank of major in Bem's army.*

In the battle at Segesvár on July 31, 1849, he was killed — in all probability by a Cossack lancer. His body was never found, and for many years several pseudo-Petőfis kept roaming the country, generously helped by the people who refused to believe in his death. The myth continues even today, as some Hungarians believe that he may actually have survived the battle of Segesvár and may have been taken as prisoner by the Russians to Siberia. In 1990 an eccentric millionaire organized an expensive expedition to Barguzin in Buryat Mongolia, where some archaeologists claimed to have unearthed Petőfi's skeleton.

Petőfi's presence still haunts the national consciousness of Hungarians — whenever there is a major political upheaval, the demonstration is likely to start in front of his statue on the Pest side of the Danube, as happened on October 23, 1956. During the years of 'socialist realism' under the cultural terror of Rákosi and Révai, young populist poets thought it advantageous to start their careers writing in Petőfi's style; eventually all of them changed their tenor. Marxist critics cynically expropriated Petőfi; he was even characterized as a 'proto-Communist.'

Although he was an absolute rebel in his age, he was also later affected by mystical visions and wanted to turn the world into a cathedral; in one poem he mentions his previous lives as a revolutionary in Rome and in France. Most strikingly, however, he predicted his own death in the poem 'I'm Troubled by One Thought' (included in this book). His poetry covered every possible form, ranging from the rhapsodical Apostle [Az apostol] *to the most delicate love lyrics; from songs in praise of wine, to ballads and idyllic evocations of his native land. He is, quite deservedly, the most widely translated 19th century Hungarian poet, and he is well known all over Europe.*

Petőfi's combined literary and historic significance led the poet Gyula Illyés (q.v.) to write a much quoted Petőfi biography.

Petőfi's significance to any literate Hungarian is comparable to a Pole's estimation of Miczkiewicz, to a Russian's unquestioned adoration of Pushkin and Lermontov, to a German's love for Heine, and for a Scotsman's devotion to Burns. Nineteenth century America, in contrast, never produced a poet who meant to the country what Petőfi did to his native land.

Petőfi was, above all, a genius of language, who mastered any form he chose. His personality is perennially fused with the national identity of Hungary.

SIR JOHN, THE HERO
(Extracts)

I.

Upon the shepherd-boy the summer sun
was shining in an ardent benison.
In such a heat, it was too warm to work;
the panting shepherd was not loath to shirk.

> From the lad's heart, the flames of love ascend;
> his sheep are grazing at the village-end;
> in all directions there they munch and pass,
> while he himself is lying on the grass.

A sea of flowers has cast its colours round,
but yet he fails to see them on the ground;
within a stone's throw flows a little brook,
and there his fervent eyes have fixed their look,

> not on the shining waters of the stream,
> but on a little lass of grace supreme,
> whose fair slim body all his love arrests,
> with beautiful long hair and rounded breasts.

Up to her knees her petticoats were pent,
for all her time in washing clothes was spent;
two pretty knees through water glimmered white
for Johnny Corncob's infinite delight.

> For who upon the grass reclined in joy
> but Johnny Corncob's self, the shepherd-boy?
> Who in the stream washed clothes with simple art
> but Julie, the bright pearl of Johnny's heart?

"My darling Julie, treasure of my soul!"
— thus Johnny spoke, his darling to cajole —
"surely in all this world, from sea to sea,
you are the only turtle-dove for me.

> Show me your dark-blue eyes, your shining face,
> come from the water, let us now embrace!
> Come to the bank; before the morning slips,
> that I may kiss my darling's rosy lips!"

"You know, dear Johnny, I should gladly come,
but for this washing, long and burdensome;
for if I cease to toil, dark trouble greets me —

I am a stepchild — my stepmother beats me..."
>   Such was the slender Julie's mournful plea.
>   Again she scrubbed the laundry busily.
>   But from the ground the shepherd lad arose,
>   drew nearer, and his wheedling phrases chose:
"Come here, my pigeon! Come, my turtle-dove!
I want a kiss at once, a hug of love;
that your stepmother is not here, is plain;
don't let your longing lover die in pain!"
>   He coaxed the melting maid with soft demands;
>   then seized her by the waist with both his hands;
>   his kisses were not one, nor yet five-score —
>   only God knew to tell how many more.

II.

Meanwhile the passing hours the pair forsook;
evening grew rosy on the little brook;
but Julie's mean stepmother choked with rage:
"where is that lazy slut? She needs a cage..."
>   Thus was the wicked dame with anger fraught;
>   the words that followed matched her bitter thought
>   (her utterance bore no hint of gentle will):
>   "if she is idling, she will fare but ill!"

Because of Johnny's amorous preoccupation, his master's sheep go astray. He loses his job and takes to the road as a wanderer. Meeting some robbers, he is forced into membership in their band, but incinerates them all in their house in the forest, along with all their ill-gotten wealth. He next meets a troop of Hungarian hussars, and enlists as a cavalryman.

VII.

On through the cold, wide world did Johnny fare;
he thought but little of the bandits' lair.
A sudden blaze of light he marked anon:
the sun on warlike weapons brightly shone.
>   Soldiers were coming now, superb hussars;
>   light twinkled on their swords like summer stars;
>   the horses pranced and snorted on the plains
>   and proudly shook their heads and tossed their manes.

When Johnny saw the cavalry draw near,
his heart went thumping with a throb severe,
because he thought: "if they would only take me,
a happy soldier it would surely make me..."
> When they approached, all straight and courteous,
> Johnny stepped forth, to greet the captain thus:
> "Hail, countryman! As you ride on today,
> does grief or devil drive you on your way?"

He spoke yet more, breathing a mighty prayer:
"Through the wide world I wander in despair;
if for an honest favour I should plead,
look graciously upon me in my need..."
> The captain answered: "You speak well, my man;
> we seek no fun but battle, if we can.
> The Turks the field of France with slaughter drench,
> and we are marching on to help the French."

"I'd like that well... I'd gladly join your force,
if I could sit in a saddle and ride a horse.
Now I kill sorrow... Why not kill in war?
That is a job I have a fancy for!
> A donkey is the most I've ridden yet
> I've been a shepherd, not a bold cadet.
> I am Hungarian born to ride, of course,
> 'twas for Hungarians God did make the horse!"

Johnny joins the troops. After many an adventure the hussars gallop after the Turks and destroy them. Johnny saves the king's daughter. They all return to France and are given a triumphal feast. The king wants to reward them:

The hussars all gave the king good heed,
that they might follow as his words proceed;
he took a drink, then coughed, and cleared his throat,
and broke the silence on a serious note:
> "Brave man, who saved my daughter from her fate,
> tell me your name, for all guests in my state!" —
> "Plain Johnny Corncob is my honest name;
> a trifle rustic, but unsoiled by shame."

XIII.
Thus Johnny Corncob spoke, in quiet pride,
to which, in turn, the King of France replied:
"Another name I'll give you hereupon:
kneel down, a peasant. Rise a knight, Sir John!
      Honest Sir John, now harken to my words;
        since you have saved my child from Turkish hordes,
        make her your wife, shelter her as your own,
        and also take with her my royal throne..."

Sir John, still faithful to Julie, refuses to marry the king's daughter and to ascend the throne of France; but the king gives him a whole sackful of gold to carry home. Setting out by ship for Hungary, he suffers shipwreck, but survives and escapes to a rocky sea-cost.

He scaled a cliff and marked above the rest
a monstrous griffin-bird upon its nest.
The griffin-bird was breakfasting its young,
as John upon the ledge fearlessly clung.
      Slowly he crept nearer, without a word;
        then swiftly jumped upon the griffin-bird;
        into its feathered sides he jabbed his spurs,
        and the strange steed in frenzy swooped and whirled.
It would have flung him down amid its babel,
it would have flung him down, had it been able;
but bold Sir John kept it in his palms' check,
clutching it closely by the waist and neck.
      God knows how often they swept through the sky;
        as they kept flying very-very high;
        but when at last they came to dawn's bright hour,
        the sun was shining on his own town-tower.
Good Heavens! How Sir John rejoiced on high;
his rapture drew the tear-drops to his eye;
and the great bird, in weariness profound,
descended ever closer to the ground.

As he arrives home, he finds that Julie has been beaten to death by the witch, her stepmother. He plucks a rose from her grave and resumes his travels.

XVIII.
Once more Sir John turned back. Above her tomb
a simple rosebush burgeoned all in bloom.
He plucked a fragrant flower from its stalk,
and left, and walking mused in pensive talk:
          "Born from the dust, o little flower of woe,
          be my faithful companion as I go.
          I must now wander to the world's far end,
          until I die without a single friend..."

*He now comes to the land of the Giants. When he kills their evil king,
the other giants choose him as their leader. As he insists on travelling
farther, they give him a whistle, by which he may summon their help
in time of need. He goes on and reaches the Land of Darkness where
the witches live. They almost overcome him, but he blows his whistle
and the giants come to his aid. But there is one witch left:*

XXI.
Then John turned back, and on his whistle blew;
the giants came at once, his mighty crew.
"At them!" cried John, "and smash them, every one!"
and as he ordered, it was promptly done.
          The darkness, with the witches, disappeared.
          Last of the hags was one he loathed and feared.
          How did the witch and John know one another?
          Why, it was Julie's dame, her ruthless "mother."

*After the giants have exterminated all the witches, one giant, at Sir
John's request, carries him to his desired destination, "the end of the
world."*

XXIV.
The giant took Sir John upon his back,
and with great legs he strode the onward trek;
three weeks at awful speed, the knight he bore,
but still he scarcely reached the final shore.
          Then in the distance, and its blueish haze,
          John's eyes saw something in a glad amaze.
          "Look, there's the seacoast!" in his joy he cried.
          "Only an island" said his mighty guide.

"What sort of island?" — was his query then.
"The Land of Fairies is its name to men.
This is the world's end that the fairies bless;
beyond it lies the Sea of Nothingness."

....

    Now when Sir John surveyed the land with awe,
    he marvelled over something that he saw,
    his eyes were dazzled by its rosy light,
    until he dared to cast around his sight.
The fairies did not run away from him;
their gentle, childlike eyes with mercy swam;
they kissed him graciously with playful speech,
and took him walking on the island beach.
    And when Sir John had viewed their sweet regime,
    he woke to sorrow as if from a dream:
    despair came hovering above his heart,
    what was this land where Julie had no part?
"Here where the very land was made for lovers' bliss
must I suffer alone in loneliness' abyss?
Everything here with happiness is blessed;
all things are happy, but my orphaned breast."
    Amid the isle a lake stood fair and trim;
    Sir John walked mournfully along its brim.
    And from his bosom plucked out Julie's rose,
    the token of her grave that with him goes.
"My own true wealth! The ashes of my dear!
Show me the way; I'll follow through this mere!"
Into the lake's clear waves he tossed the rose
and with a sigh to jump after he rose.
    But what a marvel! What a scene amazes!
    The rose is changed to Julie as he gazes.
    Frantic with joy, not caring if he sank,
    ferries the reborn maiden to the bank.
"Water of Life" this fairy lake so warm,
has power all it touches to transform.
From Julie's ashes had the rose been bred,
and so it brought back Julie from the dead.
    Would I were blessed with eloquence to say
    how John's heart almost stopped with joy that day,
    when he brought Julie from the lake with bliss

and took with thirsty lips a primal kiss.
How beautiful she was! Each fairy sprite
gazed on her beauty with amazed delight;
a crown to her, as their queen they did bring;
and fairy-lads chose John as Fairy King.
  And 'mid the fairy nation and its charms,
  encircled by his Julie's loving arms,
  His Majesty, Sir John, may still be scanned,
  the blessèd monarch of sweet Fairyland.

Watson Kirkconnell

PLANS GONE UP IN SMOKE

While homeward bound I thought about
the way, through every mile,
in which to greet my mother, whom
I missed for quite a while.
  What pleasing words to say to her?
  Dear words they need to be,
  when she, who rocked my cradle, will
  be reaching out to me.
And in my mind the thoughts caroused
more pleasing every one,
it seemed that time had halted, though
the cart was on the run.
  Then I leapt in the tiny room,
  She ran, she flew to me...
  I clung to her without a word
  Like fruit upon its tree.

Leslie A. Kery

THE CART WITH FOUR OXEN

All this did not happen in Budapest —
Things so romantic do not happen there.
The gentle members of our company
Climbed on the cart, but a cart drawn by oxen,

Two pairs of oxen formed the postilion.
And down the dusty high-road with the ox-cart
The four oxen quietly wandered on.

The night was light. A pallid moon was shining;
Wove in and out from behind tattered clouds,
Like a sad lady seeking in the graveyard
Her husband's grave in between tired crowds.
A mercurial wind came to the meadows
Stole sweet fragrance from grasses, and was gone...
Along the dusty high-road with the ox-cart
The four oxen quietly wandered on.

I myself was in that company, and
I was sitting next to gentle 'Lisabet —
The other members of the company
Were talking or singing a chansonette.
I was lost in dreams and said to 'Lisabet:
"Shall we select a star now for our own?"
Along the dusty high-road with the ox-cart
The four oxen quietly wandered on.

"Shall we select a star now for our own?"
Repeated I, dreaming aloud, to 'Lisabet,
"The star will guide us back in future days
To memories of past-time happiness
If fate should separate us from each other..."
And so we chose a star for our own.
Along the dusty high-road with the ox-cart
The four oxen quietly wandered on.   *Ila Egon*

I'LL BE A TREE

I'll be a tree, if you are its flower,
Or a flower, if you are the dew —
I'll be the dew, if you are the sunbeam,
Only to be united with you.
          My lovely girl, if you are the Heaven,

I shall be a star above on high;
My darling girl, if you are hell-fire,
To unite us, damned shall I die.   *Egon F. Kunz*

THE SHEPHERD RIDES ON DONKEY-BACK

The shepherd rides on donkey-back,
His feet are dangling wide,
The lad is big, but bigger still
His bitterness inside.

He played his flute, he grazed his flock
Upon a grassy hill
When he was told his sweetheart girl
Was desperately ill.

He rides his donkey in a flash
And races to her bed,
But by the time he reached the house
His precious one was dead.

The lad was bitter, hoped to die,
But what he did instead:
He took his stick and struck a blow
Upon the donkey's head.

                                    Peter Zollman

AUTUMN AGAIN

Autumn, once again enchanting,
has returned; I do not know
why I am so fond of Autumn,
but I love it, love it so!
        From a hill-side gazing round me
        on the patterns which it weaves,
        I shall listen to the quiet
        rustle of the falling leaves.

With a smile the sun is looking
down on earth, content and mild,
like a loving mother watching
tenderly her sleeping child.
      And indeed, the earth in autumn
      does not die, but — lying still —
      simply wants to rest and slumber,
      tired, sleepy, but not ill!
Quietly it shed its garments —
splendid garments, rich and gay.
It will dress again in new ones
at the dawn of a new day.
      Sleep, then, nature, sleep my beauty.
      let the night of winter bring
      sweetest dreams, until you waken,
      fresh and rested, in the spring!
I will softly touch my lyre
with my fingertips, and long
hear the lullaby of autumn
mingle with my quiet song.
      Sit with me, my love, in silence
      underneath the shady tress,
      till it fades, as over waters
      fade the whispers of a breeze.
If we start to kiss — then let us
join our lips without a sound,
lest we dare disturb the drowsy
sleep, in which the world is drowned.

Lydia Pasternak-Slater

[FROM *THE CLOUDS*]

WHAT'S THE MERRIEST BURIAL GROUND?
Where sorrow is buried... "Where can it be found?"
— Is this what you've come to ask? —
The drinking table is where sorrow is subdued,
The bottle in the middle is the holy rood,
A tomb in every glass around the flask...
Join this merry place of doom
In these days of gloom.

Peter Zollman

SORROW? A GREAT OCEAN.
Joy?
A little pearl of the ocean.
Perhaps
By the time I fish it up
I may break it.   *W.H. Auden*

IF ALL THE HEARTS THAT SHRIVELLED in their graves
Turned into a funeral pyre
Set on fire,
Who could name
The colours glowing in that flame?

                                                   Peter Zollman

WHAT HAPPENS TO LAUGHTER
And to weeping, after
Their sound begins to wane?
What comes of the brain
After the thoughts depart?
Of charity,
And enmity
When they decide to leave the heart?

                                                   Peter Zollman

THE FARMER PUTS HIS FIELD under the plow,
Then he harrows it even.
Time puts our features under the plow,
But won't harrow them even.

                                                   Peter Zollman

HOW MANY DROPS HAS THE OCEAN SEA?
Can you count the stars?
On human heads how many hairs can there be?
And sins within human hearts?   *Peter Zollman*

HUMANKIND HAS NOT DECLINED!
It's always been an evil kind,
It has been evil since the Fall...
Or else there was no need at all
To make up stories
Of God and salvation,
Satan and damnation,
To curb its abominable mores.

Peter Zollman

HOW WILL THE EARTH DIE?... Will she freeze? Will she burn?
I think that she will freeze to end her turn.
Those icy hearts will freeze her to the core
As they come to rest there evermore.

Peter Zollman

GLORIOUS NIGHT!
The giant moon, the tiny evening star
Walk twosome on heaven's boulevard.
Glorious night!
The velvet grass glistens with dewy spark,
A nightingale sings softly in the dark.
Glorious night!
The lover slips out to a hushed idyll...
The highwayman does likewise, but to kill...
Glorious night!

Peter Zollman

I OFTEN WONDER who will find
The answer:
Can the tears of humankind
Wash off the filth of humankind and cleanse her?

Peter Zollman

IS THE SPIRIT THE TRUE LOVER of the flesh?
Will they die together in immortal mesh?
Or is the spirit nothing but a friend,

Who does what friends do in a mere affair —
Vanish in the air —
When the other is nearing the end?   *Peter Zollman*

ON HOPE

Man, what is hope? ...a horrifying whore
Who doles to everyone the same embrace.
You waste on her your most precious possession:
Your youth, and then she leaves without a trace!   *Peter Zollman*

SOME OLD HOW

Soon we shall be truly wedded
Man and wife.
I can hardly wait to enter
Married life.
One more week is not for ever,
I wait with my best endeavour
Some old how.

My old man has seen some real
Poverty,
He shall leave me no money, nor
Property.
We shall manage penniless,
But in cozy happiness
Some old how.

I am wedding a strong-headed
Pretty bride,
I, too, have a healthy bit of
Gritty pride.
Fire running in our veins
We must try on tighter reins
Some old how.

Now I give in, next time she is
Lenient,
Why get in a petty-minded
Argument?
If by day we have a fight,
It's all settled for the night
Some old how.

Peter Zollman

HUNGARY

Cooking, it seems, is not your forte
Belovèd country, Hungary!
You leave the joint raw on one side
And burn the rest unsavoury.
So on one hand your lucky subjects
Are drowning in their plentyland,
While countless wretched folk are dying
Of hunger — on the other hand.

Peter Zollman

I'M TROUBLED BY ONE THOUGHT...

I'm troubled by one thought — to die
in bed, among pillows stacked high;
to wilt and wither, flower-like, beneath,
as if chewed by some secret vermin's teeth...
Lord, grant me, please a better end!
God, my death must be different!
Let me be a tree, transfixed by lightning
torn up by storms from its roots' deepest fastening —
or turn me to rock, dislodged from ledge or shore
by an earth-shaking thunder's loud and mighty roar!
...And when every enslaved nation
sheds in bold fight its chains' abomination
and with faces red, as its banners,
shouts out this truth that strikes like steel hammers:
"World Freedom now!"
and that's what they all vow —

and this is what they'll be shouting from East to West
and tyranny collides with them in deadly contest —
let me drop my shield
on that battle field
let youth's river flow from my heart as it's bleeding
and when the joyous "farewell" from my lips would be fleeting
let it drown in the din of the spears and the swords
let the guns and the trumpets devour my words —
let the stallions course
o'er my fallen corpse
on to the triumph we won — won at last!
...and let me lie trampled below on the grass...
Let them gather my scattered remains from their lay
when it finally comes, the Great Funeral Day,
when a processional's slow-beating rhythm
with tattered flags for shrouds will be accompanying them;
those, whose dead hulls into mass-graves will be hurled,
who have died for the Truth — the Freedom of the World!

Adam Makkai

AT THE END OF SEPTEMBER

The flowers of autumn still bloom in the garden,
the poplar's still green in the valley below,
but you surely must see how the days start to darken —
the peaks of the mountain are covered with snow.
The flames of the summer still ray in my bosom
and the youth of our springtime still glows in my heart —
but notice my dark hairs — to white streaks I lose them —
as the hoarfrosts of autumn my head's winter start.
    The flower will wilt — fleeting life fades tomorrow.[1]

---

[1] This is in all probability the single most often quoted line in Hungarian poetry, memorized by generations ever since Petőfi's death in 1849. The Hungarian original *"Elhull a virág, eliramlik az élet"* contains five /l/ phonemes, two /r/-s followed by /h/, /v/ and /m/ with a vocalic sonority built on the vowels /e u a i á e i a i a é e/, dominated by liquids and spirants. It is a perfect 12-syllable anapaestic line, whose entirety expresses a philosophy of

Come, dearest of wives, hug my shoulder a while...
You cling to me now; will you not in deep sorrow
be seeking my grave over many a mile?[2]
Should the scythe of death cut me before you — confess it! —
will you cover this hull with your tears and a shroud?
Could the love of a youth turn your head and so press it,
that you quit for his name — *our name,* once so proud?
Should you choose to discard your attire of a widow,
make a marker of it! Pin it onto my grave!
I shall rise from the darkness to veil up its window —
this, my Flag of Defeat,[3] I shall treasure and save!
It will do as a kerchief to soak up the water
my eyes will have shed at your heart's cavalier,
facile oblivion, just so that later
I can go on to love you — fore'er and a year!

Adam Makkai and *Valerie Becker Makkai*

TO JÁNOS ARANY

Now to the author of *Toldi* my spirit flies through space.
I read, my brother poet, I read your fine creation,
and I send you my warm handshake, my affectionate embrace,
to tell of heart's delight, my own's heart's elation.
Should my spirit touch you, should you feel it burn,
the fault is not mine — it is you who set it afire!

---

life characterizable as "pre-existentialist stoicism."

[2] The original says: "*Holnap nem omolsz-e sírom fölibe?*" meaning 'Tomorrow, won't you collapse on top of my grave?' The line has been deliberately changed in this translation for it is known that, demented with grief, Julia in a man's uniform, searched for weeks the battle field where Petőfi died.

[3] Petőfi's poetry cannot be read in terms of individual pieces — his entire oeuvre must be kept in sight. In another famous poem, 'I'm Troubled by One Thought' (q.v.), he predicts his own death in battle and, indicates that he wishes be buried in an unmarked grave. Although this is his most famous love poem, in it, too, Petőfi already senses the impending defeat of Hungary's Freedom War at the hands of Pashkievich's army which came to the aid of Austria.

Your book's beauty, its glittering light, where did you learn?
All that excellence, how did you acquire?
Who and what are you that like some volcanic feat
you rise up from depths of ocean thus triumphantly?
You must be given at once your laurel wreath complete,
while to others it comes, leaf by leaf, gradually,.

Who has taught you, to what school then did you go?
Alas, in no school is the lyre taught that way;
only Nature herself could ever have schooled you so,
trained you in such masterly fashion indeed to play!
Your song, like the bells of the *puszta,* is simple in its sound,
as pure it is and clear as any *puszta* bell;
undisturbed by the sin of the world, it rises from the ground,
and travels across the plains, a music no noise can quell.

And this is the true poet, he who ever lets fall
the heavenly manna of his own breast onto the lips
of his fellowmen, poor folk behind a dark wall
of cloud, from whose horizon rarely a blue sky slips.
If others do not alleviate their burdened hours,
let us, poets, be their comforters, sing
consolation, for them let the very song of ours
be a sweet dream on their hard beds, a soft wing!

These were my thoughts as I climbed the poet's sacred height,
that you, my friend, continuing my poet's story,
what I had begun, not without glory quite,
might attain through you at last its fullest glory!

Madeleine Mason

THE TISZA

When in the dusk a summer day had died,
I stopped by winding Tisza's river-side,
just where the little Túr flows in to rest,
a weary child that seeks its mother's breast.

Most smooth of surface, with most gentle force,
the river wandered down its bankless course,
lest the faint sunset-rays, so close to home,
should stumble in its lacery of foam.

On its smooth mirror, sunbeams lingered yet,
dancing like fairies in a minuet;
one almost heard the tinkle of their feet,
like tiny spurs in music's ringing beat.
    Low flats of yellow shingle spread away,
    from where I stood, to meat the meadow hay
    where the long shadows in the after-glow
    like lines upon a page lay row on row.
Beyond the meadow in mute dignity
the forest towered o'er the darkening lea,
but sunset rested on its leafy spires
like embers red as blood and fierce with fires.
    Elsewhere, along the Tisza's farther bank,
    the motley broom and hazels, rank on rank,
    crowded, but for one cleft, through which was shown
    the distant steeple of the tiny town.
Small, rosy clouds lay floating in the sky
in memory-pictures of the hours gone by.
Far in the distance, lost in reverie,
the misty mountain-summits gazed at me.
    The air was still. Across the solemn hush
    fell but the fitful vespers of a thrush.
    Even the murmur of the far-off mill
    seemed faint as a mosquito humming shrill.
To the far bank before me, within hail,
a peasant-woman came to fill her pale;
she, as she brimmed it, wondered at my stay,
and with a glance went hastily away.
    But I stood there in stillness absolute
    as though my very feet had taken root.
    My heart was dizzy with the rapturous sight
    of Nature's deathless beauty in the night.
O Nature, glorious Nature, who would dare
with reckless tongue to match your wondrous fare?
How great you are! And the more still you grow,
the lovelier are the things you have to show!
    Late, very late, I came back to the farm
    and supped upon fresh fruit that made me warm,
    and talked with comrades far into the night,
    while brushwood flames beside us flickered bright.

Then, among other topics, I exclaimed:
"Why is the Tisza here so harshly blamed?
You wrong it greatly and belie its worth:
surely, it's the mildest river on the earth!"
      Startled, a few days later in those dells
      I heard the frantic pealing of the bells:
      "The flood, the flood is coming!" they resound.
      And gazing out, I saw a sea around.
There, like a maniac just freed from chains,
the Tisza rushed in rage across the plains;
roaring and howling through the dyke it swirled,
greedy to swallow up the whole wide world.   *Watson Kirkconnell*

THE PUSZTA IN WINTER

Ah, now the puszta is indeed a waste!
For autumn cast away in careless haste
      the spring's bright gift
      and summer's thrift
squandering their many treasures, rich and rare,
and winter finds the coffers cold and bare.

Yonder no more the sheep with dreamy bell
hear the sad shepherd's pipe its sorrows tell;
      the singing bird
      no more is heard,
the raucous corn-crake's silent in the grass,
and so's the cricket's fiddle as we pass.

The flat horizon is a frozen sea,
where like a tired bird in misery
      the dim-eyed sun,
      now spent and done,
bends low to look for something, with a lurch,
and even then finds little for his search.

Empty are fisher's cot and warden's hut;
the hay-fed beasts within the byre are shut:
      when by the trough

at eve they cough,
some shaggy steer lets out a mighty roar,
longing to drink the lake's water once more.

The farm-hand takes his leaf-tobacco down
from off the rafters, and with idle frown
cuts off a stripe,
then fills a pipe,
drawn from his boot-leg and with lazy puff
fears that the manger isn't full enough.

Even in the inn a mighty silence keeps;
the landlord and his wife can take long sleeps;
their bin, well-stocked,
may lie unlocked;
the waggoners that way no longer go;
the wind has swept the highways full of snow.

Blizzards now vie for stormy mastery:
one tempest in the heights is fierce with glee —
one rises higher
in gleaming ire;
while underneath, sparkling in snowy grace,
a third world wrestles with them face to face.

If, with the dusk, the blizzards' passions fail,
mist settles on the puszta, moist and pale:
one scarce can scan
the highwayman
whom his horse carries, sneezing home to bed,
wolves at his back, and crows above his head.

Like some king banished from his former realm
the sun looks backward from the earth's cold rim —
one look askance
with angry glance,
and with a final menace of adieu,
his blood-red diadem is lost to view.

Watson Kirkconnell

NATIONAL SONG[4]

Rise up, Magyar, the country calls!
It's 'now or never' what fate befalls...
Shall we live as slaves or free men?
That's the question — choose your 'Amen'!
   God of Hungarians, we swear unto Thee,
      We swear unto Thee — that slaves we shall no longer be!

For up till now we lived like slaves,
Damned lie our forefathers in their graves —
They who lived and died in freedom
Cannot rest in dusts of thraldom.
   God of Hungarians, we swear unto Thee,
      We swear unto Thee — that slaves we shall no longer be!

A coward and a lowly bastard
Is he, who dares not raise the standard —
He, whose wretched life is dearer
Than the country's sacred honor.
   God of Hungarians we swear unto Thee,
      We swear unto Thee — that slaves we shall no longer be!

Sabers outshine chains and fetters,
It's the sword that one's arm betters.
Yet we wear grim chains and shackles.

---

[4] The archetypal political poem of Hungary, the *National Song* is on every school child's syllabus, and is frequently recited on national holidays. Petőfi first performed it in the 'Pilvax Café' in Pest standing on a table-top; two days later he shouted it to thousands from the steps of the National Museum. Translated many times in the past, former English renditions failed to bring out the natural flow and rhythm of the poem, whose aesthetic value lies less in the political message than in the fine arch the belligerent tone weaves towards the religious end. The refrain was the oil that fuelled the Revolution that began March 15, 1848; those assembled repeated it in unison.

Swords, slash through the damned manacles!
  God of Hungarians, we swear unto Thee,
    We swear unto Thee — that slaves we shall no longer be!

Magyars' name will tell the story
Worthy of our erstwhile glory:
We must wash off - fiercely cleansing
Centuries of shame condensing.
  God of Hungarians we swear unto Thee,
    We swear unto Thee — that slaves we shall no longer be!

Where our grave-mounds bulge and huddle
Our grandsons will kneel and cuddle,
While in grateful prayer they mention
All our sainted names' ascension.[5]
    God of Hungarians, we swear unto Thee,
    We swear unto Thee — that slaves we shall no longer be!

(March 13, 1848)   *Adam Makkai*

THE SONG OF THE DOGS

Loud the storm is howling
under a thundery sky.
The twin sons of winter,
snow and rain, sleet by.
    What's that to us? We have
    our hearth-side, by the grace
    of our good kind Master
    who gave us this place.
We shall not die of hunger.
Our Master wills it thus.
When he has fed his fullest
the leavings are for us.
    True, his whip sometimes

---

[5] Petőfi was only twenty-five years old when the Hungarian Revolution of 1848 started. By late July 1849, at twenty six, he was dead, exactly as he had predicted in his poem 'I'm troubled by One Thought.'

cracks, and the weals
it leaves are most painful;
but a dog's hurt soon heals.
And then our Master calls us,
his sudden anger over,
and with true gratitude
on his boots we slobber.   *G.S. Fraser*

THE SONG OF THE WOLVES

Loud the storm is howling
under a thundery sky.
The twin sons of winter,
snow and rain, sleet by.
        It's a barren plain-land
        we choose for abiding.
        Not a bush grows there
        for shelter or hiding.
Hunger gnaws the belly,
cold gnaws the bone,
two tormenters who will not
leave us alone —
        and there, the third tormenter,
        guns loaded with lead:
        on the white, white snow
        our blood drips red.
Freezing and starving
and peppered with shot — —
yes, our lot is misery...
But Freedom is our lot!   *G.S. Fraser*

OKATO-OTAIA

There's a land they call astutely
Okato-otaia;
a distant neighbor of China
and near-by Austr(al)ia.

It's a good thing that Austr(al)ia
bears such a close relation!
You can count on keeping out
western civilization!

Oh, how brave, how stern and steadfast
is mighty Austr(al)ia!
Never will she fall for evil
progress, *inter alia*.

Although China, too, is going
quietly and slowly mod,
Austr(al)ia sits unflinching
like a solid platypod.

Bless your fate and thank the Good Lord
Okato-otaia,
that you are so far from China
and close to Austr(al)ia.

Happy Land! Although you suffer
various and sundry needs,
there is one you'll never notice —
culture, that one's spirit feeds.

Human souls are modest beasts here
they don't ask for straw nor hay;
they — like asses gobbling garbage —
chew calendars by night and day.

As a result, but no surprise,
poets, artists don't abound —
folks avoiding plows and shovels
only seldom come around.

Anyone who is so foolish
to be an intellectual,
should hide in a wooden closet
his tooth, like a rare jewel,

since, should you become an artist,
teeth you won't need, nor to think —
for you won't have crumb nor feast, but
only bitterness to drink.

One of this land's greatest prides is:
serfs and gents are kept apart —
home-spun woollen and escutcheons
writ on dogskins[6] — that's *the* art!

Coats-of-arms on dogskin-parchment
that's the stuff for which we care —
small wonder... if lots of nobles
keep it on *themselves* to wear!

Even if the noble classes
get carried away a bit
with their own worth, something passes
between lord and serf, to wit:

"hold open your palm" the lord says,
"be my estate's sentinel,
hold your hands out as I tell you —
here is nothing, grab it well."

Some say there's no public building.
How about those gallows there?
Why, in every village center
you will find a pretty pair.

Oh, this nation is a proud one —
truly in matters of pride
Okato-otaia can
well in front of others ride!

---

[6] Escutcheons (coats-of-arms) were written on parchment made of dogskin.

Prosper, oh you wonderful land
you grand and glorious nation!
May you rest quite unmolested
by western civilization!

Anton N. Nyerges

'FATE GIVE ME SPACE...'

Fate, give me space to breathe, let me do
something for mankind's sake!
never let this fine flame burning in me
lie with its useless ache!

A flame burns in my heart, a flame from heaven
that seers each drop of blood;
and each beat of my heart becomes a prayer
for the happiness of the world.

If I could only say all this with actions
when words are empty forms!
Even if my actions win me at least
new cross and crown of thorns!

To die for all men's good would be a death
most happy and most fair!
Fairer and happier than all the raptures
wasted on living air!

Tell me, tell me, fate, such holy death
awaits me... And I'll make
with my own hands the cross on which I'm laid
crucified to break.

Edwin Morgan

LIKE CLOUDS

Like clouds that sail in summer skies
My feelings go and come,
Now white, now black, they never pause
To rest but always roam.

But whence they come and whence they go,
This I cannot divine;
They're borne and blown away by the
Eternal wind of time.

For lightnings showered down on me
Out of the cloud of love,
And of the cloud of friendship poured
Rain-torrents from above.

When rain and lighting both have passed,
The sky grew still and clear;
Next minute with a breath of wind,
A new cloud will appear.

And yet the clouds, however white,
Still cast their shadows dark.
If only I could see that time
When all my clouds shall part!

When on their fringe the sun shall cast
Its burning, rosy beam;
Like castles out of fairyland
The clouds above shall gleam.

Oh, this time still shall come to me,
When all my clouds of love
And clouds of friendship, too, shall leave
In rosy hues above.

But then the priest may wend his way
To bury me at last,
For when the clouds begin to glow
The sun is sinking fast.

George F. Cushing

A TIME OF FEAR

A time of fear, a time of dread!
and horror grows, fear leaps ahead.
perhaps in heaven
the oath was given
to extirpate the Magyar race...
our bodies bleed from limb to limb,
and why? Against us now there gleam
the swords of half the world ablaze.

Out on the battlefield, the war
is woe enough, yet sadder far
the plague that roams
here in our homes.
Oh, Hungary, you take full share
of every scourge of God, and death.
Rears with both hands on every heath
a never-ceasing harvest there.

And shall we perish? Every man?
Or shall survivors still remain
the tale to tell
of this black hell,
this savage age, to all the earth?
If one survivor lives, can he
describe this fearful tragedy
as each event is brought to birth?

Were he a true account to give
of these events through which we live,
Who would believe
or who conceive
that such a tragedy occurred?
Would it not seem a fantasy
a terror-stricken madman's lie
devised by minds deranged and blurred?

George F. Cushing

Imre Madách
1823-1864

Imre Madách
(1823-1864)

Madách was born at Alsósztregova (today in the Slovak Republic) where his family had an estate. He studied law in Budapest and worked as a Deputy Notary, and later as a County Court Judge. He was prevented by ill health from taking part in the War of Independence of 1848-49, but as a patriot he offered aid to his countrymen. In particular, he sheltered Kossuth's secretary from the Austrians, for which he was imprisoned in 1852. His life was embittered by a domineering mother who opposed his marriage to Erzsébet Fráter, whom he later divorced on grounds of alleged infidelity. Until 1861 Madách lived in isolation on his estate, working on his poetry and dramas, among which Mózes *[Moses] was later rediscovered and performed. He was elected to the Diet (the Hungarian parliament), and became a member of the Kisfaludy Literary Society because of the huge esteem received for his chef d'oeuvre,* Az ember tragédiája *[The Tragedy of Man], which he wrote between 1859 and 1860, and the importance of which was first discovered by János Arany (q.v.). He was also made a member of the Academy of Sciences.*

The Tragedy of Man *is justly considered the single most significant Hungarian literary achievement and one of the outstanding monuments of world literature — it is no exaggeration to set it beside Goethe's* Faust *and Milton's* Paradise Lost. *There is nothing uniquely 'Hungarian' about it, except for a single name used in passing and a handful of Hungarian expressions from the Hungarian milieu. The sheer bulk of information and reference written into* The Tragedy of Man *— without detriment to its poetry — is in itself exceptional, but that would not by itself account for the sense of involvement evident in the work, nor for its depth of profound reflection on the state of Man vis-à-vis the Universe. Madách was by nature given to reading and thinking, but personal and largely unhappy family circumstances, aggravated by the political upheaval and national tragedy in 19th century Hungary, and to some extent by the division among religious persuasions still smoldering in the country, gave his thinking a direction and relevance that impelled him to write a philosophical dramatic poem of exceptional beauty. His is not poetry in the ordinary sense, relying on known poetic devices.* The Tragedy of Man *is poetry of thought.*

Translations of this work exist in over fifty languages, including English. The latest and probably the best English translation is Iain MacLeod's, an abbreviated form of which we present below. It was published by Canongate Press in Edinburgh, Scotland, UK in 1993.

EXCERPTS FROM THE *TRAGEDY OF MAN*

(with connecting abstracts from scene to scene)

I. The Creation of the Universe is complete. The Heavenly Host pays homage to the Lord, but Lucifer disparagingly dissents. He claims to be co-creator and he demands a share in the Universe.

THE LORD: And you, Lucifer, standing there aloof,
can you not find a word of praise to offer?
Perhaps you don't approve of my creation.

LUCIFER: Approve of what? The various elements
displaying their inherent properties?
A circumstance you couldn't have seen evolving
until the fact was plainly manifest,
and there was nothing you could do about it.
Meanwhile this *matter,* kneaded into globes,
unfolds, attracts, repulses, whirls around,
till in some beast a conscious thought is kindled...
Then, all fulfilled and all its heat expended,
indifferent, the neutral dust remains.
One day, man may himself acquire the knack
and plagiarize this crude experiment,
if you allow him in your cosmic workshop,
indulgently you leave him room to blunder,
concoct and scheme and think himself a god —
until the poor apprentice spoils the broth!
Then will he rouse you to belated anger.
Yet could you blame a feckless amateur?
And as for this creation — what's the purpose?
To your own glory you composed a song
and placed the record on a botched machine,
and now you're never done with this delight,
though old the tune — the lyrics much the same.
Does this become your age, integrity,
this comedy, which might amuse a child,
to see his clay creation mime the maker,
no likeness, but a crude caricature
that flits between free will and destiny,
lacking the overall intelligence?

THE LORD:	To pay homage is your part, not to judge me.
LUCIFER:	That would be out of keeping with my nature.

[pointing at the Angels]

Your paltry hosts will give you all the praise
that is appropriate for them to give you
who gave them life, as light begets its shadow,
for I have lived through all eternity.

....

THE LORD: What's this? Rebellious spirit! Out of here!
I could destroy you, but I will desist:
I'll let you toil amidst the dust, detested,
an outcast of the spirit world, an alien,
condemned to suffer utter loneliness
with this persistent thought to brood upon:
however much you shake your earthly fetters,
futile the war you wage against the Lord.

II. Contemptuously, the Lord gives Lucifer two trees in Eden, whereupon the rebellious Archangel is expelled from Heaven. He decides to corrupt Adam and Eve, pointing out their ignorance and their potential to attain knowledge.

LUCIFER: There are a few things yet you haven't heard of,
and won't hear either. No! The Old One up there,
he didn't create you out of dust, you know,
only to share the Universe with you.
Indeed, he'll keep you while you worship him,
and tell you what to eat and stay away from,
protect you, lead you like some woolly beast...
No need at all for you — to be aware.

ADAM: To be aware? What am I not aware of?
Don't I appreciate that blessed sun
the sweet delight of being and the graces
which God bestowed on us in great abundance?
He made me lord and master of the earth.

LUCIFER: That is perhaps the view the maggots take
nibbling the fruit which you may want to eat,
or birds of prey swooping to make a kill.
What's there to make you feel superior?
In you and them there glows a tiny spark,

the stirring of the same eternal power,
which, like so many wavelets of a stream,
now sparkle for a while, then lost to sight
sink in the merging current's murky depths.
There is, indeed, one thing: the power to know,
lying dormant in your subconscious mind.
Now, that could make you come of age: the choice,
the gift of knowing right and wrong, the freedom,
to be the master of your destiny,
unshackled from the leash of providence...
Of course, you may prefer to be a worm
which breeds contented in its cosy dungheap
with not a thought till life will pass it by.
Where resignation may console the weak,
the strong will stand his own ground, resolute.

ADAM: Amazing words. You leave me quite bewildered.
EVE: Exciting, Adam, new and beautiful!
             ....

LUCIFER: Look at the eagle, soaring in the clouds,
             or at the mole, burrowing in the soil:
             each has its sphere, its point of reference.
             The spirit world's beyond your comprehension,
             therefore to your own kind it seems supreme.
             And yet, since dogs' ideals must be canine,
             dogs do you honour thinking you're a dog.
             As you regard them your inferior,
             and tower above them as their destiny
             to mete out curse or blessing like a god,
             so we consider your estate below us,
             the proud denizens of the realm of spirits.

*III. Adam and Eve fall prey to Lucifer's temptation: they disobey the
Lord, and rebellious Adam walks out of the Garden of Eden, followed
by Eve. Adam demands knowledge from Lucifer, but is appalled by
what he is allowed to see. When he asks for immortality, Lucifer gives
him an equally disagreeable picture.*

ADAM: The very ground dissolves beneath my feet:
             what once appeared solid, without a form,
             is now a turmoil of convulsive matter

struggling to take shape. Irresistible!
Coming to life: now turning into crystals,
now into buds. Amidst these whirling forces
what's happened to my independent self?
O, wretched body, what's become of you?
What folly to mistake you for a fastness
of lofty thoughts and noble aspiration!
Look at you now, you pampered child, the author
of so much pleasure and calamity,
reduced to a handful of dust as you are,
and see your better part, robust, elated,
a while before, now vapour, empty air,
dispersing with my self among the clouds.
The words I speak consume my very being,
as if a part dissolved with every thought.
I'm all aflame! O, what a baleful fire!
Perhaps that unknown spirit kindles it
to warm his ghastly mansions with my embers.
Remove this sight! This is insanity!
This fight, harassed by elemental forces,
tormented by the pangs of desolation...
Appalling, hideous predicament!
Too late to call on kindly Providence
which I innately felt but still decried!
O, tardy knowledge! O, futile remorse!

....

LUCIFER: All living things have equal share of life,
the same chance of achieving their potential:
the age-old tree, the fly which lives a day,
feel, love, rejoice and die, their stint completed.
Days, centuries make little difference.
It's not time passing, but ourselves who change.
Then be assured, you *will* fulfil your purpose,
but don't expect your personality
will linger in this human lump of clay.
Look at the ants, or take a swarm of bees.
A thousand workers throng without directive:
some, toiling blindly, fail and come to grief,
but as a whole, a working unity,
they can survive and, as of one accord,

act and assuredly achieve their goal —
until the end when all expire together...
Although your earthly body will decay,
you will survive in countless other forms,
no need to make a fresh start every time:
your sins shall visit you in your descendants,
in them you will have your disease prolonged,
whatever you've encountered, felt or learnt,
is yours to keep until the end of days.

*IV. However, Adam wants to know the future of mankind, and
throughout the following scenes he is shown samples of history
selected, invented and stage-managed by Lucifer, hoping to drive him
to disillusionment and despair, thereby undoing the Jewel of Creation,
MAN. Adam, now in Egypt, is a Pharaoh, anxious to see his glory
perpetuated in a pyramid. He feels attracted to a dying slave's wife,
Eve, who in turn persuades him to release his slaves and to abandon
the great project.*

ADAM: *[to the overseers who press forward
                   to drag Eve and the slave away]*
                                    Let them be! Get out!
                   [to himself]
                   What is this strange upsurge of sympathy?
                   Who is this woman here? Where has she come by
                   the charms which all but overwhelm the Pharaoh
                   and drag him down to join her in the dust?
                   [Adam rises.]
LUCIFER: That subtle gossamer you've seen before —
                   in which your master trapped you for a jest.
                   It's to remind you that you'd been a worm,
                   when like a butterfly you proudly flutter.
                   You must have seen how strong this fibre is;
                   so delicate, it slips between the fingers
                   and can't be torn apart.
ADAM: *[descending from the throne]*
                                    Don't try it either.
                   Although it hurts, it gives me pleasure, too.
LUCIFER: A shame to find a thinker and a king
                   enmeshed in it.

ADAM:	Then what's the remedy?
LUCIFER:	Let scholarship concoct an argument
	against the existence of these occult tangles,
	then crude materialism can shrug it off.
ADAM:	I doubt if I could stoop to either of these.
EVE:	My love, you're bleeding. Let me help you. Come!
	I'll have to wipe this blood. There! Does it hurt?
SLAVE:	Why should I live, a slave? To build the Pharaoh
	his pyramid, raise children for his bondage
	and then to die! A million does for one!
ADAM:	O Lucifer, these words! What does he mean?
LUCIFER:	Wild ramblings only of a dying man.
ADAM:	What did he mean?
LUCIFER:	Great Pharaoh, what's the matter?
	Is this indeed a thing of some importance?
	The world's about to lose — another slave.

*V. His desire to establish a free society takes Adam to democratic
Athens, where he appears as Miltiades, with Eve as his wife. However,
they meet disappointment, when a Demagogue, in the service of certain
citizens, persuades the idle and corrupt mob to condemn Miltiades as
a traitor.*

1ST MAN:	There's no excitement, news or anything.
	You'd think the army's got no one to fight.
2ND MAN:	The place is dead, not like in days, remember,
	when folk had, what you'd call them, *propositions*
	to put before us, and to — *ratify* them
	the sovereign people's throat was called upon.
	I've walked and hawked about the ruddy place,
	and not a customer to buy my vote.
1ST MAN:	A boring life! I'm tired of doing nothing.
3RD MAN:	I wouldn't mind creating some disturbance.
1ST DEMAG.:	Give way! This stand is mine. The land's imperilled
	if I don't speak.
	[approving cheer among the crowd]
2ND DEMAGOGUE:	You mean the land's in peril
	if you're allowed to speak? Get off, you hireling!
	[laughter and applause among the crowd]
1ST DEMAG.:	You're not a hireling, eh? Not worth a hire!

My countrymen! With painful resolution
I come to raise my voice against a great man,
for so I must, although it breaks my heart:
from his triumphal chariot I must drag him
before your seat of judgment.

2ND DEMAGOGUE: Hear the rascal?
He decks with flowers the sacrificial beast
before he slaughters it.

1ST DEMAGOGUE: Take him away!

CROWD: Who wants to listen to that sneering bastard?
[They pull the 2nd Demagogue off the rostrum.]

1ST DEMAG.:   It is, I say, with heavy heart I speak,
and yet I must in duty, sovereign people,
defer to you — before your general.

2ND DEMAG.:   To this, this famished mercenary rabble
which hangs about for scraps like hungry dogs
under their masters' tables? O, you wheedler!
Your preference, not mine: to each his own.

CROWD: Another traitor! Get him! Pull him down!

1ST DEMAG.:   My countrymen! I charge Miltiades
with treason!

2ND DEMAGOGUE: It's a lie! A monstrous lie!
Now, listen to me! You may be ashamed
and have regrets too late...

CROWD: Pull down the bastard!
*[Pulled from the rostrum, the 2nd Demagogue
is lost among the crowd.]*

1ST DEMAG.:   Our flower of young men under his command
had taken Lemnos with a single stroke:
at Paros now he falters... Why? He's bribed!

3RD MAN: Traitor! Put him to death!

1ST CITIZEN: Give tongue, you dogs,
or get your baggage off my property.

*VI. Abandoning his ideals, Adam, as Sergiolus, becomes a dissolute
Patrician in Ancient Rome. However, he is unable to find lasting
satisfaction in pleasure. Eve, a prostitute, dreams of her innocent past.
The appearance of St. Peter gives Adam yet another ideal to fight for.
He embraces Christianity.*

[On a raised platform gladiators are fighting.]

CATULLUS: You see the fellow with the scarlet sash?
A real fighter, that! Sergiolus,
I bet you anything he'll beat your man.

ADAM: Not he, by Hercules!

CATULLUS: What? Hercules?
It won't do. No one here believes in gods.
Swear by your concubine. It's more convincing.

ADAM: I do.

LUCIFER: Your oath is well established now.
Let pseudo-goddess beat a demigod.
But for your oath, how are we meant to take it?
You meant her beauty? Or your love for her?
Or, no, you didn't mean fidelity?

CATULLUS: Female charms fade, you know. In any case,
what fascinates today may bore tomorrow.

ADAM: It's *her* fidelity I meant. What else?
It costs me quite a bit.

HIPPIA: How wrong you are!
Can you make love to her without fatigue?

ADAM: I know, I know! Enough said, Hippia!
I take your point, but tell me: what is pleasure?
A drink of water for the thirsty pilgrim,
or an ocean to engulf the luckless bather?

LUCIFER: A proper lecture on morality —
reclining on your woman, sipping wine.
But what about your wager?

ADAM: If I lose
you have my Julia.

CATULLUS: And if you win?

ADAM: I'll have your horse.

CATULLUS: You want her back, of course?
In one month? Or I'll feed her to my eels.

LUCIFER: *[to Julia]*
Enjoy this dish of appetizing fish
before the fish consider you a dish.
[The others applaud.]

EVE: What of the worms? They'll make a feast of you.
So, have a drink! Make merry while you can!

ADAM: *[to a gladiator]*
Get on with it there!

CATULLUS: Smartly now! Come on!

Catullus' gladiator falls, and lying on the ground he raises his fingers begging for his life. Adam is about to give the sign for mercy, but Catullus arrests his hand and, with his fist clenched, he turns his thumb down towards the fallen gladiator.

CATULLUS: Recipe ferrum! He's a craven mongrel
                 I can afford to lose. Got plenty of them.
                 The carnal appetite grows all the keener,
                 and kisses deeper, when some blood is spilt.
                 [Meanwhile the gladiator is killed by his opponent.]
ADAM: I've got the horse! Come, hug me, Julia!
                 There! Take away the corpse! Let's have the dancers!
                 ....
                 Who is to sing the bawdiest song today?
HIPPIA: *[singing]*
                 Of wine and pleasure
                 we must have full measure:
                 in every cupful
                 another delight...
                 And the ecstasy! Let the ecstasy,
                 like the sunset over a broken monument,
                 enfold us in glorious light.
ALL IN CHORUS: Enfold us in glorious light.
HIPPIA: *[singing]*
                 Of wine and pleasure
                 we must have full measure:
                 another bedfellow
                 for every night...
                 And the ecstasy! Let the ecstasy,
                 like the sunset over a broken monument,
                 enfold us in glorious light.
ALL IN CHORUS: Enfold us in glorious light.
                 ....
LUCIFER: O, very good indeed! I like the message.
                 I wish I had composed the song myself.
                 ....
THE APOSTLE: O, cowardly race! You wretched generation!
                 How arrogant, while fortune smiles upon you,

how like the flies cavorting in the sun
defiling virtue, mocking God Himself!
But when disaster knocks upon your door,
or God's almighty finger points at you,
you shrivel in contemptible despair.
Why? Can't you see it's Heaven's retribution
that's bearing down on you? Look at your world!
Your city desolate; your golden harvest
all trampled down; barbarians on the march;
no order left: no one to take command,
no one to listen either; theft and murder
parade themselves unchallenged on the streets
with pallid fear and terror in their wake.
No hope, no help under your empty skies.
And yet, obsessed with pleasures as you are,
you can't suppress, you can't ignore the warning
which echoes still within your heart of hearts,
trying to stir you from your decadence.
Why can't you find contentment any more?
Your self-indulgence ends in self-reproach,
but in your fright, struggling to find the words,
you cannot pray, you have renounced your faith:
your ancient gods have hardened into stone.
[The statues of gods disintegrate.]
They crumble — and yet you haven't found a new god
to help you rise above your dustbound nature.
Go, ask what drains your city's population
more potently than any pestilence!
Thousands abandon their luxurious couches
to add their numbers to the anchorites
who seek the wilderness of Thebais
to find seclusion and a new experience
to rouse and stimulate their blunted senses.
You brood of decadence, the time's upon you:
the world must once again be rendered clean.

*VII. Adam is now Tancred, a Crusader Knight, returning from the Holy
Land. He is soon disillusioned with the excesses of the Church in
Constantinople, squabbling over doctrinal disputes, burning heretics,
selling indulgences; what is more, his love Isaura (Eve) is sent to a*

convent as a votive offering for her father's delivery from the infidels during the Crusades.

PATRIARCH:	These are dissenters who try to introduce HOMOIOUSIAN to doctrine on the Holy Trinity, whereas the church establishing the faith has clearly instituted HOMOOUSIAN.
MONKS, FRIARS:	They'll suffer for it! Burn them at the stake!
ADAM:	*[to the heretics]* Listen, my friends! Forget this letter "i": giving your life to free the Holy Land would be a more becoming sacrifice.
OLD HERETIC:	Satan, begone! We'll keep our faith untainted and shed our blood as God directed it.
A MONK:	Boast of untainted faith? What arrogance!
OLD HERETIC:	In Rimini the Synod ratified it, and others did as well.
A MONK:	They are in error. one in Nicea clearly stood for us.
OLD HERETIC:	The renegades! Trying to rival us. Have you a single Father of the Church on your side like our Father Arius?
A MONK:	And how about our Athanasius?
OLD HERETIC:	Have you a martyr?
A MONK:	More than you can boast of.
OLD HERETIC:	Some martyrs, those. The devil has beguiled them into deception and accursed death. I'd say you are that Babylon the Great. You are to be destroyed!
A MONK:	You Antichrist! That's what you are: the Seven Headed Dragon, of whom Saint John has written. You deceivers! You villains, Satan's own associates...
OLD HERETIC:	You thieves! You serpents, gluttons, fornicators...
PATRIARCH:	Take them away! We're wasting time with talking. To God the glory: march them to the stake!
LUCIFER:	Well, are you speechless? Are you terrified? You think it's tragic? Take it for a farce. A comedy. You'll find it entertaining.

ADAM:

O, keep your jests! But for a single "i"
to march unwavering to certain death?
What else so glorious, so superlative?

LUCIFER:

What might appear ridiculous to others:
a question of that shade of difference
between the two, a shift of emphasis,
as this mysterious juror, sympathy,
is drawn to eulogy or deadly scorn.

ADAM:

Why have I got to witness all this evil,
this bickering about conflicting learning?
What is to blame for all this decadence?

LUCIFER:

Success itself. That is the culprit, breeding
this fragmentation, clash of interests,
while danger brings together, makes for martyrs
encourages, witness the heretics.

ADAM:

Truly, I'd like to fling away my sword
and fly to my own country in the north,
where in my ancient forests manly virtues,
a pure and simple life will guard against
the pestilence this subtle age has nurtured,
but for this faint, persistent voice within me
which says it's up to me to change the world.

LUCIFER:

A waste of effort. You will never set
a single man against the age he lives in.
It is a stream in which he drifts or drowns:
he swims in it, but never can direct it.
Those men whom history assigns to greatness
can understand their time, can act upon it,
but don't themselves create its motive forces.
Cocks do not crow to cause the dawn to break:
they crow because the dawn's already breaking.[1]

....

ADAM:

Show me a new existence, Lucifer!
I've striven for the highest of ideals
which shallow understanding desecrated —
and offered God a human sacrifice!

---

[1] Lucifer's speech about the relationship between the individuals and
the age they live in is one of the most often quoted passages in Hungarian.

Mankind's too base to live up to my dreams!
I've given mankind noble interests,
denouncing self-indulgence as a sin,
and set up chivalry, this knightly order,
which breaks my heart... Enough! I want a change!
Too long have I displayed my worth and virtues
both in my struggles and in self-denial:
I may without dishonour leave the field.
Let nothing disarrange my peace of mind:
I'll let the world get by the way it will,
I shall no more attempt to change the course,
but watch its faltering progress unconcerned.
I feel exhausted and I want to rest.

LUCIFER: Rest while you can, although I have my doubts
that your spirit, that unremitting force,
will let you rest for long. Now, follow me!

VIII. Now in Prague, Adam is Kepler, the astronomer of the Emperor Rudolph. Against his better judgement and his dedication to science, he is forced to sell horoscopes and weather forecasts to finance excesses of his adulterous wife Barbara (Eve), an aristocrat's daughter, at the Emperor's Court.

EVE: It's hard to say, John, but I need some money.
ADAM: I've nothing left; you've taken all I had.
EVE: Shall I forever live in penury?
I must look like a pauper up at Court,
while other women flaunt their rich attire.
When every now and then a courtier
comes up to me and bows, politely smiling,
and calling me the queen amongst them all,
truly I feel ashamed for you who let
this "queen" appear in Court so poorly dressed...
ADAM: Do I not labour day and night for you,
and prostitute my art, and sell my learning?
Do I not fabricate weather predictions
and worthless horoscopes, the shame of it,
concealing my most sacred understanding
to advocate what I know to be false?
O, I've become far worse, I blush to say,

than those sibyls who did at least believe
their prophecies, for though I don't believe them,
I still concoct those lies — and all for you!
No, not for me the wages of my sin.
I've no desire, not one, left in the world,
except the night, the glimmering, starlit sky,
except the distant music of the spheres...
The rest is yours. However, my requests
for payment have been mostly disallowed:
the Treasury itself is nearly bankrupt.
You may have all that I'll get in the morning,
ungrateful though you are — which hurts a little.

EVE: *[crying]*
You would reproach me with your sacrifices.
Was it not sacrifice enough for you,
when I, a daughter with an ancient lineage,
was married to your questionable title?
If you're accepted in society,
it is on my account. Now, who's ungrateful?

ADAM: Learning, knowledge — a questionable title?
This light upon my forehead from the skies,
does this denote a doubtful origin?
What else, besides this, is nobility?
Would you affix that name to decadent
decaying puppets whom their souls disown,
while this, my title, holds forever strong?
O, woman, if you could but understand me,
if only your soul were akin to mine,
as your first kisses made me vainly hope,
you would be proud to share this life of mine;
elsewhere you would not seek your happiness;
nor would you have the sweetness of your being
so wantonly bestowed upon the world,
only to leave your hearth the bitterness.
Woman, how infinitely did I love you!
I love you still, but it's a bitter sting
mixed with honey, it fills the heart with poison,
because you lack the true nobility
of womanhood, corrupted by this age,
which holds woman in bogus adoration,

as once chivalry held her pure, divine,
while faith prevailed and times were generous.
But in these paltry days, with faith declining,
this cult of woman smacks of lechery.
I would divorce you, I would break my heart,
hoping the pain would buy my peace of mind,
and you could also find your happiness,
but our established order blocks the way,
and that authority, the Church, decrees:
we must endure together — to the grave.
*[He buries his head in his hands while Eve,
not unmoved, caresses him.]*

EVE: O, John, don't let my words upset you too much.
I may speak thoughtlessly from time to time
and still don't mean to hurt you. But, you see,
though life at Court is ever so exciting,
those women there are foppish and disdainful.
I must conform, or I may be the loser.
You aren't too angry with me, are you, John?
Good night! — I'll have that money in the morning.
[She goes downstairs into the garden.]

ADAM: What puzzling blend of gentleness and baseness
distills in women? Honey mixed with poison.
What's their attraction? Their inherent goodness
that's overlaid with vices of the times.
Apprentice, hey!
*[Lucifer enters with a lamp which he places
on Kepler's writing desk.]*

LUCIFER: I heard you call me, master.

ADAM: A horoscope's required and some predictions
about the weather. Will you make them up?

LUCIFER: Most certainly, with all the puff and sparkle.
No ready cash is rendered for the truth.

ADAM: Control your sparkle: no absurdities.

LUCIFER: There's no outrageous praise I could invent
which doting parents wouldn't take for granted.
Their every new-born babe's a new Messiah,
their dynasty's illustrious star ascending,
until he proves the villain that he is.

*IX. Adam dreams of the French Revolution. He is Danton who, in the
midst of the bloodshed, yearns in vain for the sister of a condemned
marquis — Eve. She is killed, but reappears from the mob as a de-
mented woman demanding Danton's love.*

EVE:	Be strong, brother!
MARQUIS:	May God protect you, sister!
EVE:	Here, take this head as well, no worse than Roland's.
ADAM:	These harsh words ill-become your gentle lips.
EVE:	This scaffold is no place for gentle words.
ADAM:	This is my universe, this dismal scaffold.
	When you set foot on it, a ray of Heaven
	lighted on it and claimed it for its own.
EVE:	No sacrificial beast was so derided
	while taken to be slaughtered by the priests.
ADAM:	I am the one that's being sacrificed here.
	Though some regard my power with envious eyes,
	this throne of mine has no pleasure to offer:
	joyless I look on life and death alike,
	while others fall beside me day by day
	and I await my turn amidst the bloodshed,
	tormented by the pangs of loneliness,
	trying to apprehend the bliss of love.
	If you should teach me that celestial art
	but for one day — the day after the lesson
	I'd rest my head upon that block contented.
EVE:	You dream of love amidst this world of terror?
	The pangs of conscience must torment you, surely.
ADAM:	Conscience, Madam? It is the privilege
	of ordinary folk, a circumspection
	unsuited to the man of destiny.
	....
EVE:	Here's one conspirator! Look at him, Danton!
	He meant to murder you, he did. I killed him.
ADAM:	If he could have performed my duty better,
	you have done wrong, if not, you've done the right thing.
EVE:	Suppose I have, I want to be rewarded.
	Great man! I want you. Spend the night with me.
ADAM:	Is there affection in a heart like this?

	How tender is the love the tigress nurses?
EVE:	Upon my word, you talk as if you was
	a blue-blooded aristocrat yourself!
	You talk of love, citizen? Stuff for stories.
	Have it like this: I'm young and I'm a woman;
	I fancy you're a great man, so — I want you.
ADAM:	*[To the audience]*
	A shattering sight! I must avert my eyes.
	How can I bear this most unnerving likeness?
	I can't believe it. He who saw the Angels
	before the Fall in Heaven, then saw them after,
	he might have known an equal transformation.
	The self-same features, shape, voice, everything,
	— except for something indescribable,
	intangible, yet vital, gone amiss,
	which nonetheless makes all the difference.

X. The dream within the dream ended, Adam wakes up as Kepler advising a student on the futility of learning, while his wife has an illicit affair in the garden.

STUDENT:	It's kind of you to let me come alone
	to satisfy my thirst for knowledge, Sir.
	To delve into the hidden side of things
	you haven't considered fit for others' eyes.
ADAM:	Indeed, you have been very diligent.
	Your work has earned you this prerogative.
STUDENT:	I'm here. I'm overwhelmed with my desire
	to be allowed to see the works of nature,
	to understand, to have the satisfaction
	of that superior knowledge which commands
	the world of matter and the realm of spirits.
ADAM:	You aim too high. How could you comprehend,
	a mere atom, the boundless universe?
	You look for power. You seek delight in knowledge.
	If you could live to undertake the burden
	of that achievement, you'd become a god.
	You ask for less, you may be given it.
STUDENT:	Mere fragments from the hidden wealth of learning
	you may disclose are precious gain to me.

	If truth be told I know nothing that matters.
ADAM:	I see. That sounds a likely candidate
	to penetrate the deepest walks of learning.
	Encounter truth as I've encountered it.
	Make sure there's no one listening. It's appalling

ADAM:

If truth be told I know nothing that matters.

I see. That sounds a likely candidate
to penetrate the deepest walks of learning.
Encounter truth as I've encountered it.
Make sure there's no one listening. It's appalling
to meet truth face to face, and mortal danger
to let it stray among the populace.
Yet times will come, I'd love to see the day,
when truth is freely canvassed in the streets,
when mankind will have come of age at last.
Well, give your hand and make a solemn promise
never to breathe a word of what you hear.

LUCIFER: I do — with all due eagerness and awe.

ADAM: Now, what was it you told me earlier?

STUDENT: That in effect I know nothing that matters.

ADAM: *[cautiously looking around]*

Neither do I — and no one does, believe me.
Philosophy is only a flight of fancy
elaborating on our ignorance:
a harmless discipline compared with others,
it plays about with words, aloof, secluded,
surrounded by its world of fantasy.
But there's another self-complacent teaching
which might be scrawled, as it were, in the dust,
describing lines as vortices and circles
as sacrosanct...It's quite a comedy
until you grasp the deadly fraud it is.
For many try in fear and trepidation
to get around such "outlines" of the dust,
but there are snares, and he who puts a foot
the wrong way, pays a bloody price for it.
Such nonsense is allowed to hinder progress,
unscrupulously sacred as it is,
for it supports existing social order.

STUDENT: I take your meaning. How about the future?

XI. 19th-century London. Adam is delighted to discover free enterprise, but Lucifer is scornful. Soon Adam learns to know better. Nothing is sacred. Everything is up for sale. Eve, the daughter of a London merchant, rejects Adam's approaches, but when she is persuaded by

Lucifer's trick that Adam is a millionaire in disguise, she is prepared to be his mistress.

ADAM: Now, this is it, the toilsome journey's end,
               the grand accomplishment of my career.
               It's life itself I see before me and
               the anthem of free enterprise I hear...

LUCIFER: It's like church choirs singing: fair enough —
               a long way off: hoarse voices, sighs and groans
               will blend in with the tune before they reach us.
               That's how God hears them and is so delighted
               to think that all is well with his creation.
               But where you hear the throbbing hearts below,
               I warrant you it sounds quite different.

ADAM: All doubt and scorn. Isn't this a better world
               than those you made me struggle through for ages?
               No more taboos, restrictions, segregations,
               no gruesome phantoms stalking from the past
               to be enshrined and glorified by custom,
               the curse and plague of future generations.
               No slaves to build the monumental graves.
               It's free for all, but it's for everybody.

               ....

               Ah, Lucifer, you'd let me hang around
               in that revolting place, while bliss embodied
               has nearly passed me by unnoticed. Look!

LUCIFER: It wouldn't have been the first time, anyhow.

ADAM: And she, coming from church! How beautiful!

LUCIFER: To see and to be seen, that was the purpose.

ADAM: None of your frosty gibes! Too cold to touch her.

LUCIFER: And where's that heavenly object lately found?
               The poor devil himself can't keep the score,
               the verse and chapter of your flights of fancy.

ADAM: Who would be it, but she.

LUCIFER: That was the notion
               the woodpecker had when he caught the grub:
               jealously looking round he thought he had
               the most delicious morsel in the world,
               meanwhile the pigeon eyed him with repugnance.

ADAM: How dignified she looks! How chaste and modest!

	One hardly finds the courage to approach her.
LUCIFER:	You're not a novice when it comes to courting.
	Come on! She's on the market. Bid for her!
ADAM:	Excuse me, ladies! May I come and join you?
	There's such a busy crowd: you need an escort.
EVE:	Impertinence!
MOTHER:	Please, go away at once!
	My lady daughter isn't the sort of person
	you may accost without an introduction.
ADAM:	What else is there to do? I dream about her.
MOTHER:	You dream whatever you like. This is my daughter:
	I couldn't let her waste her youthful charms
	on brazen ruffians — the likes of you.

....

EVE:	Don't waste your breath: we know you well enough.
GYPSY WOMAN:	May I find no salvation if I'm lying.
	Lord Such-and-Such is so infatuated,
	longing to have you for his — paramour.
	He'll keep you like a princess: balls, receptions,
	the theatre, a coach for you to ride...
MOTHER:	More sensible, I come to think of it,
	than getting married to a smelly cobbler.
GYPSY WOMAN:	Look! There's his Lordship. He's looking for you.
EVE:	He hasn't noticed me. How thoughtless of him.
	He has good hands, though. Every inch a lord.
MOTHER:	I wouldn't object to his company either,
	but I must go and leave you to yourselves,
	it is the best — by way of introduction.
GYPSY WOMAN:	*[to Adam]*
	The lady's there! She cannot wait to see you...
ADAM:	I fly to her at once... In ecstasy!

....

Frustrated once again. I've done away with
the spectres of the past and in their place
I've built free enterprise — to no avail.
I've taken out a vital link, religion,
without replacing it with something better
to keep the great machinery in order.
No competition where their rules are crooked:
the naked fight against fully armed;

no independence where the hungry millions
must bend to someone's yoke to keep alive.
I want a social order which protects,
does not punish, promotes, does not deter,
where everyone can work in mutual effort.
I want a system organized by science
and governed by the watchful intellect.
It's bound to come. I sense it. I am sure.
Let's see that brave, new world! Come, Lucifer!

LUCIFER: Conceited man! It's your perception only
which sees an aimless, milling multitude:
it fails to apprehend co-ordination
and system in the universal workshop.
*[A macabre Dance of Death episode follows in which
Eve rises transfigured above a pit of death and decay.]*

*XII. Adam's vision of mankind's destiny moves into the future. He and
Lucifer come to a collectivist-utopian society, governed by science. At
first he thinks he has found the answer to his problems, but soon he
realizes that the flaws in human nature have already corrupted the
system. The Earth itself is approaching its final demise, and the chief
preoccupation of science is now to prevent the global catastrophe.
Towards the end of the scene Adam discovers Eve, but it is too late.
Adam's idealism would have to be treated in a mental institution.*[2]

ADAM: Tell us, Professor,
what principle can bring mankind together
as if encouraged by a common goal?

SCIENTIST: The overwhelming principle: survival.
When man appeared on earth, the globe to him
was like a well-stocked larder, plentiful;
he only had to reach out with his hand
to gather his requirements there and then.
So, recklessly consuming that abundance,
as maggots in the cheese, he could indulge
himself in poetry and fanciful

---

[2] This scene was one of the main reasons why *The Tragedy of Man*
could not be performed under Stalinism in Hungary before 1953 under direct
orders by Communist Party chief Mátyás Rákosi.

hypotheses on his idyllic state.
But we, the late arrivals at the feast,
have long since realized we must be prudent:
the cheese is all but gone, we face starvation.
We know, in time the sun will lose its heat
and no plant-life will germinate on earth.
The intervening time is ours to learn
how to replace that solar radiation.
There is yet time, I hope, to find the answer.
Water already seems a likely source,
both chemically and mechanically.
The secrets of organic life are also
giving us vital clues towards our goal...
O, that reminds me: I forgot my test-tubes.
This is my all-consuming interest.

LUCIFER: Man must be getting on in years: he uses
             TEST-TUBES to bolster his organic life.
SCIENTIST: It's taking shape! Look! Seething, shimmering,
             swirling around, secure in its confinement,
             engendered in the warmth of my retort.
LUCIFER: What evidence? There's not a sign of life yet.
SCIENTIST: It's bound to happen. I have learned the secrets
             of every single organism on Earth.
             O, have I not a hundred times dissected...
ADAM: And come to understand a corpse, you mean?

[In a long file men march in, and in another, women. Some of
the latter, like Eve, are accompanied by a child. They form
a circle in the courtyard and a very old man takes his place in
front of them. Adam, Lucifer and the Scientist stop in the
foreground beside the exhibits.]

OLD MAN: Number Three-O!
LUTHER: [advancing one step]
                           Present.
OLD MAN: You've overheated
             the furnace of the system once again.
             It seems that your outbursts of temper are
             a hazard to the whole community.
LUTHER: I can't resist the urge: I hear the fire

savagely roar and sparkle in the furnace,
I see a thousand fiery tongues around
all threatening to reach me and devour me,
but I stand firm,[3] secure in my conviction
that I am in control, I stoke the flames.
You can't appreciate that fascination
who only kindle fire to heat your broth.

OLD MAN: His food ration to be withheld today.
He's raving.

LUTHER: *[Stepping back]*
But I'll stoke the fire tomorrow!

ADAM: Who's this? I'm sure I've heard his voice before.
This man was Luther!

....

OLD MAN: Number Four-Zero-Zero!

PLATO: *[Advancing one step]*
I can hear you.

OLD MAN: Day-dreaming once again, you've let the herd
stray and damage the crops. You must remember:
duty comes first. We'll make you clean the pigsty.

PLATO: *[Stepping back]*
Do as you will: my dreams come first for me.

ADAM: Ah, Plato! Here's your dream-society!
What irony of fate — to mind the herd!

OLD MAN: Number Seven-Two is the next.

MICHELANGELO: *[Advancing one step]*
I'm here!

OLD MAN: You left your work without permission.

MICHELANGELO: Yes,
because I'm sick of carving legs for chairs —
and of the most revolting shapes at that.
I asked permission for a change of outline,
for some design or motif on the legs.
I was refused. I begged in desperation
to be allowed at least to carve the back-rest.

---

[3] These are the words Martin Luther is supposed to have said at the
Diet of Worms in 1521, as the Reformation got under way. About the role of
Protestantism versus Catholicism during the Turkish occupation of Hungary,
see the essay by László Cs. Szabó at the end of this volume.

No use. In utmost agony of spirit
I must have gone berserk and run away.
*[He stands back without waiting for the old man's
verdict.]*

OLD MAN: For this outstanding breach of discipline —
detention in your room till further notice.

....

We have two children past their period
of requisite maternal supervision.
Bring them forward! They are to be transferred
to public nurseries.

[Eve and other women step forward with their children.]

*XIII. Disappointed once again, Adam and Lucifer want to flee from the
Earth in pursuit of the "highest ideal" in outer space. (This is the first
"space flight" in Western literature. Some of the closing lines of this
scene contain the philosophical quintessence of the* Tragedy of Man.)
*During the outward flight, however, Adam is deeply concerned, in
contrast to the relaxed and sarcastic Lucifer.*

ADAM: This reckless flight, where is this bound to take us?
LUCIFER: Well, you desired to leave the lowly dust
for a sublime existence here on high
wherein you deemed to hear (what was the word?)
a kindred spirit calling.
ADAM: So I did,
but never such a journey, grim and cold,
through empty space, this silent, alien world;
it passed for sacrilege to enter it.
I'm undecided, I feel torn apart;
I want to escape, to shed my earthly fetters,
the impediment to my aspiring soul,
and yet I'm homesick and lament the parting.
Ah, Lucifer, remember planet Earth!
At first the blossom, then the trees, the forests —
receding, everything a wash, a blur,
the countless, well-loved features of the landscape
became a vast and flat, indifferent plane.
With all that eyes could relish lost to sight,
the very mountains shrank to clods of clay.

The thunder-bearing clouds the villager
would view aloft with superstitious awe
appeared a puff of vapour round the globe
on which the seeming endless, restless ocean
itself was lost and merged in radiant blue.
There it revolves, part of the firmament,
one out of myriads. To us — the world.
But, Lucifer, to think she's there, out there!
It shatters me to think she's left behind.

LUCIFER: Our lofty viewpoint here requires adjustments,
discarding beauty first, then power and greatness,
until we're left with only one approach
to things — the purely mathematical.

....

THE SPIRIT   You've had your laughs too early, Lucifer:
OF THE EARTH: He's only touched that hostile, alien world.
No ready exit through my boundaries!
Wake, Adam, Son of Earth! Come back to me!

ADAM: I'm suffering, therefore I am — alive,
but all this pain endured is ecstasy
against the horror of annihilation.
Come, Lucifer, let's home to kindly Earth.
For all the struggles I've sustained — in vain,
I'll be content to live and struggle on.

LUCIFER: You've tried that many times. What gives you hope
of winning through this time — to no avail?
Is there a goal in sight? It takes a human
to be so childish and importunate.

ADAM: You're wrong, Lucifer. I am past delusions:
I've failed to reach the goal a hundred times.
But does it matter? Tell me, what's a goal?
Say, "goal" denotes the close of glorious battles,
then "goal" means death. But life, then, is the fight.
Man's purpose in life, therefore, is the struggle.[4]

---

[4] With these lines Madách pronounced one of the earliest statements of European existentialism in the mode of "heroic pessimism" in consonance with his slightly earlier contemporary, Søren Kierkegaard (1813-1855), Friedrich Wilhelm Nietzsche (1844-1900), and others.

XIV. Threatened by annihilation in empty space, Adam decides to return to Earth, only to find that the globe has turned into a frozen wilderness. They encounter one of the few surviving, decadent inhabitants, but when Adam discovers that the man's hideous wife is, in fact, Eve, he begs Lucifer to terminate his dream.

ADAM: I'm tired of these grim wastes of snow and ice
where hollow-eyed death stares us in the face:
no sound except the odd splash in the sea —
a diving seal alarmed at our approach.
Nothing but stunted twigs and frosty lichen,
where plants have given up the pointless struggle!
Even the moon's red face beyond the fog-banks
looks like a dismal lantern in a crypt.
Why don't you take me to the land of sunshine
where palm-trees flourish in the spicy wind,
where man, fully aware of his potential,
has truly come *of age?*

LUCIFER: That's where we are.
We stand within the Equatorial zone.
That ruddy sphere there — it's the dying sun.
Science could not avert Earth's destiny.

ADAM: O, wretched world! Fit only for the dead.
Nothing I shall regret to leave behind.
O, Lucifer! That it should come to pass!
As I stood over mankind's cradle once,
I thought I saw the promise of the future:
now, having striven long for its survival,
I watch bewildered this gigantic grave
with nature's pallid shroud spread out upon it,
the very first and last man in the world.
How was it? Did my race meet destiny
in noble strife and fall in a blaze of glory,
or flinch from fight and perish by degrees,
degenerate, unworthy of lament?

....

LUCIFER: There! Wait a moment!

MAN: *[Prostrating himself]*
                           Mercy, Lord! Have mercy!
I'll make an offering, I will, but spare me!

	I'll give you the first seal that I can catch.
ADAM:	How many of you are surviving here?
MAN:	Too many. More than I have fingers on me.
	What can I do? I've done my best to kill them.
	I've clubbed my neighbours as I love myself,
	but it's no use, you see. Too many people.
	And seals are very few. If you're a god,
	I beg of you: more seals and fewer people!
ADAM:	O, Lucifer! Let's go! I've heard enough.
LUCIFER:	No need to hurry. Come and meet his wife.
	You'll surely recognize an old acquaintance?
	Embrace her, Adam! Look, this honest fellow
	is mortally offended if you don't.
	Show courtesy to him and hug his wife!
ADAM:	Shall I who fondled an Aspasia,
	embrace this one in whom I faintly see
	remote resemblance of another woman,
	but only as if she, amidst my kisses,
	had turned into a beast?

....

[Eve throws her arms around Adam's neck and tries to drag him into the hut. Adam is struggling to shake her off.]

EVE:	Welcome, stranger! Come, make yourself at home!
ADAM:	Help! Help! Lucifer! Get me out of here!
	Back to the present time. Confound the future!
	I've had enough of sights, this pointless struggle
	with destiny. It's time to think again:
	dare I wage war against the will of God!?
LUCIFER:	Wake up, Adam! Wake up! Your dream has ended.

XV. In the final scene, once again outside Eden, Adam wakes up, staggered by the shock of his vision. He wants to commit suicide to prevent man's disastrous history unfolding. Eve, however, announces that she is pregnant.

EVE:	Adam, I think I'm going to be a mother.
	[Adam falls on his knees. A long pause.]
ADAM:	Lord, I surrender. Look, I'm in the dust.
	I'm lost without you. How could I oppose you?

	Bless or punish: I lift my heart to you.
LUCIFER:	Get up, you worm! Where is your dignity,
	the dignity that I have nurtured in you?
ADAM:	Useless. It was illusion. This is peace.
LUCIFER:	Wretched woman! What's there to boast about?
	That son of yours, conceived in sin — in Eden?
	He'll bring nothing but sin and misery.
EVE:	Please God, we'll have another one conceived
	in misery then. Let him make amends.
	Let him unite the world in brotherhood.
LUCIFER:	You spineless slave! You dare rebel against me?
	Up from the dust, you beast!
THE LORD:	To heel, spirit!
	I'll have none of this braggart grandeur!
LUCIFER:	*[bending forward in pain]*
	Curses!
THE LORD:	Rise, Adam! Rise! Do not give way to grief:
	I have restored you to a state of grace.
ADAM:	Lord, I've been troubled by appalling visions:
	I cannot tell how true, how false they are.
	Tell me: what is my purpose in this world?
	Is this brief span of life my full allowance
	to cultivate my soul with toil and trouble
	until it's drawn, a clear and sparkling wine?
	What is it for? To drench the dust with it?
	Or to be kept, a liquor for the feast?
	And then, my race. Is it to have a future,
	growing, the nearer to your throne the stronger,
	or wasting like a beast turning the mill,
	compelled to move within its narrow circle?
	Is there requital for the rich in spirit
	whose mental agony is less than paid for
	by jeering masses? Grant me understanding,
	and I shall bear my lot with gratitude.
	Knowledge is gain, however hard its burden:
	no hell is worse than ignorance and doubt.

This knowledge is denied, but the Lord encourages Adam to trust his intuition and draw spiritual sustenance from his companionship with Eve. Then he dismisses Lucifer with these words:

THE LORD: Now, Lucifer! You're part of my creation.
              Keep up the fight: I have allowed for it.
              Your stout negation and cold intellect
              shall be the leaven to ferment the mind.
              It will, in time, cause man to stray from me.
              So be it. In the end he shall return.
              But you must pay eternal retribution
              and see in every seed you seek to spoil
              the very source of great and noble things.
              ....

CHOIR OF   As you meet your hour of triumph,
ANGELS: don't, however, be complacent:
              when you render God some service
              He does it through you, His agent,
              but His acts are providential
              and He doesn't need your labour.
              When He deigns to call upon you,
              take it as a special favour.

EVE: Thank God, I hear that voice and understand it!
ADAM: I hear it too. Let it remain my guide.
              But that last dream... I wish I could forget.
THE LORD: Have faith, Adam, and fight the noble fight!⁵

Iain MacLeod

---

⁵ These closing words of the *Tragedy of Man* in the Hungarian
original *'Mondottam ember, küzdj és bízva bízzál'* [I've spoken, man, strive
on and trust a-trusting] have become proverbial in the Hungarian language.

Vilius Vajta
1827–1897

G. Burn
'72

János Vajda

(1827-1897)

Although he was born in Budapest, János Vajda, the son of a forester, lived in the country throughout his youth. Like many of his generation, he fought in Kossuth's army during the Hungarian War of Independence and found life hard to endure after the defeat. He tried a number of professions that barely paid enough to live on—he was successively a clerk, a teacher, a free-lance writer, a government official, and a newspaper editor. None of these jobs brought him any contentment. A passionate and obsessively loyal man, Vajda fought unsuccessfully to revitalize the reform-program of his youth. His pamphlets Self-criticism [Önbírálat] *and* Embourgeoisement [Polgárosodás] *caused little stir when they were published in 1862.*

With equal desperation, he clung, until the very end of his life, to the memory of beautiful Georgina Kratochwill, the only woman he was ever able to love, although she had become the mistress of an aristocrat in Vienna. His sense of double loss, of liberty and love, was further deepened in later years and revealed itself through his denial of the possibility of a divine or human justice.

His poetry, revealing an uneven but major lyrical talent, is further motivated by a deep-seated philosophical pessimism, like that of Imre Madách (q.v.), which infuses his cycle of love poems The Memory of Gina [Gina emléke], *as well as his novels written in verse:* Alfred's Romance [Alfréd regénye] *and* Encounters [Találkozások], *both of which date from 1877. Spurning official honors and rejected by literary societies Vajda, in his embittered old age, became a symbol of puritanism and political resistance to the free-for-all capitalism of the Austro-Hungarian Monarchy.*

LUSITANIAN SONG

(When the Leaders of the Romans Surrendered)

I
My country, what road do you take?
What can I think of you now?
Can I continue to love you?
Does honour allow?

I loved you in your trouble,
When you were torn by strife.
That did not turn me away from your side,
Though it could have cost me my life.

Then you were beggared, captive;
I would you had so remained.
We could have borne the pains longer;
We would not have complained.

We have endured for what's as dear
As holy, holier than yourself,
Without which life's a mockery,
Possession's a worthless pelf,

You did possess one priceless jewel,
Our alchemist's stone
That maintained your wholeness,
Though vanquished and alone:

Your honour, treasure supreme
Which nothing can restore;
You threw it away just in the hour
When liberation seemed sure.

Your best sons begged of you
A little longer to wait:
"His destiny is never lost
Who does not accept fate."

Your sons did not desert you,
You deserted them,
Thrust them from you and espoused
Those who taught you shame.

You exchanged a widow's veil
That commanded respect and glory
For a thing which honour flees
That gaudy thing — the canopy.

Oh my poor, unhappy country
Fallen woman, erring mother,
Bearer of heroes prostituted
By a mendacious procurer,

The breasts that nourished us with milk
Are fouled by alien embrace;
How can I flee the roof
That harbours this disgrace?

My country, what road do you take?
What can I feel for you now?
Can I continue to love you?
Does honour allow?

II
Oh patriot,[1] kneeling
By an overseas shore,
Looking our way, tormented
By home-sickness sore,

Patriot, unseduced by the charms
Of a new world with its claims,
Do not long to be here
To bear with our chains.

Here hope has been lost,
Faith has worn thin.
We seek life no more,
Only a grave among our kin.

Patriot, be assured,
If the new land, whose air
You breathe is even step-motherly,
Do not leave it, die there!

---

[1] Allusion to Louis Kossuth, the leader of the War of Independence, who
was living in Turkey in exile.

There, let the pain kill you,
Here the shame would, for
That fatherland for which your heart
Longs, is no more.

The land for which you bled
Itself forsook.
Chains are no longer felt;
Accepted is the yoke.

If memory called you back
To revisit its plains,
You would not even find
Your father's remains.

For they could not rest here,
The ancestors great and glory-covered;
They rose from their graves
And roam on, all scattered,

They range at night restlessly,
Seeking a sacred spot
The unmarked burial place
Of the soul of the patriot.

Jean Overton Fuller

TWENTY YEARS AFTER

As ice on Mont Blanc's frozen crest
is harmed by neither sun nor wind,
no longer burns my heart at rest
no later passion hurts my mind.

On myriad glittering stars I gaze,
which, with provoking stratagem,
vie, strewing on my head their rays,
and yet I do not thaw for them.

Bur sometimes, lost in thought, alone,
while all the world in silence lies,
upon youth's fairy-lake, now gone,
I see your swan-like form arise.

And then again my spirit glows,
as on cold nights when winter's drear,
beyond Mont Blanc's eternal snow
the first rays of the sun appear.

Neville Masterman

THIRTY YEARS AFTER

What's left now is what happened long before.
In this, our earthly life, our fate's complete.
We've met, merciful destiny! — once more,
for the last time, —before the winding-sheet!
I hoped that you would know me ultimately,
that in us then our sorrows would change place;
and even though so late, that I would see
the tear-stains of remorse upon your face.

My loss is irredeemable, immense,
which Heaven alone gave me strength to bear.
Only I see things nobody could sense;
my memory's miraculous and rare.
A moment now emerges from the past,
like a lost island from the ocean risen;
and I see your young face again at last,
as it was when your heart was still ungiven.

And this mirage, you know, affects you, too.
This soul to you your Vesta temple is.
Who, from its altar picture looks, but you?
And what I am to you, you recognise.
When I depart from this terrestrial life,
our love, then woven into poetry,
will find its own eternity in death...
By Heaven we'll be betrothed, love, you and I.

You, who so wasted all your charm and gave
treasures to knaves unworthy from the start;
I, who was this cold idol's captive slave,
and buried all the passions in my heart.
Now we are sitting here, doomed souls: at most
look at each other while the day declines...
However, in our glances, not the lost
but never-ended Eden's sadness shines.

Thus the moon, after the storm's ravagement,
sits calmly on cloud-towers the tempest cleft,
and looks about the peaceful firmament
sadly and yet with no emotion left,
but listens when the ghostly forest soughed
above the dark serenity of graves.
Meanwhile the heavy tear-drops from the boughs
fall gently on the faded, brittle leaves...

Doreen Bell

IN THE FOREST OF VAAL

Far off and deep in woodlands ways
where nettles lurk and maples blaze,
a distant valley's heart has made
a dim, serene retreat of shade.

Ah, could my wondering steps repair
to dwell within a cottage there,
how sweet would such existence be
in calmness and tranquillity!

To give the world no anxious thought
and let its evils go for nought;
to meditate in peace of soul
upon man's life, unmarred and whole.

Upon the fragrant hills to lie
beneath the sunny April sky,

and gaze upon the clouds that race
through past and future, time and space.

This, then, were better, after all,
unmarked to live, and then to fall
in silence down, unmoved by strife,
from off the dying tree of life...

And so, unknown, sepultured deep,
for ever more to lie asleep...
Such quietude at last were best,
and all we yearn for is to rest.

Watson Kirkconnell

ON THE REEDY LAKE

Above the lake the sun is high,
the boat's a shadow swinging by
the bright reflection of the sky.

Shadow slipping forward quietly,
through the ripples rolling gently,
cradled by them drowsily.

In the reeds the birds sleep.
In the boat, gun in my lap,
I rock within the silent deep.

I look around at a world of beauty.
Riddles of natural history
on every side of me I see.

Sun above me — ball of fire;
sun below me — shining glitter
in the mirror of the water.

Heaven is looking down on this
world, as if to give a kiss...
All is wonder, all is bliss.

Are we moving, or the sky?
Which of us is passing by?
Does the breeze dip, or do I?

My thought strays for from this world's fold,
on the sky's blue and the sun's gold.
Mundane life, where is your hold?

The border of the clump of reeds
bows towards me and recedes.
Present time is the circle of meads.

The sun seems to have been arrested
in its course; the sky is breasted
by its glory, where it's rested.

All's so still I wonder whether
past and future aren't together
in this moment, each in th' other.

The air does not stir; about
me, all is motionless; out
of time's march. I conceive a doubt:

what if this world, this gleam,
the life history I seem
to have — is but a dream?

Jean Overton Fuller

THE COMET

Across the night a crimson comet lies;
it ranges from the zenith to the ground;
they say its path is straight throughout the skies
and never marks through space a circling round.[2]

On where light's glittering legions flame and burn
it runs an endless race through gulfs unknown.
It cannot, or it will not, backward turn;
and so it's ever hopeless and alone.

Its steadfast worship to the moon is sent,
that fickle, ever-circling satellite —
majestic mourner of the firmament,
ah, flaring grief, I praise you in the height!

Vast sorrow, symbol of my soul's despair!
Ah, radiant brush that paints my destiny!
Throughout the boundless void you do declare
the utter loneliness of such as we!

Watson Kirkconnell

TIMES GONE BY

When from the frigid North into the woods
the viole of the wind plays such sad moods
that branches tremble and trees shiver there
and leaves are dancing, dancing in the air;

when in the sky grey clouds are seen to hover,
dark clouds like a coffin cover,
as if the weather, earth and sky would be
themselves propelled into despondency;

---

[2] The orbiting nature of comets was unknown during Vajda's lifetime.

I take my heart outdoors, hoping that I
may light upon, beneath the spacious sky,
what I cannot secure where men abound:
a sorrow that is more than mine profound.

I walk among the trees and try to guess
why it must weep, this cruel wilderness —
I fall on dead leaves, rustling, whispering,
and think of past and future... everything;

how all things pass, even Napoleon.
How we, here now, will one day all be gone.
The Son of God was crucified: therefore
the whole world is an error, nothing more.

And you, a fading but recurrent sigh,
you grieve. No doubt there is a reason why;
if I should add another, it may be
that you will have the right response for me.

Can anyone undo what has been done?
Who else will play her role? Another one?
Pray tell me, Passing Time, do all men lack
power to push the clock ahead or back?

The cicatrix on that clock's burning face!
If only somehow someone could erase
that stain which caused the heavenly virgin moon
to flame with rage! Oh, do erase it soon!

Jess Perlman

VII. CLASSICAL/MODERN HUNGARIAN POETRY

József Kiss

(1843-1921)

József Kiss was born in Mezőcsát, in eastern Hungary near Miskolc, into a poor Jewish family. His mother was the daughter of a Lithuanian Jewish cantor who moved to Hungary in order to escape the frequent pogroms. He was educated in Hebrew schools.

The year 1867, which was the year of the Compromise between Austria and Hungary and the start of the Austro-Hungarian Monarchy, was also the year of the emancipation of the Jews in Hungary, ahead of most European countries. A year later, at the age of twenty five, Kiss moved to Budapest where he soon established his reputation with his Hebrew Songs [Zsidó dalok], *in 1868. Kiss was the first major Hungarian poet of his faith.*

Closely influenced by János Arany (q.v.), he also wrote a number of ballads. He managed gradually to distance himself from the Hungarian rural tone and began to develop an urban style which, however, also showed some traces of the Secessionism of the end of the century.

In 1890 he founded a literary weekly The Week [A hét], *which exerted considerable influence on the trends of modern Hungarian literature. After 1910, however,* The Week *turned against the newly founded* Nyugat [The West], *whereupon the authorities tried to set Kiss up against Ady (q.v.). This, in turn, led to Kiss' loss of popularity.*

Kiss was elected both to the Petőfi and the Kisfaludy Societies. His first collected volume appeared in 1867, followed by Holidays [Ünnepnapok], *in 1888, which interpreted Jewish psalms and other religious poems.*

His poetic narrative A Tale of the Sewing Machine [Mese a varrógépről], *in 1884, found many readers, and so did his* Legends of My Grandfather [Legendák nagyapámról], *which appeared in 1888.*

Kiss was fascinated by the Jewish past, but throughout his literary career he remained completely Hungarian. His poetry is characterized by its transitional nature between 'Jewish' and 'Hungarian,' 'populist' and 'modern,' 'rural' and 'urban,' 'epic' and 'lyric,' and 'realistic' and 'mythical-narrative' elements.

His basically Hungarian mentality and his imagination filled with images of the native country protected his lyricism from becoming excessively cosmopolitan and general. Music plays a major role in his poetic technique, and his rhymes frequently offer flashes of ingenious virtuosity.

FIRES

Can you recall the playful brushwood fire,
Its crackle on the mud-brick fireplace,
Where flickering, the carefree flames inspire
A tale, a song and smiles on every face?
From spitting branches, from the glowing ember
I spied the secret heartbeat of the song.
Where is that fire, who can still remember?
Mine turned to ashes — others may burn along.

And where is now the lass who stirred the fire,
Her high spirits, her pretty pinafore?
And where's the lad, the dreamy young admirer,
Who wouldn't want to leave her any more?
We tossed twigs on the fire through the evening,
Some damp, some dry, till they began to sear.
Who was, we wondered, innocently dreaming,
For whom the weeping wood had shed a tear?

The sands of time weigh on those happy hours —
I left the buried brushwood past to rest,
As fires with new devastating powers
Engulfed me with devouring interest:
To burn for justice — what rewardless mission!
To burn for fame — for just to make a mark?
And as I fought for worldly recognition
My hair turned white, my mind a gloomy dark.

My corn has never ripened into harvest,
My garden is a flower in my hand,
My bliss, to see a vision in the darkness,
My kingdom is a dreamer's wonderland.
— The dying ashes softly drizzle under,
Sifting, settling in sighing monotone —
My dreams may also drift away? I wonder,
When evening falls, will I be left alone?

It's cold... I want some coal, to stoke the fire!
Just let it breathe its deadly heat on me,
As prowling cats, in ravenous desire
Blow at the frightened fledglings in the tree.
What mighty fire! Not like any other!
Not forests, the abyss did whelp it, once.
Primordial upheaval was its mother,
And revolutions are its doughty sons.

It's rumbling it's rattling and grumbling and wailing
And murmuring, wrangling in frantic travail!
As prison-bound furies would shake at the railing
To bring crashing down the walls of the jail!
Avenging god! What will befall the nations
When mighty coal asserts its native right,
The humble rock destroys its own foundations,
The seething steam explodes like dynamite?

When all that was decaying is defeated,
Bloodthirsty gods fall to oblivion,
And crawling from their holes we see the cheated,
Defrauded victims by the million...
I see the throng — what passions it arouses! —
They march to a new, fiery Marseillaise,
To toss their torches on the musty houses
Until the very last one is ablaze!

— And while mirages prey upon my senses,
And dreams of future fires start to loom
On distant skies, ablaze with luminances
At my — one day — dilapidated tomb:
I'm sitting here in silence, lonely, broken,
The hours passing faster than a flash,
And sometimes dreaming, sometimes half-awoken
I'm poking in the dying, doomy ash.

Peter Zollman

ABOUT MY GRANDFATHER
(Excerpt)

Make haste slowly, my friend, make haste slowly...
From Lithuania he came, walking
(yes, all that matters in the story!)
uninvited, that goes without saying.
Lithuania's a border country —
where? Who cares? There's no point in asking —
lice, bedbugs, and no soap to wash your hands
are the closely-guarded secrets of the land!

A bonny youth — unlike his grandson, me!
Good blood, strong bones, the finest Russian strain —
on the way he lost the family tree:
God alone knows if he'll find it again!
A laughing sage, with too much honesty
for his own good; forehead of granite grain
and blue eyes — that's how I saw him when white
winter had fringed his Moses-head with light.

His urge to roam came from deserts of old:
a wanderer's sandals bore him along,
beneath his restless feet the earth enrolled
and nothing and nowhere held him for long,
but the sounding threads reached down from his soul
and each clod clung to a new growing song.
The poet is always a mystery
and his secret lock has a secret key.

To soar, to flame in burning ecstasy —
this exhausts all that ever can be known.
Let man paint a rainbow across the sky
and then he'll never find himself alone,
and castle built on castle let him try —
if all collapse, who'll stop to count each stone?
One lesson all past centuries proclaim:
small ruins outlast castles of great fame.

With joy he drank to its last dregs his wine —
no point in my pretending otherwise.
He drank his way along that weary line
to Vilna from Moscow's tower-pierced skies.
He drank from evening to dawn's first sign,
thirst in the throat always, but calm the eyes.
Such revellers today we seem to lack —
more honor to you, Rabbi Meyer Litvak!

I understand you well, nothing resent
and only take one single thing to heart:
that heritage made mine by just descent
you left dismembered of a vital part:
to me, your singing swings with daring went,
but tell me, where's the wine to whet my art?
Oh pious Grandfather, with piety
I wish you had bequeathed your thirst to me!

Anthony Edkins

OH, WHY SO LATE

Oh, why so late, when tired leaves are falling,
When cranes gather to cruise beyond the sky:
Oh, why couldn't we meet in rose-blossom time,
In the early sunrise, you and I?

Oh, why couldn't we hark in secret two-some
As the lark was singing in the sky?
And why couldn't we meet in burning passion
Dreaming young dreams, you and I!...

Peter Zollman

THE RHYME IS RUNNING OUT

Softly, softly, the rhyme is running out:
love I used to know a song or two about.
But the wings of the years flutter fast: when
other songs came, love-songs were forgotten.

It is not the lost love that I regret:
sans youth, love is a dream to make us fret.
No, more than passing love, this makes me sad:
desertion by the rhymes that once I had.

Sometimes I see her walking down the street.
She has not changed at all: her soft and neat
figure she still retains; her hair's still gold.
Only I have changed; I alone grown old.

I stare at her, and she looks hard at me.
I feel as if she knows absolutely
that youth and song and rhyme have disappeared.
I am ashamed: that is what I had feared!

Anthony Edkins

László Arany
(1844-1898)

László Arany, son of János Arany (q.v.), followed in his father's footsteps. In the high school at Nagykőrös the senior Arany personally supervised his son's education, especially in the history of literature, metrics, and poetry. In later years he also studied law, but his favorite preoccupation was literature.

During the summer of 1860 he travelled all over Transylvania, and it was during this trip that he decided to collect and edit a significant number of Hungarian folk tales. In 1862, with the help of his older sister and his father, he compiled a book called Original Folk Tales [Eredeti népmesék]. *In these he managed to preserve the original beauty, organizational wholeness, and freshness of style of the folk tales as if they were being told by a live story-teller. By so doing he realized one of his father's goals.*

In 1867 he gave his inaugural lecture in the Kisfaludy Society on Hungarian folk tales. His work has traditionally been regarded as pioneering in folklore research in Hungary.

In 1872 he also travelled in Italy and England, where he studied the local economic systems.

His best known literary work The Hero of the Mirages [A délibábok hőse], *which describes the adventures of the central character* Hűbele Balázs [Harry Harum-Scarum], *is partly autobiographical; it depicts a character who is no longer able to serve the evolution of capitalism or the ideals of national independence, because—so he believes—no one of real stature exists in this age and he himself lacks the energy, the discipline, and the faith needed in the future. This work owes a great deal to Pushkin's* Eugene Onegin, *in whose person he found the character of a cosmopolitan dandy bored with society. These insights into contemporary Russian nobility may have helped Arany in depicting the Hungarian counterpart to that world.*

Shaken by his father's death, he soon started to put the senior Arany's literary estate into order. He published his father's posthumous works and correspondence in three volumes. This is still considered as an authentic archival source. He published an influential essay about the problems of Hungarian metrical rhythm and intonation — a work that is still considered of basic importance today. He was also an important translator of Lermontov, Pushkin, Shakespeare, and Molière into Hungarian. He also wrote extensively on politics, law, and economics.

THE HERO OF THE MIRAGES
(Extract)

Harry Harum-Scarum[1] has just contrasted his own quest for prosperity with Childe Harold's[2] quest for decadence, and now the patriotic Hero of the Mirages tries to call attention to some land which he may hold up to his countrymen as a model of progress. He says:

"Albion, teach me (and not with loud, unsubtle,
top-heavy words) to love my native land.
I do not think I'll give my life in battle,
but live and work with head and heart and hand.
The time has gone for Don Quixote's mettle:
our modern arms are metal engines and — "
with that our errant knight is running full —
tilt towards London, Albion's capital.
....

He wanders, watches, and learns, or rather...
....

He would have learned, given the savoir-faire
to be a specialist in this or that
(I mean of course some practical affair)
and been a touch more balanced, more acute;
had not his thoughts been always in the air
far over hills and valleys and what-not.
But, set upon the purpose he's just spouted,
he wastes no thought on how to go about it.

---

[1] The hero's name in the Hungarian original is 'Hűbele Balázs,' a common idiom designating someone acting rashly, without forethought. It is documented as occurring first in 1808; it is thought of having been an exhortation like 'hurry up!' János Arany in his comical epic *Bolond Istók* ['Stevie the Fool'] uses it also. It has been used for nearly two hundred years in this sense without people realizing how its popular origins were obscured by the Aranys' use of it. We translate it here as 'Harry Harum-Scarum.'

[2] Allusion to Lord Byron's famous lyrical diary, *Childe Harold*, which appeared in 1812 and was well known to literati in Hungary.

Once in this paradise Harry can see
the way the British cultivate their land;
he can admire the most ingenious way
they run a water-system underground;
but more admires the vivid greenery
than ways and means essential to that end.
Then technicalities! His backward nation
must have it ready-made, in operation.

Roaming around, through factories and docks,
he hears "delightful music" in their din.
"They get their gold from iron, their iron from rocks,
their diamonds from coal." So, taken in
(as who would not be) by his own remarks,
his fancy travels homewards and drifts on:
"Docks on the Danube and steam locomotion
would make my Hungary a glorious nation."

The skies of London change, now dark, now clear;
the streets of London, too, are changeable.
He comes upon assorted treasures here,
then there a million beggars cheek by jowl.
They put on exhibitions everywhere,
and with the same panache they starve or steal.
In Hyde Park see bewitching beauties trotting;
in Southwark see the stray and stunted, rotting.

A race without a homeland in this world,
they drag their wretched lives through factories,
or crouch in rags in fetid hovels filled
with wailing poverty and dumb disease,
where dark, alarming ignorance runs wild.
No daily bread, not even in their prayers.
No ray of hope. And not the least ambition
hinders their headlong hurry to confusion.

As sand-grains hurtle in a howling storm
to nowhere in particular, so man
loses himself here and his very name.
Conglomerated slag is melted down,

and in that mass of scraps it's all the same
if one drops out; the other scraps are soon
one molten, messy mass oozing and hissing:
and who would notice that one scrap is missing?

Harry, obsessed with matters of this kind
reads what the experts (Proudhon,[3] J.S. Mill)[4]
have got to say about supply, demand,
slums, overcrowding, labour, capital.
Perhaps there's no solution to be found?[5]
"Where is the thread in all this terrible
tangle?" — he wonders. But, no matter what he
thinks of, the problem only gets more knotty.

The mind that tries to plumb this agony
finds troubled waters dangerous to fish.
Sometimes, when storms ferment this horrid sea,
its secrets reach the surface in a rush.
Down in the depths they fight for mastery,
only to rise when everything goes crash...
He poses on the brink of this salt ocean,
until relief arrives — a fresh obsession.

J. G. Nichols

---

[3] Pierre-Joseph Proudhon (1809-1865), French economist; a petit-bourgeois thinker sympathizing with socialism; an advocate of anarchy.

[4] John Stuart Mill, English philosopher and economist (1806-1873), the famous author of *On Liberty*.

[5] Hungarian thinkers of the Reform Age in the early 19th century, particularly Count István Széchenyi, looked to England for solutions. It is no accident that Arany sends his Harry Harum-Scarum to England where, however, he finds that all is not rosy.

ELFRIDA

"Trust never to another's hand
your horse, your money, or your wooing."
My tale is strange, yet very true;
from days of old it comes to you.
It lives in song from days of yore,
from ancient Britain's storied shore.

Edgar, who ruled the English realm,
reached days of mournful widowerhood.
He wept; he wailed; he nearly died;
no balm could do his spirit good.
And yet in time his wound was healed;
a few days cured his dark despair
when word came up from Devonshire
about the Earl's fair daughter there.

The rumour came; one brought it straight;
kings do soon find their consolation —
why would they otherwise maintain
so many idle hands at station?
He came and whispered: "She who died,
deep in the grave now let her rest.
A rosebud waits in Devonshire:
go down and pluck it, in the West!"

King Edgar put his grief aside
and sent his brave knight Athelwold:
"Go, now, and spy the maiden out!
I cannot trust what I am told.
If she is fair as rumour tells,
to wed her I shall come pursuing."
Trust never to another's hand
your horse, your money, or your wooing!

To Devonshire went Athelwold;
he reached the castle of the Earl;
his heart-beat made his armour quake

when he beheld the matchless girl.
All news about Elfrida spread
was but a lie, a feeble glose.
This was no shy, half-opened bud —
this was a fair, unfolded rose.

A fair unfolded rose: the eye,
forgetful of all else, would gaze
upon her petals soft with dew
shed by the dawn of quiet days.
A shimmering blush, like down on fruit,
so lightly touched the face of her,
a breeze might mar it — 'twould seduce
the mind of a philosopher.

It is an easy thing to be
ambassador on works of state;
or lead an army to subdue
an enemy in war's debate;
but for a youth to court a maid
as proxy is his own undoing —
trust never to another's hand
your horse, your money, or your wooing!

His heart prevailed: and Athelwold
forgot the task upon him laid.
A day, two days, yea weeks at length
he dallied there beside the maid:
a handsome youth, a beauteous girl,
day after day in sweet communion —
at last they seek her father out
and ask his blessing on their union.

A wealthy youth of ancient line
the favourite vassal of the king —
in olden days, as in our own,
such wooers are a welcome thing.
A ready blessing greets the match;
a speedy marriage they obtain:

"Lo, you are mine, and I am yours
until the grave shall part us twain!"

But as they near the court, the knight
has sobering thoughts that horrify:
alas, he has betrayed the king.
Shall he confess it, or deny?
What shadow of excuse can cloak
the wickedness of his deceit?
The road is long and curved but not
as crooked as his hope to cheat.

The London road is long, and yet
how quickly to their goal they come!
Now in default of ripened schemes
the knight is near delirium.
The royal fort is now in sight,
upon it gleams the evening sun;
the knot of Athelwold's design
is caught and will not come undone.

At night they reach the city gates;
through by-ways with his dame he hies,
and seeks out a sequestered house
to hide her safe from peeping eyes.
All night he broods on stratagems,
each plan, as pondered, is replaced
by other plots; and with the dawn
he hurries to the king in haste.

"O my good king, I bring report.
I have arrived, the girl is here.
But how deceitful rumour is!
To say she's plain is but to jeer:
for she's a cripple, dwarfed and lame;
her back is humped, her mouth is cleft,
her shoulders tilt, her eyes are crossed,
one faces right, the other left.

"What could I do? They knew my will.
To leave her were a straight affront
I feared her haughty sire would rise
against my king... I bore the brunt...
and... married her myself... A man
whose sense of duty is so pure,
for such devoted sacrifice
deserves a castle, I am sure —

in fact, a castle far away
where in seclusion he might hide...
There would I go this very hour
and take my too unlovely bride.
This very hour I'd go, that none
might see and know her ugly face,
lest she and I be put to shame,
mocked by the court to our disgrace..."

"Agreed. Old Westwood Keep is yours.
You shall be hid, yet close at hand.
It lies amid primeval woods
and none shall know in all the land.
I'll let no person track you there.
There, as in night, you'll hide from view;
but I, because I love you well,
shall in good season visit you."

This was a stark dilemma now!
It was the king he most would shun.
He'd thought that in some spot remote
the court's gay pomp he might outrun;
but finds himself a slave of fear.
He tears his hair, he sighs in dread:
alas, the most entrancing bride
will yet bring trouble on his head!

That very day, without a stay,
they went; they reached old Westwood Keep, —
an ancient castle, bleak and grim;
its roads with weeds were matted deep;

its bare halls long untenanted,
its cobwebbed windows, sagging doors,
and mouldy pictures filled with gloom
the loving pair that trod its floors.

It was a mouldering ancient nest,
hidden away from human sight.
How could fair England's fairest bride
in such seclusion take delight?
And this is all her recompense
for losing queenly rank and style!
O Athelwold, you'll yet repent
in bitterness your selfish guile!

"Ah, but my lady's love is sure,
she will forgive this little plot."
So thinks he, and on schemes intent
he tells Elfrida what is what:
"My fairest love, forgive me now!
A very grievous sin is mine...
Yet my unconquerable love,
I know, will make your heart benign...

"King Edgar wished you as his wife.
He sent me forth to bring report
upon your beauty, but alas,
that beauty made my heart its sport!
Your lips bewitched me, and your face,
the peerless arches of your brows:
I quite forgot the penalties
that might pursue my marriage vows...

" 'Tis late to rue what now is done..
Forgive me, dear, for fear of harm!
And now — the devil, full of sin,
getting a finger, wants an arm.
King Edgar comes to visit us.
I pray you, help me in my scheme.
Dress, though in silk, distastefully,
and like some ugly scarecrow seem.

"Paint warts upon your face, pull down
a crookèd mouth, cross eyes in game,
stuff back and bosom out of shape,
bend standing, when you walk be lame,
pronounce your words with hideous wheeze,
pretend your wits are dull and dim.
Edgar won't come this way again;
for once, let's make a fool of him...

"Then shall we live here happily
with none to hinder or molest
and at his palace none shall dream
what beauty dwells in this old nest.
Like doves amid the quiet boughs
here in the shadow we shall hide,
happy, forgotten by the world,
and no one to our door will ride!"

You've bitten more than you can chew,
Sir Knight! Your bidding can you know?
Ask her to go through flood and fire,
and, for your sake, perchance she'll go.
But that before the world she'll stand
Ill-dressed and in discomfiture —
Let no one ever ask her this!
'Tis more than woman can endure.

She listened to his shrewd advice
and pondered in her prudent heart:
"Yea, if they call me to the throne
shall I 'mid cobwebs dwell apart?
A hovel as a hermitage
for true love very well may be
in fine romances, but alas
most lonely in reality."

She says nothing... And Athelwold
waits, whistling, for the King to come:
"how, when he sees her, he'll recoil
and hurry in confusion home!"

Impatiently he sits all day
and watches from an outlook tower.
At last the monarch comes. The thane
conducts him to his lady's bower.

He has not seen her since the morn,
and is agog with keen surmise,
holding the door back for the King,
he gazes in with eager eyes.
Where is the monster he expects?
He stares in panic round the place,
for there his fair Elfrida stands
all ravishing in form and face.

Ne'er had she seemed so fair. Her glance
lit hearts like some white fire-brand.
She curtsies gently for the King,
and then holds out her lily hand.
Head over heels he falls in love,
in swift confusion stepping back;
it took some moments ere their talk
resumed a more habitual track.

But talk than ran merrily on,
sweet wonder seized on Edgar's wits,
as compliment breeds compliment,
but Athelwold on embers sits.
Woe unto him, his end has come,
his plans are bared to his undoing...
(Trust never to another's hand
your horse, your money, or your wooing!)

But Edgar speaks no word of blame;
he doesn't seem to mind at all.
He is all grave to Athelwold,
who falls to hoping after all:
"Perhaps to him she is not fair;
or, liking me, he may forget..."
Thus he feeds hope within himself,
or rather, keeps it lingering yet.

Right merrily they spend the night.
Next day to hunt the King desires;
through all the hamlets goes the word:
a thousand beaters he requires.
All day they rouse the forests up.
The husband disappears apart,
but with the morn they find his corpse,
a dagger neatly through his heart.

Who did the murder? Who can tell?
King Edgar seeks for him in vain.
The knight is buried with great pomp,
the fair Elfrida weeps in pain.
She mourns for him for several weeks;
then, strange to say, she weds the King.
Rash youth, take never on yourself
a courtship for the atheling!

King Edgar never wed again.
In devious ways, with rash intent,
for the new Queen now wore the pants
and ran her husband's government.
Rejecting age, all posts of state,
she gave to youths in days ensuing...
(Trust never to another's hand
your horse, your money, or your wooing!)

My tale is strange, and yet it's true;
from days of old it comes to you.
It lives in song from days of yore
from ancient Britain's foggy shore.

Watson Kirkconnell

Gyula Reviczky
(1855-1889)

Reviczky was born in Vitkóc (today in the Slovak Republic), the son of an officer. He was educated in Pozsony (today's Bratislava) and later also attended the University of Budapest, though without obtaining a degree. Brought up as a half orphan, his life was an almost unbroken chain of poverty, misunderstanding, loneliness, illness, and unrequited love.

As a young man he worked as a tutor and later as a journalist. His neo-romanticism clashed with the populist-demotic literary tradition established by Petőfi (q.v.), and so Reviczky was accused of being a 'cosmopolitan,' although his pessimism and experimentations were rooted in his personal unhappiness.

A translator of Kleist and Ibsen, and also influenced by Schopenhauer, he had considerable artistic control over his medium. He could write with vigor and originality. His volumes of poetry include My Youth [Ifjúságom], *1874; and* Solitude [Magány], *1880. His collected poems appeared posthumously in 1895. He also wrote poetry in German.*

TO JÁNOS ARANY IN ANSWER TO HIS POEM "COSMOPOLITAN POETRY"[1]

I, too, bless the cradle that rocked me
Hungarian to man's estate,
and for the song laid in my heart
I bless as well a generous fate.
Above all else I would bless
the glorious world that I inherit;
I sing the ideas that spring within me,
I sing what I feel, its living spirit.

Beautiful the song, if national,
a precious treasure that is holy,
but the greatest is universal, human,
belongs to all — to no one solely.

---

[1] See the poem so entitled by János Arany.

Truth in every tongue is one,
he whose soul is great shall be
a supreme artist among his kind,
if he gives such aim priority.

Old Homer sang of a Grecian sky,
but every nation may share its blue,
and Hamlet's brooding melancholy,
uniquely his, is the world's, too.
Any Tom Fool knows that men suffer,
wherever one finds humanity,
but the greatest artist among them knows
enough to forget nationality.

In every fatherland the fate
of Don Quixote spurs bitter laughter,
but to wonder if struggling Faust is German —
man, could anything be dafter?
Molière, he was a Frenchman, yes,
but speaks a world language by any test;
his folks are cosmopolitans,
Alceste, Harpagon, and the rest.

The idea is, feeling must have greatness;
lacking this, native or not,
the song is false, to be despised
by men of truth will be its lot.
Nation on nation strive to live,
but all these nations disappear:
Rome is no more, only in Horace
humans live, exist for us here.

"The singer of great ideas is one
with people, merged are they,
each a mirror, within himself,
reflecting his nation," I hear you say.
A whole people fashions the poem,
but that which resounds with mightiest force
shines everywhere like the sun,
though it issues from a single source.

Your sun, then too, shines everywhere,
great are you among the great;
no one nation makes you so,
your eternal idea has no place nor date.
The "Wonder of the Worlds," their light
it is that makes your immortal song.
Hungarian now, when your nation is past,
you will live in that world where you belong.

Madeline Mason

THE DEATH OF PAN

Across a purple west the ship is swimming.
The sea's soft bosom heaves as if in sleep.
Light, gloaming zephyrs in their wanton skimming
just stir the dim apparel of the deep.
Warm exhalations tremble in the air,
a naked moon makes twilight doubly fair,
its globe of silver brightens into fire...
And moods of pensive calm mount slowly higher.
       But down within the ship
       resound glad song and quip,
       the mariners make gay
       and ease their mad behests,
       throw out their drunken chests
       and over long-necked wine-jars make a fray.
       Here, faithless dice are thrown, that with a sneer
       spin trecherous and fickle here and there.
       With giggling girls they flirt
       dressed only in a shirt.
       In hearts, on lips, sweet honeyed love is rife:
       "Come Lesbia, kiss me hot! Hurrah for life!
       Hurrah for pleasure's frenzy, passion's mire,
       Hurrah for all the orgies of desire!
       Drink deep the cup of laughter, for the spirit knows

no music, wine or woman where Cocytus[2] flows!"
More clamorous still becomes the vessel's hold:
in shouts more savage still, in lust more bold.
They pour the finest wine upon the floor
as tribute to the great Tiberius;
a youthful couple hide behind a door,
but playful comrades will not leave them thus.
Some dance a tarantella of delight,
and roguish, care-free satyrs, out of sight,
assist them in their circle as they buss.

But hark! The galley's helmsman hears a voice
across the night austerely call his name:
"Thamus!" — who's that? No miracle annoys:
but buzzing in my head that wines inflame.
But no! The former call returns again.
"Thamus!" — "No tricks, you rogue, I tell you plain!"
He goes to look. The night is exquisite:
the circling waves are edged by silver light;
up from the deep in trembling wonders rise
reflected stars, or wistful naiads' eyes;
far off, almost past eyesight, steep and stark,
the headlands of Aetolia lie dark.

With vexed attention Thamus looks around.
No soul in sight. Across the night, no sound.
He deems himself mistaken, turns to go
where wine and dice and women wait below —
but, from the dark that voice of mystery
a third time calls and will not let him be.
"This voice is God's, not man's; that much is clear.
Who's there? What do you want?" he asks with fear.
Then trumpet-like it speaks so clear and loud
these words are heard by all the revelling crowd:
"Oh, Thamus, hoary seaman, thou shalt be
today a prophet, though unwittingly.
When soon you sail near high Palodes Head,
proclaim loud this speech: 'Great Pan is dead!'"

---

[2] The name of one of the three rivers of the Underworld—that of Lamenting. Lethe was the river of Forgetfulness, and the Styx was the impenetrable frontier that separated the Underworld from life.

Upon the ship descends a startled peace.
From drink and wanton joy the sailors cease.
The mind of Thamus wavers and is numb;
his seamen are remorseful, filled with dread;
now to Palodes Cape at last they come,
and fronting that great headland and its mists,
he shouts, like some loud herald in the lists:
"Great Pan is dead! Alas, Great Pan is dead!"
And suddenly — a marvel to the sense! —
the trees and shrubs and even stones are stirred.
Soft sobs break forth, and faltering laments,
deep agonizing moans and shrieks are heard.
Across the dark the broken wailings go;
by every path the piercing echos spread
this universal burden of their woe:
"Great Pan is dead! Alas, Great Pan is dead!"
His silent flute forevermore must wait
in vain for him to fright the nymphs so fair;
the earth henceforth is bleak and desolate,
the playful gods no more will gather there.
The satyrs and the naiads all are gone —
from every bush a diety has fled —
from grass, tree, spring, and flower comes the groan:
"Great Pan is dead! Alas, Great Pan is dead!"
The very soul of nature has been lost.
Henceforth on earth no happy gods may dwell.
Man's thoughtless mirth shall die of chilling frost.
Self-conscious moods shall bring their pious hell.
Dull meditations and monotony...
These, Thamus, are the curses thou hast shed.
The pagan gods have gone, with all their glee.
"Great Pan is dead. Alas, Great Pan is dead!"
The sailors hear, but grasp not the intent.
"Great Pan is dead?!" — they question in a daze.
Who shall explain this hundred-voiced lament...?
Ye powers that direct our human ways,
lighten this darkness from your lucid skies
and tell what nature's sorrow signifies!
The forest wails, cold winds announce the day,
the black night wearies into haggard grey.

A fine mist sinks upon the lonely shore
and a mysterious voice breaks forth once more:
"Pan and his kin are dead!" There lives a God,
shrined in the heart, instead of tree and blood.
The wanton gods are dead, and stilled their dance,
because mere joy is full of arrogance.
Henceforth the suffering shall possess the earth,
repentent tears be valued above mirth.
The forest's calm, its gentle solitude,
shall comfort humankind in mournful mood.
An infidel is he who knows no grief —
this is Golgotha's message, from the Chief
of all sufferings, Who now begins
to take from all the earth its blight of sins.
And lo! Above the east, where dawn had birth
in blood-red ecstasies of love and loss,
over the horizon, blending with the earth,
there rose a shining Cross.

Watson Kirkconnell

ENDICOTT
1877-1919

Endre Ady
(1877-1919)

Born in Érmindszent, a village in eastern Hungary (but which today is in Romania), Ady was the most significant poet of his generation and one of the greatest lyric geniuses of Hungary. He came from a gentry family that poverty had transformed into peasants—that is, "gentlemen without means." He studied law in Debrecen and later in Budapest at his father's request, but took no degree. Full of energy and rebelliousness, he became a revolutionary poet and political journalist, blasting the establishment with great vigor. In 1901 he joined the editorial staff of Nagyváradi Napló [Diaries of Nagyvárad], *an influential organ of the left-wing opposition (today Oradea in Romania).*
He attacked feudalism, the Church, the Monarchy, and Hungary's agricultural backwardness. A few years later all of these issues showed up in his verses, transformed into exquisite poetry. In 1904 he went to Paris for the first time, an experience that left a deep mark on him. Adél Brüll, the wife of a rich merchant from Nagyvárad, was his mistress and companion.

His early love poems were written to Adél, whose name he spelled backwards as "Léda." In his poetry, Hungarian broke loose from the Vörösmarty-Petőfi-Arany line of pure, romantic love, and he added to it a dimension that he drew from the French poetry of Verlaine and Baudelaire without completely imitating them. Whatever he wrote, Ady was the center of fierce controversy. He was attacked for his explicit eroticism, for his espousal of left-wing causes, and for his unorthodox approach to God. Alcohol had taken an early toll on his health. He was an ailing man when he met the young Berta Boncza, daughter of a noble family, whom he eventually married. Their union resulted in some of the most delicate love poetry written in Hungarian. He died at the age of 42 after the Austro-Hungarian Empire was defeated in World War I. He foresaw the coming of the Hungarian diaspora. His style was so contagious that numerous imitators followed him for decades; in fact, some still do so today. Perhaps his greatest contribution is a stylistic one: he introduced a kind of rhythm, rhyme, and imagery that was entirely novel.

Translating him into any language is a major challenge. In this sense he is like Berzsenyi (q.v.). Most literary critics count the "start of the modern age" in Hungarian literature with Ady.

Communist literary historians eagerly expropriated him, but in order to do so they had to deny the fact that he was also one of Hungary's greatest religious poets, often writing in a confessional style.

I AM THE SON OF KING GOG OF MAGOG

I am the son of King Gog of Magog,[1]
I'm banging doors and walls to no avail —
yet I must ask this question as prologue:
may I weep in the grim Carpathian vale?

I came along Verecke's[2] famous path,
old Magyar tunes still tear into my chest —
will it arouse your Lordships' righteous wrath
as I burst in with new songs from the West?[3]

Pour in my ears your molten liquid lead,
let me become the new Vazul[4] of songs —
let me not hear the new songs *you* have bred:
Come, tread me down in furious, evil throngs!

But to the end, tortured, expecting nothing,
the song keeps soaring on its new-found wings:
even if cursed by a hundred Founding Fathers —
triumphant, new, Magyar, and true it rings.

Adam Makkai

---

[1] In the Book of Ezekiel, an obscure prophecy foretells that King Gog of the Magog people will start a devastating campaign against Israel, but God, by defeating Gog, will prepare the Jewish people for the arrival of the Messiah. Gog's name later became a symbol of rebellion against Divine power. A Hungarian tradition started by *'Anonymus,'* the chronicler of King Béla III, considered the Hungarians the descendants of Gog.

[2] The name of the mountain pass in the Carpathians through which the conquering Magyars, led by Árpád, entered today's Hungary in 896, A.D.

[3] Ady uses the place name 'Dévény,' where the Danube enters Hungary from the West [*Nyugat* = 'West,' the very name of the radical quarterly discussed by László Cs. Szabó (q.v.)]. The poem is Ady's Manifesto of the 'new' conquering the 'old,' because the 'new' is, paradoxically, even more ancient in its roots.

[4] Reference to the cousin of St. Stephen, Vazul (or Vászoly), who led a pagan rebellion against Stephen's Christianizing efforts. He was punished by having molten lead poured into his ears.

THE HACKNEY COACH

My Queen, the air has burst in flame,
and look, our coach begins to swing.
Today we mingle with the folk,
you are the Queen and I the King.
Beneath the lightning-gilded trees,
see how the radiant coaches stream,
see how they surge upstreet and down,
as for a glimpse of us they gleam.
Tonight we lavish wealth and boons:
my Queen, vouchsafe a lowered veil!
(The hackney coach jolts, jolts along
and we two tremble cold and pale.)

My Queen, we perish from desire.
Never before has a mortal pair
so striven for the peaks of life,
and none was ever more threadbare.
Our souls are flame, desire and sun;
and yet like beggars we must live;
we have an uncollected claim
on all the splendors life can give.
I am a King, you are a Queen,
but will our throne forever fail?
(The hackney coach jolts, jolts along
and we two tremble cold and pale.)   *Anton N. Nyerges*

THE LADY OF THE WHITE CASTLE

My soul is a castle, ancient, known to be haunted,
lichenous, lonely, and very full of pride.
(Look upon my eyes then...Aren't they huge, big eyes?
But there's no light behind them. Yes, no light inside.)
    In the empty chambers nothing, save an echo.
    Sorrows moss the bailey-wall, pierced by a pair
    of great, dark windows opening onto the valley.

(Save my eyes' weariness, what else is there?)
Ever and forever shall the place be haunted.
Mustiness and fog hold the dungeon and the keep.
Shadows only rustle through the shadow,
shadows of a damned crew, moaning deep.
    (Only sometimes, in the secret night-time,
    a taper kindles in those great sad eyes.)
    It is the White Lady walking round the solar
    or laughing from the oriel in glad surprise.

Dermot Spence and *Paul Tabori*

THE POET OF THE HORTOBÁGY

He was a large-eyed, Hunnish youth,
smitten with many a fair mirage,
and with his herd he struck into
the famous Magyar Hortobágy.
    Women and dreams have seized his soul
    a thousand times with magic snare;
    but when his heart would sprout a flower
    the herds of cattle grazed it bare.
He often thought of wondrous things,
of wine and women, death and birth;
he could have been a holy bard
in any other land on earth.
    But when he gazed upon the herds
    and on the breeched, illiterate crowd,
    straightway he buried all his songs;
    he whistled or he swore aloud.   *Anton N. Nyerges*

ON THE TISZA

I came from the banks of the Ganges
and dreamt by the sun-silted river;
my heart was a large bell-flower
my strength a delicate quiver.
Drawing well, wasteland, jumble,

sty with its dungy reeking,
wild kisses, louts, killers of dreams,
by the Tisza what am I seeking?   *Anton N. Nyerges*

THE TETHERED SOULS

They tethered my soul upon a rope
because it frisked with coltish flame,
because I used in vain the lash
gave chase in vain, gave chase in vain.

If you should see on Magyar mead
a bloody stallion flecked with foam,
cut loose his lariat, for he is
a soul — a somber Magyar soul.   *Anton N. Nyerges*

THE MAGYAR FALLOW

I walk on meadows run to weed,
on fields of burdock and of mallow.
I know this rank and ancient ground —
this is the Magyar fallow.

I bow down to the sacred soil;
this virgin ground is gnawed, I fear.
Hey, skyward groping seedy weeds,
are there no flowers here?

While I look at the slumbering earth,
the twisting vines encircle me,
and scents of long dead flowers steep
my senses amorously.

Silence. I am dragged down and roofed
and lulled in burdock and in mallow.
A mocking wind flies whisking by
above the mighty fallow.   *Anton N. Nyerges*

THE GRANDSON OF GYÖRGY DÓZSA[5]

I, the grandson of György Dózsa,
a sad peasant-noble, must cry out for my people's lot.
Ah, you masters, great landlords, perhaps you would speak
to my scythe-bearing people — for the summer is hot.

The summer is hot and the scythe cuts straight.
Ah, you landlords with fists leaden and white,
what will happen if Dózsa's vagabond people
should spill over in angry, menacing might?

Ah, you landlords, if the people come, what will happen?
From your castles of foam to what bitter fate
will your pitiful army flee? If with the crash of our onslaught
we break down the gate?

Sir Maurice Bowra

A PEACOCK TAKES ITS PERCH

"A peacock takes its perch upon the county hall —
a sign that freedom comes to many folk in thrall..."[6]

Let the proud, frail peacock, whose feathers dazzle the sun,
proclaim that tomorrow here all will be undone.

Tomorrow all will change, be changed at last — new eyes
in new battles will turn with laughter to the skies.

New winds will groan laments in the old Magyar trees,
while we await, await new Magyar mysteries.

---

[5] Leader of the Hungarian peasant revolt of 1514, cruelly murdered by the nobility who burned him on a red-hot metal throne. This defeat of the peasants weakened the country and encouraged the Turkish occupation in 1526.

[6] The lines of a famous folk song also set to music by Zoltán Kodály.

Either we are all fools, and to a man shall die,
or else this faith of ours will prove it does not lie.

New forges and new fires, new faiths, new holy men,
either you'll come to life, or be nothing again.

Either the ancient hall will fall from the flames' stroke,
or our souls will rot here, bound in their ancient yoke.

Either in Magyar words new meanings will unfold,
or the sadness of Magyar life will linger as of old.

"A peacock takes its perch upon the county hall —
a sign that freedom comes to many folk in thrall..."

Sir Maurice Bowra

THE ANCIENT "KAYÁN"[7]

Out of the East in purple robes
he entered, in the Dawn of Rhymes,
in boozy mood, astride his horse,
Old Kaján came, with tuneful lute,
and sat right down on me sometimes.
　　　The rowdy fellow sings to me;
　　　we drink and drink; I listen still;
　　　the red dawns in a long parade
　　　flit drunken past our hostelry

---

[7] Spelled *'kaján'* but pronounced *caw-yahn,* this personified adjective, 'the malevolent one' or 'the sneerer,' represents a mysterious figure, a gleefully malicious mocker, who becomes a constant companion of the poet. The *Kaján* is not a villain, neither is he the Devil, nor even a lesser demon. He is rather something of "the old Adam," Hungarian style, haunting the Magyar down through the ages. He may also represent the uncivilized *libido,* frustrating the civilized man's attempt to achieve a moral personality. And something undefinable remains in the term, stirring the poetic imagination. [W.K.]

and knock upon the window sill.
The Holy East's lost happiness,
the present's vileness, stained and marred,
and all the future's garish mists
are dancing on the boozy board.
Old Kaján wrestles me but hard.

    In my torn coat I doze and doze;
    Old Kaján's robes are purple fine.
    A cross, two candles, grace the gloom.
    A sad and endless joust is ours,
    and at the table flows the wine.

From ancient Babylon's far time
to wrestle with me he has trod.
Thus may have walked some lewd forebear;
since then he's been my bosom-friend,
my Sire, my Caesar, and my God.

    A drunk Apollo — see him leer!
    His garment slips, his horse must wait,
    but still we feast, the joust still booms.
    And on the blood-stained table-top
    my glass keeps wandering with its mate.

"Kind Sir, dear comrade of the sport,
excuse me, please get off my head!
Too much of good has sated me;
too much were sin and booze and sex;
father, love leaves me almost dead."

    With groans I yield my broken lute,
    my broken heart, but he guffaws.
    Rumbling Life wanders to and fro
    under our holy, blood-soaked, flushed
    old tavern window filled with flaws.

"Sir, wrestle with some other man.
To me that joy is joy no more,
rapture and fame are headaches now.
Proud lion-nails grew worn and blunt
in beastly dreams that I abhor.

    ...Good Sir, my sod's Hungarian sod,
    leached out and barren. Why not scorn
    your great, enthrilled encouragement?
    What worth have wine and fervent toasts?

what worth has one, if Hungarian-born?
...Good Sir, I am a wastrel serf.
A worn-out mighty fool am I.
Why should I drink till I collapse?
My cash is spent, my honour lost,
my strength is done, so let me die!
        ...Good Sir, I have a holy mother,
        I have my Léda, her I bless.
        I have the random flash of dreams,
        and some good friends; beneath my soul
        a mighty swamp of loathsomeness.
...I may yet write a song or two,
some new, great songs of lustful life,
but see, I want to tumble down
under the table, overcome
with stupor in this ancient strife.
        ...My Sir, let your sad servant go.
        Nothing is left but certainty,
        the old assurance of decay —
        don't charm me, harm me, pour me drink!
        My lord, please no more wine for me!
I feel a foul satiety;
my waist is sick and shrunk in weight.
Bowing to you my last farewell,
I dash my goblet to the floor.
Good Sir, I now capitulate!"
        Up in his saddle then he vaults,
        he slaps my back, guffaws with glee,
        and rides off on his magic steed
        with pagan songs and merry dawns
        and sultry winds of wizardry.
Farther he flies from East to West,
to further jousts he gallops fast.
And I with cross, with shattered glass,
with body chilled and frozen grin
collapse under the bar at last.

Watson Kirkconnell

ON NEW WATERS

Don't founder, my ship, tomorrow's hero guides you.
Your steersman is drunken, so the laugh derides you.
Fly on, my ship,
don't founder, my ship, tomorrow's hero guides you.
      Sail on, sail on, and sailing never falter;
      though vast and virgin seas your passage alter.
      Fly on, my ship,
      sail on, sail on, and sailing never falter.
Newer horizons ever wave before you;
new moments and a perilous life assure you.
Fly on, my ship,
newer horizons ever wave before you.
      I hate familiar dreams — I want new oceans,
      new secrets, new afflictions, new emotions.
      Fly on, my ship,
      I hate familiar dreams — I want new oceans.
You bards of faded grey will not inspire me,
let tavern-stench or Holy Spirit fire me.
Fly on, my ship,
you bards of faded grey will not inspire me.

Anton N. Nyerges

AUTUMN SLIPPED INTO PARIS

Autumn slipped into Paris yesterday
gliding silently down Rue Saint Michel,
beneath the noonday Dog and hush of trees
she met me with her spell.

I had been sauntering toward the Seine;
small-fry kindling-songs smouldered in my head,
purple and pensive, strange and smokey-hued;
that I'll soon die, they said.

Then autumn whispered something from behind.
The road of Saint Michel began to shake.
Wish, wish — the jesting leaves arose in swirls
along the gusty wake.

One moment — summer had not even blenched,
and autumn fled away with mocking ease.
She came, but that she came, alone I knew
beneath the moaning trees.

Anton N. Nyerges [& A.M.]

THE KINSMAN OF DEATH

I am a kindred spirit to death,
I cherish love in tired decay.
I cherish kissing softly those
Who go away.

I cherish the suffering roses
Wilting women's faded desires,
The autumn sun's melancholy
Dying fires.

I cherish the unhappy hours
And their haunting, cautioning moments,
Almighty Death's, all-holy Death's
Playful omens.

I cherish all people departing,
The weeping and the hardly waking,
Drizzly fields, when the frostbitten
Day is breaking.

I cherish the sad resignation,
Stoical calm and tearless crying,
The last resort of sages, poets,
And the dying.

I cherish the disappointed,
The suffering, those in stagnation,
The gloom-stricken, those without faith,
All creation.

I am a kindred spirit to Death;
I cherish love in tired decay.
I cherish kissing softly those
Who go away.   *Peter Zollman*

MATTHIAS' DEMENTED SCHOLAR

"Scholar, compose me a Magyar song,
great Dante also lived on earth!"
          And the scholar laughed, and laughed.

The song in Latin meter soared,
but not in the Magyar, never once.
          And the scholar scanned, and scanned.

A Petrarch sang within his soul,
a newer Magyar song was born,
          and the scholar dreamed, and dreamed.

But now and then through the secret night
he wrote and tore up his Magyar lines.
          And the scholar sobbed, and sobbed.
                                      Anton N. Nyerges [& A.M.]

BLOOD AND GOLD

My ear perceives no paltry difference
if pleasure pant or pain lament
if blood should spurt or gold be spent.

I know and vow that these alone endure:
all else is flotsam in the flood
save gold and blood, yes, gold and blood.

All things know death and pass to nothingness;
fame, song, high heritage, and hire
but blood and gold never expire.

The nations die and come again to birth.
Holy is he who dares to hold
my changeless gospel: Blood and gold!   *Watson Kirkconnell*

SAINT MARGARET'S LEGEND

The "Isle of the Hares"[8] confessed to me
one hush and storied night, this tale —
the king had promised Margaret
his snow-white daughter, to the veil.
       She was a dream-maid, a sigh suppressed;
       one angry word would blanch her face
       while in the courtyard there caroused
       a shaggy and barbaric race.
She awaited someone from the West —
no wild-bewhiskered, noisy boor,
a gentle, bardlike tender youth,
a tearful, strolling troubadour.
       She waited long, her heart grew sick.
       The clang of arms she heard in fright
       as Hunnish horsemen would arrive
       but never he — her phantom knight.
He never came the Danube's way,
this soft-songed youth with softer smile;
and she became a bride of Christ
and died upon Saint Margaret's Isle.

Anton N. Nyerges [& A.M.]

---

[8] The original name was 'The Isle of Hares;' it was renamed 'Saint
Margaret's Island,' after King Béla IVth's daughter, a nun. It is in the center
of Budapest spanned by Margaret's Bridge to both Buda and Pest, and is a
tourist attraction. The ruins of the 12th-century convent can still be seen.

THE MAGYAR MESSIAHS

More bitter is our weeping,
different the griefs that try us.
A thousand times Messiahs
are the Magyar Messiahs.

A thousand times they perish,
unblest their crucifixion,
for vain was their affliction,
oh, vain was their affliction.

Anton N. Nyerges

ON ELIJAH'S CHARIOT

The Lord summons Elijah-like
those whom he truly loves and tries.
He gives them racing, fiery hearts,
the flaming chariots of the skies.

Elijah's tribe rush toward the sky
toward the land of endless snow.
On Himalaya's frozen peaks
with clattering wheels the chariots go.

They are driven by winds of fate —
outcasts between the earth and sky.
Tempted by evil, chilling charms
the chariots of Elijah fly.

Their brains are ice, their souls are fire;
the earth laughs at them as her prey —
With cold and glinting diamond dust
the sun in pity strews their way.

Anton N. Nyerges [& A.M.]

JUDAS AND JESUS

I carve my defiant, raging pulse
In basalt rock on the Mount of Skulls.
My Christ, the poet I adored,
I sold you, Lord.

I dreamt every dream that pierced your heart,
I lived as your soul, your counterpart.
I crowned you, I, of all the men,
I loved you then.

Now I have sold you, almighty King,
For Life is my love, my everything,
For I have dreams, almighty too,
As poets do.

Your sacred lips don't fan my fire,
Not for me your hallowed empire,
A girl wants money, silks to wear,
She wants me there.

Am I so mean? Life is demeaning.
Has the Word lost its wondrous meaning?
Why am I lured and mortified
By paid delight?

I toss my carved rock in the abyss,
the earth will tremble for centuries
And future doomed, dejected eyes,
Will empathize.   *Peter Zollman*

SONG OF A HUNGARIAN JACOBIN

Blood from our fingertips comes welling
when, oh poor, sleepy Hungary,
we touch you with them and we wonder:
do you exist at all? Do we?

do you exist at all? Do we?
      How hopes the future to be better?
      With anguish in our souls and eyes
      we question if the slaves of Babel
      will from their slumber ever rise.
Will from a thousand sluggish longings
be born at last one mighty will?
This age-old torment is the portion
Of Vlachs and Slavs and Magyars still.
      In anguish and humiliation
      a thousand years have made us one:
      on the soul's barricade in fury
      why can't we roar in unison?
Single the voice of Olt and Danube,
a muffled murmur from the tomb.
To him, who is not lord or scoundrel,
woe will befall in Árpád's home!
      When will we join at last together?
      When will our voices speak out loud?
      Magyar or not — it does not matter —
      we are the crushed, oppressed, and cowed.
How long must we be ruled by blackguards,
poor, chicken-hearted millions, we?
How long must the Hungarian people
like caged and captive starlings be?
      Hungary's miserable beggars
      we've neither bread nor faith for fare;
      but all will come to us tomorrow
      if we but wish, if we but dare!

Sir Maurice Bowra

THE BLACK PIANO

Crazy strings: they neigh, and boom and whine.
Away with you, unless you have some wine!
This is the black piano!
The blind tickler — tears into the keys
These are life's bitter melodies.
This is the black piano.

My buzzing head, my tearful eyes,
The wake of my wrestling desires,
all this, all this: the black piano.
My drunk, crazy heart pumps my blood
Beating in time with the throbbing flood
this is the black piano.

Adam Makkai

IN FRONT OF GOOD PRINCE SILENCE

I walk the forest in the moonlight
and whistle through my chattering teeth
stalking behind me ten feet tall
Good Prince Silence —
"mercy" — I tremble, dare not turn.

"Mercy" — I tremble, dare not turn,
and dare not gaze up, up to the moon:
one false movement, one needless sound —
and Good Prince Silence
would step on me and tread me down.

Alan Dixon

I WANT TO BE LOVED

I am no heir, no proud ancestor,
I have no friend, no brother, sister,
I have never belonged,
I have never belonged.

I am, like every human: Highness,
Iceberg, enigma, strange and timeless,
Distant will-o'-the-wisp,
Distant will-o'-the-wisp.

But, oh, I can't remain unspoken,
I have to bare myself wide open,
Behold me, everyone,
Behold me, everyone.

In all self-torture, in every song,
I want to be loved, to belong.
Belong to somebody,
Belong to somebody.

Peter Zollman

TWO KINDS OF WELSH BARDS

The hatchet was buried, the table made ready,
the gentry class rejoiced at Deák's[9] skill;
fecerunt magnum gwledda[10] where the rich grape
ripened free from vine-pest on Buda's hill.

The kind lord lieutenant once more gave a party,
and the red wine flowed again at the county ball;
everyone breathed again and moved freely;
only the *plebs* were left out of it all.

There had to be gypsies, a student singer
to banish cares with paeans of praise;
the "Welsh Bards" came and greeted each other,
singing most beautiful, soothing lays.

The carouse went on for a generation;
what other than faithful Toldi's tale fitter?
But no word was sung of freedom or terror,
or concern with honour, or anything bitter.

But outside the song is free and rousing freedom;
it no longer rubs its hands the accustomed way;
had it continued thus there'd be no help left,
if it still cringed, like yesterday.

Neville Masterman

---

[9] The master-mind of the compromise of 1867 between Austria and Hungary. The poem alludes to 'The Bards of Wales' by János Arany (q.v.).

[10] The original has *fecerunt magnum áldomás,* where the last word means 'toast;' the translator here substitutes the corresponding Celtic word.

MEMORIES OF A SUMMER NIGHT
(June, 1914)

A mad angel hammered with raging might,
Drumroll alarms onto the sombre earth,
Hundreds of stars burnt out their light,
Hundreds of young brains were overturned,
Hundreds of flowers were torn, defiled.
It was a curious,
Curious summer night.
Our old beehives burst into flame,
Our loveliest filly broke her leg,
I dreamt that the dead were here alive.
Our faithful dog, Burkus, disappeared,
Our servant, Meg, mute all these years,
Shrilled the chants of a savage rite:
It was a curious,
Curious summer night.
The worthless were swaggering bravely,
Fancy robbers went out to rob,
And true-hearted men had to hide:
It was a curious,
Curious summer night.
We gathered that man was imperfect,
Tight-fisted when sharing his love,
But still, it just couldn't be right,
The live and the dead on the turning wheel:
Has man ever been a punier mite,
And the moon in a more mocking mood
Than on that terrible night?
It was a curious,
Curious summer night.
And horror leaned over the spirits
With malevolent, gloating delight:
The secrets of every forefather
Dwelt deep in the souls of the sons.
And Thought, the proud servant of man,
Inebriated, went out to join

The blood-thirsty, dreadful Wedding Feast,
And, see, he was lowly, lame, contrite:
It was a curious,
Curious summer night.
I know I believed that on that night
Some neglected God would soon alight
To take me and deliver me to death,
But I am still alive, though different,
Transfigured by that shattering event,
And as I am waiting for a God,
I remember that terror-haunted,
Devastating, world-burying night:
It was a curious,
Curious summer night.

                                    Peter Zollman

THE LOST HORSEMAN

You hear the hollow hoofbeats of
a horseman lost since long ago.
The shackled souls of ghosted woods
and ancient reedlands wake to woe.
  And where in patches here and there
  a tangled coppice used to thrive,
  inaudible and ghostly troops
  of wintry tales become alive.
Here is the denseness of the copse,
here are the blunt and brazen songs,
which lurk within the deafened fog
since our brave fathers died in throngs.
  The autumn is macabre here;
  the dwindling sums on men are small,
  and on the hill-encircled plain
  November walks in a misty shawl.
And once again the naked plain
is overgrown with reeds and trees,
hiding its bleak November self
in fogs of bygone centuries.
  Nothing but secrets, nothing but sires,

nothing but power, nothing but gore,
nothing but reedlands, nothing but woods,
nothing but madmen feared of yore.
Toward a new and tangled path
gallops the horseman lost in night;
he sees no trace of village life,
or even a glimmer of lamplight.
      Mute hamlets huddle in their sleep
      and dream of days that were more fair,
      while from the foggy thickets rush
      the auroch, wolf, and raging bear.
You hear the hollow hoofbeats of
a horseman lost since long ago.
The shackled souls of ghosted woods
and ancient reedlands wake to woe.   *Anton N. Nyerges*

AT THE FOOT OF MOUNT ZION

With his white and tousled godly beard,
puffing with cold, bedraggled, torn,
He ran, my Lord, the long-forgotten,
some place by the foot of Mount Zion
ran on a damp, blind autumn morn.
      He wore a big bell for a great-coat
      patched with red letters, mended well,
      but sad and tattered was the old Lord
      as He kept slapping the mist around him
      and for the dawn mass rang the bell.
With trembling hands I held a lantern
— the Faith sat in my ragged soul —
my long-past youth was on my mind:
and in my nostrils the Smell of God,
and finding someone was my goal.
      He waited for me by the mountain,
      flaming rocks lay in front and behind,
      He rang the bell as He caressed me,
      and washed my face with a shower of tears,
      for my old friend was good and kind.

I held his wrinkled hand and kissed it
and lamenting, I racked my brain:
"Dear ancient Lord, what do they call you,
You, to whom I so often prayed?
I try recalling, but alas, in vain...
        I, who have died, am now returning
        I, who in life, was damned to hell —
        I wish I could only pray like children!"
        and He kept ringing, ringing the bell.
        "Your name, if I could but remember..."
He waited, then ran up the steep.
The beat of his strides was that of the psalms:
psalms for the dead. And here I am left
to sit by Mount Zion and weep, and weep.

Leslie A. Kery

ADAM, WHERE ART THOU?

The misty brown of my mourning flees,
in vast white radiance comes the Lord
to subjugate my enemies.

He still conceals, He will not show his face,
but his large eye's compassionate sun
now often guides my halting pace.

And if now and then I'd won a fight,
it was the Lord who strode before
he got there first with his naked sword.

I hear his silent steps in my soul;
and as he asks "Adam where art thou?"
loud heartbeats ring the answering toll.

I've found him at last within my heart
found him to hold him in fast embraces,
and never in death to be apart.

Anton N. Nyerges [& A.M.]

THE WOODLAND CROSS

A snowed-in cross within the woods
upon a vast and wintry night,
an image marbled from the past.
We rode there in our tingling sleigh
upon a vast and wintry night.

My father was a joyful man
who sang when he looked at the cross.
I was the son of such a man
who wearied of the graven wood
and sang when he looked at the cross.

Two stiff-necked Magyar Calvinists,
like flight of time we flew along,
father and son: agreed on everything,
as we sat in the sleigh, we sang
like flight of time we flew along.

And twenty years have passed since then;
my sleigh is dashing through the night.
No more, as once, am I remiss,
I lift my hat and bow my head:
my sleigh's dashing there through the night.

Anton N. Nyerges

THE LORD'S ARRIVAL

When all have forsaken me here
and with broken soul I stumbled as I trod,
unexpectedly and in silence
I was embraced by God.
He did not come with a trumpet call of fright,
but with a true and mute embrace.
He did not come in the blaze of noon

but on a tumultuous night.
These eyes of mine that were so vain
have gone blind. My youth has ceased to be,
but Him, the radiant, I behold
for all eternity.

Anton N. Nyerges

PRAYER AFTER WAR

My Lord, I'm coming from the war —
all things surcease, surcease.
Set me at peace with myself and you.
in truth, you are the Peace.

My heart is but an aching tumor,
and nothing soothes my pain.
Please set a kiss upon my heart
that it may somewhat wane.

My sombre eyes are closed toward all
that is on earth to woo,
and they have nothing to behold
save you my Lord, save you.

My speedy legs, one time knee-deep
waded in bloody lees.
But now, behold, I have no legs,
just knees, my Lord, just knees.

I do not kiss, I do not fight,
my lips are sere and dry.
These arms are shrivelled stumps — my Lord,
measure me with your eye!

Look down at me, you too, my Lord,
all things surcease, surcease.
Set me at peace with myself and you;
in truth, you are the Peace.

Anton N. Nyerges

I GUARD YOUR EYES

With my old man's wrinkled hand,
with my old man's squinting eyes,
let me hold your lovely hand,
let me guard your lovely eyes.

Worlds have tumbled, through their fall
like a wild beast chased by fright
I came, and I on you did call
scared, I wait with you inside.

With my old man's wrinkled hand,
with my old man's squinting eyes,
let me hold your lovely hand,
let me guard your lovely eyes.

I do not know why, how long
can I thus remain for you —
but I hold your lovely hand
and I guard your lovely eyes.

Adam Makkai

BEHOLD MY TREASURES, DARLING

Behold my treasures, my darling,
they're less than the Biblical farthing,
behold the fate of a true and faithful life,
look at my grey hairs departing.

I didn't wander afar
sadly I was proud to be a Magyar,
and I got misery, woe, misfortune
and I have reaped troubles galore.

At loving I was pretty good
couldn't be outdone even by a God
as I conceived of it as a child.
Look at me now, in pain, blood, and fever defiled.

If you hadn't come my way
my lamenting mouth would have nothing to say
behold the mockers of integrity
sending me into my coffin.

Behold me with your love, my darling,
it was you I found while fleeing,
and if there's a smile left in this loathsome world
you are the smile of my heart.

Behold my treasures, my darling,
they're less than the Biblical farthing,
let them be dark and youthful to you,
look at my grey hairs departing.

Adam Makkai

Gyula Krúdy
(1878-1933)

Born in Nyíregyháza, in northeastern Hungary, into an old gentry family, Krúdy summed up his life in these lines: "I ran away from the parental home to become a journalist, I fell madly in love with a provincial actress, I was happy, I was an artist, I drank, I caroused, I made love, I don't really know what happened to me..."

He settled in Budapest in 1896 and spent most of his life in the Hungarian capital whose streets, inns, and by-ways he made his own. His first short story was printed when he was fifteen; he was not yet twenty when he published his first volume of short stories; and, except for a period after 1919, there was no year until his death that one or two volumes bearing his name did not appear.

He exhibited prodigous activity and versatility. All his work—of which the series devoted to Sinbad the Sailor, the character from the Arabian Nights, whom he made his alter-ego was perhaps the most striking—served as part of a vast autobiography. Novels, short stories, plays, articles, and children's books poured from his pen; of these, The Crimson Coach *[A vörös postakocsi], in 1913, was the first to be translated into English.*

He was, as László Cs. Szabó points out, the greatest prose-poet of the Hungarian language, hence his inclusion in this anthology.

In recent years, John Lukacs wrote about Krúdy in The New Yorker *of December 1, 1986, under the title "The Sound of a Cello."*

We present here a number of independent passages from Krúdy's writings as translated by John Lukacs. Instead of giving these excerpts their own titles, we have decided simply to number them, since they can be seen as independent prose-poems.

I.　　This city, Budapest, smells of violets in the spring as do mesdames along the promenade above the river on the Pest side. In the fall, it is Buda that suggests the tone: the odd thud of chestnuts dropping on the Castle walk; fragments of the music of the military band from the kiosk on the other side wafting over in the forlorn silence. Autumn and Buda were born of the same mother.

II.　　What somehow echo through the clanging of the town bells are memories of old kings and of ancient gentlemen who had come from afar. Men long dead, once loved or unloved by calm, indifferent women, since women customarily do not concern themselves much with history. During the embraces of her lover no woman feels any happiness knowing that a chronicler would scribble about those arms and legs and beards after they have turned to dust. Beards, breastplates, hearts disappeared, the women went on knitting their stockings; they closed their doors early in the evening, and during the night no one came back from the bridge at whose stone railing he had once gazed long at his own countenance in the mirrory water.

The historic steps were gone, new steps were heard approaching; spring came, winter came, illnesses and loves came and went, the women ripened and then grew old, the men coughed, cursed, and lay down in their coffins. A small town was this in northern Hungary, with foot-thick walls, convent windows, stoves from which smoke wafted off.

Why should people look for the heroines of this story among the kneeling women at Sunday Mass or among the ladies waltzing at the fire company's annual picnic in May? One day the heroines will die, and the care of their graves will be the entertainment of those who are still alive.

III.   To breakfast on a light-blue tablecloth, smelling of milk, like a child in the family home ... freshly washed faces, hair combed wet, shirtfronts bright and white around the table. Everything smells different there, even rum. The plum brandy men swallow in one gulp on an empty stomach is harmless at the family table. The eggs are freshly laid, the butter wrapped in grape leaves smiles like a fat little girl, shoes are resplendent, the fresh morning airing wafts from the beds the stifling, sultry thoughts of the previous night, on quick feet the maid patters from room to room in a skirt starched only yesterday.

Even the manure carts on the roads steam differently on frosty mornings from the way they do in the afternoons; the rattle of gravely ill gentlemen quiets down in the neighboring houses; the bright greens in the markets, the pink-veined meats shining in the willow baskets, the towers of the town had been sponged and washed at dawn; and a piebald bird jumps around merrily on the frost-pinched mulberry tree, like life that begins anew and has forgiven and forgotten the past.

John Lukacs

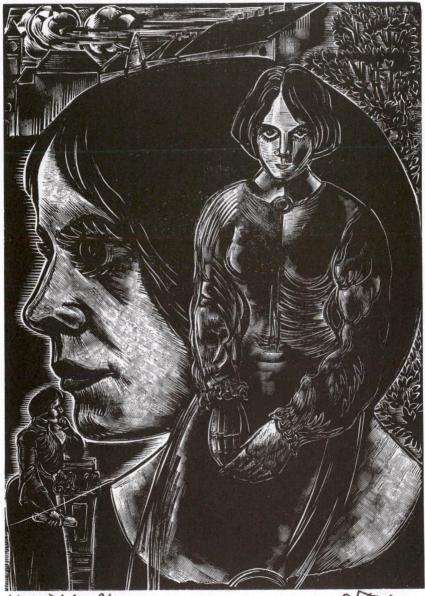

Margit Kaffka
1880–1918

G. Buday
71

Margit Kaffka
(1880-1918)

Margit Kaffka was born in Nagykároly (today Carei in Romania) and was educated in her native town, and later in Budapest. She obtained a teaching certificate for secondary schools and eventually became a teacher of Hungarian language and literature in Miskolc. She was married twice; she died during an influenza epidemic toward the end of World War I.

Her first poems and stories appeared in The Week [A Hét] *and in the influential periodical* The West [Nyugat]. *As a short story writer her delicate and perceptive talent equalled Katherine Mansfield's, although without a complete mastery of the form. Her most successful novel,* Colors and Years [Színek és évek] *which appeared in 1912, explored with insight and courage the problems of the modern woman. Her collected poetry* The Poems of Margit Kaffka [Kaffka Margit versei] *appeared in 1906. The poems cast off her age's sentimentalism and, while remaining intensely feminine, were topical and very powerful. Throughout her career as a writer she was preoccupied with two main themes — the decline of the gentry class and the fate of women at the turn of the century.*

Three main periods can be distinguished in her writings: the first was between 1901 and 1908, during the start of the periodical Nyugat; *literary scholars consider her work closely linked to this periodical and to the influence of Endre Ady (q.v.). Her second period ended with the outbreak of World War I; during this period she published two volumes of poetry* Years of Search [Tallózó évek], *1911, and* For the Last Time on The Lyre [Utolszor a lyrán], *1912; during this same period she published four volumes of short stories. Her poetry of this period was an act of self-orientation and searching for the meaning of life. She found everything floating and uncertain except the "I", her own higher Ego. Her third period is characterized by the difficult experiences that lead up to the time of her death. In her third period she wrote about the societal crises that became more clearly evident in the misery inflected by the war; she also started to be active as a journalist. Her voice was finally her own; she abandoned free and blank verse and returned to rhythmical and rhymed poetry, and her messages and style became simpler and more straightforward. As a prose writer she was a realist; in her poetry she wrote about her love for her husband and also for her son. She was Hungary's first major woman author. Her novel* Anthill [Hangyaboly], *1917, appeared in English translation in 1995.*

LITANY

My sweet, beloved companion,
what kind of treaty is this?
Which of the gods worked it out for us
when he inscribed it into our hearts?

My white, yielding pillow
on which I could never really rest,
is like the true melody of my soul
which I have never really heard yet.

My life's a book written with wisdom
which I never got a chance to study,
it is my fresh, perfect well being,
and just look for how long I've been ailing!

You're my chiming bell at day-break,
you're my fine afternoon sunshine,
my gentle evening lamplight,
my night thickly studded with stars.

You're my night, my sky's own blueness,
my sweetest ever sweetness,
my overflowing cup,
my chiming bell at dawn,
my peaceful and quiet dream,
my soothing afternoon sunshine!

We have often spoken about love
weaving prose or verse with our tears,
"love" — the very word has been cheapened,
"love" — let the word's misuse be broken!
For me you are both father and son,
my brother and my betrothed,
my small and tender nestling,
my great, earnest protector,
you're my playmate and my lover!

With faith in my own humanity
you are the very first thing I want to cling to,
avowing with words and my silent heart
that I could never deceive or betray you —
I must guard you against all harm
and for you, if necessary, I might even kill!
Tell me, my beloved companion,
what kind of treaty is this,
which of the gods has drafted its words?

Paul Tabori

DAWN RHYTHMS
(May 23, 1912. Extract)

"Dawn", said a stranger, "look, the cloud is tinted with blood.
The bud opens gorily upon the fabric of the world,
wildly the shuttle swings afresh. Perhaps the loom, too, is shaking.
Many a sultry conservatory will have its windows shattered today!
Locked treasure-chambers need airing! Dream-crowns must roll...
Tomorrow human blood will perhaps be measured by more than a
cupful, and every human heart is a Grail
when its blood spills on the street
and all kisses kissed by a whore are actually holy
if they kindle you to fight or to calling a truce!"

I listened to him as he sat opposite me
(but forgot his name and face)
no human words had ever cut me so to the quick.
"Dawn", I thought. "Above the park the cloud is indeed
tinted with blood and the faces of pale women, haggard soldiers,
or young literati with fresh voices are all pink.
Oh, my sisters, you poor girls with your strained lips
in this exhaustion at dawn!
My kinsmen, you tired lads! My kith and kin, you boys with such
wise, sad eyes!

Let my heart fill today to the brim! Let everything
rush into it, like thunder! Maybe blood won't be spilled in the streets
by the cupful after all...
I think a time will come when petty feminine troubles
will be shameful and laughable.
"Men", I said softly while looking into their fine, alert eyes,
"if something bad should happen, do not forget
to send us word, too!
Today we still trifle with our hearts, for our hearts
are the narrow jails of our fate, we keep washing it with tears,
and decorate it with all kinds of love-roses, silly as we are.

But for a little while at such times you can loosen our shackles
it would be far better for us to rush into battle than to wait,
weep, tremble with fear and bear your children;
do not forget, men, that female blood, too, is worth much more
for loving than for fighting,
so just go ahead and summon us, as during earlier revolutions,
right up to your barricades.

Like dried-out haystacks, the heat of our surplus lives
will do just fine bursting into flames and casting brands
so you can boldly use our poor, exploited corpses
to fill the gaps in your heroic ramparts.
Listen, you men, should something bad happen —
        don't you dare forget to send us word!"

Paul Tabori

Mihály Babits
1883-1941

Mihály Babits
(1883-1941)

The son of a judge, Babits was born in Szekszárd and received his education at the Cistercian secondary school in Pécs and at the University of Budapest. He became an accomplished classicist. He taught at the high schools of Baja, Szeged, and Újpest as well as in Fogaras, a city in Transylvania (now Făgăraş in Romania). He felt banished to the outer provinces there and wrote the poem Letters from Tomi, *which evokes the exile of the Roman poet Ovid. Back in Budapest, he published his first poems in* Nyugat, *the journal of which he was later appointed editor. Babits read a vast amount of world literature in the original and wrote a most erudite* History of European Literature. *Hungarian literary historians to this day, perhaps not unjustifiably, call him 'the Hungarian T.S. Eliot.'*

Although extremely widely read, he never became anyone's imitator. Instead, he became the teacher and spiritual father of a whole generation of poets such as L. Szabó, Weöres, Pilinszky, and Nemes Nagy (qq.v.) who are sometimes characterized as the 'urbanites.' A master translator of unsurpassed skill, Babits rendered the entire Divine Comedy *by Dante in 'terza rima;'* Shakespeare's The Tempest; *and a large number of Latin medieval hymns collected in the volume* Amor Sanctus.

He also published a selection of erotic poems translated from different languages, Erato. *Babits became the supreme arbiter of Western-oriented Hungarian literature and the chief administrator of the prestigious Baumgarten Prize. As a novelist he wrote brilliant books such as* The Stork Caliph *[A gólyakalifa], 1912, which treated the Jekyll-Hyde theme in modern, Freudian terms;* The Sons of Death *[Halálfiai], 1921, depicts the decaying gentry and middle class, while* The Son of Virgil Timár *[Timár Virgil fia], 1921, deals with the problems of a priest's protegé. His brilliant discursive essays were collected in several volumes.*

His books of poetry start with Leaves from the Garland of Iris *[Levelek Irisz koroszorújából], 1908; But Prince, if Winter Should Come [Herceg, hátha megjön a tél is], 1911; Recitativ, 1916; Island and Sea [Sziget és tenger], 1925; and In Race With the Years [Versenyt az esztendőkkel], 1928. His enduring masterpiece is* The Book of Jonah *[Jónás könyve], published shortly before his death. He describes the spiritual agony of Jonah, the Prophet, who doesn't like what God wants him to do but who is morally obliged to cry out against sin and corruption. This was a warning against Fascism. He died of throat cancer with his long agony transmuted into creative integrity and human dignity.*

AGAINST HORACE
(In Horatium)

I loathe you: keep your distance, you lowly crowd!
and hold your tongues: for I am about to sing
   (priest of the Muses) yet unheard of
      poems designed for the young of hearing.

Look at the sky and notice the Gypsy clouds —
look at the waters whereon the foamy waves
   rejoice over constantly changing
      shapes — singing praises of fair Aiolos.[1]

For flames are waves, too. Phoenix-like flames our world,
blazing incessant. Nothing can ever live
   that never died. Oh, flora, fauna,
      life is a gift you receive from dying!

For everything on earth is eternal flow.
All things rush past like floods of a rustling brook.
   "One can't step twice into the same stream":
      so willed it Thanatos[2] and Aiolos.

So let the songs, too, be of a new design,
let old ideals change in a thousand robes,
   let old styles come back in, to fashion
      suitable dress for a new idea.

If Tibur's[3] farmer-poet did often boast
contentment, in a metre akin to this,
   I take it, in my turn, to ring out
      hymns of eternal dissatisfaction!

---

[1] The son of Poseidon, the lord of the winds in Greek mythology. He had to imprison the winds in a cave and then let them loose at Zeus's orders.

[2] The god of death in Greek mythology.

[3] Referring to Horace, who like Maecenas, had his summer home there. (It is today's Tivoli in Italy.)

For everything on earth is eternal flow,
all things rush past, like floods on the mountain peaks,
   like breaking waves, like avalanches,
      lava or flames. You should also, therefore,

throw off the armour-plates of your indolence,
throw off contentment, jettison modesty,
   and be as light as foam, or cloud, or
      birds of the air — be as light as death's wind.

Let bent modesty, virtue of serfs afraid,
no longer press your neck, sick of all the yokes:
   you're frail indeed, but you were meant to
      sail on the ocean and leave behind you

the port of Golden Mean — you must join with zeal
the secret forces weaving the endless wreath
   of hundred-hued, kaleidoscopic
      change that is labyrinthine, eternal.

Adam Makkai and *J.G. Nichols*

THE LYRIC POET'S EPILOGUE

I am the only hero of my verses,
the first and last in every line to dwell:
my poems hope to sing of Universes,
but never reach beyond my lonely cell.
     Are others there outside, to bear the curses
     of being born? If God would only tell.
     A blind nut in the nutshell's dark traverses,
     I loathe to wait for Him to break the spell.
A magic circle binds me like a chain,
and yet, my soaring dreams defy the weight —
but wishful dreams, I know, may tell a lie.
     A prison for myself I must remain,
     the subject and the object. Heavy fate:
     the alpha and the omega am I.

Peter Zollman

MEMORIAL

No-one has ever seen me. And the seasons
sail by. Each year I shed another veil
but still, my soul is: veils within a veil
amid retreating melancholy seasons.

Slick like a fish, they never catch me live.
I'm Proteus, I change and melt away
like sea foam. Oh, I change, I melt away
and slip their grasp as long as I'm alive.

But when I die I leave my coffin, naked
to stand erect upon my grave forever —
I shall remain a monument forever
for all to see me motionless and naked.

The birds come, fly around me: I'm just standing.
The sun comes out, I smile, and then a great cloud
looms over me, I darken with the grey cloud;
even the rain falls harder where I'm standing.

Peter Zollman

THE TOMB OF HEGESO
(On a Greek monument)[4]

My heart's true bride has slept two thousand years;
Dead for two thousand years, she waits for me.
A Greek girl, Hegeso, sedate to see
from head to foot pale marble she appears.

---

[4] A marble grave-stone in the National Museum, Athens. Dating from
about 425 B.C., the relief carving shows Hegeso seated in a chair, sorting out
jewels from a casket held by a slavegirl.

Living, I swear, though none her breathing hears,
Her robe, conceals a heart's grave systole,
Thoughts in that curly head flow full and free
As bowed she sits, pale, pensive, and sincere.

Before her stands a slave, a little girl,
Who holds a costly casket, from whose freight
She sets out gems, rare amethyst and pearl;

Perchance (I dream) she means in jewelled state
Her treasured virgin beauty to unfurl
When I, hereafter, come to be her mate.

Watson Kirkconnell

QUESTION AT NIGHT

As twilight softly turns to sombre brown,
you see a velvet-silky eiderdown
spread slowly by an otherworldly nurse
to coddle warm the sleepy universe
so caringly, that not a periwinkle
is blemished by as little as a wrinkle,
that butterflies remain perfectly painted,
their double wings so delicately decked
and not a single blade of grass has fainted
wrapped in the shades that comfort and protect,
in sombre soft repose they meditate,
unconscious of the velvet-silky weight:
at nights like this, wherever you should roam
or muse inside your melancholy home
or in a tearoom, by the setting sun
watch as they light the gas-lamps one by one,
or walk the hills leg-wearied by the climb,
you with your dog, and see the moon to wane,
or drive along a dusty country lane,
your coachman nodding off from time to time,
or sail upon the swell, as pale as parchment,
or spread along the bench of your compartment,

or amble through a foreign city square,
entranced by gazing idly at the glare
of street-lamps stretching many-many miles
in accurately even double files,
or cross the Grand Canal, towards the Riva
where opal mirrors split the sunny flames,
to brood upon the blush of bygone fever,
remembering the sweet and sorry games
of seasons past, which like those lamps of yore
loom up some time and then they disappear,
remembrance that will linger ever more,
remembrance that's a burden, yet so dear:
then lower your remembrance-burdened head
to contemplate the marble floor you tread.
And yet in this delightful Paradise
the craven hearted question must arise:
why all this beauty, jewel, graven marble?
— you ask the question with dejected eyes —
oh, why the silk, the sea, the butterflies,
and why the evening's velvet-silky marvel?
and why the flames, the sweet and sorry games,
the sea, where farmers never sow a grain?
and why the ebb and tide of swelling waters
and why the clouds, Danaos' gloomy daughters,
remembrances, the past in heavy chain,
the sun, this burning Sisyphean boulder?
and why the moon, the lamps shoulder to shoulder
and Time, that endless ever-dripping drain?
Or take a blade of grass as paradigm:
why does it grow, if it must wilt in time?
why does it wilt, if it will grow again?

Peter Zollman

THE DANAÏDS[5]

In the silent halls of Hades, down the windless halls of Hades, in the
   dells of asphodels, where asphodel leaves never tremble,
   mourning bows will never bow and poppy petals hold forever,
   for the wind is fast asleep there, sleeps in beds of asphodels,
   sleeps and will not say a word,

where the lakes are marble mirrors, motionless, inertly dozing, eyelids
   permanently closing, for the lash of languid eyelids, for the whip of
   wavy waters, there the wind has never stirred:

into urns of alabaster, giant urns of alabaster fifty guilty sisters
   filling, draining, straining, never spilling, fifty doomed and wretched
   widows lifting fifty slender vases pouring water down below,

fifty doomed, tormented sisters into urns of alabaster vainly drain their
   priceless liquid, water from the precious Lethe, never-ample costly
   flow.

Mourning trees in dreamy drowse will never shake their mighty boughs
   (for every bough is but a ghost, a suicidal, ghastly ghost, growing
   there upon the tree;

wakeful, yet without awareness reaching out into the airless, merci-
   lessly reeky, rank riverbank,

to the bank along the Lethe, — for this bank is on the Lethe, — reeky
river   rotten, swilled with ancient, long-forgotten guilt, soiled with
   ancient guilty secrets, never draining in the sea,

as in seven coiling girdles endlessly the Lethe circles round and round
   and round again): there the fifty wretched sisters strain and drain
   their priceless liquid into urns of alabaster but in vain, but all in vain

---

[5] Babits translated Poe's *The Raven,* which has been a favorite recital
piece ever since in Hungary. *The Danaïds* was his reply to the genre.

filling, straining all the day the fifty sisters vainly wrestle as each
  alabaster vessel mercilessly drains away, like the ocean ebbs away,
  with the tears and Lethe-water that the urns of alabaster,
  vicious vases, can't retain.

Fifty alabaster sisters, raven-haired, tormented sisters, wakeful, yet
  without awareness chant a song half-understood;

those tormented widow-sisters, fifty plaintive, pale choristers, chant
  their half-understood verses haunting from their half-remembered
  bygone sunlit sisterhood:

"We have murdered, we have murdered fifty valiant wedded husbands,
  for we loved and freely lusted, heaven knows for whom we lusted,
  drained the juices of desire, draining, spilling, ever willing, in the
  glorious golden sunshine, on the earth beneath the sky. —

Long lost words are dimly glowing in our souls' decaying fire, as if
  streetlights vaguely gilding shadows in an unlit building; long lost
  words, how could be trusted as we chant them never knowing what
  is *loved?* and what is *lusted?* what's the meaning of *desire?* Deep the
  darkness keeps its secret and the shadows don't reply.

So let us chant *we have murdered* — and remember well: — *our
  husbands* — just keep chanting, never knowing, ever draining, ever
  filling, ever straining, never slowing, keep echoing without knowing,
  otherwise the world is silent and the silence so harrowing, and the
  silent deadly darkness never, never says a word." —

Thus the fifty sisters chanted, doomed widows of deep resemblance,
  pallid shapes of alabaster, fifty wives with raven tresses, by the bank
  along the Lethe, in the midst of poppy flowers, never-trembling
  asphodels, where mourning trees will never bow and windrustle is
  never heard;

in the silent halls of Hades, there the wind, in haunted Hades, sleeps
  in beds of asphodels — sleeps and never says a word.

Peter Zollman

LIKE A DOG...

Like a dog in his lowly corner,
always last in the pecking order,
battered and bruised, mud on his shoulder,
faithful, bold, defiant soldier,
howling away, ever louder, bolder,
cold, as the winds turn even colder:
that's how I howl as I grow older
in solitude, in dark disorder,
kicked and muddied from flank to shoulder,
trembling, but ever louder, bolder.

I am left alone, all on my own,
my voice is like the old dog's monotone
or the echoes of a wheezy groan
from a gaping prison catacomb
deep below. (I am the catacomb.)
When it leaves my lips, the tone
is hushed by hundred walls of stone,
for life has washed me in the filthy foam
whose dulling, dumbing mud and loam
has silted up my windows. I'm alone.

Sometimes in my cluttered cupboard
I find ribbons, fancy, coloured
nick-knacks. Faded, quaintly puckered,
fashion fossils, re-discovered
bygone wealth: a sombre record.
And I say: "My children, voices,
pick some ribbons, pick your choices,
cherry-reds, yellows, turquoises!"
And they pick their fancy choices,
my children, the faded voices.

Even so, they remain unsightly,
more awkward, as they fidget shyly
— in hand-me-downs — stilted, untidy,
my beggarly begrudgers deride me,

but the voices just come and hassle,
they come regardless, hatch and nestle,
stumbling but new, in virgin vessel,
struggle through stone and mud abyssal,
they drown and drill and work and wrestle
until their rags drop all in a frazzle.

I question them: "What are you trying
dimmed and drowning, shivering, shying?
Why show your shame to all the prying?
Why should you come here stammering, crying?"
They reply: "Though straying, stammering,
we must come, a word we're ushering,
a word will come forth after our stammering,
we are envoys, road builders, labouring:
A great word, a great word is our future king!
We stammer, but one day he comes conquering."

Peter Zollman

BEFORE EASTER
(1916)

If my lips shred to pieces — oh, courage!
this wild, wild burgeoning month of March,
drinking excitement with trees all excited,
drunk with seething, tantalising,
intoxicating,
blood-bearing, salt-scented March winds,
by grey, heavy skies,
enmeshed in the murderous mill wheel;
       if my lips shred to pieces — more courage!
       if bleeding raw with the song, and if
       drowned by the thunderous Mill, my song
       cannot be heard but merely tasted
       by tasting the pain,
       even so, give me yet more courage
       — oceans of blood! —
       blast the bitter song of bloodshed!
God, we have now heroes to glorify!

the mighty giants' blind, bloody victories,
engines and red-hot gunbarrels
busily packed with cold compresses
for their dreadful exercise:
but I will sing no paean to victory,
the rough-shod iron tread of trampling triumph
is paltry to me,
as the deadly mill of the tyrant:
> the teeming, pregnant winds of March, mighty rush,
> fresh tingling blood, forbid me to sing the mad
> death-machines, monstrous mills, rather
> lovemaking, people, the living
> swiftly flowing, racy blood:
> and if my lips are torn to shreds — give courage!
> in tantalising, salt, blood-scented March winds,
> by grey heavy skies,
> enmeshed in the murderous mill wheel,
where mighty thrones and nations grind to dust,
century old boundaries,
iron shackles and ancient beliefs
crumble into smithereens,
flesh with the soul of twofold demise,
as gangrenous sores
are spat in the face of the virginal moon
and one rotation of the wheel
ends a generation:
> I will not sing the mighty machine
> now in March, when in the air,
> excited by the blustering wind
> keenly we sense the moistness,
> taste the sap rising, precious Magyar
> blood to awaken:
> my mouth, as I swallowed the salty spray,
> flaked into sores, and
> I am aching, weak as I'm speaking.
But if my lips shred to pieces, oh courage!
Magyar song soars in the month of March,
blood-red songs fly, ride the tempest!
I scorn the victor's glorious fame,
the blind hero, the folk-machine,

the one, who spells death wherever he goes,
whose gaze can maim, paralyse the world,
whose touch betokens slavery,
but I'll sing, anyone who may come,
      the one, the first who comes to pronounce the word,
      the one, who first will dare to say it aloud,
      thunder it, oh fearless, fearless,
      that wondrous word, so waited for,
      by hundreds of thousands, holy,
      mankind-redeeming, breath-restoring,
      nation-salvaging, gate-opening,
      liberating, precious word:
      it's enough! it's enough! enough now!
come peace! come peace!
peace, oh peace again!
Let us breathe again!
Those who sleep shall rest asleep,
those who live keep coping,
the poor hero buried deep,
the poor people hoping.
Ring the church-bells to the sky,
glory, alleluia,
new March, bring us fresh blossoms,
bountiful renewer!
Some shall go their work to do,
some their dead to witness,
God give blessing, bread and wine,
give wine to forgiveness!
      Oh peace! come peace!
      we want peace again!
      Let us breathe again!
      The dead do not seek revenge,
      dead souls do not mind us.
      Brothers, if we stay alive,
      leave the past behind us.
      Who was guilty? never ask,
      plant the fields with flowers,
      let us love and understand
      this great world of ours:
      some shall go their work to do,

some their dead to witness:
God give precious bread and wine,
drink up, to forgiveness!

Peter Zollman

PSYCHOLOGIA CHRISTIANA

Even as the praying statues of the sainted,
facing to the outside smoothed and finely painted,
but towards the recess in the wall around them
scraggy rocks, as once the quarrymen have found them:
      such front-chiselled saints are we!

Since our souls were carved out of the ancient bedrock,
stubborn stones still cling on, in unbreaking deadlock,
half-born filthy fragments, sharp and adamantine,
never seen by eyes and never reached by sunshine.
      Help your people, Christ our Lord!

We have heard of carvers, of those pious ancients,
who carved every part with equal care and patience,
whether it was seen, or hidden from the viewer. —
All is seen — they knew — by God, the mighty Hewer.
      Oh, if we could be like these!

Through the eyes of all men we are seen by Jesu;
fear my soul, and tremble, for He truly sees you,
and beware, the shame you see in your behaviour
through your very eyes is seen by Christ the Saviour.
      Help your people, Christ our Lord!

Where can you take cover, your own terrifier,
and a spy too, in the Holy Judge's hire?!
In a drifting sand blow, sightlessly embedded,
unprepared, when Death comes for the ostrich-headed?
      And what will befall us then?

Unconfessed, unseeing, sullied and guilt-ridden
as the years go by, you end up on the midden,
tossed among dull potsherds — till the day is ended,
thrown back in the dark earth, unwashed, unattended.
        Help your people, Christ our Lord!

Who will ever carve us to be whole and simple
if our chisels cannot cut even a dimple,
if we have no hammers, burrowing wheelbraces
reaching in our deepest pain-tormented places?
        We were made for suffering.

Suffering amounts to triumphing in glory:
Oh, the hardened chisels, they will stab us sorely
ere we may deserve it that the King of Heavens
wants us to be statues in his Hall of Presence.
        Help your people, Christ our Lord!

Peter Zollman

A KIND OF CULTURE

You belong to the tired, modern kind
who have forgotten how to think about things.
Words are buzzing, to shroud the things from sight.
Delirious words are prancing, entrancing.
They play, join hands, to form a chain
inside you,
to dart and vanish,
somersaults to turn, headstands to make,
and sometimes you cannot help giving them a shake:
"Culture!"
"Clue: Rut!"
Most profound symbol!
Sound the cymbal!
                *
Things are worth thinking about.
Things go on... go on...
on their own.

As you go too, as you walk in the street,
battle-weary, aimless, loafing,
with a crippled pocket and brain
in which the words are whirling,
and all you see is words.
"Superstout!"
Doesn't it shout!
In letters of fire!
But very soon others begin to tout:
"Lager"
becomes "Regal" when it flips about.
                    *

"Lager" and "Regal": are they linked some way?
Not a bit.
But one can always
have a stab at it,
the same way as the poet links his rhymes. —
For all things are linked,
it's even handier
today, when Belgrade and India
are tied together by one huge metal web
— you too are tied inside it: where's your self-defence? —
two random words cannot be more absurd
than this world
of metal-webbed murderous random events.
                    *

Go then, loaf about, you poorest of them all,
and jangle merrily
not your empty pocket but the small change
of words in your jammed brain!
Fresh words jangle jaded ones,
and crazy words, old brass farthing!
One is worth as much as the other.
Dumb toy.
"My doubt!"
Cry: doubt!
Oh Word! sigh, cry, defy, crucify, shout!

                                        Peter Zollman

A GYPSY IN THE CONDEMNED CELL

There was time when my fingers could shape the world
as the Lord may have created the winged, shiny
articulated, armoured ladybird.

Later, the poem was shaped on my lips in a burst
of brass clarions, as the clarion call
hangs on the soldiers' lips chapped of shivering thirst.

But now as the poem tremblingly, softly appears,
it seems to flow out of sunken eyes
like trembling, shimmering tears.

I do not weep for myself: I have companions,
strangers to joy even in their dreams,
my poor brothers, those pauper millions.

My brother would build a hut in the woods: but logs are not allowed.
He is lucky if they give him a small box
in a huge grim concrete box among the city crowd.

And he is lucky — when all is shattered and he needs a rest
— if he can step over the corridor railing
and good mother earth hugs him to her breast.

The world is bleak! Frightened poems have trembling tunes to play
like a gypsy in the condemned cell.
Humming, fluttering, shiny wings, shoo, shoo away!

Why should the clarion sound, if not for waking the dead?
Only the tears, the tears, the tears keep flowing,
they don't ask why they are shed?

Peter Zollman

THE BOOK OF JONAH

I.

The Lord said unto Jonah: "Rise, go down
to Nineveh and preach against the town!
The stench is high, sin flows in every street,
the filthy foam has fouled my holy feet!"
Thus spoke the Heavenly One, and Jonah went,
but not to Nineveh, the insolent,
for he was loath to wear the prophet's mantle,
he shunned the town and coveted the gentle
piece of the desert and to live without
a stoning by the reprimanded crowd.
So he went down to Joppa's port and found
a vessel for the port of Tarshish bound.
He paid his boat fare to the chief of sailors
to flee the Lord as thieves would flee their jailers!

But lo! The Lord brewed up a mighty storm
and turned it loose some mighty waves to form,
and from the sea arose a hundred valleys
of lofty waves that bounced in rage of volleys,
as though a new Nineveh were built upon it
and collapsed on its own ruins every minute.
The mast broke, the boat tipped, it all but sank,
no plank remained attached to 'nother plank.

The panic-stricken sailors, almost mad,
had now thrown overboard all freight they had;
with faces lashed by horrid brine and foam,
each of them howled his own god's sacred name.
Jonah, having puked as much as one might,
with staggering feet into the 'tween-deck climbed,
down the stairs, to the bottom of the ship;
at last he fell there into dazed half-sleep
rolling to and fro on the shaking floor.

And there the steersman, coming to explore
the damage, stumbled over him and said:
"What are you doing here, you slug-a-bed?
Who are you? Rise and cry the bloody name
of your god — he may help us all the same!
Or have you no god? Which land bore you, stranger?
Is it not you that brought on us this danger?
Which town claims you her citizen, you rascal?
What made you cross the foul waves in our vessel?!"

And Jonah answered him: "I am a Jew,
'tis from the Lord of Heavens that I flew.
What have I got to do with this world's sin?
'Tis only peace my soul seeks pleasure in.
Let it be God's concern and never mine,
I answer not for others' pain and crime.
Let me hide in the bottom, for I think
that I would rather drown here when we sink.
But should you choose to put me ashore, it should
be by some distant, shaded, lonely wood
where I could starve on acorns, cherries rotten,
but live in peace and of the Lord forgotten..."

But yelling mad, the steersman retorted yelling mad:
"Confound you! What's this talk of 'shore' and 'wood'?
Where is the wood? Where could we let you out?
Into the sea alone — and we, no doubt,
will do so, for my boat shall carry none
whose soul is by a secret sin undone!
Now I feel sure our fate was caused by you,
didn't you say it was your god you flew?
No devil can protect whom gods pursue —
hey, men! Come quickly! Let's throw out this Jew!"
And eight hands grabbed his feet, his arms and throat,
lest he should cause the sinking of the boat,
for lead is heavy but the heaviest
is he who by some secret sin is pressed.

But Jonah cried and wailed and groaned as he
was fiercely swung well high above the sea.

"Heave-ho! Away with this unwanted one!"
A splash...The sea calmed down as he was gone,
a gravid monster that just bagged her food.
As for the sailors, they just wept and stood
or knelt and bent their heads in thankfulness,
making rash vows to gods and goddesses —
the rainbow then appeared far in the East.
The marble-smooth sea stirred not in the least.

II.

And the Lord had the foresight to prepare
for Jonah a big whale and bade it fare
his way, mouth open, for to swallow him
in a wash of salt water, scales, and fin,
so that Jonah slipped headlong through the throat
unbroken, lengthwise down that slimy route
to the stomach, and not a single hair
was lost from his head. Soon he woke up there,
dimly conscious, and then with dizzied sight
he blinked into a soft, fish-reeking night.

And so he came into a monstrous thing,
a living cradle that did blindly swing,
and dwelt there three days and three nights alone,
in the whale's belly where midnight and noon
were both alike, where only thoughts did rise
and with serpentine flames soar to the skies
like wild fire from a stifled cave's floor.
And Jonah did then his dear Lord implore
out of the fish: "To you I send my cry
from the depths: hear me, oh my God on high,
see, I am shouting, cursing, I am wailing,
from the mouth of my live coffin I am howling.

"Into the darkness you have tossed me down,
and on the whirlpools of Your sea I'm thrown,
surrendered by the perils of Your brine,
my poor head is by seaweeds all entwined.

Your ample billows have me overridden,
in the depths of your Universe I'm hidden,
into the pit of your world fallen down
who used to perch on top of its high crown!
Once I was Jonah, but who am I now?
I knew your secrets — now what do I know?
Your bouncing waves keep tossing this huge fish
and I am locked up in its slimy flesh!"

And he would breathe, but his lungs could not fill
by sucking wildly at the fish's gill
which was a throng of palpitating flutter,
the breath was scarce he filtered from the water.
The bulky beast did roll and pant in pain
throwing its burden up and down again,
while Jonah, vexed by nausea and hunger,
could hardly bear that foul dark any longer
and howling like a wolf caught in the trap
he groaned: "My Lord! Why have You locked me up?!
You have put me in the darkest depth of mire
from where Your radiant face I can't admire.
And yet, the blind caves of these eyes of mine
don't cease to gaze upon Your Holy Shrine.
I've shot the arrow of my yearning glance
and all this nightly darkness split at once.
Through faith my sharp attention has gained strength:
I see You, God, You cannot hide at length!
It was in vain I tried to hide, for, lo,
You followed me through sea-storms, down below.
You have tortured your sluggish servant hard,
you broke my horn of solitary pride.
The fouler depths I'm falling into, though,
the brighter will Your face come into view.
I see that fleeing You puts one in trouble,
he who shuns suffering, must suffer double.[6]
But neither can You flee me, Oh, my Lord,
though in this whale I've turned into salted lard!"

---

[6] These two lines have become proverbial in Hungarian.

The whale then jolted with a violent shock,
with both feet Jonah gave a mighty kick.
Both of them felt a torment new and fresh —
the fish hurt Jonah, Jonah hurt the fish.

And Jonah said: "Who made me dance like this?
Who will not let me find my death in peace?
You have pickled me in your brackish brine,
you whip me like a top, scarce worth a dime.
The soul in me has utterly diminished,
but my Dear Lord He does not let me perish.
The Shepherd wishes me to be his dog,
and saved my soul from rotting in some bog.
You come, Oh Lord, to unlock all my locks —
so I'll run with baying words to steer Your flock.
My prayer has climbed the steep and airy Height,
and got as high up as Your Holy Might.
Whip me, oh whip me, Lord, for You are wise,
whip, lest I should forget my earnest vows,
for he will find no happiness whatever,
who wastes his precious time in false endeavour."

Thus Jonah spoke. The fourth day came then, and
the Lord, He bade the huge whale swim to land,
it went and spat out Jonah on the shore,
vomiting with him oil and bile and gore.

III.

And God said unto Jonah once again:
"I am your God! You shall rise and be gone!
Go to Nineveh, don't stop on the way,
and preach the words I've given you to say!"

And Jonah rose, to Nineveh he went,
where one could walk about three days on end,
three days along her winding streets and ways
without finding one's way out of their maze.

And Jonah went and on the first day there,
crowded with tents, he found a star-shaped square
and stood among the vendors who at the sight
of his wild beard and sticking, sludgy suit
of ragged clothes, derided him and roared.
But Jonah cried as ordained by the Lord:

"Hear the words that the God of Heaven has sent,
reform yourself, Nineveh and repent,
or you will be by brimstone set ablaze
and swallowed by the ground in forty days!"
Thus Jonah spoke, and stood with eyes blood-shot,
his tortured face bathed in a flood of sweat,
but the vendors around him went on laughing,
bargaining, eating, quarrelling, and chaffing,
and Jonah, sad and frightened, had to steal
away in stench of melons and of oil.

The second eve he found another square
with actors and with mimics playing there,
moving on sand with snake-like nimbleness,
before the folks they shamelessly did kiss.
There Jonah, climbing to the topmost row
of seats, loosed from his shaggy mouth a howl
that made the people think a bull had come;
they all fell silent, shocked, and stared at him,
while God kept roaring from him in a blast:
"Dread, Nineveh, your Lord, repent and fast!
The sun will set still thirty-nine days more,
the town will then be drowned in fire and gore!"

Some women gathered round him; he stopped, and
a foolish flock followed him where he went,
they smelled his stench of fish, clinging to him,
with dreamy eyes they sniffed at his soul so grim.

The third day, with the women all around,
the square before the royal house he found.
They knew him there and waited for him; they
showed him to the hall where the Mighty lay

beside their golden plates and cups and knives,
attended by a host of slender slaves,
and other slaves were dancing naked or
were killing one another with their sword
for fun. On top of an ornate and rich
pillar, Jonah was then put up to preach,
to prophesy them that the world was ending.

Then Jonah cried a terrible, soul-rending
curse on the king and on the royal court,
on the women and on the palace fort,
a curse on mimics, on the actors' band,
a curse on vendors, a curse on craftsmen and
a curse on entire Nineveh he roared,
and hopping down he broke loose through the guard,
and ran across the hall's statues and wardens
through chambers, corridors, and gaudy gardens,
he swam across a pond, climbed down a grid,
all down the gutter's channel then he slid,
through streets, up ramps, along the walls he ran
right out of Nineveh to open plain,
with just one vision in his raging heart:
this town must be destroyed and torn apart.

And he went to the desert where the grass,
devoured by locusts, became very sparse,
where the traveller who the hot sand trod
had his sole burnt, unless with sandals shod.
And there he made a vow that he would stay
there for thirty-eight days, would fast and pray,
and would not leave until with brimstone's flames
the far horizon would be red in blaze,
until a mighty rumble would be heard
and the big castle's towers fall to earth,
and no one in Nineveh would survive,
each one would die with father, mother, wife,
with brother, sister, daughter and with son,
like Jeroboam's family had done.

Thenceforward, coming down from thirty-eight
he kept a careful counting of the date,
crying to his God: "Hear my voice, Oh Lord,
renowned Avenger! Listen to my word!
A vile worm unto worms You did me send:
they lived 'gainst You, without Your punishment.
I would have rather sat in a desert, though,
starving on roots and locusts as I'm now.
But fast and chant to You is empty mime:
for silence midst the guilty is a crime.[7]
Kin will be made responsible for kin;
each man must go the way that You send him.
But the wicked will sneer at what is good,
see how they mocked me, Oh Heavenly God!
They pilloried Your servant, yes, this happens,
for truth and sermons are too weak as weapons,
fine words and prayers here do not much avail,
while battles and Powers' arrows never fail.
I, Jonah, who have never loved but Peace,
of war and ruin now am forced to preach.
Wage war on them, my Lord! And strike them down,
kill the warped race, destroy the wicked town,
because we can have neither peace nor truth,
till Nineveh's flames have scorched Heaven's roof!"

One, two, three, four, and five weeks came and passed,
and the thirty-eighth day had come at last.
The morn, the noon, the evening came — all day
Jonah kept staring where the huge town lay;
it sank into the night then, still there came
from all Nineveh not one single flame.

---

[7] These two lines have become proverbial in Hungarian, especially since
World War II had just erupted. It refers to what Julien Benda called *La
trahison des clercs*.

IV.

For Jonah's words, as God could well perceive,
had sprouted in some hearts buds of belief,
like the good seed that falls onto good ground,
like hidden embers stirred up by the wind.
And He thought: "I have time, I'm in no haste,
the centuries, my servants, do their best;
they shall blow of my spark a mighty flame,
though silly Jonah shall not see this come,
Jonah shall go, others come in his stead."
But Jonah did not know the thoughts of God,

into a mighty fit of rage he fell
and said: "Since I first came out here to dwell,
people have daily come to me from town
to ask me, first with mocking mien or frown,
then more and more repenting and afraid,
how many days were left — to these I said
the number. Lord, You threw me into slander,
for I did lie, and so did my calender.
And God did lie, too. Was that Your intent?
You have confounded those who would repent.
But it was plain! I should have known it, yea!
That's why to Tarshish I would wend my way...
For you are He who turns all bad to good,
He who diverts all evil from its road.
But back unto You now my soul I give,
for 'tis my wish to die rather than live."

To make the tale complete: when Jonah had
left Nineveh for good — here we must add —
he turned round towards the East, facing the town,
and there beside a big-leafed gourd sat down,
whose tendrils webbed the branches of a tree
which had dried out from the heat, so that he
had shade for his parched head, and from below
this bower all day he watched Nineveh glow
through the radiant veils of distant blaze.
And with his gourd Jonah was greatly pleased.

And then one morning the great Lord did form,
early at dawn, a tiny little worm
and sent it to the gourd its roots to gnaw,
so that the trailing tendrils should hang low,
so that the leaves should curl and twirl anon,
the plant should droop, withered before the sun.
It dried as thin as it had grown so tall,
and was then no more bower or shade at all.

And next the Lord He shaped a mighty heat
and scorching, parching Eastern winds with it,
and it happened that the sun's torrid rays
struck Jonah's head and made him faint and dazed,
they made him languid and he felt the ground
and sky begin to sway and move around,
as if once more at sea. His maw was sick
with nausea, and of thirst his tongue was thick,
and thus he moaned: "Oh Lord, my soul receive,
for 'tis my wish rather to die than live!"

The Lord said unto Jonah: "Do you deem
it just to grieve thus and to put the blame
on me, because of that one broad-leafed gourd,
whose foliage has ceased to give you shade?"
And Jonah answered in a burst of wrath:
"Indeed, I'm justly angry, unto death!"
And God then answered him: "You deem it right
to pity a gourd that grew up in one night
and that has withered away in another,
about which you have hardly had to bother,
to which no care, no attention you have paid,
so long as you could loll in its cool shade.

"Should I not pity Nineveh far worse,
that has been built for many hundred years?
Whose towers raise to heaven their rival heads?
That like a conquering army has far spread
into the desert, and where every street,
like a picture book that History has writ,
lies open? Shall I Nineveh not spare

that points right to the future with each spire?
The town that like a giant torch has burned
through ages and generations have learned
their lessons by her light? That long could stand
the fierce assaults of desert winds and sand?
Where many hundred thousand folks have dwelt
who have their homes with toil and patience built,
not knowing — and who could tell it aright —
what they wrought left-handed, or with their right?

"Leave it to me: I will distinguish fine.
Yours are the words — the arms they shall be mine.
Your task, Jonah, is to preach, mine, to act.
Nineveh will perish some day, in fact,
as will the gourd and Jonah. There will come
new Ninevehs in the long course of time;
new Jonahs will come, too, as from the seed
of this plant new gourd-tendrils will proceed,
and forty days or years or thousands more
do mean the same on the lips of God the Lord."

Thus spoke the Lord — Jonah made no reply.
The sun was jogging on across the sky.
Afar and swinging in the heat and haze
the terraced towers of Nineveh did rise.
The monstrous town lay, like a panting and
exhausted beast, all stretched out in the sand.

István Tótfalusi [& A.M.]

JONAH'S PRAYER

Abandoned by my words I'm left alone
or I've become an aimless, overflown
drifting river and in my murky mud
I drag the flotsam washed up by the flood:
old idioms with tired, vain pretences
like broken hedgerows, signposts, maybe fences.
Oh would the Master wisely grant the force

that channels deep, to lead a steady course
toward the sea, and would He fit the rhyme
to fringe my verse perfectly every time,
ready for use by me, his good disciple,
(for prosody I'd read his Holy Bible),
as lazy Jonah shirked to no avail
and then for three days languished in the Whale,
I, too, went down and shared those deadly bays
of hot throbbing pain, but for thirty days,
for thirty years or three hundred, who knows,
to find, before my book will firmly close
and an even blinder and eternal
Whale swallows my last departing journal,
my real voice, to marshal every true
word into action, as He gives me cue,
to speak up loud as it is right and fitting
for all who hear (my sickly throat permitting)[8]
until the powers, cosmic and Ninevean
will silence me and send me to oblivion.

Peter Zollman

---

[8] Two years after this completion of the poem, Babits died of cancer of the larynx.

GYULA VÍHÁSZ
1853-1937

F. Bíró
'71

Gyula Juhász
(1883-1937)

One of the major Hungarian lyrical talents of the first half of the 20th-century, Gyula Juhász was the eldest son of a family of artisans; his father was a postal clerk. Juhász was educated at the Piarist high school in Szeged. He studied Latin at the University of Budapest where he became a friend of Babits (q.v.) and Kosztolányi (q.v.).

He was one of the first writers to recognize Ady's (q.v.) significance. Given to depression, he tried to commit suicide on two occasions. Next to Attila József (q.v.), one of Juhász' protegés, and Lajos Kassák (q.v.), he was the most significant sympathizer of the workers' movement. A social democrat, in 1918-19 he associated himself with the extreme left and even wrote some programmatic papers for the National Theater of Szeged; his poem Hungarian Summer [Magyar nyár], *featured in this anthology, expresses best his revolutionary expectations.*

His love poetry centers around the figure of "Anna," partly influenced by his love for the actress Anna Sárvári (1887-1938), but it is also an expression of a deep-seated general sadness and renunciation. He was a nontraditional religious poet as well. In the figure of Christ he celebrated man's having risen to divine heights; moreoevr, a cult of the Virgin Mary is noticeable in his Anna poems. His lyrics were driven by the music of form; three hundred of his poems are sonnets, but he also cultivated the couplet and iambic free verse.

He is traditionally thought of as "the best artist of the Hungarian landscape — a painter who was working with words." His work did not go without recognition. He won the Baumgarten prize, the most coveted literary award Hungary could offer between the two World Wars, on three separate occasions. In his lifetime most of his books were published in his native Szeged, such as This is My Blood [Ez az én vérem], *1919,* Forget-me-not [Nefelejcs], *1921, and* Testament [Testamentum], *1925.*

Juhász committed suicide at the age of fifty four. His collected works were published in Budapest in 1963 for the first time.

As the poet of Szeged, a major urban and university center in Hungary comparable in size and importance to Debrecen, Miskolc, and Pécs, he is rightfully considered one of Hungary's major poets whose life was marked by World War I.

WHAT WAS HER BLONDNESS LIKE...

What was her blondness like, I can't remember,
but I do know the meadows fair and blond —
when summer yields its wheat, golden and tender,
this blondness makes me feel her spirit's bond.

What blueness was in her eyes? I can't remember,
but when autumn skies open their manse,
in languished twilights of a soft September
I see her eyes' hue as if in a trance.

Her silken voice? Nor could I this remember.
But towards springtime, when the meadows sigh,
I feel I can hear Anna's voice re-enter
from a springtime that's distant like the sky.

Adam Makkai

HUNGARIAN SUMMER
[1918][1]

The fire-charms of summer's flaming legion
Brand poppy-flowers onto the lazy region.

The Tisza almost boils, a muted cauldron,
Hugged by its gleaming banks that grant no pardon.

Silk-blue the skies, whose languid sorrows burn us —
In depths of our rambling desires' furnace.

And in the blond light of the endless prairie
Haystacks heat up. They languish fat and dreary.

---

[1] The year of the Hungarian Revolution after World War I, that resulted
in the short-lived first Communist regime followed by the twenty-five year
Horthy regime lasting until the end of World War II.

The silence cooks as when a silo closes —
In Eastern laze[2] the Magyar summer dozes.

What will it be like when the haystacks' mire
Will catch a spark, putting the world on fire?

When tired of its hundred lazy warlords
The Magyar summer plows a storm with warped swords?

Adam Makkai

LOST BEHIND THE BACK OF GOD

Our provincial city's narrow streets send me a
Tremendous longing for distant India...

The clubhouse is so sad, Gvadányi's[3] portrait hurts —
The Far East's sun-embroidered landscape teases, flirts.

Maybe I should vanish silently in Japan,
Where life is noiseless and death gently greets a man.

Maybe in the New World in an island jungle
I could forget my tortured nerves' aching bundle.

Could it be proud Berlin's cascading sentiment
Giving my spleen musical accompaniment?

Maybe there's a foothold in the distant oceans
Which, like sleeping seagulls, subdues all emotions...

How about returning to the Middle Ages
Finding rest 'midst wafers, chalices and sages?

---

[2] Hungarian poets feel a traditional ambiguity towards the 'easternness' of all things Hungarian, once nostalgic, once resentful.

[3] Allusion to József Gvadányi (q.v.), a minor Hungarian poet (1725-1801), descendant of an Italian count, whose name was Guadagni. Juhász's nostalgia was not directed at Gvadányi's poetry, but his Italianness.

Could it be that there is no spot on this whole earth
Where my yearnings might yet quench their sorry thirst?

Maybe it's the spirits of dead friends — dismal link —
Pulverized hearts' magnet, from yonder, that's calling?

Adam Makkai

ONE FOR THE "ANCIENT GYPSY"...[4]

Where is that old "feast of reconciliation"?
I just cannot see it...Well, maybe our grandsons...
Only in death can I reckon jubilation,
"Feasts" above the surface? How measly their joint sums!

Many a proud dream is vanishing forever —
But it is forbidden to weep by the manger...
It is held against me that I hide and sever
Ties — within my homeland, I've become a stranger.

So I'm outshouted by clamoring nobodies?
— Silently my pain sobs, for I am exhausted —
Mine remains a fate of true Magyar oddities,
Homeless humanity — I'll keep it undaunted!

Adam Makkai

THE DEATH OF SHAKESPEARE

Now in the Golden Stag's mossy courtyard, where
the heartache, the natural shocks just aren't let in,
a merry set who meet each evening here
sit watching the April night as it settles down.
In front, the grey water of the Avon flows,
on the banks, willows sway in a line of grey;

---

[4] An obvious allusion to Mihály Vörösmarty's famous poem 'The Ancient Gypsy,' featured in this anthology.

but slowly the wine bring colour into their eyes,
conjuring up enchanting scenery;
and the early spring and the late drunkenness
make them believe a harp is sounding; they feel
as if the far-off Forest of Arden lies
over the elves like a flimsy veil.
It's nine o'clock, and he comes in just now,
the light of the lamps reflecting cheerfully
on the bold enormous dome that is his brow,
his eyes blue violets, blue sky, blue sea.
And with a gentle gesture, just like one
waving away the whips and scorns of time,
      he raises merrily, as he settles in,
      the cup that always helps a man to dream.
      He says that the evening's very calm; says that
      April's the gentlest month; he mentions his son
      Hamlet, or Hamnet, whom he can't forget;
      his sad voice has the cello's tone.
And now the parson puts away the cards,
and the country magistrate lights up his pipe,
and they're all hanging on Master William's words —
words that resound, bringing the past to life.
When suddenly he clutches at his heart,
and the precious light of his eyes is suddenly dimmed
      like a torch charred, once its flame has flickered out.
      The innkeeper wants to know "What's wrong, my friend?"
      His voice is ringing like an empty barrel.
      He sinks his yellow face onto the table,
      and quotes himself: "The rest is silence."

J.G. Nichols

TO LORD BYRON

It is a child of a subjected land
who leans across to speak to you today,
freedom's hero, whose fate is fine, whose end
not death at last, but immortality!

This land of profiteers, proud Albion,
disowns you, you the best of all her race,
and you belong to peoples trodden down,
your poetry their hymn and means of grace.

Till sighing poplars and sad willow trees
send you this song, this hymn of our resistance,
where rash intruders will not keep their distance.

So even in your grave you find no peace;
at no time have there been such bolts and bars,
so many jails and chains beneath the stars.   *J.G. Nichols*

SONG ABOUT KŐRÖSI CSOMA[5]

From Transylvanian peaks to far Tibet
he sought the ancient homeland of his race;
past holy old Himalayas he set
his feet on paths more old than time can trace.
Onward he marked the runes that told his quest;
he left on desert sands his bloody track;
hunger and suffering his way oppressed,
but forwards till he moved his bivouac.
New light kept dawning on that ancient home
as ever on he walked towards years of yore;
up on the bright old summits would he roam
and fill his parchments with increasing lore.
A colleague he became of Hindu lords
and holy princes in monastic calm;
so from a vanished world he craved rewards,
as August leaves might yearn for April's balm.
Wrinkles on wrinkles spread across his brow;
sorrow on sorrow battled with his peace;
and still the hour-glass would disallow
with its slow curse all chance of death's surcease.

---

[5] Sándor Kőrösi Csoma (1784-1842) walked across Asia to Tibet in
search of an ancestral homeland for the Magyars. He published the first
grammar and dictionary of Tibetan. His bust stands in the British Museum.

He did not thread his homeland's hidden spell;
the road to reach its gates he could not trace.
Ancient and deathless Magyar, who can tell
if an eternal homeland claims our race?

Watson Kirkconnell

VILLAGE NIGHT

Asleep beneath the cold and virgin stars
the house and households heal their daily scars.
    Asleep the clamorous and the strident cocks;
    Empty chicken-runs dream of absent flocks.
Asleep the lumbering freight of trains; and fast
asleep the pub — it dreams about the past.
    Asleep upon the plinth the Virgin stands,
    she holds her smiling son in loving hands.
The sanctuary lamp throws shadows on the walls;
the old night watchman sings out his ancient calls.
    Poor seething brain, you too should heal your scars,
    asleep beneath the cold and virgin stars.

Anthony Edkins

A MAGYAR SCENE THROUGH MAGYAR EYES

Cows on a narrow fringe of marshland browsing,
blurred in the dusk of evening, dim and dumb.
Grey willows hunched forlornly on and on
beside the stagnant water, brooding, drowsing.

All gaze afar, and from the far beyond
a gramophone makes music. The ear catches
a sorry tune in squeaking, scraping snatches.
An old duck waddles in the muddy pond.

The evening, a dreamy painter, as they set,
tints all the clouds in hues of violet —
a blood-like gold on barks of grey trees lies.

The river Tisza borrows the whole palette;
its shining light transforms the silhouette
of my native land, seen through my Magyar eyes.

Godfrey Turton [& A.M.]

HUNGARIAN WINTER

The window of the little inn shows light —
white flowers like a graveyard's, where the sun
sets in the blood-mist of oncoming night
with the moon's faint arc a slowly waxing one

The night drawn near; for us white crosses yield
their overwhelming peace. This loneliest,
this deepest, this most ancient burial field
where all the generations find their rest.

Resplendent sky's campfires, one by one,
are slowly lighted up. Under the sky,
through yard and inn, the noise still going on,
a silent angel softly passes by.

Old tipplers and those sad ones in the still
for one brief moment hear the fluttering wings.
Poor Bodri[6] whimpers, scratches snow, until
abruptly the cuckoo-clock no longer sings.

Stupidity and spirits...What a din!
Grief, superstition, songs and curses' spate

come pealing forth from out the brawling inn
and pound the graveyard's portals until late.

Jess Perlman

---

[6] A typical Hungarian dog's name, like the English 'Rover.'

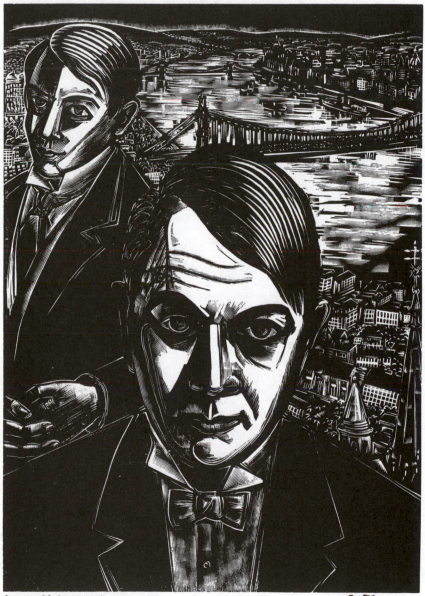

Dezsö Kosztolányi
1885-1936

G. Buday
'41

Dezső Kosztolányi
(1885-1936)

Born in Szabadka (today Subotica in the north of the former Yugoslavia) where his father was the headmaster of a secondary school and where he also studied before attending the University of Budapest, Kosztolányi's first literary works appeared in The Week [A hét], West [Nyugat], *and* Life [Élet.] *Throughout his life he was a popular newspaper columnist in various daily newspapers. He was far less committed to radical reform than Ady, Babits, or the others of his generation. He was a novelist with a keen insight into the human psyche of both men and women. His novels include the dramatic* Nero, the Bloody Poet [Néró, a véres költő], *which appeared in 1921;* Lark [Pacsirta], *1924, a tragedy of parental love for an ugly girl, and* Anna Édes [Édes Anna], *1926, the tale of a servant girl. A brilliant short story writer, he created the character of* Kornél Esti, *an alter ego for himself through whom he was able to project his wishes and fantasies.*

His volumes of poetry include Within Four Walls [Négy fal között], *1907,* Magic [Mágia], *1912,* Laments of a Poor Little Child [A szegény kisgyermek panaszai], *1910,* Poppy [Mák], *1916, and* Bread and Wine [Kenyér és bor], *1920,* Laments of a Sad Man [A bús férfi panaszai], *1922-1924.*

A superb master of his native language, which he zealously guarded, he also had a great talent for innovation. He wrote a great deal about linguistic and stylistic problems. One of the greatest and most successful translators of world literature into Hungarian, his work in this field was of an extraordinary nature — it was more a matter of re-creation than faithful rendering, though he often succeeded in combining both elements perfectly.

His own poetry is dominated by extraordinary sensitivity and by an early preoccupation with death, against which he kept protesting throughout his life. He was an inveterate punster and avid player of language games. He and Frigyes Karinthy (q.v.), would sit in the Café New York in Budapest for endless hours giving each other difficult puzzles hidden in the game of 'Twenty Questions' where the answers could only be 'yes' or 'no.' According to a Budapest legend Karinthy one day announced the death of his wife through this game, and Kosztolányi got to the solution on the seventh question.

As a critic, Kosztolányi objected to the outspoken emotionalism of his great contemporary, Ady (q.v.), calling himself a "homo aestheticus" in contrast to Ady, the politically committed "homo moralis."

WOULD YOU LIKE TO PLAY?

Tell me, would you like to be my playmate?
How would you like to play always and ever?
With a child's heart, looking very clever,
would you like to hide in the dark till very late?
Solemnly to sit at the head of the table
pouring out water and wine with restraint,
yet throwing around beads and pearls and be able
to enjoy trifles and clothes that look funny and quaint?
All these things that make life — would you like to play
a snowy winter and a long-long autumn day,
together, silently, sipping our cups of tea,
with yellow steam, the drink the colour of ruby?
With a pure, full heart, would you like to live
and between long silences sometimes to give
a sigh of fear, when this old man, November,
is strolling on the boulevards and under
our window he whistles now and again?
Would you like to play being a serpent or a bird,
a long voyage on a ship or on the train,
all the good things, a Christmas and dreams
and a happy lover, too, who only seems
to cry, who only pretends feeling blue?
To live inside a play which has become fully true,
how'd you like living like that forever and ever?
And here is a scene: between flowers you lie
on the ground....Would you like to play that we die?

Thomas Kabdebo

TO MY DOG, SWAN

Sit here and guard the household
you, wolf's descendant, tame and milky-white,
you — man-hater of old, to whom our footsteps
cause nerve-wracking alertness, day and night.
Do not allow irreverent destruction

of what was built by hand from brain and soul,
so that your master may, a few weeks longer,
daydream in his tight circle, his closed hole.
Those far from me and alien to my writing
must never come across the wall: outside
the street lies, anyway — the street, this horror
my solitary heart cannot abide.
Stretch out, as a stern statue, on the threshold
and guard the frontier faithfully within
this truthless world you, truthfulness' symbol,
wise Hungarian sheepdog, guardian of my kin!

Now come to me...Just listen to my lesson:
open your dull, shortsighted eye that spells
such goodness, mixed with permanent suspicion:
ensure, guard noiselessness — above all else.
Chase rapidly away those who destroy it
who rattle on, and will not understand
that yet a long, long road stretches before me,
demanding tireless labour, pen in hand.
Do not be angry with the harassed beggars,
who — poor and thin — stand gazing at the gate
in moonlight silhouetted: they are harmless,
and theirs is not an enviable fate.
No, rather watch the literary climate!
Should some sly fellows loiter here, please bark,
and if you notice that they bark about me,
then, be so good, and at them, loudly bark!

Lydia Pasternak-Slater

THE DARK FATES

The fatal sisters — death and cards and women —
stand sadly on life's torturous road.
Inscrutable veiled destiny, what secret,
meant for me, do your robes unfold?

Be you a witch, a fairy — never mind —
you'll be my lover for a hundred nights.

I'll find you in my Friday of misfortune,
to lay my worried forehead on your knee,

and pray to you for help, in exultation,
pray for the word, the meaning, for the key.
My life is slow: enhance it, multiply it
with burning fevers, hotter still than hot!

So secret is this treasure-box — unlock it,
make it let fall the hard, unyielding lock!
Allow fast spinning then to every spindle,
show, brilliantly transfigured, to my mind

life — from the cradle to the coffin dwindle,
and, touching fate with fairy-gentle fingers,
allow the thread of my slow life unwind.

Lydia Pasternak-Slater

LAMENTS OF A POOR LITTLE CHILD
(Excerpts)

Like someone who has fallen between the rails...

and re-senses his ephemeral life
while glowing wheels are throbbing in their strife,
before his eyes wild zig-zag pictures roar
and sees, as he has never seen before:

Like someone who has fallen between the rails —
I farewell the far, the infinite life trails,
for they can become like distant fairy tales,
like someone who has fallen between the rails.

Like someone who has fallen between the rails —
wild panorama, pleasures, shrieks and wails,
between the rails and between many wheels
above my head while sad life's sorrow reels
and death roars into distance, I am grasping

for one second that which is everlasting:
butterflies, dreams, allness and details:

like someone who has fallen between the rails.   *Egon F. Kunz*

Inks of all colours are filling my dreams;

yellow's the nicest. In letters galore
I'd choose it to write with, to write to a little girl;
I'd choose it for her whom I truly adore —
scrawling Oriental signs I would draw her
as well as a sweet bird with lovely curly wings...
Then I'd be wanting the colours, the colours
of bronze and silver, and green and gold.
More than the hundreds and even the thousands,
and more still to follow, a million, a crowd:
fun-loving lilac and grey that is wine-like
and chaste ones as well as the racy, the loud.
I would be needing a sad looking violet,
brick-brown, but also a blue that is squinting
at the shade of the moon through the stain of the window
as August is painting the doorway with its singing.
Also the blood-tones and red ones a-blazing,
like those which the sunset in anger keeps raising
and then I'd be writing, unceasingly writing.
Blue to my sister and to my mother all in gold —
ink that is pure gold would I write to my mother,
in flames like the sunrise the words would be told.
Ever untiring and writing and writing
I'd dwell in my steeple for time and again.
Joyful I'd be then, oh God, I'd be joyful:

colouring all of my life with a pen.

Leslie A. Kery

Dear mum's old picture.

Charming photograph.
She is so young still. Sixteen and a half.
She wears a large cross made of ivory
but secret future sufferings imbue
her sombre hair and velvet finery.
Against the weight of rings and golden bracelets
her dreamy hands are nesting slightly curved,
she rests an elbow lightly on the table
head gently leaning, countenance reserved.
She looks a stranger, quite unknown to me,
the bride of secret fairy-story dreams,
only her eyes, those wistful violets,
they smile at me their melancholy beams.
I see my own self in those wistful eyes,
misty with future dreams she would encounter,
those anxious eyes, fixed gazing in the void.

My soul is circling there around her.

Peter Zollman

I want to kill myself...

Life is so dark.
One nasty leer at me, the slightest one,
and there I'm hanging in the City Park,
or do it like a grown-up, with a gun.
Just let them cry and feel sorry for me,
adorned with roses, draped in inky lace,
with frozen eyes and ivory grimace
I lie asleep in silence evermore.
The young'un gets my humming top, the bells,
the stamp collection goes to some one else.
My little sister or a village boy
can have the puppets and the cuddly toy.
When I am gone, they never, never find me,
my cardigan may ask: where is he, please?

I leave this world it has been so unkindly,
a bitter, disillusioning disease.
They whisper softly: "Sorry little lad,
a tiny angel flew up to the light",
at once I feel so sad for me, so sad
and join them, sobbing: "poor, unhappy mite"...

Peter Zollman

LAMENTS OF A SAD MAN
(Extract)

I am an entry in all kinds of books:

they keep account about my every move.
Some grey and aging form contains my data

where dismal smells of ink fill every groove.
Oh, gnash of teeth, how they have mortified me!
My fetters, shackles are but slavery.

My hands and feet are my members no longer,
my head is but an entry for their count.
I would prefer to live in distant wastelands,

or rot in greasy soil, hid underground,
for I'm an entry in all kinds of books
they keep account about my every move.

Leslie A. Kery

THE CONDUCTOR

Towards evening time,
with few left in the car, he takes his ease.
Would take a seat whilst the tram runs along
with joyous abandon midst the wintry trees.

He stares at the floor of his swaying home;
may well have turned his thoughts to life's elapse —
rattling hollow tokens of memories
he's like a man — a passenger, perhaps.

Leslie A. Kery

FUNERAL ORATION

Brethren, behold, how suddenly he died
and left us here alone: we are cheated, denied.
We knew him. Neither great nor of marked powers,
he was a heart, and that heart beat close to ours.
But now he is gone.
He is dust returned to dust.
The treasure house that could not last
has tumbled down.

Learn wisdom from this sad example.
All men are so. Each a unique sample.
Not one more of his kind has lived or lives
and as no tree has two identical leaves
no other like him shall grow out of a great time.
Look at this head, observe the shine
fading from the eye. Look at this hand,
dissolving into a fog not to be named:
now, turned into stone,
it becomes a relic whereon
scratched in cuneiform, is the rare, brief
archaic secret of his single life.

Whoever he was, he was light, he was heat.
One knew and said it was he, there was no doubt.
How some particular food appealed
to him; and how with lips that are now sealed
by silence, he spoke, and to our ears it would sound
like the chiming bells of churches that are drowned
in the sea's depths; how he said not long ago,
"Darling... I fancy some cheese, I really do...";

or else he would drink wine and gaze content
at the smoke of a cheap cigarette that burnt
in his loose fingers; and he'd run about and phone,
spinning her dream along like a coloured thread:
his unique sign shone clear on his forehead
marking him from the millions, a human alone.

Look for him where you will, it is in vain.
Neither here, nor in Cape Colony, nor in Asia,
not in the past, nor in the abundant future,
will you find him. Anyone can be born
but he. Now ever more
will the vague light of that rare smile be seen.
Fortune with all her magic is too poor
to recreate those miracles again.

To me, dear friends, all this seems to recall
the man, in the fairy tale.
For suddenly life conceived of him, and thus
we began his story: *Once upon a time there was...*
Then the terrible sky broke in on him, and we can
only continue in tears,... *there was no man...*
There he lies now, who fought toward the better:
he is frozen-dumb, transformed into his own statue.
Words, tears, drugs do not wake him, nothing can.
But once upon a time... there *was* a man.

Clive Wilmer and *George Gömöri*

SONG ABOUT BENEDEK VIRÁG[1]

How in the sad depths of old centuries,
back in the long ago, I yearn to be,
when souls in virtue blossomed, and not today,
in this dull era of Modernity!
Weeping, I seek my spiritual home
in a return to long since vanished hours

---

[1] See Benedek Virág in this anthology.

when eyes looked up in worship to the sky
and hearts were like an altar heaped with flowers.
Then people only died when old and grey.
Smiling their withered autumn years away;
with hearts as true as in their years of June,
they whispered loving words beneath the moon.

Among good men would then have been my lot —
yes, even here, where now I note them not.
With Tabun's water-colours on my wall,
I would have lived at peace with one and all.
Here in the window-corner I would sit.
I would go walking with a pale sweet maid,
mutely old-fashioned, or on Gellért's hill
would gravely hunt for insects in the shade.
Frothy new wine I'd drink, still mild and bland;
then, door-key and a hand-lamp in my hand,
I would go home along the dark, deaf street
with rakish shadows round my plodding feet.
Then just to wait — for Death will soon keep tryst —
to read my Horace in the evening mist,
deeply to dream and lazily to rest
and dance on winter nights in Little Pest.
Today, when Earth laps up our blood and tears,
I'd like to hasten back across the years!
Here, 'mid the mottled hills, my neighbourhood,
the "old saint" Virág lived, serene and good.
He'd light his candle with a flint, and then
would scribble Magyar songs with goose-quill pen.

Folk did not recognize his gift divine
that wrought with fervor the poetic line,
smoothing the harsh gnarled words with burning eyes
or gazing in distraction at the skies.
Often I pause where long ago he dwelt
and humbly ask, with pathos deeply felt,
what still remains, his life's lean after-crop? —
A worn old door-step and a tramway-stop.
But oft would I have sought an interview
that with his words he might my soul bedew.

I would have gazed at him with burning cheek,
to hear his priestly mouth austerely speak.
Bohemian in hair and in attire,
I, old-fashioned novice of the lyre,
would, by the hour, have read him what I'd planned,
my poems on *The Ether* and *Our Land*.
Daphnis and Chloë and in lines sedate,
(hexameters of course), *Our Magyar Fate*.
He would have nodded, fatherly and proud,
and I, to take his blessing, would have bowed.

He was a wrinkle-handed preaching sage.
A braided jacket was his worn old suit.
His room was like a snug old priest's retreat.
His cabinet was stored with wines and fruit.
Praising the poet's art with which I grapple,
he would have handed me a rosy apple.

Watson Kirkconnell

THREE SATIRES

1. EMINENT PUBLIC FIGURE

He must attend two dozen funerals
and thirty banquets every year. Assistants
and tape recorders take down his dictations:
condolences and greeting telegrams.
The subject of the economic crisis
"attracts his deep concern". He moans about it.
Meanwhile he puts on weight and tries to lose some
on holidays in Marianské Lazné,
which cost him much more than the yearly upkeep
of two-three families. To start the day
he boxes with his English language tutor.
At work he scrawls his signature — in person —
a number of times, and on these occasions
he turns his tired gaze towards the window,

his misty eyes are dazzled by the light.
He must endure his endless work schedule,
and hold his post to serve the public good,
ignoring reasoned medical advice,
for in these hard, disturbing times his duty
is "work and work" without a moment's rest.
His blood pressure is high. He was instructed
by famous German specialist professors
to rest, and lead a life of moderation.
So now he smokes a nicotine-free brand
from longer holders, seventy a day.
He reads sometimes, especially confessions
by brainless army chiefs or presidents,
"substantial" works on something "serious,"
not poetry or novels. Every night
he straps his earphones on his puffy head
and falls asleep with music in his ears
provided by a jazz-band from Vienna.
He speaks Hungarian, German and some English,
in every language, every time the same old
insipid clichés. That's his mother tongue.
He's said six hundred thousand times: "my pleasure,"
when pleasure was the last thing on his mind.
His memory is vague. On busy days
he cannot tell his mother from a stranger,
and oftentimes her Christian name eludes him.
But then he can remember other things:
the odd phone number, files, some shabby hackwork.
His lifeless face is ashen grey. His time
is up. What are you waiting for? Return
his ashes to the ashes. Bury him.

Peter Zollman

2. THE SOCIETY WOMAN

Six stone in weight and so disconsolate,
she plucks her eyebrows with a tiny tweezer
in public. Tossing back her bony head,
she looks intently in her hand-mirror,
and with a practised movement of her lipstick

she shapes her mouth as scarlet butterflies.
She almost had her breasts removed one day,
(a fashionable surgeon was selected),
but she was dissuaded in the end.
Mind you, she had her way some years before,
when her appendix and some other organs
were found superfluous and had to go
to help reduce her weight. So nowadays
she is quite empty, like an unpacked suitcase,
or like a novel written by Dekobra.
She swims, she flies, keeps fit. She plays some bridge
and rummy too. Of course in better circles.
She played the piano when she was young,
but gave it up. She gives up everything.
She goes for long walks with her tragic life,
and people sympathize. She is the woeful woman.
She's often cold when she is warmly dressed,
and hungry after lunch, "misunderstood
by all," including him, "that decent man,"
— her phrase for husband, father, bread-winner,
although she never touches bread at all,
just aspic, grapefruit, lumps of caviar,
therefore she's independent of her husband.
The poor woman is ill. She has her "syndromes,"
some twenty outfits, thirty love affairs.
Exhausted all the time, her voice is lifeless,
impersonal. The very early talkies
had soundtracks like this, neither close, nor distant,
addressing no one in particular.
Oh Eve, oh sweetest Eve of all the ages,
I see you Eve, when she comes into view,
your silky mane, your lusty, lazy thighs,
your mellow, milky mounds, your moist embrace,
I see you lying, mother of us all,
in Paradise, among reptiles and roses,
beneath the shelter of your shiny hair.
She shows her fancy fingernails to me,
her purple-lacquered, curving fingernails,
and promises to tear me into shreds.
But all this fails to wake my interest.

Not so her maid. When I am asked for tea,
the maid receives me, opening the door,
then in the hall I kiss her on her lips.
And hours later, when I leave the house,
I bow my head and kiss her on the hand.

Peter Zollman

3. THE REVOLUTIONARY

He walks among us. He's a gentle soul,
and very kind. He grows a Christ-like beard
in tangled shaggy fringes. On his jacket
he wears his sympathetic, throbbing heart,
as punters sport their tickets at the races.
His "backward Asiatic country" grieves him,
"they drive this precious land to wrack and ruin,"
instead of leaving him to do the same.
He married young, his bride was thin and ugly,
unlike her dowry which was fat and handsome,
allowing him to "dedicate his life
to high ideals." Yet he is resentful.
His build is definitely on the short side,
his nose is weak, his forehead rather low.
His goal in life is full equality,
a grand re-distribution, in the hope
that next time fate will bless him with a tall
and princely spine, a noble aquiline nose,
and grey cells from the brain-capitalists.
His aim is simple, nothing could be simpler:
to bring salvation to the Human Race.
This is his god. What's family to him,
his children, or his poor neglected wife?
He treats her with unfeeling cruelty,
and lets his mother languish in a garret
while he is junketing in luxury.
He is the great friend of the Human Race.
He ties a mourning band around his sleeve
and cannot sleep for weeks in his distress

when it is rumoured that the Human Race
has hurt its toe, or has a runny nose.
It seems, they do get on extremely well:
the Human Race is modest after all,
it won't knock on the door to beg for handouts
such as warm clothing, money, shoes. Like neighbours,
they live in peaceful quiet co-existence,
a love affair that never fades away.
He doesn't give a penny to the beggars
who stretch their hands of skin and bone towards him,
but gladly gives those hands a friendly shake,
as man to man. This is his principle.
He dreams about the day of reckoning.
On Sundays when the capitalist flowers
are blooming, pimply bank clerks have a pint,
and little ladies, widows on a pension,
are sipping at their tea, after a hard week
of scrubbing floors, when groups of little lads
and little lasses in their Sunday best
are gaily promenading in the street
balloons aloft, and nibbles in their mouths,
he grimly watches their extravagance
and gives his friends a prod as a reminder:
"There will be blood here, soon there will be blood."
Because, as you have daydreams of the future,
of sitting in an orchard of your own,
or reading in the quiet of the night,
he plays with blood, with lamp-posts for the rich,
with rising peasants brandishing their scythes
in deadly parlour games. He runs a blacklist
with everybody entered into it.
He smells a corpse, and hangs new candidates,
not out of hate, but of "historical
necessity." His madness is a threat
to public safety. He is not at risk,
he never harms himself. For this we praise him.
In fact, the public couldn't care a cuss,
this drives him up the wall. On one occasion
he tasted happiness: As he was strolling
along the promenade, a kind detective

walked right behind him, as a mental nurse
would guard his patient, caring for his life,
prepared to save him from an accident.
Then, suddenly he raised a mighty row,
appealed to God and to the Human Race,
to every free and cultivated nation,
the stars, the world, the firmament above.
With blood-shot eyes and manic gaping nostrils
he shouted thus: "Reactionary plot!"

Peter Zollman

MARCUS AURELIUS

Rome still lies gleaming in a yellowish-golden hue
but the sunset smoulders like a wounded lion
while you keep riding above the
Capitol's time-honored summit,
Marcus Aurelius!
Bronze-headed Caesar, bearded in thick gold,
your shining, though blind, metallic eyes watchfully
keep watch, and behold, here I stand before you.
Majestic Emperor,
greatness dignified,
immense heathendom's eternal truth,
who would withdraw from the tumult of stultified mobs,
lonely on the lofty heights of your throne;
you beggar of an Emperor!
You were no fanatic apostle,
no insane follower of some eastern hocus-pocus,
but a royal fellow writer,
with heart and head together,
with a sorrowful sadness and a far-sighted wisdom.
Lonely is the man who in this broad, tormented world,
lives all fear-ridden and who, though trembling,
sees the law, yet calmly walks to the tomb
with the lamp of reason still lit in his firm hands
disgusted with the barbarous,
and everything that reeks of falsehood.

For I will never embrace anything
barbarous, nor will I ever hanker for the witless.
Neither can I fancy the man who secretly talks to
the heavens through his radio, a magician, a sooth-sayer,
or some slip-shod trickster who floats around in nebulous
vapors of fantasy; the crowd-pleasing jerks,
who are fooled while fooling others and who fall down at any sign
with contorted grimaces,
radiating insanity in their looks.
    What I am seeking is one true, proud man,
I yearn for someone who fearlessly senses the soil under his feet,
touching with both hands the awesome, stony truth
of Medusa's slimy reality
and declares: "this exists!" "this does not exist!"
"this is truth!" "this is falsehood!"
and finally throws his own corpse to the worms.
Show me one hero, who in the noontime's glaring splendor
dares to confront the apparitions,
who sheds his tears in the sunlight
while he boldly wears his crown of
splendid, glittering sadness.
    I've been swept away far from the worthless,
trivial sounds of the musicians; my soul flutters
between the South and the West Wind,
but this is how I become freer all the time.
    Here I throw away my mask, then put it on again,
and walk on with a smile, learning endurance,
the not-so-humble virtue of conscious self-abasement,
suffering dirt, harassed, and hurriedly hiding
my regalia which have been torn into shreds.
    May I still lift up my unbelieving, clean,
questingly hesitant, humanly mortal spirit toward you?
I, who came from the hills of Pannonia,
and who live there between the far shores
of the brown Danube and the fair Tisza?
    May I still lift up my heart to
your brotherly heart once more,
                Marcus Aurelius!

Earl M. Herrick

DEEP ARE THE WELLS

What end did she meet, O my God, what end?
Useless to ask, I do not comprehend.

I only know that sad winds pass and blow,
and forests sing and hours come and go.

I only know as fast as fancy's ride,
the timeless cogwheels' rotations abide.

I only know her cleansed shadow is deep
where swaying bays and surging breezes weep.

I only know on life's path sorrow dwells,
and life is deep, and deep, deep are the wells.   *Egon F. Kunz*

THE SONG OF "KORNÉL ESTI"[2]

Start my good song,
start my brave song,
let him who spits in your traces
glint at your flighty graces:
all the pains that throng.
    Keep turning on the top of Life,
into the upper levels of light,
be like Everything,
you, the Big Nothing!
    Don't say either this or that
don't speak lies, give no tit for tat,
what hurts you, you must not admit
beg no comfort — be adamant.

---

[2] Kornél Esti, 'Cornelius of the Night,' was Kosztolányi's famous alter-ego: the court jester, whose task it was to speak masterfully rhymed, paradoxical truths and insights about the eternal and the ephemeral.

Be alive like the grass and the trees,
a wonder in itself, yet one who wonders and sees,
be one who doesn't divulge
his secrets, keep flying, stoop at no bulge.
Be that which is the outer crust
of wise pleasure, the fruit-rind's trust
in its excellent clothing, colored green
on a tree, as the surface of the sea is seen
the appearance of the depths' thrust.
Well then, just run with the drunken wind
zigzagging up and down along the beach
inside and out, both night and day —
everything that flares up and exists
you must reach.
Negotiate with whimsical insanity,
shake hands in mortal danger with the enemy,
and laugh at the busy-body
who yearns for profundity.
What can a diver bring you
when he emerges from the surf?
Mud-soiled his paws on the turf —
this is all that he's brought you.
He sees nothing, when the magic
of the bright waters is dancing,
he keeps groaning once he's reached the surface,
his own chains make him fall on his face,
his gloves weigh a ton,
an officious, frost sternly won
sits in his eyes' glassy gaze
 — Every diver's face is a maze —
where can he go
with his swollen ego?
O woe, how shallow the depths and bare
and how deep can be the shallows —
and how dense wateriness can be
and how morose merriness can be!
We've known for the longest eons
how light it is what folks call 'heavy,'
and how heavy 'lightness' can be
scorned by the grizzly bear.

O, holy emptiness of the clowns
with the haughty paint on top of the heart,
so that it can ridicule the wounds,
when they are still raw, unhealed and bleeding!
O, you hero, whom a merry mask
shields from the scare
of a death-face's mark,
O, how a vagabond rattle
is music good enough to settle
the torments of wheezing
which calms you down by soothing;
imitates jokingly and hits upon real pain
with the prettiest rhyme.
    You should be painting the whorishness of life,
that which you truly are, you should but mime:
how can you still acknowledge a superior
despite your kingly nature?
Laughingly toss aside
the stiff, lazy weight of bored, frozen matter,
and blow into oblivion the failing chatter
of the paralysed, contempted body
with the exercises of the spirit.
    Be then light and empty, rid it;
stay empty, forever playing,
be a seer, but who is seen from afar,
with the silk of a hundred deeply-hued
colorfully fluttering words in the air
like a streamer, or like a soap-bubble,
up, up, be light and start bouncing
in the sky, between the many winds,
and stay alive as long as the soul bids
as beauty and whimsical flights of fancy
because — so help me God — me, too,
I too will only walk that stretch of road.
    Go and be the daybreak above the squalor
dipped in many a playful color,
be like Nothing, you who are Everything.

Adam Makkai

Árpád Tóth
1886-1928

A. Bara
'72

Árpád Tóth
(1886-1928)

Born in Arad (today Oradea in Romania), a poet, translator, journalist and critic, Árpád Tóth was the son of a sculptor in Debrecen, where he spent the first half of his life. He attended the University of Budapest where he studied German literature. After his graduation he earned his living partly by tutoring private students and partly as a theater critic.

During the 1918 revolution he acted as secretary of the Vörösmarty Academy for writers—a temporary post that soon disappeared along with the revolution itself.

After several years of free-lancing and joblessness his poetry caught the attention of Mihály Babits (q.v.) and the critics of the Nyugat *circle, and he obtained a job at the newspaper called* The Evening [Az Est]. *His poems are always cast in impeccable metrical and rhyming form. His favorite form was the "Nibelungian Alexandrine". He suffered from tuberculosis, and as the then fatal disease progressed towards its final conclusion, Tóth's poetry gradually deepened in content.*

The two volumes he published during the last decade of his life were Serenade at Dawn [Hajnali szerenád] *and* From Soul to Soul [Lélektől lélekig]; *in these he clearly emerges as one of the major poets of the first* Nyugat *(Ady-Babits-Kosztolányi-Tóth) constellation.*

Tóth's skills and reputation as a translator equal the very high level of his own original output. The poets he translated include Milton, Keats, and Shelley from English; Flaubert and Maupassant from French; and with the collaboration of Lőrinc Szabó and Mihály Babits (qq.v.) he was instrumental in creating a definitive Hungarian version of Baudelaire's Les fleurs du mal. *He also translated Goethe and Lenau from German, Chekhov from Russian, and many more authors. Babits called Tóth's translation of Shelley's* Ode to the West Wind *the most beautiful Hungarian poem ever written. In his interpretations these poets spoke to Hungarian audiences with great beauty and authenticity. The critical edition of his complete works started to appear in 1964. As a poet he is best remembered for the basic sadness of his disposition reflected by his most frequently used words: 'sad', 'quiet', 'meek', 'shy', 'tired', 'sick', 'dilapidated', and 'languish'. He was familiar with both world literature and Hungarian literature and this profound erudition, added to his natural talent, made him a major 20th-century master.*

RETREAT

Have the gods then loved me here on earth?
Or haven't they? — I do not know.
But golden sun and blue storm were spent
along my road below.

Here have I plucked both flower and weed
that from the moist earth feed their leaf —
the fragrant female pleasures of the spring
and man's autumnal grief.

And I have sung at times. But while
my song grew masterful and deep,
a spur of pain was rowelled in my flanks
and forced my flesh to seep.

A hundred times within my heart
there died, and then was born again,
that fair celestial orphan of our earth:
true Love, born out of pain.

Among hyenas, jackals, dogs
I've boldly striven with all my might;
learning that one must bear, and be maligned
in life's heroic fight.

I have become a murky dusk
who was once radiant as dawn —
even of song I have grown tired at last
my lip is mute and drawn.

You powers above, was this your plan?
Celestial bands, is this your boast?
Escorted by my silent woes I come,
a grim triumphal host.

A darkened spirit, guttering fast,
decked in imperial rags of rout,
I stand before the sentinel's barred gates;
my silence, too, cries out:

"What penalty is this for a man?
In such defeat, what justice lies?" —
And still the icy gods stare mutely down
with their silent, starry eyes.

Watson Kirkconnell

THE PENDULUM

Hoarse is the husky tickling's muffled chant
as often through the night my sad eye sees
eternity, it seems, sway there aslant,
and whittle futile Time to atonies.
> How softly, right and left, it seems to tread
> within the compass of its crystal walls;
> and on my spectral life's parading thread,
> like the Grey Sisters' shears, its knife-edge falls.
Then would I cry to men: "Rise up! Beware!
But Silences within the darkness break
and choke my words. Through leagues of midnight there
> only a myriad pendulums are awake:
> blind, swaying splendours and mysterious miens,
> relentless sickles, golden guillotines.

Watson Kirkconnell

BERZSENYI

Minstrel austere, I honour you with gloom,
you, a colossus out of swooning times,
old Ossa that from Magyar prairies climbs,
dark cape where clouds of Scythian sorrow loom.

The lavas of your heart upon me rest;
out of the flashing of your lightning's bruit

I gather power for my gentle lute,
and hear the panting of your granite chest!

Trembling, I summon up your evenings' mood
as tippling, tired and still, beneath a beech,
you urged your soul to soar to better ages.

Your servants, meanwhile, fearful and subdued,
awaited, Daniel, your sad Magyar speech,
a lion proud that from your lone cave rages.

Watson Kirkconnell

SERENADE AT DAWN

Dawn...and the city's lifeless dirt turns grey.
Beyond it, in the clear and airy distance,
fresh canvas is spread out across the sky
by Dawn, that eminent impressionist.
He draws capricious clouds with a silver crayon
and dreaming them, paints them aquamarine.
Then brilliantly the moon, with pins of gold,
attaches the heavenly picture to the void.

Darkness, unlovely vestment of the night,
falls from the trunks of trees without a sound;
and in the cool eternal forest stands,
voluptuously naked, shivering.
And now, before presenting to the world
its comely body, silently it stretches
until the Sun, that rich old lecher, places
a golden comb in its far-flung green hair.

Imprisoned here among the narrow streets,
grey-coloured Dawn is dreary and defiled.
The flickering gaslight, solitary bloom
of night, has shed its monstrous yellow petals;
and only here and there, queerly ailing,
aflame within the vague and heavy darkness,

a trustful tree or two, a pale green torch,
now blindly swings around the soundless squares.

Sleeping, little Ann? Through the sorrowing streets
alone I saunter in the sad, lamenting dawn;
and to console me, my imagination,
lone Gypsy, plays a quiet violin.
With woods and skies and your smiling lips,
it mutes its music whilst I stroll about.
It would be good to stop now by your window
and sing a sweet and poignant serenade.

I give my heart...Let it be the violin...
My heart from which sadness and desire cry out.
May it transfuse mild sorrow into your heart
and vague desire that flits about forlorn,
so that within your quiet virgin dream,
without suspecting that you shed a tear,
that in your dream, which you'll forget by morning,
you may perhaps lament my broken life.

Jess Perlman

SOUL WOVEN OF SHADOWS

It is my joy at evening to be gazing
at calm large tree-shadows on golden heights:
bodiless body of shadows beyond praising,
whose secret texture with my soul unites.
God wove that soul perhaps from shadows, raising
pinewood and sweetness through the evening lights,
and pensive bliss began to be amazing
and over gentle folds make timid flights.

A dear weaver is God, the soul a treasure.
How often have I drawn its quiet veil
round me, and charmed away — times without measure —
the harsh world's thorny glare; it could avail
to change into companionable pleasure
the selfish din of life; and the grim tale

of hours of hell become a dream of leisure
in a tranquillity of hill and dale.

If sometimes from a brother's blow I smarted,
if one believed most loyal turned out worst,
if idle blood all other toil deserted
for evil's mill, and even God could cast
a jealous look — in dreams the veil reverted;
a mystery cried, "We're all abandoned"; past
all hunger of revenge forgiveness started;
the hissed curse died; sympathy smiled at last.

The trees I loved, the marvel of flowers caught me,
and over books of peaceful mood I shed
the honey-coloured lamplight, which has brought me
still Sesames, when the weary day has fled:
an hour perhaps when trouble vainly sought me,
a cavern which the stream of tears had made
and warmed. In such a hermitage I thought me,
and felt life's sadness need not make me afraid.

With a quiet cigar at dusk it was amusing —
yellow forms moved across a checkered field;
outside, the millstream was already freezing;
upon the hearth an old oak hummed a mild
woodland refrain; its mossy beard was oozing;
somewhere far off it seemed, accordions growled;
Orion moved his huge wings, slowly rising
above the pinewoods in a gleam of gold.

The village doctor and I were always saying
midnight adieus, then lighting up again.
Like trees on which increasing snow is weighing,
my mind was strangely altered by the strain
of knowing, as I left, I'd soon be trying
to make a poem. Bed tempted me in vain.
At last I'd laugh to hear my own voice crying
youth's tortured sweet desire out into rhyme.

So like a timid sailor — shy Ulysses

of tiny scattered shores — I was consoled
by gentler happenings for the storm and stresses
of harsh reality, deceived and lulled,
even to gratitude, by cowardly blisses:
tobacco-smoke, a dirty glass half-filled
with gritty wine, the touch of dreamy tresses,
and several quiet lines my mouth has spilled.

Why then has life become so very painful
and so alarming in this new world? Why
must the last Trump sound every day its baleful
warning, and fatal lightning strike, while I
cast uselessly around myself that veil, full
of comfort once, wild storms tear off? And why
is every cavern, once so soft and soulful,
a crooked mouth now with a hideous cry?

Oh, grey-haired God, by whom our souls are woven,
look at this precious fabric you have made,
until your wiser eyes distinguish even
through tears the separation of each thread.
Oh, will there come a time when they're re-woven,
once this obstreperous hurricane has died?
Or must I flutter into bits, wind-driven,
dark flag fixed on a shore long since decayed?

Edmund Blunden and *J.G. Nichols*

NON PIU LEGGEVANO[1]

Again he made his way through bloody hell;
but as the circle, wrapped in purple cloud,
where sorrow wandered, there he mused aloud.
A sigh rose to his lips; his pen stood still,

---

[1] Italian for 'they were no longer reading' quoted from Dante's *Inferno,* and often quoted in Hungarian as a complaint against cultural deterioration.

as they were reading, he recalled the way
Francesca and Paolo sinned; and how
voluptuous words assaulted them. But now
they read no longer on that tearful day.

As in the darkness of a well's dry base
a bucket glows that sank there long before,
in Dante's eyes a strange grief gleamed unsure.

A hot belated tear coursed down his face:
oh young desire, accursed yet sweet and pure..!
The poet on that evening wrote no more.

Jess Perlman

ELEGY ON A BROOM BUSH

Prone, I stretch myself upon a mountain where it's grassy,
and above me heaps of flowers like little boats unfold;
the blossom of the slim and gentle broom bends over me,
aerial myriads swing, gems of fretted gold;
then like an orphaned giant I gaze upon them there,
when from my heart's depths through my lips I sadly heave a sigh;
to them this is a storm, this unexpected gust of air,
convulsing the defenceless barks, this golden argosy.

Oh happy, happy ships that float upon the airy blue,
with joy in an enriching and late summer afternoon,
endure it kindly, if a lazy giant startles you
with an unexpected sigh, since with life he's not in tune;
endure it kindly, if a stormy gust of sorrow
comes swirling up with sudden strength from worlds you cannot scan;
deep-dug pit-shafts are found there, and no words can make you know
what lies within the depths of this orphaned brute — a man.

Quietly you swing so that cool and silvery showers
as well as thick sunshine with its heated golden beat
seep right down into your depths, enriching carefree hours,
while stocked with scent and honey your frail holds are made replete.
You gather up the dew of dawn like heavy precious pearls;

not for disembodied treasure have you purposelessly striven;
on impossible ambitions no flag of yours unfurls;
not by the stubborn captain, Self-Awareness, are you driven.

I also am a vessel in which the last iota
is compressed into the body by iron nails which flay,
steered on journeys quite insane by a savage mariner,
who will not let it rock to rest its grief in some calm bay;
but the hidden magnetic mountain of being-beyond-being
already is attracting with its spell the aching nails;
no more the rattling wreck's torn by restless journeying,
but on a silent roof in peace disintegrate its sails.

And what about the others... our brother human beings?
The tossed and broken persons, or the greedy boats that creep;
those driven by worn-out sails, by a current carrying
through sorrowful seas of blood, pirates, orphans made to weep.
Oh, how ghastly is the lot of those human vessels, flung
on the modern flood of bitter tears and bloodshed by harsh fate;
perhaps we shall all perish, and there'll be no Noah among
the soiled, whom on Ararat that pure one might await.

Perhaps we will all perish and the world will learn silence,
and only gentle vessels, the countless flowers, will swing;
a rainbow spreads on the grass, on the branches, too, no violence;
and this dumb post-human world will enjoy a silent spring.
Then, quivering with primeval delight, aching matter
will, sighing, spread the happy news that pain's begun to cease;
while trembling virgin lips of an opening lotus stir,
and sweep through that fresh and joyous air on snowy pinions' peace.

Neville Masterman

AN EVENING HALO OF LIGHT

In front of us the road's turned misty-grey
bodies of shades were falling 'cross the park,
but still a soft halo of light's delay
wove through your hair within the twilight's dark.

It shone with a faint, discreet and lovely glow
which was no kin to any earthly light —
'twas filtered into silent scent below
by transmigrating objects of the night.

Yes, scent and silence — secret's eerie scent
was glowing in your hair, stillness and peace,
and it felt good to live, though reticent,
my wondering eyes, drunk with your light, could cease
questioning mutely whether *this* was you,
or was your blessed body The Burning Bush
in which a God came down to earth to renew
his covenant through the tremblings of your flesh?

In deep enchantment silently I stood
and minutes passed, millennia cavorted
you touched my hand, as if you understood,
my heavy eyelids to seeing resorted;
and I could feel: my heart is filled again
with deep, cascading music sounding through
— like flows of blood rousing a sleeping vein —
the earth-made feeling: how much I love you!

Thomas Kabdebo [& A.M.]

UNTIL NEW SPRING OR DEATH

Once more by the roadside fallen, Lord,
I ask myself of my own accord
On this winter night: what did life afford?

What is there then for me to muster —
Barriers, limits, a hopeless cluster
Of colorless drudgery, lack-lustre.

Skies overcast, with scanty blue,
For companions, beggars, a grandee or two,
On broken strings faint songs and few.

Wild raptures in an occasional bed,
One or two months warm-lipped and red,
All over now, heart calm instead.

Here in huge mountains at the last,
Among the diseased another one cast,
I sit facing death, my back to the past.

Can it be otherwise, or no?
Expectant, unexpectant, slow
In the dimness moods and desires go.

And following after in their trail
The old swineherd, black-furred and frail,
Resignation wordless, pale.

I live under quilts of silence, see,
The season of great tranquillity:
I can feel God taking care of me.

Like bushes whose dark berries glow
Aromatic under the snow,
With cool, good things my heart fills, no.

What is their use will then be seen
When the fleece of snow peels down to green —
To a new spring or to death, I mean.

I muse my fate, idly resigned,
And God looks down on me from behind
The infinite night, musing in kind.

Madeline Mason

FROM SOUL TO SOUL

I stand beside my window in the night
and through its gulfs, immeasurably far,
there gathers to my eye a quivering light,
the gentle radiance of a far-off star.

A billion miles or more it came to me
across the chill, black darknesses of space.
Thousands of years it sped untiringly
with none to rack off its celestial race.

Its heavenly message has arrived at last,
safe in my sight from wandering through the skies,
and dies content when I upon it cast
the coffin-cover of my weary eyes.

But through prismatic crystals lured and bent
the self-same ray reveals its parent flame,
and gives us news of many an element
related to our earth and my sad frame.

I drink it in. Locked in my veins it throbs.
And dreamily, in silence, I can feel
what ancient sorrow to my blood it sobs,
when timeless griefs the heavens to earth reveal.

Perhaps the stars feel pangs of lonely heat,
being a million orphans lost in space?
Perhaps they mourn because we cannot meet
across the icy night through which we pace?

Why weep, O star? No further do you stand
than human heart of earth from human heart.
Ah, who can tell if, at my own right hand,
my friends, or Sirius, move more apart?

Alas for friendship, and alas for love!
Alas for the impervious road from soul to soul!
Rays from our weary eyes unceasing move,
but icy voids of night between us roll.

Watson Kirkconnell

Frigyes Karinthy
(1887-1938)

Hungary's greatest modern humorist and satirist, Karinthy, who was of Jewish ancestry, was a prolific short story writer, essayist, and playwright and a strikingly individual poet. Much of his life was spent in journalism and in writing short theatrical sketches and other ephemeral material for the minor theaters of Budapest. *His brilliant sequels to Swift's* Gulliver's Travels— Journey to Faremido [Utazás Feremidóba] *in 1916 and* Capillaria *in 1921— together with his haunting autobiographical* Journey Around my Skull [Utazás a koponyám körül], *1937, are integral parts of world literature. Karinthy was a magnificent parodist and a ruthless but never pompous social critic. His poetry was a mixture of carefully polished, effectively classicist and broadly-rolling, Whitmanesque verse. It was collected in the two volumes* I Cannot Tell It to Anyone [Nem mondhatom el senkinek] *in 1930, and* Message in a Bottle [Üzenet a palackban] *in 1938. He is one of the most widely translated Hungarian writers.*

Hungarians remember him for his extremely witty volume of parodies Így írtok ti [This is how YOU write], *in which, for the first time in Hungarian literature, the major Hungarian poets were held up to a funny mirror. Karinthy succeeded in characterizing the peculiarities of each of the poets so powerfully that generations of Hungarian readers first learned about the poets from Karinthy's parodies rather than from the originals. Many of Karinthy's parody lines have become proverbial.*

He was particularly successful in poking fun at Endre Ady (q.v.), who was fond of repeating lines; at Mihály Babits (q.v.), who showed an excessive fondness for alliteration; at Gyula Illyés, Attila József, and Lőrinc Szabó (qq.v.). Together with Dezső Kosztolányi (q.v.), and a few other writers, Karinthy would sit in the famous New York Café and hold literary court. Being invited to his table meant instant fame and recognition. Karinthy and Kosztolányi played extremely sophisticated verbal games.

His own poetic language is a unique blend of elevated Biblical diction and colloquial turns of speech taken from modern usage. He sensed the approaching age of Fascism, which he chastised from the point of view of radical bourgeois liberalism. His son, Ferenc Karinthy (1921-1992), who became a well-known novelist, contributed to the spreading of personal anecdotes about his famous father, whose name cannot be separated from modern Budapest wit and Hungarian humor in general.

THE MESSAGE IN THE BOTTLE
(The Poet Is Asked Why He No Longer Writes Poems)

(A few illegible lines, then:)
"...my fingers
are frozen. This bottle's in my left hand. The right
holds the joystick. It has grown very stiff.
There's thick ice on the wings. I don't
know whether the engine can take it. It makes Queer
snoring noises in here. It's terribly cold.
I don't know how high up I am
(or how deep? or how far?)
Nearness and distance — all empty. And all
my instruments are frozen: the scales
of Lessing and the compressometer of the Academy;
the Martinetti altimeter, too. I think
I must be high enough because the penguins
no longer lift their heads as my propeller
drones above them, cutting across
the Northern Lights. They no longer hear me. Here are
no signs to see. Down there's some rocky land. New land?
Unknown? Ever explored before? By whom? Perhaps
by Scott? Strindberg? Byron? Leopardi?
I don't know. And I confess
I don't care. I'm cold, the taste
of this thin air is bitter, horribly bitter...
It could be that my nose has started to bleed.
I'm hungry... I've eaten all my biscuits.
Some unknown star keeps blinking
at the point I gaze at. The pemmican
has gone maggoty... What star can that be?
Perhaps already... from the beyond...? And what's the date?
Wednesday? Thursday? Or New Year's Eve? Who could be
sitting around the homely hearth? Little brothers,
singing birds,
beside the anxiously guarded hearth
of petty feelings; bird brothers in the depths
of the human heart's jungle... Hallo! Hallo!
Is there no one to hear this exiled fellow-crow, myself?

A little while ago
something crackled through the rusty antenna of my radio...
I hear that Mr. D. has found a fine adjective
in Banality Harbour
while C. has discovered a new metaphor
between two rhymes in Love Canal.
The Society's reporting it. Congratulations!
I'll...tell you all...that I...
when I get home...and...land...
all that I...felt up here....only when
he escapes.....can.....the traveller....relate it.....
But does he ever escape to return?
Now I put these few confused lines
into the empty wine bottle
and drop it through the hatch. Like rolling dice!
If an uncouth pearl-diver should find it, let him
throw it away, a broken oyster,
but should a literate sailor find it,
I send this message through him:
    "Here I am, at the Thirteenth Latitude of Desolation,
the Hundredth Longitude of Shame,
the utmost Altitude of teeth-gnashing Defiance,
somewhere far out, at the point of the Ultimate,
and still I wonder whether it is possible
to go any farther...

Paul Tabori

MENE TEKEL

First hear, then repeat what I say; it's rhymed
The better to keep it fixed in your mind.
        I engrave it within your heart: no doom in
        This world could be worse than being human
In this age, whose book-keeping records cheat:
False entries each day on your balance sheet.
        The man was enticed in the midday light
        And the phantoms howled in the deep of night.
They lamented Christ on his cross of pain
But hailed the killer as hero again.

He guzzled the blood, and the brain she swallowed,
While out on the pavement the poet bellowed.
The dead were adorned in silk and brocade;
The living puked blood and their clothes were frayed.
The graves were garnished with garlands of rose;
The living hunched frozen under the snows.
Loud promises on the coffin were made;
The dead wailed softly while they knelt and prayed.
With eyes open wide the child looked around;
The old people crouched and uttered no sound.
But he — a disciple in days gone by —
Mean cutpurse — he spat in the master's eye.
Frigates went speeding through fiery seas
And the whore's gaudy rags flapped in the breeze.
But the best and brightest of the lot
Was left like a dog on a dunghill to rot.
Now, tearfully clenching my hands, I implore you —
Take care, the account's being entered for you.
Safe in your heart, in your ears, let it stay —
You'll know how to read it, on the right day.
MENE TEKEL — you may not comprehend it,
But take note: it is for you I intend it;
My words in the dark, so hushed and so small,
Are written like flame on Belshazzar's wall.
Today they may seem to be grey and blurred,
But mark them carefully — mark every word:
When I'm stilled, they'll be heard.

Aaron Kramer

DANDELION

Towards your hand,
Towards your hand, your hair
Towards your hand, your hair, your eyes
Towards your hand, your hair, your eyes, your skirt
Why this snatching? — You ask me always,
Annoyed and loudly, or shaking your head in silence —

Why not soft and gentle caresses,
Yes, well behaved, like others would do it,
Why this snatching, and in my eyes a twinkle
And worse still, I am laughing — impudently!
It is so strident, rude and ear-splitting!
You'll leave me here at once, or smack my hand!
Flower, don't leave me, I rather tell you
I tell you — I breathe in your ear, wait,
Just smooth this curl away now.

Towards your hand,
Towards your hand, your hair
Towards your hand, your hair, your eyes
Towards your hand, your hair, your eyes, your skirt
What keeps snatching — you still cannot remember?
What keeps snatching — you still can't think of it? —
Though you've this same expression
Always when, annoyed, you try to fend it off
Holding your hair, your eyes, your skirt against it.

Towards your stem
Towards your stem stamen
Towards your stem stamen pistil
Towards your stem stamen pistil petals
What keeps snatching, flower? — The wind!
The wind, the wind, impudent, fickle wind
Chirping cheerfully, seeing you annoyed.

Flower, what next?
This was just a light breeze
This can only snatch and chirp away,
But now I have to speak to you about my family,
Listen, I say!
Proud, Trumpeting Tempest was my father —
          The famous Typhoon of Arkansas my mother,
A whirling tornado married my sister —
Fair flowerfluff, have you ever wallowed exalted — exhausted
Hoisted on a heaven-piercing hurricane?
So don't smack me now on the hand, dear.

                                                          Peter Zollman

STRUGGLE FOR LIFE

Brother, it seems, you have been beaten.
As Law decrees and Precept goes —
Your corpse is sniffed round by hyenas
And circled by the hungry crows.

It's not the pack who were the stronger,
Smaller beasts beat you to tatters —
And who fights now over your carcass:
Jackdaw? Jackal? Hardly matters.

Your fist when it was time to use it
Always stopped halfway in the air —
Was it Charity? Weakness? May be.
Fear? Pride? Modesty? I don't care.

Or mere disgust, perhaps. So be it.
Good. Amen. I accept the terms.
I prefer that worms should eat me
Rather than I should feed on worms.[1]

Peter Zollman

---

[1] These two lines have become proverbial in Hungarian.

Lajos Áprily
(1887-1967)

Born in Brassó, Transylvania (today Braşov in Romania), Áprily studied German, Hungarian, and classical literature at the University of Kolozsvár (today Cluj-Napoca in Romania), and became a teacher in the high school of Nagyenyed. In 1923 he received a diploma as teacher of French in Dijon, France. He subsequently settled in Budapest in 1929, where he became a teacher in the Preparatory Academy of the Hungarian Reformed Church.

He belongs to that generation of Transylvanian Hungarian poets who, born in the Austro-Hungarian Monarchy, had to live through the tragic dismemberment of Hungary in the wake of the Versailles Peace Treaty of 1920. He also had to live through World War II, and witness the ill-fated return of Transylvania to Hungary for a short six years as a questionable gift from Hitler. He lived through the Hungarian Uprising of 1956, dying ten years later. As a result, his poetry is what may be termed quintessential Transylvanian pessimism, but not without an occasional outburst of irrepressible joy in life, as can be seen in his poem 'March in Transylvania.' *This poem, which was written in rhyming dactyls, poses an unusual challenge for any translator. It appears in English here for the first time.*

A brilliant translator, he rendered Ibsen's Peer Gynt, *Pushkin's* Eugene Onegin, *and numerous Romanian poets into Hungarian. His son, Zoltán Jékely (q.v.) was an equally brilliant and prolific translator.*

His poetry gave the classical forms a supple, individual life with a special "Transylvanian flavor." His volumes include Abel's Smoke [Ábel füstje], *1957, poems and one-act plays, and* Report from the Valley [Jelentés a völgyből], *1965.*

Although he belongs to the generation of Nyugat [The West] *in terms of his birth date, in Hungarian literary history he is considered as one of those poets whose career started after the collapse of the Austro-Hungarian Monarchy in 1918. Áprily's poetry is like the craft of his Saxon goldsmith ancestors: polished to perfection. As editor of several literary magazines, he developed the reputation of "Elder Statesman of Hungarian Poetry."*

His popularity was so great that in order to satisfy public demand, an entire residential district north of Budapest, near Szentendre was named Áprily Park [Áprily Liget] in his honor.

ANTIGONE[1]

The sun, dear Haemon, in its far domain
unties the hawser of its crimson boat;
across the dew-bright grass of Dirce's plain
the ocean breezes of the morning float;
and when night comes, the yellow dust will blow
and hide my footprints that so lightly lie —
      black is the sand of Acheron[2] below;
      here, my dear Haemon, we are doomed to die.

What should we seek for, we, a lonely pair,
where hatred reaches to the sky above?
I was not born to hate, this I declare,
yet here it is not possible to love;
my forebear's curse, alas, a wail of woe;
shrills through my destiny with evil cry —
      black is the sand of Acheron below:
      here, my dear Haemon, we are doomed to die.

Here we are doomed. Who knows the face of Fate
and in what space of time its light, now dim,
will brighten to give man release from hate
so each may love the brother true to him?
Though downwards, cursed by laws, my soul may go,
of a new world I'll dream with pensive sigh —
      black is the sand of Acheron below;
      here, my dear Haemon, we are doomed to die.

Watson Kirkconnell

---

[1] The allegorical borrowing of the tragic figure of Antigone from ancient Greek drama is characteristic of Transylvanian indirectness. Áprily is comparing the fate of Transylvanian Hungarians to Antigone, the heroine of the famous play by Sophocles (442 B.C.), who buried her brother despite King Creon's orders not to do so. Antigone has thus become the symbol of unwritten moral law as opposed to the false rights of external powers and the state.

[2] The name of the main river of the underworld in Greek mythology.

MARCH IN TRANSYLVANIA

The sun-flames of springtime
turned student to wind-chime
he climbed up the mountain
he stands on the peak.
Bursting with laughter
his mood circles after:
his ancient "Hurrahs" the light-giver seek.

Waves from a dry lake
swell like a mud-cake,
water erupts from the wells with a burp.
Coal-headed titmouse
chants in its playhouse
beats dithyrambs with its dactylic chirp.

Silks of the catkin
peer through its flat skin;
dogwood's in blossom, all yellow and pink.
Light dashes streaming,
noontime's a-beaming
glaciers grow gluey and gulp as they shrink...

Brown rivulets scream
filling the main stream
floods to the lazy Maros[3] river dart.
Songs shake the high ridge,
songs fill the rain-ditch —
does a song, silly song, happy song, fill your heart?

Adam Makkai

---

[3] The Maros river, which originates in Transylvania, is the largest left-bank tributary of the Tisza, which it joins at the city of Szeged in southern Hungary.

NIGHT IN KOLOZSVÁR

Soft moonlight shines upon the corner store;
with acacia flowers the cobble-stones are strewn —
The old town does not know me any more,
    nor the old moon.

Stones of the old path worn so long ago
I pace with eager steps, mourning my lot.
And the acacia branches whisper low:
    "We know him not..."

Out through an open window in the night
a song wings softly like an autumn bird.
Both song and voice are unfamiliar quite,
    till now unheard.

I lift the latchet of a garden gate.
"Stranger!" — it clicks in metal monotones:
and at the sound my breaking nerves vibrate
    in stifled moans.

Roofs in moonlight, flowers' delirium,
love-song and fire and wonder in the heart —
no longer mine! Ahasuerus, come...!
    Let us depart!

                  Watson Kirkconnel

NIGHT SONG

Indoors I sat, with my two sons,
upon a couch, a fire-light plain;
night, the brown beggar, sad and blind,
crept slowly in, as if in pain;
upon the window pattered loud
the drum-beat of the autumn rain.
       My arms on either side embraced
       the slender bodies of my boys.
       A three-fold shadow on the wall

behind us seemed to shift and poise.
And with the night, the Tales of Grimm
to merry thoughts had turned out thought,
although, outside, the morning wind
with notes of boundless grief was fraught;
will they — it seemed to say — aspire
in a new world new Spring to find,
with proud eyes worshipping the light
upon the summit of mankind?
Or dropping into whirling tears
will each dream perish after all?
And plucked of feather, clipped of wing,
so near the summit, will they fall?
From the soft lawn will life's path sink
down to the wild and horrid fen,
to treacherous swamps, appalling mud,
to blood again, oh blood again? —
Indoors I sat with my two sons,
and like a giant python near
shadows behind our fire-lit couch
within the chamber seemed to rear.
My arms were held protectingly
about my boys, so slight and small.
(The shadow grew immense and black;
it grew behind us on the wall.)
Hawk-headed pain swooped down on me,
blood-kin to pangs now past and gone —
and on the walls, as dark as fate,
above us loomed Laocoön!

Watson Kirkconnell

THE VICTOR

The loot the legions sent embraced these three:
treasure, and slaves, and slips of cherry-tree.
    The treasure sank like mercury from sight
    amid the orgies of the city's night.
The slaves were slain to make a holiday,
with blood and flame and gladiatorial fray,

or nailed to crosses by the highway's side;
in endless choking lines they writhed and died.
But still, across the gardens, fires of spring
burst from the cherry-tree's white burgeoning,
until my little son in wonder stands:
"Ah, pretty, pretty!" And he claps his hands.

Watson Kirkconnell

NOSTALGIA

How strangely beats my troubled heart
'midst blare of noise and blaze of light,
to seek my cave of calm again
I greatly yearn to take my flight.
I crave those quiet vaults of stone,
the darkness of my ancient lair,
amid whose labyrinthine peace
I heard my pulse upon the air.
My now enkindled cavern fires
where pain was by the rocks concealed;
my grief within the darkness loomed —
stalagmites, shapeless and congealed.
And if a murmur reached those depths
from outer worlds, I heard the race
of rainy tempests, and a stream
poured downward through my hiding-place.

Watson Kirkconnell

THE STAG OF *IRISORA*[4]

Dawn broke. The pile of clouds kept growing softer
as it slid downward toward the silent trees —
'twas in the jungle of wild and lofty fir

---

[4] A mountain in the Carpathians, today in Romania. The poem is a further manifestation of the 'stag' theme of Hungarian poetry — in this instance it symbolizes captivity, alienation, and the unexpected discovery of one's ethnic and cultural roots.

that mountain shepherds found the little beast.
      So soon enough a mountain-dwelling trapper
      took him down on his back to see the boss —
      they shook hands on it — 'twas a simple matter —
      some mountain-gin, tobacco — no one's loss.
The Simmenthal-cow made him her own gladly
strange though he seemed behind her smallish fence,
the orphan suckled eagerly and madly
forgot his past and sensed no difference.
      And he forgot the tiny mountain river
      which laughed and made summersaults in the air
      hiding his body in cool twilight's shimmer;
      and he forgot how free he had been there.
And he forgot the small pool of the fountain
whose mirror gave a cool, seductive puff,
and when, succumbed to dehydration's taunting,
he drank from his sun-beaten, lukewarm trough.
      He could not see his noble mirror image
      reflected, when his youthful antlers grew —
      had no idea of his proud lineage:
      grew up a calf among calves in his mew.
And he became an antlered barnyard creature
causing the hunters' hearts to skip a beat —
and he just gazed, not guessing at the feature
that made the tourist eyes stare at the treat.
      But toward summer's end when from the glaciers
      the autumn poured down winds and blueish fogs,
      from unseen heights of moist, slippery dangers
      stags' mating-calls were bellowing from the bogs.
And then: his mouth started to wheeze and tremble
his cows' corral became foreign to him
stepmother-cow, calves he'd no more resemble,
and boomed in the fog like organs boom a hymn.

Adam Makkai

ON THE WALL OF MY AGE

I lived here, too. On prison fare and water,
here I revolted and here I finally broke
in this grim time-cell, on my wing and fire,
a blind warden turned the key in the lock.
> But sometimes beyond the iron-barred time
> meadows of stars lit by a distant race
> a wind rose and my flagging lungs were filled
> with the pine-wood scent of unending space.
I shook my shackled wings at such rare times
and would have soared into free and great domains,
and looked to the ancestors, free and wealthy
old masters who moulded their precious gold.
> And thought that after a good hundred years
> the new world's sun shall shine upon his face
> and he whom his age plundered, made a beggar
> will find compassion in his grandson's gaze.   *Paul Tabori*

PLEA TO OLD AGE

Old age, wise curber of the blood's ebullience,
teach me to come in silence to my Silence.
> Do not incite me to complain or bellow,
> from a blustering make me into a taciturn fellow.
And, unlike the loquacious swallow, even
let me be a rare talker like the raven.
> Of my communicativeness fill the well,
> let me be a Carthusian in a cell.
Only the rumbling streams chatter ceaselessly,
rivers arrest their turbulence near the sea.
> Save me from people with mouths like gushing brooks,
> and from the dense forest of words in books.
Give me only words with roots. And smooth and rough
a short word at the end would be enough,
> the question "Are you ready,?" in one stress,
> while seeing the shore yonder, answering "Yes."

Doreen Bell

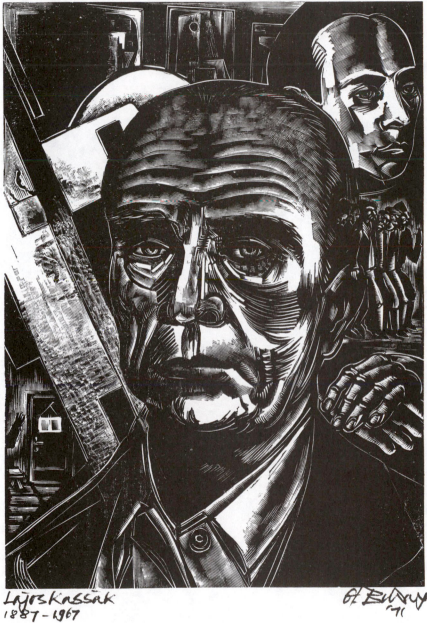

Lajos Kassák
1887 – 1967

Gf Buday
'71

Lajos Kassák
(1887-1967)

Kassák was a completely self-educated proletarian poet who also became the most original and the most daring leader of the early Hungarian avant-garde. Working in an iron foundry, he became an ardent Socialist while only a teenager. At the age of twenty-two, he walked through Austria, Germany and Belgium. He was eventually repatriated to Hungary by force. He was an active participant in the short-lived Soviet-type Hungarian Communist regime, during which he engaged in bold polemic with Béla Kun, the Head Commissar of the dictatorship.

After the 1918 Communist revolution he went into a long exile. His review, Today [Ma], *provided the necessary forum for many experimental and progressive writers. In 1926 and founded a second review* Work [A Munka] *and managed to survive the long, harsh years of the Horthy régime and of Nazism. He had meanwhile become a much-honored poet of the post-1945 years, but was silenced during the Stalinist era in spite of his firm left-wing credentials.*

His closest links to world literature were through Walt Whitman, Apollinaire, and Georg Kaiser. His rhetoric is never empty pathos and, at his best, he has given the age-old themes of protest, pacifism, and humanism new meanings in new forms. His main prose work is an autobiography in eight volumes. His poetry has been collected in the volumes Bonfires Sing [Máglyák énekelnek] *in 1920;* The Horse Dies, The Birds Fly Away [A ló meghal, a madarak kirepülnek], *1922;* My Mother the World [Világanyám], *1920; and* The Book of Purity [A tisztaság könyve], *1926. He also wrote numerous short stories, several novels, and a number of plays.*

Kassák was also a successful and prolific painter, typographer and graphic artist. Literary historians enumerate four periods in his stylistic evolution. In the first, he deliberately turned against literary traditions. In his second phase he developed free verse to its utmost limits, not only in terms of form but in terms of content as well. His social disenchantment was reflected in the amorphousness of his writings. His third phase was that of extreme formalism. Finally, in his fourth phase, he broke with the avant-garde and became more balanced and classicist in style. He also wrote lyrical pieces reflecting mature old age and making his peace with the world. Today he is mainly popular among the younger poets of the avant-garde.

MY POETRY

I ought to hurry up in order to save what can be saved
but instead all I do is sit
heavy, like a slab of stone
or like that big bird
I once killed when I was a youngster she bled to death in the shade of
a willow tree wounded and dumb.
In an unknown part of the world in deep silence
I write my poetry which is simultaneously on the customary side
and outside the grooves of habit
which the fools adulate.
To hell with pre-manufactured beauty
and inherited hand-me-downs —
my poetry is not the product of hazy dreams
but out of geometry's logical order
it peels off the rind of fruits
arranges the object in space
sweeps away the garbage of the past
and promises a happier future.
This is the essence of my poetry, its truth, this is the content of my
words the meaning of my testimony some regard as meaningless
my poetry is a fire-fall
and a tinkling of icicles
which due to the law of opposites
fills and evens out
the world's unknown regions.
      It's not my heart alone that sings now
      neither is it language alone.
      The blue tears of my eyes
      the white calcium of my teeth
      my body's classic frame
      the indecipherable convolutions of my mind
      the millions of hairs on my head
      my hand's ten fingers
      ten mesmerized members
      of an orchestra playing in unison
      to tell the world that I exist.

I sing both in light and in the dark
for the benefit of all who were born under an adverse constellation
or came to grief as they got older
for those who can't hear
for those who can't see
for those who have lost their faith
for those possessed by foolishness
for those who commit suicide by leaping from a mountain top
for those who're too scared to emerge from their caves.
> I sing
> so that others
> may pick up on my tune and echo it
> from the depths of their fate
> and be fortified
> so they can head in for the shore
I sing wherever the womb of life is in labor
I sing wherever the seed planted in the soil starts to swell
I sing wherever the barn-door doesn't have a padlock
I sing wherever the shepherd doesn't abandon his flock
I sing wherever humans can recognize a brother
who takes matter and tools in his hand
> to create signs
> scarlet red like blood
> black with pain — talking about the meaning of his life.

Adam Makkai

THE FACTORY

Its expanse is gigantic
a structure of engineering hot and cold continuously emitting
eager and frightful sounds like herds of elephants.
Once it was my home;
today it is the river of the past contaminated with oil and soot;
home to the people of tools and materials
who rebel at times
to tear a piece of bread
out of the iron

from the merciless machines
and from safes.
Its walls and gates
are black from the curses of generations.
Its huge chimney stacks
feed smoke to the wandering clouds.
Neither flowers nor birds live in their vicinity.
Humans alone are capable of survival hereabouts.
          Once it was my home;
          the source of anguish and sorrows —
          I have not departed too far from you.
          I still have no glasses with gilded frames
          nor white collars with black bow-ties
          I do not loiter about staring at shop windows
          where lace panties and blood-red nail polish chant in unison.
          With my glance
          I guard your indigenous laws.
My weakened lungs
the ten fingers of my hands
the bent contour of my back
and one thousands five-hundred poems
born inside my heart
are blooming now with a reddish-black colour
and they all remind me of you.
          Often on my I turn back to see
          with open eyes with more of a gleam in my eyes
          to see that you're not the old monster
          of stones and iron any longer.
          You bathe in the rays of the sunlight
          and dry yourself in linens of smiles.
          You disgorge your filth
          like someone who's overstuffed himself
          and you kindle the lamps
          and prepare a bed for those who're exhausted.
You're no longer as merciless
and so neither are you so heavily bombarded with curses.
Those who enter your gates
aren't heading for the torture chambers any longer
and those who leave coming through your gates

aren't trying to escape any more.
>Leaning against a post
>I look at the streets stretching in front of the people
>and the houses that welcome them.

Michael Kitka [& A.M.]

TO A HOOLIGAN GIRL

If there is still some room left in your heart
for a bird
for the bird of love with a beak purple with blood
you listen to me.
If there's still some room in your heart
for tormented love
listen to me
you, with the pony-tail hairdo
and those black stockings
you, wondrous craze of our age.
>Listen to me
>with your lips shut tight and your eyes closed.
>Listen, just listen
>I'll guide you over to the country
>that I dreamt for you — yes, for you alone.
>Long is the road I say the road is long
>cracked up by rocks and dark is this road —
>the poor folks tread there, barefoot
>their faces are wet with tears, their voices
>choked off by cursing
>yet held high they carry an invisible flag in their hands
>on which the words 'freedom' and justice' are plainly
>inscribed.
>This was the road I, too, walked throughout my life
>burdened by the wretchedness of dirty little games
>I refused to play.
I am no source of happiness
nor was I born into this world as a white sheep
but you listen to me nonetheless

you fluttering sprout of a hazel-bush
exulting in the mirror of flattery
you heart-wrenching goodness
I guide you to the country
that I dreamt up for you — for you alone
one night
when I had no bread or water.

      Here I go re-living my childhood
      restlessly ensconced in the warmth of my mother's lap
      and I'm crying so beautifully as if I were singing an aria.
      It's this crying-and-singing voice of mine that calls you now
      I'm talking about the country that I dreamt up for you
      with all of its building that I also dreamt up for you
      with all of its buildings, dense vegetation and railway stations
      and its harbours —
      all this for you to find your home once you arrive
      in the house with the garden
      where an ebony-black cat purrs in the profound silence.
      You wouldn't understand what the cat's saying yet you can
      rest assured that it's singing a hymn in praise of you
      in its own special way while also consoling me
      who am waiting for you at the gate with my hands in my
      pocket and sigh occasionally so deeply from the depth
      of my heart that the quivering leaves of the trees
      and the flight of the birds echo it back as music.
I look at the stairs and you seem to appear
walking towards the porch
cheerful and scented with cheap perfume,
the odour of poverty and ill-conceived dawdling
they pass me by as clouds charged with thunder
but you are getting nearer and nearer
and I don't see you as a silly teenager any more
but as a large red rose
waving to me from a pot of black earth as one
inebriated with the strong spirits of loneliness.
Oh, you with the pony-tail hairdo
and those black stockings
you wondrous craze of our age
if there is room left in your heart

for a bird
for the bird of love with a beak purple with blood
you listen to me!

Michael Kitka [& A.M.]

THE DICTATOR

He's sunk forever. There's no doubt.
Never has there been an uglier death,
never more implacable hate —
the cowards deserted him
and the flatterers betrayed him.
>He stepped out from the forest of banners
>and yelled and stamped his feet ominously —
>those who had eyes he sent to their death,
>those who had tongues he sent to their death,
>he wanted to spill
>the blood of an entire nation —
>finally at last he lies crushed
>in the snow, in urine, or under the flaming ruins.
Was he punished by having to kill himself?
Is he, who killed him, guilty?
Has the world become any poorer
without those slave-driving days
and those devastating nights?
No! No!
>Now the black sky has split.
>Now the new seed
>quickens into life.   *Paul Tabori*

BAFFLING PICTURE

Where did I see this region before with its bleak earth
its blind stars at the back of the clouds?
It all shakes and shimmers on butterfly-wings
and yet everything is so surely in its place.

Beyond the reed a Gypsy keeps playing his hook
and while the wind cries for its wild brood
the moon is a silver raft and drifts, drifts
dead it drifts on the black mirror of the lake.

Edwin Morgan

YOUNG HORSEMAN

The horse he sits on is saddleless
and he himself is naked.
Marvellous boy
as his thighs tighten
and his sunburnt chest
heaves up and down.
>   My mate whom I
>   can't sing well enough ever,
>   burning youth, unconscious pride,
>   let me praise you!

Edwin Morgan

LIKE THIS

Neither the interminable patches of land
nor crags with frozen stone-geometry
my true home is the city
with its gangrened damp-walled houses
with its chimney-stacks to scrawl the sky black
with its endlessly swarming crowds
with its knots of children yelling and squealing
with its half-bald dogs
with its amorous cats
with its rats emerging from nocturnal sewers.
And I love the feverishly clattering machines
bathed in oil
gorged in flames
workmen's wood and iron constructions

looking like fearsome fireside pets.
Idols of my early days
that made me leave my birthplace
my school and church.
I have served them and praised them.
They became
goal of my vagabondage
seed of my verses.
Day and night I drum out their rhythm
and write my books
with my brain's eternal discontent.

Edwin Morgan

SNAPSHOT

Everything but everything
has to be smashed
including even
what lurks in the dark walls of the womb.
    The fury inside me has reached flash-point.
    Impotence hour.
    Red-hot.
    Ice-cold.
    My ashen faith's
    in a cave of my heart
    crouching.
If I open the window
of my room nothing happens.
No wind.
No din.
    Beside
    the tram-rails
    an old dog lies
    dead.
    His right eye
    and his muzzle
    gape.

Edwin Morgan

I AM WITH YOU

In front of you I go
you in front of me
the early sun's gold chain
jingles on my wrist.

Where are you going — I ask
you answer — how do I know.

I speed up my walk
but you speed all the more.

I in front of you
you in front of me.

But we stop in front of a gate.

I kiss you
you give me a kiss
then without a word you vanish
and spirit my life away.

Edwin Morgan

Milán Füst

(1888-1967)

Poet, novelist and critic, Milán Füst obtained a law degree but became a high school teacher until forcibly retired because of his left-wing views. In 1947 he became Professor of Aesthetics at the University of Budapest. Closely linked with the review Nyugat *from its earliest days, both his poetry and prose have been a unique blend of classic imagery, Whitmanesque vers* libre, *and a powerful pessimism that finds its closest equivalent in Robinson Jeffers.*

His first volume's title You Cannot Change It [Változtatnod nem lehet], *which appeared in 1913, sums up his attitude. Other poetry volumes by Füst include* The Choir of Oblivion [Az elmúlás kórusa], *1920, and* Selected Poems [Válogatott versei], *1935. He published two important dramas,* The Unhappy Ones [Boldogtalanok] *and* King Henry IV, *which were both produced after 1945, while his novels* My Wife's Story [A feleségem története] *and* Advent [Ádvent] *have only later reached a wider European audience through translations.* My Wife's Story *was translated into English by Ivan Sanders and published in New York.*

His aesthetic studies are contained in Vision and Passion in Art [Látomás és indulat a művészetben] *published in 1948. His autobiographical works include* All This I Was Once [Ez mind én voltam egykor], *published in 1957, and* Reminiscences and Studies [Emlékezések és tanulmányok], *which appeared in 1956. He has also produced a remarkable translation of* King Lear.

His own recitals of his poetry have been the subject of interesting studies. Professor Iván Fónagy, a Hungarian linguist living in Paris, had a number of readings by Füst of his own poem 'Old Age' *transcribed in musical notation and compared them with readings of the same poem by others. The results were published in a trail-blazing study by Fónagy called* The Voice of the Poet [A költő hangja], *Budapest 1975. Füst was a spellbinding lecturer whose* viva voce *renderings of his own poetry amounted to acts of co-creation.*

An entire generation of younger Hungarian poets considered themselves disciples of Füst. His lamenting voice is reminiscent of the prophet Jeremiah in the Old Testament.

SELF-PORTRAIT

I, too, want to be
  a spare old man with a convoluted mind
    like the Lord himself...
And if he called me to account for my children,
  I should have to turn away in contempt,
    for I have no children — I had no share in such pleasures —
      quite like the Arabian donkey
        which upon smelling the soil of its birthplace turns suddenly
          onto a new path thus have I set out once upon my safe road.
Neither did I choose the road of joy — but that of the barren Desert
  where the surface is red and no flocks graze at all —
    but where the test is made as to who can stand how much.
And if the Heavenly Father does not feed me, shall I endure it?
  Shall I not wail because of my thirst?
    Shall I embrace evil in my days of an outcast?

And in all knowledge I sought constantly new knowledge
  and glory always greater glory
    and where the sky was light, greater brightness
      and a more burning, greater darkness than that in the lap of
        women...

It looks as if I would not become an old man.
  And now should I still continue the old life?
    Woe! I would perhaps shout from a window
      but I'm afraid of a sneer and hide myself within.
Only four fiery walls stare at me,
  the reddish anger of the Lord God —
    then, nodding, slowly I shall go away
      and like the man who has carried death in his heart
        for a long time, a damnified steward, an insulted, old servant,
          who's gone looking for justice but never found it.

Paul Tabori

OLD AGE

O my eyes where are you, you that found a face so wonderful?
And o my marvellous ears where are you, you that grew sharp as
  donkey's from some bitter-sweet laughter?
And where are you my teeth, ferocious teeth that drew blood not just
  from strawberries, but from richer and redder lips also?
And where are you, dreadful song in my breastbone?

And where is the pain and where is the delight I go after emptily in my
  distraction, clutching a crooked stick as I wander?
Mad helter-skelter? Chasing the deer, a doe-footed girl, lying down
  somewhere to whisper to her, not her but the moonlight...
About the enigmas no one unravels beyond their changeless name —
  anguished happiness...
Where are you swirlings, sooty oaths? Everlasting scuttlings?
Where is the ravening mouth and where is my laughter?
God, where is my laughter, where too is the great motiveless sobbing:
When again and again — O blood-drained webs of reverberating
  daybreaks! —
I grovelled in the darkness before you!

Listen to me o youth. Remember the old Greek who lifted
Both hands like a statue and calling for his youth to return to him
Cast that Aeschylean curse on the one who gave old age to the living.
Half blind he stood on the hill, wrapped round with radiance, his hair
  blown back with the wind and
The tears coming down from his stammering eyes at the steep feet of
  the Deity.
And still his voice roared, his words transfixed the mill-wheel, shook
  the hill-side
And even made the five-year ram lift up his head. — But the Deity
Did not look at him, said nothing to the old man, nothing.
The Deity wept. For it was like drums beating in his ears, a dull
  drumming,
And the drumming answered by the landslide and the landslide
  answered by the sea-surge...

The immortal wretchedness of old age had swept up so huge before
    him, and so sacred.

For he was standing by his own grave and arguing with the wind
    incessantly
and aching to declare his truth once again before he crumbled...

And then of course he moved on — silence at last took that territory.
But by then everything in his heart was also silent, we should not
    forget, and another still vaster attention...

And round his head the wan half-daylight.

Edwin Morgan

IF I HAVE TO YIELD MY BONES

This wild team rushes at a savage pace,
and it seems to carry me to a safe goal, a secure roof:
It rolls into the zones of old age, sickness and toothlessness
and stops finally between the happy aborigines of Non-Being.
No matter, I shed no tears...Oh, run on, wild horses,
and gallop along with me that the forest of men shall rumble,
let me neither see nor hear. Let my heart be full of savagery
like the hunter's who sets out to kill, without fear —
without regard for the Creator above,
does not watch His face, whether it's clouded and how He shall judge
when the bullet starts to fly...

But speaks thus: This is the law! I must make a sacrifice, I must die
I who was hungry like the snakes,
Lazy like the crocodile,
and with a bent for destruction like the Yellow Rider of the Apocalypse
and the wild spots of greed stirred in my eyes.
So you mourn your own misfortune?

Consider the bird of the sky, who helps it when it screams?
Take the oak, the giant, when it falls groaning in the storm,
consider the calf that would still suckle and is taken to the slaughter-
house and all the others who move sadly towards their undesired goal...

And finally compose your hymn in this world
about the screeching vultures and proclaim that here the glazed eye
was judged more beautiful
    then the bright one.

Paul Tabori

GHOST STREET

Everything rubs me the wrong way. I can't stand dancing any more;
and brother, you can't show me a new one; even a Knidos
dance instructor can't invent one.
    Can't stand music either. What's it mean to me? Why, I used to
make up my own tunes! I hum them, but they don't mean a thing to
me. I stay quiet. Most of my life I've been living in darkness,
you know, the deep and secret silent type, that's me.

Ah, a cool breeze! Like when a guy walks at night on soundless,
dangerous streets. Even if sixty torches were to throw out wild flames,
they would all flow into nothingness...because nobody is there!
    This is Ghost Street.
    Walk a few more steps and you'll turn chicken, too;
and your old soldier's heart is sure to go bad on you.

There was a time when I loved lots of things: sailors' chanties,
the golden roses of dazzling consummate sunshine...
I can't count them any more, all the things I've loved.
The fire of earth was a joyous warmth for me,
it burned its way all through me, it made me tremble;
and still quivering with that heat, I dreamed of cold, cold nights.
Now the nights alone are my integrity. Don't think I'm being modest.
No, I want to forget my past and hide...
no, immerse myself in everything that is still mine by rights.
    Surely I'm entitled to that much!
I must get to know you. Who are you? Are you dark?
You whom I have faced so long in darkness,
you, my silent king,
        your mysterious Impermanence!

Jess Perlman

THE DRUNKEN MERCHANT

Two crones were giving a whipping to a drunkard in the fog;
While through the fog a sturdy cart rolled leisurely along,
Bearing two oafish country youths: one hefty lad
And by his side the gentle moonshine.

To begin with, the devils fought with me,
They were invisible. Later they were consolidated,
Crystallised by the air; they started to beat me
With incorporeal blows and they berated me.

One peeled a turnip and threw the rind at me
And from a rounded turret the other leered at me
And blustered frightful things I'd known about a long, long time.
That one exposed his private parts to me.

"Ugh, the head man's mouth is full of filth!
And those who ate liver and nuts on New Year's Eve
And gorged themselves on luscious fruit out of the panniers,
Their souls, like the fish, are asleep in the deep."

"Once I wore a dunce's cap though I had been a merchant.
I used to plunge my stumpy legs, in those days, in the snow;
And once I caught a cold on New Year's Eve...
But those who witnessed my disgrace, they died long, long ago."

No matter how fast I ran, he never stopped pursuing me,
But what he whispered to me I cannot remember now.
"Aye, aye, thou sly one, give me money for my news,
Or smell me if thy nose is able to!"
    That was his farewell. And then the earth sucked him in
and the drunken clouds of night swallowed him.

Jess Perlman

THE WINEGROWER

Look where the Great Bear glows; he beats his son to teach him
    silence,
While down below, the Swan, like a water-lily, glides away languidly.
The blue grows darker here, spreads over the luxuriant mountainside,
Where hundreds of small white houses have been hurled haphazardly
By a monstrous sling among the blackened sterile vine-shoots.

The autumn winds on cloudless nights fly far below the moon,
Propel the hasty luminous clouds...
For a moment his eyes pass over the hill as he walks about;
Then he, too, says farewell, safeguarding the heavier grapes,
Now that winter is on its way.
The winegrower withdraws in silence.

Now he comes striding down the hill and lays away his pannier
And all the other tools, back in the cool cubicles
Drenched in a heavy wine-cellar smell;
And till the winter wanes and the gurgling wine in the casks ferments,
Merrily he lolls about, cheerfully quaffs his wine
And tastes the joys of purest wisdom.
Meanwhile, the snow keeps coming down. Outside.

Jess Perlman

A LETTER ABOUT HORROR

"Upon my chest the Cross of the Knights' Order,
violet braid upon my loose-swinging cloak,
and with the light sorrow of horsemen upon my face
I trotted recently with my companions towards Madrid —
as the first news of peace arrived.
Wherever we passed, even the waters seemed to draw back.
The people locked their doors — my wild dogs
were cursed at the village outskirts — of course, no one else knew my
secret, that they had nothing to fear for I remained soft even
amidst rude hands. See. Just like the beast of the forest as it stirs

or when the twigs crackle under your feet — is the fear
so great here then? That your nights should grow pale and outside
your houses the watchman to mask his terror, cries out,
a horrible cry? Is that it? That a man steals himself one more day,
one more kiss, a mouthful of wine, star-fires? And flees with it
like the thieves? Until now I believed existence more orderly.
Today I despise it. Does one have to hurry?
And be afraid? Oh, men! Can't I look leisurely at the moon?
This beautiful world isn't mine then?...Oh, let me! Let me still
weep over this... For yesterday I was still young... My heart was so
young... And today it is like waters sleeping upon drowsy,
heavy dawns. Dark and taciturn. My life has swung out of joint...
Oh, some visions are worth a millennium! No matter. Nothing wrong.
And I shall not run."

Jess Perlman

DEATH OF SAGITTARIUS

Autumn is here and darkness comes earlier now; the rain is falling.
Time grows old and tears roll down his beard.
The soul is lonely. It shivers in the foggy night,
quieting only when the dawn is foggy, too, when the scurrying
sea-green clouds swim across the sky. Dead then
lies the soul, and it rejoices. A kind-hearted ghost,
an unfamiliar ghost approaches, holding
a sea-green grape before his sorrowful eyes.

He fetches cool green apples; and he devours them, too.
Dead lies the soul and the quivering tears keep rolling down.
O what joy to sleep away the rainy days!
The wind will no doubt breathe a sigh
among the cool cascades, with water overflowing,
surge down into the brooks from forests long forgotten.
The wanderer roams the smoky hills
and in his grief-stricken soul the autumn's
well of sorrow bubbles noiselessly, without end.

Among the barren bushes of the flowing ravines
the green-eyed wildcats and the sand-hued wolves are hidden...
And where the virgin light of dawn paints gold-leaf
on the flying clouds, a slim celestial maiden draws a veil over
her beautiful, flaming countenance. The lady is ethereal,
transparent, like golden wine in a crystal chalice;
like a grape, the fruit of her breast, is transparent,
beautiful, sweet.

Woe is mine! I go to Persia or anywhere else, to any far-off place.
In the morning I quit this evil, ruthless town of my
intolerable anguish. I dreamed my dreams on this misty autumn
night...
But, oh, in my soul's humility, enfeebled tears flow once again.
Like a frail dry branch a night-owl alighted on,
the sorrowing soul is impotent and keeps on withering.

Jess Perlman

MISSISSIPPI

What do you aim at? Or have you grown deaf and dumb?
The river thunders three miles from you,
breaking its black waves under the fan-shaped reef
at the feet of the Rocky Mountains. — Copses murmur
along its course, but you don't care a bit, old chum, you do not
    even shake your ears,
you smoke right and proper — and don't give a hoot to the water...

You do not swim in its waves, you do not rest on its shallows,
you do not place fish-baskets either to catch some pink salmon
and to dry them with cut-up bellies in the hot summer sun!
Are you so much content with what you've reached: the pleasures
    of your bungalow and the steady run of the months
that you would not be pleased even if Jupiter came down with its
    nine moons to drink from your well?
(See, Abraham too got up when the angels came, he washed their
    feet and had a kid killed for them
"and prepared for them a savory meal" — by gosh, why should I

explain it at great length?
Well, you are used to angels and devils alike — I know you by heart.)

But, see, it is otherwise with me, — I, like Abraham, still am
enthusiastic about God. And I dream of distant great rivers.
  And, see, when I die
and that good judge from beyond lays his hand on my heart
and asks me about my reward, my due claim, about what I want
  as wages for my heart-consuming work,
I'll mention Mississippi then, old chum, for there and then I'll
  open my mouth, be sure,
I will speak up and stop being ashamed as I have always been. —
  Take me to the Mississippi, far away,
oh, very far away. Because my home is there where I am loved by
  all since none knows me,
and see, I also can love but those whom I don't know.

My life has been a long black day. — Whom shall I complain to?
  It's over now.
I feel as if I'd never seen a bright and sunlit sky...
Oh you distant river, oh you distant and grim wilds of America! —
  I am afraid...
that there is no good judge at all and I shall never see you!

               István Tótfalusi

Sándor Sík
(1889-1963)

Poet, translator, literary historian, theologian, and editor, Sándor Sík completed his university studies in Budapest in Classics and later obtained a doctorate in Hungarian literature. In 1903 he entered the Piarist order and rose to eminence as an orator. Eventually he obtained high civil and ecclesiastical offices. Exceptionally learned and many-sided, Sík had a lasting influence on his younger contemporaries, among them Miklós Radnóti (q.v.), because of his critical observations, his views on aesthetics, and his special methods of tutoring.

At age seventy-two, when Sík celebrated the fiftieth anniversary of his priesthood, the composer Zoltán Kodály dedicated his 'Te Deum' Mass to Sík.

Sík's poetical works include Facing the Sun [Szembe a nappal], *1910;* Silence [Csend], *1924; and* God is Young [Az Isten fiatal], *1940. His collected poems were published in 1941 and his posthumous volume of poetry was issued under the title* Blessing [Áldás] *in 1964.*

The famous Catholic monthly The Vigil [Vigilia], *which was founded in 1935 and survived both Nazi and Communist oppression, was restarted in 1946, after a pause during the war, with Sík as its Editor-in-Chief. He consistently published high quality essays, short stories, and poetry, along with many translations from western languages, a tradition he passed on to his equally talented successor, György Rónay.*

Sík's poetry was enriched by the world of Latin hymns and psalms, of which he was one of the most successful interpreters.

THE ENGLISH

High in the mountain mist, a world apart,
alone, obscured, remote the hotel stands,
the sun no longer with its golden wands
suffuses all and lends its charms to art.
> In heated rooms which they infest like kings,
> a group of English who regard this earth
> their natural home, divinely theirs from birth,
> command the service, food, and everything.

They trust, they dance, waiters to their demands,
dear God! The ping-pong bats rise up at the commands
of little English girls with rosy faces.
      Choke back my tears! 'Tis useless to bemoan.
      O, Hungary! My love, my life alone,
      what know these of thy mystery and graces?

James Turner

SUMMER AND DAWN

Summer and dawn. It's Visitation Day.
And living wreaths of mowers crown the fields.

Behind the hill, Our Lady's summer-day
resounds already upon golden chords,
as, in the wind of dawn, breathes tremulous
the destined fire of the summer noon;
yet dew still quivers on the lilac-leaf,
and scythe-blades gleam with yet unsullied steel.

Mowers already, sober and sedate,
extend their slow, brown phalanx through the field;
and after them the maiden gleaners stoop,
their kerchiefs dancing like a wind-blown posy
of party-coloured wild-flowers. All is peace,
save as a whetstone clashes on a blade

and a young colt, from far off, whinnies clearly.
One mounting lark, a living shaft of song,
pierces the morning blue above my head;
while tingling through my body and my soul
I feel, within me, Earth's deep, flowing song
rise, ever rise, to greet the o'er-arching Heaven.

Watson Kirkconnell

Zseni Várnai
(1890-1981)

Poet and novelist, Zseni Várnai was born in Nagyvázsony. She studied to be an actress, but chose a secreterial career instead of the stage. She married Andor Peterdi (1881-1958), a poet, translator and journalist; their daughter Mária Peterdi (1919-1970) became an Egyptologist in Paris, eventually co-operating with her mother on a joint autobiography.

Zseni Várnai became instantly famous in 1912 when she published her poem 'To My Soldier son' [Katonafiamnak!], *which is presented here. She wrote it on an occasion when the workers were planning a major demonstration and the news spread that the military would be brought into action against them. This also became the title of her first collection of poetry which appeared in 1914.*

Her poetry is dominated throughout by pacifism, an intense desire for peace, anti-fascism, the role of women in society, and a yearning for a just social system. In 1942 she published her autobiographical novel One Woman Among Millions [Egy asszony a milliók közül]; *it was followed by a trilogy.*

In 1956 she was awarded the Attila József prize. She has been translated into several languages.

TO MY SOLDIER SON

My precious heart, my handsome soldier son,
I write this letter with my blood to you.
Since you've had to take the Kaiser's shilling
our world has turned red of a fiery hue.
The big decisive battle is approaching
and you will be our enemy, beware!
When they command you to attack your own blood:
don't shoot at us, my son, I will be there!

The fertile womb of Mother Earth is stirring,
she eyes the armies of the worker-slaves
who'll sow the seeds of life in virgin furrows,
she wants those vital reproductive waves.

Now soon we'll test our formidable forces,
we'll leave the cornfields mercilessly bare,
the living soil shall be our insurrection:
don't shoot at us, my son, I will be there!

My soldier son, I carried you inside me,
I suckled you and cradled you to sleep,
I gave you day and night, my every moment,
now read these shaky lines and hear me weep;
flesh of my flesh, blood of my blood, I ask you,
how could you fire when you hear the prayer
that I will scream and wail towards your army:
don't shoot at us, my son, I will be there!

You are our hope, our life, you are our fullness,
Messiah, Christ, who gloriously reigns!
My son, you hold our fate within your power
the blood of slaves is raging in your veins;
the heady fever of the revolution
shall sweep you gloriously in the air,
and whip the oceans in a roaring tempest:
don't shoot at us, my son, I will be there!

The seas run high now, bitter storms are raging,
the haughty ship is struggling on the course,
but think... the tides could breach the old defences,
and conquer with an overwhelming force!
Just think... if every mother sent a letter,
each to her son, to soldiers everywhere,
awakening, inflaming, agitating:
don't shoot at us, my son, I will be there!

Peter Zollman

László Mécs
(1895-1978)

Born in Hernádszentistván, Mécs completed his university studies at the University of Budapest, after which he entered the Order of Premonstratensians in 1914, teaching at various schools of his order. From the publication of his first volume of poems, Bells at Dawn [Hajnali harangszó] *in 1923, through* The Slaves Are Singing [Rabszolgák énekelnek] *in 1925 and* Glory [Megdicsőülés] *in 1935, to further volumes, his popularity, enhanced by accomplished readings and recitals of his own poetry, increased year after year.*

He spoke up against social injustice and the influence of Hitlerism in Hungarian political life before 1945. In 1953 he was arrested on false charges and spent three years in prison. After his release, he retired to Pannonhalma, the seat of the Benedictines in Hungary. He was rehabilitated after the Uprising of 1956.

His collected poems were published in Budapest in 1940, while three separate collections of his works were issued in the United States, one in Hungarian and two in English: I Graft Roses on Eglantines [Vadócba rózsát oltok], *Toronto, 1968, and* The Golden Fleece [Aranygyapjú], *in 1971.*

His poetry represents a new kind of humanism in which the dominant voice is a sense of mission.

PRAYER FOR THE GREAT LUNATIC[1]

Night of nations. On a death-dense bassoon,
like a satanic ghost, now plays the Moon.

And on Europe's historic sooty peak
towards the Moon sleep-walks a lunatic.

His assured gait appears to lend him wings;
around his head a bloody rainbow swings.

---

[1]   Written in the 1930s against Hitler.

He never falters — his brain fire-possessed
by a Guardian Demon, all his steps are blessed.

Woe to the sober burghers who did not
share his drunk state and like a lemming-lot

set out when he appeared among their ilk!
A hero he, unflinching like Old Nick.

Thus he leads millions, all of them obsessed,
as if his words were all with charm addressed.

On the towers of Europe's history
like water down the rain-pipe blood runs free.

Let us now pray for him then, fellow men:
"While he stares at the Moon-phantom, we can

survive somehow! Meanwhile let our own rage
remain contained by saint, poet, and sage,

God, do not call him, for he might be stirred
into waking — and so perish the world!"

Paul Tabori

WHO CAN UNDERSTAND THIS?

The Sun descended on the top of the mountain
And drank up the sea of night.

A dove drank from the marshes
And the water became mountain clear.

A swallowful of good news landed on my heart
And drank up my ocean of sorrow.

Ken Thomas

MY DEAR LITTLE FELLOW

I believe in the chance behind which God smiles
as I do behind the window-panes
in the winter to feed the tomtits,
or when, passing in the streets
where some poor children are playing,
    I furtively drop a few copper coins and smile to myself.
Thus by chance from its little nest
on the roof of the Budapest station
a sparrow fell, at nine o'clock in the evening.
    It was no great matter to be sure, but a poet noticed it,
a reporter of the newspaper
"The Way, the Truth, and the Life,"
of which God Himself is the manager.
Over that sparrow there will be a great hubbub in Heaven,
and the Angels will chatter:
was he chased by his brothers? That is possible,
for sparrows are bad-tempered, like men,
dogs, foxes, hyenas, and magpies.
    It is also possible that he couldn't stand the hard winter,
or that he had eaten nothing,
or very little, that evening, and fell dizzily
into the sack of a newspaper-vendor, blind and one-armed,
into the very midst of the news of the world,
among the seven deadly sins with their potion and hate,
into a sea of sins that cry out to heaven,
into the arrogance of the French,
the five wounds of crucified Hungary,
the endemic misery of the Germans,
the fireworks of the Geneva circus.
    It was into this that the little sparrow fell.
At first the blind news vendor trembled at it,
then he felt it, held it, caressed it,
repeated a hundred, a thousand times:
"My dear little fellow, my dear little fellow,
dear little throbbing heart, I shall give you drink at the fountain,
at the fountain of fairy tales, with the crystal water,
I shall feed you on diamond-wheat, on lentils and honey;

awake, my little fellow, my joy, my treasure!"
Then put it in his pocket with his money, and,
with his hat in his hand, he seemed to murmur a prayer.
    I watched him from behind a pillar
covered with notices; my heart trembled
and my astonished heart overflowed:
"O red-nosed tatterdemalion, blind man maimed by the war,
you, who have only a borrowed pallet for all your wealth
and the scant furniture of the poor,
grizzled greyer than the sparrow,
my dear little fellow,
where have you been hiding your story and its fair colours?
    How has such a lily grown from your squalid lodging?
My dear little fellow,
where have you been hiding all that gold
with which you could cover
a hussar's equestrian statue,
making this world's winter shine with its brilliance,
or hammering it with your miraculous hand,
creating a summer more brilliant than gold?
My dear little fellow,
while you were gazing at God with your blind eyes,
I missed my train,
but never mind! I hastened to Budapest on foot,
asking myself nothing, seeking nothing,
but stammering like someone who has fallen in love,
whistling to the rhythm of my steps:
"My dear little fellow...My dear little fellow!"

    I should love it if, when we fall in the agony of death,
like the little sparrow, God with a caress
would soothe the throbbing of our hearts
and say: "My dear little fellow!"

Watson Kirkconnell

GOING DOWN, PLEASE

The Eiffel Tower, on the topmost platform.
A spring breeze imprints its kisses on me.
The pleasure of the ascent in the lift.
When arrived on top, I only said: "My God!" In no other city are
greatness and beauty blended on such a vast scale
as in ancient Lutetia, today's young Paris.

The mists from the rainbows and the city are now
all green and opal. The sun is overhead;
over Hungary a dark cloud hovers
but there, too, the sun warms its rainbow-arch.

I strut enthusiastically in its rays and fancy
that I could reach the Moon.
(Insatiable heart, where then would you stop?)
— But behind me the tower-attendant calls me back:
"If you please, the ten minutes are up. We are going down."
The lift sinks, slowly. My back
has goose-flesh in that silent fall.

The rainbow becomes unhooked, comes down, its scale is reduced,
as if by an order in the heavy silence.
The masculine Sun goes down along with me,
sowing the gold of his kiss on the lift.
Yesterday at the famous Sorbonne I recited poetry
before a fine, large audience, to a storm of applause.
And standing there I distinctly noted, knocking at my heart,
the deep voice of the lift-man calling out behind me:
"If you please, my good Sir, we are going down.
Ten long minutes are up."

The lift glides down; here I am neatly on the ground.
A bit dizzy, a bit shaky in the knees,
but it is well, it will do. I am going to breathe again
my few sprigs of violets. I am going to embrace again
my white-haired mother and all my friends.

A final greeting, if I am granted the time, and at last
the terrible voice will whisper: "If you please,
we are going down, a few feet under the ground!"

Watson Kirkconnell

ON THE TOMB OF THE UNKNOWN SOLDIER

The hero is a good lad. He causes no anxiety.
He died modestly, without trying to pose.
On the battlefield, he became a flower, his country's toast.
The peace-banquet is good: Hip, hip, hurray!
    The mutilated soldier lives on. He is a bad fellow.
He shows his wounds shamelessly.
He has no modesty. He shed his blood for the fatherland
but he lacked tact — and came back.
    As if in a beauty show, he displays his hands,
his shattered limbs; and there is no Taygetus
from which to throw him down. Speeches, statues, laurels
don't go with him: this barbarian wants to eat!
    He needs bread (not a rich man's cake)
and gets the right to go from house to house
and on the street in an eddy of traffic
to sell shoe-laces.
The sentimentalist sobs, the people weep and dream,
the angels of the revues dance in heavenly style,
and our dreams are pierced by the creaking
of millions of wooden legs and cries of hunger.
    Thousands of soldiers march,
they parade in public squares in Paris, in Berlin,
and the cripple, this grey ghost of fear,
hobbles past and cries *Mene, Tekel, Upharsin.*
    The people love the hero: in the rainbow of blood-vapours
he has become an ethereal ideal.
But the war-cripple subversively rots
on the threshold of the door to a fairer future.
    The hero is watched over by the flame of worship.
A pale anemone kissed by the nimbus of glory.
— The sight of the war-cripple annoys and makes the blood boil.
For the hero is dead,
                but the cripple
                    wants to eat.

Watson Kirkconnell

József Erdélyi
(1896-1978)

Erdélyi was born in Újbátorpuszta in Transylvania into a poor peasant family. His father was Romanian (named Árgyelán); his mother was Hungarian. He was discovered by the periodical Nyugat [The West] *and the liberal newspaper* Az est [The Evening]. *In 1915 he graduated from high school and was sent to the Russian front. In 1919 he enlisted in the revolutionary Red Army. After the defeat of the first Communist régime he served in the university militia, but in 1920 deserted the military. He tried to survive as a poet, but he was so penniless that he had to roam the country on foot. In 1921 he revisited Transylvania, then under Romanian rule, where he was captured and jailed in the old fortress of Fogaras [Făgăraş in Romanian].*

Erdélyi was a pioneer of the populist literary movement. During the years preceding World War II, he was, like many of his generation, somewhat under the influence of right-wing propaganda which he later truly regretted. His political vicissitudes which took him from Red Soldier to quasi-Nazi sympathizer, then anti-Hitlerist and spokesman for the downtrodden peasantry, constitute an unfortunate footnote to his otherwise very beautiful nature loving poetry. His poem 'The Sons Changed into Stags' bears comparison with Ferenc Juhász and László Nagy (qq.v.). Erdélyi came into Hungarian literature in the post-Ady era, bringing with him a voice of innocence, somewhat like Jean Giono in France who, with his Quelqu'un des montaignes [Someone from the mountains] *shocked the urban sophisticates of the mid-thirties. Erdélyi represents in Hungarian lyrics the "revolution of the country" in an age increasingly dominated by big cities.*

His books include Ibolyalevél [Violet-leaf], *1922;* Világ végén [At the End of the World], *1924;* Délibáb és szivárvány [Fata Morgana and Rainbow], *1927;* Kiáltás a Dunán [A Shout Across the Danube], *1938; and* Visszatérés [Return], *1954, a volume of self-criticism which rehabilitated him under the Communist rule two years before the Hungarian Uprising of 1956. One of Erdélyi's side lines was a highly inspired but amateurish etymologizing which he wrote up in a fascinating but strange book entitled* Árdeli szép hold [The Beautiful Moon of Ardel] *which appeared in 1939. In it Erdélyi sets out to seek the "ancestor of all languages" which, he says, he once knew as a poet but forgot and for which he is now endlessly searching. Erdélyi now enjoys a quiet renaissance in Hungary. His collected poetry was recently published in Budapest, omitting his politically compromising weaker writings.*

THE SONS CHANGED INTO STAGS[1]
(After a Transylvanian and Romanian Folk-Ballad)

Once there was a father
who begot exactly
nine in virile offspring,
handsome, well-built striplings.
Never did he teach them
any trade or calling,
taught not plowing, sowing,
herding hairy cattle,
herding heavy horses,
only took them hunting,
climbing savage mountains.
Once the nine fine fellows
hunted till they chanced on
stags, a herd unequalled.
These they kept pursuing
till they lost their bearings,
then were changed into
nine stout mountain-stagfolk.
For them now impatient
rose their grizzled father,
seized upon his rifle,
turned again to hunting.
What did he discover?
Nine stout mountain-stagfolk.
Down he knelt instantly
so that he could shoot them.
Quoth the biggest stag-son:
"Stop, my dearest Daddy,

we will snatch and grab you
up upon our antlers,
ever we will toss you,
ridge to ridge we'll throw you,
summit onto summit;
precipice to valley
we will hurl you downwards
till you smash to splinters!"
With a mighty outburst
speaks their grizzled father:
"Darlings of your father,
little lads I long for,
do come home, I beg you,
where your ma awaits you,
there she waits with longing,
with the table laden,
with the candles lighted,
with the glasses brimming.
In the house she's sitting,
fills with wine the chalice,
fills the house with sorrow."
Word for word replying
speaks the biggest stag-son:
"Good and darling Daddy,
homewards go directly
to our darling mother!
We shall no more go there,
for our branching antlers

---

[1] Both László Nagy and Ferenc Juhász (qq.v.), years after Erdélyi, returned to this haunting theme. Also the Transylvanian-born Béla Bartók's (1881-1945) *Cantata Profana,* which exploits the legend in its modern musical form (just as the composer's "Romanian Dances"), is both Romanian and Transylvanian-Hungarian, generated by the mystical atmosphere of the Carpathian mountains. Erdélyi's version antedates both Juhász and Nagy.

do not fit the doorway,
only fit the mountains;
neither will our footsteps
seek the hearthstone's ashes,

they will walk in brushwood;
nevermore our lips will
drink from kitchen glasses,
but only from spring-wells!
But only from spring-wells!

Watson Kirkconnell [& A.M.]

THE SPLENDID STAGS[2]

Once upon a time an ancient man had fine
        male children, yea, an ancient man,
with splendid offspring nine.
        But he failed to teach them trades of any use:
plowing, sowing, weeding; trades like stallion breeding,
        even cattle feeding — but he taught them, hunting skills
high upon the savage hills. His splendid offspring nine
        went right on with the kill, high in the hills until
they came upon a herd of deer and chased it, chased it night and day,
        after which they just lost their way.
Lo and behold, they then became all stags, the splendid nine!
        Their father grew worried, troubled, impatient,
he took his rifle and went out hunting,
        he went out for searching and hunting.
All of a sudden he found the fine
        stags in the mountains, the splendid nine!
The ancient father raised his rifle,
        knelt down and took his aim —
but the proudest stag confronted him boldly
        and from his mouth the words of a hunter came,
'twas a hunter who spoke, behold,
        grave words he spoke and boldly told:
"Our belovèd father,
        against us dare not raise your rifle!
For our antlers will impale you,
        they will hurl you on high, skyward,

---

[2] This is the same poem as the one above in another interpretation.

from one savage hill to 'nother
         from one jagged peak to 'nother,
from ledge to ledge, from rock to rock,
         until upon a grey and bleak
and mighty cliff we nine will thrust
         you down into the distant depths
and smash your body into dust..."
         Their father spoke in sweet reply:
"Belovèd sons of mine, all fine,
         my splendid male offprings, you nine,
hark your mother's yearning
         for her sons' returning —
she waits with candles burning!
         She waits with table laden,
cups filled and ready bed...!"
         That's what their father said.
"While up here in the wild you roam,
         she fills her cups with wine,
her sadness fills the home..."
         The eldest and proudest of the fine
stags, all his sons, the splendid nine,
         said to him in reply:
"Belovèd father, go, turn home!
Return to our ma alone!
For here we must remain...
Our heads of horns have grown
wider than any door —
they travel through the sky.
We shall never again
step into your hearth's warm ashes,
only into the forest's green;
         nor can our lips drink from a cup as before
         only from spring water clean,
                 only from spring water clean..."

Thomas Land [& A.M.]

CHERRY-TREE

The cherry-blossoms may be white,
a pure and snowy flood:
but cherry-fruit will ripen red,
the hue of human blood.

Such cherry-crops have always been
since first the world was made.
Beneath their blood-red weight the trees
bend down in every glade.

When does this dark and blood-red flow
come forth? From this our earth?
This soil has seen enough of war
to bring such fruit to birth.

The cherry from the deep blue sky
brings bloody dew and rain,
through such a battle-gush of blood
no warfare could attain.

The cherries with pure drops of blood
shine bright upon the tree,
but where (they cry) are lad and lass
to pick the fruit for me?!...

The juices of the cherry-fruit
can quench their burning thirst;
with dreams of hills in cherry-time
the kissing young are cursted.

They dream of hills in cherry-time,
and still they follow after;
and visions of a fairer world
come back in love and laughter.

However blue the hill may be,
however far withdrawn,
the cherry with its blood-red fruit
still lures the young pair on.

The young lad shakes the tree above;
the lass picks up below;
her apron and her basket both
are full, and overflow.

She heaps the basket to the brim;
the heart is likewise filled;
and blessing on her womb's fair fruit
from gods of love instilled.

O cherry-tree! We cherish you,
our own dear native tree;
a model for the life we seek
you evermore could be.

If we desire a fairer world,
let life's true course begin:
Let us love bravely, without fear,
for love is not a sin.

If we desire a better world,
let death be still withstood, —
heroic courage can achieve
the triumph of the good.

Watson Kirkconnell

BLACK KŐRÖS

The Kőrös was our river, we would go
throughout the summer months to bathe in it.
The high barrage seemed like an endless well
imprisoning the river out of sight,
as a tall fence holds a leaping lion,
containing it life-long, a strong fortress,
though it was still impossible to hide
it from the blue sky and bright watchfulness
of sun, the moon, the thousands of the stars,
or dull its memories — unhindered flow,
freedom, or lessen unabated strength,
or tame its wish to break a gap and go;
nor can they take away essential life,
dare not deprive it of a natural death —
it can still flow on, the same Black Kőrös,
to give the boundless Black Sea all its strength...

We could not wait to be upon the dam.
We ran at once. This was the splendid prize:
the first one up would see the Kőrös first...
Before we reached it we would shed our clothes,
then gallop wildly in the sunburnt dust
towards the water's edge, like thirsty foals
released from stables into the meadow,
stretching to water with their parched nostrils...
As if victorious on a castle wall,
panting we stood on top of the dam...
Below us, shimmering, the Black Kőrös,
dry summer light reclining in its stream.
It slunk along its bed, the cunning one,
the ample valley's undersized inmate,
as if it would never press its muddy
foaming flood against the water-limit...

Young men approached, muscular harvesters,
as strong bulls, with hirsute loins and chests,
they jumped into the water from steep banks

to wash the sweat of workaday pursuits.
Hiding among young birches, girls undressed,
disturbed by prankish glances from the boys.
The silver-bellied fishes splashing break
the stillness with their sharp innocent cries.
And they bathed modestly, kept on their slips,
which, wet, clung to each supple breast and thigh.
They took their time and then began to wring
soaked hair, lifting their arms, then let it dry...
Some women walked there from surrounding farms,
one carrying a baby; her small son
stepped to the river, clutching at her side.

Slowly they walked into the river and
wading up and down the shallow water
seemed to resemble melancholy cows.
Everywhere the water took them deeper.
Deep in the river they would lift their skirts
so that the water washed above their thighs,
rose to their waists, plainly they did not care
if womanhood was clear to any gaze...
Coolly their thighs were soaked by Black Kőrös
as round about the water spread the rings
which measure time and bring into the world
all beauty and the death that beauty brings...
The water-mother scattered with her waves
their images, their sad reflected heads;
perhaps she pitied them... They crossed the ford
like ill-fed cows returning to their sheds.

To the right and left, away from the dam,
and on its wall in a continuous line,
telegraph poles stand constantly and guard
the earth, which once had been a marshy plain
over which the Black Kőrös spread its flood,
the gift of melting mountains every spring
for thousands of years, which would continue
except the dam is high, the levee strong...
Man is strong, too, he took the soil away
and marked a narrow path for the river;

where once the water rose among the reeds,
woods and bird-song, now grain waves everywhere.
Estates subdue the ground to right and left;
Armenians, priests, Jews are masters there;
the surplus people of the villages
live in that wilderness, eat servants' fare.

The river still remains part of their lives:
they are afraid when it is flushed and strong,
can bathe in it, or stand upon the dam,
when they have time — the heat can choke and cling.
In it they pound their sweat-soiled underwear;
their pigs, cattle and horses are allowed
its water, but the unmolested fish
cannot be caught, either with net or rod —
game wild in the fields, game-birds in the sky
belong to masters, they cannot be snared;
sun glints on the waters of the Kőrös
and on the bayonets of the river's guard...
The people built it, people moved the earth,
unhappy Nimrod steps into his traps,
ensnares himself in a hunter's tackle...

He could liberate the captive river,
allowing it to soak into the parched
and splitting earth, to wash out the soda,
drown salt-flowers finger-thick, the accursed
fields upon which the dew no longer falls
in the expectant dawns, where in the heat
of summer, on bare grazing, the starving
cattle collapse in heaps, so much gaunt meat.
He could spread an abundance of fish ponds,
bring the floods again to the plains that choke
in clouds of dust, where tuberculosis
wheezes and harvests the sallowing cheek,
where the cowherd's pipe now makes no music
and folk-tales and song are renewed no more
and the earth is outstretched beneath the stars
like a wreathless coffin upon its bier...

By the Danube my summer is now spent,
I wander sadly in Buda and Pest.
Why am I here? I ask myself and think
about the land which is familiar —
on the embankment of Danube, which boils
through the Black Forest, into the Black Sea,
think of Black Kőrös which like my sadness
has fluctuating moods, must change to be
itself, forced by its dams and banks — the veins
which channel our desires; deep in my bones
this is the urgent need: to liberate
the country poor, redress oppression's pains,
gather together a holy army,
all people of the water and the land,
to fight until the whole great globe becomes
one shepherd's willing flock within one fold...

Alan Dixon

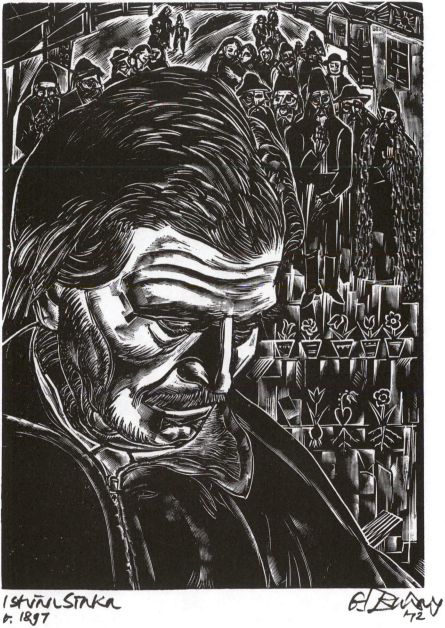

Istvál Stáka
b. 1897

István Sinka
(1897-1969)

The son and grandson of shepherds, Sinka started life as a shepherd's aid. The family was poor, and Sinka was unable to get any schooling. It is said that he would stay out in the puszta for periods as long as three straight years without a roof over his head. He taught himself to read and to write at age sixteen, using a Bible and a volume of Petőfi's poetry (q.v.). His poems, short stories, and novels reflect the struggle of a self-taught, self-made man. Under these adverse circumstances, he still managed to give a lyrical yet realistic description of his birth place, Nagyszalonta (today in Romania), and the surrounding countryside. At the beginning of his literary career, he wrote a number of hymns imagining himself to be an ancient shaman, an intermediary between the living and the dead.

In his songs and ballads an immediate and realistic view is combined with surrealistic elements, giving an almost magical effect. He expresses the awesome depths of the world of the nomadic shepherds with a strong admixture of social emotion by introducing a hard, almost Asian world-view into 'populist literature.' He felt very strongly that he had a mission to speak for his people; his position as chosen messenger brought to the surface an archaic heritage which revealed itself not only in his themes but also in the depth and originality of his language.

Sinka's most active period was the late 1930s and early 1940s, when he joined the populist movement and wrote his most memorable books in verse and prose. His volume of poetry Accusation [Vád] *appeared in 1939, and in 1943 his* On the Road of the Landless [Hontalanok útján], *along with his* Book of Ballads [Balladás könyv]. *After the war he could not publish anything more until after the Revolution of 1956. He died in 1969, and most of his works appeared only after the collapse of Communism, brought out by Püski Publishers, who had sustained him during his years of silence. In his mesmerising* Book of the Islands [Szigetek könyve], *he uses the names of actual friends and acquaintances, reminding one of the American Edgar Lee Masters'* Spoon River Anthology. *Sinka's linguistic contributions to Hungarian are considerable, and translating Sinka into any foreign language is a most challenging task. Instead of interrupting the flow of his verses with his original Hungarian names of villages and people, similar sounding, roughly synonymous English words were created for the translations included here.*

ONLY THE SUN

Far away from all those
she loved, the shepherd's little wife
with eyes of blue
died on a hospital bed.
Heaven knows why every rose
shivered just then;
that afternoon not one mignonette grew.

Joy, gloom, hair-clasp,
little casket are another's instead.
No more across the springtime grass she'll wander
to carry a wicker basket out to the pen;
when the poplar flowers, no newborn kitten to ponder.

She has gone, among drowsy grass,
mounds in repose.
She no longer climbs on the cart
to gaze at the view.
In the evening that pinned-up
crown of hair flows
down to her shoulders no more
at her fingers' cue.

In autumn she no longer echoes
the wild geese overhead.
Empty landscape.
                    Only the sun forever glows.

W. Price Turner

THE SHEPHERD'S WIFE'S FAREWELL
TO THE OLD PASTURE

I gaze over the landscape, clouded and dark,
but oh! I search in vain
for the so well known meadow, where my sheep
once grazed; there's no familiar mark,
I've lost my youth on the green autumn plain —
I shan't find it again.

And yet here once, with noisy bells, fine clothes,
my wedding party passed,
beribboned carts drawn by Kunili's horses,
so silently they went, where the Bara flows —
so beautiful in the leaf-fallen past,
a rosy dream at last.

And in the course of years my babies, too,
were coffined one by one
and there, by the floating vapours of the Bara,
were swallowed, down where the elders grew,
by the green land spread beneath the sun
where the flat meadows run.

I stand here now, an old bent shepherd's wife,
unseeing, with my eyes
blind to the carts with milk, deaf to the fluting
and the black Pan pipes, on ground where, out of life,
beyond the meadow trees each little one lies,
dusty for eternities.

I take the thin gold loop from off my ear
and wrap it in my shawl,
to remind me of this day and my resolve
never again to wear it or come near
this landscape, in the spring or in the fall —
or visit it at all.

                                                        Gavin Ewart

MY MOTHER DANCES A BALLAD

Mother's dance blossomed in beauty at last
when she threw down her shawl on the grass
at Prairie Meadow,[1] near Plow-Rest Brook[2]
while her wingèd feet by the bonfire took
insubstantial, flower-scented flight,
to my tall, husky father's delight.

But no happy figure, no merry caper
shone through her exquisite dance —
all she could do was signal by swaying, as if in a trance,
how her ancestors swooned into meeting their Maker.
For 'twas the same song crying o'er the meadows
that they all died without a prayer
with beards grown long, hanging from the gallows.

And towards dawn, in the fluttering breeze
when light burst forth from her sultry summer-eyes,
the men placed ten candles all around her
and six more candles were set in a circle
in whose midst my mother shone and reflected
while on her dainty boots the flames' sheen deflected.

The shepherds whistled in ancestral rhythm.
By the twos, they took their places at her side
signalling, how the mocked ancestors sighed
as their ghosts broke loose, being no longer with them.
And when they would "close the eyelids of the dead"
this endless and eternal dirge
was performed by the fire under a stand of birch.

---

[1] 'Pusztapánd' in Hungarian; an invented English place name for reasons of euphony.

[2] 'Korhány' in Hungarian, an antiquated regionalism: 'two-pronged wood used as a plow-rest.' (The locality may have resembled its Y-like shape.)

And when it was time to start and "dig the grave"
my father joined their ranks as number six
whose steps were watched by the five other dancers
as if he'd entered on special purpose and gave
new sense to the ritual with his masterly fix.

When the candles had burnt into a neat
heap of ashes, my mother fashioned a final pirouette.
As for the shepherds, they were just gazing at
the Moon as it sauntered through the sky
admiring, awe-struck, with its giant, pallid eye
the Ballad on my mother's nimble feet.

Adam Makkai

THE BOBBIN STOPS

The hills, the bridge, the country, the squeaking wheelbarrow,
the blind ploughman who wandered without a cane
and my house that fell into dust, I've forgotten long ago —
a tale has grown over my past.

I've forgotten the poppy-seed's blueish juice
and the old soothsayer, as she shut her greenish eyes
and bent over me with her strange, sleepy face
with wine for dreams in her cup,
old midnight fortune teller that she was.

And I forgot the spinning wheel, and the skein
as we used to sit, all ten of us, 'midst the noiseless wonder
as we just sat there, all ten of us,
in the reddish nothing
          and the barnyard intoned a song
                    in its merry mood...
The barnyard was singing while the women were spinning
secrets and fates — but they got punished by death,
all of them... Only I grew up big, and now
I'm whispering about the secrets of the twilight,
so that no other woman, nor my sister should ever

indulge in it...
                Let them see that there,
                in that world the size of my palm, blood runs out,
                the bobbin stops, and the spinning wheel
                        rambles on
                                threadless.

Adam Makkai

MEMORIES OF MUDLAND-MEADOW[3]

    You may ask the world
who he was, the man who lived next to the waters of
Complaint Creek[4] in that forbidding wilderness,
while the spider on its dusty thread descends
and the wine goes sour in the glass,
the stars turn their faces away;
and the knocking of the autumn rains stops,
and the Moon just turns its face away and gives no answer.

                        *

    Valentine Hadabash,[5] too,
broke a loaf of bread into two
as he learned it from his father:
he made the sign of the cross over it, or rather
he blessed it, so it may become part of the body.
And he ate... And the lamp-light
or the light of the sun kept playing hide-and-seek
in his hair.

    He, too, was a serf-tenant
by the craggy banks of Complaint Creek.
There were reedy marshes, willows, birds

---

[3] *'Sártalló'* in Hungarian. 'Mud-Meadow' comes closest in English.
[4] *'Panasz'* in Hungarian, which means 'complaint.'
[5] *'Hadabás'* in Hungarian; 'Valentine' is *Bálint* in the original.

and fish — that's why he went to live there.
There was reed a-plenty; he cut it with his scythe
and he would use it for fuel in the winter when snowy clouds
were swaying above, and sickly flies
kept whimpering under the master beam.

It was a narrow world in any event,
whatever he could hug up in the vast space —
it was wheatless, meadowless and tiny: a pillory.
And there was born as a last, bitter-sweet smile,
as the seventh child among six others, the little Hilary.[6]
And as when a tree
sprouts one more bouquet of flowers
before the leaves start to wither and fall
and keeps showing them to the Sun, to the High Noon
that chides away at empty space
ferociously howling — so did her mother, Rose Benedict,[7]
defend her last-born child.

They gave her every new fruit's first-ripened piece;
they carried her to the meadow, to the wheat field,
and they knew that they would be eventually bereaved,
when the little rose-bud grew up,
when the late violet becomes a flower of spring-time.
How fragile are those pieces of fruit too, which,
when their skin is still velvety,
sit in the cup of a wood-flower,
why, even a flea may eat or destroy them.

But if it grows to maturity — it's a separate life,
bed for honey in which the earth, the mother-soul, lies down
and becomes redeemed right along with the soul of a tree.
Then does the struggle start. How much danger must pass
until the apple becomes a new tree, a hidden soul, that
blossoms forth with a song in the palms of the earth.

---

[6] 'Karola' in Hungarian, which rhymes with the word for 'pillory,'
'kaloda' in Hungarian.

[7] 'Rózsa Bence' in Hungarian. Bence comes from the Latin 'Benedictus.'

And so — Hilary Hadabash, too, grew up, and
wove a ribbon into her hair;
and she was beautiful as was the earth;
and beautiful was that summer day when Lazarus Rider[8] took her
home to his court near Mud-Meadow-Island.

How could the world ever find out what sorrow hovered
over her head, as she became more and more disappointed
and everything turned into deadly boredom?
Ill-fate had sullenly clung to their door,
and just kept standing there, a stubborn sentinel
in both hot and cold; all terrestrial
pathways were heavily restricted —
forbidden ditches, forbidden distances,
only towards the sky was the road wide open.

*

O charm, let your voice once more be heard,
remember, all you dear people, now trying to remember —
do not wave in memory's fog, O you, vast prairies along Snail
Brook;[9] get up, O forest, and you, the region of Mud-Meadow,
low-lands of Hoarfrostville,[10] who drank up so many heavy rains;
little hut, tornado, and you ancient hay-stacks,
little river's foot-bridge, bucket of an old well,
bitter paint of sumack, black and uninviting,
smoke that oils the cauldron with layers of greasy soot;
sorrow weighing you down, joy that flies to heaven,
heavy, grave poverty of an ancient footpath —
— O, how many are the memories one has to carry!

Now, when we are all placed
under heavy judgment

---

[8] Translated as 'Lazarus Rider,' the original has *Lázár Lovas*.
[9] *'Csigla'* in Hungarian. *Csiga,* skipping the /l/, means 'snail.'
These localities are generally all unknown to Budapest Hungarian readers.
[10] *'Hór'* in Hungarian, sounding like *'hoar'* in *'hoarfrost.'*
The word has no recognizable meaning in Budapest Hungarian.

so that life may hurt us equally —
will my old fate return to haunt me?
Will my erstwhile paths come running back under my feet?
And is there no hope under the vault of Heaven
except that I may once more clasp my
smoke-blackened fingers?
   And can all this complaining cake in my mouth
sentencing me to having to listen
to the sobbing of the fallow till I die?

   Let it be so.
               But may I still learn what I have lived for?
May I know that I shall become mud, fertile soil
producing wheat for the folks and for the birds,
and may I know that I shall become the one
who eventually wanders home every now and then
out of the fairy tales
like a fugitive ghost from a cemetery.

   May I know that I was alive
to keep on living in tales and inside the bread,
for which I now burn up my great, big stupid heart.

   Let it be so.
               But you, Memory of Distance,
Beauty, Song and Life, you should accompany me,
as long as I am still alive —
"You", who were my reason to exist, there, once upon a time
in the dust of Hoarfrostville,
since it was "you" who spoke to me
in the most beautiful language,
teaching me that there are boys and there are girls,
and where, after several centuries,
I became cognizant of the secret
that it's in your smile that I am alive once more —
the smile of the sky.

   When the wind doesn't blow and yet the twigs go on trembling,
only then can they dream such beautiful dreams
about the one and only flower

which they hug with their foliage
and hide from everyone's eyes; they'd rather
bury it into graves of ice; they'd bend over the flower's memory
and, like the human soul, just keep mourning for it in silence,
for a long, long time.

   Not only trees: the *puszta,* too,
can dream such dreams — in its memories
beauty increases, it stretches out its big fertile arms
and conjures back to life those it saw while dreaming,
so that there may be some hope
in the sadness of mortal humans.
— Susie Soldier[11], too, was such a hope.

   It was as if she had
neither father nor mother, or so it seemed;
but instead, as if it had been the gold of the sunsets
that became incarnated in the palm
of the Angel of life,
and became neither rose nor elm tree,
neither grape nor honey,
but a seedier form of Mother Earth:
a girl, the enemy of blood-thirsty Death,
one who provides the soul wanting to get dressed in a body
and after that backs into the grave only one step at a time.

   To be an orphan on the *puszta* by
Complaint Creek next to Hoarfrostville
can be as sad as when one laments over all hope vanishing,
or like the lost war fought with the slinging of mud.
But a little calf will walk up to you
        if you have the sign
             of loneliness on your forehead, yes,
not just the little calf but the foal, too,
and lovely blond doves will make conversation with you:
if a girl of the *puszta* should stare under your hat,

---

[11] The name is *Zsuzska Katona* in Hungarian; 'Susie Soldier' is an
accurate translation.

her eyes will grow as big as a star and turn into day-dreams
and into a seven-secreted rainbow.

And she will wish to unite with you
like one brook with another,
so that you may flow on together
throughout the whole world
and that you two may have one name,
far away, even in the night of life,
when you will cover yourselves with silence and snow.

To be united with him, just as two
brown lumps of earth unite, and when they're already one
the soul of flowers sits down in your warmth
and demands a sprout, and begs for such a body
as is needed for an earthly beginning
in which it can wander off towards higher goals
— life and wandering never cease, they're eternal —
and though motionlessness, can penetrate all motion.

To be united with him, as sweetness with its honey.
The bitterness of life must be conquered
by the girl's entering the vineyard of the sky
and her making a *future*-bed for a boy of the future.
And she steps in harmony with the one she's united with,
for bitterness is a-plenty and sweetness is mighty scarce;
the earth is no good — loneliness
            is not our goal,
                        — so they enter together the bed's Garden of Eden.

O man, rise up and grovel no more,
you, who'd been cast down into the dust,
you, who were once the son
of the skies, a soul soaring on wings;
then became fallen innocence; then a body
identical with the earth, and still later the bearer
of earthly wounds — move on, and try to seek some comfort!
Why, here and there life gives you a few pleasures, too,
and sometimes even a smile or two.

But who among all men could step into his grave with a hurt
as deep as mine; me, whom the Avenger
thinks of as the Original Loser even today?

   True, I no longer roam
the old *puszta*'s desert regions,
but it's today that I really live in a desert.[12]
And how utterly alone, alone with myself.
Time, though trying to soothe me, won't lie.
I am traversing this loquacious, noisy world
without taking my chagrins along as weapons,
all I carry with me is a smile, the smile of those
who would preach even unto the birds.

   And my paths will always turn into autumn
but I'll be encouraged by pure hopes, no matter
how desolate life's *puszta* is today;
all the past distances draw near,
even the Moon... and lo, the Moon, too, becomes the old
acquaintance; Susie N. Soldier steps out from its spheres,
the past crying on her face, and beautiful ancient meekness in her eyes
— did she become flesh-and-blood again now that she's
lived down her torments through sleep?

   But yes, O Charm, you do still exist,
you, who're still loved only by the stars,
the distant ones, that break into shreds in the foam of the
brook at night with memory trembling between its shiny slivers,
or are there other secrets, too, in the silent stars?
You do live, O Charm! Little by little I'm beginning
to remember you... And I fetch you up in my
tired, old arms, and bathe you in pure human sorrow.
   Do keep on wearing your youth,
like a broken crown, behold: I return it, it's yours,

---

[12] Sinka wrote this poem in 1951 during the height of Stalinism in
Hungary without the slightest hope of ever seeing it in print. It eventually
appeared in 1967 as the introduction to his volume *Mesterek uccája* [The
Street of the Craftsmen.]

so that you may step over ages and times
with it — for you are that blessèd one
on whom memory bestows eternal youth —
for, see, my own heart by now has grown so very quiet.

  You do still live, O Charm sublime,
with the sorrow lifted from your face.
And gone will be all the old landscapes,
gone forever, if not right away, surely later.
The winds will have blown far away the ashes of Mud-Meadow,
there's no such thing as "years," and upon earthly sorrow
        there she sits, the World's own Brooder,
              the Great Bird of Time.

*

… And how good you were, too, heat of the summer time,
sometimes you'd give me bread,
and occasionally even a bed,
and pointed my way to where
the Flower of The Smile grew; and it was you
who would look for me, when I would lose sight of you.
Please be kind to me, you too, wind of the autumn air,
keep whistling away on top of the hills, but way down there,
in the depths of the glen, where humans live in their tiny huts,
hush, please! …Not a word about how we used to
        wander and stumble and stagger together
              along so many paths and mud-caked, hardened ruts.

Adam Makkai

DEAR STARS, ROCK ME TO SLEEP...

A. Smith, I. Brown and my own self
were walking away from Peak's-Bed
while the dust flew under our soles
like the yellow smoke of our Fate's eternal dread.

Indeed our fate sits in primeval twilight
it smokes and this smoke is choking —
just as the autumn's fog suffocates
a destroyed ant-hill's self-pity in joking.
There we walked, all three of us,
everything we had was stuffed in our bags;
we each had a pitch-fork, a knapsack,
and some lamentable, torn and dirty rags.
Anyway, when you're so orphaned and poor
that you consider a pinch of salt of great value,
all you can make music with is your finger nails   ;
no fancy embroidered pants will derail you.
So how long did our journey last?
Journeys like this have no mileage-markers.
There were many farms, many mud-roads,
all the way to Lake Adobe's[13] waters.
See, how much men have got to wander
and always on foot, as long as they're alive;
A. Smith, I. Brown,[14] and me, Steve Sinka,
as long as we've got a slice of bread for our knife.
Hey you, Lake Adobe's waters! There we stood
on your banks where there's a lot of reed.
And what the hell were we? Eager and unemployed
unhired hands, wanting to make haystacks or pull up some weed.
We stuck our pitch-forks into the ground,
three migratory birds, wild and brave.
The sky was blue; so were the waters of Lake Adobe,
but for us the region was a huge, blue grave.
...Remembrance! Memory! Whatever happened
to A. Smith and what befell I. Brown?
O you stars, should their souls fly in your direction,
rock them to sleep; you bed them down!

Adam Makkai

---

[13] 'Adobe' and 'Peak's Bed' are Anglicizations appropriate to the Hungarian original.

[14] 'Brown' and 'Smith' are equivalent Anglicizations of common Hungarian surnames.

Margit Mikes
(1897-1976)

Born into a literary family, Margit Mikes was the daughter of Lajos Mikes (1872-1930), a major figure among Hungarian editors of the Nyugat *generation. Her elder sister married the poet Lőrinc Szabó (q.v.); she married László Kemény, a noted post-impressionist painter. The two families lived in the same house in Buda, where a great deal of Hungarian literature was happening both socially and artistically.*

Her poems and short stories appeared in journals such as Nyugat [The West], Magyarország [Hungary], Az Est [The Evening], Budapest Diary [Pesti Napló], Pest Gazette [Pesti Hírlap], New Times [Új Idők], Life and Literature [Élet és Irodalom], The Contemporary [Kortárs], *and* Vigil [Vigilia].

Miklós Radnóti (q.v.) characterized her poetry in these words: "...She is a highly disciplined poet, whose poetic motifs develop organically from one another, forming a close unity. She has a great deal to say about the feminine soul and the trials of the spirit, often with spectacular poetic solutions..."

An early feminist, she gave voice to the fate of oppressed women in the general context of speaking up against poverty and exploitation in the humanistic manner.

Her single volume published in Hungary is Költő a konyhán [Poetess in the Kitchen], *which appeared in 1938. In 1976 she and her husband left Hungary and joined their daughter in New York City. She published two volumes living abroad,* Üvegpohár [Drinking Glass], *1971, Cambridge, MA., and* Csillagtalan ég alatt [Under a Starless Sky] *in Munich, Germany in 1974.*

POET IN THE KITCHEN

The sun bursts through the window.
Shall I write? Go out?
Spring calls, but the work says:
"Just look around; pots and pans
and dishes in a dirty bunch;
beneath the cabinet lurks the dust

and you are thinking of poetry for lunch?!"
"Come on, you hired hands!" I nag —
"It's time to work! Snag the dish-rag,
grab the broom,
with nimble fingers make them dance
within the sink, around the room!"

Still, little time remains for what has worth,
and maybe little energy as well.
My hands are servants,
but they call me 'Lady.'
You working-class lady, smile and tell
how life has brought you down to earth!
While still a girl, upon a shady
riverbank you read and dreamed
and played the piano while your father worked.
You read your book,
and never thought how time is money,
and someone has to cook.

The sun bursts through the window.
No use crying over what I was;
life goes on... And I burst out in song!
(In the spring a mood doesn't last very long.)
Friday is Pasta Day! Now that's important.
A fine spaghetti dinner! So let's see — I toss
flower and eggs together — there! To be
your own maid means that you're the boss!
I knead and pull the dough
(how rich that smell)
and fold a sunbeam in
(now watch it swell!)

Sun, golden sun, golden future,
brighten my day.
Brighten these ground-floor lodgings
where I stay.
The past is gone, so let the present shine;
most people's lot is far worse than mine.

Spring comes, and deep within me is displayed
a newborn world, and a new maid,
one who no longer bows and scrapes
(except perhaps in front of dirty dinner-plates)!

Suzanne K. Walther

IDENTITY

Without my mother tongue and my country,
without my familiar community,
what good is my nationality?
I don't know, but still
O guard it with fierce loyalty.
That's me... but who am I?
My identity is the same.
I know I will remain
— be it foolish or brave —
Hungarian to the grave!
I am a leaf torn from the Magyar tree,
blown here by the storm.
The leaf is ripped free,
it tosses, turns and cries
until it dies.

Suzanne K. Walther

TO MY DAUGHTER

Once Death has spoken, the words are final.
The lid of my coffin is firmly down.
You call, but in spite of your denial,
I can no longer shelter you from harm.

I listen to a New Law: time is now shaped
in Earth's cradle, where I'm a new-born dead.
I sleep, I wake: I finally escaped
life's desire, struggle and constant dread.

I have reached my Maker. You should be seeing
eternity as my Savior. Be brave,
don't cry and mourn too long over my grave.

I keep watch over your earthly being,
from afar. Don't stay locked in your misery;
then it's better — to have forgotten me.   *Suzanne K. Walther*

GLASSWORKS

The temperature is zero below.
On the kitchen window the snow
sticks in flower patterns;
memory and fantasy together bring
the illusion of a white spring.
As I search for some matches,
a water glass shatters in the cold.
My breath catches.
What a painful shriek, a piercing sound!
A dangerous transformation of matter.
As I turn around
it clatters to the ground
and a cylinder of ice rolls out.
Before it was clear water, refreshing potion,
now, in this temperature
it has become a miniature
frozen ocean.

You transparent, dead glass
our fate is the same.
Indifference engulfs us.
The tears that gushed
on my face freeze;
the pain numbs,
in the frozen vice of apathy
my heart is crushed.

Suzanne K. Walther

György Sárközi
(1899-1945)

Born into a non-religious Jewish family, Sárközi was the descendent of country school-masters and millers. His father was an office clerk, and the family moved away from Budapest in 1909 for financial reasons. The following three years spent in Vác, not too far north of the capital and on the Danube, proved very important in the life of Sárközi, because he attended a Catholic college there and converted to Catholicism.

Returning to Budapest, he was fortunate to continue his literary education under Professor Marcell Benedek, a first-rate scholar, essayist and critic. Hungary's foremost literary periodical, Nyugat [The West], *published several poems by Sárközi as early as 1917. Soon after graduation from high school, still in Budapest, Sárközi became a publisher's reader and remained in publishing for the rest of his life. "Lyric poetry is not dead, after all" wrote Mihály Babits (q.v.), upon reviewing Sárközi's first volume,* A Fight of Angels [Angyalok harca], *which appeared in 1926. His next volume,* With a Relayed Soul [Váltott lélekkel], *1927, shows a mature poet who is deeply concerned with social problems. By the mid-1930s Sárközi had become not only a well-known literary figure, but also—because of his position with one of the country's largest publishing firms—the center of a large circle of writers. He became editor of the populist movement's literary magazine,* Response [Válasz], *and initiated the socio-geographical series* The Discovery of Hungary [Magyarország felfedezése] *which, after several interruptions and changes, is still active today.*

He married Márta Molnár, the daughter of the famous playwright and Hollywood screenwriter Ferenc Molnár (1878-1952). Sárközi and his wife lived a few happy years until World War II broke out. He translated Goethe, Thomas Mann and Petrarch. His third and last volume, Hope for a Miracle [Higgy a csodában], *appeared in 1941. In 1944 he, like his friend Miklós Radnóti (q.v.) and others who were considered Jews according to Nazi "laws", was conscripted for forced labor.*

Because of his immense popularity, Sárközi was offered several chances to escape and live through the end of the war in hiding, but he proudly declined. He died at Balf concentration camp in March of 1945, another innocent victim of the Nazis.

THE UNKNOWN WORLD

If I but stretch out my hand, someone grips it. I feel this is certain.
If I but lift up my head, countless stars tremble afar in night's curtain.

During the dark, I can hear axes thud in the depths subterraneous,
Sense, at the dawn, lights invisible flash by spontaneous,

and, as if deep-hidden mice gnawed my heart and were hungry to tear
   it,
know some perdurable grief — the perpetual pang of my spirit.

Why should I roam in the forest, if there too the autumn is sleeping?
Why stop for flowers in the meadow? The meadow with graves in its
   keeping?

Why should I gaze in your mirroring eye — soon but dust all
   unseeing?
Why know this butterfly-life, folding back once again in non-being?

Baffled with veils of eternity, sightless I gaze and deplore me:
Where, oh my God, have You hidden the face of the world from
   before me?

Watson Kirkconnell

RAINDROPS

A day must bring an ending of the self,
and change me to a slim book on the shelf:
the joys and sorrows of my life embark
to the print's silent and eternal dark.

Occasionally, a hand will reach for me,
and from my rustling leaves, surprisingly,
a word will glow, a far world glimpsed by men,
and he who sought me starts to live again.

The choking mists of black and turbulent ages
will blot the lines stretched lifeless on my pages:
but hold these same leaves up towards the sun —
a hidden symbol's pressed into each one!

So even after death I'll live as long
as paper's mercy holds, and the old tongue
in which the song was uttered's not consumed
by chance in epochs troubled, warring, doomed.

The memory of me that's left, one day —
breath on a winter pane — will waste away,
and like a dost-mote by the desert's face
time will possess and not reveal my place.

Roy Fuller

FOG

Fog: big doped cats lazily
padding around; they lick
me first, then spit on me.

I can't see a thing — just hear
footsteps waddle and stop,
coughs from the invisibly near.

Shadows, who are you? Old pals?
New enemies? Is it you, God?
Or just sawdust, dangling dolls?

There's an eerie demi-light,
like this hour sandbagged earth
topples over into night.

Where are my son, my wife,
my country? Where are my heroes?
The fog fills earth and heaven, both.

What once was solid — fog-rivers;
cold fog one's heart's blood also;
and the sun feverish on fog-feathers.

Roy Fuller

LIKE GULLIVER

Like Gulliver in Brobdingnag,
scared as a kitten in a bag,
Somehow I find myself at large
in realms where giants are in charge.
Their shadows can eclipse the sun;
when they stamp, awful fissures run;
should one of them feel peeved with humble
me, his great boot could make me crumble.

Like Gulliver in Lilliput,
I wander, melancholy, mute,
where everything's of midget size,
and everything of greatness lies
shattered to particles of dust.
In this dwarf universe I must
be frightened to lift up my bent
head, lest it burst the firmament.

Roy Fuller

CURSED IS A MAN

Cursed is a man in his forsaken years.
The naturally happy birds will never
build on a hollow tree shivered by lightening's spears.

One of its arms still stretches to the stars,
but only irascible and growling bees
find honeyed use for its wide, grimy scars.

Cursed is a man in his forsaken years.
How carefully he guards his empty heart!
Aged stag-beetles hear his secret tears.

He's irrelevant to new storms that arise,
and when his breast is touched by the cool, rough hooves
of foal-like winds, he merely faintly sighs.

And to the last creaking of a cloven bough —
a bough with dry and fading, rustling leaves —
he topples, and earth crashes on his brow.

Roy Fuller

HOPE FOR A MIRACLE

When the sultry air is ripped by a wind
and suddenly the sky shouts to the land,
and the trees with their delicate boughs become roots,
hope for a miracle!
> When the hot night hushes the village, and
> before the threshing floor wheat sheaves stand
> dreaming of flames, like phantoms from Hell,
> a slopping butt on a cart, and loud bell,
> hope for a miracle!
When the earth grunts and the walls fail to meet
and you feel the floor alive under your feet,
and your scared wife runs to get the boys,
and your horse cries at the unknown human voice,
hope for a miracle!
> When armies' swords are broken, thrown down,
> because the bright comet will strike the town;
> when the poet, in a fix-hole, sings his last,
> and new bosses ride on an old country's past,
> hope for a miracle!

Roy Fuller

THE HYMN OF LOVE

My brother,
staggering amidst the shiny glass mountains of the North Pole,
riveting your fixed gaze unto the frozen lake of the sky;
   and you, the other,
emaciated, swarthy traveller of the desiccated, dreadful Sahara,
with tongue hanging out while you gallop on a crooked, skinny camel;
   and you, too,
bronze-skinned, morose son of America, kicked a hundred times;
   and you, too,
opium addict, roaming your sleepy, lukewarm house with tipping gait;
   and you, you all, all of you,
brothers and sisters, millions, wind-swept seeds of the same ear of
      wheat;
   you, who're alive now, or will live in the future or have lived in the
past: Love one another!
   Look:
A Light flashes in the sky and flamingly shouts: Love one another!
And the heart of the earth answers throbbing back: Love one another!
   Listen:
The oceans roar out, they roar: Love one another!
Thunderbolts drum it among the mountains: Love one another!
Suddenly,
millennia flicker away over our heads like rapid lightnings;
the industrious scythe of the Grim Reaper clatters in its rush —
   Brothers and Sisters!
Let dark hatred not hurl mud on the treasured moment,
while our immaculate lips are still able to touch one another!
When in the far-off future
the earth, gone cold, will dash around like a tossed snow-ball
around a hoarfrosty sun with the planets shuddering all over,
let one single orphan ray of light,
that of the erstwhile world-illuminating Love of Being in Love,
still shine into the darkened void!

Adam Makkai

Ödön Palasovszky
(1899-1980)

Poet, actor, novelist and stage director, Budapest-born Palasovszky finished his schooling in the capital and in Eger; between 1916-1920 he studied at the University of Budapest and at the Drama School of Budapest. In the 1920s he was the leader of avant-garde theater movements and intended to reform Hungarian theatrical culture. He was a member of the Social Democratic Party from 1921 on, but also kept in touch with the illegal Communist Party as a distant sympathizer. He was hauled into court more than once before 1945. He organized diction choirs for workers and was also interested in the artful movement of the human body. From 1927 onward he was a faculty member at the Madzsar Institute of Dramatic Arts. His articles and essays appeared almost exclusively in Társadalmi Szemle [The Social Review] *and in* Korunk [Our Age].

Although his left-leaning past could have guaranteed him success after World War II, Palasovszky, who retired early, kept a low profile and did not participate in the cultural opportunities afforded those who declared their loyalty to the Soviet Union. His name was heard rarely. In 1977, however, he won the Robert Graves Prize for "best poem of the year," a prestigious award founded by Robert Graves from his Hungarian royalties.

His works include Manifesztum [Manifesto], *1922;* Új stáció [New Station], *another Manifesto from the same year;* Reorganizáció [Reorganization], *a volume of poetry published in 1924;* Punalua [Punalua], *also poetry from 1924;* The Daughter of Ayrus [Ayrus leánya], *a drama, 1931; and* Thousand and One Nights [Ezeregyéjszaka], *1949, the classical tales presented in new versions. A collection of his poetry entitled* Opál himnuszok [Opal Hymns] *was published in 1977; a collection called* The Theater Aiming at the Essential [A lényegretörő színház] *in 1980 contains his essays on drama; in 1987 his* Selected Poems *were edited by János Parancs.*

This modest and often self-effacing man has enjoyed much less visibility than he deserves. We are able to present his poem that won the Graves Prize 'Susannah Bathing,' along with 'Lapiade, Opus 3' and 'Humiliating the Laser Beam' thanks to the interest taken in him by Kenneth McRobbie in the pages of the Hungarian Quarterly.

SUSANNAH BATHING

From blue sky to green forest, bathing
The morning of the stream is bathing
Susannah's in a cool stream bathing.

Ancient eagles circling in the sky
Rocks with human faces looking on
Into-spring sprouting adolescent bushes
Tree-branchingly slender centuries.

Susannah's bathing — and everything that's living
Young and old does gaze on her.

Rustlings in bushes: word is passed
That now she takes off butterfly shoes
That now her breathy panties float down.

Draw nigh, ye aged

A silver church doth bathe
A gold-brown steed doth bathe
An embrace is bathing
A flower bathes

Draw near, you young, drawn nigh, ye aged
Draw near, to espy her nakedness.

A prayer has bared itself to bathe — just look at that —
Impudent youngsters, sniggering oldsters
Devoutly the high forests look on
Young machines circle in the sky
A porno hymn is bathing — amen.

For her deer she's bathing
For her birds bathing
For poets' rhymes bathing
For painters' brushes bathing
Before form-restructuring cameras she's bathing

To humour the daily round bathing
Come see, come see

Now she's under the falling water
Spume-foam's force slaps at her
Splashes on her shoulders, on her fore-parts fair
From silken belly to posterior —
Round her slender waist flowing
She'd be like this if you caressed her
Spume-foam's force slaps at her
She'd be like this if you teased her
A water-spurt jets right into her lap
She'd be like this if you forced in there.

They stare, and stare
The dolphin-numberers, the atom-fireraisers
The town-builders, the defoliators
Susannah does bathe — the naked dream
The from blue sky down to cool stream bathing —
From yellow skies at time's four corners —
Her breasts two red-capped determined guerillas
Her lap the burning bush of our fate

They're watching—they can see her
And they shake,

You can't tell whether they're snickering or praying

Kenneth McRobbie

LAPIADE, OPUS 3

The train tears along, I'm on my way
leaving behind days, the nights
the days, nights are left behind
the train tears along, day and night
a hundred thousand kms. on the clock
we're on our way, I'm on my way
our train's tearing, tearing on.

Next stop a swarming station
we've ten minutes, a Friday, we'll get water
there's still water just once a week
ten minutes and I get off, I drink
would have, but my water-voucher's expired
mister your water-voucher isn't valid
the computer doesn't accept it
please get it stamped at the embassy
or drink from the brandy tap
mister if you need any LSD—
go to hell, I'm in a rush—

      still lots of time
      says the uniform.

That's my train over there, I can see
I mustn't forget my compartment's that one
up on the roof of car number three
there's a small speckled bird, singing.

      Mister your water-voucher isn't valid
      and your oxygen voucher's also expired
      but if you need a woman
      if you want some marihuana—
      mister if it's oxygen you need
      the computers, hey mister
      they're sounding immediate smog-alert.

I'm on my way
my train's leaving
still several hundred thousand kms. to go.

      Hurry along
      says the uniform.

I'd start back, but from left and right
newly arrived trains come whistling in
with snorts and hisses that stop across my path —

but that's my train over there, I can see

up on the roof of car number three
a bird preening itself.

> I'd start back — not valid —
> a blond for ten bucks, mister
> would you believe, you've got no shoes.

Smog-alert! Gas masks on, everyone
the sirens wail, smog-alert.

> The station's empty suddenly —
> I'd leave but where's my train gone to
> silence surrounding me.

The town to the right disappears suddenly
to the left the hill with clouds disappears suddenly
the station's collapsing
the rails vanish —

I am walking through slag and debris
rags paper thin splinters
and I've got no shoes on.

> I'm alone in the wasteland
> refuse in pyramids — still growing —
> junked cars, phased-out hymns
> plastic bags in the garbage
> the down-at-the-heel truths —
> god, where did I put my sunshine-voucher?

Night falls, the moon creeps on
mister your drinking-water voucher's not valid
mister your moonlight-voucher's up soon —
O for a tree! Or just a bush —
I beg to state
your greenbelt needs ran out long ago
the bird-voucher
will be validated for another thirty seconds.

I'm alone in the wasteland
only a single desiccated tree still stands
god god
there sits the bird.

Then on impulse
it flies away.

Kenneth McRobbie

HUMILIATING THE LASER-BEAM
(Lament in these our dark days)

Servant of the world's welfare once were you — god bless
the air's poisoning cannot be ascribed to you — god bless
the water's polluting cannot be blamed on you — god bless
the prosperity of all of us was served by you — god bless
our knowledge was made more exact by you — e.g. how far we are
    from the moon

bloodless operations were performed by you — god bless
the tunnel's path ran more exact, thanks to you — god bless
data-bank, you, hologram's life and soul, again you — god bless
the lightwave-telephone, credited to you — god bless

most terrifying murderous of weapons, this you've become
making death more exact — god bless
god bless

Kenneth McRobbie

VIII. CLASSICAL HUNGARIAN POETS BORN IN THE TWENTIETH CENTURY

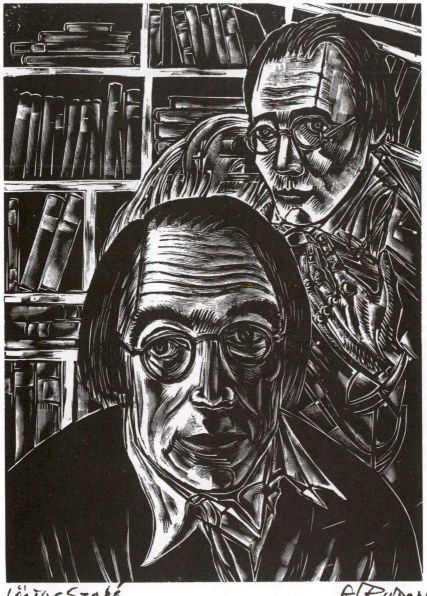

Lőrinc Szabó
1900 – 1957

Lőrinc Szabó
(1900-1957)

An outstanding poet and translator of the second Nyugat *generation, Szabó studied in Debrecen and Budapest and published his first book of poetry* Earth, Forest, God [Föld, erdő, Isten] *in 1922. He was heavily influenced by the German poet Stefan George (1868-1933), whose right hand in plaster form Szabó kept on his desk as a relic. After a revolutionary "Sturm und Drang" period of anarchistic revolt against the money-making ethics of society, Szabó made his "separate peace" with reality, turning to philosophy and to less topical subjects. In 1944 he won the Baumgarten Prize, in 1954 he was given the Attila József Prize and, in 1957 he won the Kossuth Prize.*

His literary style shows a unique blend of intellectual perception and sensual experience; few poets lived as passionately in the present as he did. Cricket's Music [Tücsökzene], *in which he told the story of his life in a brilliant sequence of poems, appeared shortly after World War II in 1947. He devoted a major lyrical requiem to his dead lover in the volume entitled* The Twenty-sixth Year [A huszonhatodik év], *which appeared in 1957 shortly after his death and contained one hundred twenty sonnets. He also excelled as a writer of poetry for children.*

Szabó's output as a translator from foreign languages is staggering. Best known are his translations of Baudelaire, Shakespeare, Pushkin, Tyutchev, Coleridge, Omar Khayyam, Villon, Kleist, Goethe, Hölderlin, and Molière. His collected translations appeared as a two-volume set bearing the title Our Eternal Friends [Örök barátaink] *and was reissued more than once. Because of his long-standing involvement with German poetry, he was mistakenly accused of having been a Nazi sympathizer.*

In 1955-1956 the influential socialist-populist Gyula Illyés (q.v.) wrote a major essay on the "missing Hungarian bourgeois novel" and presented the theory that this lacuna was filled by Szabó's revolutionary poetry. Illyés's argument was accepted by the officialdom, and Szabó's collected poems were thus able to appear shortly before the Hungarian Uprising of 1956.

He developed the rhyming technique of the Hungarian language to an unprecedented degree; assonances and enjambments of a highly sophisticated nature became Szabó's personal trademark and signature.

FROM *THE MUSIC OF A CRICKET*

THE TRANQUIL MIRACLE

You have nothing to do with me, alas,
I know, you simple crickets in the grass,
yet it is pleasant to have deemed, with pride,
when, now at night, I throw the window wide,
that you send word, my fateful little friends,
that the world's beauty to all lands extends —
just as the meadow through my bedroom's calm
sweeps in its soothing, aromatic balm,
breathing the soft, warm scent of new-mown hay,
mingled with sparks from out the Milky Way,
the fire-bright moon — all this your symphony
sends in its trilling messages to me;
thus you do, out of gentle music shed,
weave hither, with your notes, around my bed,
over the ruins of the day's merry ploy,
the draperies of what was once our joy,
this tranquil miracle of shared delight,
the happy and melodious summer night.

Watson Kirkconnell

WITH FLUTE, WITH VIOLIN

With *ű,* with *i,* the overture begins;
all afternoon the flutes and violins
already play; but when the night's silence falls,
within it freshen fairy madrigals:
i chirps and *ű* resounds, now low, now high,
an answer flashes and at once will die,
kri-kri and *ű-rű-krű,* as if the grass —
a thousand voices in a magic mass
tune more intensely, forming rings of sound
as wreaths of foam an island's shores surround;

the music swells, it floods and presses on
in criss-crossed notes, cadenzas come and gone;
the *ü*-s and *kri*-s that sparkle in the night,
their shafts of sound, their rings of crystal light,
this fairy-trumpet-battle skyward rears
to the bedazzlement of nerves and ears;
even tomorrow you're all *ü,* and *i,*
pure flute and cricket-fiddle ecstasy.

Watson Kirkconnell

ON A RAFT

A new flood came, transcending Ipoly's[1] banks.
A door I salvaged bore me on its planks,
my paddle was a branch. The water spread
above the pot-holed pasture as its bed;
the mighty lake of light transparent ran,
here a half-metre deep, there but a span;
in a blue summer day, sparkling in flame,
in diamond silence as the ripples came,
I floated above path and grass and flowers —
over the whole wide earth in those bright hours.
I did not even close my eyes, I deem,
before through all my senses flamed a dream,
a dream like that which opium bestows,
a dream that silent joy's caresses knows,
a dream that carries one through living walls,
a dream where mirrored wantonness enthrals,
a dream where earth and sky are wholly bright,
and all our body is a mute delight.

Watson Kirkconnell

---

[1] A left-side tributary of the Danube on the Hungary-Slovakia border.

BABITS[2]

What did I see in you? King, hero, saint.
What did you see in me? Lawless restraint.
What did I see in you? My destiny.
What did you see in me? The start of a way.
What I in you? Secrets, loneliness, mourning.
What you in me? Curses and spite and scorning.
And then, what I? My future of nightmares.
And then, what you? A hairy beast's desires.
Then I? A god in great need of salvation.
And you? The looming standards of damnation.
And later? That I'm your antagonist?
And I in you? One never to be lost.
You, ten years later? After all, your son?
I, after twenty years? Blind but divine.
You, after twenty? Pity about that one...
While I? Sad there is nothing to be done.
You, finally? That's how it had to go.
I, now and always? There's no one but you.

J.G. Nichols

THE MOMENT

As from a shell, a husk, I stripped you bare,
and not from garments only, for your stare
up in my eyes before the final strait
when you beheld the onset of your fate
yet still protested, yes, devoid of arts
you then looked up and in your heart of hearts
continued to undress: your offering eyes
then took to flight, reflecting wild surmise
and inner struggle in a fright so vain

---

[2] The poem is addressed to Mihály Babits, the poet, (q.v.), and is characteristic of the immense influence Babits had on his younger colleagues.

that my own heart contracted from your pain.
But slowly love won out; a quivering smile
of pensive trust your lips did then beguile;
victorious deadly joys your cheeks bedeck,
you raise your arm and clasp it round my neck:
how beautiful you were! That look to me
with which you yielded your virginity,
your future, and your heart without regret;
that was a gaze I can never forget.

Watson Kirkconnell

TO FORGET?

Up-flaring through your nerves, you know the flash
of mighty lightnings whose resounding crash
melted you, blinded you, and with its jars
widened that minute out to match the stars
and swept along the highway like a fire,
consuming all the tinder of desire,
while loud reverberations of its anger
soothed your numbed members with delightful languor;
then came the rain, relaxing limbs that thresh.
Describe the sweet explosion in your flesh,
that climaxed moment of our shared delight
beyond the power of language to endite,
except for faith, for thus, with me to aid,
you died and were reborn, my little maid.
Tell me that minute's spell, in accents mute;
tell me that minute, dear, and all its fruit
(tell not in words, your smiling will suffice) —
could you forget it, short of Paradise?

Watson Kirkconnell

ENGLISH POETRY

"Wilde is the easiest", said my master, one
fine morning. So we settled down upon
a sofa, spent an hour or so on grammar,
then with no more ado began to hammer
some meaning from *The Happy Prince*. We felt
saying it properly was difficult.
Even Babits had doubts. "It's quite the thing,"
he chuckled, "ever since Arany's time,
Hungarian poets study Shakespeare's tongue,
and never hear it..." The end of that day came
with Swinburne and some Browning (just a taste).
This way seventy hours, a whole week, passed.
He was translating only with his eye;
sometimes he changed the sonant made by */t/*
and */h/* into */ts/*; all with his own
strange but successful way of scanning. Then:
"You try it now: the English have at least
ten men as great as Goethe at his best."

J.G. Nichols

SHAME

Today when I came underneath the spell
(a sort of nervous spasm, *petit mal*)
with someone present, why, I kept a leash
upon myself. That's what first made me gauche
in front of girls: I battened down that pressure
which could be painful yet gave so much pleasure;
as my emotion rose, I grew ashamed
at being vulnerable, and most alarmed
at what my flesh was rising to, at the
excitement, sin, and the uncertainty,
the mad compulsion and (already known
well in advance of action) shameful pain;
such shame, such shame I swear a gentle game

of chess made my teeth chatter; such great shame
of any personal matter, from this spasm,
of any doubt, of all enthusiasm,
such shame I turned to writing poetry —
a childishness that lingers to this day.

J.G. Nichols

LÓCI BECOMES A GIANT[3]

Like giant with a dwarf who thwarts him
I quarrelled with my little son:
stop hammering the sideboard Lóci!
What have you got? What have you done?
Come straight away down from the gas stove!
Give me the scissors! Can't you see?
Terrible child — again you threw off
the rose-pot from the balcony!

In vain I threatened, he ignored me,
I could have spoken to the moon.
He mountaineered my sacred book case,
he ruined my whole afternoon.
He shaved the blossoms off the cactus
and dissected his latest toy.
I am as tall as you! — he boasted
and jumped on my desk full of joy.

He wore me out. I felt quite hopeless,
but still I liked to see him gay,
and lest I should be forced to spank him
I settled down with him to play.
I squatted down, the giant dwarfing
for ten, fifteen minutes or so.

---

[3] The nickname of the authors son, Lőrinc Szabó, Jr.

(What would happen — I thought — if like him
we always would live down below?)

And as I cowered down to Lóci
the world grew high and filled the air:
around me towers soared and wandered
and legs and legs were everywhere,
and heights increased, distances grew,
the wardrobe, table, and the door,
I felt a hapless tiny captive
locked in the jail-pit of the floor.

And frightening it seemed from down there
that all the grown-ups were so tall,
that they were strong and knew the answers
while I was powerless and small.
Humbled and frowned on by the big world
a tall desire sent me high
— up! up! like him the first aeronaut
who dared his wings against the sky.

Then slowly anger overcame me
that I could neither fly, nor grow,
like a walled-in unseen time bomb
I readied myself for a blow.
I longed for revenge, for some action
so that all would stare and see...
Just ten minutes passed and I hated
the world that was suppressing me.

I hated, oh how much I hated...
Then suddenly I heard a crash:
The table-cloth flew off the table
and Lóci made tracks in a flash.
I jumped to my feet: oh, you scoundrel!
— And later: Never mind at all —
and lifted high the little fellow
to make him a giant, mighty tall.

Egon F. Kunz

PRIVATE TRUCE

If I had always known what I've learnt
      over the years,
if I had always known that life was
      squalor and tears,

I wouldn't be whistling now in the street,
      walking so tall,
I would have surely hanged myself, to
      finish it all.

With most other prodigal dreamers
      I once believed
that the world and the human species
      could be reprieved,

I thought that by force or by saying
      a gentle word
many of us working together
      could change the world.

Everything is much ghastlier than
      I thought before
but, thank God, I am not so squeamish,
      not any more,

now I can face life's abominations
      with open eyes,
that time and apathy succeeded
      to immunize.

I've seen now all the old disguises
      and flimsy veils,
my thirty-three years cannot be fooled
      by fairy-tales:

I see now, life is much more evil
   than I had guessed
when as a young man I was about
   to leave the nest,

I see how the sucker gets cheated
   day after day,
poor sucker can't do anything else,
   try as he may,

I see how reason becomes the whore
   of interest,
how villains dress up like Galahads
   on holy quest,

I see the noblest causes soiled by
   the too-many,
I see that only death can bring us
   true harmony, —

and since this isn't a fact to despise
   or to deplore,
and since the seed of all human things
   is bloody war:

I look at life, with calm resolve
   and patience steeled,
as a doomed leper colony, or
   a battlefield.

If I had learned about these perils
   all at a blow,
I would have certainly hanged myself,
   some time ago.

But fate must have planned a part, it seems,
   for me to play:
it taught me everything, but slowly
   the gentle way:

This is why I signed a private truce,
  myself alone,
and this is why I do my duty
  without a moan,

this is why I think there are moments
  worth living for,
this is why I am writing poems,
  in times of war,

so I whistle among the lepers,
  and smile inside,
and I am growing very fond of
  the simple child.

          Peter Zollman

HAY WAGON

The hay wagon passed through the town at night.
Along our street it travelled in the pale
moonlight beneath the watching eyes of rows
of stuffy houses, under the lopped trees
that reached from the pavement longingly.
The hay wagon passed through the town. It came
and went, swimming and floating in the sweet
scent that had come with it; in a haze of light
it swam, and as it swam it told a tale.
Told it to me. For me it conjured up
the moonlit village, dumpy chicken coops,
the shaggy sheepdog and the meadows and
the deep song of the mowers, the brown skin
of country girls, the plow, the pails of milk,
the gypsy's fiddle and the wailing pipes;
all this brought back to my memory
and the fierce glare of sunshine in the eyes
of the black-coated bullocks, heaps of dung,
and pouring skies and the rain-freshened hills,
the grinding toil, the vigour and the stern

endurance — it brought it all back to me.
Everything it recalled as it rolled on
through night-hushed, lamp-lit streets, through the dead town
and listening with a breathing heart I felt
trees, grass, and woods growing around me, and
from distant hills that quivered with the breath
of giant limbs outstretched in ageless dreams
I heard the wild oak-crested mountain god.

Godfrey Turton

THE DREAMS OF THE ONE

Since you are this way and they are that
and his interests are different
and truth's a sort of nervous fact
on verbal front
and since nothing out there pleases me
and since the crowd still has supremacy
and of the framing of rules I'm utterly
innocent:
it is high time now
that I escaped your net.
    What should I go on waiting for any longer,
timidly scanning days to come?
Time hurries past, and whatever lives
is true to itself alone.
Either I am sick, or you are; and
am I not to recognize the weapons in the hand
of love or hate that comes to stand
before my face?
If I am for ever only to understand,
where is my own place?
    No! No! No! How can I bear to be
no more than a thread in a mad web:
to understand and honour the guard
and share his pain, his pain!
All who could, have long got out of the snares,

they go freely through and about the wires.
I and the world, there go the two of us,
captive in the cage,
the world with the limelight on itself,
like me on my own stage.

We're escaping, my soul, we've sprung the lock,
the mind has leapt away
but is careful to paint itself
with the bars of appearance.
Inside it is one that outside's a thousand fragments!

Who knows where the man ever went
that saw the fish, and still the net is
intact?
Forbidden? By some one else! Sin! To them,
if caught in the act!
Within us, inside, no divisions or frontiers,
nothing is forbidden;
we are only what we are, each one a solitude,
not bad, not good.

Hide in the depths of yourself! For there,
the great and free dream, you'd swear,
lies abandoned still, as were our mother, the unbounded
sea appears like a memory
in the sharp taste of our tears and blood.

Back into the sea, into our selves! Only
there can we be free!
We needn't look out yonder to see
anything coming to us from the Many.
If ever we are hucksters with the crowd,
truth crumbles down to powder;
only the One is our home ground,
never undone:
let us dream, if we still can,
the dreams of the One!

Edwin Morgan

THEY SAY SHE IS LOVELY

They say she is lovely, and I say nothing.
They say, her fiery bronze hair is the glow of down,
and the radiance of the stars in her eyes;
that she is proud and willful and would
ignore an ugly, swarthy guy like me.
As she just laughs, they gaze longingly at her
scornful lips and the graceful curve of her chin.
They don't know that yesterday she kissed me.
When she is quiet they can't guess that she
is thinking of yesterday, of the drizzling mist,
the mist that fell on us, on her and on me.
Even the thrushes were drunk with happiness
when they saw our joyful coupling;
diving low beneath the green branches
they burst into a delirious love song.

Suzanne K. Walther

MATERIALISM

Sometimes I stop on the street afraid,
observing what is newly made.
New gods spawning everywhere
while old ghosts haunt the very air.
The pavement is no longer there,
I lift my foot yet do not dare
to put it down.
For that would ruin the illusion
that all things labour just for me.

My birth was wholly miraculous,
but my teeth chattered in the iron of the winter.
So, the mountains gave me coal and wood
that made itself a fiery sacrifice for me.
Then came the stone and scraped up to the skies,

forming a perfect cave to please my eyes.
Iron came every day, turning
to hammer and to tools while learning
how to be its own blacksmith, and beat
itself in white frenzied heat.
Iron has arms that never tire;
some that heat up in the fire
while others cool and flatten,
shape and bend to circles.
Sweating, wearing-out and breaking-down,
workers in ultimate poverty,
lower than the lowest of the animals.

Rubber tires huddle the wheels of my car,
the metal begs to carry me far,
petrol explodes so that I can fly.
And all the others, clothes and shoes,
chairs, cups and pencils, all I use,
my pens, my lamp, my books, my dish,
yes, everything that does exist
for comfort, health, mobility,
food and fire — nobility
of soul, and music's perfect whole,
all swarm upon me and consume my soul.
My flesh inside, my flesh without,
the soul's exposed and torn about
quite pitilessly, cruelly degraded
to rags, to rubbish, and to dirt.
I do believe in matter,
that takes a thousand forms,
minds not this self-immolation,
celestial self-sacrifice.

My friends, I do believe that there's no more
than this; that matter *is,* and is the core
of truth and every goodness;
that there is only matter, now and now.
A million times a moment humbled
for its sad sister, called "the soul."

The suicide of matter is life.
Is there more goodness or a beauty
that I can love with greater gratitude,
that lies in pure and patient matter?
Abused by mindless priests
dismissed by men of little thought,
never asked "why?" It runs or pants,
why flesh, wood, glass and metal work for naught?
And plants, filled with a thousand kinds of blood,
that labour on despite the cruellest odds,
they have the secret strength of matter and their roots.
A sacred strength that gives survival.
Why should it always work for us?
Why should it be so patient and so humble?
Why should it work for us, for thoughtless Man?
O, why should matter work, just for the Soul?

Laurence James

ALL FOR NOTHING

It is terrible, I admit that,
            but this is how it's true.
If you love me, let your life be
suicide, or almost that.
You will never see me pause
for today's people, today's laws;
within, the man is master who
            was prisoner out there,
and I take gladness only through
the law I own and cannot share.

You are not mine till you are yours:
            in love? — not yet.
If it's still me-for-you you choose
you hang weights upon my neck.
Business, though sacred, is business: the thing
I need now is: All for Nothing!

Anything else is two selves running
                a hidden fight;
I want more: you, becoming
a part and parcel of my fate.

I am tired, I am sick, I am suspicious
                of one and all;
my faith has given up its patience
though I perhaps desire you still.
If you would allay my fears,
all my disgusts, this is for your ears:
show me how the last humility
                and sacrifice
are for joy, show me your ability
to contradict a world I despise.

For until you need one minute
                with yourself alone,
till you dare think you could win it,
till you regret the life you've known,
till you stop being an object,
lying there dead and abject:
till then you are no better, no more
                than all the rest,
till then a stranger at my door,
till then irrelevant at best.

Let the law save those who are
                good as their fellow-men;
beyond the law, like an animal,
be like that, I'll love you then.
Like a lamp that's turned off, you
mustn't be if I don't need you to;
don't complain, don't even see
                a prison that's invisible;
and I in my mind will guarantee
that you forgive my ruthless rule.

Edwin Morgan

PRISONS

Still in one body, locked and barred
still me? Never a new image?
Nowhere a thoroughgoing change?
How do you all endure these bars?

A different man! Why for once
can I not be my anti-self!
My soul, what is out there? It spells
other days, another order, other skies.

My brain is like the shell of a hall,
the word flies through it and returns;
and unless my fate concurs
even dying's impossible.

I am an engineer who sits
in the prison of his own works
fumbling blindly, and in the dark
some day will throw a fatal switch.

Edwin Morgan

NIGHT ON THE BOULEVARD

What can I do, now there's nothing to say?
There's no fire
left, no desire.
I loved you first because you seemed
so fresh, like a rare spark gleaming.
        Now, all at once, I feel leaden, tired.
        And my childhood days
        are a darkened maze.
        Everywhere there's grinding poverty
        and grasping hands are all I see.
So many lives are spoiled forever!

Alone, in the cold, blue
February night you
came to me in your beauty and youth,
making it difficult to see the truth.
>   Walking late, I saw young, ragged animals
>   labouring in the streets,
>   opening the world beneath our feet.
>   A charnel smell whirled into white steam
>   bubbling up from the teaming
main sewer of Budapest.
A wraith led me down,
led me below the town
and I saw the unseen flood
of rushing water, filth, and mud.
>   This world of excrement,
>   a temple to the bowels
>   of the bourgeois; foul
>   beyond imagining, starker
>   than the inside of my mind, and dark
as a medieval Hell. Children,
most of them who labour there,
their bodies rotting, their hair
matted and plastered to infected heads,
who pass their days as fearful, living dead;
>   complaint is futile in that lifeless world,
>   though well I know their thoughts
>   like rats are caged and caught
>   knowing nothing but despair
>   and never seeing sunlit air.
Thinking of those doomed, abandoned people,
left by Christ, condemned by Man,
I pondered on our love. Can
it stand to be compared
with anything but this dull despair.
>   I heard fingers scrabbling,
>   nails breaking on frozen earth;
>   swearing and coarse, gallows mirth.
>   Suddenly, you were far away from me,
>   and our love became disharmony.

You have grown a world away
from me and from this place.
The blood streams down my face
from the torn furrows where nails
have marked my failure.
> A failure to see you for what you were.
> I wish to God they had you here,
> to feast on your soft body and tear
> your white breasts.
> I would not move to save you from those beasts.
No hand, no word, not even a look
would make me turn to spare
you. I no longer care
of your genteel charms,
your facile laugh and clinging arms.
> What should I do, what can I say
> to you? What once we knew
> is gone, no longer true.
> Those darkened sewers stripped off that false disguise
> of love. At last, long last, they opened wide my eyes.

Laurence James

QUARTER-HOUR BETWEEN GOD AND THE OFFICE

Blessed be you beautiful
morning, as you splash warm waves
into my face
when I step out of my
melancholy doorway.
> Left behind me is
> God's peace, yet still
> blessed be you beautiful
> quarter-hour
> which flies me on speeding tram
> towards the city,
> towards work,
to factory, office, towards

the jail of a coolie work-day
yet still, through souls and through windows
you pour in the sunshine!
      For only at such time
      am I who I am;
      only at such time can I steal
      into my young eyes
      the warmth of the sweet life,
      from hurrying girls' feet
      the stockings of sunshine,
      the forbidden ways of young desire,
      — only at such time
do I still belong to myself,
only at such time to my brothers,
to everyone,
who here and everywhere
scurry with me on bustling
trams
towards the money
towards the city, towards the torture chambers
of envied employment
and thinks over all that is beauty
and weeps over all that is pleasure;
for this is the final
parting from ourselves; this minute
preceding work on sunbathed crescents:
this minute is ours, the revolt of
relaxed instincts, freedom's
day-to-day recurring hope,
single, sacrosanct quarter-hour
between God and the Office.
      Be blessed you beautiful
      tram-route, golden
      morning, for you at least
      remained — and return the greetings
      of those
      who are going to die.

Egon F. Kunz

THE DREAM OF TSUANG TSI

Two thousand years ago the Master Tsuang Tsi,
pointed at a butterfly and remarked rather musingly:
"In my dream" he said, "I was this butterfly,
and now I wonder if it is he, or, actually, I."

"A butterfly, yes, a butterfly was I!" He would often tell,
"and it danced and frolicked in the sun merrily
and didn't even suspect that he was Tsuang Tsi...
And I woke up... And now I cannot tell,

now I have no idea!" He continued wistfully,
"What is the truth? Which one could I really be?
Did Tsuang Tsi dream the butterfly,
or was it the butterfly that was dreaming me?"

I had a good laugh: "Stop kidding me, Tsuang Tsi!
Who else could you be? You are: Tsuang Tsi! You, of course!"
He just smiled: "The butterfly within your dream
believed, just like you do, in his own truth!"

He smiled and I shrugged my shoulders. Then,
something or other made me shudder, nevertheless.
I've been trying to figure this out for two thousand years
but my certainty is fast dwindling to less and always less.

And so I came to believe that 'truths' don't exist as we know them;
I think that everything is either an image or a poem.
Tsuang Tsi dreams the butterfly — that's how it now seems —
the butterfly dreams him, and the three of us are but *my* dreams.

Adam Makkai

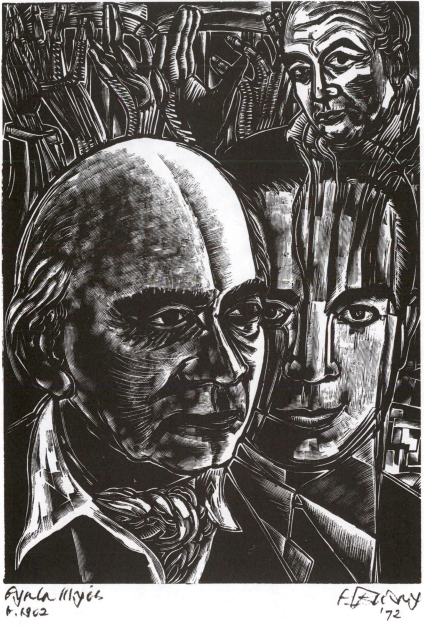

Ayala Illyés
r. 1902

F. Bródy
'72

Gyula Illyés
(1902-1983)

Perhaps the most important, politically committed Hungarian intellectual of the 20th century, Illyés was born in Felsőrácegrespuszta of poor peasant parents; his father worked as a machinist on a large estate. As a young man, Illyés became a convinced Socialist and participated in the student and worker movements of 1918-19. To escape arrest, he moved to Paris in 1921 where he became fluent enough in French to pass for a French poet; his friends were Éluard, Aragon, Tzara: the "left élite." He returned to Hungary in 1926 after a general amnesty. Concerned with the fate of the oppressed Hungarian peasantry, he became an engaged spokesman for the rights of the landless; his searching sociography The People of the Puszta [Puszták népe] *is an enduring classic of its genre.*

He published his poetry in Nyugat [The West] *starting in 1927 and he eventually became one of its editors under Babits's tutelage. He made a trip to the USSR to the Soviet Writers' Congress in 1934 which gave him a chance to look for linguistic relatives of the Hungarians in Siberia. He won the Baumgarten Prize in 1936. As an active anti-Fascist, he was in hiding in 1944. After the war, he was elected member of the new parliament. His standing was so high that the Communists tried to co-opt him rather than muzzle him. As Communism became uglier and viler, so Illyés's disenchantment with his erstwhile ideals grew. When the Uprising of 1956 broke out, his poem* 'One Sentence On Tyranny,' *featured herein, was published in* Irodalmi Újság [Hungarian Literary Gazette] *and has been regarded as the key poem of the uprising ever since. When the Soviets labeled 1956 a "counter-revolution," Illyés protested in a plenary session of the Hungarian Writers' Association and called this opinion an "historical error." He escaped imprisonment by seeking refuge in a mental institution for a few months.*

His attention turned increasingly towards the downtrodden Hungarian minorities in Romania, Czechoslovakia, and Yugoslavia. This was a taboo subject which no one but Illyés dared approach. It was thanks to his outspokenness that the United Nations in Geneva took note of the human rights abuses against the Hungarians in Romania. When French President François Mitterrand visited Hungary in 1981, Illyés headed the reception committee. In short, he became the conscience of the entire nation.

As a writer and poet, he was prolific. Apart from poetry, he wrote novels, plays, and enduring biographies, such as his book on Petőfi *(q.v.). His plays deal with historic events, such as that about György Dózsa, the leader of the 1514 peasant uprising, which was performed shortly before 1956. He paid a great deal of attention to other minorities in Europe as well, such as the Cathars of medieval Provence and the Basques.*

As a poet, Illyés was the undisputed master of the Grand Ode, written in a free-flowing but rhythmical style full of unexpected rhymes.

He won the Attila József Prize in 1950 and the Kossuth Prize three times (in 1948, 1953, and 1970). Austria gave him the internationally coveted Herder Prize in 1970; France bestowed upon him the Grand Prix International de Poésie in 1971 and in 1978 the Prix des Amitiés Françaises. He was a successful mediator between contending extremes. He explained that he could do this because, during his early years, he had been exposed to the different religious ideas of the Catholics and the Protestants. He was also a prolific and highly skilled translator.

Although his poetry started in the atmosphere of the Paris avant-garde, he became more and more of a classicist and a post-modernist in later years. In a sense there is a 19th-century-like grandeur in his major odes, such as the one written about the Hungarian language. These remind one of the older Vörösmarty (q.v.).

Illyés's funeral in Budapest in 1983 almost amounted to a national demonstration, with novelist András Sütő of Transylvania, a Romanian citizen, giving the eulogy.

BONDAGE

The human race would die out all
if women were to hear how males
talk about them — amid what gales
of obscene laughter they recall

the moment that bestowed the boon
sought for as for oasis water;
and the body they'd adored, that after
became for them just a spittoon!

How many of us have been true
to thank our sisters as was due
to them following their bondage?

We have just lain low and bleeding,
downtrodden fighters in receding
faith, hope, blind battle, carnage?!

Doreen Bell

SACRIFICE

The lines I fashioned yesterday
I have destroyed completely,
if they be found and I confess,
I will disown them neatly.
Today another thought arose,
an image longs to greet us,
but I am strangling this one, too,
this living poem-foetus.
Still kicking, sense stirs inside you?
To life do you feel driven?
Are you a poem? Would you speak?
Then shout, corpse, up to heaven.

Marie B. Jaffe

THE APRICOT TREE

I
The apricot tree
shoulder-high or less —
look! An apricot
at branch-tip ripens.

Stretching, straining,
holding out a prize,
the tree is a maiden
offering her closed eyes.

You stand and wonder,
will she bend and sway
her slender waist or
step back, run away...

With quick breath she shudders,
either from heat or passion,
fans herself, and signals
right in the high fashion.

Shakes the shimmering
pomp out of her dress,
then blushing she waits
for your compliments.

This garden, a ballroom,
she gazes about,
anxiously, constantly,
wants to be sought out.

II
I spend each evening
all evening with her.
'Come again tomorrow,'
she says in a whisper.

She rustles softly
when I salute her.
It seems my poetry
can still transmute her.

Sweet apricot tree,
in a dream I saw
the cool arbour, and you
on the crackling straw.

First you glanced around
anxiously, then left
the dark hedge, the well,
in your moon-shine shift.

Your stepping increased
the silence gently,
brought me your body
soft and sweet-scented.

Since that dream I glance
towards you, flushing.
Please look at me too,
askance and blushing.

Christine Brooke-Rose

FATHERLAND IN THE HEIGHTS

A time may come, when to remember
shall ask more courage than to plan,
to claim the past more than the future
in seeking a new fatherland.
What do I care? My land already
holds, more than any height, all steady.
I walk, look around, live, nothing else —
I have found a weapon, magic spells!
I already share it, too, if I come
to tell you its nature, this secret home.

Murmur a line of Petőfi,[1] friend;
in a magic circle at once you'll stand.
  If this pure land's overrun by invaders,
  a new Tartar horde or a horde of traders,
  if our paths are twisted and made to squirm,
  just as when somebody treads on a worm,
then speak of yourself, with eyes closed,
just speak the words which at one time caused
sands drifting, peoples, houses
to compose the pattern that Hungary rouses.
  Enraged rivers learned gentleness,
  or defiant cliffs — do not forget this —
  if we go back, proud-lipped, unscarred,
  into our fortresses, our secrets.
For mere chilling horror cannot chill us,
the merely murderous cannot kill us;
weave your bullet-proof vest of language right,
declaim our Berzsenyi[2] into the night!
  Gather, friend, all you learnt to see
  when you walked in meadows which then were free,
  all the spoil of the heart's and the mind's dominions,
  in merry dispute, with girls for companions.
As Noah into the Ark brought all kinds,
bring every type of thought of human minds,
the number of yearnings, orphaned, tell
and your dreams' menagerie, as well.
  Though for a thousand years to come,
  like an echo unchallenged, they lie quite dumb,
  your words shall answer the questioners' wonder
  then with the more surprising thunder.
Watch, then, and take the lesson to heart
which is mute, though it reaches places apart —
clasping my book in close embrace
I look and laugh in my enemy's face.
  For if I stand nowhere, I still can be
  at home, at the heart of what I see,

---

[1] Sándor Petőfi (1823-1849) (q.v.), was Illyés's favorite national hero.

[2] Dániel Berzsenyi (1776-1836) (q.v.), whose use of Hungarian was uniquely beautiful and all his own.

> even if there my world is shown
> like a fata morgana, upside-down.

So I remain a messenger here
with the precious graveyards in my care.
If the order to shoot me through the forehead is given,
whatever there nests, escapes into Heaven.

Vernon Watkins

HORROR

I saw Budapest burning —
around every head
before a fall, a glowing
wreath of fire; war; war dead.
> I saw — as if someone else —
> amid wild briarbush
> of exploding shell, a corpse,
> a nightmare carcass, crushed.
There was moonlight that morning,
six o'clock, New Year's day;
the housewreck I was standing
on, at dawn, turned grey.
> Like Moses' bushes, burning,
> each shell, with rapid shriek,
> burst, screaming something — —
> God or Fate tried to speak.
In the icy snow of the street
I saw a human head,
a bas-relief trampled flat
by some inhuman tread.
> I saw a baby, still blind,
> close to its dead mother —
> not milk to suck but blood,
> blood, not wool for cover.
The baby raised its bloody face
and cried out to the dead.
His mother was — this very place;
himself — the years ahead.

Anthony Edkins

THE MARKED ONES

The tram bore along, my eyes
interstraining like a net
the passing crowd, it had become
an obsession with me to pick out
those older than I, this face, that,
the other, reading my future in
the ruins of their faces; the heart-alarming
similarity stabbed me — they were my kin!
Together with them, I was given
a mother tongue, an Eden, a native land,
(and these, my children of the Spice Islands,
southern and brown-skinned.)
   With them I held a common ideal
   my illusions, my heaven, my faith;
   with them I burn in a common hell,
   if we ever lose our faith
   in this: that, though Eden is lost,
   fruitful soil and work remain to us;
   though Heaven fades, the future towers
   above us, wonderfully populous.
Between Chinaman and Chinaman, or
Negro and Negro, there can be no greater
bond of colour, blood, or fate
than the one that binds *our* lives together.
We find, alas, of the same
age, a common road, a common aim.
We bear a yellow star, more communal than
the one worn by the outcast ones of late —
already, I walk with them in procession
towards the brickyard of our fate.
   This I thought, and this, too — so I
   must share with these their joy and care;
   the others are just gawking idlers,
   whether they pity us, throw some money or sneer,
   always different! Their food, manners, fate
   all different, alien! No kin!
   Defiantly, indignantly, I thought this

for a long time. Now I begin
to see that I was wrong... For those,
who just now strutted boldly by
on the side-walk, will bring up the rear
of our procession presently.
Just a few minutes; then, oh! What wild
panic will break loose, what blind
terror will link those who must
"produce identity papers on demand."
I feel I want to call out to them:
"For God's sake, run — go quickly and pack;
as for escape — don't even think of it!
Throw into your bundle bread,
aspirin, blankets, butter, cotton wool,
and (quickly) a kiss for those to whom farewell
without a kiss isn't really farewell.
Then let's go. Our luggage is enough,
even too much, however little..."
So I would speak. But I do not speak.
Any warning is quite futile.
I, too, was given the alarm
once — and given it uselessly;
though it was not just anybody,
but poor Babits[3] who gave it to me.
I stare at the people on the side-walk
silently, uncaring whether
they understand or not. I greet them
as one condemned man greets another.

John Brander and *John Wilkinson*

---

[3] Mihály Babits (q.v.), Illyés's mentor, the Editor-in-Chief of *Nyugat*.

ON SEEING THE REFORMATION MEMORIAL IN GENEVA

I paced the length of it — one hundred and forty-three
paces from end to end. As a messenger
bearing the last salute of murdered millions
I passed along the line of stony faces —
Calvin, Knox, Farel, Béza! And those great bull-heads,
grim captains of embattled faith,
all those Williams, Colignys, and Cromwells,
Bocskai[4] with his battle-axe — how they stared at me!
It was all too much; I couldn't take them in!
I had to step back towards the garden, back
among the trees, back into the soul,
into the coolness, where alone it is possible
to see a thing objectively and entirely.
                And now, standing before me, at attention,
                like so many soldiers on parade,
                they seemed almost
                on the point of stepping forward
                out of the rock face
                in which they stood,
                out of time, which had set
                solidly on their backs.
Once they could move. Then they stiffened and became
stones in the sunlight. Their voices died away,
their words remain only in the form of deeds,
to provide a kind of explanation
somewhere in time... You who are dead,
you who stand at attention, speak!
                Or am I to speak first?
                Must it always be with you as it always was —
                "Here I stand; I can do no other..."
                No compromise, whatever cause you serve,
                for the lukewarm are spewed out of God's mouth,
                while the right intention shall survive
                like an object? How much truth is left

---

[4] István Bocskai (1557-1606), Prince of Transylvania, Protestant thinker, and anti-Turkish and anti-Habsburg warrior.

in those great fists which once, four centuries ago,
grasped the Bible and the sword?
What did you think you saw
in the goal towards which you hastened,
pushing on with the rage of a lover
as you drew near?
Do you sometimes wonder?
But suppose the answer should not be to your liking?
Well, I shall give it anyway.
It's just as bitter for me as it is for you.
You stood there, burning with the truth of God,
while the opposing camp burned with the same fire;
then, the thousand-and-first time,
instead of reason,
weapons of flame resolved
how the soul may reach eternal bliss;
bodies writhed by the million
on battlefield and scaffold.
The wheel, the stake, and all the new
master devices for inflicting pain,
and opposing forests,
forests of the cross of Jesus
sprang up all over Europe.
People burned
in order that paintings, "idols," should be burnt,
and the "false book" of the opposing party.
Cities and villages burned!
Half-savage mercenaries
devoured the flesh of men, fire met with fire,
crime with crime, until the final — Victory? —
time, which awaited you, sagely, patiently,
with a touch of humour.
Now, today, in my country, as in yours,
the same two camps face each other still,
opposing fortresses gaze on opposing fortresses.
From ancient towers, austerely white or gold,
ornamented, opposing bells, like cannons,
peal out defiance to opposing bells,
every Sunday. And, inside, the priests
still thunder as they used to; but, after service,

they wave across the street, signalling
at what time and at what house this evening
they'll meet for a game of cards or a nice fish supper
with a few drinks.
          Fair enough! I approve!
          If I were a clergyman, I'd do the same!
          'Live and let live,' by all means...
          And yet... you know...
          those Thirty Years of killing... wasn't it just
          perhaps a little too high a price to pay?
          D'Aubigné's fury, Coligny's death, the Night
          of Saint Bartholomew still unavenged,
          Germany, all of Europe torn apart,
          and the Turk in our country
          a hundred and fifty years...
          So this was "victory"? God's way
          of "proving, like the sun," that the fight was not
          for Him, but *because* of Him?
          Was this the prize decreed to you by the future,
          — since there could have been no victor whom He
          had not *predestined* to His triumph?
          You won.
          The Devil won with you!
          You were mugs, the lot of you! About turn!
          You have no right to take even one step forward.
          Crumble with your stone and with your Time —
          Crumble! For the fight was lost
          before it had begun.
Or perhaps I spoke too harshly, like one who first
castigates himself with his own truth.
So you failed.
The net result, written upon the blackboard
— the continent you wiped clean with your armies —
was the mere answer to a foolish riddle,
and that is only possible in Hungarian,
where Protestants call themselves *"Keresztyén,"*
and Catholics call themselves *"Keresztény,"*
both meaning 'Christian.' And so the riddle runs:
"Why is a *Keresztyén* more than a *Keresztény*?"
Did you really require all the blood

of so many millions dead, before
you could distill this particle of sense:
the little 'y', and when, forgetful of
your duty, you took up the sword and hacked
the Gordian knot of Christian brotherhood,
(*Keresztyén* hacking *Keresztény*.)
And when you had cut so valiantly
through the tangle of your own perplexity,
did you find it there, that little 'y'?
And were you satisfied with your "result"?
But suppose none of this
had ever been? Then only inside myself
the two opposing bells would toll,
calling up for the thousandth time
the old, bitter conflict, hardly less bitter
for finding expression only in the old
vile opposition of the words, a kind of "word-wrestling,"
then the shepherd of Tolna[5] would have kept the old faith of his Lord;
then the rebellious preacher of Sárrét[6]
would have had to endure the battle — inside his own breast.
   What made you take up arms?
   Does not a virtuous man in his own right
   furnish a proper answer to the wicked?
   And if the battle had not been fought? If, wordless,
   the Faith had perished in the "Roman Filth"?
   If the world and the ideal together,
   led by the "Church vendor with the tiara,"
   had gone where it was no longer possible
   to speak against unrighteousness? Well, of course,
   virtue would have made its sacrifice!
   But hopelessly! And what would then have happened
   to us? Would we have been spared the conflict,
   the bloody sacrifice of the Inquisition?
   If — albeit "in vain,"
   Gustavus Adolphus had not ridden,
   if the Puritans of Toulouse had chosen

---

[5] A county in southwestern Hungary where the shepherd ancestors stayed
mostly Catholic, while the rest of the population became Protestant.

[6] A region full of lakes, where the population became mostly Protestant.

    to submit rather than take up arms;
    if the Vaudois, the Hussites, and the free men
    of Bocskay, who knew no word of Scripture
    nor yet of prayer, had said "We will not fight" —
    do you suppose we should then have had peace?
    I almost see a patronising smile
    crossing your stony faces at the thought of it!
    And would we Magyars have been quite the same
    if there had been no Calvin?
    I don't think so.
Or, put another way: would you have had
electric light, had not Giordano Bruno
gone to the stake? Here was the beginning
of nuclear power — and when, some time tomorrow,
you take a rocket and fly out into space,
you will have these to thank for it, men
who were not daunted by the stake or the galleys
or the certain prospect of defeat,
the "in vain" that waits on every step.
They saw; they saw it well
that there is no road leading to the past;
the past collapsed in smoke, hurling them forward
as the powder hurls the cannon ball.
They undertook the burden of their Fate;
then say with me: Glory be to them!
        I stood before them, a speechless messenger,
        hardly caring now what explanation
        their deeds might have to offer, deeds, which like
        a child, can be reasonable for themselves
        only when they're grown up.
        Finally, as a self-consolation, I said:
        "Whoever was responsible for the intention,
        not even God could have made it otherwise..."

John Wilkinson

FAITHFUL MIRROR

I caressed your face with my fingers —
Let my palm be your mirror!
You may have much to suffer,
My failures bring you wrinkles...
Let your face's skin behold it
What your youthful image moulded —
Increasing in beauty's balm
In my faithful, loyal palm.

Donald E. Morse and *Adam Makkai*

A PIECE OF ADVICE

That you belong to the 'folk', sonny-boy, had you not better show us
Less by the village you left, than by the road you will take?

Adam Makkai

BARTÓK[7]

"Cacophony?!" — Let it be that! If in
their dismay
we find our medicine!
Just that! Let violin
and singing throat learn
the din of curse in breaking the glass at the inn;
for they turn between the teeth of saw and file —
let there be no peace, no joy for any while
in the gilded, night-charred

---

[7] Although the Communist regime prior to 1956 eagerly expropriated Bartók's name, it forbade the performance of some of his works, e.g., the ballet opera *The Miraculous Mandarin,* as it was considered 'offensive to Socialist morality.' Illyés's ode to Bartók appeared in 1956, a few months before the Uprising. It became the aesthetics of the post-1956 generation of Hungarian artists. Illyés argues for telling the truth, no matter how unpleasant.

vastness of the concert halls, until they part
the dark of pain from every single heart!

"Cacophony?!" Let it be that! If in
their dismay
we find our medicine,
that in the 'people' there still lives a soul —
that they are still alive
the 'people,' and do call!
The theme of clashing stone and steel
in crushing cursing variations to reveal
through the well-tuned chords of instrumental or vocal tone
the cruel truth of flesh and bone
since such cacophony alone
has coined
a counterpoint!
For it is this
precisely this cry of pain
— through so many falsely merry melodies —
which from fate has claimed its harmonies
that very order, without which the world would fall into the abyss
unless we learn again the language of the eagle.

Strict and great musician, great Hungarian,
('infamous' — like so many in your company),
how was it decreed that you should plumb the depths
of soul and spirit among these men and send your cry
across the megaphone of this still so-narrow
mine-shaft into the brazen, frozen
megalithic concert hall,
whose chandeliers are the star-lit Heaven?

My sorrow is offended by the melody
of pampered comforting.
Our mother's corpse must not be cheapened
by gaudy farewell feasting in a comic opera.
For it is countries that have perished; who will dare mourn them
with the circus-like tunes of barrel-organs?
What hope can, then, still spring from the human race?
When in such solicitude the struggling intellect is mute

YOU must speak,
the musician, stringent, strong, strict, and astute,
that in spite of every strife
we have the right to hope and life!

And we do have the right
— since we're all mortals and givers of life —
to face all of that
which we cannot avoid, try though as hard as we might.
For he, who hides what's wrong increases it![8]
It was once possible, but is no longer
to keep us with our ears muffled and our eyes shut
while the raging storm razes our country flat,
and then to blame *us* for that very fact.

For you have paid us homage by revealing
what had been revealed to you,
the good and the evil, the virtue and the sin.
You have made us grow
by addressing us as equals, long ago...

This, indeed, is consolation!
Speech like yours — how differently you repair!
Honest humanity — no cheap fabrication —
enfranchises us to use the ultimate deterrent,
our own despair.

Our thanks
to you for the strength
to prevail even against the gates of hell!

Behold the end — the future's sentinel.
Behold the example that he, who artfully pronounces
the name of the cancer, by so doing, reduces

---

[8] Similar to Babits's line written in the 1940s against Nazism.
"For among sinners 'silence' means 'accomplice'", Illyés's line has become
proverbial and in a sense the slogan of the new aesthetics.

its black magic-hold.[9]
Behold the great soul of a true artist, which must be bold
to have been through damnation, return, and live to tell.

For there were sights we've seen and voices we've heard
for which there is no human word.
Only Picasso's double-nosed virgins,
or his six-legged steeds
could have forced a cry adequate to such torture,
for what we have endured in sickness
could not be understood by normal men
who did not live to see beyond their ken,
there is no language known on earth to witness,

except for music, music, music that you made
with Zoltán Kodály, your great soul-mate,[10]
yes, music, music alone
which transplants the ancient heat of mines into the marrow,
while dreaming of the 'people's future song'
creates a future triumph's orchestral throng
and knocks down all the prisons by tomorrow
toppling phoney altars to the ground
and praying through the very wounds
inflicted by the cursing sound;
music, which transports
into a better world
those who can discern the good
in what they've heard.

Work on, good surgeon, shunning cheap enchantment,
you, who keep poking at our souls with measured bars,
you're always touching on the unhealed scars
that pain has rent.

---

[9] This sentence, according to critic and literary historian Zoltán Szabó (1912-1984), life-long ally and friend of Illyés, sums up the new aesthetics of the post-1956 generation.

[10] The original mentions a 'great pair of twins.' It is obvious, however, that Illyés meant Bartók and Kodály's earlier period of co-operation, during which they worked together on ethnomusicology.

Oh, what strangely working medicines you urge
by striking up your 'cacophonous' dirge,
which should be welling up in our breast,
but cannot, while our hearts know neither peace nor rest;
oh, what lamentation serves
to be the instrumental music of your nerves!

Robert C. Kenedy

ONE SENTENCE ON TYRANNY[11]

Where seek out Tyranny?
there seek out tyranny,
not just in barrels of guns,
not just in prisons,

not in the cells alone,
where the third degree goes on,
not in the night without
challenged by sentry-shout,

not where in death-bright smoke
prosecutors' words provoke,
not just in the emphasis
of wall-tapped Morse messages,

---

[11] A 183-line version of this poem first appeared during the Hungarian Revolution in *Irodalmi Újság [The Literary Gazette]* on November 2, 1956; an amended 200-line version appeared in 1971 in Zagreb in a volume entitled *Poezija*; in Hungary the complete version first appeared in the journal *Tiszatáj* (Szeged, 1987:5), published in an article by László Péter called 'Parallel Analysis of a Poem.' The poem was considered too dangerous for inclusion in Illyés's several volumes of collected verse during the Kádár regime. We present the complete 200-line version here.

not in confession told,
not in the judge's cold
death-sentence: 'Guilty!!'
not in the military

'halt' and the snapped-out 'aim!'
'fire!' and the drums of shame
scattering the squad, as it
drags the corpse to the pit,

not in the furtively
guarded, and fearfully
breathed words the message bore
passed through half-open door,

not in the 'sssh' revealed
on mouth by finger sealed,
nor confine tyranny yet
to rigid features set,

peering through bars that still
show, through that iron grill;
cries that dumb throats retract
stopped in the cataract

of inarticulate tears
deepening the silent fears
in pupils griefs dilate
darkened by looming fate;

not in the van with that slight
noise gliding through the night,
where it draws up and waits
throbbing in front of gates;

in the silence when you can hear
a stranger's intruding ear
listening on the phone
when you say 'hello';

nor in the telephone wire
Laocoön's own quagmire;
trains, planes, railroads
are fetters and tie-ropes;

track down all tyrannies
not only in the 'hurrah!' cries
surging on tiptoe, strong,
in the acclaiming song;

not just in mustered bands,
tirelessly clapping hands,
fanfares and opera-stalls,
just as crude, just as false;

monuments, art galleries,
though cast in stone, speak lies;
yes, a framed lie can crush
even in the painter's brush;

for where there's tyranny
it's there omnipresently,
everything to it will nod
more than to your ancient God,

you will find tyranny
in the school and the nursery,
in father's counselling rule
as much as in the mother's smile,

in the way a child will stammer
answers to a probing stranger,
in the way you look and listen
all around before you'd whisper;

not just where barbed wire twines,
not just between those book lines;
but worse than the border-guards guns
in the paralysing slogans;

there, more discreet, it is
in a wife's parting kiss,
near you and at your back:
'when, dear, will you be back?';

in the words that folks repeat,
the 'how-do-you-do' in the street,
in the then suddenly softer
handshake one moment after;

making your lover's face
found at the meeting-place
freeze in an instant of
tyranny; it gnaws at love;

not only in the interrogation
but also in love's confession,
in love-drunk words, your appointment
is like a dead fly in the ointment,

for even in your dreams
tyranny's first; it precedes,
in the bridal bed
and in the desire it bred;

nothing you think is fair,
— like your bed — didn't it share;
it had already preclaimed
its spoils when love was first named;

it sits on the plate, the glass,
in the nose and in the mouth,
it stalks in the cold and dark
outside air; inside your house;

as if through an open window
oozed the reek of carrion
or somewhere in the house
there was a leak of gas;

talk to yourself and hear
tyranny, your inquisitor;
you have no isolation,
not even in imagination;

the Milky Way through it becomes
a border terrain scoured by beams,
a minefield, and the star
a spy-hole in a war;

the swarming canopy of the sky
is a monstrous labour-camp:
the orator, Tyranny,
shouts from the bells on the ramp;

from the priest to whom you confess,
from his sermons, too, no less,
Church and Parliament — all these
with the rack: stage properties;

open and close your eyes,
still its scrutiny lies
upon you like a sickness,
following you with memory's quickness;

hark at the wheel of the train,
this is their refrain:
"you'll be taken prisoner, prisoner;"
on a hill, by the sea, you inhale the same;

in the lightning of a flash it's seen
in every little unforeseen
sight and noise, its poison dart
lights up your astonished heart;

where you rest, why, there it is
inside boredom's manacles,
in showers that forge nearby
bars that reach up to the sky;

in the snow, whose fall
sheer as a cell wall
hides you in its murky bog
through the eyes of your own dog;

for it is in all that you intend,
in your tomorrow it is at hand,
before your thoughts it is aware,
in your every moment it is there;

as water cleaves the river-bed
you follow and form it; but instead
of peering forms that circle anew,
out of the mirror it looks at you;

in vain you try to escape its wrath;
prisoner and jailer are you both;
it will corrode and furtively go
into the taste of your tobacco,

into the very clothes you wear,
it penetrates you to the marrow;
you detach your sense from it, only to find
no other thought will come to your mind;

you would like to look, but can only see
the holograms of tyranny,
what tyranny decides to do
works like magic in front of you;

you look around — what prompts your gazing?
you use your eyes, but what do they catch?
already a forest fire is blazing
fanned into flame by the stick of a match,

where carelessly you threw it down
as you walked, and forgot to tread it in,
and now it guards you in the town,
in field and home and the factory's din;

you feel no longer what it is to live,
you cannot have desire, nor love,
you don't know your meat and bread,
hugging arms are stopped by dread;

thus the slave forges with care
the fetters he himself must wear;
you nourish tyranny when you eat,
you beget your child for it;

where find tyranny? think again,
everyone is a link in the chain;
of tyranny's stench you are not free —
yes, you yourself are tyranny —

it turns your very own kids
spiteful and hard in their wits,
while your wife inside your hut
weighs in your lap like a scheming slut;

like moles on a sunny day
walking in this blind, dark way
we walk and fidget in our rooms
making a Sahara of our homes;

because, where tyranny is,
everything is in vain,
every creation, even this
poem I sing turns vain,

because it is standing
from the very start at your grave,
your own biography branding,
and even your ashes are its slave!

Vernon Watkins,
Adam Makkai, & Károly Nagy

A WREATH

You can no longer
soar. And yet you blaze,
wind-slit Hungarian tongue, sending
your snakelike flames along the ground, hissing
at times with pain,
more often with the helpless rage of the humiliated,
your guardian angels forsaking you.

Again in grass,
in weeds, in slime.
As through all those centuries, among
the stooped peasants. Among
the tight-lipped old, keeping their counsel. Among
girls trembling under coned reeds as
the Tartar hordes swept past. Among children
lashed together
while mute lips shaped their words;
for the Turks, if they heard a sound,
would bring whips down in their faces.
Now you show forth
truly — and to me as well — your use,
your pedigree, your coat-of-arms, the stone-biting
strength in your veins.

Language of furtive smiles,
of bright tears shared in secret, language
of loyalty, lingo
of never-surrendered faith, password of hope, language
of freedom, briefly-snatched freedom, behind-the-prison-guard's-back
    freedom,
language of master-mocked school boy, sergeant-abused rookie,
dressed-down plaintiff, of little old ladies boring clerks,
language of porters, odd-job hired men, being a language
of the no-good-for-the-factory, no-good-for-test-passing proletariat,
language of the veteran stammering before his
young boss; testimony —
rising from depths even greater

than Luther's — of the suspect
beaten up on arrival at the station;
language of the Kassa black marketeer, the Bucharest servant girl,
the Beirut whore, all calling
for mother, behold your son, spittle
on his rage-reddened face,
master of many tongues,
held worthy of attention by other nations
for what, as a loyal European,
he has to say:
he cannot mount any festive platform,
cannot accept any wreath,
however glorious, which he would not, stepping quickly down,
carry over to lay at your feet, and with his smile draw forth,
on your agonizing lips,
your smile, my beloved, ever-nurturing mother.   *William Jay Smith*

REFUGE

You try to hush me, and hearten me
to put up with this small matter;
I know that I am ill, it's useless
pretending: I can't get better.
I fell ill with a deadly ailment
and not just some few days ago,
no treatment has been found to cure it,
it is congenital, you know,
there isn't any medication
to ease the pain and help me cope —
a foregone case, so say the doctors
and they abandon every hope;
no drug can shoo away this spectre
not even for a single day;
all that remains now: brave acceptance,
resignation to sure decay.
    For old age is this ancient ailment.
Its symptoms are a sad disgrace,
so worrying that I am frightened
to look the mirror in the face.

The poor man, whose cheeks are yellowing
with cancer, knows what grieves me now,
or the wretch with syphilis, bearing
the sentence of death on his brow;
I see fate might call any day. When
you see me, think of this remark:
the pangs of death haunt sooner, later,
all of us past the fifty mark.

    You do not help me, or restore me
by shrouding my eyes to the sight
of the threat which, as time is passing,
perhaps no longer gives me fright.
To face what cannot be avoided,
without a craven sinking heart,
I need, sweet hushing-heartening one,
your mystical womanly art;
to know, caught out in that last dogfight
where fate will strike the final blow,
to run backwards and find Mother's knees
without looking, like long ago;
to know — and hear these ancient verses:
te spectem suprema mihi
cum venerit hora — "in my last
hour, to hold my eyes on thee"
and also — *te teneam moriens*
deficiente manu — "let my
declining, poor arms embrace you
when I am called away to die."

    With your angelical advantage
you know, you women, how to lave,
how to treat the blood-soiled hero
as you would treat a tiny babe;
since death and love are both the same bed,
whatever ends all our troubles,
by death we are denuded always,
debased as foul untouchables,
and since we have shared every secret
for many long years already,
with mother-patience help me over
the shame of my mortality.

Peter Zollman

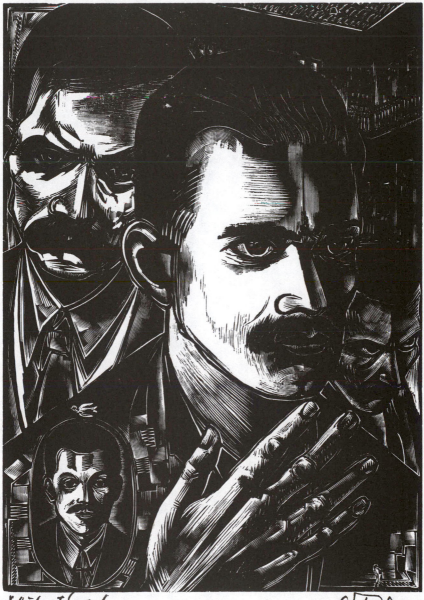

Attila József
1905-1937

Attila József
(1905-1937)

Endre Ady (q.v.), was often quoted as saying that there would not be another Hungarian lyric poet comparable to himself for more than two generations. He was wrong. Attila József, the son of a laborer and a washerwoman, reached equal, or perhaps even greater, heights as a poet and is now generally recognized as one of the most original exponents of modern European poetry. His own Curriculum Vitae *reads like an indictment of the have-nots against the haves, for deprivation and misfortune, fate, and class conspired against a proletarian nonconformist who came too soon.*

His Romanian-born father deserted the family when the boy was only four; the mother, crushed under the weight of raising three children, farmed young Attila out to foster parents in the country. From there, among peasants, he periodically returned to his home environment, the industrial suburbs of the capital. The family was supported by his elder sister's husband, a lawyer, who became Attila's guardian after his mother's death. Attila tried his hand at various trades but cared only for poetry. He became a student in Szeged where he was to major in French and Hungarian philology, but his poem 'Song of Innocence' (1925) cost him his university career. He was accused of advancing atheistic and revolutionary ideas. Yet leading critics hailed him as the spokesman of the new generation. He moved to Vienna, where he read Marxism and Freudian psychology voraciously. Next, he moved to Paris where he tried to write in French, not unlike Gyula Illyés (q.v.). The two met only in Hungary later and, in spite of a brief period of friendship, became rivals. His first volume was The Beggar of Beauty [A szépség koldusa] *and the last* The Pain Is Sharp [Nagyon fáj]. *He became a member of the illegal Communist Party, but was later expelled for his "mysticism and Freudianism." Later he developed schizophrenia and finally committed suicide by jumping under the wheels of a train. The Communist régime expropriated his poetry and his name like no other — a major prize, a street in Budapest, and the University of Szeged were named after him, but his poetry was instrumental in preparing the 1956 Uprising. His greatest love poems were written to intellectual women, one of whom was a psychiatrist who later married Gyula Illyés (q.v.). His is an incandescent intellectual poetry, rich in forms ranging from the sonnet to Alcaics and Sapphics, replete with a new vocabulary, a tactile imagery and lulling rhythm, playfulness, philosophy, and wisdom; here man is an atom who knows both his constructive and destructive energies.*

SONG OF INNOCENCE

I have no God, I have no land,
no father, nor a mother's hand.
I have no crib or coffin-cover;
I share no kisses, I have no lover.

Three days I have been starving numb
for lack of either feast or crumb.
My strength: I'm twenty, whole and hale,
my twenty years are up for sale.

If no one wants to have a try,
then let the Devil come and buy.
And I will jimmy safe and fence,
kill, too, if need, in innocence.

Upon a noose they swing me high,
then in the good soil will I lie —
and tips of poison grasses start
to prick above my splendid heart.

Anton N. Nyerges, Thomas Kabdebo [& A.M.]

ON MANKIND

Humankind, that my broken mother, fooled,
increased to woe and couldn't figure out —
I take no fright at rebirth for your crowd,
you, billions of coupled solitude![1]
  I saw you sob by frozen river-falls
  like sore-bedazzled kids on flames of ice —
  I saw you kill and die and agonize,
  framed in splendor on great cathedrals' walls.

---

[1] The line has become proverbial. Attila József wrote 'two billions of coupled solitude,' referring to the earth's population at that time.

I saw you stand on mountains, stoop in stables,
your hapless lot; languishing, lifeless fables —
that you deserve Death as forbear is plain!
　　　Bloodless, you wait for your blood to be shed,
　　　but mating-folly props you up, instead,
　　　which finds you swell in every kind of pain.

Adam Makkai

THE THREE KINGS OF BETHLEHEM

"Praised be God, and Lord Jesus, Lord Jesus,
We're the 'Three Kings' as God sees us,
　　　come afoot to hie the quicker,
　　　following a bright star's flicker —
　　　by a lambkin we were greeted
　　　'here dwells Christ!' — with force it bleated.
　　　　　King Melchior is my name,
　　　　　your great glory I proclaim."

"Son of God, we wish you a Good Day!
We're no old priests, this we dare say,
　　　we have heard that you had landed,
　　　king to all the poor and branded,
　　　so we thought it meet to bob in
　　　at your place with hearts a-throbbin'.
　　　　　Gaspar am I called, by right,
　　　　　a mere king on earthly plight."

"Good Day to you, fair Redeemer,
we have come from lands far greener.
　　　All our sausage ran out early,
　　　our boots, too, are worn and knurly;
　　　but we brought gold, six full measure,
　　　frankincense, too, for your pleasure.
　　　　　King Balthazar 'tis, the Moor,
　　　　　who is knocking at your door."

Blushes, flushes blessèd Mary,
prettier than any fairy,

bursting in tears every instant,
hardly sees her holy infant —
"Stop it, shepherds! Music, rest! Heed!
what this babe needs is a breast-feed!"
          Adds in a voice that softly rings:
          "Good night to you, dear Three Kings."

István Fekete [& A.M.]

ODE

1.
Here I'm perched on a sheer cliff.
The luminous breeze
of early summers wafts by
like the memory of familiar
suppers come back to tease.
The heart is quiet; the head is bowed.
It's not too hard
to get used to solitude.
The past crowds the present
and my hands dejectedly dart
about.

I gaze over the rocky terrain —
each leaf in the mountain's main
reflects your glistening brow.
There is no one, no one on the road,
but I can see how the wind
intending to flirt
has gently furled your skirt.
Beneath the fragile foliage of leaves
your hair tumbles and your quivering bosom heaves.
As the brook bubbles through the pebbles,
I see anew how — like rebels —
the sparks of your pearly smile
escape from your teeth.

2.
Oh, how I love you!
You, who could put into words
(with equal ease) the treacherous curse
of cavernous loneliness,
and the mysteries of the Universe.
Who, as the Niagara tumbling,
escapes his own rumbling thunder
departs to join a quickening yonder;
while I thrash about
in the ebb and flow of life
ever nearing the past,
and proclaim in a scream
that I love you, you sweet step-wife!

3.
I love you as a child loves his mother;
as a dank cave threatens to smother;
as time and space need one another;
as the body craves rest and the spirit wants to fly!
I love you as the living love life
until they die.

As objects are collected by gravity,
I guard your every word, smile, and gesture.
With my perceptions I reforge you in my memory,
seared into metal, like images of iconography.
You sweet, lovely figure!
Your essences fill my senses.

The minutes rattle and rumble,
but You remain quiet in my ears.
The stars ignite, then tumble,
but you still stay in my eyes.
As dampness permeates a cave,
your taste lingers
in the nave of my palate.
The back of your hand
is criss-crossed by fine veins
as you take the glass in your fingers.

4.
What am I made of? What material is this,
what kind of spirit and light,
that your glance can cut and shape me so?
And what delight
that I can travel on the mist of infinity
the rolling landscape of your fertile body?
I penetrate the mystery behind
as The Word enters the receptive mind.

The circuitries of your arteries deliver
a current, the rush of blood
that, like so many red roses, quivers
and makes your cheeks flush with a blush
and your womb flood
to prepare for the blessèd fruit of love.
In the pit of your stomach,
to nourish your body,
fine roots keep weaving a pattern
and feed every cell of your matter.
The branches of your lungs with a hush
whisper their own glory.

Contentedly Eternal Matter
burrows through your ducts and as a sign of health,
the stones of waste in your ardent kidneys shatter
into streams of hot and golden wealth.

The industry of nature works in your entire being;
in You, the constellations achieve their meaning;
billions of creatures jostle, the earth heaves into mountains;
singing cicadas,
strangling lianas,
nature's abundance and cruel beauty
shine in you as the sun and the dusky northern lights;
within You Unconscious Infinity lies.

5.
These words drop
at your feet

like clots of blood.
Existence stutters in defeat,
only The Law can speak clearly.
My busy senses,
that renew me day to day,
are already prepared for muteness.

But until then they shout —
to You, whom I have singled out
from among millions in the crowd,
You, singular entity,
You, soft cradle, tough grave and living bed,
receive me inside your body...!

(High in the morning sky
like emblems of an army
a multitude of stars shine.
My eyes are smarting from their glimmer,
I think I am lost...
I can hear above me my heart
flutter and quiver.)

ENVOY

(I travel by train
and keep struggling to maintain
an appearance of calm; for we may
yet meet and you could say:

"The bath is drawn, take this towel to dry!
The meat's on the stove to fry!
Eat to ease your appetite!
My body is your bed tonight...")

Suzanne K. Walther

FOR MY BIRTHDAY[2]

VERSION 1

VERSION 2

Today I have turned thirty-two:	I am thirty-two and wise,
Methinks there is a poem due	Poem, be a big surprise
a meet	pretty
and neat	ditty.

A joy, a modest gift with which	Gift that shall my spirit rouse
I pamper in this tea-room niche	in the lonely coffee house
myself —	who? me.
myself.	who? me.

Yes, thirty-two years flitted by	Thirty-second whizzing by
but a monthly hundred ne'er had I	Ten a week? I only try
how grand	hunger me,
my land!	Hungary!

By now I might well hold a chair	Could have been an educator
not be my fountain-pen's despair,	but became a pencil nibbler
so poor	sure
a boor...	poor.

It happened that in Szeged town	One fine day they ousted me
from college promptly sent me down	from the university
a queer	fool
emir.	school.

His admonition was bestowed	They expelled me forth and hence
for "Fatherless,"[3] my bitter ode,	for my "Song of Innocence"
with steel	fending
and zeal	sending.

to guard the land against my kind.	He defended Hungary
I let my lute conjure to mind	rules of the academy
his name	name
and blame:	shame.

---

[2] Although it is considered untranslatable, we present four versions of this poem.

[3] Called 'Song of Innocence' in this book.

"I trust, Attila, you won't try
to graduate and qualify!"
he screamed
and beamed.

If Mr. Horger leaps for joy
that teaching ain't my grand employ
his bliss
's amiss —

to all my folk I'll teach the plumb
truth, they in no curriculum
confined
can find.

Version by
István Fekete

VERSION 3

Am I thirty two? That's nice.
All I need now's a surprise
just a nick-
nack;

can my spirits I cheer up
with another coffee cup
by my self
myself.

My thirty-two years flew away
without ever decent pay
— some grand
homeland!

I could have been a fancy teacher
not some lonely pencil-chewer
oh well,
what the hell!

But in Szeged the varsity
dean opted to get rid of me,
bad omen,
old man!

"Long as I am teaching here
stay clear of this hemisphere"
gloating
bloating.

If Professor Horger's glad
poet's grammar turns out bad
little
spittle.

Mine's a school for all the people
not to high school pap and nipple
each in
teach in!

Version by
Anton N. Nyerges

VERSION 4

Now that I've kicked in thirty-two
I wrote this without much ado
a slight
delight

a party favor to myself
in this café beside a shelf
very
merry.

Like wind my thirty-two have flown
not once two hundred, nor a loan
this field
did yield.

A teacher I could have become
not a pen-chewer, no not some
ruddy
buddy.

But Szeged University
had no use for diversity:
the dean
with spleen

His warning hit me tough and rude
for my "Fatherless" attitude
his stick
our hick-

town saved with great alacrity.
I quote here for posterity
his word
absurd:

"As long as I have any clout
you won't be teaching," he ran out,
huffing,
puffing.

Should Dr. Horger gloat with glee
that teaching grammar ain't for me
spit
on his wit:

my words will teach the nation whole
beyond a high school's meager role
with a bomb's
aplomb.

Version by
Earl M. Herrick

objected to my poesy
accusing me of heresy
he raved
and saved

the country with his dagger drawn.
My spirit conjures with a frown
his ire
and fire:

"As long as it is up to me
nowhere will you a teacher be!"
he huffs
and puffs.

If Dr. Horger jumps for joy
that grammar ain't my daily toy
his lust
goes bust:

I'll teach the nation as a whole
over a high schools' daily role
poet:
know it!

Version by
Adam Makkai

LULLABY

The sky is letting its blue eyes close;
the house its many eyes closes, too.
The quilted meadow lies in a doze —
　　　go to sleep softly, little one, do.

The wasp and the beetle are both asleep;
their heads are down on their feet, and through
darkness, a drone in the dark they keep —
　　　go to sleep softly, little one, do.

The coat is sleeping across the chair,
the trousers are sleeping where they're worn through;
no more today will it stretch the tear:
     go to sleep softly, little one, do.

The tram has fallen asleep as well,
and while it's still rattling, it slumbers, too,
it tings in its sleep a little bell —
     go to sleep softly, little one, do.

The ball and whistle are both at rest.
So is the wood where the picnic grew.
Even your sweets are by sleep possessed —
     go to sleep softly, little one, do.

All will be yours in the crystal ball —
you'll be a giant, it will come true;
but just let your little eyelids fall,
     go to sleep softly, little one, do.

A fireman, soldier, herder of sheep,
you'll be all three, and each will be you.
See, your mother is falling asleep —
     go to sleep softly, little one, do.

Vernon Watkins

THEY WHO ARE POOR

If God as a scribe were to write
unceasingly all day and night,
He would not be able to cover
all that the poor have to suffer.

They who're poor are the poorest. The chatter
of their teeth they give to the winter,
their sweat to the summer, and in haste
their vain life to the land that is waste.

Looking forward to Saturday, toiling,
they are plagued by a hundred things spoiling,
and if Sunday cheers them and gladdens them
Monday is near them to sadden them.

Yet within them singing doves nest,
doves starry in feather and crest,
but griffins at last they'll become,
bringing the hawk-folk to true justice home.   *Vernon Watkins*

HUMANS

In our family goodness is a guest.
Interest arranges all things like a host
foolishly, but the rich were long aware
of this, and now it dawns on most of the poor.

Every entanglement works loose at last.
While we are sure of our truth and hold it fast,
our lives gloss over those with bad designs.
A change of setting does not change the lines.

Yet at the top of our voices we all sing,
borne on the gusto wine and powders bring.
Mouth empty, our spirit sinks — we drain the vats.

He is best who, bearing disillusion, pauses.
We are as full of small and mordant causes
as the murmuring willow grove is full of gnats.   *Vernon Watkins*

MOTHER

For over a week now, again and again,
thoughts of my mother have wrecked my brain.
Gripping a basket of washing, fast,
on, and up to the attic she passed.

And I was still frank and released my feeling
in stamps and yells to bring down the ceiling —
let *someone else* push those baskets of laundry
and let her take *me* with her up to the pantry!

But she just went on, gave me no look or thrashing,
went on, and in silence spread out all the washing,
and the kneaded clothes, rustling blithely,
kept twisting and billowing up brightly.

I shouldn't have cried, but it's too late for this.
Now I can see what a giant she is.
Across the sky her grey hair flickers blooming,
it's in the sky's seas she dissolves her blueing.[4]

Vernon Watkins [& A.M.]

HUNGER

The engine stops. Dust in a weary threat
hovers above it like fall vapour's grey,
and settles on bent necks of men a-sway
who are now eating. Soiled shirts soaked in sweat
      cling to their arms as to their meal they set.
      Cucumbers, bread make up their lunch today,
      and each eats so, that not a crumb can stray;
      as bite for bite their teeth by teeth are met.
For count of time they do not care at all.
Almost continuous are the bites they take,
yet every mouthful has been chewed complete.
      With peasant lungs, still sound, they suck the pall
      of dust and hay-scent as without a break
      they eat, they eat, they do not talk, just eat.

Watson Kirkconnell

---

[4] The old-fashioned European ancestor of modern liquid bleach.

BY THE DANUBE

I

I sat there on the quayside by the landing,
a melon rind was drifting on the flow.
I delved into my fate, just understanding:
the surface chatters, while it's calm below.
As if my heart had been its very source,
troubled, wise was the Danube, mighty force.

Like muscles at work, when lifting the axe,
harvesting, welding, or digging a grave,
so did the water surge, tighten, relax
with every current, every breezy wave.
Like Mother, dandled, told a tale, caressed,
laundered the dirt of all of Budapest.

A drizzle started, moistening the morning
but didn't care much, so it stopped again.
And yet, like someone who under an awning
watches the rain — I gazed into the plain:
as twilight that may infinitely last,
so grey was all that used to shine, the past.

The Danube flowed, and like a tiny child
plays on his musing, lively mother's knee,
so cradled and embraced and gently smiled
each playful wave, waving hallo to me.
They shuddered on the flood of past events
like tombstones, tumbling graveyard monuments.

II

For a hundred thousand years I have been gazing
and suddenly I see what's there to see.
A flash, and time is fully-grown, embracing
what generations scan, and show to me.

I see what they've not seen, for they defended,
embraced, dug, murdered, their living to ply,

and they see now, in cold matter descended,
what I can't see when I'm to testify.

We all relate, like blessèd to the damned,
mine is the past and theirs is the today.
We write poems — my pencil in their hand,
I sense them and remember what to say.

III

Mother was Kún,[5] Father was Székely, partly,
and half, or maybe pure Romanian.
From Mother's lips the food was sweet and hearty,
from Father's lips the truth was radiant.
They embrace again when I am stirring.
This fills my heart with deep melancholy —
we are all mortal. It's me, re-occurring.
"Just wait, we'll soon be gone!..." — they say to me.

They call, we are now one, I know: this oneness
has made me strong, for I remember well,
that I am every parent in the boundless
succession to the primal lonely cell.
I am that First, who splits, proliferating
till I become my father and mother,
then father and mother split, procreating
the multiplying me — and none other!

I am the world — the ancient endless story:
clan fighting clan for creed or crazy greed.
I march among the conquerors in glory,
I suffer with the conquered in defeat.
Árpád and Zalán,[6] Werbőczy[7] and Dózsa —
Slavs, Mongols, Turks and other variants

---

[5] An Asiatic people (Cumanians), who settled on the Great Hungarian Plain seeking protection against the Mongol invaders in the 13th century.

[6] Leader of the Slavic people living in the southern part of the Carpathian Basin before the Hungarian Conquest in A.D. 896.

[7] István Werbőczy (1458-1541); he wrote the repressive laws of 1514.

in me, we shall redeem the long foreclosure
with gentle future — new Hungarians!

...I want to work. It's hard for human nature
to make a true confession of the past.
The Danube, which is past, present, and future,
entwines the waves in tender friendly clasp.
Out of the blood, our fathers shed in battles,
flows peace, through our remembrance and regard:
creating order in our common matters,
this is our duty; and it will be hard.   *Peter Zollman*

HOW LONG THE LORD

How long the Lord,
how short the lard.
How sick the poor,
how rich men are.
>   He bends and turns
>   where dairy barns
>   open their doors
>   to milking girls.
How long, how hard
the bishops' God,
and still the poor
would trust his care.
>   A sausage ring,
>   a wifely dress,
>   and they would learn
>   to bear the Lord.
With summer eyes
he sees, surveys —
the poor are where
the dangers are.
>   If to this day
>   he's not our Host,
>   the wasted poor
>   cannot rest there.

Anton N. Nyerges

WELCOME TO THOMAS MANN

Just as a child, already by sleep possessed,
drops in his quiet bed, eager to rest,
but begs you: "Don't go yet; tell me a story,"
for night this way will come less suddenly,
and his heart throbs with anxious little beats
now wholly understands what he entreats,
the story's sake or that yourself be near,
so we ask you: sit down with us; make clear
what you are used to saying: the known relate,
that you are here among us, and our state
is yours, and that we all are here with you,
all whose concerns are worthy of man's due.
You know this well: the poet never lies.
The real is not enough; through its disguise
tell us the truth which fills the mind with light
because, without each other, all is night.
Through Madame Chauchat's body Hans Castorp[8] sees.
So train us to be our own witnesses.
Gentle your voice, no discord in that tongue;
then tell us what is noble, what is wrong,
lifting our hearts from mourning to desire.
We just buried Kosztolányi;[9] cureless, dire,
the cancer on his mouth grew bitterly,
but growths more monstrous gnaw humanity.
Appalled, we ask: more than what went before,
what horror has the future yet in store?
What ravening thoughts will seize us for their prey?
What poisons, brewing now, eat us away?
And, if your lecture can put off that doom,

---

[8] Famous characters from Thomas Mann's novel *Zauberberg* ['The Magic Mountain'].

[9] Dezső Kosztolányi (q.v.) was a close friend of Attila József. He died of cancer of the tongue in 1936, the year of Thomas Mann's visit to Budapest.

how long may you still count upon a room?[10]
Ah, do but speak, and we can take heart then.
Being men by birthright, we must remain men,
and women, women, cherished for that reason.
All of us human, though such numbers lessen.
Sit down, please. Let your stirring tale be said.
We are listening to you, glad, like one in bed,
to see you now as they switch off the lights
a European — among the whites.

Vernon Watkins

I HAVE DONE MY RECKONING

Right from the start I have stood on my own feet;
with nothing to call your own, you've nothing much to forfeit.
        You've no more to lose, and that's a fact,
            than an animal when it drops dead and that's that.
I may have felt afraid, but I have never been cowed:
I was born, I mingled; I have emerged alone from the crowd.
        As my debts fell due, I paid them off;
            and to the generous I responded with my love.
When a woman led me on, perhaps only to tease me,
if it would please her, I took her seriously.
        I have hauled up buckets and scrubbed decks down:
            in a world of clever masters I have played the clown.
I have sold toy windmills, been a vendor of bread
or books, papers, poems, whatever could be had.
        For me no death in battle, nor the end of a rope:
            bed is the place I would finish up, I hope.
Come what may, I have closed my reckoning.
I have lived. Others, too, have died of living.

Michael Hatwell

---

[10] The welcome to Thomas Mann was prophetic indeed, as Hitler had been in power for three years in 1936 and just three years later World War II was to start. He opposed the Nazis and spent the war in the United States.

ARS POETICA

I am a poet — so why should I care
for the art of poetry as such?
Once risen up in the sky, the star
of the night river is not worth much.

> I've done with the milk of the story book;
> time's slow seeping will never stop.
> I quaff great draughts of truth in every nook,
> a neat world with foaming sky on top.

Bathe in it! — Pure and sweet is the source!
Calm and tremulousness embrace
each other; from the foam wise discourse
rises with elegance and grace.

> Other poets — what concern of mine?
> Wallowing in fake imagery
> belly-high and fired with bogus wine
> let them ape out their ecstasy.

I step past the revels of today
to understanding and beyond.[11]
With a free mind I will never play
the vile role of the fool in custom's bond.

> Be free to eat, drink, make love — and sleep!
> Weigh yourself 'gainst the universe!
> I shan't hiss my inward curse to creep
> and serve the base bone-crushing powers.

The bargain's off — I want to be happy, devout,
Or else insult me, all you mighty and high,
growing spots of red will mark me out,
and fever will suck my fluids dry.

> I will not hold my disputatious tongue.
> I cry to deeper knowledge and to truth.
> The century responds "yes!" — booms its gong —
> the peasant ploughs, thinks of me, and approves.

---

[11] This line is proverbial in Hungarian: *Az értelemig és tovább* — 'to reason [rationality] and beyond' and serves as the ideological motto of post-materialistic, non-Marxist philosophy. It is also thought to be proof that the Communists expropriated the poet without understanding what he meant.

The worker's body resonates my being
between two of his movements stiff with pain;
the slip-shod, shabby youth lingers in waiting
for me before the movies in the rain.
       Where villains scheme, encamped, about
       to attack my poetry's battle-lines,
       divisions of brotherly tanks start out
       rumbling abroad its mighty rhymes.
I say that man is not grown-up yet,
but, fancying he is, runs wild.
May his parents, love, and intellect,
watch over their unruly child.

                           Michael Beevor

BELATED LAMENT

My fever's over 98 point 6, and still
mother, you're not with me.
Like any loose, easy girl when called at will
you have lain down by death's side readily.
From the gentle autumn landscape and many
kind women, I try to piece you together,
but there's no time left as the all-consuming
fierce fire grows hotter.
       As I was returning home for the last time
       the war had just come to a grinding close,
       in a ransacked and twisted Budapest
       many shops were left breadless and empty.
       Crouching on train-roofs I brought you potatoes,
       while the sack was filled with millet and other grain;
       stubborn me, I had got a chicken for you in vain,
       for you were nowhere to be found.
Your sweet breast and self you took away from me
and gave them to the worms.
Remember how you consoled and chided your son? But see:
false and deceitful were your kind words.
As you blew on my soup, stirring it, you said:
"You're growing big for me, eat, my precious, eat."
But your empty lips taste oily dampness now —

greatly you misled me, and how!
> If only I'd eaten you!... You brought me your supper,
> but did I ask for it?
> Why did you bend your back over the washing?
> That now in a box you should straighten it?
> See, I'd be glad if you should box my ear once more,
> now I'd be happy for I'd return your blow;
> you are worthless for you're trying not to be,
> you spoil it all, you insubstantial shadow.

You're a greater swindler than any woman
who deceives and betrays...
Stealthily you deserted your living faith;
you bore out your loves amid your wails.
You gypsy! What you had given, cajoling,
in the final hour you stole back the lot.
The child feels a quick impulse to swear; mother,
don't you hear it? Please, tell me off.

> Slowly light enters my mind as the legend
> vanishes like a dream.
> The child that clings to the love of his mother
> now realizes how silly he's been.
> Deceit awaits him who's born of a mother:
> he's either deceived or to deceive he'll try.
> If he struggles on, he'll die of this, but if
> he gives in, of that he'll die.

John P. Sadler

THE CITY LIMITS

On the city limits where I live
in twilights of fallout and glow
the soot settles like tiny bats,
it flies on softish wings and alights
and ossifies like guano
hard and slow.

> Thus weighs this age on our chests.
> Like gray mops of rain
> swabbing
> the jagged roofs of tin,
> a sorrow in vain

poultices the crust of our pain.
You may try blood, but
we are a new breed and from a new soil.
Our talk is different, our hair
is barbered a different way.
We are rolled not of God or reason royal,
but coal, iron, and oil.

> We are basic stuff,
> sloshed in the appalling mould
> of a society
> seething and savage,
> and it's our task to uphold
> mankind on this enduring wold.

We succeed priests, soldiers, and the middle class.
This is the latest scene.
We are the sensitive recorders of history.
Within us moans
whatever the works of man may mean,
like a bass violin.

> They never destroyed
> under a system of the sun
> more indestructibles
> though long is the past,
> and our homes were undone
> by famine, bigotry, cholera, and the gun.

The humiliation
was never sealed
for so many future victors
under the watching stars.
We fixed our gaze on the field
where the secret was revealed.

> Look at how our precious animals,
> the machines, run amock.
> Fragile villages crumple
> like thin ice on a winter pool.
> Plaster falls from the town's mortar
> when the heavens leap, struck by thunder.

But can the landowner subdue
the shepherd's wild cur?
The machine's childhood was ours.

We were raised in one school.
A well-trained animal... So try to command her.
We know her name, Sir.

> Soon your machines will see you polishing
> the floor on your knees
> worshipping your
> very own possessions,
> but the machine only sees
> who feeds him fodder, not pleas.

Children of a world of matter,
here we are, together with the scars.
Lift up our hearts! They are his
who will lift us up,
and he alone can raise the bars
whose heart is full of ours.

> Fly it above the factory
> black and round,
> like the sun
> asphyxiated in a smoke of its own,
> and booming with the sound
> of the earth's deep underground.

Up! Up! all over this staked-out world
as we blow
the fences squeak and sway
in the gale.
Up with the heart! Blow below!
Above the sky let it go!

> One day, and soon, it will illumine
> our beautiful gift for order and the real[12]
> by which the mind will know
> the finite frontiers of infinity —
> the forces of production, without, they reveal
> and the instincts, within, unseal.

This poem is pitched to the city limits.
A poet — your brother, you know —
is watching as it sifts

---

[12] This line has become proverbial. In Hungarian it is: '*Míg megvilágosul / gyönyörű képességünk, a rend*' meaning 'until our [splendid] beautiful ability, [which is] order, becomes a reality.'

the soft and lipid soot,
and ossifies like guano
hard and slow.
        The song rattles on the poet's lip.
        But he (the engineer
        of the spells of the concrete world),
        sees into a conscious future
        and creates inside of himself a harmony of cheer
        as you, later, out in the objective sphere.

Anton N. Nyerges

A TRUE MAN

My eyes, peasant women milking the light
into pails, turn out your pails,
my tongue, you whooping jaunty boy,
try giving up your endless navvying,
beast, run from me, out into Asia,
down to the sweaty jungle-roots,
my spine, go giddy under the Eiffel Tower,
let your harpoon swerve from the smell,
my nose, Greenlander, fisherman-sailor,
my hands, run a pilgrimage to Rome,
my legs, kick each other into the ditch,
deliver up the cymbals,
my ears, the cymbals!
my thighs, spring to Australia,
you dewy rosy marsupial,
my belly, you airy balloon,
fly to Saturn's orbit, fly to Saturn!
for even as it is I'll stand on my mouth's edge
and with a high shout throw myself into your ears,
for the stalled clocks are now wound up,
for the villages will blaze like floodlights,
for the towns will glow with whitewash
and my vertebrae will roll wildly over the world
for even then I shall still be erect on my feet
among the dead sprawling twisted all around.

Edwin Morgan

Jenő Dsida

(1907-1938)

Jenő Dsida was born in Szatmárnémeti, Transylvania, (now Satu Mare in Romania). He died in Kolozsvár (now Cluj-Napoca in Romania) at the age of thirty-one. His father was an officer of engineers in the Monarchy's army; his mother came from a family of wealthy landowners. The family moved to Budapest in 1910, but moved back to Szatmárnémeti in 1919, where Dsida finished high school. His first poems appeared in Cimbora [My Pal], *a children's journal started by Elek Benedek, the dean of Transylvanian Hungarian literature.*

He studied law at the University of Kolozsvár, but did not graduate. He made his living as a journalist, editing a Hungarian language daily, Keleti újság [Eastern Newspaper] *in Kolozsvár.*

The most accomplished Transylvanian poet of the inter-war period, Dsida was a virtuoso of the Hungarian language. His lyrics have a musical quality of great perfection imbued with a Rococo nostalgia. His exuberant love of life was seen by some critics as a compensation for his persistent fear of premature death due to a weak heart.

Dsida became a Christian mystic: he compared the fate of the poet living in minority status to Christ's ministry on Earth, as seen by the title of his first volume, Maundy Thursday [Nagycsütörtök], *which appeared in 1933. With his posthumous volume* On the Zither of Angels [Angyalok citeráján], *which appeared in 1938, Dsida reached the heights of a "poeta angelicus," through several poems written in the face of impending death. He was greatly concerned with the survival of the Hungarian minority in Romania and the Hungarian language: he echoed Zoltán Kodály's sentiments in his famous, longer, emotionally charged poem* Psalmus Hungaricus [Hungarian Psalm]. *He urged national unity in the face of divisive minority status. As a stylist, he was able to unite in his poetry the bold associations of the avant-garde with such time-honored classical forms as the Graeco-Latin hexameter. He was a major translator of world literature: he interpreted French, Latin, German, Italian, and Romanian poets; of particular significance are his translations of the Austrian poet Georg Trakl. He was also a steady contributor of essays, travel, and criticism to the various journals he worked for, primarily in the city of Kolozsvár which, although under Romanian rule, was the second capital of Hungarian literature between the two World Wars.*

His premature death was due to severe influenza and pneumonia which his congenitally weak heart was unable to withstand.

SERENADE FOR ILONKA

I was a child and she was a child
In this kingdom by the sea:
But we loved with a love that was
More than love
I and my Annabel Lee.
[Edgar Allan Poe]

The willow leans into the water
and ripples splash it round and round,
caressingly, with their brief fond chatter,
a kiss for each down-hanging frond.
The moon, lone wanderer in the sky
keeps silent vigil overhead,
can she from her high station spy
where a young girl is lying dead?

Gentle Ilonka lies below,
white in her grave she lies;
her spirit tossing to and fro
as the waters towards her rise,
like the branches of the willow-tree
dipping in the waters below,
she is bending gently over me,
splashed with water-music flow.

A song about her, feather-light,
with her cataract of golden hair,
and her eyes are all shining bright,
her lips are full of kiss-desire.
I see again her lovely face
the sweet face of my belovèd
I hold her again in my embrace
her hand like a snow-flake soft.

Once among violets she lay
we lay together in the grass
the violets unfolding all the way
unfolding, opening over us,

then with a smile she opened to me
a moment blissful and blest,
between the hum of insects, happily
I fell asleep on her breast.

I saw her sink down in the grassy land
the dark hole opened under my love
she sank down, the lyre in her hand
she sank slowly into her grave —
into this silence like a strange
intruder, the merry bird-song rose
and in the silent depths came the change
of insects, in red and green hues.

— The willow-branch leans down in the water
the water-splash is a psalmody,
the water goes on with its chatter
it murmuring repeats in me,
the song is overcast and sad —
a nuptial prayer, a colourful spread
but the chattering is past,
the opening violets are overcast.

Gentle, heavenly Ilonka,
your image lives on in me,
I see you now as when you lived
— blue butterfly on the greenery
from your soft mouth wild strawberries grow
all among the swaying grass
from your soft mouth a Seraph laughs now
and the young grass murmurs over us —

I lie in the grass, on a bank
the bank holds me in its lap
a thousand insects, bitter, rank
towards me are moving up
they move up to me from the depths
and on a thousand instruments played
I taste the music of your lips
in an endless serenade.

All my kisses since I had yours
are bitter and ugly and coarse
they only brought back to me
your wonderful memory
the kisses died, have faded away
under my shadowy years
among my grief and my cares
the kisses of your dead lips stay.

Ilonka, my sweet, gentle Ilonka
to me you are always the same
your soft, caressing voice, Ilonka,
still keeps calling me by my name,
and in the darkness I answer you
I see a path of light break through
the water-reeds shiver and over the lea
a sound of sobbing calls to me —

What can I do for the future
I, who have held your white hand,
where shall I look for the future
now that you eyes are dead and blind?
I shall stay here forever now
inert, numbed hopelessly,
while the soft mould sinks below
and the dark hole opens under me

coming to this bank at night
I followed a flickering light
that led me to this willow-tree
I felt your soft hand leading me
here I shall lie in my grave
I shall sleep, as you sleep, at your side,
I will die, as you, Ilonka, have died
I will die with a happy laugh

life lessens amid the chatter
of the frothing, swishing water
like the skeleton of an ancient crow
that died centuries ago,

my body dissolves, fades away
but the soul stirs, as the branches sway
I am barely alive; but memory
vibrates in me, dreamily.

In the waters of the Lethe now I bathe
they splash and swirl around me
they splash out on the open path,
washing round me caressingly,
from the bright shine of the moon
comes a sudden trumpet blast
and with the roar of a mighty host,
the fanfare of the rising sun.

The music of your lips has weakened me
I am awake, *miserere!*
The music of your heart rises in me,
burning, a great light, gloriously —
we rise together in the blue air
like the feathers flying there
and in our embrace, holding tight,
we rise up to clouds of light.

Joseph Leftwich

A CONFESSION

Where I live is like an island.
Each day what can I do
but kneel — preoccupied
by nothing except you?
It may be the sun cools,
it may be the moon will fall
this resonant otherworld
dissolves me, absorbs me whole.
It has sweet fragrances,
the light has its own tricks,
the laws governing it
are happy as they are strict.
What elsewhere would be measured

by the tick of a small clock
here by the steady throbbing
in your breast is marked;
you speak and each soft word
that, dreamily, you yield
becomes a silver flower
set in a blue field;
and your sigh is the wind
stirring in my hair,
and your face has the moon's glow,
and your face has the sun's glare.

Clive Wilmer and *George Gömöri*

THE POET'S RESURRECTION

The candles are burning
around him;
lux æterna, shine where he goes.
— A veil on his face!
— A cross in his hands!
— Dark, heavy wreaths at the toes!

The air is sultry,
the flesh is decaying,
billows of incense are wheeling afloat,
coughing and crying,
some secret sighing,
the vicar is clearing his throat.

Suddenly,
look, He rises again,
staggers to the door
and out to the plain.
Drunk on the bracing air
His blood runs racing
a-rush to the brain,
while giant firs in a chain
blow fanfares up

to the sky.
He's off in the dusk to run after
a fiery gold butterfly.

Peter Zollman

MAUNDY THURSDAY

No connection. The train would be six hours
late, it was announced, and that Maundy Thursday
I sat for six hours in the airless dark
of the waiting room of Kocsárd's tiny station.
My soul was heavy and my body broken —
I felt like one who, on a secret journey,
sets out in darkness, summoned by the stars,
on fateful earth, braving yet fleeing doom;
whose nerves are so alert that he can sense
enemies, far off, tracking him by stealth.
Outside the window, engines rumbled by
and dense smoke like the wing of a huge bat
brushed my face. I felt dull horror, gripped
by a deep bestial fear. I looked around:
it would have been so good to speak a little
to close friends, a few words to men you trust,
but there was only damp night, dark and chill,
Peter was now asleep, and James and John
asleep, and Matthew, all of them asleep...
Thick beads of cold sweat broke out on my brow
and then streamed down over my crumpled face.

Clive Wilmer and *George Gömöri*

THE VERSE OF DARKNESS

The time of vigils comes, alas, to blight!
Grimly the pen-point leaves a heavy mark.
At six the rusty juices of the night
already ooze on foliage in the park.

The lymph of rotting trees comes trickling slow,
and then you think: how many years till death
are left, alack? Your footstep fears to go,
lest paths mistaken lead it to the end.
...Have you, I pray, just dipped a sugar-cube
(its snow-white corner) in a fluid brown,
the bitter night-damp of a squat glass tube,
a glass of *café noir* that darkles down?
And have you watched the heavy liquid soak
most slyly, lazily, relentlessly,
up through the crystal cube and so revoke
its clearness with a dark lividity?
And even so see night now penetrate
and soak into yourself with ruthless reign;
the dank smell of the grave will saturate
your being, every fibre, flake, and vein,
until one murky evening, mucky-wet,
it soaks your heart to melting in its stink,
that you may sweeten, as you pay life's debt,
some ruthless godhead's dark and bitter drink.

Watson Kirckonnell

WHAT WILL COME OF THIS?

Everything fades, turning into grey.
We're losing our hair.
The apples are not as red as they were yesterday;
the grass is not as green-gleaming as it was day before yesterday.
Our smile of today is cooler, darker,
weak and emaciated:
a scared and sad imitation of the earlier ones.
Day after day our words turn out to be more sooty and charred.
The arms of love grow wider, turn lax, lose momentum, then release...
What will come of this, my love?
Night? Black silence? An overcast coldness?
Or is it exactly along roads pulverized into ashes
that one reaches the eternally smiling, brightly gleaming meadows?

Adam Makkai

László Szabédi
(1907-1959)

A distinguished poet of the era between the two World Wars, Szabédi was born in Sáromberke, a village in Romania today. (His family name was originally Székely.) He acquired a doctorate in Language and Literature at the University of Kolozsvár (today Cluj-Napoca in Romania), and he also studied in Strasbourg. After 1932, he lived in his home town where he worked as a journalist, librarian, and publisher's reader. From 1947 until his death, he taught aesthetics at the Bolyai University of Kolozsvár. After the forced Romanianization of the University, now called Babes-Bolyai, he committed suicide by throwing himself in front of a train. His poetry is characterized by intellectual clarity and depth, but his real genre was the essay rather than lyric poetry. His selected poems were published in Bucharest in 1955; his work on Hungarian prosody, The Forms of Hungarian Rhythm [A magyar ritmus formái], *1955, is a major contribution to a knotty problem.*

CREATIVE POVERTY

Our home is all too fragile, rather like
some delicate glass cup, some highly wrought
carving in wood — Oh, curious works of art,
outstandingly expensive bric-a-brac!
> For fear it might break, we take but half the chair;
> we barely touch the carpets with our feet;
> and — truly terrified of falling out
> of immemorial beds — we dream with care.
Among these precious items polished thin
by our creative poverty and care,
like cautious connoisseurs we live and move.
> Lest one expansive gesture bring them down,
> we live our lives out in continual fear.
> And so we hardly move and hardly live.

J.G. Nichols

IRRATIONALE

Like a rope that has been snapped,
like a vessel that has cracked,
like a clock that has run down,
like a tramp, his journey done,
     like a madman who has stowed
     reason and faith in one small word,
     like a dead man whose tortures live
     on in the deaf and eyeless grave,
like a god, bored with himself,
who has created, but in vain,
a man of mud, to find the filthy
mudface but reflects his own.

J.G. Nichols

THE MARRIAGE OF DEATH

     New moon! New king!
     Death is marrying!
     Who will be his bride?
Let him take the heavens' dead,
take the old moon for a bride,
let him take the dreadful black
of the night without a star,
let him take the hopeless ache
of the creature who is poor,
if he has to take a bride.
     New moon! New king!
     Death is marrying!
     Whom to fecundate?
Oh, this generation's womb
is barren. Let the poet teem,
he who dearly loves to make
promise of life and sacrifice
for a better future's sake —
only let death not for us
breed but death upon himself.

J.G. Nichols

Anna Hajnal
(1907-1977)

Member of an orthodox Jewish family, poet, translator, writer of children's literature and married to the critic and writer Imre Keszi, Anna Hajnal edited the short-lived literary review Argonauts [Argonauták] *in 1937-1938. From 1949 onward she worked as an editor for a major state publishing house.*

Her poetry has great formal discipline and an almost masculine simplicity; much of it is devoted to psychological exploration and the gentle but inexorable synthesis of emotion and thought. She sought to express the cosmic fullness of existence in her myth-creating poetry. Her objective view of the world absorbs the throbbing exuberance of things — dissolving the world of plants and animals into hymnal forms of music.

The poet Miklós Radnóti (q.v.) wrote of her: "This constantly searching, and attentive poetry, which is always thriving to create a synthesis, communicates in every moment of its existence with the totality of the universe..."

She belongs to the third generation of Nyugat [The West]. *She won the Baumgarten Prize in 1947 as well as the Attila József Prize in 1966.*

Her books of poetry include Awake in Me, Dream! [Ébredj fel bennem, álom!], *1935;* A Century of Giants [Óriások százada], *1952;* The Rain Falls [Eső esik], *a book of children's poems from 1954; and* Oil Jug [Olajos korsó], *1961.*

TO THE CREATOR OF MY BONES

Where convex and concave
turn incandescently into one another,
bone, turning joyous joint
the marks of your hand shine upward.
Ring and moon! Stars to each other
it's all your doing, that the sweet ribbon
its constant and unfading magnetism
will hold me and I can't leave you,
as long as my thoughts twist and turn.
And if I move out of my body
in which I am caught now
ready to rot, put into a dark grave
for another thousand glimmering years,
in the darkness, shining only to you
in the happiness of work
you built up on centuries,
you shaped for beautiful serious purposes,
for me to be, see, I am!

The frame is yours, and the throbbing too
which softly surrounds it like clothing,
mesmerizes petals into its circle
like a spring whirlpool.
See, I am overjoyed with your smile,
enraptured with the burning lights around me
and what you planned for the brief tomorrows,
I am joyously filled with your traces
I am guarding you and I am yours.

Jeanette Nichols

THE DESERTED ANGEL

His howls flow patient and slow,
through the small window a square of light lies in the dusk
and he waits, slowly turning his hazy head,
his large lumbering wings crossed in front of his forehead.
He stands, waits, but no hand aromatic of stars comes,
no fresh wind opens the door,
no warm arm hugs his head,
no magnetic gaze looks into his ragged eyes.
The one he awaits —
who was ordered to guard him closely by their master —
as a guard and as a servant, was taken away,
collapsed, by his gentle male nurses.
He lies stiffly, his fever racing
like a wild chariot careening on a cobbled road,
moaning and twisting, from a widening distance
looking backwards, the closed eyes see:
he listens to the patient, slow howling,
he sees the manger, its empty glow,
the angel waiting in the soft dusk,
his large lumbering wings crossed in front of his forehead.

Jeanette Nichols

AFTER LIFE

It bends the trees and floats them,
runs timber throughout the summer,
thus within its new home the soul
makes for itself a castle.
It crouches like a beaver
under the thick crusted ice,
while the cold winter squeaks and splits
the new-born beautiful lakes.

Then it begins wandering
the beautiful spring weather,

around each naked tree a silk
chemise begins its new growth.
Soft fur begins to emerge
on its light and spotless limbs,
the penniless soul is thus blessed
gently trodding through its days.

The nights are now transparent,
springtime with its fair weather,
he with nothing urgent to do
is the true raptured lover...
A bird feather floating thus
by us on shiny mornings,
it plays and starts, flies up and rests
and is what creates love there.

This then is the soul's coolness,
its light and lazy tiredness,
like a bright lacquered cherry tree's
shiny reaching towards the sky...
So light is the spirit there
with the bubbling birch bush,
and the foam-skirted blackthorn tree
blossoming by the pathway.

My life is here such a cold,
windswept and drafty gateway,
like a spider caught on its thread
fear holds me a tight captive,
a breeze stirs and trembles in me...
Weeping lingers on this side,
but sometimes a door is opened
and afterlife shines through here.

Jeanette Nichols

CYCLONES

Far beyond the chalky plain,
high above the cloudy plain,
great sighs pass a night,
breaths disturb the night.
Giant women stride the skyways,
giant women walk there lonely,
cross their legs and sit in silence,
fold their arms while sitting silent.
Waiting for a dream that sings,
bids them to unfold their wings
rising from their rest.
Fluttering at the edge of stars,
edging past those starry peaks,
stretching, spreading high above us —
circles around the moon.
Up and round the circle spins,
always spinning, spinning, soaring,
whirling, whipping in a circle,
single-sided in a circle.
And the circle is unbroken.
Annabella starts the year,
walking with her wings outspread.
From her feet the earth is whirling,
from her arms the sky is boiling.
Quicker steps from man to heaven,
circling back from sky to land,
see her turning, lightly leaven
fatal whirlpools, awesome, grand,
drawing up to her embraces
fishers, farmers, mud, and sand.
From the valley, from the mountains,
goatherd, eagle, love her well,
rising at her eldritch knell.
Barbara sets out to follow,
burning with a silent flame.
Burning forests as she passes,
melting mountains with her breath.

In the desert palm-trees smoulder,
screaming lions rush for the sea.
In comes March and here's Cecilia,
summoned by that distant song,
stepping proudly, hands out-reaching,
stepping proudly, head held high.
Blue-black hair that trails behind her,
sweeping clouds down from the sky.
North she flies and brings the thunder
breaking up the skeins of geese,
barring them from Southern sun.
And she draws the fishes with her,
nets them in her blue-black hair.
May brings Diana and Esther,
giant women striding skyways.
Then comes Flora, reaching earthwards,
crushing groves of trees to splinters.
With one hand she lifts them higher,
sprays them through the air uncaring.
In her palm a forest dies.
When the call comes she goes walking,
walking with her face turned earthwards.
Gazelles cower as she whirls by,
and elephants scream.
None of them can turn back safely,
none of them can safely hide,
Flora never, never looks back.
Grace begins in dreadful rage,
Hatty blasts in while the skies crack,
spinning cities in her cage.
Sea-spume dribbles from her nostrils,
countries tremble at her anger,
from her feet the steeples sideways slip.
Burning daughters of the skyway,
from the plains of chalk they run,
when the cry sounds through the seasons,
out of mist their lives begun.

Their awesome bodies hugely towering,
sounds the ears cannot believe, reject.

Arms invisible, twisting, threshing, pulling
with a pressure that circles irresistibly.
A cone of power dashing high an albatross,
breaking an eagle's wing, stark above the sea.
An embrace of majesty, the love of a universe.
Those arms that reach from sky to earth —
who do you seek?

Laurence James

APRIL IN THE OLD PARK

There they go. Slowly they saunter.
I rush to catch them, far ahead. I know
that we shall never meet again.
I ask myself, what use to hurry so?
   I know that far off there, it's we
   who walk together gaily, hand in hand
   among the firs' low-drooping boughs,
   down a lane where rows of dark trees stand.
   The path we follow winds through meadows
   strewn with crumpled leaves, and fades away:
   the gilded cupolas of beaches
   at the slightest touch of breezes sway.
Across the rustling forest floor
they amble through the thickets' ruddy light,
around their heads a silver halo;
then, as the trail bends, they pass from sight.
   I know that as they stroll there, arm in arm,
   they do not even notice me.
   Another turn — and now they reappear
   still farther off. They smile, they see
   only each other, with their heads inclined
   still closer. Now, hypnotically
   they're lured into the dreamy mists. Along
   the way they shared so joyously
   I follow slowly, step by halting step,
   alone.

Daniel Hoffman

MAKPELAH

The path leads up to your house, and stops.
There's no going further.
Grass covers your dwelling-place, and quietness.
And you are lying in princely snow-whiteness.
I could whisper, I could whimper,
could cry out, sob aloud,
you can't hear now,
it's all the same to you.
So many layers
and envelopes
cover you, light
grasses, thick roots.
Weight. Solid soil
caving in, pressing
splinteringly
the plank-hulled ship,
compresses you,
bears down above
bears up below.
You feel nothing,
it's all the same to you.
In there, deep down
between the sheets
the body dressed all in white:
robe, long coat
of white linen,
white your skullcap,
— your sacred earth-filled cushion, white —
your shawl white, too,
long stockings on your legs
fit closely about your shins, in white
and according to the Law
there's the prayer shawl.
Hiding, covering,
enwraping you
— sacred is death —
covering your sacred head

and hiding it
the ancient shroud;
in your ancestors'
sacred burnous,
sacred tallith
they have dressed you.
From your cheeks'
bone-passages
in-dwelling pain
has ebbed,
changing into
stiffly frozen
cold majesty.
— Sacred are the dead. —
These are your bones,
you have been gathered.
You have returned.
Like Abraham,
like Isaac once upon a time,
like our angel-wrestler ancestor Jacob.
Forget the grief,
your cave of Makpelah grave
you'll with me share soon,
I'll with you share soon.

Kenneth McRobbie

IN PRAISE OF THE BODY
(A Grateful, if Conceited, Song)

1. June, 1977

Bobs on the water. Boat-like can cleave it.
Walks on dry land, turns, does pirouettes.
Has there ever been a better building?
Am I its owner? Or just a tenant?
Have you ever seen a palace of marble
which is such a self-cleaning marvel?

Up-to-date, its hot-water and heating system!
Well-designed machine for living in!
Exactly sensing electro-mechanism
faithful to its original programme.
Absolutely tireless its thinking
both in- and outside self-adjusting:
apportioning materials and power well,
decorating this, letting these grow, or those peel.
Will this architect never be done with it?
This art-fancier for ever toy with it?
Although, he's already thinking of the day maybe
when he'll simply leave off doing any of these
— pity!

       The place, I declare, is quite intimate!
       But where can I get something more select
       with a lease in perpetuity!

It would be worth whatever money
the owner would ask — i.e. me, and yet not me
the one who shines within, and yet above me.

2. Winter, fur-coated

A silkily-fluffy fur, an *étui*
like the case is for the jewel — protector
of the soft breathing secret of my being,
my master's most masterful masterpiece,
of which I am no more than keeper.

Kenneth McRobbie

Ferenc Jankovich
(1907-1971)

Jankovich was born in Székesfehérvár; his father was a bricklayer at whose side he learned the family trade. He received his diploma in French and Hungarian Language and Literature at the University of Budapest. After this he continued his studies in Paris at the École Normale Supérieure. From 1931 to 1933 he worked as Assistant Professor at the École des Langues Orientales. After his return to Hungary, he enroled as a voice major at the Franz Liszt Academy of Music.

He was a contributor to most of the leading Hungarian literary magazines. His poetry is forcefully realistic, preoccupied with the life of the poor and with the Transdanubian landscape, with a rich variety of expression but not without a serene playfulness. Jankovich wrote a number of novels with contemporary themes and several historical ones, among them a trilogy of the long Magyar-Turkish wars of the 16th and 17th centuries. His poetry has been collected in the volumes Roamer [Barangoló], *1937;* Elegy [Elégia], *1941;* On the Shore of Szántód [Szántód partjánál], *1956;* Those Who Wait for the Sun [Napvárók], *1960;* In Starlight [Csillagfényben], *1970; and* The Song of Restlessness [A nyugtalanság éneke], *which was published posthumously in 1987. He edited several popular anthologies of poetry and translated plays from the French by Dumas, Molière, and Romain Rolland.*

IN THE COURTYARD OF THE SERVANTS

When the great acacias spread upon the sky
like cedars, opening their blossoms wide
for winds to whisper in, melting, brush by
gigantic forms at eventide,
      the little girl flits from the house; a small
      angel in a lilting dress,
      she starts to dance; her white arms lift and fall
      in one beseeching tenderness.
Her song, like a rivulet sparkling, flows
and laves her every moment,
her arms uplifted seem to be gathering those

invisible threads some god might spin,
 and from impalpable hands let lightly down
 for her to take on flying knees
 like foam on lighted foam an instant shown,
 gone in a splash of foam like these.
And while she dances airily, each stress
swings out to meet in its descent
an enchanted palm's invisible caress,
or was it the grapevine Bacchus sent?
 Open wide your mortal, wondering eyes,
 drink in the sight of her, elate,
 and learn from reeling gods' immortal guise,
 swill visions down, inebriate.
As flowers change the jousting into dance
under assault of their heavy wind,
learn to savor each mysterious chance
of rhythm, the tunes all yours to find.
 The moment shines, forgotten, on the girl,
 and now the night, as if to trap,
 the dancer with the moon in darkling pearl,
 spreads under her a deep, kind lap.
Crowding upon one another, stars
rush out to look from balconies
of sky; in a stable window an old cow stares
and moos, moved by what she sees.

Madeline Mason

ON THE SHORES OF SZÁNTÓD[1]

I with the mind then of a child squandering
my youth's thirty pieces of gold, carefree,
stop now for a little self-pondering.
Paris I've seen, Baranya[2] I did not see;
I have seen Monte Carlo, and Avignon as well.
And now like a gambler whose money has run out, gains few,

---

[1] A small town on the southern shores of Lake Balaton, famous for its ferry that crosses the lake to the Tihany Peninsula.

[2] A county in southern Hungary neighboring the former Yugoslavia.

startled, I ask: "What did you win, fool? — Tell!"
"Avignon's gone, and Somogy[3] is left for you."

When Mihály Csokonai Vitéz[4] wrote his song
of reproach, when here on the shores of Szántód he sat,
casting his almond eyes broodingly and long
towards Tihany,[5] he already knew more than that —
he hadn't seen Watteau, nor had he seen Boucher,[6]
but life cried out in its cradle at his feet,
and he dreamed as beautifully as ever they,
and all the world was his to go and meet.

But at my feet the cradle is empty now.
Perhaps, World, you are just waking up, are in labor still,
as I come back again, a fine new-born, to vow
amidst fervent tears my soul to you, my ardent will,
you who already with ugly birthmarks come near,
summoned by pain and pride, and feared in stupid error,
perhaps by tomorrow, my country ever so dear,
you will be born in defiance and in terror.

Mother of a hundred breasts, hold me tight.
Land of hills, who slumber now sadly,
perchance you dream of me, that fever-scourged night,
with arms that tremble reaching for me madly.
And halfway through your moon-enfolded sleep,
your foliage, flutter-lipped, whispers of me,
your wandering son, ah, yes, and sighing deep,
my Transdanubia, your breath comes yearningly.

Love me! I love you! And listen here:
The western wanderers are drawing nigh.
Your soil, your sward, your waters disappear,

---

[3] A county in southern Transdanubia, bordering Lake Balaton in the
North; its capital city is Kaposvár.

[4] The famous 18th century poet (q.v.).

[5] See Csokonai's poem 'To the Echo of Tihany' which is included.

[6] Antoine Watteau (1682-1721), French landscape painter, and François
Boucher (1703-1770), French painter, protegé of Mme. Pompadour.

but there's still a token left for such as I,
to gird us who return from far away.
Can you give us a hand-out? We left you then,
in order to come back to you one day, —
as ghosts return — come back as conquering men!

I who with the rest have learned to fight outside,
in pages' quarters admiring the knightly art
of great masters, must wield my pen with pride.
See me now with a youthful mind about to start;
a shining, pinioned sword, I unsheathe this pen of mine.
Though on my lips no loud, victorious march may roar,
yet I am bound to win under your sign,
Pegasus, horse with unfolded wings that soar!

Dazzle me no longer, Paris, with your pearls flaring
as you roll them out upon a flaming sky;
and farewell, Notre Dame, which once stood staring
at my sweetheart in my arms — a long goodbye.
Your slender telescopes, through which I spied on life,
fires of long ago no longer in view,
stars with hide-and-seek eyes, now dim, now rife,
I bid you one and all a firm adieu.

Vanished ladies of my old life, it's time to go,
the valley of Bakony[7] is calling me.
Goodbye, Croiset and Lisieux,[8] I leave you so,
for time commands accounting urgently.
It folds me in its meshes, golden-eyed,
guarding there my future's glorious face
that in time's net forever must abide,
and neither life nor death shall pluck me from my place.

Madeline Mason

---

[7] A mountain range in Transdanubia north of Lake Balaton; its highest peak is 713 meters.

[8] Famous tourist attractions in France; Lisieux is particularly famous as a place of pilgrimage on account of St. Thérèse, who died here in 1897.

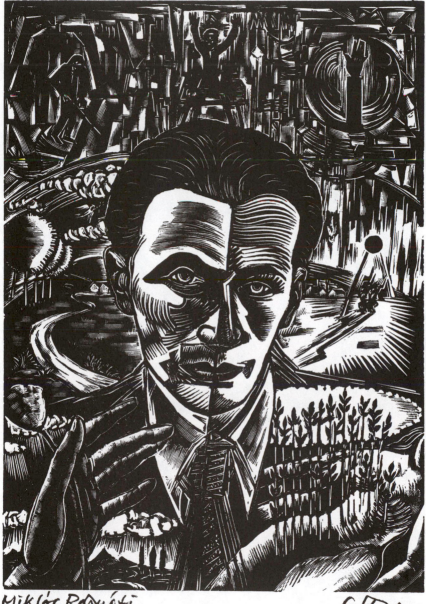

Miklós Radnóti
1909-1944

G. Barany
72

Miklós Radnóti

(1909-1944)

A poet, translator, and essayist, Radnóti attended elementary schools in Budapest, studied textile-technology in Liberec, now in the Czech Republic, and then returned to Hungary to study French language and literature at the University of Szeged, where he obtained his doctorate in 1934. Two years later he married the love of his youth, Fanny Gyarmati, and the same year received his teacher's diploma. In spite of this, he was unable to receive a teaching post in a secondary school. He made his living by writing and journalism, contributing mainly to liberal or left-leaning newspapers and periodicals. In 1937 he received the Baumgarten Prize (delivered by Mihály Babits [q.v.]), a prize awarded to the "most promising writer of the given year."

That same summer, accompanied by his wife, he went to Paris and participated in demonstrations in support of Republican Spain. Being a Jew, Radnóti was not drafted into the regular Hungarian army during World War II, but into labor-camp service. After the German occupation of Hungary in 1944, he was taken to Serbia to a camp near Bor, where he was forced to work mining copper and building roads. In October of 1944 the Germans evacuated Serbia, and Radnóti's labor squad was driven in a forced march to Abda in northwest Hungary. There, with twenty-two others, he was shot dead by guards on the ninth or tenth of November and was buried in a mass grave. Several volumes of his poetry appeared during his life, but Radnóti's popularity, indeed his world fame, is due to the posthumous volume Foamy Sky *[Tajtékos ég], published in 1946. When his body was later exhumed, a notebook of poems (including several included in this collection) was found sewn into his clothing.*

Radnóti's greatness as a poet is often attributed to his profound morality and keenness of vision, the sincerity of his love, and his lack of self-pity. His works have been widely read, making him both one of Eastern Europe's best-known Holocaust victims and the most translated Hungarian poet. His Post Card #4 *['Razglednica'] is one of the most incredible seven-liners in world literature: in a way both ironic and clairvoyant, the words seem to predict the poet's own execution, which would take place only seven days later. We present several versions herein. There exists a monograph on Radnóti, written by Emery George (New York, 1986).*

PORTRAIT

I am twenty-two years old. Christ
might have looked like this in the autumn
when he was the same age: his beard
hadn't sprouted, he was blond, and girls
dreamed of him nightly.

Thomas Land

THURSDAY

Manhattan, a small hotel.
T. hangs in his own noose.
Footloose for years, how can he
ramble another step?

In Prague, it was J. M.
Killed himself, lost at home.
And P. R.? No news for a year?
Is his body cold, root-clutched?

A poet, he went to Spain.
There sorrow dimmed his eyes.
Poet, freedom-lover: can his voice
ward off the long flashing knife?

Can his raised voice ward off
eternity? The finite road
ends here: homeless, in chains,
can his voice save his life

in times like these, when sheep
and doves feed on raw meat,
snakes hiss along the path,
and the chill wind sings high?

John Wain

JUST WALK ON, CONDEMNED TO DIE

Just walk on, condemned to die!
in woods where winds and catscreams wail,
sentence in darkened lines
shall fall upon the pines;
hunchbacked with fear the road turns pale.

Just shrivel up, you autumn leaves!
shrivel, most hideous of worlds!
cold hisses from the sky;
on grasses rusted dry
the shadow of the wild geese falls.

O poet, live as clean as those
hill-dwellers in their windblown snows,
O live as free of sin
as baby Jesus in
an ikon where the candle glows,

as hard as the great wolf who goes
wounded and bleeding through the snows.

Zsuzsanna Ozsváth & Frederick Turner

PARIS

Where the Boul' Mich' meets the Rue
Cujas the corner slopes perceptibly.
Lovely wild youth, I have not left you,
your voice, like echoes in a gallery,
a shaft, beats through the caverns of the heart.
At Rue Monsieur le Prince the baker plied his art.
In the park, leftwards, one of the tall

trees has shimmered yellow to the sky
as it felt the chill of Fall.
Liberty, long-thighed nymph, O lovely shy

one clad in your dusk-goldening chemise,
are you still hiding in the veiled, the shrouded trees?

The drums of summer marched and beat,
sweated, and raised the dust upon the road.
Cool vapors followed; soft and sweet
from both sides now a subtle fragrance followed.
Noon was full summer; cool in the evening
with rainy brow the autumn came a-visiting.

I took my pleasures where I found
them, like a child, or like an erudite
old sage who knows quite well the world is round.
How green I was! my beard was snowy white.
I wandered where I would and no one frowned.
Then I descended to the torrid underground.

Where are you now, echoing metro stations:
CHÀTELET-CITÉ-ST. MICHEL-ODÉON!
DENFERT-ROCHEREAU — sounding like imprecations?
Maps flowered on the dirty walls. How long,
how long! I cry out. Hush, I'm listening:
that smell of sweat and ozone starts its whispering.

And O the nights! the nightly wandering
from the far outskirts to the Quartier!
And shall the strangely clouded dawn yet bring
to Paris once again those pales of grey
when I'd undress for bed so sleepily,
dazed and still drunk with writing poetry?

Had I but strength, O would I might go back
against the heavy current of my fate!
The vile cave downstairs employed a black
cat that climbed the rooves to copulate.
And shall I hear again that yowl and croon?
That was the very moment that I learned how great
a din there was when Noah swam beneath the moon.

Zsuzsanna Ozsváth & Frederick Turner

IL FAUT LAISSER

Il faut laisser maison, et vergers et jardins —
A late verse of Ronsard opens with this line;
I hum it to myself, the brown lane's listening,
And from a garden rose a few dead petals fall;
Two denuded shrubs forward lean in wistful brood,
It seems a little French here might be understood;
Il faut laisser, a dreaming oak repeats the sound,
And a tired acorn drops on the misty ground.

      The sun sits in a cloud, a goat tied to a rope
      Walking round and round, like a bearded ghost of gloom.
      It treads among the pools that in the meadows lie,
      In a 'V' formation birds swim across the sky,
      Are lost, one after one, as the light begins to fail,
      Between sparse leaves cool rain, while falling like a veil,
      Whispers, *il faut laisser;* just as Ronsard was laid;
      Your beads of sweat will freeze one day, don't be afraid.

Neville Masterman

THE FOURTH ECLOGUE

Poet:

You should have asked me in the cradle: oh yes, then
I knew for certain that I didn't want the world. How
I howled "It's rough! Take it back again!
The light's too sharp: darkness clubs me." Ah well, now
I've survived this far, my skull's grown thick:
my lungs got stronger as I cried myself sick.

Voice:

You've been lucky. Afloat on the red waves
of blood-boiling childish fevers, you bumped ashore.
You couldn't even drown in a cold lake. Slaves
work for you inside: heart, liver, lungs — that poor
machine, hidden, drenched that no one knows!
Is your flesh waiting for cancer's pain-rooted rose?

Poet:

Look, I don't know. No one consulted me.
But here I am, a grown man. I can't explain it.
Guards kept my way safe. I longed so much to be free.

Voice:

You've been on mountain-tops the wind caressed:
and among mountain grass and leaves; as dark
came, you watched the wild doe kneeling to her rest:
seen pearls of resin stand on the pine-bark:
a girl, swimming naked, pulled herself up to land,
and, once, a fine big beetle landed on your hand.

Poet:

That's something else you can't see from a cell.
Why wasn't I made in another shape — a bird,
a planet, a mountain...? Such thoughts please me well:
save me now, freedom, with one magic word!
Lead me to the peak, the forest, the trees, my wife:
show me gold-misted dawn, a second birth, new life!
Silence. But far off the storm is there.
On the twigs the doomed fruit lolls at ease.
The late butterfly is tossed in rougher air:
already death breathes amid the trunks of trees.
And I, too, know I shall be ripe for death soon.
Time's wave lifted me, then beached me here.
I'm a captive. As the slice of the moon
grows bigger, my loneliness shines out just as clear.
But the earth finds me not guilty. I shall go free!
Above the level of soil, all's ruination:
desks and pens smashed, the world burning slowly.
Rise on your heavy wings, imagination!

Voice:

The ripe fruit hangs a while, then falls. You'll lie
at peace in the deep and memory-packed soil.
But till then, let the smoke of your rage climb the sky.
Write on the air! That's something they can't spoil!

John Wain

IMAGES

You're like a bough, so silky-whispery
arched over me,
and poppyseed to taste,
spice and mystery,
     and like the seasons' ever rippling waves
     you are exciting,
     and so soothing, serene,
     like tombstones on their graves,
or like a lifelong friend, with all to share,
yet I'm still mystified
when I inhale the scent
that haunts your heavy hair,
     and when you're blue, I fret, don't leave me here
     wayward willowy smoke —
     and when you are lightning coloured
     you give me quite a fear,
and like the tempest when the sun breaks through:
dark golden glow —
when you get cross, you are
exactly like an 'oo',
     a booming, looming, long and gloomy sound,
     and in response
     I sketch sunny loops out of smiles
     to circle you around.

Peter Zollman

FRAGMENT

I lived on this earth in an age
When man fell so low he killed with pleasure
And willingly, not merely under orders.
His life entangled, trapped, in wild obsession,
He trusted false gods raving in delusion.

I lived on this earth in an age
That esteemed informers, in an age whose heroes

Were the murderer, the bandit and the traitor.
And such as were silent — or just slow to applaud —
Were shunned, as if plague-stricken, and abhorred.

I lived on this earth in an age
When any who spoke out would run for it —
Forced to lie low and gnaw their fists in shame.
The folk went mad and, drunk on blood, filth, hate,
Could only grin at their own hideous fate.

I lived on this earth in an age
When a curse would be the mother of a child
And women were glad if their unborn miscarried.
The living — with poison seething on his plate —
Would envy the grave-dweller the worms eat.

. . . .

I lived on this earth in an age
When poets too were silent: waiting in hope
For the great Prophet to rise and speak again —
Since no-one could give voice to a fit curse
But Isaiah himself, scholar of terrible words.

Clive Wilmer and *George Gömöri*

SEVENTH ECLOGUE

Darkness descends, do you you see our hutment slowly dissolving?
Barbed wires fences float in a mist, vanish into the evening.
Those monuments of our captive life grow dim to the eyesight,
only the brain, this brain is aware of the tight, heavy wires.
Dear, do you see as the night liberates our fantasy freely:
our lacerated limbs, restored by dream-medication,
take us, poor prisoners, on a freedom march to the homeland.

Rag-uniformed bald men, fly snoring into the night, from
Serb savage mountains back to the homes so peacefully nesting.
Peacefully nesting home! Oh dear, is there such a home still?
Missed by the bombs? Intact ever since we went to the call-up?

He on the right, and the man with the whimper, will they return
   home?
Tell me about such a home where they still fancy an eclogue!

Undotted, uncrossed symbols grope and join to the last one,
feeling my way I write as I live, condemned to a dark world,
sightless, probing along my page, imitating an inchworm.
Torches, books and the rest were taken away by the warders,
post never comes, just the mountain fog drifts into the building.

Rumours and rodents mix with a few Serbs of the Resistance,
Frenchmen, Poles, with the pensive Jews and noisy Italians,
feverish and fragmented, yet one in the desire —
for happy news, soft words from a loved one, dignity, freedom,
and for an end, difficult to predict, a miraculous easement.

Beast in a cage I lie with the vermin, spine to the hard plank,
fleas on a frontal attack, with the horseflies scarcely retired.
Evening time, one day has again passed of the detention
and of our life. The camp is asleep. The moon as a searchlight
beams on the wires drawn, do you see, as tightly as always,
while silhouettes of guards and rifles pace on a grey wall,
and busy night-time noises float from every direction.

See, my dear one, the camp is asleep, dreams rise on a whisper,
somebody wakes with a start, then snorts, and squeezes a tight turn,
soon he's asleep with a flushed, sweaty face. Just I sit awake here,
tasting upon my lips a half-smoked, foul cigarette butt,
not your kiss. The soothing sleep is slow to arrive, for
I cannot live and I cannot die any longer without you.

Peter Zollman

LETTER TO MY SPOUSE

From deep below a world of eerie silence
roars in my ears, I cry out in defiance,
but I get no reply, no friendly sound in
this battle-weary grim Serbian mountain
and you're so far. Your voice weaves through my dreams, —

by day my heart will tell me what it means, —
so I listen while rustling ferns so proudly
stand like a guard and cooling shade around me.

When shall we meet again, I ask the question;
you were my weighty psalm, my sure direction
and beautiful like light, and like the darkness,
I'd find my way to you speechless and sightless.
You hide now but the mind comes to the rescue,
upon my inward eye I can arrest you;
you were once real, now I dream your presence:
I fall back in the well of adolescence

and ask "You love me true?" jealously, vainly,
and "later, in the prime of youth, once, maybe,
would you become my wife?" — I hope again
and in the sober waking state the brain
confirms: you are my wife, my friend, my angel,
but caged by borders, distance, deadly danger.
It's autumn soon. Will it forget me, traceless?
I will remember always your embraces.

Some time ago I still believed in wonders,
above my head a bombing squadron thunders;
up in the sky your blue eyes looked back at me
then blue turned dark, the bombs were desperately
trying to dive. I live for mere survival, —
and I'm a slave. No act of self-denial
is too daunting if it can reunite us;
for you I marched with sinners and the righteous

in distant lands; I'd walk on glowing embers,
for you I'd force my poor reluctant members
through walls of fire, but I'll be returning,
I shall be further toughened by the burning.
Fierce men who live in danger every hour
are calm, serene, (this is their shield and power),
that calm now weaves a spell and I am able
to be as sober as the 2-times table.

Peter Zollman

ROOT

The root stirs with rushing power,
soaks up earth and rain below,
and its dreams are white as snow.

Struggling upward to the daylight,
wisely creeps, cunningly gropes,
look, its arms are sturdy ropes.

On its arms the worms have slept,
on its legs the worms have rested,
the whole world gets worm-infested.

And the root just goes on living,
but not for the world at large,
just for the boughs in its charge:

Nursing, pampering the boughs,
sending tastes for them to savour,
every sweet, heavenly flavour.

I, too, have become a root now,
worms and I a home we share,
this poem is written there.

Now a root but once a flower,
dark, heavy earth weighs me down,
I have reached my final hour,
a saw is weeping in my crown.

Peter Zollman

À LA RECHERCHE

Intimate evenings, times long past, refined to remembrance,
glorious table, young poet-artists and pretty spouses
slowly you slide in the silent swamp where history ripens.

Warm summer night, when sparkling, noble wines animated
sparks in noble minds, dear friends, oh, where do we find you?

Verdant verbs climbed up to the lights, adventurous adverbs
bounced on a crest of crisp anapæsts in graceful abandon
and the dead were alive, the captive free, busy writing,
long disappeared dear friends, many known as fallen in action,
weighed down by heavy earth in Spain, Ruthenia, Flanders.

How many were, who just clenched their teeth, leapt into the fire,
soldiering purely because they could not see other options.
While the platoon lay under the foul sky fitfully sleeping,
they had a dream of that room back home, that warm, steady shelter,
their little island circled by society's ocean.

How many went in sealed cattle-trucks like beasts to the slaughter,
they had to stand there, frozen, unarmed, flung into the minefields;
how many went there freely to join up, gun to the shoulder,
they had a cause down there, that war stood for liberation, —
angel of freedom, you guard their great vision under the night sky.

How many... Leave it! Where do we find those intimate evenings?
Fragments of verse multiplied as the call-up notes were arriving
and very soon a few sorry wrinkles grew by the smiling
lips and eyes of those pretty spouses, whose sunny, sylph-like
steps have grown heavy in these silent, unhappy war-years.

Where do we find that night, that table under the lime tree?
And those men who may still be alive, that downtrodden army?
Their words beat in my heart, my hand holds their steady
     handshakes,
I recollect their lines, their shapes unfold to me slowly,
Serbia weeps and I analyse (caged, muted assessment).

Where do we find that night? That night cannot be recaptured,
death gives a new perspective again to the men who departed. —
They sit among us, keeping warm in a soft, feminine smile,
taking a sip from our glass of wine who, unburied, unmarked
slumber in faraway silent woods and alien uplands.

Peter Zollman

EIGHTH ECLOGUE

Poet:

Peace be with you! Savage mountain roads don't seem to retard you.
Are you endowed with wings, good sir, or chased by opponents?
Hoist by wings you are spurred by rage, your eyes very lightnings,
wanderer, old man, I know your kind, your fury betrays you:
thundering old prophet, that much is clear, but which one, I ask
    you?

Prophet:

Which prophet? Nahum am I, a Jew and native of Elkosh,
I am who preached to vile Ninevites, and Assyrian harlots,
blasting the word of God, like a fiery furnace of anger!

Poet:

I am acquainted with all your words, your Book is alive still.

Prophet:

Yes, it's alive, but sin kept breeding and ran a-riot
as we have failed to divine God's will and His very purpose.
He said that all rivers and all seas shall parch to a dust bed,
Carmel, Bashan, and high Lebanon shall ruefully languish,
mountains shall quake and melt as the earth is burnt to a cinder.
It came truly to pass.

Poet:

        Swift nations wage bloody warfare.
Like Nineveh, our own souls too, are vilely denuded.
Tell me what has been achieved by locusts, blustery sermons?
Basest among all beasts, mankind is a shame to creation!
Suckling babes are slung to the wall by broad sunny daylight,
church to a torch and house to a stove and men to the ash-heap,
factory buildings soar to the sky in loud detonation.
Streetfuls of fleeing people aflame succumb to the sirens,
craters of air-bombs spew to the sky like foul frothy cauldrons,
wide city squares are strewn with a host of dark bloody corpses,
shrunk like cowpats after a week. The world is again as
you had depicted it in your Book. — From peace everlasting,
tell me, what brings you back to this earth?

Prophet:
                My fury. The people
are little orphans still, pressed into the army of evil
man-shaped beasts. — I came to harangue this age as a witness,
and to be here when the sinful walls abjectly surrender.

Poet:
We have heard you. The Lord hath said, through you as a
    mouthpiece:
woe to the greedy, rich city walls, from corpses erected.
Tell me, besides, what fed your rage through so many thousand
years, what has kept it alive with fierce invincible ardour?

Prophet:
Once in a bygone age my unclean lips were anointed,
instead of oil with a glowing coal, as once were Isaiah's,
by the Almighty, who probed my heart; the coal was alive and
held in a pair of tongs by an Angel: "Lord look upon me!"
— my very words — "Send me to preach thy Word to the people."
Once sent forth by holy command, we men become ageless,
restless too, the divine coal keeps us eternally glowing.
What's to the Lord, a thousand years? The blink of an eyelid!

Poet:
Father, I envy you, you're so young! Though my petty few years
are but a day to your awesome age, I'm already worn down,
small pebble in heavy seas that fleeting time has eroded.

Prophet:
Fear not. I know your recent work. Rage sets you afire.
Rage like yours is akin to ours: it's food to the people
and drink too, to sustain all those who wait for the Kingdom
long foretold us by a rabbi, a holy disciple,
who fulfilled what we prophesied and all the Commandments.[1]
Come, we announce that the time is ripe, the birth of the Kingdom
is very near. Let us go, gather all good people around us,
come, bring along your wife, and cut some sticks for the journey.

---

[1] This allusion to Jesus Christ is one of the many indications of Radnóti's
strong Christian undercurrent.

Walker and staff make a great old team, look, there is a fine tree,
cut me a staff from there, good friend, I fancy a gnarled one.

Peter Zollman

FORCED MARCH

He's mad, who lying half dead   gets up to march again,
a walking heap of torment   bends ankles, knees, the brain,
with secret wings to help him   he is back on the way,
the ditch is so inviting   but he's afraid to stay,
and if you ask the reason   he will perhaps reply,
at home his wife awaits him   and wiser ways to die.
But poor man is deluded: at home, above the house
the ashes fly in circles,   a scorched wind comes to browse,
the wall lies flat in silence,   the plum tree had to shear,
back home the night is tousled   in restless, shaky fear.
If I could still believe it   that it's not merely dream:
my home and all the good things   I hold in high esteem,
if only!... on the cool porch   just as it used to be,
the jam cooled in the jam jar   to tease a bumble bee,
the late summer were basking   in sleepy semi-shade,
the apples in the soft breeze   nakedly, slowly swayed,
and Fanni's blond hair greeted   before the tawny hedge,
and shadows slowly doodled   a lazy, lacy sketch, —
but wait, there may be hope yet!   the moon is strangely large!
Oh, friend, don't leave, just call me!   and I get up to march!

Peter Zollman

RAZGLEDNICA (1)[2]

A raging cannon-thunder rolls from Bulgaria,
it hits the ridge and lamely falls in our area;
the men huddle with beasts, carts and thoughts in muddy maze,
neighing, the highway shies back, the moon's mane is ablaze.
I live in this mad turmoil but you are permanent,
still light deep in my mind, star on my firmament,
you glisten like the Angel marvelling at the Fall,
or glow-worms in a dead tree on their sepulchral crawl.

Peter Zollman

RAZGLEDNICA (2)

The houses and the haystacks are on fire
a mere six miles away,
and poor folk sit scared, smoking in silence
on the edge of the hay,
while here the pond still drapes its lacy flounces
on bathing shepherd girls
and lambs still drink the clouds and lick the water
to frill the fleecy curls.

Peter Zollman

RAZGLEDNICA (3)

The oxen's muzzles drip with bloody slaver,
the men's urine is brown with bloody traces,
we stand in knots, the stench is hard to bear.
as dreadful doom is driving in the air.

Peter Zollman

---

[2] Serbian for 'postcard.' These four short pieces culminate in Radnóti's own death poem, presented here in several versions.

RAZGLEDNICA (4)[3]

I tumbled next to him, his body turned
and tightened like a string about to go,
shot in the head. — This is how you will end,
I breathed, — just lie rigid from top to toe.
Now death blossoms where patience perseveres. —
"Der springt noch auf!" — sounded above me.
A sludge of gory mud clotted my ears.

Peter Zollman

RAZGLEDNICA (4)
(additional versions)

I.
I fell beside him and his corpse turned over,
tight already as a snapping string.
Shot in the neck. "And that's how you'll end too."
I whispered to myself; "lie still; no moving.
Now patience flowers into death." Then I could hear
"Der springt noch auf," above me, and very near.
Blood mixed with mud was drying on my ear.

Zsuzsanna Ozsváth and *Frederick Turner*

---

[3] There are several outstanding versions of Razglednica (4) which, for obvious reasons, has become one of the most famous Holocaust poems. This anthology presents four more. Each one brings out a different nuance. The sentence in German means 'this one will jump up yet' i.e., 'this one's still twitching.'

II.
I fell beside him. His body — which was taut
As a cord is, when it snaps — spun as I fell.
Shot in the neck. "This is how you will end,"
I whispered to myself; "keep lying still.
Now, patience is flowering into death."
"Der springt noch auf," said someone over me.
Blood on my ears was drying, caked with earth.

Clive Wilmer and *George Gömöri*

III.
I dropped beside him. Taut as is the cord
before it snaps, his body twitched and fell.
Shot in the neck. "That's how you'll end up too,"
I whispered to myself: "Lie low! Keep still! —
For patience this time blossoms into death."
"Der springt noch auf," I heard a fellow call.
My ears were crusted with blood-sodden earth.

Iain MacLeod

Istvān Vas
b. 1910

István Vas
(1910-1991)

Poet, essayist, and translator, he studied in Vienna where he absorbed the twin influences of Marxism and Freudian psychology, not unlike Attila József (q.v.). He returned to Hungary in 1929 and, after various civil service jobs, became a full-time writer and publishing consultant. He was the descendant of Jewish rabbis, but embraced Catholicism, became the husband of Lajos Kassák's (q.v.) daughter, Etel, before World War II, and became somewhat of a mystic. He survived the war, thanks to the help of his friend, the novelist Géza Ottlik. After the Communist takeover he could not publish because of his allegedly bourgeois attitudes and had to survive for several years on translations.

As a poet he belongs to the third generation of Nyugat [The West]. *He was a close friend of Miklós Radnóti (q.v.), whose tragic death haunted him to the end of his life, somewhat as Arany (q.v.) could never forget the death of Petőfi (q.v.). His poetic role models were János Arany, Mihály Babits, and Dezső Kosztolányi (qq.v), but he was also attracted to Illyés (q.v.). A master of many verse forms, Vas was a deeply conscious, rational artist, one of the new contemporary poets who was able to transform abstract ideas into perfect artistic expression.*

His autobiographical volumes Difficult Love [Nehéz szerelem], *1964;* The Interrupted Investigation [A félbeszakadt nyomozás], *1967; and* Why Does the Eagle Screech? [Mért vijjog a saskeselyű?], *1981, are not only brilliant chronicles of Hungarian literary life, but urbane and yet pitiless self-revelatory documents. His narrative style unites exactitude with irony; he is equally at home in the regions of the soul and actual, documented history. His prose provides invaluable portraits of many contemporary writers and poets.*

He has translated, with great artistry, Shakespeare and other English poets such as Donne and Marvell, as well as Villon, Racine, Molière, Schiller, and several contemporaries.

He was the first critic in Communist-ruled Hungary who managed to publish an appreciative review about the exiled poets of the 1956 generation. His volumes of poetry include Letter About Freedom [Levél a szabadságról], *1935;* Double Path [Kettős ösvény], *1946;* The Created World [A teremtett világ], *1956;* Collected Poems [Összegyűjtött versei], *1963;* The Underground Sun [A földalatti nap], *1969; and* It Doesn't Count [Nem számít], *1979.*

His wife, Piroska Szántó, is a major artist, painter, and book illustrator. She illustrated several of Vas's books, including Burglary in Rome [Római rablás], *in 1962. His last selection of poems,* Elegy of Szentendre [Szentendrei elégia] *appeared in 1990, and the last part of his autobiographical reminiscences* After That [Azután] *in the year of his death, 1991. The prose volume* Remembrances [Visszaemlékezés] appeared *in the same year. He was much loved for his integrity and appreciated by poets of various generations as a sympathetic critic and role model.*

A selection of his poems in English, Through the Smoke, *by several translators, was published by Corvina of Budapest in 1989 with an introduction by George Szirtes.*

COVENTRY CATHEDRAL

This cross is the most sublime:
these two surviving beams
crosswise bound with wire,
roof-beams, charred by the fire.

What fire could not destroy
huge nails sustain the church,
they pierce through the world's body
even in lands where the cross
is an alien mystery.

The broken arch now kneeling
in dust is of red sandstone,
blackened, but not by yesterday's
German bombs alone:
you can sense the acrid odour
of new fires from Asia.

Clive Wilmer and *George Gömöri*

THE DEAF MUTE GIRL

Between the stone huts of the vineyard hill
of vines and boulders many children played
children of charm and beauty and of strength.
At first I did not notice that she spoke
no word, but that she was more beautiful
than all the others, nor could I surmise
what caused the earnestness in her big eyes,

deep blue, or what had shaped her warming smile,
what cruel, twisting turn of nature made
this wonder not alone of sculptured head
but every tiny sinew which, at five,
already reached that rare maturity
great actresses display in their sublime
triumphant moments; why, up to her forehead
in dirt, barefooted, every glance of hers
should be significant and every move
she made should bear a grace more than itself,
as if some human link had blossomed bare
in beauty only. What her smile was like!
It had the dazzle of the cool landscape
of lava origin before the grape
was harvested, with all its promises
of earthly giving and of happiness.
Her questioning eyes, her querying finger stretched
no more were child-like, curiosity
painful and faced with all the mysteries,
so that when she would signal *no,* it was
she who was mystery and love itself,
the unattainable, still aching-sweet
and in her *no* all that our life denies,
even the fruitful knowledge: "we must die!"
and as she ran to someone with her *yes!*
as she would put her little hand in mine
her gaze so open and so vulnerable
was a gift of surety and trust
that hope still lived between two humans so.
And her *goodbye!* She stood there in the road
above Lake Balaton beneath the rocks,
the landscape all around from which she grew,
her house behind her nestling in its hill,
her family, her dog — her lovely hand
waving as if it hoped that Time itself,
the irregainable, could be retained!
For me this was far more than sparkling bay
of castle ruin crumbling at the top
of fabled Szigliget, more than the full
grape clusters hidden by protecting leaves

where crumbled basalt marked the terraces
between the vine-leaves. Lovely spirit grown,
for me you are attainment, nature's own
grown beyond nature and beyond the pain
of its destruction, gathered in your being
the meaning of the world, its fuller sense
of beauty, born of all humanity.

Charles A. Wagner

UNDERSTANDING

You understand him not. Christ does not claim
submission like a party boss from those
who follow him. He knows him best who knows
that kingly as a beggar king he came.

He Magdalene, not Martha, praised. To all,
to every heart a different path he shows,
and some by ways without a path he chose
like doubting Thomas, persecutor Paul.

Each will a heaven find such as his own
imagination pictures. Yours will be
impersonal and vast and undefined;

but I in terms to sense familiar known
shall apprehend the final mystery,
and ever live the life I leave behind.

Godfrey Turton

XENOPHON'S SONG

All these undertakings!
We always get the worst of it.
This handful of us, we who were let down.

Once we have pitched our tents,
where have the big armies disappeared to?
We have usually been forgotten.

We, the forgetful ones.
We regret behaving heedlessly, we do.
A thought that sparks too late is a dog's thought.

And then to thrust to cut to strike
hail of arrows sharp glitter of lances.
All that — and just for a retreat.

The tents are put up they are taken down
hot days freezing nights
and then, wave upon wave, the Persians.

Our manner of retreat is always to advance.
And march upon march.
But in the end the gleaming sea, *thalatta*.[1]

To break out of ourselves into ourselves.
Eyes words and silence, drawn and ready.
It was no conquest, merely *anabasis*.[2]

Clive Wilmer and *George Gömöri*

SANTA MARIA ANTIQUA

On the side of the vaulted library of Augustus
stands the most ancient of Christian altars,
the ruined church of the Virgin, "Old St. Mary."
Built nearby the square of the temple of Vesta,
even disfigured, it stands as a memento:
what every Rome must expect as necessary.

---

[1] Greek for 'sea,' in Attic Greek. A dialectal form *thalassa* also exists and has found its way into several English compounds with the [ss] spelling.

[2] A 'going up' or 'military advance', especially that of a Greek mercenary army, led by Xenophon, which retreated from Persia to the Black Sea after the claimant to the Persian throne who had hired them was killed in battle. Xenophon later wrote the history of their retreat.

On its walls Eastern saints and Western saints
side by side lived and fell into decay
through rains and wars that flailed them to corrosion;
but, even now, on one bare wall's illumined
a holy picture which, though blurred, is blazing:
life and idea, colour and devotion.

Both ruined long, they still stand side by side,
and the Vesta temple, just as the temple of Mary,
has with centuries — not stone — been overlaid.
All things survive, though in some other form.
And even the joy of God — who is eternal —
in change, in revolution, is remade.

Clive Wilmer and *George Gömöri*

ARMAGEDDON

And already they are beginning to witness that Armageddon,
where the Dragon and the false Prophet
open up to them their throats filled with blasphemy;
where the great Whore arrayed in purple and scarlet
sits upon the scarlet beast
with its seven heads and ten horns.
But the seven angels are also there and each in turn
pours out a vial brimming with pent-up wrath,
and the sea will become like molten blood.
And every living creature will perish in it,
and then there will be great resounding voices.
And lightning and thunder,
and stones will hail down, smiting to death
everyone that hath the mark of the scarlet beast on him.
And the scarlet Whore will be torn into three pieces
and thrown into the sea of molten blood.
And then a man seated on a white horse
will capture the scarlet beast with a laser beam
and chain it up for a thousand years.
And there will be great rejoicing and all the just
shall fall on their knees before him seated upon the mustang.

The Lord of Hosts will cover the world
with an enormous cowboy hat beneath which
will stand churches and factories.
And then there will be great silence, and peace on earth
and good will toward men. Amen.

William Jay Smith

FROM THE ADMONITIONS OF
ST. THERESA OF AVILA
(In lieu of an 'Ars Poetica')

Those who have not been chosen for any higher call
are best advised not to attempt to climb up by the wall.
This you would well to note since if you try it,
you're more likely to lose than profit by it.
The soul will manifest herself in her true essence
providing she be in her Saviour's presence,
may cling in love to Jesus and His blessed humanity,
and dwell for ever in the Master's company,
may even have converse with Him, and so confide
to Him her sufferings and what she lacks beside,
and if she does not forget His presence in her bliss
she may rejoice with Him, though not with artifice
of formal rhetoric, but words that come to hand,
or such as her immediate necessities demand.
That is as much as we can do: if this will not content
a man, if his soul would venture the ascent
to that place where they will not let him through
he forfeits everything. That is my own view.
For the mind is paralysed once it breaks through nature's band,
and the soul too quickly withers in the desert sand.
In any case what is the spirit's corner-stone or basis?
Humility, nothing else. And humility increases
as we approach God's throne — or we lose what we had won.
But no one should believe that I would have them shun
those noble thoughts by which the human spirit mounts
so it may feel the goodness to which God has set no bounds,
or by which it may see the miracles of heaven.

It's true that I myself have not been given
such high capacity. Yet notwithstanding
I say again, it was God's mercy helped my understanding:
in my continual poverty I should not have presumed
to set my soul to earthly tasks. So how could I assume
that I might freely meddle in affairs of heaven then?
And yet there is no shortage of such able men,
particularly of those who, by dint of education,
are fitted to conduct a higher investigation.
For in this field such knowledge, provided with a measure
of genuine humility, I hold to be a treasure.
And yet I still maintain we should not try to climb,
that God, if He will, will raise us in His own good time.

In any case the mind will sometimes simply fail:
in mystical theology God waits — then draws the veil,
I condemn this only when our self-conceit has swollen so
we draw the veil ourselves. No, let the engine go,
else we grow cold and foolish, and we lose for ever more
the goal at which we aimed, as well as what was ours before.
If God suspends the intellect, have faith in His decision:
He wants to make us think again or lead us to revision.
At such times a mere credo will blaze forth with greater light
than whole years of solicitous labouring day and night.
But that we ourselves should wish to curb our spirit's energies
or stop the engine operating — that way madness lies.
It may not be a sin perhaps, but the punishment's all the worse:
you let the man prepare to leap, then grab hold of his purse.
Again and again he tries, grows tired eventually:
the will is ineffective without humility
that, once it enters the engine, so functions in the whole
that disgust accompanies the actions of the soul.
For those of you who understand, the matter is quite plain,
and as for the others, I, for one, will certainly not explain.

George Szirtes

RHAPSODY: KEEPING FAITH

1

READING RADNÓTI'S DIARY

So little there is of Life: of Letters, page on page!
And how the life strikes through the barren verbiage!
Three days I've watched and listened, while days that have long died
gather and strike and leave their froth upon the tide.
A disembodied light, a sieved and flickering screen,
permits one ghostly dusk to filter in between,
as if again we sat and looked down on the same
Danube with her bridges, and all our days of shame
gathered and struck through words and the heart's animus.
In whom did that shame burn so fiercely as in us?
Our country's! The whole world's! His voice is furious:
is this to be our youth? this bitterness? this test
of character, this shame of intellect oppressed,
this time of baited traps and tortuous arguments,
these awkward situations, these filthy lineaments
of shady confidences, this terror of events!
    And behind these literary chaste
tantrums with their helpless hiss, the waste
of steam, vain intellectual effort. Not enough:
Our limbs grow loath and leaden in the spreading slough.
However much we differ, days and events combine
once and for all to weave our lives to one design,
the monster-breeding river, the past-for-present years,
my name bobs in their foam, appears and disappears,
the war's first autumn turns all suffering to stone,
and there's the catafalque, and there the dead march on!
In a subordinate clause night rattles out her dirge,
and shows us walking home together from the verge
of someone's grave. O world, where death-rattles resound!
Our agonies, like brothers, are each to the other bound,
and in the pages where another's life winds down
I see the creeping on of death — this time, your own.
If I should once forget, but once, your agony,
may no-one ever owe fidelity to me.
Never may I enjoy a moment of relief
should I but once betray our bond or our belief.

May I be stricken down, as senseless as the sod
if I once curse the cause, of death's obedient rod.
You poor, you saintly ones, the kind and brave and true!
Dry bones be all my brains, should I be false to you.

2
TWO DAYS LATER

   If ever I denied desires dear to us...
But did you desire what we did, on your precipitous
and evangelic route, that final beaten track?
I'd try to see it through, but intellect starts back.
For you a painful death and final cleansing wait.
I flee through realms of filth, escape the well-sprung bait.
How much of hiding, feigning, tricks and trickery!
Till Götterdämmerung and, lastly, liberty!
Later, the sulphurous marsh, the pestilential pool.
The fever that kills by stealth, and more perfidious rule.
Fulfilment soiled intentions, the disgrace soaked through,
shame courses in our veins, the curse still circulates,
and each one falls and sinks obeying the dictates
of his own nature, since the will that should defend
turns counter: even fear finds guilt a nagging friend
who lathers in his spittle the clear untainted head —
must I keep faith with this to keep faith with the dead?
   I fled and I escaped and so I stayed alive.
Friendly hands and unknown hands had helped me to survive!
Since then how many a faithful or faith-restoring face,
fresh heart or eye has blithely preserved me in its grace.
How often fresh hope folded me round in close embrace,
and new friends through new terrors strengthened in their place!
And that, for which we longed, is an opposing tide,
which slowly kills them off or drowns the spark inside,
as it would kill you too, the best parts, the most true —
how can I not break faith, and yet keep faith with you?
   Up here and down below are much the same to me,
the living ones, the dead ones bind us equally,
it's not enough to keep faith with things for which we long,
since everything that happens ties new knots just as strong,
in vain to know each act of trust means something new,

that fierce opposing armies claim service as their due,
since it isn't my affair to put the world to rights,
my heart and mind keep faith with equal opposites,
each moment has its twin that moment grafted on —
dry bones be all my brains, should I be false to one.

3
SUMMA FIDEI

Each moment has its moment grafted on its back
and I am stretched both ways on an eternal rack,
now I observe it calm, precise, where not self-consciousness,
but faith, the axis of my being, splits under the stress.
They say the ancient Magyars could afford a type
who, though impaled upon the stake, contrived to puff a pipe —
so self upon its rack, takes bitter comfort in
the moment split asunder striving with its twin.
They cancel out each other in mutual endeavour:
choose this or that! cries pain. But I'll choose neither. Never.
Not while I am myself, or sense my single core,
I'll not surrender faith to any Either/Or.
If one terror oppresses me and consciousness wears thin,
or my sphere of being starts to whimper and gives in,
if trembling and fear protest, "Anything but that!",
if even my will surrenders and turns confederate,
or, scared of what might come, when dark runs through my brain,
I cry to the passing moment, "Let that which *is,* remain" —
it's only fear in action, not I myself that act,
my faith is what it was, timeless, whole, compact.
Maddening, faith-destroying, infernal Either/Ors —
dry bones be all my brains if I walk through your doors.
  Each moment has its twin grafted on its heart —
O all preserving Pity, let them not fall apart,
and you, Affection, true to each as is his due,
be one to whom new hearts in new ways might be true,
you mysterious Sympathy, you radiant Secret, be
the ones who turn betrayal to fidelity,
you to whom a hundred different loyalties lead,
accept the contradictions my own fidelities breed,
O you, in whom erratic knowledge seeks to know

O you, in whom erratic knowledge seeks to know
itself, show my stray paths the way they ought to go,
you pastor of kept faith, accept me at the gate
where those things are made whole which now disintegrate,
where Either/Ors, those tyrants, may not gain passage through,
where I'll discover all I owe allegiance to,
that those once rent asunder may never be undone,
be, all transforming Love, a thousand shapes in one.

George Szirtes

THROUGH THE SMOKE

Through cigar smoke, through
night's fogged cloak, through
wreaths of the winter moon, through shawls of rain,
in the opening dream's light and uncertain
golden-dream
purple and ebony
stage scenery
between reckoning and translation,
in brief relaxation,
when tired brains like spiders weave their screen
it's always you I've seen,
the impossible, the brilliant green fly
I catch as it flits by.
You're every picture, all the thoughts that rise
under the lids, behind the eyes.

George Szirtes

BEETHOVEN'S OLD AGE

This is not in German, nor in the tongue
of another barbarous tribe held together
by credence and secretion, nor in the intelligible Latin
of order and loveliness in which they flatter you —
those sounds, in unspoken speech, you must understand this.

in me art conquered itself,
vanity, coquetry, prostitution.
This should tickle nobody's itches,
make nobody's guts tremble,
nor stir those to dance who are frigid.
Let no lofty impotence
sublimate its failure through me.

An in A-minor, nostalgia's noble key,
like Mozart when he wanted to sob sweetly.
But no one should sob for me, no one
should say of me, the poor deaf man.
This torment is not my concern,
this death is not my death,
this viola chills the tears welling up in the eye,
this Quartet in A-minor refutes A-minor,
this saturation lays everything bare.

You must answer this, this you must answer to,
and question upon question, charge upon charge
and why, and why, and how could you do this?
And suddenly the melody sweeps clear, and I could do that too,
but I don't want to continue it, we are not singing.
I challenge you and, if you don't reply, I'll disqualify you,
and the violin strives, the viola grates,
the cello moans: an answer must be given.

Daniel Hoffman

IN THE ROMAN FORUM

The stones no longer interest me
neither does history
these days it's hard for
my eyes to make out
the Latin texts on the stones
nothing interests me any more
only what I can credit
when it happens to come along
yet I only vacillate alone

yet I only vacillate alone
on the way I started
where have the Romans gone

Bruce Berlind

THROUGH TIME'S SEGMENTS

Nearly midnight. Windows open. Summertime.
Moths cover the neon bar in my room.
I stand at the window. This solitude becomes
chronic. I feel this room contains old rooms
from here, from there. The time, the space
of rooms criss-crossing one another's place.
This person, and that, the lodgers reunite
through time's segments. To them
I speak in several kinds of time.
Alone. Speak to the overflowing night.

Daniel Hoffman

ROMANUS SUM

Romanus sum — and I held my hand in fire;
Through twenty years it has burnt me to the bone.
I played the part of Mucius Scaevola
Before what would, though yet unborn, be Rome.

And suddenly it was here. All that the past
Has spewed ferments between its malformed walls.
Rome has not yet been built but in its place,
Bloated with lies, a new Byzantium swells.

And the Crucifix is debased to a gilded bauble
And the flames of Pentecost lap a martyr's stake.
It was such a waste to have burnt one's living flesh
For a stillborn City's sake.

Clive Wilmer and *George Gömöri*

UPON A DRAWING[3]

These feet and hands, two pelvises, this movement
Is unmistakeable. But who was it had
Such a narrow face? Who between mouth and brow
Such a long, narrow cavity? This skull, balding,
Yes, this one I know — but who looks through these eyes?
This one, and that one. They are making love —
Not two, but many of them. Those dead
Lovers and wives move in their intimate
Movement. In these lines men and women,
Irreconcilable once, now come together.
What lines! What an embrace!
This coitus of line that is poured in white across
A background of black, how richly laden it is,
Rich in its purity, pure too in its lust!
Such lust is available only to those who already
Are no more, who exist in these lines alone, hidden
In this embrace. In this framework, translucent, yet
Ingeniously solid. And in all the signs of life
Of this exclusive multitude, only they, only they
Can be named, these two. You and I, you and I.

Daniel Hoffman

THE INVISIBLE ELEMENT

To that invisible element which claimed
A part in our becoming fact not fiction,
Which turned what knowledge and desire had framed
Against itself in direct contradiction
       What could you possibly say? That our schemes ripen
       To performance, that thoughts petrify
       To form? The bonds of contemplation tighten
       From cradle to the grave, and so we die.
At what point did the fatal germ infect
The process of becoming with its lies?

---

[3] On a drawing by the poet's wife, the artist Piroska Szántó.

Or was it bred within the intellect?
We hoped for more? No, this was no surprise.
>   What do you know? If you were still alive
>   What could you say? Or were you wrong as well?
>   No answer. Yet the very germs which thrive
>   Are sweeter than grace although they give us hell.

George Szirtes

THE LION

The Lion of the stars is losing power,
His incandescent heat is on the wane
And after velvet nights of shooting stars
The latish-summer sun can take it easy,
Like that declining lion in the cage.
It wasn't his desire but the female's:
Perhaps the last lovemaking, final *encore,*
Her sturdy ochre body softly snuggling
Against his flank in flirting invitation.
He stretched his lazy limbs, stood up at last
And clambered ponderously on his mate
Whose rump was gently lowered for his comfort.
He tried to roar, but gave up with a wheeze.
The act was rather quickly consummated,
As best he could manage. Then sliding down
He rested on the ground exhausted, panting.
The female was revived, got on her feet
And gave him loving licks of gratitude.
He too was grateful, resting head and mane
Upon the lioness. They shared a smile.
We stood there, fresh-faced lovers, by the railing
And felt a wave of electricity
Sweep over us! Come quick! Come home! To bed!
But stayed there quite a while and watched the lions:
There's beauty in the love of aging hunters,
In cooling bodies kindled into flame.

Peter Zollman

László Kálnoky
(1912-1985)

Poet and translator, Kálnoky was born in the historic city of Eger in northeastern Hungary, famous for its resistance to Turkish capture in the 16th century, commemorated in the famous novel The Stars of Eger [Egri csillagok] *by novelist Géza Gárdonyi. Kálnoky served as mayor of his native city in 1939-1944. He studied law and obtained a doctorate in political science. He was a prolific contributor to the leading Hungarian reviews. He left a veritable treasure trove of translated literature mostly from German, French and English. He suffered from tuberculosis from early childhood onwards, and this left a hue of pessimism over his outlook on life.*

He disliked injustice and oppression and helped many persecuted friends during World War II. He worked as an editor after 1953; from 1957 he supported himself as a free-lance poet and translator.

His own poetry is filled with nostalgia for wider horizons, with the revolt against the monotony of small, provincial towns and their life. The two poets who seem to have left the most visible mark on him are Dezső Kosztolányi and Árpád Tóth (qq.v.). He was a pessimist and brooded upon man's biological and social helplessness as well as the cosmic catastrophe awaiting all humankind. He was also affected by Jean-Paul Sartre's (1905-1980) philosophy of pessimism and by the British astronomer Sir James H. Jeans (1877-1946), the founder of catastrophe theory.

Kálnoky's poetic style changed from formal poetry towards freer and freer forms until he abandoned rhyme and emphasized thought and content; toward the end of his life his diction even approached that of the avant-garde. His volumes include The Garden of the Shadows [Az árnyak kertje], *1939;* Elegy from a Sanatorium [Szanatóriumi elégia], *1942;* On a Feverish Star [Lázas csillagon], *1957;* In the Shadow of Flames [Lángok árnyékában], *1970;* The After-life of a Hyena and Other Stories [Egy hiéna utóélete és más történetek], *1981;* The Glass Hat [Az üvegkalap], *1982;* Beached Whales [Bálnák a parton], *1983; and* Deed of Heroism in the Bathtub [Hőstettek az ülőkádban], *1986.*

A late-starting member of the third generation of Nyugat [The West], *Kálnoky was a shining island of taste, culture, integrity and humanity in one of the most difficult periods of Hungarian history.*

WHAT MAN CAN DO ON THIS PLANET

To kindle fire so that flame,
when flaring, should bite our hands.

To suffer thirst so that after the first gulp
the glass should absorb water.

To run along a corridor
streaked by shrill lunatic cries
without losing our sanity.

To fall down ensnared by lights
waiting for the weapon to strike
or for a reprieve granted by the mercy
of him who misunderstood our countenance.

To nettle indifference with provocative words
just when it was turning away from us.

Vegetating in the colourless matter
of danger that you get accustomed to,
to find a secret window
and to divine the blurred picture
of the town five hundred years from now.

Even with plugged ears
to listen to muffled, unknown voices
and answer them
even with your mouth gagged.

George Gömöri

HEART ESCAPING

Under a rain of blows, the heart
plunges blindly forward,
trying to break a path
through friable rock
which the futility of flight
softens into compassion.
Thus the worm, boring into
the dark night of the toe.

Kenneth and *Zita McRobbie*

HAMLET'S LOST MONOLOGUE

Denmark sleeps soundly.
Its bays and meadows are sunk in night.
I'm alone now, sleepless prince prowling
that moonlit glimmering stairway
where once I followed in the steps of the ghost.
I summon it again; but it doesn't come.
Shall I go back to the palace then?
Listen to the murderer's drunken
snoring behind iron-bound doors?
Or wait outside under the open sky
and stare at the scenes devised in misty air
and shapes set there by invisible hands,
beyond mind's understanding?

Or should I perhaps await those nightmares
befalling mortals in the small hours
when breathing comes in fits and starts,
when the heart begins violently to beat,
its palpitations shattering the thickly
encrusted layers of disquietude?
Shall I conjure faces of the guiltless,
their dust now jealously enclosed
within funerary urns of stone

whom it was my mission to deliver up,
casually playing some ball-game perhaps
even as they trustingly cried out my name,
their final accusing convulsions going to my head?
No! For I dread seeing them again
when the autumn rains, the claws of winter
disintegrate the fence of too
too perishable flesh about the bones.

As if I were sitting in a tossing barque
on all sides the drowning cluster,
hands reach up, clutching at the gunwales,
and they couldn't know that I, the boatman,
already count myself among them...
You rulers of earth and sky,
who for your amusement formed
brightness of stars from lightless clay,
what do you care if some mistaken principle's
at work in your insignificant creation!
Anyway, it's I who's doomed to perish,
I who proclaim your shame to your face.

My witnesses are the fallen millions,
imprints of primeval ferns in shales,
bone fragments turning up in soils
of gigantic reptiles, wingless birds,
and mothers' wombs opening amid pain
from which like bones from earth's belly
emerges already destined for death
pulling livesome life.
My witnesses are those illusory
miracles of nature, those blinding sparks'
fiery freckles on the cheeks of dawn,
my witnesses the denizens of evening gardens,
and darkening flower-rage in scarlet calyxes
when the sun plunges to its
waist in the ocean.

My witnesses are the shells in gravels
of eroding rivers' estuaries,

as snails' empty houses. And my witnesses
are the holiest concepts conceived
by wisdom, which will burst in the air
like seedpods, blown as far as they can go,
without anything living reaching into them.

No, I'll not submit to punishment
from such a quarter, though pecked fragments of liver
fall warningly at my feet.
Peering out to sea, I know
I'm no sinner; it's your ship
that with its cargo of alluring bait
has entered port, so that eager hands
of the vulgar, of milady, of the haughty councillor
may rummage through its goods.

And I despise this tawdry trash
with which you lead astray.
Not for me this business practice.
I'll die free. And if, before,
I couldn't be your adversary,
I'll not be an accessory...

Kenneth and *Zita McRobbie*

WANDERINGS ON A HEAVENLY BODY

Lifeless plains at the foot of
ash-bluely slumbering mountains.
Arriving in cities, saddest
are the piles of bones yellowly
littering the back-street alleys,
stumps of reddish brickwork
in the last flare of evening light,
and stone steps to the harbour
from which caked blood was washed off
at high-tide long long ago...

A rain of ash has fallen on corpses
of the light-minded who'd yielded
to misleading impulses.
                    In the centre
raged an epidemic more terrible than plague,
though the stars were shining in the same way.
And they'll do so, even when
run-wild vegetation overgrows
the statues and topmost tower-roof mouldings.

Spelling failure, its blackness was not
without a certain gleam of heroism,
because those who failed had reached for the heights.
Ending pathetically, their shame
could never wipe away sorrow.
Here now humility abases itself
and covers with kisses the soil's wounds,
remembrancing's hook in its heart.

Kenneth and *Zita McRobbie*

SWEPT AWAY

Again and again that scene, enthralling in ordinariness,
its banality breathtaking, the overwhelming greyness
of Eger's main street in the 'thirties,
the bustling evening Corso's short stretch
between Lyceum and cinema,
the pool of yellow lamplight, washed-out faces,
the stately gait of a middle-aged gentleman with corporation,
heavy gold watch chains of office-managers or well-to-do merchants
looped across buttoned waistcoats,
I see their buxom or scrawny spouses' mill-wheel hats,
hear the gigglings of sailor-suited schoolgirls
swarming out from the English Misses' chapel after the May litany,
here a whiff of cologne, there of wine or cigar,
the magistrate and his wife each taking an arm of their idiot
daughter who otherwise would paw the boys,
with silver-headed cane the frock-coated

land-titles registrar takes his evening stroll,
the church's greying choir-master pursues chits of girls,
a lilac-sashed canon drives off in a glass-doored coach,
and six or seven church towers all of a sudden
together ring out vespers,
and already the scene begins to waver,
flood-water tollings making it tremble
the narrow street tapers to a mountain torrent,
swelling waves of sound bear passers-by on its current,
flailing arms, carp mouths, catfish whiskers breaking surface,
the splashing of the drowning, gasped agonies of fear,
all carried on the tide toward the pitch-black mouth,
I, dead trout among them, but my silvery bruised scales
are shining still, there in the twighlight
on housewalls or cliff-face shore.

Kenneth and *Zita McRobbie*

SVIDRIGAILOV'S[1] LAST NIGHT

I'm waiting for sleep, but it won't come.
Why keep tossing on this rickety bed
in an inn of dubious repute?
What is it that settles on my soul, like dust
sifting between pages of a book,
blotting out characters?
Why so terrifying the high wind's sighing
through nearby trees?
How remote now my country estate,
my well-rubbed pipes, my furniture,
comfort that was such an assumed necessity,
priest-cursing brandy on an empty stomach,
a well-basted roast pheasant and partridge,
hearty breakfast chubby little woodcocks,
the pantry's sides of bacon, hams,
pianoforte evenings in the salon,

---

[1] One of the negative characters in Dostoevsky's novel, *The Brothers Karamazov.*

pianoforte evenings in the salon,
hands of whist, seducing of girls
their protestings stifled by embraces,
so many secret wickedly sweet cuddlings,
the sleigh jingling down the road's incline,
little grey horse's shadow on the snow.

Why should this still interest me,
upon whom the dead have come to call?
Nothing remains here any more
except dark patches where objects used to be,
leather-smell, mouse-think, soiled bedclothes
and a meal tray's nauseous leftovers'
feast for flies.
I've been distributing my money.
Do they deserve it? Better not ask.
This way it's easier to leave,
and I've a premonition of where the road will end.

Yes — yes... Eternity's neither
heavenly bliss nor fiery hell.
It's a dusty alcove, with nothing
but a dirty window you can't see out of,
a dilapidated cane-bottomed chair, walls sooty
like those behind some hovel's stove,
cobwebs thick across the corners.
There one can yawn, then nod off
for a thousand years, and then another.
Occasionally waking with a start. Fancying there's
a knock at the door, though it's only the cold heart's
spasmodic flutter. An irritable wave of a hand,
heavy head again falling forward onto chest.

Kenneth and *Zita McRobbie*

DE PROFUNDIS

No towers tremble now at the blast of my sighs,
the red stream of my blood makes no roaring through the lands.

No giants with stone-axes
huge hands all thumbs slash
my likeness in rock.
Love's Christmas tree
struck once with coloured candles of desire
has glided into unknown far-back childhood,
and any tears that fall for me are falling
not on fresh body but on mummy-cloth.

      Where have all the young women gone
      who spirited off in such sweet oil
      the rosy salmon-slices of my heart
      and shut up in a pin-box
      my feelings twisted on a spool?
      Where have those girls gone
      who stepped out on their starry trajectory
      shining down on my dim and always dusky sky?

When I soak my lonely looks
in the green veins of neon signs,
when I flounder on
like a lumpish-headed diver
deep in the seas of the past, I feel
my shadow quietly flaking off
from my heels and vanishing
in reverse. I feel
fate has stopped waiting for me
neighing, stamping, bridled.

      More and more impossible
      the lavatory-brush moustaches
      below noses like carrot-stubs,
      the flatfish faces swimming on TV
      and the ears that sail away.
      More and more I panic at
      the rattling detritus in the skull.
      More and more I linger musing
      over letters spelt in ashes.
      If no one overhears me,
      more and more I let it out —
      the crippled cedar's shocked and whistling cry.

Edwin Morgan

MEETING

Sometimes you appear in the swampy twilight.
In the yellowly reflecting ring around the moon, your face
withers light-sensitive plants.
Between us rises invisible barbed wire.
The table's glass of red wine slowly bleeds away,
and a signal cracks in the furniture.

I start off, sea-green waves of rain in my face.
I'm trying out other-worldly navigation, awkward sailor
always blown off course by some sardonic squall,
battling malevolent currents to the end.
Or like one who wakes in a pitch-black room
and gropes his way blindly in one direction or another,
knocking into chairs his fumbling hand
upsetting meaningless objects arranged on the table,
looking for the door long since bricked up...

Kenneth and *Zita McRobbie*

REMEMBERING

And he sees them, sees their faces
as they rise from the surface of a puddle
to beat frenziedly at his window
and dissolve into long dribblings.
     And there's no preventing their coming,
     wandering up and down on the wind;
     he knows it's impossible not to hear
     murmuring voices in the walls,
and their rising rhythmic drumming
goes right through his aching temples,
like an abruptly slammed down
piano lid, snuffing out
skittish sparklers of roulades.

Kenneth and *Zita McRobbie*

Sándor Weöres
4.1913

Sándor Weöres
(1913-1989)

The son of a gentry family from western Hungary, Weöres was the intellectual and artistic heir to everything that Babits, Kosztolányi, and Milán Füst (qq.v.) knew and stood for. He burst on the Hungarian literary scene fully formed and possessing a talent which enabled him to write in all possible forms of Hungarian poetry including sonnets, Alcaics, Sapphics, blank verse, and free verse. He won the Baumgarten Prize in 1936. He studied law, then Hungarian language and literature at the University of Pécs; his doctoral dissertation (1939) bears the title The Birth of the Poem [A vers születése], *which is significant both as a theoretical treatise and as the meditation of a truly great poet. His first volume* It Is Cold [Hideg van] *appeared in 1934 and was followed by other highly successful ones such as* The Praise of Creation [A teremtés dícsérete], *1938;* The Portico of Teeth [A fogak tornáca], *1947; and* The Tower of Silence [A hallgatás tornya], *1956. Weöres was unable and unwilling to go along with the dictates of "socialist realism," as he was drawn to a spiritualist world-view encompassing ancient China and Japan, along with the Epic of Gilgamesh from ancient Mesopotamia. He survived during the Rákosi era mostly as a translator and a writer of children's verses which were, however, eagerly read by grown-ups as well. Like Babits and Kosztolányi, Weöres also became a master translator, who particularly excelled in rendering Chinese and Japanese poems. He travelled to the Far East, including Malaya. He had an uncanny ability to wear any mask he chose to. He published a collection entitled* Psyche, *in which he reproduces the poetry of an imaginary poetess from the nineteenth century, called 'Erzsébet Lónyai.' "The best feminine poetry in Hungary was written by a man"—one woman poet wryly remarked. He was a poet of extraordinary inventiveness, earthy eroticism, and insatiable curiosity. His search for meaning constantly led him into the area of metaphysics. His collected translations were published in the volume* The Conjuring of the Soul [A lélek idézése], *published in 1958. In Weöres's poetry the "urbanist-populist" distinction disappears forever from Hungarian poetry and yields its place to a community-minded spiritualism. Weöres handled Hungarian folk rhythms with as much ease and elegance as any Latin or Greek meter or other western European verse form. He left a legacy which, in terms of formal virtuosity, is very hard to surpass. An English selection of his poems entitled* Eternal Moment *appeared in London in 1989, edited by Miklós Vajda.*

THE BRAMBLEBERRY

Eves of autumn
Gleam with the brambleberry's
Gleam with the brambleberry's
Shimm'ring dress.
Thorns a-rustling,
Winds scurry hither-thither,
Trembles the brambleberry
Comfortless.
Should but the moon let lower her veil,
Bush turns maiden, starts to wail...
Eves of autumn
Gleam with the brambleberry's
Gleam with the brambleberry's
Shimm'ring dress.

Adam Makkai and *Valerie Becker Makkai*

THE FOUR ELEMENTS

Embers of wood in fire I'd be —
Soft moss on stones in ponds I'd be — —
Swaying poplar in wind I'd be — — —
On Earth my father's son I'd be — — — —

Donald E. Morse and *Adam Makkai*

THE DRAGON-STEED

I dashed around on a Dragon-Steed
I bathed a bird with diamond feet
I kept chasing the sky's Great Bear
and married a girl with moonlight-hair

Donald E. Morse and *Adam Makkai*

SHEEP SCHOOL

Once there occurred a miracle:
a 'sheep school' — what a spectacle!
only bleaters got the praise
talkers weren't allowed to graze.

Those who never showed up there
got medals sewn into their hair —
therefore, not one sheep attended
and the 'sheep school' was suspended.

Donald E. Morse and *Adam Makkai*

TIME'S COME UP PEARLS...

Time's come up pearls — let us wander,
we've got no cart, so let's saunter;
where the lazy river billows
let us walk in groves of willows.

Tired feet wear out by evening;
we make our cots in the clearing —
dreams come on grasshoppers' ankles,
worlds soar on butterflies' mantles.

Donald E. Morse and *Adam Makkai*

WINGLESS

When I was dropped out of my mother
who dared rob me of my flying?
No more 'human rebirth' — ever!
life without wings ain't worth living.

Donald E. Morse and *Adam Makkai*

STORM FROM THE FAR HEIGHTS

When storms swoop down from the far heights
don't you shun me, little brother —
when the moon stirs in the foliage
you protect me, little sister!

Our shack sits near the clearing
through the shrubs you'd never notice;
but the Angel, when alighting
eats her supper where our door is.

Donald E. Morse and *Adam Makkai*

A DISSOLVING PRESENCE

I'm of no interest to myself
only the certainty of my death
can save me from the uninvited clown,
although if a mask is trampled on, it hurts.
Is it the Great Nothing I will reach through my death?
I'll have no more longing or trouble.
Will I continue after death?
I endure it now — I'll endure it then.
Neither life nor death interests me,
all I need is that harmony
which matter cannot carry
and of which reason knows nothing.

Donald E. Morse and *Adam Makkai*

ANOTHER WORLD

Sent by another world, I wonder
what it was like, but can't remember,
although it's broken, boding glimpses
shine on a veil that lost its color.

And as across these earthly visions
my erstwhile home offers a view,
I'll catch sight of joy and suffering
harkening back from over there too.

Donald E. Morse and *Adam Makkai*

RAYFLOWER

Rayflower
About the head
So flickery
Then fled
     Above the shoulders
     Below the chin
     A lonely night-light
     Is carried in
In front of the chest
Lace-foam flying
Already the fire there
Fading dying
     In the swelling
     Of the belly
     A shadow spreads
     Enormously
In a dark sea
No foot lingers
Fearing to leave
The Lucifer fingers

Edwin Morgan

MOON AND FARMSTEAD

Full moon slip swim
Wind fog foam chord hum
The house empty
     Rampant
     Thorn fence
     Eye blaze
Moon swim flame

Grass chord twang
Cloud fling
      The house empty
      Door window
      Fly up
Chimney run
Fog swirl
Full moon circle

     The house empty

Edwin Morgan

TO DIE

Eyes of mother-of-pearl, smell of quince,
voice like a bell, and far-off violins
and hesitant steps hesitating, thickening,
heavy-horned twins of emptiness snickering,
sinking, cold brimming, blue, wide over all!
Wide magnet blue, ploughs flashing on,
and burning thorns in naked storm,
earth-wrinkles, dropped on pitted soil,
shaking the wild sweet nest, the bright
dish flying in its steady-spread light.

Edwin Morgan

WHISPER IN THE DARK

From a well you mount up, dear child. Your head a pyre.
Your arm a stream, your trunk air, your feet mud. I shall
bind you, but don't be afraid: I love you and my bonds are
your freedom.

On your head I write: "I am strong, devoted, secure, and
home-loving: I have eternity."
On your trunk I write: "I am poured into everything and
everything pours into me: I am not fastidious, but who is
there who could defile me?"

On your feet I write: "I have measured the darkness and
my hand troubles its depths; nothing could sink so deep that
I should not be deeper."

You have turned into gold, dear child. Change yourself
into bread for the blind and swords for those who can see.

Edwin Morgan

CLOUDS

In the mirror of the open window the mirror-cloud drifts
facing the cloud. Cupids melt off at its edge, the heavy
centre writhes with the lumbering bodies of monsters, a satiny
blueness retracts and spreads bitten between gaping rows of
beast-fangs. A violet coach flakes off, hurries away into
the blue and quickly vanishes: yet it is easy to imagine it
galloping there out of sight. Gods are sitting in it, or the
no-beings of non-being, or the dead we have heard the earth-thudding
down on and know nothing about any more.

The clouds drift and the mirror-clouds face them; and for
anyone watching, nature drifts face to face with thought
in the depths of the skull.

Edwin Morgan

INSECT

Soft murmur in the walnut leaf:
six legs, four wings, light *leitmotif,*
two pearl-tipped feelers probe the veins
for pathways on the leafy plains.

Peter Zollman

VALSE TRISTE

The evening's getting cold and old,
vine-branches tremble and infold.
Songs of the vintage-days subside,
inside their corners old men hide.
The steeple starts to flare
the church's foggy lair;
across the meadows, stark
showers are running dark.
The summer songs subside,
old men retire to hide.
The evening's shade is cold
as thickets clatter bold.
The hearts of people wear and smother,
each summer looks like any other.
It does not matter, old or new,
our memories are frozen, too.
Red fever on the trees,
inside, a maiden weeps;
her lips need lipstick, too,
the evening's pinched them blue.
Whether it's old or new,
our memories are few;
the hearts of people smother,
one summer's like the other.
The thickets' hair dress clatters well
as autumn rings the autumn-bell.
Upon the sloe, frost lays its hold —
the evening's getting cold and old.

W. Arthur Boggs

ETERNITY

The Earth that creates all that lives,
the tomb that swallows what it gives,
the plains, the seas, the mountain-pass
appear eternal — but will pass.

The cosmos and the firmament
gyrating, celestial cement,
legion of fire-balls' hot mass
appear eternal — but will pass.

What's buried by forgetfulness
the lizard's leap, bird-wings' caress,
tremors which trickled long ago
appear to pass — but never go.

For some things that had taken place
no order can change or erase —
neither God nor the Ancient Foe:
they seem to pass — but never go.

Donald E. Morse and *Adam Makkai*

ETERNAL MOMENT

What you don't trust to stone
and decay, shape out of the air.
A moment leaning out of time
arrives here and there,

guards what time squanders, keeps
the treasure tight in its grasp —
eternity itself, held
between the future and the past.

As a bather's thigh is brushed
by skimming fish — so
there are times when God
is in you, and you know:

half-remembered now
and later, like a dream.
And with a taste of eternity
this side of the tomb.

Edwin Morgan

TWENTIETH CENTURY FRESCO

Cuckoo-bird-castle-in-the-clouds —
it's been filling for three thousand years with garbage and ornaments,
huge boxes full of it, their inscriptions: "I!"
"Mine!" "Me!" "For me!" — its walls have been pushed out
everywhere by "my treasure," "my fever," "my salvation,"
at last it tipped over and fell into the dung collected underneath.

Its inhabitants
jostle and bustle in the filth below,
they don't understand what has happened to them, they cannot see in
the night, moaning they writhe on top of the trash-heap, or running
around and treading on one another they drag their creaking, broken
belongings, or they want to build something, pillaging the rubble.
But there is One among them who can see,
and rolling in the tar he sets himself aflame so that the others, too,
may see: desperation-light, live torch!

A few are pointing at him: "Behold the fool,
he has dipped himself in tar and he'll turn into ashes
instead of trying to help us in our rescue work."
Others shout: "By his light we can see!"
and they push and drag the broken trash even faster.

What could they see? What would the live torch show them?
the rubble, the dung,
and above it the black nothingness
whence cuckoo-bird-castle-in-the-clouds is already gone
with all the Angels having disappeared,
the Angel of Security, the Angel of Freedom, the Angel of Justice, and
the others, even the Angel of War
(for what's "war" for these is but an endless quarrel of those
who bump into each other in the dark;
where are the times when free decision would start a real war?)
and gone is the Angel of Hatred as well
(for everyone bites the ankle he can catch;
but where is real "hatred" now?)

There's but one left in the sky, the idle, indifferent soul,
the Angel of Disgust. For it is only Disgust that has a soul left.

If they should see by the light of the Live Torch
they would see him, the Angel of Disgust,
as he dangles his legs for the dogs
or pisses on the ruins while he whistles,
and they would not believe that he is an Angel,
that he is love, transformed, which would rather smile than be angry,
and if they were to see him near at hand: they would not believe
that he is the Angel of Disgust
because of his beauty comparable only to the woman carried in
the depths of our dreams,
the murderer would get drunk if he saw him, sobbing with desire
he would fall on his fists,
taking vows and making promises,
and even the pure would be astonished in front of him: what is beauty
that its drift is so strong ?

And the screaming, flaming torch, and this final sweetness: Are
one and the same.

If they ask the Angel, he answers:
"Quit meddling!" — pouting, it says: "Don't meddle." And for the
third time: "Don't meddle!" — and falls silent.

The live torch dashes around and screams:
"Have you heard it? Quit meddling!
These two words are the Great Book,
The Word flung into your faces, this short commandment is the one
that would relieve the convulsions
of the world!
Quit meddling! Quit the flag-waving,
stop waving agitatedly with constructive-destructive and rescuing
motions, forget the slogans, officious principles and jerking ideologies
tearing at you!

Hear this: Desire no advantage,
set no store by the value of advantage,

and you'll shed the hundreds of madnesses, all offering advantage,
and you shall be like the heart-beat:
its calm its function, and its function its calm..."

So shouts the live torch, then finally collapses,
soot and flue-ashes pour forth from its mouth,
even its bones are black.

And the Angel of Disgust
plays on top of the ruins
with equanimity.
Waiting.

Adam Makkai

MONKEYLAND

Oh for far-off monkeyland,
ripe monkeybread on baobabs,
and the wind strums out monkeytunes
from monkeywindow monkeybars.

Monkeyheroes rise and fight
in monkeyfield and monkeysquare,
and monkeysanatoriums
have monkeypatients crying there.

Monkeygirl monkeytaught
masters monkeyalphabet,
evil monkey pounds his thrawn
feet in monkeyprison yet.

Monkeymill is nearly made,
miles of monkeymayonnaise,
winningly unwinnable
winning monkeymind wins praise.

Monkeyking on monkeypole
harangues the crowd in monkeytongue,

monkeyheaven comes to some,
monkeyhell for those undone.

Macaque, gorilla, chimpanzee,
baboon, orangutan, each beast
reads his monkeynewssheet at
the end of each twilight repast.

With monkeysupper memories
the monkeyouthhouse rumbles, hums,
monkeyswaddies start to march,
right turn, left turn, shoulder arms —

monkeymilitary fright
reflected in each monkeyface,
with monkeygun in monkeyfist
the monkeys' world the world we face.

Edwin Morgan

COOLIE

Coolie cane chop,
Coolie go
  go
     only softly-softly
  Rickshaw
  Car
  Dragon-carriage
Coolie pull rickshaw.
Coolie pull car,
Coolie pull dragon-carriage
   only softly-softly
Coolie go foot.
Coolie beard white.
Coolie sleepy
Coolie hungry.
Coolie old.
Coolie bean poppyseed little child
big wicked man beat little Coolie

only softly-softly
Rickshaw
Car
Dragon-carriage
Who pull rickshaw?
Who pull car?
Who pull dragon-carriage?
Suppose Coolie dead.
Coolie dead.
Coolie no-o-o-t dead!
Coolie immortal
only softly-softly

Edwin Morgan

ON DEATH

Don't mind if you die. It's just your body's shape,
intelligence, separate beings which are passing.
The rest, the final and the all-embracing
structure receives, and will absorb and keep.

All incidents we live through, forms we see,
particles, mountain-tops, are broken down,
they all are mortal, this condition shows,
but as to substance: timeless majesty.

The soul is that way too: condition dies
away from it — feeling, intelligence,
which help to fish the pieces from the drift

and make it sicken — but, what underlies,
all elements that wait in permanence,
reach the dear house they never really left.

Alan Dixon

ARS POETICA

Memory cannot make your song everlasting.
Glory is not to be hoped from the evanescences:
how could it glorify you, when its glitterings are not essences?
Your song may flaunt a few embers from eternal things
while those who face them take fire as a minute passes.

Sages suggest: only individuals are in their senses.
All right; but to get more, be more than individual:
slip off your great-poet-status, your lumbering galoshes,
serve genius, give it your human decencies
which are point and infinity: neither big nor small.

Catch the hot words that shine in the soul's estuaries:
they feed and sustain countless earth-centuries
and only migrate into your transient song,
their destiny is eternity as your destiny is,
they are friends who hug you and hasten soaring on.

Edwin Morgan

IN MEMORIAM GYULA JUHÁSZ[1]

Let beasts whine at your grave my father
whine at your grave
let the beasts whine
between the byre and the blade
between the slaughterhouse and the dunghill
between the clank of the chain and desolation
my mother as Hamlet said
let the old hunchbacked women whine
between the hospital and the glad rags
between the asylum and the lily-of-the-valley
between the cemetery and the frippery
and the wretches with buried ulcers

---

[1] The poet (q.v.) whom Weöres regarded as one of his role models.

between stately doctors and strapping priests
all those paralysed by deferred release
on the far side of hope on the near side of confrontation

Let butterflies twist above the stream
Ophelia who drowned before we were born
the roseless thorn is yours
the profitless pain
the lacklustre ghost in a mourning frame
the falling on knees face in the mud
the humiliation boundless and endless
the dead body without a cross
the unredeemed sacrifice
the hopelessness that is for ever hopelessness

Let rabid dogs howl at your grave
let hollow phantoms hoot
my starry brother my bearded bride
the good is only a moment's presentiment
evil is not eternal malice
in the meantime blood flows
lacerated life cannot die
death is deathless liberty   *Edwin Morgan*

SATURN DECLINING
(In memory of T.S. Eliot)

They took my flock away. Should I care? I have nothing to do now,
no responsibility; easy an old man's life at the poorhouse.
Firstly they chased the priest, that antlered rambler,
off his springboard, from which he took to the sky daily — fool! —
and appointed more clever priests; then deposed the king, the defender
undefended, and welcomed the sabre-rattling kings; then the sage,
saying, We have enough scholars as it is; lastly the poet:
What is he counting his fingers for anyway, prattling? Singers,
styled to requirement, flock in his place as a consequence.

So I stand, face turned to the wall, with broken crook.
My flock jostles at the trough: how many bright, brand new,

away — should I care? It's not my vocation any more;
they stick teeth in me if I look; what will happen to the enormous
progeny, the scraped womb, ravenous,
stupefied, quickening, and the murderous rays,
the explosive left at the doorway — As it is when a train
rushes towards the deep with no shore on the other side —
should I care? — maybe they'll stop it at any moment;
there could be tracks to carry it over the chasm, perhaps I am blind;
perhaps, at the edge of the abyss, it will open its wings, and fly;
they know. I do not. Their problem, if they do not.
All the same to me now: my shepherd's crook broken,
so easy to lie about in the straw, resting
from centuries of toil. They can't see, their heads in the trough;
I only see their rumps and flapping ears.

Alan Dixon

NEVER AGAIN ANOTHER GARDEN...

Never again another garden like
the seventh one, where the clock among lilies stands
          and has no hands;
where numbers for time, like shadows, have no place;
that is hemmed round by foliage like starlight.
How long will he stay who's beckoned by an angel?
          Perhaps he'll often retrace
his steps to the sunny haven with a stone bell
inditing its diary, and the marble columns whereon
round and round reels gentle oblivion.

Eye to eye even, it's their backs the people
stand there showing, they're whispering distantly
          in the garden. There won't be
tomorrows at all if they're not bold enough
for the flames of dawn, for noon, for the beams of nightfall,
          there'll again be yesterdays if
our handkerchief by a lucky chance was left there,
which more than willingly would be torn to pieces,
impaled and rent on the spears of the brass fences.

A soothing garden — even so, sheer sorrow.
Although from happiness anyone here would
          weep if tears could
flow from the dew-drenched statues that we are...
Let me go on always longing for you,
who burned me, figure slim as flame; from here,
          home of silence, lead me far
away so that I can worship you forever,
clutching onto your green sparks, royal princess,
like an infant onto the thread of his mother's dress.

Bruce Berlind and *Mária Kőrösy*

THE SEVENTH SYMPHONY
— *The Assumption of Mary* —

(To my mother's memory)

1
Shadow, stone, linen, lime, the
pillow under the skull's vault,
iron padlock, swaddling clothes,
the knocking sundering clod,
do not see ascend the dark of the body
over the final flame, the world pried open
by the smouldering chaplet of sweat.

Foot protrudes from the brindled shroud,
its clotted veins coated with wax,
a violet beam on the nail.

Shins ensheathed are sleeping,
the tendon straight, the knee relaxed;
olive trees line the path.

Hail to you, shrivelled womb!
An armored insect in the wall's fissure
scratches the lip of the blind abyss,
flowers its ensigns, its arms.

Hail to you, prayer-locked hands,
plunging arches of a shrine,
two rows of casketed tapers,
ten swans' wings immersed in dew,
enfolded night-blooming flowers.

Hail to you, seven-pained heart!
The scream, from the start its neck weighted with stone,
falls down a bottomless well, fails of its journey.
Narrow neck, tilted head, sticky hair,
lead-coin of the final ransom on the pale face,
around the mouthhole and sunken eyes
the senses' cooled-off scatter of wrinkles,
twig-knots of trampled-down acanthus,
spoors of galloped-off steeds.

    2
    Shadow, night,
    silence, cold,
    crack, crackle,
    clay flies,
    beam cleaves,
    dust signs —
    Two new moons in
    the sky culminate,
    blazing mesh
    descends,
    spider-legged
    glowing coals race
    up, wings hover on
    gleaming roof,
    flock of lambs,
    harps, flutes,
    violin screeches,
    bell peals,
    horn replies —
    For faceless,
    ashy ancestor,
    face of gold,
    assembles bones,

> leans on an elbow,
> rears up,
> gives ear —

Chorus
Wailing, wailing, wailing
for her own at the edge of dark!
We saw her with her child in starlight;
we were grazing our plump sheep,
with the coming of spring we sheared the fleece,
when winter came we flayed the hide;
slowly, cloud-like, we drifted
on the mirror of water filled with fleecy hills,

> our boat
> came ashore,
> she saw
> who we were,
> brambles tore
> our thin shoes,
> earth
> painted our brows.

We're shepherds, also sheep.
Now for the shearing,
now for the skinning,
strew it in her path.
Wailing, wailing, wailing
for her own at the edge of dark.

3

Alternate choruses
The drone of oars infuses
the infinite clear stillness,
the curly breath-hue, faintly purplish,
churns in the glistening white,
a maelstrom of mast, a whirlpool of sails
looms through,
ferry of flame, bridge of haze, golden ark,
fever's nether side on a diamond mirror,
circles, in the distance ripples,
the rush and scurry of small ones,

on the rainbow a smiling tear,
veiny swish of milk-foliage,
the woman's festival alive in the world...
> (But we always cried.
> We were starving.
> What else could we do?
> We always cried.)
...her skiff sparkling in the rush of spume,
on the lusterless yellow sickle of heaven,
on the giant azure scales of the eye,
on the red wheel of the war-car,
on the crest of the green monster,
on the black mouthhold of cold,
and at night she turns down your white bed,
through every inferno she follows you,
though the nest be razed she summons you back...
> (Bottom-up stumps
> with our roots upwards,
> earth cast us out.
> Nobody stoops for us.)
...she kneels within you, my dear, and you become her,
forsaking your chaplet whence
color comes to the rose and light to the eye,
and you feel her as you cover your chalice
with the vagrant foggy shapes of the chasm
and the numbered centuries of years
with frenzied omens on their foreheads,
impassioned, drank from...
> (Flowers crawling with worms,
> who wants the tattered petal
> while the spring dawn rains down?)
...from the crusty dark ascending
the distending moon's shimmers,
aroma that under the rind
gathers to flame in secret veins,
under the heart a regal star-crowned dream
in the shade of a warm bower,
falling clusters of grapes, red wine,
the flame of the mother ablaze in the world...
> (Whom have I killed? Myself.

Whom does it pain? Me.
Leave me alone in her lap.)
...the lovely hands close-clasped in prayer,
clinging columns of kindness,
a hazy roof-row of fingers,
ten mother-wings of live silence,
naked fingers in a sea of petals,
the tenfold soundless ringing
gleams, dispensing its brightness,
its light, beamlessly, pathless as a kiss...
(The salt of sweat in our bread.
The taste of death in our meat.
Around us the coffin-wall.)
...she who stood under the cross
unbroken by misery, stares
with a child's scared blue eyes
at the frothing world on the cross,
sobs at the sill of hell;
in festering dens the dead
wrapped in closely watched night
wink at the wounding light...

(Take from our hearts the dripping poison,
take from our hearts the black maggot,
take the ember from our hearts,
take from our hearts the dark.)

...the gleam of the pure blue eyes
pierces through all the circuits
mirrored in the curving hoop of space
and the hundred-tunneled race of time;
like a sweet drop on the nodding sedge,
a sparkling bead of mutability,
it is always replenished, always rolls off,
the peace of the Virgin flows over the world...
(We shiver, draw close our cloaks,
have mercy on us, Blessed Virgin,
pray for us, have
mercy on us.)

4

Over the spring
down spins off
from fanning wings;
light snow falls;
young wine makes
in big basins;
on a thousand balconies
a thousand armies;
the shackled rage of
the earth is still,
everything fills
with the clamor of wings:

Chorus

Through flame, through light
wings the dark earth's virgin,
never are shadow and night
more violently flung open,
valley and peak, by the looking-dance,
assault-waves of mazes of flowers
setting the greyness ablaze.

Vein of rose, blood of dove,
brimming chalice of wine,
where the mountain-shadow plunges
faith harvested the vines;
blood-pearls of chamois in snow
calls the hunter, where he climbs
the trail is narrow, the space wide.

Dear mother, bashful bride,
our blushing tender maid,
our wings billow toward you,
their thick combs quake like the sea;
are you flying toward us, do you see us?
we are rugs laid in your path,
dear mother, be our spring.

Mary
I glorify him I conceived in my womb
who raised to the sky my sickle of moon
and set on my forehead a string of stars
who made my cloak to be borne on the milky path
who made my veil to be blown by the storm of sweetness
who made my triumphant car to be flown by the living fires
who peoples with armies my victorious progress
who raises around me towers of endless song,
as it pleases him; and it cannot be explained
by the fiery armies, the misty generations
turning under the furrows where I walk.
My father from the beginning, I brought him forth
who towers, three-headed pillar,
with his triple forehead's glory
over the far-flung void, above
the glistening crystal silence
surfacing from the wake of creations,
like a roof of lightning he covers me.

> *Chorus*
> Queen of flowerbells,
> assembled before you, welded around you,
> bell-hearts beat in a thousand bodies,
> a cupola of rays wavering,
> a tower of haze quavering,
> they peal for you, appeal to you:
> when our bell-metal chips,
> silence it out of your power.

Mary
It is not mine to judge; the scales, the sword
are someone else's; I never learned to strike,
only to stroke; nor to starve, only to feed;
to be hurt, but not to hurt; nor to take, only to ask.
In the resonant silence, the anonymous silence,
larvae and wedding-gowns blossom alike on me,
the lion lies down with the lamb in my bosom.
The babe defiles me, no stain is left,

he scratches my breast, a necklace of blood flows out,
the heaving sea has more and will not miss it.
The killer spatters me with blood, I wipe it off;
revile me, I do not turn away my face.
I am no stone wall returning caresses and blows
measure for measure;
I am no clay road returning steps and turnings
measure for measure;
I am no fountain of fire that exposes body and space
as they manifest before it;
I am only a nest that sheds what warmth there is.
You who see me shining forth in glory,
think for a moment: it does not come from me;
a tear is my only treasure; so with you;
my son's wound my immeasurable possession
and the agony of this world my gateless garden.
The luxuriant tree of life lies in my lap,
and if, torn off, you fall down under it,
your powerful fist clutches my apron, you fell
your head's log on my knee. Do not fear:
you are watched over by silence, tears, and me.

> *Chorus*
> There where there is no light,
> my heart is born among thorns,
> down where the nightingale nests,
> in the jungle of numberless moans;
> new threats buffet the planets,
> but the blest sleep on in peace,
> nectar-drops on their lips.
> Down there a rose-tree blooms,
> dawn spreads out on the hill,
> fingers — weak and strong —
> proffer a feast; debris
> of ashes litters the hearth,
> but a purple flood in the depth
> proclaims eternal dawn.

Fields of roses swaying
wisps of flame in the wind,

bewitched by her bright eyes;
she comes, turns slowly again,
a rose-sea of waving babes
clutches, clutches at her hem;
death and time stand still.

> Mutability, wire-like
> grows taut;
> cooled-off ancestral coal
> glows hot;
> patriarch
> from tomb's dark
> hums to himself
> fulfilled words;
> the clod is quiet,
> lips stuck together;
> the sound of wings
> outspread forever.

Coda
Lady of orbits, Mary,
protect Mary my mother,
lest, torn from my sight,
sorrow befall her.
You who have heard this song,
a fragment only of the song
that wrung the world's heart:
you who have heard this song:
wake up from your sluggish dragons.

Bruce Berlind and *Mária Kőrösy*

Zoltán Jékely
(1913-1982)

Poet, translator, art historian, librarian and teacher of French and Hungarian literature, Jékely was born in Nagyenyed, Transylvania (now a part of Romania). He is the son of Lajos Áprily (q.v.). (The original family name is Jékely; it was the father who used Áprily as his pen-name.) The family moved to Hungary in 1929, and Jékely completed his education in the secondary school of the Hungarian Reformed Church. He studied French and History of Art at the University of Budapest. He wrote his dissertation on the beginnings of Transylvanian Hungarian literature after World War I in 1935. The years 1937 and 1939-1940 saw him in Italy and France. He spent most of his summers back in Transylvania. In 1939 he won the prestigious Baumgarten Prize.

A frequent contributor to leading Hungarian literary magazines, he also produced translations of Shakespeare, Racine, Dante, and many German, Italian and Romanian poets such as Eminescu and Caragiale. During the short-lived return of Transylvania to Hungary (1940-1945) he moved to Kolozsvár (today Cluj-Napoca in Romania), where he married Adrienne Jancsó, the well-known actress.

In 1946 he moved back to Budapest. In 1948 he was able to go to Italy once more, but the Communist takeover prevented the publication of his collection Dream [Álom]. He was then expelled from the Writers' Association and had to survive on translations. He was rehabilitated after 1956 and then could publish his selected poems after being reinstated as a member of the Writers' Association.

A lonely, highly cerebral, tragic poet, much occupied with death and oblivion, he devoted many a poem to the steadily worsening situation of the Hungarian minority in Romania, a taboo topic in Hungary until the late 1970s.

His books include Nights [Éjszakák], *1936;* Towards a New Millennium [Új évezred felé], *1939;* Forbidden Garden [Tilalmas kert], *1957;* Exorcism of the Will-o'The-Wisp [Lidércűző], *1964;* In the Star-Tower [Csillagtoronyban], *1970; and* In Search of the Last Word [Az utolsó szó keresése], *1985. His collected short stories appeared posthumously in 1986, and his collected poems two years later. In his plays he dealt with events of Transylvanian history; in his lively and brilliant essays he described Transylvanian poets and novelists, many of whom were his personal friends and contemporaries.*

ODE TO CHAPLIN
(For his 50th birthday)

Little man, whom I love so much,
knowing that you will die grieves me more,
gives me more pain and sorrow
than the death of the ancient Kings
caused their loyal followers.

After so much laughter I want to weep.

I count myself among the few
who — like Cocteau —
know who you were.

Truly, truly the world is made of iron.
And man annihilates man with machines.
The noise of the turbines will penetrate
the quiet of our lakeside graves.

Keep pulling at your little moustache for a long time yet,
to make us laugh — to laugh at ourselves —
and shed tears after our laughter
when Chaplin weeps and his frayed trousers show.

Who will take your place? Will our grandchildren
have anyone to comfort them like you,
as you have comforted us in this confused century,
when with all its abundant riches,
even the rich live in poverty,
and often in fear?
There can be no one to succeed you.

When we're no longer alive,
when our bones will have been crushed by machines,
will the counterpart of our beloved Charlie Chaplin
be shown to people wearing a different kind of trousers?

Who could he be? Then, horror-struck, disconsolate,
I ask myself — who am I?
And who are we, who chaotically
live and die on this vagrant globe of mud?

Joseph Leftwich

FOOTBALLERS

The football thuds upon the green field
with a peculiar jungle beat —
rising, falling — heroic message
from childhood, landing at my feet.

Always the same kind seem to kick it;
they rush full speed ahead, these powerful
thick-thighed rapid adolescents,
their youth just breaking into flower.

I used to rush in this same manner;
I dared to strike out for the goal,
and when opponents overtook me,
I beat my head just like a fool.

The match for which I was preparing
was with the folk of Uruguay,
I think — at any rate a battle
which we must either win or die.

What happened to our team? A storm-wind
scattered us all, made us retreat
from playing fields; the ball was quickly
passed to the urchins in the street.

And now this thudding jogs remembrance
which causes me both joy and smart:
I seek out in this novel scrimmage
the way we threw ourselves about.

Their fine and accurate passing causes
a quiver in my ancient thews,
as Toldi's[1] ancient warhorse kindles
hearing remembered battle-noise.

There'll always be, outside great cities,
a meadow with cropped grass where one
may hear in the cool hours of evening
this music thudding like a drum.

From miles away it works, like magic,
on youngsters mad to touch the ball
and an odd greying fellow leaning
and dreaming up against the goal.

J.G. Nichols

IN THE CHURCH OF MAROSSZENTIMRE

Dust and old plaster on our heads descend
as "Zion, City of our God" we bellow;
under the pews a mouse is running around;
sometimes an old owl issues from his hollow.

We are the congregation, just we ten
(though, if we count the priest, it is eleven)
singing as many hundreds were in tune,
which makes the dust and plaster fall from heaven.

We rouse a bat, so loud a hymn's ascended,
and some worm-eaten beams up there work loose;
the priest is the eleventh, unattended;
the Lord Himself brings it to twelve of us.

---

[1] The hero of János Arany's (q.v.) epic poem, included in abbreviated form in this anthology.

We sing, we sing, we few who still remain —
"whom the Lord loveth He chastiseth" — yet
we hear beneath the creaking boards join in
those whom old time has viciously wiped out.

J.G. Nichols

TOWARDS THE NEW MILLENNIUM

It's not the year two-thousand, my poor love,
the new millennium has not come upon us;
we're asleep in the deep though the old blue above
is buzzing with a strange new apparatus.
The house where we were born has been knocked flat,
whole districts downed. Our beds and chairs are dust.
Our books are gone (foul hands have seen to that),
our likenesses are likewise lost.
New shoes are squeaking down the avenue:
the girls are different, their clothes different too.
Our dreams, like old wine too long bottled, thicken
and grew sweet, till their very flavours sicken.
Time dangles the sun on its slow pendulum
above the earth. And when at last we come
to sleep, it's as if in some distant zone
like long-boned Incas swaddled in the stone.

George Szirtes

TO MY BONES

I live my life day today as if
about to sleep for ever, dreamily
watching bones that have jogged along with me
and which my soul's so rudely set to leave.

My skull which has been of little or no use
these hundred years under its weight of clay
now cracks in three, a spring shower sweeps away
dusty heaps of poems like so much refuse.

My teeth corroded over twenty years
by rich food, eaten through by acids, glow
uncannily in row by rotten row
under the earth, sad timeless souvenirs.

My spine, with its length of crackling vertebrae
through which blood pounded, now the marrow's gone
is hollow, perhaps a snake might try it on
or roots provide a line to dangle by.

My poor hand, which I used to love to sniff
after it had explored another's skin,
no use you beckoning to the man within,
poor hand, for you, like him, are trapped and stiff.

And you, my legs, young puppies, you who'd squeeze
a female leg, or kicked a football high,
for ever at attention now you'll lie
nor graveyard sergeant give you the 'At ease.'

George Szirtes

DRAGON SLAYING

That hideous overgrown toad again!
How it croaks through the night, in the silence!
It blares in my ear, it fills my apartment —
already I see its dull yellow eyes before me.
But where is it hidden, what nook, or what sewer?
Where's its rolling belly, that monstrosity,
show me so I can kick it or grind it under!

How soundly the town sleeps,
the panting spirits of tired humanity
tumble softly across the wide pavement,
their dreams are fumbling at clouded
windowpanes — are joined in one outsize
dream of peace rising slowly to heaven.
And look, we must hear that terror again
right from the beginning, in the silence!
Is it rutting mood, seeking a loathsome partner
to reproduce its repulsive image? —

From a gateway it belches into view, its huffing
belly in full croak — I see it! Disgust and fury
pursue me as I run, and I
grab at a half-brick, and smash it as hard
as I can, into his horrible body — death to all such! —
and I can still see its guts spilling out,
how they ripple in coils in the half-light,
and its monstrous eye keeps staring at me,
I, who was born on the day of St George who
once slew the dragon, and has again slain it.

George Szirtes

IN MEMORY OF THE FUNERAL HORSES[2]

Where have you disappeared to, horses with the trembling top-knots,
you splendid funeral palfreys?
Can I ever hear the thumping of your feet again
on the roads of cemeteries, as you dart at the harness
and start with someone on his last change of location? —

The sluggish carriage hits a bump, the horse-shoes grind against the
    cobble-stones;
the flashing bundles of muscles twitch under your raven-colored skin,

---

[2] Before the age of automobile hearses, coffins were taken to the grave
site in ornate funeral carriages drawn by specially decorated horses.

the petals of flowers fly in the air, a wreath with ribbons rolls into a
    bush,
and a little boy envies the dead amidst this solemn procession
as he lies up there among the silver-spoked, crackling wheels!

The wind tears at a mourning veil; sobbing breaks out every here and
    there;
heads bent low while folks support one another with stumbling feet and
sinking of knees — no, no, we haven't got the strength, we
    thought,

to keep on marching to the gaping pit of the fresh grave!
At times like this your horse bellies would pour out
the golden dung of your innards — due perhaps to the effort,
right in front of the black shoes of the mourners, on the road,
with animal simplicity — and this was the ancient signal from this
    world

that no matter it shames and humbles: survivors must keep on living,
they must live on,
until such time that you come to fetch them too, until
the drumming of your silver-spoked carriage is heard,
you, splendid funeral palfreys with your trembling top-knots!

George Gömöri and *Adam Makkai*

János Pilinszky
(1921-1981)

A poet who wrote relatively little and yet exerted a major influence on Hungarian literature, Pilinszky was born in a family of intellectuals. He was educated at the high school of the Piarist Order, after which he studied law, literature and the history of art at the University of Budapest, but did not complete his studies. His first poems appeared in 1938. Between 1940 and 1944 he was one of the editors of Élet *[Life]. He was drafted into the army in 1944 and stationed in Harbach, Germany, where he saw the horrors of the concentration camps—an experience which he would carry with him for the rest of his life. He became, in fact, one of the few non-Jewish intellectuals (he was a Roman Catholic) who contributed to the cannon of European literature a number of poems which told the stories and honored the memories of those killed in the Holocaust. His famous 'Oratorio for a Concentration Camp' became a universal symbol of the tragedy of human existence.*

Between 1946 and 1948, during the short-lived post-war democracy, he served as co-editor of the Budapest literary review Újhold *[New Moon]. His first volume of poetry,* Trapéz és korlát *[Trapeze and Crossbars] appeared in 1946. It won much critical acclaim, and in 1947 it received the prestigious Baumgarten award. In the 1950s, dogmatic Communist cultural policy forced Pilinszky, along with many others, into silence; only after the Hungarian Uprising in 1957 could he join the editorial staff of the Catholic weekly* Új Ember *[The New Man]. In 1959 he published the volume* Harmadnapon *[On the Third Day], and in 1963 the volume* Requiem. *In 1972 his last poems were published under the title* Szálkák *[Splinters].*

His work was translated into English by Ted Hughes and János Csokits, and into French by Pierre Emmanuel; these translations brought him international fame. He visited London several times and read his poetry there at international poetry festivals.

Pilinszky's terse and beautiful poetry expresses alienation with a rare evocative force; in most of his poems, Catholic existentialism is manifested in hermetic forms. Even the commonest of words have a volcanic effect in his poetry; silence and things unexpressed become an integral part of his texts. The chief philosophical paradox of his poetry is the simultaneous experience of absolute Catholic faith and the absurdity of being cast blindly afloat in the sea of human existence. In Pilinszky's own view the apogee of poetry is the Augustinian soliloquy of the soul with God.

FISH IN THE NET

We writhe in a star-net
fish, hauled onto land;
we gasp into the emptiness
we bite dry nothing's end.
The Element we've left and lost
whispers in vain to return,
'midst prickly stones and pebbles
suffocating, we must
live and die next to each other!
Our hearts tremble and burn.
Our writhing wounds and suffocates
ourselves and our brother.
The cries of one outcrying the other
no echo can adjust,
for all this fighting and killing
there's no reason, yet kill we must.
Although we're doing penance
this is no punishment,
no suffering can bail us out
from our hell's banishment.
We keep writhing in the immense net
of a cosmic fisherman and maybe by midnight
we'll turn to food in his frying pan.

Adam Makkai

THE FRENCH PRISONER

I wish to God I could forget the Frenchman.
I saw him from my window in the dawn;
he sneaked among the shadows in the garden
as if he had been planted on the lawn.
He looked around and peered in every corner,
then found at last a secret hideaway
where now he could enjoy his new possession!
He wouldn't leave this shelter, come what may.

The man was feeding, gorging on a turnip,
he hid it underneath his army coat.
The bites were raw, but swiftly chewed and wolfed down
to tumble feverishly past his throat.
His tongue was both delighted and disgusted,
he sensed the sickly sweetness of the food:
a ravening voluptuous encounter
between damnation and beatitude.

I can't forget his shiver-shaken shoulders,
his starving hand reduced to skin and bone,
his fingers clinging to his lips like limpets
to feed him — and to eat some on their own!
The hopeless shame and anger of his organs
engaged in bitter fights of jealousy
as hunger forced them slowly to surrender
the last remains of solidarity.

The monkey-chatter of his happy munching,
the way his clumsy legs were left behind
and squatted humbly while his body wallowed
in wild delights and pains of every kind.
His gaze — if I could but forget the Frenchman! —
he nearly choked but went on slavering,
and gobbled on regardless, yes, he feasted:
on this, that, on himself, on everything...

But why go on? — The man was soon recaptured,
the prison camp was just across the way...
I'm roaming in the shadows of my garden
as in that garden on that other day.
I look into my notes and quote the entry:
"Could I forget the Frenchman...!" so I wrote.
And burning in my eyes, my nose, my eardrums
the memories come crying from his throat:

"I want to eat!" — At once I sense the craving,
the everlasting hunger that he felt,
the hunger that the poor man doesn't feel now,
— by earthly food such craving can't be quelled.

He feeds on me! With ever-growing hunger
and I am less and less good for the part!
The man would once put up with any morsel,
but now he claims the title to my heart.   *Peter Zollman*

ON THE THIRD DAY

And roaring then the ashen skies resound,
as trees of Ravensbruck when daylight breaks.
And roots sensing the light will then respond.
The wind comes live. The world cries out and shakes.
     For paltry mercenaries may have killed
     him, and his heart could stop — but lo, see a
     real wonder, in three days he conquered death
     et resurrexit tertia die.   *Adam Makkai*

INTROITUS

Who shall open the closed book?
Who shall make the first cut in unbroken time?
Turning and turning, from dawn to dawn
lifting the pages and letting them fall.

Which of us dare reach into the flames
of the hidden? Who shall dare to grope
among the dense leaves of the sealed book?
And how shall he dare, bare-handed?

Which of us is without fear? Who would not fear
when even God's eyes shut
and all the angels fall flat
and every creature darkens.

Among us, only the lamb has no fear.
He alone, the lamb — who was killed.
And he is jogging along on the sea of glass.
He climbs up onto the throne. He opens the book.   *Ted Hughes*

THE PASSION OF RAVENSBRÜCK

He steps out from the others.
he stands in the square silence.
The prisoner's uniform, the convict's skull
blink like a projection.

He is horribly alone.
His pores are visible.
Everything about him is so huge —
everything so tiny.
And that's it.
           The rest
the rest was simply
that he forgot to cry out
before he dropped to the ground.   *Ted Hughes*

THE DESERT OF LOVE

A bridge, and a hot, concrete road —
the day is emptying its pockets,
laying out, one by one, all its possessions.
You are quite alone in the catatonic twilight.

A landscape like a bed of a wrinkled pit,
with glowing scars, a darkness that dazzles.
Dusk is close. I stand numb with brightness
and blinded by sun. This summer will never leave me for a
    moment.

Summer. And the flashing heat.
The chickens stand, like burning cherubs,
in the boarded-up, splintered cages.
I know their wings do not even tremble.

Do you still remember? First there was the wind.
And then the earth. Then the cage.
Fire, dung. And every so often
a few wing-flutters, a few empty reflexes.

And thirst. And when I ask for water —
even today I hear the feverish gulping.
Even now, helplessly, like a stone,
I bear and quench the mirages.

Years are passing, and years. And hope
is like a tin cup toppled in the straw.

Ted Hughes

THE REST IS GRACE

Fear and dreams
were my father and mother —
the corridor was
my unfolding landscape.

This is how I lived. How will I die?
What will my destruction be like?

The earth betrays me. She hugs me close.
The rest is grace.

Adam Makkai

AGONIA CHRISTIANA

The daybreak is still far away
With its rivers and blowing winds...
And I put on my shirt and suit
Buttoning up my death within.

Adam Makkai

STONE WALL AND FIESTA
(Homage to Robert Wilson)

Is it the motion of the stabbing knife, and
after the unhappy stations of the hand?
Is it the interrupted melodies,
the dishevelled fiestas and this beyond
the lights of the confused chandelier?

Before the wall? Or behind the wall?
What happens, what is it that really happens
during the unhappy and horrendous
time of every one of our actions?

Adam Makkai

YOUR DEATH AND MINE

The humming will put you to sleep
the prematurely darkened night
its devotion and attention
meeker than a mother's milk.

For she's the bosom burglarized.
An outsider, she is the nurse.
The stranger come home by accident.
Eternal humming will put you to sleep.

Adam Makkai

CRIME AND PUNISHMENT
(For Sheryl Sutton)

Imagination all walled up
keeps on, keeps on repeating this —

On the electric-chair-throne of the moment
the face is still there,
the nape of a neck dipped into rock,
a splendid hand —

your gappy, porous presence.
The summer's still on.

Queen, let go of your sceptre.

Adam Makkai

HOMAGE TO ISAAC NEWTON

We commit what we do not commit,
and we do not commit what we commit.
Somewhere there is a terrible silence.
Towards that we gravitate.

Peter Jay

AUSCHWITZ
(to Erzsébet Schaár)

I can be no more than four or five,
and at my age the world
or — if you like — reality,
in a word, everything that exists
— two years or eighty years,
a shoe of a hundredweight
a jacket of several tons,
and above all, what lies ahead —
is exactly five or six years old.

Peter Jay [& A.M.]

RELATIONSHIP

What a silence, when you are here. What
a hellish silence.
You sit and I sit.
You lose and I lose.

Peter Jay

DEPRESSION

I look at my mother's photograph on the wall,
and even her once loved
glance is stiff now,
stiffer than a pebble. And what is worse,
just as indifferent as
my look, facing her.

Peter Jay

DIFFERENCE

Between a centipede and a flamingo,
between an electric chair and a marriage bed,
between the crater of a pore
and the brilliance of a gleaming forehead:
there's no difference. The only difference is
if someone says, 'I am good',
or — which is rare — someone says 'You are good',
but this is only such a difference
that God says to himself:
both the same.   *Peter Jay*

VEIL

No son. No moon.
And no childhood.
And above all no earth, no mother earth.

No coffin and no fatherland.
No cradle and no bed made,
death slipped into place under your head.

Whoever lives turns on a needle-point,
and our peace is nothing else
than a drooping wing that faints,
like a wedding-veil removed

or not removed, swooning onto the nail.

Dangling.

We are dangling.

Not even a cemetery.   *Peter Jay*

LIFE SENTENCE

The bed shared.
The pillow not.   *Peter Jay*

ORATORIO FOR A CONCENTRATION CAMP

An empty stage or concert platform. The choir stands surrounding the two sides of the stage, leaving a narrow passage way in the middle. Hung above, there are horizontally positioned concert reflectors.

Dramatis personae: LITTLE BOY; OLD WOMAN; M.R., a young girl. All three are Concentration Camp inmates.

While the orchestra is tuning up, M.R. appears first, then the LITTLE BOY; the OLD WOMAN is last. M.R. is wearing striped prisoner's fatigues, her hair is cut short like a boy's; the Old Woman is wearing black; the Little Boy has a grey dust-robe on. Each holding a lit candle, they assume their positions in front, in the middle of the stage. They have music stands in front of them on which there sits the score whose pages they themselves are turning as the oratorio gets under way. The Little Boy stands in the middle, the girl to his right, the Old Woman to the left. The orchestra grows quiet. Pause.

M.R.:   I am from Warsaw.

OLD WOMAN: I am from Prague.

LITTLE BOY: I don't know where I'm from.

OLD WOMAN: *(Picking her head up suddenly):*
It's as if they'd been shaking nails.

M.R.: Yes, as if they'd been shaking nails!

LITTLE BOY: That was when I first saw the night!

OLD WOMAN: The nails didn't wake up.

M.R.: It was me that kept on yelling inside the box!

OLD WOMAN: I never woke up again.

M.R.: I am from Warsaw.

OLD WOMAN: I am from Prague.

LITTLE BOY: I don't know where I'm from.

OLD WOMAN: It was the middle of the night when we left the city.

M.R.: All lit up and forgotten.

OLD WOMAN: The ice-empty stars were knocking.

M.R.: The ice-empty light bulbs were knocking.

OLD WOMAN: It was as if they'd been shaking nails.

M.R.: Faces and hands. Exhausted smithereens.
Stuff from the open yonder raining in.

OLD WOMAN: And lights upon a face forgotten.

M.R.: Wrinkles on a face never seen.

OLD WOMAN: Tell, Prague, is this all you ever were?

M.R.: All lit up and forgotten.

LITTLE BOY: You mustn't talk to me from now on!

M.R.:   I never saw a house in my whole life!
It stood amidst pine trees at the end of a row of trees.
Its windows were glittering.
I didn't touch it with my hand.
I'll touch it now, very carefully.

Forget me, forget me, my love!
Who cares about an animal leaning against a tree-
trunk?

OLD WOMAN: There are scribes in the moonlight.

M.R.:   Churches and graveyards.

OLD WOMAN: Walnut trees, peasant jail-guards.

M.R.:   Dossiers in half-dream; needle and thread.

OLD WOMAN: Deadly silence.

M.R.:   Gothic letters.

OLD WOMAN: Germany.

LITTLE BOY: Very far away and very near
someone was stretched out on the table of stone.

OLD WOMAN: It was as if it had been a greenhouse for flowers
but there were no flowers in it.
A single, long corridor;
adobe walls, but still with the warmth of the earth.
The corridor widened out toward the end
and gave off light like an altar monstrance.

M.R.:   *(With increased simplicity, as if in another story)*:
Once upon a time
there lived a lonely wolf,
lonelier than the angels.

Once he drifted into a village
and fell in love with the first house that he saw.

He'd already fallen in love with the walls of it, too,
and the caressing of the stone masons,
but he was stopped by the window.

There were people sitting inside the room.
Except for God, nobody ever
saw them as beautiful,
as this pure-hearted animal.

During the night the wolf entered the house,
stopped in the middle of the room,
and never again budged from there.

He stood there all night with eyes wide open,
even in the morning, when they beat him to death.

LITTLE BOY: Surely we're dead, aren't we?

M.R.:   It was as if it had been a greenhouse for flowers,
but there were no flowers in it at all.
One single, long corridor;
adobe walls, but with the warmth of the earth.
It was in the afternoon, about three o' clock.
The corridor widened out toward the end,
and shone brightly like an altar monstrance —

The top of it must have been made of glass,
because the sun's rays got stuck in it.
Somebody was stretched out on the table of stone
with naked finality.

OLD WOMAN: There were scribes in the moonlight.

M.R.:   Churches and graveyards.

OLD WOMAN: Walnut trees and peasant jail-guards.

M.R.:   Dossiers in a half-dream, needle and thread.

OLD WOMAN: One gigantic blow!

M.R.:   The dead in flames of magnesium.

OLD WOMAN: Deadly silence.

M.R.:   Gothic letters.

OLD WOMAN: Germany.

M.R.:   It's getting late. All I have with me now
is an unravelled thread from my jail-fatigues.
I tear it off and put the thread in my mouth.
Here I lie dead on the tip of my own tongue.

OLD WOMAN: Don't be judgmental, my beloved ones!

LITTLE BOY: There are seven cubes.
I know nothing about the first.
The second one: roads and distances.
In the third one: soldiers.
And the fourth? It's we who're inside it.
And in the fifth: hunger and bread!
In the sixth cube there is silence.
The seventh cube remains unknown to me.

M.R.:   I dream that I'm waking up.

OLD WOMAN: Try it, my treasure, what's there to lose? Maybe!

M.R.:   I'm terribly afraid that I may lose it. *(Pause.)*
I'll hurry through the deserted courtyard.

OLD WOMAN: You are lost! While you have nothing to lose!

M.R.:   I have the impression he's here, very close.

OLD WOMAN: As near as only we are able to love.

M.R.:   He's here. My heartbeat's stopping.

OLD WOMAN: Break down the door on him! We've already earned the
                right to.

M.R.:   I'm crying. He has landed on my face.
                Everything's here, what's mine, and what's not mine.

OLD WOMAN: Yes, if we could only know one thing,
                that's whether we can finally break
                the solitude, not ours, but of the other;
                that of the victim, who's scared,
                that of the killer feels not he has killed!
                of those who no longer dare to know we lived.

M.R.:   Everything running down my cheeks like a waterfall.

LITTLE BOY;   The first cube I know nothing about.
                The second: roads and distances!
                Dark roads and an empty distance.

OLD WOMAN: *(Leaning against the air with her hand, as if it were a
                wall):* It's starting to snow.
                In Prague it is winter now.
                There's a small table standing under a glass roof.
                One of its feet is tipping off balance.
                The clockwork is turning inside.
                Once I used to think that I am here.

LITTLE BOY: It's us who are inside cube number four.

M.R.:   All lit up and forgotten.

OLD WOMAN: I hurry across St. Venceslas Square. *(Pause.)*
                (As if talking to herself): People,
                have mercy!

M.R.:

Alone at last, totally.
        All that's left is
the thread unravelled from the prison garb,
it put on the unwritten fate of a line.

There's nothing but the time and the location
where ultimately they keep track of us.

There's only me and them. *(Pause.)* Who're still
asleep.

OLD WOMAN:

Don't be judgmental, dearest ones!
We have been living here like cattle.
Like pigs, we have been kneeling in the dust,
yet when food reached our desiccated tongues,
'twas meek just like the body of the Lord.

LITTLE BOY:

In the sixth cube there is silence.

M.R.:

I am dreaming that I'll wake up.
The night is dark, so incredibly deep.
I barely am.
        There's but a single room,
light shines in but one window: it is his.
That's empty, too.
        And like a broken mirror
his room keeps falling, cannot reach the ground!
I have to leaf my way through page by page
across this soft forest. It's nothing but wounds.
When from the midst of leaves soaked into mush
I liberate his handsome head, I faint.

Comelier than the fairest youthful maid —
There's no more woods.
        What else you want from us?
Our death, no way, that we will not give up.
We hug it tightly and won't give it up.

(Continues after a short pause):

How soft the air is!
The leaky eaves, the barrack-walls, and the distance.
Devastation slowed into happiness.

LITTLE BOY: There's silence inside the sixth cube.

M.R.:   Weak beyond belief,
                some pulses strive on
                to stay alive.

M.R.:   Everything halts. It is evening in Warsaw.
                My bed had a white woollen bed-spread on it.

OLD WOMAN: O, my sweet ones! My dearest ones!

M.R.:   My dark Heaven.
                (The vertically placed reflectors are turned off.)

OLD WOMAN: It was like a loaf of bread punched full of holes.
                Its windows were glittering.
                It shone brightly at the end of the row of trees.
                There were people sitting in the room.
                We were marching along the highway.
                The house is hidden by the trees.

LITTLE BOY: I don't know the seventh cube.

M.R.:   There's only me and they who are asleep.

OLD WOMAN: There were scribes in the moonlight.

M.R.:   Churches and graveyards.

OLD WOMAN: Walnut trees and peasant jail-guards.

M.R.:   Dossiers in half-dream, thread and needle.

OLD WOMAN: A single, huge blow!

M.R.:   The dead in magnesium light.

OLD WOMAN:	Light-patches on a forgotten face.
M.R.:	Wrinkles in a face never seen.
OLD WOMAN:	It was as if they had been shaking nails.
M.R.:	As if I had been shaking nails.
LITTLE BOY:	It's for the first time I see the night!
M.R.:	It was me who was yelling inside the box.
OLD WOMAN:	Never again will I wake up.
LITTLE BOY:	*(He steps forward a couple of steps. He holds both of his hands in front of himself, as if examining them; he now stands apart from the others):* Unhappy is the moment, when the orphan discovers himself and thinks that this hand, this crookedness may be important to someone else, too, and from now on is yearning to be loved.
M.R.:	I am from Warsaw.
OLD WOMAN:	I am from Prague.
LITTLE BOY:	I don't know where I am from.

(The overhead reflectors are turned off.)

Adam Makkai

Ágnes Nemes Nagy
(1922-1991)

Ágnes Nemes Nagy graduated from the University of Budapest in 1944, obtaining a diploma as high school teacher of Hungarian, Latin, and the History of Art. Until 1957 she was employed as a teacher. She is generally considered to be Hungary's most important woman poet of the 20th century, whose output was modest in quantity but always of true depth and brilliance. Her verbal magic transmuted everyday experiences and things into universal and enduring beauty. A prolific translator whose output actually surpasses that of Mihály Babits (q.v.), she produced excellent Hungarian versions of Molière, Corneille, Racine, and Bertolt Brecht for the stage. She has also published a number of children's poetry books. Her volumes of poetry include In a Double World [Kettős világban], *1946;* Dry Lightning [Száraz-villám], *1957; and many more.*

Nemes Nagy was one of the great intellectual and moral passive opponents of 'socialist realism' and the Marxist philosophy of art, but she disliked politics so much that instead of attacking the prevailing policy, she wrote poems about the Egyptian Pharaoh Akhenaton, the initiator of monotheism. In lines such as 'and now the tanks came', or 'the juice of beef seeps through the newspaper on which it says "dialectical"...' — tucked away in a poem which she wrote on a crowded Budapest street car and dedicated to Sidney Keys — Nemes Nagy developed a philosophy of art which puts her in the very front of world literature in this century.

After the war and before the Communist take-over of 1949-50, she was a member of the The New Moon [Új Hold] *intellectual writers' group together with Weöres, Pilinszky (qq.v.), and several others. She was not allowed to publish her own poetry between 1949 and 1957, but this enforced silence only deepened and condensed her talent. She is one of the most translated Hungarian poets; Bruce Berlind, Hugh Maxton, George Szirtes, and others have presented her poetry in English. She uses classical meter and rhyme as often and as effortlessly as she writes free verse. Translators have chosen to render her poetry formally or in free-flowing English. She visited the United States under the International Writers' Program at the University of Iowa and in a posthumous diary described her impressions of the USA.*

Her poetry unites lyrical sensitivity with historical consciousness — morality, erudition, and intelligence with blazing passion. She gave numerous lectures at the University of Budapest on aesthetics and older Hungarian poets such as Csokonai (q.v.). She had a large number of dedicated followers.

TO LIBERTY

Cathedral. Full of awe and reverence.
Garlanded Angels. Looks of beatitude.
From down here their feet's circumference
seems Gargantuan — and their heads minute.

Up there majestic pillars splice the dome's view,
fake heavens flame like varnished amethyst.
What good if you exist but I disown you,
what if I praise you, but you don't exist?

Left-over God. Your wayward fascination
binds me no more. I tired long ago.
Some of my friends have just died of starvation —
haven't you heard? I thought I'd let you know.

What kind of straw did they last clench their teeth on?
What kind of skulls sank to what kind of dust?
A few odd crumbs might have been within reason;
some small miracles would have been august.

I long to see their lips again in smiling,
their soft, round chins that were ground underfoot:
I long for Rome. For beautiful, beguiling
gardens, and for rich, luxurious food.

Give meat! Bananas! Be the world's Provider.
Naples at night... A clear Swiss morning scene...
False love of all my yearnings' wild desire,
give back the vibrant air above the green.

Give marvels! Faith! A new Heavenly Sign!
Break all the laws! Offer yourself to us!
That racketeers should not constantly dine
and that the dead may rise up from the dust!

— — In a vase on the table: a peony,
her ornate beauty's like a diadem.
Around the brim, magnificent and stony,
her gorgeous petals cascade off the stem.

If I could still find worship exultory
upon my crumbling knees to her I'd crawl:
on her alone pin your triumphant glory!
She's beautiful, alive — and has no soul.

Ila Egon

TOWARDS SPRINGTIME

Hewn out of faith and composite politics
the Tropic of Capricorn radiates the light.
The Summer forages on towards the North.
Lift up your head, lift up your sun-soaked sleepiness,
your latent strength, your iridescent weakness
my Self — spell out where does the Sun strike forth?

In the deep of night heavy engines rumble,
deep in the earth buried guns germinate
fish ever slimier rows of roes beget.
Slimy bodies. I don't revere my species,
my cells don't ooze with past eternities,
yet how does Order spread her vital net?

Not blood alone in hundred forms subsistent,
not mere existence only feed my brain.
Order revitalises my vital eyes.
And intertwined like climbers of twin foliage
intentions will bear Gods to their own Image,
and pure intellect its own self fertilise.

Ila Egon

CARBON DIOXIDE

Only the plants remain sinless and pure,
for they cannot categorize.
Yet it's the plants that sinful CO_2
during the night, resynthesize.
      The firmament glitters pure in the mornings
      from mute redemptionism wrought by oak trees.

Adam Makkai

WINTER TREES
(Three Versions)

1.
You have to learn. The trees in winter.
As hoarfrost dresses foot, top, centre
curtains of white that nothing moves —
      You have to learn those secret grooves
      where crystals start to turn to vapour
      and trees fade over into fog
      just as bodies flow into memory.
And the river behind the trees
flapping mute wings of skeins of geese,
the blues of blinding ice-white nights
in which some hooded objects linger —
this is our task: We have to seize
the trees' inexplicable deeds.   *Adam Makkai*

2.
One ought to learn. The Winter Trees
Bound in their frosted silver sheaths.
Consolidated draperies.
      One ought to comprehend the plane
      where ice crystals begin to smoke
      and where the trees drift into mist
      like bodies into memories.
And the river behind the trees,
the wild fowl's silent, gliding wings,

the blind, opaquely white-blue night
where hooded objects stand around;
one has to perceive here the dark,
unspeakable deeds of the trees.

Ila Egon

3.
Learn. The winter trees.
Hoarfrosted from crown to root.
Immovable curtains.
            And learn too of the zone
            where a crystal steams
            and trees merge into mists
            as the body in recollection of it.
And behind the trees the river
mute wings of the wild duck
the white-blind blue night
of hooded objects standing:
it is here we must learn the trees'
inexplicable deeds.

Hugh Maxton

CONVERSATION

— 'Set me free, flagpole, why must you deny me the free wind?'
— 'A useless rag, you alone, — but a banner, a banner on me!'

Adam Makkai

LAZARUS
(Three Versions)

1.
As slowly he sat up, near his left shoulder
Each muscle of a lifetime weighed a boulder —
his death, like gauze, torn off. Everything hurt.
For Resurrection's just as difficult.

Adam Makkai

2.
Round his left shoulder, as he got up slowly
everyday's muscle gathered in agony.
His death was flayed off him, like a gauze.
Because second-birth has just such harsh laws.   *Hugh Maxton*

3.
By his left shoulder, as he sat up again
each muscle of a complete life throbbed with pain.
His death ripped off, like lint or plaster guise
for it is the same agony to arise.   *Ila Egon*

STORM

A shirt blows across the field
Freed from a clothes-horse
at the height of an Equinox,
stumbling now above Saint Swithin's Grass
it is the bodiless dance
of a veteran.

And there they go, the sheets
running under the recoil of lightning
in battalion manoeuvres
even as they flee — flags, sheets,
a top-sail, a rag — each
ripped to its own hissing sound
on the open green field
diving and rising
their movement unveils
the winding sheets of mass-graves.

Without moving, I step
outside my contour,
a somewhat more transparent runner
body taut behind among them
like a half-wit whose birds have flown
like a naked tree whose birds have flown

calling them back with my beckoning arms —
And now they fall.
And with a motion white-winged, wide,
the entire flock takes wing as one,
takes wing like an unmoving image
takes wing like the bodily resurrection,
eternity called up
from the water, at the crack of a gun.

Nothing left in the field but that beckon
and the dark green colour
of the grass. A pond.

Hugh Maxton

CONCIOUSNESS

Should I return to consciousness or stay
still numb in the dense, early summer heat?
In falls the world with sharp, colliding streaks
beneath my forehead: sunshine, side-walk, trees,
are ripping up the fog in front of me.

Should I return from such a streaky burble?
Get up already from behind my shutters?
What can I tell? What can the semi-circle-
shaped sand do, which would indeed be total
for me, if meanwhile the land perishes?

There is no chance for action. My desire:
the thought, and agony pulls me back from thought,
since decay germinates with every hour,
and petal by petal, even as from a flower,
ideas, hair, fingers fall and come to nought.

Flower of leprosy. I was not born to be sick,
but rotting takes me now, ah, cell by cell.
How can I tell? My mind cannot forget,
and the swarms of nameless, secret roots as yet
are stronger, they dig into deeper soil.

The fleshy, tepid petal-leaf falls off,
all fall off, all, how sweet and frail, the frailest,
my desire lives like a dry-stalk, but does live,
and in my closely cropped mind there revive
road, memory, moral: an unfellable forest.

Doreen Bell

ICE

Slowly the world freezes into me
like clumps of reed into a wintry lake
in ice-bound blocks the jagged fragments ache,
a patch of sky, a scene, a sound, a tree...

I believed in you, you Silent One,
you'd spread out your two warm palms for my sake,
they'd shine above the ice, above the lake
in twofold glory like a small Twin Sun.
The ice would break, the surf awake,
and all the objects leaping high
would gleam against the morning sky.

Ila Egon

LAKE BALATON

I

A bitsy cotton bathing-costume
tattoos her body with the century's badge
but her delicate breasts assume
light like a Naiad in the sedge,
dark head deep in the stumpy fronds
curls streaming from the gentle neck,
and float-weed links her arm in bonds.
In summer haze, you might mistake
her for some Ophelia in the lake.

The boy arrives. Seeks and strides
through his sleeve of yellow hair;
gathers the tidal impact there
around his marbled sides.

II

Who would believe, beneath the surface
above the surface of the lake
the dead and deeds of settlement
drift between biplane and wreck?

A marshy lake. Like sugar cane
pours slowly into the moon
soon to be boiled away
by a southering noon;
only in autumn, when water clears
and vapours take to hills untrod,
do pendulant grapes slake
the gentler gods.

III

Behind the promontory.
A small lake the larger
once tenanted; its stone-memory,
mapped fields of lavender.

Crushing the hills in throes,
collapsing humus
of fire-pits unearths
its sandalled Titan-toes.

IV

How warm the boards are! Almost steaming hot
in the foam and light that meet in the place.
Slowly take off the straw bonnet
and place it slowly over your face.

Below the boards stretch like a drum.
Water tingles in the trap.
Sound drowned in float-weed geranium.
Yet, hear the boards snap.

Sleep, fisherman. It is three exactly.
This is Christ's death to a second.
The sun smites the lake abstractedly,
halves the reckoning.

V

Neither a moon nor a path. The eye stares
loosely in a high jungle of stars.

Deeper and yet see a stone parapet
seeming bright with phosphorescent.

And brushing against breasts of the hill,
hand alights on a grape-spill.

Sky able to remain intact!
Able to endure its climax!

And its horror — noon of midnight —
able to endure its ultimate?

VI

Copper-cut and grey
etch each other,
engraven dusk shivers,
the wide clouds smother.
Unmoving, stipples
a motley shambles,
rising the ripples hold
storm's incisive cold.

VII

rising ripples cut the wind
dusk shivers behind
the night-moon none may see
cover your face slowly
girl is dead none may see
the body hidden perished
but shallows ferried
being no depths but time
small lake hot marsh-mud
how very hot the board
over the face everywhere
ecstasy and terror
twin-breasted grape-spill Naiad
sun smites bitsy costume
the dreadful Titan-toes
ovoidal grapes on the northern
jungle of stars deluding night-sky
able to endure its reckoning
the moon unrisen that none may see
this is Christ's death to a second —

Hugh Maxton

TO MY CRAFT

Craft of mine and delight
how you sustain me
between morality
and dread, dark and light;

those giddy landscapes
of lightning and outlandish
clouds — the image of brains! —
when a jet of fire escapes

and with it begins
my endless siege,
Jericho and Buda
of my origins,

all in between tottering,
tacked up, tattered
while the heart ravels,
word beats on a thread,
word oscillates a rhythm
slumbering, loud,
between field and heaven
takes its contraction for those clouds'.

Between morality and dread
or with immoral dread,
craft of mine and pleasure
you match the unmeasurable,

a rocking pendulum
to tick off solo time.
This, my craft, may rhyme
light distinct from night.

Hugh Maxton

THE GARDEN OF EDEN

I

One fat poppy dawdles
where field meets forest,
just one poppy its lug
droopy as a rabbit's.

It's the country. Fern swaddles
an arm-long hedgehog:
he tumbles into the glen
a pot-bellied bruin

printing the sand
with his soft, spiky skin.

Vines dive under undergrowth
till they come on a log
and press their breasts
between leaves of a laurel.

Greenery shakes like water,
breaks in a solid wave
on trembling cliffs and caves —
a glint of bone
visible and then gone, a landscape altered:
sleek, bleak.

Below, the glen expands
and everything appears to melt
lightwards into a cloud-belt;
there a screen of vertical timber
(slivers that blackedge the field)
unmelts, unmoves, and never yields,
thrusting a last light into the clay,
bearing the heat — between
gapped infinity...

between those silver-trees, a sea reflects.

***

Where are you going, frail and weak-boned?
Don't you hear the sky
softly ping above your eye
as glass clangs on silver
or the sky's vault echoes, don't you hear
starlings cheer?

As these swoop, don't you see
the shuddering vinery?
Fruit's thick scent as it spills

from the cluster
under their shrieking bills?

Or feel up there a deeper dark
behind the heavenly lights?
They have just begun to sparkle,
traceable on flowing screens;
pale signs of a farther sky
assume now further signs.

A minor jounce:
earth begins to turn, to bobbin Time,
germinating every thing —
boughs tacky with resinous heat —
sense your leaf-mulch bed seethe
sense you lie on exploded fruit?
How young you are! To endure your passion!

Don't you fear for your eyes?
The year's turning, cover them while you can.

Don't you fear for your gentle lips?
Too sticky for the honey of grapes.

And fear for your shoulder?
Forever tanned in appearance
with its India-copper freckles.
Don't you fear the heavy trance
of an Indian summer will lean and murmur?
And you will fall and stay fallen
a heap amid a scorching midden,
and then will fall with a fearful shout
into a flailing grove it bound with twines.
And in that torment yet you'll taste the sting
of wild chicory its meth-lamp hissing
near invisible in the huge sun's haze,
and know your flesh blaze of its lightest clinker —
don't you fear for your eyes?
There's the Girl. She doesn't look at you!

Don't you fear for your unsullied mouth?
She's standing up to the knees in grass, green
mirrored on the palimpsest of her skin
like green exterior sunlight dallying
on a white ceiling
while the sun sits in the boughs of trees —
don't you fear for your shoulder?

                                        *

And so, dusk.
          A large chilly sky.
The clouds charge in a final muster.
Scattered nightfall equips itself
with a mane silently lashing
with light sharply piercing
with foaming drifts
with titanic gestures
with hounded muteness silent
like ineffable passion.

Languishes. Silence. Two still figures sit
at the hill-top, resting their backs
against the gruff surface
of the tree, one each side of it.
Around about them, several empty
minute volcanoes are floating
from the level plain waist deep in fog.
Lunar foothills mute in moonlight.
Which grows sharper
the night ever deeper.
Stirs the wind betimes.

                    Above them
answering the breeze
the Tree trembles.

II

Cooling night's vapour drops onto the ground:
an Angel saunters in the darkened grounds.
His mantle catching in the clinging wood
sets it to murmur, as the new wind would.
He halts. And thrusts the point
of his man-sized staff into the clay;
wrapping all his fingers round the handle
resting his chin upon his hands.

Thus he can see between two bonds of green
shadow on shadow on the earthly scene.
And if he pull a single shade away
new shadows in their shades display
new shadows
ready for pulling. A lumbering predator...

But no. Enough
now of this picture and its stuff.
Deeply he sighs. The ceaseless torrent
of shadow on shadow is a torment.
If other figurations others furnish,
his eye beholds the earth to be a fish:
the waters of the universe
break on its arched and shining scales:
steam spouts from its back in gales
and in a liquid hectic furnace
breaks it forth from waters icy, beingless.
          "What of the blood," the Angel said,
"that seethes yet, can'st thou hear it, Lord?

For I am alone who lives silent,
I am alone who crosses space
in most dangerous passage
shrouded in darkness from hair to toe
wrapped in my own frosted wings.
So what do I care? But he who is
divided male and female, in whom blood sings,

claps the back of fish or pullet,
his breath rattling in his gullet
and bare arm outstretched in terror:
a gummy-eyed infant primate.
It is he whom you fix and focus
on as he fixes on lake and locust.
And why? What's your business for him?
What purpose has divided flesh from spirit,
what purpose has the night sky overhead
spin-drifting in the spheres, his eyes;
petals wafer-thin racked on ligaments?
To what end disposable delight?
When bakelite and multi-storey
stagger and rise, cable and zinc...
why should he hang, a rag upon a stick,
hang on a cable, hang on a world of cable?
What's the use of a finger scored for art
that fits the runnel of a bloodied sword?

Why vaulted chambers
beneath the bone?
An infinite living network
squared off by nerves
with horoscopes incised?
What use Being beneath Being,
order of things, species of grass,
slates, stones?
Yes, blind him now, blind let him grow,
or throw him to the hurricano,
he's just electron-detritus!
And thou art mercy —"

Thus spake the Angel.
                    And his shoulder
swayed the branch of a young elder
gathering its shy fragrance
in the emptiness of his glowing fist.
Thus spake the Angel, while the round
and hand-sized moon fell to the ground.

Thus spake he, while between the trees the light
disposed itself as density and height.
There were a million armless, white
and luminous silver palms upturned
and rippling, a million tiny balances —

Thus spake the Angel. Meanwhile through the leaves
many-branching Libra heaved and burned,
oscillating, weighing up the night —
Thus spake he, thus was quiet.

Hugh Maxton

BETWEEN

The air's enveloping capacious sleeves.
The air on which the bird disports,
with ornithology supports,
wing on the ragged edge of arguments,
foliage bearing astonished reports
a minute of the sky takes, leaves,
the trees of the tremulous mist, spiralling
their longing to the upper branches,
each minute breathing twenty times
the huskiest angels of the frost.

And here below, the weight. Upon this plain
vast chunks of mountain tremulously moan;
rocks, ridges of rock, peaks, though they lie
are able to kneel upon one knee;
sculpture, geology combine;
the valley, a distraction of a minute,
is displaced by blocks, the restless volumes
muscling an outline on the chalky bone,
identity crumpled into stone.

Between the sky and ground.

Loud dislocations of the rocks.
As the translucent ores within sun's heat

almost metallize, if glowing stone
is stamped on by an animal, its claw
spitting out smoke, above the rocks, rise, soar
the twisting ribbons from the kindling hooves,
and then the night in desolation,
the night as it extinguishes, reaches in
to the spine, intrinsic rock, the glacial night,
and as the ligaments, joints, stone blocks
wrinkle and fissure, cleaved to racks
of aggravated endlessness
in a splitting ungovernable trance,
habitually in black and white
the forging hammerings of the lightning strike —

    Between the day and night.

The devastations, lacerations,
the visions, the drought, the privations,
the disproportionate resurrections,
the verticals intolerably taut
between the lower stretchers and the high —
    Meridians. Conditions.
    Between. Stone. Ruts of tanks.
    Scribbled reeds across the desert-margin, black,
    two lines, in the sky, on the lake,
    on two blackboards, a system, a coding,
    accents of stars, reed lettering —
    Between the sky and sky.   *Alan Dixon*

DEFEND IT

Defend it, call it a thing of worth,
worth all the effort, call it best,
worth climbing, putting it to the test,
the high benevolence, the strife,
the hidden edge on the lagging knife,
the brave death at its stealthiest,
say, say that it was worth the love

of mind traversing a dark recess
flashing its streaky beam to prove
it worth the gasping, the distress
of breath withheld, the postulates
of intellect, the dumb world's gist,
the abstract nouns, distinction, the chest
stiffening as the heart digests
its flame in cloud gravid with snow,
internal cloud, snow biting, to last
in a city where the flames must grow,
say it was worth it to our time,
while on two shoulders not to cease
and on two wrists and on two feet
irrevocable injuries teem
and burst apart, infliction's waste,
continuous blood, a blackened stream —   *Alan Dixon*

A COMPARISON

One who rows a storm at the inception,
quadriceps aching to the uttermost,
who strains to push away that rock, the footboard,
whose right hand loses, all of a sudden,
substance and effort as the oar bends backward
appropriated from a fractured handle,
whose liberated body then
convulses — can get my meaning.   *Alan Dixon*

THE SHAPELESSNESS

The shapelessness, the endlessness.
I almost fall before I cut away
my statement from the timelessness.
With sand I wall a bucketful of sea
against a waste of nothingness.
Perpetual indifference should be
intolerable to consciousness.

Alan Dixon

László Nagy
b. N 25

A. Barux
'72

László Nagy
(1925-1978)

László Nagy was discovered by populist critics after the end of World War II and was hailed as a 'son of the working peasantry.' Little did anyone guess that he would soon become a visionary, resembling in some ways both Yeats and that other great Celt, Dylan Thomas. He has also written some of the most moving love poems of his generation, and with his poem 'The City's Coat of Arms' [A város címere] and others he protested against the Soviet army's brutal intervention in Hungary in 1956. (This poem is presented here in English for the first time.)

He was surrounded by art during all of his life in more than one sense. Himself a most talented painter and graphic artist, Nagy married the talented poetess Margit Szécsi (q.v.). His love poems were inspired by her. His younger brother István, another talented poet, changed his surname to Ágh.

Together with Sándor Weöres (q.v.) and Ferenc Juhász (q.v.), Nagy has become known in English translations during the past two decades; a selection of his poems entitled Love of the Scorching Wind [A forró szél imádata] *was published in 1973 by Oxford University Press. Newer publications of his poems include* A Hymn for All Seasons [Himnusz minden időben], *1965;* Hiding in Poems [Versben bújdosó], *1973; and* The Bells Are Coming to Fetch Me [Jönnek a harangok értem], *1978.*

His poem 'The Young Miracle Stag' [A csodafiú-szarvas], which is included here, retells the story of the 'Miracle Stag' from a modern, Christian point of view. Nagy's poem is the critical link that ties this shamanistic, heathen tradition to the new vision of the 'Miracle Stag,' — the one representing a Cathedral, Jesus Christ, and Hungary's eternal journey towards both the political-geographical and the intellectual-spiritual West.

Despite his early disenchantment with socialism, apparent from his Love of the Scorching Wind, *he was awarded the Attila József Prize three times and the Kossuth Prize in 1966.*

For his translations from Bulgarian folk poetry he received the Botev Prize in 1976, while for his original work he was awarded a poetic prize in Struga, Macedonia in 1968. Apart from translations from the Bulgarian, he translated the Polish Zbigniew Herbert and also Dylan Thomas. His poetry developed from populist and idealist socialist beginnings into a universal vision of both the splendor and the frailty of the human condition.

FROSTS ARE COMING

Hard frosts march together —
white rage, a ruthless guard
snapping down the shoulder
like pretzel in their tread.

Where to live without you?
That makes fibres shiver.
Your nearness a refuge
dawn's slow fires discover.

I can't bear the sight of
that winter-cold platter.
Take it! Feed me with love
now my shadow wears thinner.

Let me put the roof on
our love's burning-tower;
unfasten the skirt on
your hip's gold and lustre.

Alan Dixon

HYMN FOR ALL SEASONS

You, with your rainbow-brows woven of light,
Daughter of the sun, with your lap glowing bright,
A diamond-whetstone for lances fit for the fight —
           You guide me, my Vision of Beauty!

Shepherdess, you, of the nightingales,
Strummer of noontime's radiant tales,
Palace of marble — the holiest place:
           You guide me, my Vision of Beauty!

Fresh dates to eat in the Valley of Tears,
Smiles hidden under the canvass' veneer,

Golden cupola topping the church-nave's tier —
   You guide me, my Vision of Beauty!

A racing mare, whipped to the frenzy of a win,
Banner of the Uprising that streams in the wind;
Star, who squints through jail-windows, looking in —
   You guide me, my Vision of Beauty!

Healer of battle-scars out in the field —
Home for the countryless, fending with your shield;
My sweet superstition in honey-wine sealed:
   You guide me, my Vision of Beauty!

Open-air fleamarkets' drowsy beggary,
Dancer of poverty and of misery,
New Year's Eve's trumpet-blown, raucous reveille —
   You guide me, my Vision of Beauty!

You, who were known to me at every turn of time,
You, who stay pregnant with hope and design;
You, who through charm and guile received strength divine —
   You guide me, my Vision of Beauty!

You, who my arm have been holding eternally,
You, who my pillow have always shared with me,
You, who can kill the black, beastly crows, singingly —
   You guide me, my Vision of Beauty!

When I am dizzy with fright and repugnance,
When I am thundered at with dastardly arrogance,
When I must do battle against my own militancy —
   You guide me, my Vision of Beauty!

If there are rights to be had, they are *my* rights;
All power on Earth is but mine alone, by rights,
So I shall don my sword and shield of the old knights —
   Just guide me, my Vision of Beauty!

Behold how my court starts to glisten anew,
Black soot and red blood will turn into silvery dew —
The doves on my shoulder begin to coo,
        If you guide me, my Angel of Beauty!

Adam Makkai

WHO'LL FERRY LOVE TO THE YONDER SHORE?

When down the deep-six I'll be stored,
will crickets' fiddles still be adored?
Who will breathe flames on frosty twigs' to glow
crucifying himself into a rainbow?
Hugging and crying, who'll change the rough rocks
into soft meadows, and gentle hillocks?
Who'll have a nickname to christen the crawl
of hairs and arteries sprung in a wall?
Who will erect for all faiths devastated
a Cathedral from swear-words thus consecrated?
When down the deep-six I'll be smothered,
Who'll have the guts to scare off the buzzard?
        And who — like a retriever doing its chore —
        will ferry Love, in his teeth, to the yonder shore?

Adam Makkai

THE CITY'S COAT OF ARMS

  For the bees keep buzzing around the meat
and the carcass-flies, murmuring, nibble at the grapes:
      The Black Soldier cometh and cometh.
  For there arose so many a male whore
under the gaudy canvasses
and also under cupolas of ancient patina,
that the Earth is spitting up laughter.
And because fate listens only to these whores:
      The Black Soldier cometh and cometh!

For Lake Balaton sorely misses
the sight of some black sails
and the mountains and the fir-forests
keep howling their psalms for the pale-white dead
and the stench of the dead;
because the meat-grinder of the Bakony[1]
can't have enough of our love-affairs on the run:
   The Black Soldier cometh and cometh!
 Because the towers have gotten fed up
with the doves, as did the doves with
their own petrified droppings in their own nests,
and the bells, that went insane from the silence,
want to resound, even if consumed by flames;
well, then let the exalted bells melt like wax flowers;
let the dysentery of bronze overflow the cobble stones
and the gleaming hot walls,
and so that pigeons may never alight again:
   The Black Soldier cometh and cometh!
 For the flour brought in the freight cars
refuses to turn into bitter bread,
let the trains bring
black wounds instead;
because the milk refuses to turn
into water time and again:
let the dairies suddenly burst a-bleeding —
and because the candy wafer-like planks
in the lumber-yards are crushed into dust
by the heavenly wheel —
since everything here is screaming "NO!":
   The Black Soldier cometh and cometh.
 Yes, the Black Soldier Cometh —
a huge black velvet bat is he,
his wings are soft cupolas with a muffled roar,
he has gigantic roller skates on his
legs covered with pants woven of loose hair,

---

[1] A mountain chain in western Hungary, north of Lake Balaton, where the outlaws used to hide after the 1848 Hungarian War of Independence. 'Bakony' in Hungarian literature is synonymous with the hide-outs of political refugees and rebels, and also with nonconformists in the arts.

he kicks his skates forward and alights in the city;
we go blind; the calendar, too, goes blind
and so does history; — blind, too, go all of my loves,
the artist's long mane; the golden curtain
of your thighs shrinks into wind-blown ashes,
and I, who knew all about hell, keep twisting my fingers
in utter amazement: for I would never have believed,
I would never have thought it possible
that you, virgins, should lie in your beds
hugging an ice-cold weapon; never,
that you, street urchins, should suddenly drop your baby-teeth
and let them turn into horrendous carnations on the pavement —
with dreadful horizontal lines
the city's coat of arms is thus drawn anew,
smoke and prayer the decorative strokes around it,
      for The Black Soldier cometh and cometh,
      the Black Soldier cometh and cometh.

Adam Makkai

BARTÓK

To keep him with us, feasts are not enough —
he was a lover merciless and tough;
love him, without losing yourself thereby!

When cheap "Hurrahs" make of his name a fuss,
he vanishes riding a blade of grass
and sweats his blood on distant ocean shores.

He is a judge — he won't put you to sleep;
always awake, inexhaustibly deep,
he conjures a fairy, the future;

to sew it up, he spins sun-flower suture
and shapes Niagaras from a cricket's string —
on these he soars up to the Sun-dial's ring.
Inside him rage a million splendid bees;
but he waits patiently for his triumph's sake —
he doesn't relax; he summons you to a wake.

His splendor throbs inside my nights, ever since
I recognized Him as the frosty-bitten Fairy-Prince...
When will You, at last, rest within my heart?

Adam Makkai

THE YOUNG MIRACLE STAG

Spring is a-rising,
Buds are a-glowing
A shiny pair of antlers
Charge at the jasmine tree:
The Miracle Stag-Boy
Charges at it fiercely,
Charges at it fiercely.

'The flowers of the jasmine tree
I'll chew up by first light;
On the bow of my sinews
I'm hurled into the noon Sun —
There I'm roasted skinny, scrawny,
All alone and lonely,
All alone and lonely.'

'Hunters stalk and shoot me down
Bullet in my shoulder —
All the waves of Balaton[2]
Tears from mine eyes smarting —
Crying I howl, howling I cry;
Haste is no good — I'm falling behind.
Though I'm the Miracle Stag-Boy,
It is all for nothing,
It is all for nothing.'

---

[2] Hungary's 'inland sea', in fact the largest lake of Europe, 75 kms. long
and 5 kms. wide.

Heralded by dew and snowfall
Christmas is a-coming;
Lo and behold the Miracle Stag-Boy's
On the altar standing.
His fine antlers burst aflame
  Candles they are thirteen,
    ...Candles they are thirteen!

Adam Makkai

GRASSHOPPERS ON THE BELL

Here they caper all over the scarred bronze
here hiss the tiniest of words they have to tell
and the grass, the grass, the grass is surging
massively on into the heart of the bell.

Kenneth McRobbie and *Júlia Kada*

CSONTVÁRY[3]

That's him: head reared above the Babelic ramp,
red eyeball gigantic beyond all doubt,

comet-brush's blur across a canvas big as the world,
peppered with everyday-calibre smallshot from below,

from everyday kings, preposterous poppers-off
for he is God's Leviathan, mini-men's monster-fate,

radiant pure power, madness through a transformer;
plug in your city gentlemen — all the lights come on;

inimitable miracle, Sun's son, who has on his mind
the burning Carpathians for a crown!

---

[3] Tivadar Csontváry Kosztka (1853-1919), Hungarian painter. He projects his pantheistic, magical world view into monumental compositions.

It was slander — death knocking him down in a corner
of his room on a heap of one hundred times stewed tea-leaves,

who hurtles from north to south, feet fending off
the meridians, horizon askew, equilibrium gone;

slander's world, that cats should have tyrannized our painter
when today lions sink back inert beneath his wrist!

Look here where he parades a wormless glory,
his flesh mere memory, needless mere reality.

Transmitting on frequencies of the world's marrow
he became alpine snow, virginity, music in the leaves,

mountain torrents, a sudden charge of azure boars,
a new vision across the plain, a mirage-erasing storm,

even in contemplation a corrosive mirrored changeling,
white spectre of a bull in pale marble and cambric.

Listen, now the abandoned self-mortifying master is speaking,
his a new beauty in a desert age, his beard steel strands,

his hand pages through great epochs back towards pain,
searing cramp and drought Mona Lisa's womb.

The artist can be a sulphur-and-cobalt peacock's sky-shriek;
by some law from million-rooted loneliness the cedar grows.

He's here, his erupting summit a swing for stars,
for ever creating pain for himself, for us shocks of vertigo.

Kenneth McRobbie and *George Gömöri*

THE COALMEN

In the outer suburbs the coalmen race their carts,
they forget the decorum proper to men of trade;
"G'd yup" they roar, and hoofs strike sparks from the dark,
"G'd yup" and the jolting cart lamps leap and fade.

The carts are coaches! Their drunken, heroic burdens
rolling and grabbing — hold in a splendour of black,
billow wrath-blooms of rum on the jangling air, —
dangling to watch the wheels, or lolling back

in a dog-tired daze, beyond the constellations,
with nothing above but the depths, the empty spaces;
they obey no law, they're numb to the tumbling hailstones
pocking like birdshot at their coal-grimed faces.

Steam flies, foam flicks! — The mighty, drenched dray-horses
thunder back to the stables, guided by instinct and desire;
but that Palace is far from lust for the dusty lads,
who will find sharp draughts, damp hay, and a guttering fire.

No wives await them, no girls that are game for fun
will wiggle wide hips and giggle behind the beams;
saltpetre will limn their lecherous lips all night,
the ammoniac stink of horses will plague their dreams.

Cold comfort for those who must lose the kind Kingdom of Booze,
— for such is their fate: even booze will be taken away.
So remember the lads on the carts; their rough-hewn hearts
deserve more than the coal-ash burned on a winter's day!

Tony Connor and *George Gömöri*

Margit Szécsi
(1928-1990)

Descendant of a Gypsy family, a fact she often mentions in her original and vital poetry, Margit Szécsi was born in Budapest. Having risen from disenfranchised, poverty-stricken outcasts, she was a willing believer in the cause of radical Socialism in her younger days. In 1948 she entered the University of Budapest on a special scholarship for "proletarian students."

Her early poems started to appear in 1949. She joined the editorial staff of the periodical Csillag [The Star], *the successor of* Nyugat [The West], *which also appeared for a while under the title* Magyar csillag [Hungarian Star]. *In 1951 she volunteered for manual labor at a village called Duna-pentele, which the Communists renamed Sztálinváros 'Stalin City.' The idea was to display one's enthusiasm for the new social order.*

Her poems from this period were, accordingly, about the inspiration she felt about "building Socialism." She managed to make a living exclusively from her writing as of the year 1953. Her first independent collection of poems March [Március] *appeared in 1955, but already in her early work under the Socialist rhetoric there throbbed the heart of a genuine poet whose real, lasting inspiration came from Hungarian folk poetry.*

Her celebrated marriage to one of the greatest poets of the era, László Nagy (q.v.), only deepened the underlying attraction to the traditional Hungarian 'Flower Song' and the almost mystical visions of life that came to characterize her later, mature poetry. Although she was influenced by Nagy's circle which included Ferenc Juhász (q.v.), she also represented the lasting influence of Attila József and Lajos Kassák (qq.v.). Szécsi paints the desire for completeness, and tension of the awareness of being threatened, by using an original set of suggestive symbols and images. Her volumes of poetry include Angyalok strandja [The Beach of the Angels], *1956;* A trombitákat összesöprik [They'll sweep up the Trumpets], *1965;* A Nagy Virágvágó Gép [The Great Flower-Cutting Machine], *1969;* A Rózsaszínű Dzsip [The Rose-colored Jeep], *1982; and* A Betlehem-blues [The Bethlehem Blues], *1986. The* Great Flower-Cutting Machine *symbolizes her resistance to anti-social and anti-humanitarian attitudes prevailing during her youth and throughout the Kádár régime. In 1960 she was awarded the Attila József Prize. Toward the end of her life she consciously chose to return to her Gypsy past and to folk-songs expressive of love for nature.*

LETTER

Even the wind that should listen hums something lovely.
Gently throbbing eggs are warmed by the golden-necked hen.
Buds in the orchard boldly each day more and more open.
Pussy-willows sprinkle sweet pollen-weddings daily.

This spring ripens very slowly — like a snowy
goose softly biding her time in the straw, nestling
there till the marble egg cracks apart and the gosling
under her tummy flowers like a yellow lily.

Time flies! Self-reproducing's the rage of everything.
It's through love in their lives that humans can carry on.
The rustling field-crops from bright red seeds have come —
even the bird is thrown down to earth by great loving.

Kenneth McRobbie

LOVE'S FOOL

It happened before my eyes:
grass sprouted miraculously,
and rancid oil on my tongue
didn't taste bitter to me.
The world of all that is not
was setting light to my hair,
in my rags just like some saint
fiercely I preached at the air.

I know now he was laughing
at me for being a fool;
O how lovely my blindness,
believing was impossible.
And you came, mud-stained flower,
with such dreaming agonized;
when the sky came crashing down
it was myself I recognized.

Kenneth McRobbie

ONLY WITH RADIANCE

When we know we are on the way out,
  our desperation is what's ugly.
Last year's bark peels from the tree
  humbly, like scabs from a body.
Roots raging, veins glistening, old
  trees extinguish by an act of will,
still putting out leaves to the useful sky,
  a yellowing last smile.
O were there some sombre enough clothes,
  a transcendent uniforming,
skirts of iron to toil in place
  of me! I'll cease struggling,
I'll never again be sold on common
  self-deception, nor crawl
snake-pliant, nor wriggle after
  life running away downhill.
I'll stop... Women, women, if your shoulders
  are shapely still, chances are you're offhand
in tiny-stringed scornful maliciousness;
  this is a thing you can't understand,
old crones too: wobbly sergeant-majors
  who have already been advised
of mortality, the same revulsion stares
  out at you from my stone-cold eyes.
You without the dignity of misery,
  curlered, flabby-breasted,
you long ago settled up with corsets,
  you arthritis-knotted, withered!
And you too whom I knew at school
  how pot-bellied and bold you've grown!
In front of the meal-ticket window
  how quietly you've settled down!
What have you now to do with me
  who wouldn't play the hand she was dealt,
who wished to win every heart
  by making others radiant!

God pelts me with little stone
   stars, friends grow more vain,
jealous cats tease of course,
   old admirers long went down the drain.
I've been left with nothing to do
   — but, thank you, I'm holding quite still,
I'm keeping an eye on my body, lest its
   dying be a public spectacle.
Is it so shameful to trudge up with nothing
   to the heights that are only death's?
Watch me: putting off all I once thought mine
   now I wear only timelessness;
away with my vertigo of shallow
   society's gossipy depths.
My sinewy brown legs are means
   of carrying on for a while yet;
then, then, fire alone the food
   my lungs' rose-bushes will get,
the heart will live only by song,
   stone-steady eyes by radiance.
I shall not play the bitch
   sniffing the pantries of the rich.
Even as I curtsied I hated them all;
   I scorned, that's why I was quiet;
everything about their culture's cheap,
   tombs with tears running wet.
I've got all I ever needed,
   now let me be free,
and though my fall is but a breath away
   I'll celebrate openly.
I am all the purer
   by what makes me ever poorer.
It's not my falling, I am sure,
   but everything I dreamed of: Life.

Kenneth McRobbie

TWILIGHT

We dissolve — away from daytime, away from the sun,
down we float, burying ourselves into fairy tales,
we shine up from underneath the earth
like Jóska,[1] the outlaw, in his black sheepskin coat.
      Immortally we crumble into dust
      and our amber-nosed herds of stallions,
      our ancestors playing at being locomotives,
      choo-choo full the ears of silence.
There's only us here: your father, your mother;
keep running, you, our crumbling worn-out rags
breath-like over our shimmering knives.

Agnes Arany-Makkai

GENIUS

I wear the scaly skin of frequent fevers;
my pulse is beating like the lizard's throat.
The plummet of my heart pulls me to the ground,
and I can feel how the earth is turning.
There were dense curses, there were thin friendships,
there was whatever there was — I am a fiery rock;
seas boil up from my surface onto the sky,
showers and seasonal frosts.
    But a snowman radiates forever
    in sunshine, in heavy rain.

Agnes Arany-Makkai

---

[1] *Jóska* is the Hungarian nickname for 'Joseph.' The Robin Hood-type outlaws of the Hungarian plain were considered romantic figures. They were often clad in sheepskin coats.

JULY

He who shut off the rain
will come in the image of The Lion —
the night shines through his mane;
he's a cloud that makes no promise.
The rye sends beggings of gleaming spears
towards the suction of his throat,
my big shock of hair rises and bursts aflame —
O, summer, the painted river
catches fire on the ironed shirts.

Agnes Arany-Makkai

NOAH

I didn't let the blue ship run aground a wreck,
for the Earth has to have an end.
Idly it loiters on Mount Ararat
— waiting for your hearts.

Agnes Arany-Makkai

OLD TREES WITH HANDS SAWING THE AIR

The wind is blowing from side to side,
the clouds keep fleeing higher and higher.
Signs of an electric combat,
dry thunderbolts are flaring up.
        A roll of thunder roams the immense
        sky with a dull rumble.
        The dry curtain of dust is shivering,
        and the tuning-fork goes wild.
The thirsty, cracked soil sounds hollow,
the wall hiding emptiness resounds.
Old trees with hands sawing the air
would like to negotiate with the storm.

Agnes Arany-Makkai

János Székely
(1929-1992)

Poet, novelist, dramatist, and essayist, János Székely attended the military academy of Marosvásárhely (now Tirgu Mureş in Romania). Toward the end of World War II he was taken to the front while still a teenager. He was captured on the Western front. Thus it was only with great delay that he could graduate from high school in Marosvásárhely in 1948. He wrote up his wartime experiences in an essay-novel entitled The Western Division [A nyugati hadtest]. *In 1952 he graduated from the Hungarian Bolyai University of Kolozsvár (now Cluj-Napoca) as a Literature and Philosophy major. He worked as one of the editors of a Bucharest-based Hungarian language publisher's Kolozsvár office; he retired in 1989.*

In his essays he pronounced the harsh view that "poetry is dead;" [Ars Poetica], *1973; poetry has lost its ancient function of expressing the essence of life; it no longer carries it former role in mankind's culture. He went so far as to refute and denounce his own poetry as lacking any real function. He symbolically declined the prize offered him by the Hungarian Literary Society of Kolozsvár for his above-mentioned novel,* The Western Division. *Yet he kept active as a poet and even as a translator; he translated the works of Romanian authors M. Beniuc, I. Calovia, and the writings of the expatriate anthropologist Mircea Eliade living in the U.S.A. Székely also translated poetry from Russian and German. He was greatly embittered by the Ceauşescu régime's systematic discrimination against the Hungarian minority in its own native habitat. The date 1968 of his poem* 'Nothing-Never' *featured here is significant: the Ceauşescu régime, which was in its early phase, announced a partial amnesty for those imprisoned for their political views.*

His books include Profane Passion [Profán passió], *1954;* The Lieutenant of Caligula [Caligula helytartója], *1972;* The Protestants [Protestánsok], *1978;* The Merciful Lie [Irgalmas hazugság], *1979; and* King Béla the Blind [Vak Béla király], *1981.*

Székely's poetry is quintessential Transylvanian pessimism at its best. Due to insufficient cultural exchanges between Romania and Hungary, Székely's work, with the possible exception of his dramatic work and the long poem Dózsa *about the leader of the peasant rebellion of 1514, which appeared in 1964, is less known in Budapest than he deserves.*

NOTHING-NEVER

Ministers are rehabilitated.
They were shot and harmed in other ways.
"Not shame, but glory to their names!"
That's great, I agree; I am elated.

But I remember other things.
My mind still hears the hoot
Of black limousines; they haunt
Me like a nightmare of the past.
I can recall the roughnecks
Who've pulled the strings behind my vote;
Some German families who flew
Away in the wind like straw;
I recall death-cries and screams
From the cellars of the police.
Some thin peasants who were persuaded
With clubs which beat them round the head.
I recall the slaves who built
The Danube Canal with their hands,
And how well I remember empty slogans,
Trials of kulaks, labour camps.
Letters which were routinely opened,
Phones which were always bugged and tapped;
A whole people whom fear compelled
To adulate its murderers;
I remember my own life and
My father, dressed in prison garb.
And since it's only me who remembers
And no one else seems to take up their cause,
I'd like to suggest that the whole people
Should be rehabilitated at once.

And tell me who will ask forgiveness
From me, and who'll give consolation
For watching to the bitter end
This world-disrupting horror-passion?
Who'll make up for my barren years?

For the terrible fear in which I've lived,
For the poems which I've never written,
For those ones which I have destroyed?
For the insolent and stupid lies
Which I had to swallow unprotesting,
For the shame that to this very day
I had to shun my native language?
For the curse that ignorant fools
Have watched and pushed my pen on paper;
That those blatantly untalented
Could poke and fumble in my brain,
That I could not have become
What I could have been, who was awaited —
Who can make up for all this loss,
When will I be rehabilitated?

[1968]   *George Gömöri*

ANALOGY

Now I was thinking of those bacteria
which make their home within the human
body, inside, in the caverns
of the living flesh, finding
such a comfortable and naturally temperate
abode and such an abundant larder, too,
that they double their size every minute
and breed unhampered all the time.

Greedily, they eat and multiply,
until, full of vigour, at the zenith
of their power, suddenly: a blow —
they all have to go, they must vanish,
for having turned their own soil toxic,
for having killed what nurtured them before.

All this came to my mind when in the papers
I've read the boasting news that we, humans,
by 2007 — right in this extremely friendly,

cosy and domesticated world —
will exactly double our numbers.

George Gömöri

GALILEO

I've solved the riddles of the planets.
My brain has reached and felt the deepest points
of space, where wise attractions of the stars
unite in order, keeping up the balance.

Now, too, I turn my eyes towards the heavens
so I won't see the demented flock of priests
who'd, torch-like, send me to my death of flames,
while barking in their hunger fearful words.

My lips reveal, showing my inner self:
what was my reason may fall into pieces —
so I've recanted... Come, judge me anew!

Beware, posterity, that comes to shame me,
with a sarcasm that's worth a hundred deaths:
life's more important than eternal glory!

[1951]   *Adam Makkai* and *George Gömöri*

Géza Páskándi
(1933-1995)

A Transylvanian poet of the second post World War II generation, Páskándi was born in Szatmár (today Satu Mare in Romania). He studied law at the University of Kolozsvár (Cluj-Napoca). His first book of poetry Red Bird [Piros madár] *was published in 1957, but soon afterwards Páskándi's career was interrupted by his imprisonment, a result of the anti-minority repressive policies of the Gheorghiu-Dej régime. Although he was the descendant of a working class family, he was never affected by the Socialist-realist schematism prevailing in the area of Stalinism.*

He reappeared on the literary scene in the mid-sixties and published an interesting book of poetry entitled Moon-Boomerang [Holdbumeráng] *in 1967 and a collection of short stories entitled* Bottles [Üvegek] *in 1968.*

Páskándi's intellectual qualities did not limit the directness and the vividness of his poems; he shaped the language with admirable skill and a genuine sense of humor. He kept a strong attachment to the Hungarian poetic tradition, but his sense of literary mission made him a strong ally of the avant-garde at the same time. In one of his most significant collections of poetry The Eye of the Needle [Tű foka], *which appeared in 1972, he gives up the instruments of classical lyricism such as rhyming and allows the elements of heterogeneity, the grotesque and the dissonant to appear. Many a poem is a veritable puzzle for which readers have to find their own interpretation. His clusters of words and associations are so rich that the resultant poems give the impression of being unfinishable and unalterable.*

After his release from prison he worked in a book depot as a physical laborer; from 1971 to 1973, however, he was the chief editor of Kritérion, *a Bucharest-based Hungarian language publisher. He repatriated to Budapest, Hungary, in 1974 where he became the poetry editor of* Kortárs [The Contemporary]. *In 1977 he was awarded the Attila József Prize and in 1993 the Kossuth Prize. According to his own statement about his work, he was always inspired by the emotional thrust of his intellect. His poetry reflects a synthesis of sensuous and intellectual experiences. As a dramatist Páskándi pursued the kind of "theater of the absurd" whose aim was to search for the meaning of human existence. As a short story writer he concentrated on presenting a central thought surrounded by "absurd" situations reminiscent of his plays and of some of his unique poetry. His last volume* The Great Dilettantissimo [A nagy dilettantissimo] *appeared in 1989.*

LAST WILL AND TESTAMENT

I have a little pipe that I
will leave to Gussie when I die.

I have a book: please give it him
slyly whom I stole it from.

My friends some night (a dreadful pack!)
ought to break open this new deck.

My fee for this verse (should it come)
is Coloman's to waste on rum.

My room and all its furniture
to him who happens to live there.

My elvish lair I leave to him
who squeezes through the window-frame.

The mouse beneath my bed (squeak! squeak!)
to pussy, only if she's quick.

To the envious nose, a horse-radish root
as pungent as my pungent fate.

My poems must not lay down laws:
I leave my readers a rude noise.

A gorgeous set of rhymes — what takers?
Ideal for dogged doggerel makers.

All novelists without a theme
will find I've left a list for them.

And that exam I never took?
I leave some schoolboy better luck.

My lover, if she still loves me,
must hold on to my memory.

I leave to all aspiring Adams
this windfall: apples for their madams.

To the lugubrious, my grin;
and to the frolicsome, my frown.

My heart my mother may retain,
almost as gentle as her own.

I trust my father will look cute
in my not-half-worn two-piece suit.

I leave the belt to him, since he
so very often belted me.

A box of fat cigars for me,
in case I can't think what to say

when people ask me why on earth
I bothered to draw living breath.

J.G. Nichols

FIRST RESURRECTION

First resurrection, move forward —
second resurrection, move forward —
third, fourth, hundredth resurrection, move forward!

I too have risen.
All my resurrections have risen;
not counting the hours they have risen
from their grounds — my brothers.
They were counting their fingers with a lingering doubt
counting the pieces of their hair
and when it was done

they danced and feasted
each looking at an organ of his or hers
from which he would not
from which she would not part.
The slut gazed at her own lusty hillocks
the mother caressed her own breasts
the poet went to sleep on a little hedgehog
and looked up at the two women.

I took part in every feast
I wiped off the kisses of good companions
I shoved the Muse off
since her lips were sucking brains.
Somebody said: sports can only decline, not die.
A shout was heard: a resurrection for sale!
(But no one stated what the price was.)
I was just looking at the great noisy crowd
nectar dripping from their mouths
lukewarm fat crystallized as candle drips
and lilac-shaped beer-froth.
I watched them sharing the roast
quarrelling, screaming, shrieking.
Some were trampled to death in this primordial orgy —
I just looked on this buzzing whiz
and from my head Pallas
Athene sprang forth: Horror.

I knew then
than I am here
not because God had planned it
that my soul rose
not because there could be no world without
that I can walk, run, or dance
not because the rivers would stop for the want of me
I knew then
that my body rose
not for proving the flame of my spirit
that I rose
not to prove you
but because He is proved through me.

I came as bone-proof
that He is almighty here
and I knew then
that I will leave my feasting friends
and God
and will say to the world:
here I am Lazarus, who departs
here I am, going towards the people
he who dances through the minutest
eye of the needle
since it is terrible terrible terrible to picture
that the purpose of my life is just to be a carpet
under God
that I be loaned out like a *perpetuum mobile*
rent free
to prove a higher existence with flesh.
Since it is terrible terrible terrible to picture
that I should have no purpose of my own
and that I should just get a loan-existence
to be the aim-servant of my existence.
So here I am Lazarus, who departs
just walking towards the people
just dancing through the minutest
eye of the needle
and hissing up to God
but blessing men on the way —
          I forbid my resurrection!

Neville Masterman

FROM *THE EYE OF THE NEEDLE*

LANGUAGE MEMORY

22.
Close your eyes over my sins,
— after all, you do have lashes on your eyes.

52.
My shirt got torn to rags,
you patch it up!
Short are my pleasures,
you shore them up!
Tie a knot on my tie,
for it went bust;
lift up my heart,
it fell in the dust.

55.
You don't even have any sins!
How, then, could you possess the truth?!

118.
Mother of God, you tired Mary,
your fair hair is but matted glory.

129.
I have killed a virgin by being born,
yet so doing I managed to give birth to a mother.

166.
In the grass of the twilight: the seventh day is God.
I'm watching the balancing act of
insect acrobats.
The tune of the tough laments of nomads kicks up
to the sky.
A stamping of horse hooves —
they, like drum-sticks, strike up a thunder in the cosmos.
O you slumbering heavenly dulcimer!

Agnes Arany-Makkai

Ferenc Juhász
(b.1928)

The most prominent poet of his generation, Ferenc Juhász was born into a working-class family of peasant origin. Together with László Nagy (q.v.) and István Simon, he enthusiastically welcomed the socialist transformation of Hungary after 1945, but like the other conscientious reformers, he was deeply disturbed by the political atmosphere of the 1950s with its inevitable explosion in the Hungarian Uprising of 1956. While his personal fortunes changed little with the years, he moved from being a free-lance poet to the editorship of the monthly periodical Új Írás [New Writing].

His poetic style started to take on complex, indeed often visionary, overtones while extending to epic dimensions in terms of length. It was obvious to both his critics and his admirers that Juhász had built up an intensely personal poetic language, a private universe inhabited by biological monads, a cosmic world whose richness is unparalleled, but often difficult to penetrate.

His books include My Father [Apám], 1949; The Prodigal Country [Tékozló ország], 1954; The Force of Flowers [A virágok hatalma], 1956; The Land of Profusion [A tenyészet országa], 1957; The King of the Dead [A halottak királya], 1971; and The Underground Lily [A Föld alatti liliom], 1991. He was translated into English along with Sándor Weöres (q.v.), as well as into French.

George Steiner, the author of After Babel, considers his poem 'The Boy Turned Into A Stag Clamours at the Gate of Secrets' the best long poem ever composed, while the Canadian poet-translator David Wevill correctly identified Béla Bartók's Cantata Profana as Juhász's musical inspiration. Considering the millicentenary theme of the present volume, it would have been negligent not to include this extremely striking paraphrase of the 'Miracle Stag' theme, which persists on all levels of society in spite of its age.

Ethnomusicologist and anthropologist Irén Lovász has found even recently Hungarian shamanistic folk poetry in present day Slovenia, a now independent country that was formerly part of Yugoslavia but which has also been inhabited by some Hungarians from long before the days of the Austro-Hungarian Monarchy. (See the first piece in the 'Folk Poetry' section of this volume.)

Ferenc Juhász is the only living poet whose work is included in Volume I.

THE BOY CHANGED INTO A STAG
CLAMOURS AT THE GATE OF SECRETS

The mother called to her own son,
cried from far away,
the mother called to her own son,
cried from far away,
went to the front of the house:
from there she cried,
unwound her heavy knot of hair
dusk wove to a shimmering bride's veil
that flowed down to her ankles
a flag, tasselled, black, for the wind
the firedamp dusk smelled of blood.
She knotted her fingers to tendrils of stars,
the moon-froth covered her face,
and like this she cried to her dear son
as once she'd cried to her child —
stood in front of the house and spoke to the wind
spoke to the song-birds
to the love-cries of the wild geese
shouted across the wind-fingered reeds
to the luminous sprawled potato flower
to the stocky, cluster-balled bulls
to the sumack tree, shade of the well,
she called to the jumping fish
to the welding rings of water —
    Hush! you birds and branches
hush, because I'm calling
    be still, fishes and flowers
be still, I want to speak
    be quiet, breath of the soil
    fin-quiver leafy parasols
be still, deep humming of sap,
rumours that seep from the atoms' depths
    bronze-chaste virgins, wool-breasted flock
be quiet, because I'm calling,
I'm crying out to my own son!

The mother called to her own son
the scream rose upward, writhing
spiralling in the vortex of the universe —
its blade glittered in the light
like the scales of a spinning fish,
like metal in roads, nitre in caves.
The mother called to her own son:
come back, my dear son, come back
I am calling you, I, your mother!
I am calling you, I, your river-bed
    I am calling you, your fountainhead
come back, my son, come back
    I call you, your memory's teat
come back, my son, come back
    I call you, your ragged tent
come back, my son, come back
    I call you, your guttering lamp.

Come back my son, I'm always knocking against things,
I have bruise-stains under my eyes, on the skin of my brow,
my calves, my thighs —
objects charge and butt me like angry rams,
the garden stake, chairs, the fence gore me terribly,
doors thump me like Saturday drunkards,
the light's broken, the switch gives me shocks,
blood crawls in this skin of veins as through the beak of a
        stone-bruised bird,
    the scissors swim off like metal craps,
matchsticks hop like sparrows' legs, the bucket handle hits back —
come back, my dear son, come back
I can no longer run like the young mother doe,
    my legs are ripe with bindweed,
    knotty, purplish roots grew in my thighs,
my toes swell with calcium-mounds,
    my fingers stiffen, with flesh tough as shell,
like snail's horn scaly, like old shale-rock,
    my branches are sickly, dry and ready to snap —
come back, my son, come back
    for I'm spellbound,

haggard, and fool of visions —
they flicker from my decaying glands
as the winter morning cock-crow
pings of the frozen shirts hung on a fence —
I call you, your own mother,
come back, my son, come back —
give meaning to all these things,
control them again: tame the knife,
   make the stubborn comb show itself,
for I'm just two green gritty eyes,
bubbles of light: like a dragonfly,
   which as you know, my child
   carries between its nape and jaw
two crystal apples that fill its whole skull,
I am two huge eyes without a face,
and their vision is not of this world.
Come back, my son, come back —
   breathe life into things again.

      The boy listened,
      he tossed his head,
      with nostrils like pails he
      sniffed, his dewlap quivering —
      his veined ears pricked at the sound
      of that crying voice, his body tenses
      as if sensing the hunter's footstep
      or a whiff of smoke in the forest
      when the smoke-blue forest
      mourns its own burning, whimpering.
      He swung his head that way
      hearing the familiar voice cry,
      suddenly stiffened with fear —
      on his rump he noticed the fur,
      discovered the split hooves,
      stared at his cudweed shanks,
      at his furry buck-apples
      hidden there, where the lily shines.
      He galloped across to a pool,
      his chest plowed through ferns,
      body a muck of foam

gouts of leather smacking the ground;
his four black hooves
stamp life from the flowers,
a tiny lizard is squashed, its
crushed neck-bib and tail grow cold.
He stoops over the pool,
stares into the moonlit water —
a beech tree with the moon its hair
shudders — the pool reflects a stag!
Then he sees that the thick fur
covers his body all over —
fur covers his knees and thighs,
his tassel-lipped penis sheath,
and antlers grow from his head
where the bone branches have budded,
his face is furred to the chin,
the cut of his nostrils slanting in.
He whacks his antlers against a tree,
his neck a rope of veins,
paws the ground, his nerves strain
choking to bellow a cry —
but it's only the voice of a stag
his mother hears echoing back —
he'd weep the tears of a son,
and blows till the watery monster is gone,
blows, and in his breath's whirlpool
in the liquid midnight sparkle
little fishes with petal fins
scatter, their eyes like diamond-bubbles.
When the water's feathers settle again
it is a stag that stands in the moon-foam.

Now the boy shouted back
    bellowing, stretching his neck
the boy shouted back
    a stag's voice wildering through the fog —
mother, mother
I can't go back
mother, my mother

don't call me back
my nurse, my nurture
mother, mother
marvellous foaming spring
roof I grew up under
breasts with swollen buds
tent sheltering me from the frost
mother, my mother
don't ask me to come
mother, my mother
my one silky flower
my bird of gold
mother, mother,
don't call me back!
If I were to go back
my antlers would spear you,
my horns, tip to tip,
I'd toss your old body —
if I were to go back
I'd tumble you on the ground
with these hooves I'd squash
your little breasts
my horns would stab you and stab
you, I'd bite you —
I'd trample your loins
if I went back
mother, mother,
I'd rip you soul from body
bluebottles would flock to it —
the stars would gape
in shame at your soft lily-cleft,
though this gave me once
such lovely, tender warmth
in its lustre of oils,
warmth such as the breathing
cattle gave Jesus.
Mother, mother
you mustn't call me —
you'd turn to stone
you'd die, if you saw

your son coming.
Each branch of my horns
is a coil of gold rings
each twig of each branch
is a candlestick-cluster
each fang-sharp tip
is a fine funeral candle
each lace frond of horn
is a gold altar-cloth.
Believe me, you'd die
if you saw my sprawling
antlers filling the sky —
as on All Souls' Eve
the graveyard is lit
by candles, leaf by leaf,
my head is a petrified tree.
Mother, mother
if I found you
I'd scorch you to
a blackened stump,
I'd burn you to a lump
of greasy clay,
I'd roast you to chunks
of charred black meat.
Mother, mother,
don't call to me —
if I went back
I'd eat you up
I'd wreck the house
with my thousand-tipped horns
I'd slash
the flowerbeds to pieces
I'd rip up the trees
with my stag's teeth
I'd swallow the well
in one gulp —
if I went back
I'd set fire to the house
then I'd gallop off

to the burial-plot
and with delicate nose
and all four hooves
I'd dig up my father —
I'd tear off the lid
of his coffin with my teeth —
I'd scatter his bones!
Mother, mother,
don't call me back,
I can't go back.
If I did go back,
I would kill you.

So the boy cried with a stag's voice,
and the mother answered him,
   come back, come back my son
I'm calling you, I, your own mother
   come back, my son, come back
I'll cook you sour-cabbage soup, you can slice onion rings into it,
they'll crunch in your teeth like bits of stone in a giant's jaws,
I'll give you warm milk in a clean glass,
in my cellar the lair of fire-bellied frogs
in my cellar blinking like a giant green toad
I'll gently pour wine into heron-necked bottles,
with my stony fists I'll knead bread — for I know, I know
how to bake round little froth-bellied loaves, and Sunday twists —
         come back, come back my son,
I plucked the crops of live, shrieking geese for your feather bed,
I cried, I plucked, the geese cried... The feather-wounds drooled white
     fat,
I sunned your straw mattress, I shook it out,
the clean-swept courtyard is listening for you, the table is laid.

         Aiii, mother, mother
            I cannot go back,
         don't give me your twist of milk-loaf
            or sweet goat's milk in a flowered glass!
         Don't make my bed springy and soft
            or pluck out the throats of the geese —
         throw the wine away, pour it over your father's grave,

weave the onions into a wreath,
fry your frothy doughnuts for the little ones now.
> For the warm milk would turn to vinegar in my mouth,
> a stone would squat in place of the milk loaf,
> the wine in my glass would turn into blood,
> each soft bed-feather become a flame,
> the small drinking mug a blade of blue sword-lily.
Aiii mother, aiii, aiii mother —
> I can't go back to my birthplace now.
Only the green forest can hold me,
> the house is too small for my huge, furry horns,
the courtyard has no space for my graveyard antlers,
> the shaking world-tree of my branching antlers
with stars as its leaves, the Milky Way as its moss.
> I can only eat sweet-smelling grass,
the tender young grass is my cud —
> I can no longer drink from a flowered glass,
only from a spring, only from a clean, fresh spring!

I don't understand, I don't understand your strange talk, son
you speak with a stag's voice, the soul of a stag moves in you,
> my poor one.
When the turtle dove weeps, turtle dove weeps, the little
> bird calls, little bird calls, my son
why am I, why am I in all creation the unhappy one?
Do you still remember, still remember your little mother, my son?
I don't understand, I don't understand your piteous crying, son.
Do you remember how happily you'd come running home,
> with your school-report,
you dissected frogs, nailed their speckled webby hands to the fence,
lost yourself in your airplane books, helped me in with the washing?
You were in love with little Irene B.... V.J., and H.S. the painter,
> his beard like a wild orchid, was your friend.
Do you still remember, Saturday nights when your father
> came home sober, how happy you were?

Aiii, mother, mother, don't remind me. My sweetheart and friends,
> they swam from me cold like fish. The poppy-throated painter,
> who knows where he went, mother? Where my youth went?

Mother, mother, don't mention my father. Sorrow flowers,
  blossoms from his flesh of earth. Don't mention my father —
  he'll get up from his grave, gather up his yellow bones
  and come staggering out — his nails, his hair sprouting again.
Aiii, aiii! Old Wilhelm came, the coffin-maker, runt with a doll's face.
  He said I'll grab your feet, will put you nicely into the box —
  but I started retching with fear. I'd just come back from Pest,
  you used to go there too, by train... a caretaker... the rails got
      twisted.
  Aiii, I have cut myself to pieces, the candle puddling shadows on
      your taut face —
Latzi, our new brother-in-law, the barber, shaved you. The candles
      drooled like babies,
  their innards melting out, dribbles, the bowels gleaming, the nerves
      shining through.
  The Choral Society stood around in their purple caps, lowing your
      death like cattle,
  and I touched your forehead, your hair was alive,
  I heard it grow, saw the bristles beginning on your chin —
  by morning your chin was black, next day your throat was spiky
      like stalks of viper's bugloss,
  a slice of hairy melon, a yellow caterpillar with a blue-cabbage
      skin.
Aiii, I thought it would outgrow the room, the courtyard, the whole
      world
  your beard and hair, the stars in it humming like vermin.
Aiii, aiii! In the dense green of rain, the red horses pulling your hearse
      whinnied in fear —
  one kicked out at your head, the other pissed helplessly, its purple
  cock flopped out like a hanged man's tongue, the coachman swore,
  rain washed the blare of the brass band, your mates were blowing
      and sobbing,
  stood blowing by the thorny, thistled chapel wall,
  blew out a basket of silvery breath from their puffed black lips,
  blew the tune with cracked bloody lips and bloodshot eyes,
  blew the card games, wines-and-sodas, the bloated and withered
      women,
  blew the minted planets of coins, baksheesh, up into the void after
      you,
  blew the thick dust of hopelessness away, sobbing. The tune

blared from the hard, glinting O-mouthed horns into a void stinking
    of corpses —
petrified loves, decaying women, the mouldering militias of
    grandfathers,
cottages, cradles, enamel and silver onion pocket-watches,
Easter bells multiplying redeemers like a bird's wing fanning,
trumpeting briefcases, train-wheels, brass-buttoned ratings stiff with
    salutes.
They blew with gum-pink teeth, the friends, with black puffy liver
    lips,
and you led them: That's it, lads! That's great! Aiii, don't stop
    playing —
your hands, crossed, a pair of gold spiders, long legs, jointed,
    hinged spokes of your heart.
Your shoes in the cupboard await for the next-of-kin, your
    breadcrust-callous feet look childlike, helpless in their white
    socks,
and your mates blew on in the dashing rain, the trumpet-stops
    hiccupped like steel Adam's apples,
like claws of the reptile bird, Carchadoron's teeth, the brass
    trumpets glittered.
Aiii, mother, mother, don't speak of my father.
Leave him be, his eyes stare from the earth like buds.

The mother called to her own son,
    cried from far away
come back my son, come back
    come away from that stone world
stag of the stone forest, smogs, electric grids and neon glitter.
    The iron bridges and tramlines, they thirst for your blood,
        a hundred times a day they jab you, but you never hit back —
    I am calling you, I, your own mother
        come back my son, come back.

There he stood on the crest of all time,
there he stood on creation's highest mountain,
there he stood at the gate of secrets —
the points of his antlers played with the stars
and with a stag's voice he cried,

cried back to the mother who'd borne him —
    mother, mother, I can't go back
the hundred wounds in me weep pure gold,
I die every day, a hundred bullets in me
every day I get up again a hundred times stronger
I die every day three billion deaths
and three billion times a day I am born,
each prong of my antlers a twin-legged pylon
each branch of my antlers a high-tension wire,
my eyes are ports of cargo-ships, my veins are greased cables,
my teeth are iron bridges, my heart is a thrashing ocean of monsters,
each vertebra is a thriving city, my spleen is a chuffing stone-barge,
each cell is a vast factory, every atom a solar system,
my testicles are the sun and moon, the Milky Way is my spine-
    marrow,
each point in space is one grain of my body,
each galaxy is an inkling of my brain.

Son, my lost son, I still want you back —
    your mother's eyes, like a dragonfly's, won't rest until you come.

To die I'll come back, only to die.
To die I'll come back,
mother — only to die will I come.
Then you can lay me out in my childhood home,
with your age-veined hands you can wash my body,
close my eyelids, swollen glands with kisses.
    And when the flesh falls off me,
and the stench it was sweetens to flowers,
    I'll be a foetus drinking your blood,
I'll be your little boy again —
and this hurts only you, mother,
    aiii, hurts only you, mother.

David Wevill

IX. "A NATION AND ITS POETRY"

by
László Cs. Szabó

A Nation and Its Poetry
by
László Cs. Szabó

(This study deals primarily with literary and other artistic trends and with the links between the nation's history and its poetry. As such, it is not intended to be a complete history of Hungarian poetry, much less of Hungarian literature as a whole.

In this first volume we cover only those authors whose lives' works are now complete, plus a single poem by a living author without which the theme of the 'Miracle Stag' would be incomplete.

Volume II, which is forthcoming, will present in detail the work of living Hungarian poets, regardless of their domicile or citizenship. [A.M.])

***

"When a Pole wants to explain some facet of his work, he starts by giving one a lecture on Polish history. And he is probably right, for in Poland very little is understandable except by reference to the past. Thus, the first thing one is told at the studios of Łódż in Poland is that for two hundred years the nation's real leaders have generally been the artists."[1]

Within these few sentences, the basic attitude of typical Central Europeans, including the Hungarians who are friends and neighbors of the Poles, is established through the eyes of an outsider. Ask a Hungarian about the weather and he will look up at the sky and reply

---

[1] *Poland,* by William Woods, London, 1972, p. 146. The present essay was first completed by the author in 1972. A rough translation of it was subsequently prepared by Paul Tabori and has since been edited by Earl M. Herrick. Shortly before his death Professor Cs. Szabó asked me to make sure it was up to date when it finally appeared. I have therefore added events, names, and movements after 1972, as well as references to the development of Hungarian poetry beyond the early 1970s. I have also added all of the footnotes. [A.M.]

with an added sigh, which automatically contains the memory of the conquest of his country; then he sighs again, and in that sigh the disaster of the battle of Mohács is encapsulated.[2] Both the Pole and the Hungarian are, alas, entirely correct.

Turning to his poets, the Hungarian's respect is accorded in equal measure to a poet's attitude and to his work; to call someone a "great character" is just as much of a positive evaluation as calling him "The Great Master." It would make little sense to couple these two possible views—the social and the artistic—in the case of Leopardi,[3] Keats, or Baudelaire; but in the case of Petőfi (q.v.), both his past and his present compatriots actually expect it.

Nations often know little of each other, even if they happen to be neighbors. In earlier times, it was the painfully overcome distance alone that nourished these misconceptions—more recently, it is the jet-plane throng that only sits on the hot sand of a beach during the daytime or in a strumming tavern in the moonlight.

Whatever the world knows about Hungary and the Hungarians is largely the decaying remnant of cheap pulp novels. In the imagination of foreigners, the country offered some cosmopolitan "pashas," who were the aristocrats, and some picturesque "bedouins," the herdsmen and the highwaymen, just like in the Egypt that disappeared but yesterday. A modern biography of Haydn still maintains that fate must be capricious because (lo and behold!) the intellectually demanding, new form of the Classical symphony was shaped not in the urbanized West, but on the Hungarian *puszta* (the Hungarian prairie), where Classical Viennese music came of age.

Yet the Austrian musician who served his Hungarian patron never actually experienced the *puszta*. The landscape where he lived was very much like the environs of Vienna. Of course some small and great

---

[2] In 1526, the Ottoman emperor Suleiman the Great, leading one of the world's most modern and powerful armies, which was armed with guns, wiped out the Hungarian army, composed of only light cavalry and infantry, near the city of Mohács in southern Hungary. Thus began a period of 150 years during which Hungary was divided into a Turkish-dominated south-central part, a western part under the Austrian Empire, and the independent Duchy of Transylvania in the east, which paid taxes to the Sultan.

[3] Giacomo Leopardi (1798–1837), Italian poet and scholar who wrote superb lyric poetry despite a life filled with frustrations which led him to an attitude of extreme pessimism; he also edited the works of Cicero.

pashas still existed, and so did the herdsmen and the highwaymen. It was the tragic twist of Hungary's national history that turned such characters loose on a land which, at the end of the Middle Ages, had a different, much more civilized look to it, well planted with Romanesque abbeys and Gothic parish churches. In addition, there were some fanciful Hungarian writers who, albeit innocently but by no means harmlessly in their effect, romanticized such bandits and robber barons. Yet ever since the last third of the 18th century, the hotbed of Hungary's burgeoning national consciousness has been its intellectual middle class, with its revolutionary spirit, not unlike the one that set the Young Turks' movement ablaze at the beginning of our century and after World War II transformed many former colonies into neo-nationalist states. It was this class, too, that launched Hungarian romantic poetry in its time.

A nation that is certain of its identity rarely thinks of itself. If it should be unsure, it is concerned with almost nothing else. Who am I? What is a *Magyar?* The Hungarians have spent as much ardent passion on this question as, say, Oxford has spent on disputes over moral philosophy or linguistic logic. The nation was worried and uncertain of itself by its isolation in the middle of Europe, while from the outside it suffered a series of historical blows, partly of its own doing, but also because of ill fortune. For a good four hundred years, Hungary was a considerable power along the Danube. Its kings fetched their wives from Bamberg, Byzantium, Paris, Kiev, and twice from the Norman court in Palermo; but since the middle of the 16th century, it has not been as independent as England or Spain.

The idea of "Fate" has always played a more important role in the faiths of nomadic populations than in the religions of agricultural nations. It made it easier to accept the incessant struggle for the *puszta*'s grazing territories. Such a spiritual heritage has also survived among the settled descendants of the formerly nomadic Hungarians. Like both the besiegers and the besieged of Homer, chosen for death, they do not budge from the battlefield, for no one can escape Fate. And if one must make a stand, let it be made with one's head held high and with a defiant smile on one's face, cracking a joke.

And so, indeed, after frequent destruction, Budapest rose from its ashes as often as did Jerusalem.

From the Beginnings to the Disaster

"Are we Orientals or Occidentals?"—the self-searching Hungarian, brooding over his identity, asks. And if the essence of a Hungarian is Eastern in its origins, to what extent has it been spiritually transformed into a Western mold? The roots of this pondering are more emotional than rational, and after so many tribulations, it is linked to a nostalgic dream which says that Magyar fate might have been better and easier to endure elsewhere. This "elsewhere" might be some place west of present-day Hungary, or, paradoxically, back in the East whence they came to their present location in the Carpathian Basin. It is significant that the kindred Finns, living on a similar level of civilization, are not tormented by this question.

A partial answer can be found in Hungary's centuries-old folk ballads. Their Eastern and Western elements had already been firmly amalgamated by the end of the Middle Ages. Faithful to the unwritten, international laws of this *genre*, the great majority of these ballads are deliberately harsh, but they also include certain Christian visions, probably due to a pronounced Franciscan monastic influence. Otherwise, Hungary remained outside the upheavals of the mystical and heretical movements within Christianity, and it is quite understandable that the Hussites,[4] too, made only minor theological inroads into Hungary from the Bohemian North, because, beneath its upper current of a religious revolution, some contemporary Hungarians were more swept along by its early nationalistic undertow.

Although the first Hungarian king had established pilgrims' homes in Rome and Ravenna, Hungarian family names do not include any such name as *'Pálmás'* (which would be the equivalent of the English surname *'Palmer,'* frequently found in the English speaking world), and among given names one seldom finds *Christian,* common enough in French and Danish. Nor are there any Hungarian names like *Gottfried* or *Gottlieb,* which are rather frequent in German. There were several centuries of European madness during which witch-hunters

---

[4] Jan Hus (1369–1415), founder of a revolutionary movement against feudalism and the Roman Catholic Church, was sentenced to death at the Council of Constance in 1414 and was burned at the stake. Emperor Sigismund and Pope Martin V launched a crusade against the Hussites in 1420. Hussitism is generally regarded as a forerunner of the Reformation.

tried to indoctrinate Hungarians with their theology of intolerance, but their success was scant. The Hungarian loved the Lamb, but the Devil he treated rather like a joke, making no attempt to use flames to drive Satan out of his fellow Hungarians.[5]

Numerically speaking, folk ballads represent but a fragment of popular poetry. The immensely rich trove of ballad material began to be collected systematically near the end of the 1820s, with the major impetus coming from John Bowring,[6] a man of universal interest and adventurous life who was well-versed in Hungarian literature. Additional impetus came from Scotland and Finland and—with the blessings of Goethe—from the general influence of German Romanticism. For the Germans not only encouraged the work of British amateurs, but rounded it off with a Rousseaunian theory. A song, this theory said, was the purest mirror of the uncorrupted, ancient, national soul.

Musicologists and ethnographers, closely allied, still continue to collect anonymous songs and verses, not only in Hungary, but also in other Magyar-speaking settlements, particularly in Romania. This treasure-boat, now dangerously close to sinking because of discrimination against the Hungarian language in the successor states of the Austro-Hungarian Monarchy, has inspired generations of researchers in their rescue work. Before it finally disappeared, Bartók and Kodály[7]

---

[5] King Coloman the Learned (Könyves Kálmán, 1068–1116, reigned 1095–1116, issued an edict in Latin which said *"De strigiis, quae non sunt, nulla questio fiat."* ('About witches, who do not exist, there shall be no discussion.')

[6] (1792–1872). He travelled all over Europe and visited Hungary in 1837, where he befriended Ferenc Toldy and Mihály Vörösmarty. In his anthology entitled *The Poetry of the Magyars* (1830), he published English translations of 64 folk songs and 96 poems by 26 poets including Zrínyi, Kazinczy, Sándor Kisfaludy, Csokonai, Berzsenyi, Kölcsey, and Vörösmarty (qq.v.). In 1866, he published a volume entitled *Translations from Alexander Petőfi, the Magyar Poet*. He used German translations in order to better understand the Hungarian texts. When he died, he was translating Jókai, the novelist.

[7] Béla Bartók (1881–1945) and Zoltán Kodály (1882–1967) were composers who started out as colleagues and close friends. Bartók left Hungary in protest against Nazism and spent the years of World War II in the U.S.A., where he died. Kodály remained in Hungary as a focus of intellectual resistance against both Nazism and Communism. His music remained more traditional. They jointly discovered the "Eurasian Pentatonic Melody Circle."

gave it a new, powerful impetus; their specialist knowledge was laced with an immense amount of love and care, which extended to foreign music and folklore as well as to North Africa and to Anatolia in Turkey.

The collecting of folk poetry was immediately extended to poetry in general. This in fact was an international phenomenon, for in the eyes of the Romantics all over Europe it counted as an outstanding merit if a *Lied*, although signed by an individual, spoke as though it had originated anonymously, emerging from an imaginary "national psyche." Later, this initial inspiration became cheapened and bourgeois, changing into a lower-middle-class *genre* typified in art, for example, by second- or third-rate paintings that featured landscapes studded with people dressed in peasant costumes. But this did not last forever. Under the all-pervading effect of Bartók's music, poets with a modern feeling for life turned, this time without any imitative intention, to the deepest pre-Christian layers of poetry to search for formal and linguistic elements.

This phenomenon is, to a certain extent, characteristic of British literature as well. In the atmosphere of a formal, enclosed, aristocratic society, the songs of Burns still mingle only with the upper layers of folklore materials, showing stylistic affinity with Baroque and Rococo. But when, in the neo-barbarian atmosphere of an atomized, permissive society, Auden began to depict the voyage of contemporary man through the winter of solitude, he dug his way back for linguistic help to the granite foundations of archaic Iceland and Anglo-Saxon poetry.

Did the Hungarians have an epic dealing with their ancestral deeds? A saga about battles, the capturing of the land, and their leaders? Surely they had to; even African tribes have such epics. Alas, everything that Hungary's illiterate bards preserved from one century to the next seems to have disappeared. Yet at first the professional *regős*es—Hungary's bards—even had their own villages. But the literate priests found their songs 'devilish' and actually persecuted them; and so these songs were never written down. The royal chronicles, how-ever, were written in Latin and served dynastic interests, and Latin legends devoted to ecclesiastical purposes were preserved. Between these two, the Hungarian epic, sung or recited in Magyar, was the silent victim. The clergy had also attacked the "wicked flower-songs," which were actually the old, genuine Hungarian folk poetry. But these pieces of folk lyric turned out to be far more enduring. As if mocking its indignant enemy, this folk poetry absorbed several vagrant songs, as well as the musical testimonials of itinerant priests, drop-outs, and tumbleweeds. Also absorbed into such folk lyrics were the songs of educated but drink-sodden customers of the inns, singing about the pleasures of the flesh and the world.

About the same time, in the 15th century, recorded literature in their native languages began to burgeon with great vigor in Hungary, Bohemia, and Poland. This contemporaneity is understandable, for these three countries were not only neighbors tightly linked through commerce, but around the end of the first millennium of the Christian era they simultaneously developed into independent kingdoms under three separate dynasties. Following the slow urbanization that characterized the region, a new kind of intense religious life, the *devotio moderna*,[8] flowered in the cities, with its main centers in Flanders on the Atlantic seaboard and in Prague in Central Europe. In the latter place, its gentle initial smouldering was fanned into Hussitism, which lit up half of Europe. Universities were founded—belatedly, of course, as compared with their founding at Padua, Cambridge, and Paris. But the first Hungarian printing presses were already functioning two years before Caxton's[9] London enterprise. In the sunset years of the Middle Ages, although not for long, Central Europe seemed to have caught up with the West.

This was the period of Hungary's sudden, brief flourishing under its king Matthias Corvinus.[10] He was a contemporary of Louis XI of

---

[8] Founded by Gerhard Groote (1340–1384), a Dutchman who was educated in Paris and Prague. He demanded a deepening of religion, criticizing the abuses of both the priesthood and the laity. *De Imitatione Christi* [The Imitation of Christ], the main book of the movement, may have originated from Groote's diary. It had a strong effect on the Humanists of the Netherlands, on the Reformation, and particularly on Erasmus.

[9] William Caxton (1422–1491), the first English printer. He learned printing in Cologne, Germany, and in 1475 he produced at Bruges the first printed English book, his own translation of *The Recuyell of the Historyes of Troye,* by R. Lefevre. He then moved back to England, where, before his death, he printed more than 100 books, 24 of them his own translations.

[10] Matthias Corvinus (1443–1490, reigned 1458–1490). He was the son of János Hunyadi, of Serbian ancestry, who had defeated the Turks at Belgrade (called Nándorfehérvár in Hungarian) in 1456. In memory of this

France and Henry VII of England and similar to both. Leaning on the support of Hungarian and foreign mercenaries, he organized a national kingdom upon the ruins of feudalism, just as the Valois king had. But while the life-style of the secretive and cunning French monarch was still medieval, Matthias, as if anticipating the manner of Henry VII's son Henry VIII, united under a golden canopy the royal idea of his own time with the shining idea of *virtus,* the glory of ancient Rome. The proper framework for such an attitude had to be imported from Northern Italy. Among the greatest scholars of his age, the exceptionally learnèd Philippe de Commynes,[11] the chronicler of Louis XI, also paid tribute to Matthias. It is an infernal joke of fate that he mentioned the Hungarian king in the same breath with another great man—none other than Mohammed II, the conqueror of Byzantium who, over the ruins and the trampled bodies of that city's defenders, opened the way for his successors to conquer Buda,[12] Matthias's capital. There was a Florentine bookseller, Vespasiano da Bisticci,[13] whose records of his international clientele were the Sotheby catalogue of his age. Just as today's art collectors vie for paintings, the jealous medieval princes competed in their bids for painted codices. A rival of the Prince of Urbino and of Lorenzo di

---

victory the Pope ordered the church bells rung at noon throughout Christendom, a practice that continues to this day. Hunyadi's victory delayed the advance of the Turks into Europe by half a century. His son, Matthias, was Hungary's 'Renaissance King.' His short 32-year reign constituted Hungary's golden years of culture, and his library, the *'Corvinae,'* was the largest in Europe with the exception of that of the Prince of Urbino. Matthias imported noted humanists from Italy, such as Galeotto Marzio (1427–1497), who wrote a great deal about his host, and Antonio Bonfini (1434–1503), who wrote a history of Hungary commissioned by Matthias.

[11] (1447–1511). Because of his mature and objective judgment, he is regarded as the first French historian in the modern sense.

[12] Today's Budapest originally consisted of two separate entities, Buda and Pest. Buda was the name of a son of Attila the Hun; the word Pest is Slavic in origin and means 'oven' or 'furnace.' It is known to be a Slavic cognate of the English words *bake* and *bakery.* The letter 's' in *Budapest* is pronounced like English 'sh', or /š/ as in *sugar* and *sure.* Buda and Pest were united to form today's Budapest in 1872.

[13] (1421–1498). He wrote the biography of Janus Pannonius (q.v.) and also wrote a great deal about Matthias. He employed some sixty copyists in order to be able to supply the demands of the courts.

Medici, Matthias was one of his most eager clients. Nor was Matthias the only collector in Hungary—he was equalled by some of his own high-court dignitaries, especially the Primate of the country, the Cardinal János Vitéz.[14] During this period Italian humanists and miniaturists moved to Buda, while the king and János Vitéz—acting for his king in the same way as Cardinal Wolsey would do in England—sent talented Hungarian youths to famous professors in Ferrara and Padua to obtain a superior education. Just as Polidoro Vergilio acted as Henry VIII's chief of propaganda, so did Antonio Bonfini act for Matthias. Their task was the same: following Livy's style of presentation, they constructed an inspiring, smoothly moving national myth out of the misty depths of the past to support their patrons' tyrannical organization of their respective countries. They carried out their tasks brilliantly, especially Bonfini. His history, a consoling Magyar gospel, became a second Bible in the hands of later generations when, with the Turks pressing them hard, Hungarians had to adjust psychologically to their new, tragic situation. Hungarians eagerly embraced the legend of Matthias. With the aid of this Italian court chronicler, they created within themselves an unimpaired, virtual fatherland, under different sovereignty, upon the soil of their dismembered country. Janus Pannonius (q.v.), the first significant Hungarian poet, was one of the youths sent to Italy for a finishing course. He was a Hungarian centuries ahead of his age, especially in his nostalgia, since he felt like an exile in his own land after his return. In this 'barbarian' setting he longed for the magic garden of the "Great Female Magician" (meaning Italy and her culture), but at the same time he improvised heart-rending poetic miniatures of his native Hungarian landscape. Through oratory and correspondence, humanist Free-masonry had its own international state, which, nevertheless, soon accepted within the jealously guarded frontiers of its Ciceronian Latin the enthusiastic, brainy Hungarian, Janus Pannonius.

He was deliberately elegant, vain, and educated—a typical humanist poet, whose constant ailments cast a dramatic shadow over his rhetoric, as did the bitterness which, after a spoiled, carefree youth, begins to gnaw at all sensitive people if they feel they have been slighted. His

---

[14] His exact birth-date is unknown; he died in 1472. In 1465 he founded the *Academia Istropolitana,* a university in which the teachers were renowned humanists. He was the personal tutor of King Matthias and of the poet Janus Pannonius (q.v.).

hurt feelings swept him into a conspiracy against the king, but his weakened health could not stand the excitement, and death overtook him while he was escaping. Janus Pannonius can be compared to the Latin satirical poet Martial.[15] Imported humanism might have become rooted in Hungary, and it might have led to a defense of the native tongue by expressing its superiority, after a generation or two, over Latin. This is what Du Bellay[16] did in France, and Sir Philip Sidney in England. But the death of Matthias destroyed his political edifice, and once more feudalism gained the upper hand, especially after the failure of the 1514 peasant uprising.[17] Yet amid the growing anarchy, the circle of the second generation of humanists still expanded for a while. They turned, not to the south, but to the north, drawn by the magnetic field of the newest, most brilliant star, Erasmus.

The Battle of Mohács, on August 29, 1526, was fateful. After it, Hungary was never again what she had been before. The king[18] fell, and his widow, a Habsburg princess, fled to the Netherlands, where she became the deputy of her brother, Emperor Charles V. Erasmus tried to console the lonely woman with a little book,[19] and his despondent spiritual disciples, who were Protestant village preachers, began to try to console the forsaken Magyar people.

It was in this manner and at this time that Hungarian literature was born.

---

[15] Marcus Valerius Martialis (38 or 41–104), Roman poet, who wrote sharp, epigrammatic satires. He had an influence on Janus Pannonius's early style.

[16] Joachim Du Bellay (1522–1560) who, together with Pierre de Ronsard (1524–1585) and Lazare de Baïf (1496–1547), formed the French school of the 'Pléiade,' whose goal was the renewal of French cultural life in an antique, Dionysian style.

[17] Led by György Dózsa (his birth-date is unknown), who was cruelly executed by being seated on a white-hot metal throne, after which his officers were forced to eat his flesh. Dózsa was the chief officer of a crusade, originally intended to fight the Turks, which changed into a major peasant uprising against feudalism. This civil war, which was won by the nobility, devastated the country and thereby contributed to Hungary's weakness, which became evident at the disaster of Mohács in 1526.

[18] Louis II (1506–1526) of the Lithuanian-Polish Jagiellon dynasty. He ascended the Hungarian throne in 1516.

[19] Entitled *Vidua Christiana* [The Christian Widow], it appeared in 1529.

Song during the Rain of Blood

Throughout Europe, modern literature crystallized in the sixteenth century, with the help of printing ventures around two poles—the capital of the country and the court. The two were not always identical. Imagine Shakespeare without London, or Ronsard without Fontainebleau, and both of them without printers! Their works would probably have been almost entirely lost. In this age, for the first time, the writer began to feel the presence of an anonymous public apart from his patron. It was not his financial circumstances that changed so radically—in these he was still a helpless and exploited partner. It was his acoustics that had changed.

In Hungary from 1541 on, Buda was the seat of a Turkish governor, while the remnants of the national kingdom were shared by two rulers. In the west, with Vienna as his capital, a foreign Germanic king ruled; in the east, ruling in Transylvania, was a Hungarian Prince, a vassal of the Sultan of Turkey.

Literature took refuge in the castle and in the parsonage. Sometimes the latter had a hand-press, for the village priest was often both a poet and a printer in a small way, but the majority of the books by Hungarian authors were printed abroad, in Cracow, in Vienna, and, the finest of them, in Switzerland.

In the castles a new epic of heroic deeds and exploits was born. There were so many sieges in the eroding border zones that they supplied an inexhaustible source for an uncouth, lesser Iliad. Their authors were rhyming war-correspondents, their life-style that of a singing front-line service for very meagre rewards. In those days, wine was the universal medicine, although the throat-burning plonk and the people who doled it out in the fortresses were abused even worse by the students and soldiers who drank it than by the Turks. One of these warrior-minstrels acquired nation-wide fame: Sebastian, a student from Tinód (q.v.), whose native village had been destroyed. He and the others composed for the ear, not for the eye; without the accompaniment of the lute or lyre and the human voice, their texts seem spiritless, even if some of the better known extant examples were later printed with musical notation added.

Hungarians complain to this day among themselves that, while their ancestors were relegated to the bastions and cellars and to the lute-picking of itinerant students, the protected West, behind the shield of Hungary, delighted in Monteverdi's madrigals. But, judged by the grim public mood of the second half of the century, the West did not feel itself invulnerable, either. And even if the West was defended against the Turk, who could defend it against itself? Hacked-off heads were sometimes served on silver platters to the accompaniment of Monteverdi's madrigals, and even in the West, music-making was mostly restricted to the blissful intervals between the perennial battles. At other times people were occupied with Spanish and French military maneuvers, the naval exploits of English pirates, and the tumult of the various wars of religion. Although no one would gladly risk a visit to Hungary, Monteverdi accompanied his patron, the Duke of Mantua, on an expedition there in 1595. Hungary's world was, it would seem, not entirely alien; after all, the children of the century staged St. Bartholomew's Days in the protected half of Europe—one big one and many small ones—and music was often drowned out by screams rising from torture chambers.

If the singer of the frontier fortresses was on the move because of the sieges, the incumbent of the parsonage was made homeless because of the battles. Sometimes he was the only one of his tiny flock and his burned village to escape alive. In England, too, the parsonage had been the nest of poets, a quiet nest like George Herbert's.[20] Its Hungarian occupant does not fit with the 'gardening mystics'; rather, he shared the fate of the jail-bird Bunyan,[21] persecuted unto death.

The Turks were outdone by multiple religious schisms within Hungary itself. These divisions created three kinds of literature to satisfy an urgent but none-too-extensive demand. The kind that was addressed to the Prince and the landed aristocracy was moralizing in tone: Let them treat their subjects humanely, for after death they all

---

[20] George Herbert (1593–1633) was a parson and an outstanding singer who could also play the lute and the viola. His baroque-style poetry, rich in various forms and images, dealt almost exclusively with questions of religion and faith, and was published only after his death. He is considered to have influenced Coleridge.

[21] John Bunyan (1628–1688) had become a Baptist and insisted on preaching without the permission of the Anglican Church, which was then considered a criminal activity. His audiences, therefore, often consisted of his jail-mates. His religious autobiography, *Grace Abounding to the Chief of Sinners*, appeared in 1666. His best known work is *The Pilgrim's Progress from this World to that Which Is to Come* (1678), which has become internationally famous and has even influenced Hungarian novelists.

would have to render account of their earthly reign in the realm of God. The second kind, poetry intended for the people, sounded the prophets' cry of woe and reproved and confessed sins. The Turk was seen as the scourge of God—whom the straying 'pagan' and 'idolatrous' Hungarians deserved. Although the poet-preacher knew just as well as his flock of serfs that there were many country-wide robbers among the great lords, there must be no revolt, even against evil masters, for judgment belonged to God alone. The third kind of literature consisted of polemical, crude accusations and counter-accusations for the love of their country among Catholics, Lutherans, Calvinists, and Unitarians. Their arguments were borrowed from the Hebrew scriptures, from Isaiah to Daniel—for the Calvinists had possessed a complete translation of the Bible since 1590, and the Catholics since 1626—and this fact had the same effect on the Hungarian language that Luther's version had on German and the King James Version had on English. But even if they drew their argumentative warnings from the Bible, they borrowed their words from the stable-yards, from the foul language of the coachman. They all had a splendid talent for inexhaustible, spicy abuse. Almost all of them had read Erasmus, for some of them had visited Dutch and German universities. It was through their writings that the preachers received the admonition of St. Augustine: in worldly matters, the congregation must obey the authorities. (He, of course, was thinking of the Roman Empire.) The trials of this world would not last long, anyhow, for *in hoc maligno seculo* ('in this malignant age'), man was only a passer-by, a *peregrinus*.

But was he really? It was in the midst of this rain of blood that the greatest affirmer of life—Bálint Balassi (q.v.)—lived. He was educated by a furious preacher who thoroughly implanted in him a sense of guilt and a passionate inclination to confession. But he could no longer quench the flames of his wild baronial blood. Like Hutten,[22] Luther's humanistically trained soldier, Balassi was the Hungarian version of Germany's *Reubritter* ('marauding knight'). War had mobilized his previously feckless instincts, and this dangerous man became a hero defending his country. There are ages in which, within a scant thirty

---

[22] Ulrich von Hutten (1488–1523), German knight and humanist poet who espoused the cause of the Reformation. He is regarded as the poet in whose work humanism moves from the theoretical to the practical. His outstanding works were five orations written in Latin.

years, the blasphemous Promethean soul consumes an entire century. Its thirst for life breaks through all moral barriers, but its heroism remains legendary.

Balassi is one of the greatest Hungarian poets, not only by Magyar standards but by any independent foreign test as well. In the rainbow of his work, Eastern and Western elements merge—from the Turkish *ghazele*[23] to the Italian *siciliana*[24] and the 'vagrant songs' of the goliards.[25] Balassi also wrote poetry to be sung. His life-style was deceptive—behind the restless adventurer and the wounded soldier, there was a learnèd, multilingual poet who was conscious of his peerless worth. It is only recently that people have begun to realize that he not only wrote single poems but, like the greatest poets, succeeded in creating a connected, coherent, mature body of work with fine, proportioned divisions in the Renaissance manner. Only he, of all his compatriots, knew that a poet is an artist of the language, setting his own laws, and that the form of a poem is a reliquary that has to be shaped with a goldsmith's care, for he alone knew what was happening beyond the frontiers. If he wished, his poetry could be grim like a psalm; if he desired, it was embroidered with merriment or sparkling with precious stones. Hungarians still relish and imbibe his language in the way that the English feed on Shakespeare's sonnets. None of his

---

[23] A kind of Turkish love lyric that originated in Persia and was practised at its best by the Persian poet Háfiz (1325–1390). In its original form it consisted of a limited number of stanzas having the same recurring rhythm. In Europe this genre was imitated by Goethe, Pushkin, and the Hungarians Csokonai and Arany (qq.v.). Balassi must have heard the *ghazele,* which was thought to have reached Turkey in pre-Islamic times, sung by Turkish prisoners of war kept for exchange purposes in the various Hungarian border castles ('végvár' in Hungarian).

[24] Also called *strambotto poppolare;* a stanza with an ABABABAB rhyme scheme; there is also a shorter version with only 6 lines. Thought to have originated in Sicily in the 13th century, it functioned as a folk art form until the 15th century, when it was also used by learnèd poets. Its popularity lasted until the first half of the 16th century when it was overtaken by the madrigal.

[25] The goliards, *scholares vagantes* or *clerici vagi* in Latin, were wandering poets who moved through Europe for several centuries; their own names are usually unknown. The topics of their songs include fights, drinking, and amorous exploits. Their songs often use vulgar words, often ridicule the clergy, and often mix Latin with other languages such as Middle High German, with their 'innocuous' parts in the vernacular language.

poems were printed during his lifetime; they were only distributed in manuscript form. For a century and a half, Balassi's style endured. His heritage could be molded and bent in different ways; his immediate successors, dulling his brilliance, used it at the turn of the century to interpret *tacitismo,* the somber outlook of Tacitus, to express the idea of 'destiny' in Hungarian. But even a full century later, the songs of the *kuruc,* the Hungarian freedom-fighter guerillas, imitated on the popular level, and sometimes with original variations, the great poet Balassi, whose true home was the war-tent and whose only true, equal partner was a comrade-in-arms.

Balassi fell in 1594, during the Fifteen Years' War (1591–1616), which might have expelled the shaken Turkish power from the land if only the land had not been torn apart territorially in Turkey's interests. But the battleground, whose vanishing and self-deceived people now called it sometimes 'the protecting shield of the West' and sometimes the *antimurale christianitatis* (the 'advance bastion of Christianity'), was in reality a secondary front in the clash among the Western powers. It was here that the Protestant world alliance confronted in battle the Catholic world mission of the Habsburgs. To explore the possibilities of the planned alliance, Sir Philip Sidney came on a secret mission to Hungary after St. Bartholomew's Day. A generation later, the Transylvanian Prince Gábor Bethlen[26] fought as a member of this powerful alliance—and with Turkish permission!—against Vienna. Between these competing forces, the liberation of Hungary was delayed for eighty devastating years.

It is possible to accommodate oneself to decay. The front lines grew rigid in the country; gradual erosion set in behind the grandiose propaganda façade of strength and power. From the open and flexible humanist way of thought, the churches, in defense of their acquired or regained rights, adopted closed, hierarchical attitudes. Both sides had a haughty Establishment, and the secular side also had somewhat humbler allies. Amidst the skirmishes of the warring parties, Péter

---

[26] (1580–1629). He became Duke of Transylvania in 1613 and fought successfully on the side of the Protestants against the Habsburgs in the Thirty Years' War. He organized the best army since Matthias and attempted to liberate Hungary proper in three separate campaigns, but failed to achieve his goal.

Pázmány,[27] the Jesuit champion of the Counter-Reformation, argued verbally from the pulpit and in written pamphlets against the Protestant world alliance.

One of his pupils was Count Miklós Zrínyi (q.v.), the greatest Hungarian poet of the 17th century. His faith was that of a fighting Christian missionary, but without a fanatic's hatred of those who believed differently. He was chivalrous even to the Turkish foe because of his respect for Ottoman culture, which stretched at its zenith from Persia to Austria. This culture left its influence upon Zrínyi as well. And he saw plenty of Turks, armed, on horseback. Yet just like Satan's hosts in Milton's eyes, so for Zrínyi, the Sultan's was not a contemptible army.

But the struggle against the Turks was a Holy War. The Turks were seen as the scourge of God—they had been let loose from Hell upon the 'corrupt' land so that, under their incessant blows, the blood of self-sacrificing, voluntary warrior-saints should gain grace for the nation. These soldiers were 'Magyar martyrs,' saviors and captives of Hungary, protected by the Holy Virgin. But they were not all speakers of Hungarian; Zrínyi himself was bilingual in Magyar and Croatian. His family considered Pannonia, Croatia, and Dalmatia its homeland in equal measure. I use those Latin geographical terms deliberately. The Jesuit professors instilled in Hungarian and Croatian students a Catholic spirit tempered with Roman-style patriotism.

The similarity of Polish and Hungarian weapons and tools is striking in this age, and so is the kindred orientation of the two nations' minds. Under the crucifix in their prayer-stools, they kept Livy's book about the Roman heroes who defeated the Etruscans, together with Machiavelli's pamphlet about the National Army, an essential national political and strategic asset for which Zrínyi kept arguing desperately and, alas, in vain.

Whereas Balassi, the brave soldier, never lost his lyric vein, Zrínyi was driven before long from poetry to prose by his urgent political and strategic ideas. For he was not only an outstanding officer, but also a great general—alas without an army. The Habsburgs did not trust their

---

[27] (1570–1637). Cardinal of Esztergom and Primate of Hungary. He was the chief Catholic ecclesiastical polemicist. He founded a University in Nagyszombat (now Trnava in Slovakia) in 1635—it was the ancestor of today's University of Budapest, named after him in 1922 and renamed the Eötvös Loránd Tudomány Egyetem (ELTE) in 1949 after the Communist coup.

miles christianus (their 'Christian soldier'). All he had left was paper, quill, and the excited urgency of his writing.

He wrote his masterpiece while young, during a single winter; it was about his great-great-grandfather, the commander of Szigetvár. This fortress fell to the Turks in 1566, a year after the world-famous, unsuccessful siege of Malta. That great event had been recorded by the illuminators of the Sultan's court in a painted chronicle in Turco-Persian style.

After his Italian pilgrimage, the young poet Zrínyi was encouraged in his great undertaking by Tasso's[28] celebrated epic *Jerusalem Liberated*. But what he learned from his master was neither the linguistic magic nor the atmosphere of witchcraft, but the powerfully ideological and dome-like crowning of lyricism, the spirit. After all, apart from his vanity and the encouragement of enthusiasts, Tasso, the bucolic Italian poet, was inspired to glorify the first crusade against the Arabs by the more recent victory at Lepanto[29] over the Turks—a belated chronicle of the Crusaders' battle. This was how and why *Jerusalem Liberated* was born.

Zrínyi's verses were once considered clumsy and rough-hewn. The critics demanded polished, shiny surfaces from the painters, brightly polished marble from the sculptors. Since then, the order of values has changed. Today, in our eyes, Michelangelo's *Slave*, half-frozen into the marble block, and his chunky fragment, the *Rondanini Pietà,* are considered superior to his mirror-smooth *Madonna* in St. Peter's, which was a bravura performance of his youth.

Zrínyi's poetry certainly has a deliberately abrasive surface, and it has Latin word order, with frequent inversions, but this was probably done intentionally for the sake of emphasis. His rhythm is rich and varied with more movement than Tasso's. The Hungarian poet immersed himself in the reigning baroque style, but he also remained faithful to the 16th century and its tradition in Hungary, shaped by the Turkish menace. From this past, his Catholic epic absorbed the

---

[28] Torquato Tasso (1544–1595), author of *La Gerusalemme Liberata* [Jerusalem Liberated], which he wrote between 1570 and 1575 in Ferrara. Tasso's epic influenced Lope de Vega, Dryden, Collins, and Byron. Zrínyi, although independently inspired, was also influenced by Tasso.

[29] The Battle of Lepanto, fought on October 7, 1571, ended Turkey's naval domination of the eastern Mediterranean. The commanding admiral of the united Western navies was Don Juan d'Austria.

homilies of Protestant psalmists and the historical songs of the frontier singers.

We have mentioned that Zrínyi was bilingual. He learned from his Croatian predecessors, as well as from the Hungarians and from Tasso. The Croatian poet Karnarutić[30] from the coastal city of Zadar had devoted his poetry to the fall of Szigetvár, the future topic of Zrínyi's great epic. Earlier yet, the Ragusan poet Gundulić[31] had written a heroic poem entitled *Osman*, filled with Slavic pride about the struggle of the Poles against the Turks. Thus Zrínyi's work united Catholicism with Roman-style heroism, Italy with Dalmatia (because of Tasso), Dalmatia with Poland, and, (last but not least) Hungary with Italy.

It was a curious world. Evliyā Çelebi,[32] the peerless Turkish traveller, while thoroughly exploring the Ottoman Empire, also visited Zrínyi, his formidable foe. The count received Çelebi kindly and provided him with magnificent entertainment. He also gave him a guided tour through his museum-like castle and lavished presents on him. The notes of this Turkish eyewitness are half colorful Oriental fairy-tales, half a spy's report. He promoted Zrínyi to royal rank, partly as a genuine mistake and partly due to his personal impressions of the man. During his visit, Turkish prisoners of war spaded the symmetrical garden in which chopped-off Turkish heads dried on stakes.

Zrínyi's fame spread to the West as well. In the book entitled *Sim-*

---

[30] Brne Karnarutić (ca. 1520–1572 or 1573) was a Croatian poet whose greatest work was *Vazetja Sigete Grada* [The occupation of Szigetvár], 1548, describing its capture by the Turks. *Szigetvár* means 'Castle on the Island'; it was an important Hungarian fortress that was captured by the Turks. Karnarutić's work was the most significant forerunner of Zrínyi's own *Szigeti veszedelem* [The Disaster of Sziget].

[31] Ivan Gundulić (1589–1638) was a Croatian poet who enthusiastically desired the liberation of the Christians in the Balkans from Turkish rule; he was inspired by Tasso's *Jerusalem Liberated* to write his own epic poem *Osman*. Ragusa is the former name of the city on the Dalmatian coast now known as Dubrovnik.

[32] (1611–1687). He was a Turkish world traveller whose writing was often of a fictional nature. His reports are, nevertheless, interesting, because other sources often confirm his statements. His main contribution was *Sejāhatnāme* [Book of Travels].

plicissimus,[33] one of the best-selling novels of the century, a veteran mercenary thinks of entering Zrínyi's service. Zrínyi was only 44 years old when a wild boar killed him during a hunt.

In 1686, the Western allies, with Hungarian auxiliary troops, retook Buda after a gory siege. Within a few years, they rolled back the 150-year-old occupation, and the country was liberated from the Turks. In 1690, the Magyar principality of Transylvania lost its semi-independence, but the Habsburgs did not reunite it with Hungary; they governed it separately. There was little joy in the liberation. In the eyes of Vienna, Hungary, with two-thirds of its population exterminated, was a colony to be resettled. The court only regretted that its wild, restless subjects had not been liquidated completely. It had no reason to worry about the obedient Germans who had immigrated there or about the inhabitants of other nationalities. But in the eyes of the court, revolution was an incurable Hungarian disease.

Until 1680, the 17th century, equally tragic from the military, political, and demographic points of view, was by no means a desperate one spiritually. In Holland, wandering Hungarian Protestant students were happily infected by a tolerantly religious pluralism, and by the philosophy of a French exile in Amsterdam whose name was Descartes. After their return from Holland, several of these young Hungarians came into conflict with the rigid, reactionary Establishment. Mainly through Jesuit channels, the Catholics were swept into the current of the international baroque style. There were plenty of poets toying with amorettoes;[34] they were shallow entertainers of aristocratic amateurs and great land owners. On a deeper level, there were mystics with burning imaginations and tongues of flame who cast themselves into the fiery furnace of celestial love like their Spanish, French, and Silesian fellow poets. Hundreds of poems in manuscript form were preserved, both with and without musical accompaniment. Many of them are excellent, but most of them are anonymous.

---

[33] Written by Hans Jakob Christoffer von Grimmelshausen (1622–1676), German novelist whose chief opus, *Abenteurliche Simplicissimus*, appeared in 1669. It is now considered to be the best piece of German fiction before Goethe. Its hero, Simplicissimus, spends his youth as a mercenary in the Thirty Years' War, and at one point in his career considers entering Zrínyi's service.

[34] An Italian style of love sonnet.

From the Reformation to our own days, Hungarian literature has had to go underground more than once. The first such underground period occurred from about 1680 to 1730. That was the period during which England finally became a civilized, modern country. Could one conceive a more crushing judgment of the liberation?

In 1703 the Hungarians, full of bitterness over the forced colonization of their country, crossed the border to the east and gathered under the banner of Prince Ferenc Rákóczi II of Transylvania,[35] who led Hungary's Freedom War (1703–1711) against the Habsburg Empire. Rákóczi's Hungarians received only limited aid from the French. The pro-Austrian English government disapproved of the war, and its hired pamphleteer, Daniel Defoe, wrote a series of articles condemning the defeated Hungarians. After his defeat, Rákóczi first went into exile in France, then into Turkish exile with his retinue.

Saint-Simon depicted Rákóczi in his *Mémoires* with sympathy and occasionally with a bit of irony, as a basically sad, dignified, handsome individual who could always count on Louis XIV's tactful favor. Rákóczi's attitude never relaxed. In his little court in exile, even in the most remote location, he still demanded order, discipline, and Christian piety. He deserves special respect if we compare him to another exile, Bonnie Prince Charlie,[36] who, after the final defeat of the Stuarts, drowned his sorrows as an unsuccessful pretender in drink.

The guerilla freedom-fighters under Prince Ferenc Rákóczi II were called *kuruc*. The priests and students who served in their ranks were the ancestors of the urban guerillas of later times. The anonymous songs which they composed lit up with flashes their strategy of ambush and surprise.

---

[35] (1676–1735). He is generally considered the greatest of all the Transylvanian Princes. He was an outstanding prose writer himself; his *Confessiones* (1716–1719) were written in the monastery of Grosbois in France and later in Turkey, where he died in exile. He was a Jansenist.

[36] Charles Edward Stuart, the 'Young Pretender' (1720–1788). He was the last Stuart claimant to the British throne and leader of the unsuccessful Jacobite rebellion of 1745–1746. He wandered around Europe, trying to revive his cause, but his drunken behavior alienated his friends. After he settled in Italy in 1766, the Catholic powers abolished his title to the throne.

The first collector of these songs, Kálmán Thaly[37] in the last century, smuggled his own excellent forgeries into his anthology—out of naive patriotism rather than for selfish gain. In this almost timeless genre, from the Greek *klephtai* ('thief') ballads to those of the Australian highwaymen, the persecuted have created their anonymous masterpieces in various languages and at various times. The original *kuruc* songs permeated the Hungarian culture so much that they are still sung, without any educational pressure—especially with the help of some wine. Endre Ady (q.v.), one of the greatest Hungarian poets of the 20th century, used them for marvelous paraphrases of his own times and thoughts. After Rákóczi fled at the end of the war, the country was barely breathing. A hundred years later Ferenc Kölcsey (q.v.), the author of the Hungarian national anthem, looked back upon the ruins and wrote:

> *Chased, we ran and hid. The foe*
> *Probed our caves with armed hand.*
> *We looked 'round, but could not find*
> *Our home within our homeland.*

These four lines, perhaps the grimmest ones ever written in the Hungarian language, make any detailed description unnecessary.

A Quiet Century with a Bloody Epilogue

Centuries do not start with round numbers. In Hungary the 18th century arrived in 1711, when the House of Habsburg and the Hungarian people made an uneasy peace. Prince Ferenc Rákóczi II never recognized their peace treaty, but an exiled prince and politician is only the subject of spies' reports, not of diplomatic correspondence.

Some quiet century! The country changed from a battleground into a military storehouse. South of Hungary, the Turkish wars continued, with cholera claiming more victims than did the arms; in the north, the War of the Austrian Succession and the Seven Years' War devastated

---

[37] (1839–1909). Historian and Member of Parliament for the Independence Party. He specialized in the age of Prince Ferenc Rákóczi II, espousing a romantic, aristocratic, and nationalistic philosophy of the Hungarian nobility.

the best cultivated territories of Central Europe.

There had to be mass immigration to replace the losses of human life. After 1711 the Magyars no longer formed a decisive majority within Hungary as they had before. However, they did not collectively tyrannize their Slavic and Romanian fellow-citizens, as earlier 20th-century propaganda has claimed. The feudal system ruled both Hungarian and non-Hungarian serfs. On a lower level, there were the middle ranks of the nobility, the 'country squires' who were locked into the minor principalities of the various counties. On a higher level, there were the barons, counts, and princes, the landed aristocrats who preferred spending their lives circling the sun of the court in Vienna.

Quietly and gradually, the rebuilding of the country proceeded. Under the patronage of the prelates, South German and late Austrian baroque culture penetrated the formerly Turkish-occupied territory that had been laid waste. Hungary's northern and eastern borderlands (now the Slovak Republic and the western edge of Romania) are medieval in their art because they were never occupied by the Turks. The Gothic monuments in these parts are therefore still standing. Today's Hungary, on the other hand—that is to say the central portion that was liberated by the Austrians from the Turks and was the former battle-ground—is largely baroque, even in its folk art. The last several decades of the 20th century did change this picture somewhat, since a systematic restoration of monuments has gradually rebuilt the fortresses of the Turkish period and some of the ruined Renaissance castles as well.

Hungarian historiography, as one might expect, began in Latin, because the schools were under the conservative, Catholic leadership of Piarist, Cistercian, and Jesuit Fathers, and Protestant teachers were also heavily influenced by Latin. By this time, Protestantism had become a minority on the defensive; the Counter-Reformation had reconverted most of Hungary to Catholicism. Progressive thinking, which in earlier times was a Protestant trait influenced by Erasmus, had by now passed to the small Hungarian vanguard of the Enlightenment. Initially this new ideology seeped in only through the libraries of wealthy aristocrats, since the censors conducted a successful purge of what they called the 'Plague from Paris.' But the censors were unable to search the libraries of influential personages who were attached to the Habsburg court.

The 'century of elegance'—as the 18th century was called in Western Europe—was rather a fallow one in Hungary, especially before the 1760s. There were, however, two brilliant writers of prose: the exiled Kelemen Mikes[38] living in exile in Turkey with Prince Ferenc Rákóczi II, and Ferenc Faludi (q.v.), who became a Hungarian author in a Jesuit monastery. Bessenyei (q.v.), the first outstanding Hungarian Voltairean, became a poet while in Vienna as a member of the Noblemen's Guard serving the Empress Maria Theresa. All three, in fact, matured abroad. Paradoxically, the country was more alert and more open intellectually around 1560 than it was two hundred years later!

Balassi, as we saw, was not a single day behind his age; instead, he was the Danubian poetic counterpart of the English Petrarchists. But when Voltaire's Hungarian contemporaries looked around the Hungarian capital after their stay in Vienna, they were astounded by the cultural backwardness that greeted them at home. Theirs was the same shock-treatment that the young Russian Officers' Corps experienced during the Napoleonic Wars. In the fullness of time, the tragic personal consequences of this awakening of the respective consciences were also similar—the Russian Decembrists[39] ended up on the scaffold, the Hungarian Jacobins in prison or on the executioner's block.

The Hungarian Enlightenment was complex. First it advanced forcefully, then it retreated in fear. It was an ambivalent movement under the strain of opposing forces. It was no wonder some literary historians, such as the British G.F. Cushing,[40] considered it altogether the most exciting age. The country, as mentioned before, prospered—in fact, Hungary had plenty of resources to contribute to the Habsburgs' military ventures on distant battlefields. The decades that Haydn spent at Eszterháza were financed by massive sums that were originally intended as contributions for support of the army. Count Eszterházy could more than afford his own orchestra, replete with Haydn as its renowned resident composer and conductor.

But in the meantime, there was an unremitting tug-of-war between

---

[38] (1690–1761). Known as the father of Hungarian prose, he wrote letters to an imaginary aunt. He was private secretary to the exiled Prince Ferenc Rákóczi II. His real, lasting effect came as late as the 19th century.

[39] Russian revolutionaries of noble ancestry who organized an uprising (which was defeated) in December 1825 on the accession of Tsar Nicholas I.

[40] George Frederick Cushing (1923-1996), professor of Hungarian language and literature in London; author of *Hungarian Prose and Verse* (1956).

the king and the nobility. Which of the two would exploit the peasantry more thoroughly—Vienna, in order to support a rationalized administration, or the aristocrats, for the sake of luxury? That is to say, the greater masters who frequented the court, or the lesser ones who chewed on their pipes in the courtyards of their mansions in the country? In the long run, it amounted to the same thing. The poor had not stirred since the abortive peasant revolt of 1514. The 'quiet century' was dreadfully quiet indeed.

Some of the aristocrats forgot the Hungarian language, but they were, nonetheless, book collectors. Compared to the collections of the monasteries, a personal library of ten or fifteen thousand volumes was no rarity—except, of course, that their bookshelves were lined with different 'church fathers,' mostly the newly banned ones, written in French and English. For the progressive spirit of the aristocrats exhausted itself in fashionable anti-clericalism. Their attitude, of course, had a political edge to it. The aristocrats wanted to eliminate, with the help of the king and Monsieur Voltaire, their feudal rivals, the landed squirearchy who ruled over the counties and towns. They therefore acted as intermediaries, bringing the censured Western ideas to the poorer middle nobility, to the literate but poor public servants, and to the few members of the bourgeoisie. They achieved this act of *Kulturschmuggeln* ('smuggling of forbidden cultural goods') through their private libraries as well as through their Masonic lodges, into which censorship was unable to penetrate.

The feelings of the lesser nobility and the middle classes were divided because of their anxiety that Empress Maria Theresa's absolutism would deprive them of their treasured traditions. Her son and successor, Emperor Joseph II, seen as the prototype of a slightly tyrannical 'Enlightened Despot,' instilled similar fears in the same classes. Because of their intellectual inclinations, these worried sections of Hungarian society sided with the king. This was especially true of the Protestants. Paradoxically, it was the lower echelons of the Catholic clergy who provided the most belligerent shield of the national spirit against their Catholic ruler, being fully aware that the ecclesiastical *status quo* was being assured only by political immobility. Even if the constitution had been amended, church policies would not have changed along with it. Protestants and Jews still remained second-class citizens.

Voltaire's 'noble savage,' as presented in *L'Ingénu* and some of his other works, was the archetype of all anti-clerical nationalists everywhere in Central Europe, but it also cast a longer shadow, reaching as far as an awakening Greece. These stirring but still backward nations knew little about each other, but they had the well-springs of their salvation in common. These were the university cities of Tübingen, Paris, London, Edinburgh, and Zürich, from which all the imported books, ideas, doctrines, and slogans kept coming. Few middle-class intellectuals had a chance to travel; most of them saw the world beyond their frontiers only while soldiering.

Serious stirrings only started to ripple the water's surface between 1780 and 1794. But even during this comparative intellectual effervescence, publishers could only recruit four or five hundred subscribers for a periodical and no more than two or three hundred for a book, which, of course, did not even cover their costs of printing. The only exceptions were occasional anonymous political pamphlets, such as those which sold thousands of copies at the beginning of the French Revolution. Although official literary historiography dates the Hungarian Age of Enlightenment as starting with Bessenyei (q.v.) in the middle of the 18th century, his initiative soon ran out of steam. Few of his writings appeared in print during his lifetime, and he withdrew into the life of a village hermit.

At the death of Joseph II, it still seemed as though all modern desires could be fulfilled. It was hoped that the new Encyclopedic gospel would triumph; that in politics and in literature the Magyar tongue would prevail over Latin; that in economics English rationalism would gain the upper hand. 1790 was a year of promises—a veritable Hungarian *annus mirabilis*. The atmosphere was as electric as it was during the summer of 1956 at the debates of the Budapest Petőfi Circle.[41] But in Paris the radical Jacobins had seized power after ousting the Gironde, and Louis XVI's head had rolled. The terrified Hungarian nobility came to an agreement with their king, and the police were given a free hand. In 1794–1795, the Martinovics trial crushed the spiritual awakening which had been so full of hope just a few years before. Tamino fell; the Queen of the Night cast him into prison with the consensus of the Sarastros, all of whom were retreating in fright. And Tamino was no longer the pious, unarmed idealist that

---

[41] An organization of writers, poets, journalists, young intellectuals, and university students, the Petőfi Circle became a hotbed of discussion and criticism of the Communist Party and the Secret Police prior to October 23, 1956.

Mozart's opera *The Magic Flute* had depicted in song.

In Hungary at this time there were neither literary stirrings nor regular publishing; neither patrons nor a flock of readers—in fact, not one intellectual focus could be found anywhere! After its brief expectation of a 'Pentecost,' Hungary had become a startled, silent country in which the printed word was suspect because it smelled of 'Jacobinism.'

If a true genius happens by accident to be born into such a desert, it is a great misfortune, but there did happen to be such a person. His name was Mihály Csokonai Vitéz (q.v.). His challenge was this: Create and inspire in such a wasteland, if you can!

As a young college tutor, he quarreled with the fossilized, old masters of the Calvinist school, and, as a result, he had to subsist without any regular income. Branded as a trouble maker and living on charity, between stretches of near starvation he staggered from one feast to another across the country. He could find no wealthy patron for his writings, and at age 32 he was cut down by tuberculosis. But in spite of his disappointments, he was always full of plans.

Due to the age in which they lived and also because of their fragile physical constitutions, Hungarian historians of culture have sometimes compared Csokonai to Mozart. As artists they stepped lightfootedly and gracefully across abysses and whirlpools with great intellectual assurance. Their faith was unbroken in spite of their broken bodies—their faith in the victory of light over darkness during the Century of Lights. They personally reaped no reward for their faith. It is we, their admiring posterity, who are increasingly indebted to their unflagging hope.

The essence of a genius can be either a peerless originality or an immense talent for assimilation. (It is in this latter sense that Joyce became one of the greatest writers of this century.)

Csokonai, as a poet and writer, was a great assimilator. In his work one sees the amalgamation of folk songs; of bucolic pastoral idylls, which were very fashionable for a few years in Hungary; of *Anacreontic songs,*[42] much the favorite of several contemporary

---

[42]   Named after the Greek poet Anacreon (ca. 570–ca. 490 B.C.). Only a few of his short epigrams and songs, written in iambic heptameter, have survived. He is considered the successor to Alcaeus and Sappho. Much later, in 1554, Henri Estienne, a French printer (1504 or 1505–1564), published a collection of sixty poems which came to be called 'Anacreontic songs' because

Germans; of Oriental, especially Persian, poetry; of Swiss landscape poetry; and of English rationalism.

Alexander Pope was Csokonai's *vade mecum*. There was hardly a poetic form which Csokonai did not attempt: learnèdly, but with playful, imitative panache, as though a poem were only a kiss of the Muses rather than painstaking and exacting work. Csokonai's lyricism is essentially pre-Romantic. He was enamoured of suffering and the subject of Artemis, the Moon Goddess, rather than Apollo. In his *Lilla* songs, we constantly sense that, in the depths of his soul, he was far more frightened of blissful fulfilment than of unhappiness. And so, of course, his choice of subject, with fitting poetic instinct, fell upon a woman who, in all probability, stimulated his fructifying disappointments to perfection. There was a keening tone in his references to his personal fate; Rousseau, the hermit of Ermenonville, was his proclaimed spiritual kin. Yet his personal misfortune did not destroy his serene faith in humanity and the Hungarian people, with whom he became acquainted in all their shapes and forms, from reckless shepherds and singing students to penny-pinching counts. From the raw material of his poems, one can draw a dictionary of local idioms, including everything from botany to philosophy, and he would still be remembered for the mere music of his verses. For Csokonai, however, something greater and different is involved: the splendid balance of an effervescent soul.

The reader feels joy in reading his poetry, even when he complains. It is one of the most arguable open questions about Hungarian poetry whether its later multiple rebirths found their respective inspirations in Csokonai or in the works of the Romantics.

Among those who were accused and condemned at the Martinovics trial were Kazinczy and Batsányi (qq.v.). They had previously launched a periodical for spreading the ideas of the Enlightenment, although from the very start they never really got along with each other. Their natures, both bent on wanting to be the leader, would not let them remain under the same roof for any length of time, even for

---

of the topics they treated—love and wine, with pastoral settings full of nightingales, flowers, and happy lovers. The genre was also influenced by Horace (65 B.C.– A.D. 8) and by the Persian Samszu'd-Dín Muhammad Háfíz (ca. 1325–1390). In France, the authors belonging to the 'Pléiade' reflected the influence of the 'Anacreontic Songs'; in England the term was first used by the poet Abraham Cowley (1618–1667) in his work *Anacreontiques*.

short stints of editing. Their ways of thinking were different: Kazinczy was an accommodating snob with a lukewarm political temperament; Batsányi was a haughty, radical plebeian. Yet both remained attached to the Emperor, Joseph II. Kazinczy was a Freemason, but only Batsányi clung faithfully to the French Revolution; he was a dictatorial character who completely approved of the Jacobin dictatorship.

After they were freed from prison (they were both arrested in 1794, but Batsányi was released in 1795, while Kazinczy was released only in 1801), their destinies diverged. Kazinczy went back to farm his estate, while Batsányi moved to Paris and became a librarian working on Ossian,[43] with a stipend received from Napoleon. (It is well known that the French Emperor loved the legendary Celtic bard.) When the armies of Napoleon's enemies entered Paris in 1815, Batsányi was arrested and imprisoned in several jails in the West.

Ferenc Kölcsey (q.v.), who lived in eastern Hungary, was the best informed Hungarian poet of his age, and Dániel Berzsenyi (q.v.), who farmed near the Austrian border, acted the part of a nobleman of great Asian ancestry. They were both students of German works on prosody. Their financial resources were undermined by the great inflation that followed the Napoleonic Wars. No wonder that, under these bleak circumstances, a few members of the privileged class, infected by culture, should have fallen prey to manic depression in their isolated mansions. We are not only in the age of Gogol[44] but in his very world. Kölcsey was an aesthetic poet controlling inspiration with the sensitive radar of 'poetic principle.' His criteria were sometimes in

---

[43] The name of this legendary warrior-poet, the hero of two cycles of Irish hero-tales, is also written as Oisín. However, the works that Batsányi would have been working on would not have been genuine folk-takes but the spurious, so-called "poems of Ossian" that were published in 1762 by the Scottish writer James Macpherson (1736–1796). These "poems of Ossian" were largely Macpherson's own work, although they contained small bits of authentic Irish legend; but they were the works that were then being acclaimed by the pre-Romantic movement.

[44] Nikolai Vasilyevich Gogol (1809–1852), Russian novelist and playwright. His most famous novel, *Dead Souls* (1842), revolved around the fact that, in Russia, one could own serfs, even though they were dead. His internationally famous comedy, *The Inspector General,* was written in 1835, but is played even today, after the collapse of Communism in the former U.S.S.R., because it depicts the main symptoms of the maladies of Russian society: fear, greed, and corruption.

error when applied to others, but never when applied to himself. He transmuted his misanthropic melancholy into polished marble. At the same time—like Csokonai before him—he was among the first to salvage folk poetry by transforming it into literary art, well scrubbed and consonant with the rules of contemporary taste. He lived on the edge of a district inhabited by minorities; not all of his peasants could speak Hungarian. Though he was a man of deep, humane feelings and spoke at the Diet against the burdens that the serfs had to bear, the nobles who sent him there as their spokesman considered him far too revolutionary. He was, before long, enveloped by the spectre of the national debt, for he identified the preservation of the Magyars with the survival of the nobility. What would happen if and when all serfs—Hungarians, Serbs, Wallachians, and Slovaks—were freed? This was the question that weighed upon his mind. And yet they were sure to be liberated sooner or later. It was this spiritual agony that inspired his poems which had the most profound effects. His was a heavy heritage indeed, and its shattering visions probably heightened the dramatization of Hungarian destiny throughout the nation's literature. Berzsenyi, on the other hand, was an instinctive poet and perhaps the greatest Magyar verbal genius. He was inspired by Horace, and much like Goethe's contemporary Hölderlin, worked in the Alcaic meter.

Horace's phrase 'let us praise the vanished times' was an ideal common to members of Berzsenyi's generation. But 18th-century Hungarians believed that the Hungarian equivalent of Horace's patrician Roman republic would consist only of the Hungarian nobles, with their escutcheons and their family trees which they traced back either to the conquest of the land or to Romulus, the founder of Rome.

Berzsenyi felt right at home in such a setting, as though the world and the various Classical poetic meters had been hand-tailored for him. Otherwise, he was a kind, simple, unassuming man, living like a peasant among his serfs. Like his Latin master Horace, Berzsenyi emphasized form over content; the one can be separated from the other only by taking considerable risks. Berzsenyi's discipline amounts, in fact, to a double triumph: first over the subject matter, and second over his own nature, which was not in the least 'Horatian.' His poems are inner volcanic explosions; no contemporary of his could depict the overwhelming effect of the distantly thundering Napoleonic wars merely by the power of words piled upon each other as well as Berzsenyi could. But then he unexpectedly quieted down. This once vociferous poet now wrote the quietest poem about the quiet steps of autumn. His successors did not take his example sufficiently to heart. He knew when to stop in a poem—sooner than its actual end, an effect he must also have learned from Horace.

Until 1825, the official language of the Hungarian Diet was Latin. Those who did not know French read Montesquieu[45] and Rousseau's *Contrat social* in Latin translation, not in Hungarian. But let us not exaggerate. The Latin that most Hungarians knew was not that of Cicero or Horace, but a popularized, Hungarianized Latin. Classical tongues are nourished at a high level only in communities where their native literature is also of superior quality, as at English, Scottish, and German universities. The critical edition of Homer's Greek text with Latin commentary was published in Cambridge, not in Buda.

Great Expectations and Another Disaster

Beethoven composed two short overtures for the inauguration of the permanent theater at Pest. One was about King Stephen, the founder of the country; the other, *The Ruins of Athens,* foretold the resurrection of the Greek nation decades before its War of Liberation. The day of the small nations was approaching. They looked back upon their ancient days with aching pride, their embellished past being the springboard for their belligerent nationalism.

The situation was rather similar in Hungary, because the nation was not independent. Its king was enthroned in Vienna, which also housed his supreme offices. Yet, starting in 1825, political and intellectual ferment was in full bloom. For the first time since Mohács, i.e., since 1526, the Hungarian capital became a focal point for young writers who had moved to Pest, on the eastern side of the Danube. Printing firms grew; periodicals and illustrated fashion magazines were

---

[45] Charles Louis de Secondat, Baron de La Brède (1689–1755), who inherited the name Montesquieu in 1716. One of the most important philosophers of the French Enlightenment, he wrote the influential *L'esprit des lois* [The Spirit of the Laws], 1748, in which he developed the concept of governmental 'separation of powers' that influenced the system of 'checks and balances' incorporated into the constitution of the U.S.A. He also influenced many European democratic constitutions written during the 19th century. In Hungary he exerted a major influence on Kelemen Mikes, Batsányi, Csokonai, Berzsenyi, and Kölcsey (qq.v.).

founded, following the trend set in Paris; readers and writers met regularly in the streets and in small cafés; and for the first time there were many women among the reading public.

At the end of the 18th century and the beginning of the 19th, the cult of history tended to dominate Romanticism. England led the way, but without any ideological or political motivation. In British historiography, the stylistic reëvaluation of medieval Gothic architecture became combined with the discovery of ancient folk poetry. On the other hand, in Germany, the same cult was nothing if not political.

It is not difficult to see the cause of the difference between the two kinds of historicism. The British had nothing to compensate for psychologically, but the Germans most certainly did: their series of defeats at the hands of the French in the Napoleonic wars.

Understandably, Hungary was receptive to the German version of such historicism. Without any ill-will, Herder,[46] the most respected advocate of the concept of the *'Volksgeist,'* considered Hungarian (Magyar) to be a vanishing tongue, and he prophesied a great future for the Slavs in Eastern Europe. Understandably, the reaction was electrifying. To justify itself to itself and to other people, Hungarian Romanticism also reached back into the past.

As a rule, every nation tends to extract a flattering self-portrait from its storehouse of historical memories. The Germans selected their Christian age of chivalry, the Age of the Emperors. Hungarians, on the other hand, preferred the pagan times. The history of the 'Taking of the Land'—Chief Árpád's conquest of the Carpathian Basin in A.D. 896—became a veritable national obsession. It was at this time that the search for the Hungarian Primeval National Epic, presumed to be lost, got under way.

Poetry proved to be an encouraging forum, and the stage even more so, since the effect of the latter was more tangible than that of books. It became a public, political concern that the nation should have a National Theater as soon as possible. After it was finally established

---

[46] Johann Gottfried Herder (1744–1803), German Romantic poet, essayist, and philosopher of history; the leading figure of the *Sturm und Drang* ('Storm and Stress') period of German literature. This movement was characterized by vehement emotions and the recognition of instinct. Natural talent meant more to its practitioners than taste and rigid adherence to rules, the virtues extolled by the Classicists. The movement's other leading figure was J.W. von Goethe.

in 1837, it was fed by inspiring historical dramas. The country did not possess the kind of multi-layered, urbanized society that would provide enough raw material for a Balzac-like tapestry, although they tried to imitate him; instead, on their stage ancient heroes portrayed by actors in historical garb acted out the tasks of the present in exemplary fashion. Because of the influence of the stage, novels on historical topics were preferred over social ones.

Shakespeare, Walter Scott, and Robert Burns, who gave mankind royal dramas, belletristic archaeology, and folklore, respectively, provided the three-fold inspiration which the English and the Scots projected upon Hungarian literature. The fact that the Hungarian imagination was particularly stimulated by Scotland is, in all probability, due to the fact that their emotional relationship to Vienna was rather similar to that of Edinburgh to London, and *mutatis mutandis,* also akin to the feelings of the Irish towards the British Empire.

In those years the reputation of England was immense outside the field of literature as well. To show this, the career of a single man, István Széchenyi,[47] suffices. His personality was uniquely Hungarian in every respect. In order to make up for the excesses of the majority of the aristocrats, Széchenyi set out to modernize Hungary on the model of Britain. On the surface he was like a pragmatic English lord; and his soul, permeated with Jansenism,[48] was strikingly different from that of his fellow horse-breeders. Profoundly Catholic, he inclined towards martyrdom. It is largely due to him that, to this very day, the Hungarians look back upon the years between 1825 and 1848

---

[47] Count István Széchenyi (1791–1860) founded the Hungarian Academy of Sciences (officially so called, although it covers languages, history, and literature as well as the natural sciences) through a generous donation. He delivered the first speech in Hungarian to the National Diet, where Latin had always been the official language. He was the central figure of the pre-1848 reform movement. He traveled to London and imported the engineer Adam Clark, whom he commissioned to build the first permanent chain bridge over the Danube. He oversaw the regulating of the banks of the lower Danube, he served as Minister of Transportation, and he wrote many influential treatises on economics. His diary reveals him to be a literary genius as well.

[48] A religious movement within the Roman Catholic Church during the 17th and 18th centuries which, like Lutheranism and especially like Calvinism, emphasized St. Augustine's teaching that God has predestined every person either to salvation or to damnation.

with undivided respect and nostalgia.

Hungarian historians call this period the 'Age of Reform.' It had British witnesses, too: Julia Beverley Pardoe,[49] the popular authoress of Oriental travel sketches, and John Paget,[50] who settled among the Hungarians. His sympathetic, serious, and reliable book that deals with the years of great expectations can still be profitably read today.

It was during this time that the still-prevailing public belief crystallized, according to which the true law-givers of the country were its poets and not the authorities in power. Yet the government had to be obeyed, no matter how reluctantly, since it was, with or without constraint, the tool of an external power.

Spiritually, the Hungarian people 'emigrated into poetry' in order to escape their history. From childhood onward, such an attitude tends to educate Hungarians to become eager consumers of poetry, although not without some danger to themselves and to the rather frequently misunderstood authors. Hungarians, especially in the 19th century, tended to believe that it was impossible to create a fatherland worthy of human habitation other than the one that sparkled inside poetry. In Hungarian literature the type of Victor Hugo was far more frequent than that of Mallarmé. But English literature, too, had the great romantic Shelley, deeply impressed by the French Revolution, according to whose well-known statement "poets are the best legislators of public affairs." This view was not generally accepted by the British public, because they always had more or less reliable public servants. A distrust of politicians in favor of writers is frequently seen elsewhere in Europe as well. Think of what the English visitor heard in Łódż, Poland, and what was said at the beginning of this essay.

Vörösmarty was the noblest embodiment of the new type of Hungarian literary personality. He amounts to a genuine European pheno-

---

[49] (1806–1862). After travelling to Portugal and Turkey, she also visited Hungary, and wrote about it in her book *The City of the Magyars* (1839–1840). A poem which Vörösmarty (q.v.) wrote for her in distich form in her keepsake album appears in this anthology.

[50] (1808–1892). English traveler and writer who arrived in Hungary in 1835. His book entitled *Hungary and Transylvania* appeared in 1839 in London. He married the widow Bánffy and became a Hungarian citizen in 1847. He actively participated in the 1848–1849 Hungarian War of Independence, becoming General Joseph Bem's adjutant. He had to go into exile in 1849, but returned to Hungary in 1855.

menon who had his kindred contemporaries in the Norwegian Werge-land[51] and the Greek Solomos.[52] Their patriotism was multi-phased; the mystic love of the fatherland soared into a winged solar hymn about World Freedom; then, becoming softer, it finally settled again upon the local landscape, which it experienced religiously. Their style reveals them to be typical sons of the age of the Great Spring of the Small Nations—the Europe-wide movements that surrounded 1848.

The young Vörösmarty was an escapist, full of longing for a para-disiacal island somewhere far off in misty space, but he succeeded in overcoming temptation. He tasted death, and he chose life for the sake of others. This nostalgic poet carved into marble the ideals of the Age of Reform. This was the gold reserve of his poetry kept for his fellow citizens.

The Romantics, as a rule, lived at a higher rate of metabolism than their contemporaries, but even during their accelerated internal combustion, the best of them still managed to develop a clear vision which was rooted in self-irony, previously something unheard of in European literature. How clearly Vörösmarty saw himself becomes evident in his enchanting play *Csongor és Tünde* (approximately 'Galahad and [the] Fairy,' although actually untranslatable) with its hidden autobiographical references. The famous 'Monologue of the Night' from this play appears in our present anthology. The play itself has been regarded as a sort of Hungarian *Midsummer Night's Dream*.

Vörösmarty was the first to have written in the Hungarian language as though for a symphony orchestra, a style which was helped by his stage experience. For a long time he provided the National Theater with historical dramas, some of which are successfully revived today. It is not far-fetched to say that Vörösmarty is spiritually related to Verdi, who in his operas from *Nabucco* to *Don Carlos* displayed similar sentiments—the idea of a great nation degraded into smallness by a hostile history.

Perhaps it had never been such an elevating feeling to be a

---

[51] Henrik Wergeland (1808–1845), Norwegian poet. He cultivated a typically Norwegian style, which is difficult to translate. His main works are *Man and Messiah* and *The Creation*.

[52] Dionysios Solomos (1798–1857), generally regarded as the first great poet of modern Greece. His *Hymn to Liberty* (1823) has become the Greek national anthem. The comparison of him with Vörösmarty is particularly apt, although they had no knowledge of each other.

Hungarian poet as it was around 1835, although there were already signals of a coming storm. In 1832 the suppression of the Polish uprising inspired Hungarian poets, among them Vörösmarty, to write a few great poems of sympathy. In his poetry, a sense of duty always struggled with demonic forces of self-destruction, sometimes openly and sometimes under the surface. The time finally came when, under the effect of nerve-shattering events, the negative forces within him gained the upper hand.

In 1848 the Great Spring of the Small Nations was drowned in blood throughout Europe. The Hungarians held out the longest, until August of 1849, against the combined forces of Austria and Russia, with an improvised army in which British, Polish, and even liberally inclined Austrian volunteer officers were serving. The disaster broke Vörösmarty, the nation's poet. His few last half-crazed poems were the measure of a country's deepest point of depression. Time rarely changes the rank that a genius has achieved—but the evaluation of one's life's work may change considerably. Around 1900, during the *belle époque,* Vörösmarty's fellow countrymen were unable to appreciate his quasi-Shakespearean style (it was he who translated *King Lear* into Hungarian), whereas today he is appreciated as a living contemporary.

The Hungarian Age of Reform washed away several centuries worth of differences between counts, country squires, burghers, and peasant lads who succeeded in joining such company through education. Many minority youths speaking a language other than Hungarian also joined. The kernel of the movement could be best described as a Republic of the Intelligentsia. The situation was the same in Russia, where the tremendous intellectual ferment wiped out all the differences in birth between the urban-bred Herzen,[53] Turgenev, a country-bred nobleman,[54] Chernyshevsky,[55] and Belinsky.[56]

---

[53] Alexander Ivanovich Herzen (1812–1870) is best known for his editorship of *Kolokol* [The Bell], which featured literary and political writings from exile.

[54] Ivan Sergeyevich Turgenev (1818–1883), novelist, poet, and playwright whose works brilliantly portrayed Russian life; *Fathers and Sons* is perhaps his best known novel.

[55] Nikolai Gavrilovich Chernyshevsky (1828–1889) viewed literature as a means to social action. His book *What is to be Done?* (1863) became the Bible of young Russian revolutionaries.

Following Széchenyi's initiative, many entrepreneurs set out on trips to the West for study—going even as far as the U.S.A.—and they published reports about the industry and commerce which they found there. These are not literary works but serious suggestions concerning an agenda for national salvation. Those who travelled to the West were concerned about the future. At the same time, interest in the past was keenly shown by the Hungarian Orientalist Sándor Kőrösi Csoma,[57] who travelled as far as Tibet. He is buried in Darjeeling, high in the Himalayas.

This was also a time of the gradual awakening of the plebeian class. The young poet Petőfi (q.v.) was one of these young plebeians. His early career was generously helped along by Vörösmarty. It is characteristic that Petőfi should have chosen *Coriolanus* as his first translation from Shakespeare. He did it because of the opening scene, which portrayed the plebeians and gave him a chance to voice his own social criticism.

Petőfi's father had been a village inn-keeper and butcher who was once well-to-do but later was completely ruined financially. The family lived at first above the social standards of the peasant community and later below them, but always outside of them. The young Petőfi quarrelled frequently with his father and left the family home at an early age; he therefore felt that he was a 'prodigal son' driven from his home. From this background he emerged as a born rebel, much like the young men who fell in Paris on the barricades of 1848 and during the 1871 commune. He is the easiest of all Hungarian poets to visualize as a French Revolutionary.

Petőfi was an expert not only in poetry but also in the technique of revolution—indeed, he was the only Hungarian poet whose life's work showed a synthesis of words and action. Not for a day did he take a leave of absence from history. In Hungary Petőfi has become the ultimate symbol of revolution and the country's fight for freedom to the extent that large groups of young people habitually gather by his

---

[56] Visarion Grigorievich Belinsky (1811–1848) is best known for his contributions to Realism in Russian literature.

[57] Alexander Csoma de Kőrös (1784–1842), linguist, Orientalist, and traveler, wrote the first English–Tibetan dictionary and a grammar of Tibetan that was published in Calcutta in 1834. The Royal Asiatic Society erected a statue over his grave in Darjeeling and a bust of him in the British Museum.

statue whenever the country faces severe oppression, as it did in 1956.

Petőfi's poetic faith was both plebeian and democratic. In his fairy tale 'Sir John the Hero,' he created a favorite figure of national folklore whom every generation feels to be its merry contemporary, and who has grown as close to the Hungarians' heart as Ulysses is to the Greeks'. The English literary historian D. Mervin Jones[58] has discovered that these two characters are also similar in a narrower and deeper sense. Both Sir John the Hero, a shepherd, and Ulysses, a tribal king, become wanderers, and they are equally bound by their final loyalties to Juliska and Penelope, respectively. Neither blind fate nor any change of fortune can break the shackles of their hearts. Petőfi's pioneering predecessor and model was the Scotsman Robert Burns, whom he greatly admired.

Petőfi travelled all over the country on foot and by cart. He knew it to its most obscure corners. He painted his birthplace in the Great Hungarian Plain with such force and personal flavor that, ever since then, all the landscapes of Hungary have become identified in foreigners' imaginations with its prairie-like *puszta*.

Strong light casts a sharp shadow. He was good at hating, while at the same time he had a great talent for love. No one sang more tenderly about what he loved—democratic freedom, his own birthplace, and the woman he won for his wife at the cost of a hard struggle. For Petőfi, a woman was an equal life-companion in the modern sense, but his friends disapproved of his wife, Julia Szendrey—they considered her to be a 'blue-stocking' like George Sand.[59] When she married for a second time after Petőfi's untimely death at the age of 26, the whole country turned against her, as though she had betrayed a national legend.

For Petőfi did actually become just such a legend. He disappeared forever in one of the last battles of the failed 1848–1849 Hungarian War of Independence. His body was thrown into an anonymous grave, together with many others, like a common soldier—a fact he foresaw and prophesied in one of his most famous poems. Fate fulfilled his

---

[58] (b. 1922). British novelist and theater critic; see his book *Five Hungarian Writers,* Oxford, 1966.

[59] Pseudonym of Amandine-Lucie-Aurore Dupin (1804–1876), French novelist. She was a prolific writer who in the 1830s already portrayed emancipated women and spoke on behalf of the moral rebellion of the individual. She also was an advocate of free love.

wish to the letter. Many people who refused to believe that he was dead sheltered and fed impostors—pseudo-Petőfis—and talked for decades about a greybeard who, keeping his name a secret, returned from Siberian captivity.

Vörösmarty, who was in extremely poor health, survived him by only a few years. Széchenyi shot himself, and Kossuth,[60] the organizer of the 1848–1849 War of Independence, fled to Turin in Italy, where he died in exile. Walter Savage Landor[61] was his admiring bard.

Compromises

There was a man named János Arany (q.v.) who could never quite forgive himself for surviving Sándor Petőfi. These two were truly devoted friends who never quarrelled, and they carried on a correspondence in verse that is still taught in Hungarian schools.

Petőfi was an extrovert, belligerent, and a brilliant improviser, while Arany was a retiring and self-tormenting poetic artist. Both Petőfi and Arany also wrote longer epic poetry and satirical plays, and in this way both can be said to resemble Heine. Both of them, but especially Arany, were excellent translators of poetry from foreign languages into Hungarian.

Both Petőfi and Arany wanted to raise Populism to the heights of national Classicism at a time when Populism was still strongly identified with the peasantry. Mihály Csokonai Vitéz and Ferenc Kölcsey (qq.v.) had already tried such a transformation of the Popular style into a national Classicism—they both wrote in the Rococo or Neoclassical style. But for Petőfi and Arany, the situation was far more

---

[60] Lajos Kossuth (1802–1894) was the chief figure in the 1848–1849 Hungarian War of Independence against Austria. He became Governor of Hungary, and in that capacity he officially deposed the Habsburgs from the Hungarian throne. He taught himself English from Shakespeare and from the King James Version of the Bible. After he went into exile in 1849, English-speaking audiences both in Great Britain and in the U.S.A. were electrified by his speeches—in the U.S.A. he was invited to address a joint session of Congress.

[61] (1775–1864). English poet and novelist who was a Radical in politics; at Oxford he was called a 'crazy Jacobin.' He wrote a trilogy entitled *Andrea of Hungary* (1840) about the marriage of the brother of King Louis the Great.

concrete, because they lived at a time when the country-wide collection of folklore had begun in earnest. Both Petőfi and Arany clearly saw the links between the linguistic and political revolution of Populism; however, their realization did not take the form of some joint manifesto or newspaper article, but is to be found only in their teasing, jocular correspondence.

Arany's career is mirrored in his trilogy *Toldi, Toldi's Love,* and *Toldi's Evening*. It centers around Miklós Toldi, a legendary medieval folk hero, who is the disinherited younger son of a nobleman —somewhat like Orlando in Shakespeare's *As You Like It*.

When *Toldi* was published, Arany became famous overnight, and it won him the sincere admiration and friendship of Petőfi, who was already well established and celebrated. The genre of this first epic is old-fashioned but filled with a new kind of feeling. Its tone is a miracle all by itself, for it appeals both to finicky gourmets and to peasants gathering in the market place. This epic obviously has a political message as well, for it contains the symbol of a popular giant who is about to be liberated from being a common man and made triumphant.

In the second part of Arany's trilogy, its hero turns old and savage after Hungary's defeat in the 1848–1849 War of Independence[62] against Austria and the Habsburgs. Arany was broken-hearted—living under police surveillance and hounded by a stupid, bureaucratic censorship. After a long pause he returned for the third time to his favorite character—this time under the pressure of public demand. After the famous 'Ausgleich' or Compromise of 1867 with Austria,

---

[62] The 1848–1849 Hungarian War of Independence against Austria began with a popular uprising on March 15, 1848, during which Sándor Petőfi emerged as a leading figure. He aroused the people with the powerful words of his 'National Song.' This uprising became a full-fledged war against Austria, which the Hungarians were winning until the Habsburgs asked for, and received, massive help from the Russian Tsar. A huge Russian army led by Prince Pashkievich intervened on Austria's behalf, and the war ended with the Hungarian army's surrender to the Russians at Világos on July 31, 1849. Thirteen years of vengeance and retribution followed, which are known in Hungarian history as the 'Bach Period' (named after Alexander, Freiherr von Bach, the Habsburg's Minister of the Interior and no relation to the great composer). This was ended by the 'Compromise of 1867,' which established the Austro-Hungarian Dual Monarchy that lasted until 1919.

wrought by Ferenc Deák,[63] a period of relatively stable relations set in between Vienna and Hungary, during which the upper classes made rapid gains. The last instalment of *Toldi* was hailed by the whole country—bankers, serfs, and literati. The first part of the trilogy was like an explosion of Arany's spirit at the time when he wrote it; the third part he wrote slowly and reluctantly.

Arany abhorred playing the role of the leader, but his artistic perfection made him a leader against his will. For decades his faultless language and prosody were the standard against which all others were judged, and his poetry was justly called a second Hungarian Bible. This simile happens to be doubly apt, because of the way he expressed his ideas. Its first ingredient was his style; its second was the Calvinist puritan heritage of the 16th century which reached its stylistic apogee in him. Arany's literary authority was shown by the fact that, even in the field of poetic translation, he set the standard of unprecedented perfection. Even today it is a daunting task to improve his translations of *Hamlet* and *A Midsummer Night's Dream,* though it has been tried.

There was a duality in Arany's approach to life. On the one hand, he was a truly urban poet who occupied the position of Secretary General of the Hungarian Academy of Sciences. On the other hand, he wrote poems in the style of Horace, full of nostalgic sighs for a secluded country cottage. He obviously hated the crude, jostling, elbowing capital. Yet it is impossible to imagine him elsewhere than in the principal city of the nation, with its dust, stink, and crude lust for life, shouting in mixed languages—which the saintly man, prematurely aging, derided with resignation.

As Hungary approached the year 1896, the millennium of the founding of the country in Europe, some irresponsible orators suggested that the 'Horsemen of the Volga'—a name given to Hungarians in symbolic reference to their nomadic origins—would once again achieve a leading role in Central Europe.

At this time, all of Europe was undergoing a psychological crisis,

---

[63] (1803–1876). Trained in jurisprudence, he entered Hungarian politics and wrote numerous articles. He was the main intellectual architect of the Compromise of 1867, which established Hungary and the remaining parts of the Austrian Empire as two equal states under the Habsburg dynasty, and which put an end to the 13-year period of persecution of those who had participated in the 1848–1849 Hungarian War of Independence. He earned the name 'The Wise Man of the Fatherland.'

caused by determinism and Darwinism, which were never in harmony with the increasing desire for economic development or with the balance of power among the states of Western Europe. More railways were built; tunnels were drilled through the Alps; the French science fiction writer Jules Verne sent his characters soaring to the Moon and into the depths of the ocean. All of this furious activity created, as its own reaction, a kind of philosophical pessimism which made people ask 'Why are we here?' 'What is the good of all of this furious activity?' 'Is humanity also a species that is doomed to extinction?'

In Hungary it was János Vajda, the lyric poet, and Imre Madách, the playwright-philosopher (qq.v.) who reflected this pessimism. The lives of both men were unhappy. Their disillusionment about women and politics made it easier for them to justify to themselves their somber images of the world.

Imre Madách, who was born in the same year as Petőfi, had a tyrannical mother and an unfaithful wife. He was imprisoned for his participation in the 1848–1849 Hungarian War of Independence. Later, living on his family estate in Alsósztregova, which is today in the Slovak Republic, he wrote a dramatic poem that is arguably the single most important piece of Hungarian literature. Its title is *The Tragedy of Man*. This play has been frequently compared to Goethe's *Faust* and to Milton's *Paradise Lost,* but for the wrong reasons, because, although *The Tragedy of Man* shares with Goethe and Milton the Fall from Heaven through Lucifer's rebellion, Madách actually produced in it the first piece of existentialist, philosophical drama in 19th-century Europe. (For the full plot of this centrally important piece of Hungarian literature, see the section on Madách.)

During the first space flight in European literature, Adam says:

> *The goal is death, life is nothing but strife,*
> *And the goal of life is this strife itself.*

Could the true antidote for despair caused by forbidden knowledge be found in stoicism? Although Madách had read the optimistic Hegel, he already foreshadowed Spengler in his vision of a haughtily stoic, indeed existentialist, historical philosophy of defeat.

The Tragedy of Man can be interpreted in a number of different ways. It can be seen as an internal dialogue conducted by a Manichean heretic with himself, all the way to the edge of suicide. Lucifer, Adam's companion who bears hardly any similarity to Mephistopheles, the God of Evil whom we see at Faust's side, is actually the true master of our created, material world—he is the great shadow between the splintered, spark-like human soul and the brilliance of the hidden, Primeval World Spirit. Adam, the eternal exile, thrown aimlessly into repetitive cycles of history as though he were playing out a script written by Giambattista Vico, can never escape from Lucifer's grasp. It is notable that a hundred years later Gyula Illyés (q.v.) wrote a play about the Manichean Cathar[64] movement in Southern France, for which he appears as the spokesman and partisan. (It is quite likely, of course, that Illyés had the National Uprising of 1956 in mind.) It, too, constituted a defiant glorification of defeat.

Unlike his great contemporary Madách, Gyula Juhász (q.v.) had no coherent philosophy to offer. He was a collision point between the rebels of 1848 and the compromisers of 1867. The former overrated him; the latter underrated him. In reality, he was simply the Great Indignant, fighting an everlasting personal battle against the Establishment. He uttered puritanical outbursts amidst the tumult of life's commercialism as though he were trying to preserve Petőfi's virginal revolutionary faith at the sick bed of a nation that was spiritually only half alive. He resembles the British Arthur Clough.[65]

János Vajda (q.v.) was a unique genius. Inspired by Schopenhauer, his kind of pessimism turned towards a Buddhist-like Nirvana; but, strangely enough, he was afraid of death. His greatest merit in Hungarian literature is that he was able to express his true love, continuing through several decades, for one woman.

In this regard he may be compared to his contemporary, George Meredith, although comparing him to the Russian Turgenev makes better sense, since he was an East European, not a Westerner. Vajda lived with his dark moods in an agrarian world, on a reedy lake accompanied by no one, waiting with his shotgun for wild ducks. His main cultural role was the heralding of the great literary renaissance that was then in the making.

---

[64] The Cathars, also known as the Albigenses, were a heretical Christian sect that flourished in France and Italy during the 12th and 13th centuries. They were neo-Manicheans, believing in the coexistence of equal (or almost equal) good and evil Gods. They were suppressed by crusades and by the Inquisition.

[65] Arthur Hugh Clough (1819–1861) was sympathetic towards the revolutions of 1848. He wrote poems about the conflict between dogmatic faith and free thinking and about the debate between atheists and believers.

The Sun Rises in the West

In 1895 there appeared in Madrid, Spain, a book entitled *En torno al casticismo* ('In Search of Authenticity'). In this bold work, the young Unamuno[66] presented a philosophical challenge to the nationalism of the wounded Spanish people, fearful of change and loaded down with sickness and hurt pride. In 1906 a volume by Endre Ady (q.v.) called *New Poems* [Új versek] was published in Budapest, and only two years later, as if answering the call of a larger circle of resonance, there appeared the most important Hungarian literary review, *Nyugat* [The West], which was to become the home of an entire generation of truly superior geniuses. While there had been earlier Hungarian reviews that had greeted the 20th century (one of them was actually named *20th Century*), the voice of *Nyugat* was not only new, but radical as well—it provided new manifestos, both political and literary, for an entire generation. It immediately provoked the anger of the established political and literary interests as well as the well-intentioned guardians of the old traditions. The fight was tough, but without such confrontations there can be no viable intellectual life—only court poetry, and an official kind of it at that.

During King Matthias's reign, as we saw earlier, a narrow circle that enjoyed nationwide power entered the blood circulation of the Italian Renaissance without appreciable delay. As we also saw, such simultaneity of Hungarian events with the mainstream of European culture was exceptional rather than usual, although Hungarian culture does, by and large, manage to keep pace with the alert peoples of the borderlands of Europe. This was certainly true during the 15th century, as we saw in the case of the Hussites. Later, from the 16th to the 19th century, Polish literature provided the Hungarians with a good model, and during the high tide of Romanticism, Southern Slavic and Greek literature provided, to some extent, good suggestions as to what the Hungarians might be writing at the same time. Between 1895 and 1905, a decade of ferment by any standard, a feeling of backwardness

---

[66] Miguel de Unamuno (1864–1936), Spanish writer. His main works include *The Tragic Sense of Life* (1913) and *The Agony of Christianity* (1924).

haunted the peoples on the periphery of Europe; their common idea, which first matured in the consciousness of their writers and was then expressed in their writings, was 'we must catch up with the West.' Although Spain is geographically part of the West, it was culturally much less so at that time. It is therefore significant that the Spanish 'generation of '98' (spearheaded by Unamuno), the Greek Kavafis,[67] the Russian Alexander Blok,[68] the Turkish writers who published in *Servet-i-Fünun,*[69] and the founders of *Nyugat* in Hungary were all contemporaries. In every case, their driving force was the same: They were all deeply involved with self-searching, with iconoclasm, with their consciousness of a mission, with the cult of the poet's personality, and with frequent changes of sides from one faction to another, studded with various and sundry law suits. But they agreed on one thing: They excoriated provincialism wherever and whenever they found it.

In Hungary, also, there was plenty of bickering among various groups of the *Nyugat* generation, but their later influences merged to shape the next generation's psyche. It had rarely happened before that sons and grandsons should so readily accept their fathers and grand-fathers as their literary role models. Hungarians' literary goals have changed many times since then, but they have always acknowledged that it was *Nyugat* which gave their values their correct priorities. And it was this loose association of writers, variously branded as 'symbolists,' 'decadents,' 'cosmopolitans,' and 'apers of the West,' which guided Hungarian thought from self-deceiving dreams back to reality. It was the educated, multilingual translators, poets, and

---

[67] Konstantinos Petros Kavafis (1863–1933), a Greek poet whose poem *Ithaca* was translated by T.S. Eliot and published in his prestigious periodical *Criterion.*

[68] Alexander Alexandrovich Blok (1880–1921), a significant figure among the Russian Symbolists. His first volume, *Poems about the Beautiful Lady,* appeared in 1904; his masterpiece, *The Twelve,* appeared in 1918. Among Hungarian poets, Dezső Kosztolányi and Attila József (qq.v.) have translated his works. Both Kosztolányi and József were educated by reading *Nyugat.*

[69] *Servet-i-Fünun* [The Treasure Trove of the Sciences] was a Turkish literary review, the leading organ of the new Turkish literature. It was inaugurated in 1891 and, although it survived only until 1901, its founders did achieve their basic aim of bringing Turkish literature up to the contemporary European standard. Their most famous poet was Tevfik Fikret; their most significant prose writer was Halit Ziya Uşaklïgïl.

essayists of *Nyugat*, reading and speaking French, Italian, German, and English, who managed to dismount the 'Horsemen of the Volga,' toppling that old, glory-seeking, national phantom from its greasy saddle.

The leader of the rebels was Endre Ady (q.v.). His behavior was ambivalent: on the one hand, he knew, proclaimed, and insisted on his role as a standard bearer; but on the other hand, he felt no obligation to be loyal to anyone but himself. Modern Hungarian poetry already possessed quite a few inherited symbols—there was Mihály Vörösmarty's 'Csongor,' a quasi-Shakespearean fairy-tale prince at the crossroads between dream and reality; there was Petőfi's 'Sir John the Hero,' 19th-century Hungary's merry proto-Ulysses; and, finally, there was Arany's ever-popular 'Toldi,' the victorious son of the people. In contrast to these well-known and extremely popular symbols, there now appeared in Ady's works a new symbol, projected right out of his own brooding and prophetic personality: 'The son of Gog and Magog' from the Book of Ezekiel in the Old Testament. Ady called himself 'The Monster of God.'

The aging Delacroix once painted 'Jacob's Fight With the Angel,' a mural in the Church of Saint-Sulpice in Paris. The more one looks at that painting, the more one understands the essence of Ady's poetry. The human's desperate efforts to assail the angel amount to nothing; the angel deflects his efforts with ironic pity, while the human obviously knows that he cannot possibly win.

Ady came from a strong Calvinist background. He was born in the same district of Transylvania, known in Hungarian as the *Szilágyság*, where Ferenc Kölcsey (q.v.) had been born. The Ady family belonged to the country-squire nobility—they were proud, ancient, and quite poor. Ady, as a young man, often clashed with his father, as had Petőfi. Later, as a beginning journalist in Nagyvárad (now Oradea in Romania), he did a great deal of reading. The German philosopher Herder, who predicted that the Hungarian language would die out and the Slavic languages would flourish, was one of his favorites. He reacted strongly to this prediction and enunciated a program in which his Hungarianness would be emphasized ever so strongly. In his works his native land played a decisive role. Being the Petőfi-like rebel that he was, he considered his own social class to be doomed—and if it was, let the Dance of Death be accelerated! Flouting death rather than fearing it has always been a particularly Hungarian escape mechanism for its national consciousness—an almost shamanistic ritual, which allows the participants in the dance to jettison their ballast and thereby gain a new lease on life. It should be mentioned that, for Ady, the term 'nation' no longer meant only the nobility, as it had for Berzsenyi and Kölcsey (qq.v.)—he included in it the peasants, the proletarians, and the rebellious urban intellectuals.

One can tell a great deal about a person's inner drive by seeing whom he picks as his main enemy. For Ady, the enemy was not the Habsburg monarch who still ruled Hungary; it was his fellow countryman from the same Transylvanian county, the Prime Minister of Hungary, Count István Tisza.[70] It was almost like a family feud—a fight to the death between brothers—as though Arany's epic had turned into Ady's real life. In *Toldi,* the valiant younger brother, Miklós, who comes from the people, fights for the truth, while the villainous older brother, György, is a member of the ruling establishment and is one of the oppressors. In Ady's life script one may think of him as Miklós, the hero of the people, with Prime Minister István Tisza as György, the elder brother. In reality the Prime Minister was not the evil monster whom later Marxist historians have depicted; he merely lived an anachronistic existence as though he were still a member of Kölcsey's generation, full of outmoded anxieties for his nation.

Ady's style evolved gradually. His early diction still carries some of the signs of the dawning century, showing the influence of the German Romantics, and particularly that of Nietzsche. In this he may be compared to the Greek author Nikos Kazantsakis,[71] whose contemporary he was. Ady's early poems show a bit of Secessionism and self-indulgent outbursts of a yet immature mysticism. He was wooing his public by swinging between Narcissus and Satan. He was egged on in this by a married woman with whom he had a notorious love affair, Adél, whose name he spelled backwards as Léda when he dedicated his first book of poems to her. She was wealthy and urbane and introduced the young poet to life in Paris. Ady thus skipped

---

[70] (1861–1918). He was Prime Minister of Hungary from 1903 to 1905 and again from 1913 to 1917. Tisza was seen by the progressives as a reactionary who represented the interests of the aristocracy and approved of the Monarchy's military alliance with Kaiser Wilhelm II. It is generally agreed that the battle between Ady and Tisza was the most important ongoing adversary relationship in Hungary at that time.

[71] (1883–1957). Noted Greek novelist and Nobel laureate; author of *Zorba the Greek, A Sequel to the Odyssey,* and *The Last Temptation of Christ.*

Budapest and moved from Nagyvárad directly to Paris, fulfilling an old romantic dream that all Hungarians traditionally nurture about 'la vie parisienne.' Because of Ady's frequent trips to Paris, some critics developed the notion that he was an imitator of Baudelaire and Verlaine, but this is not true. Their effect on him was only minimal and superficial at best, although the praise of wine and drinking, the pose of living like a habitual bohemian drunkard, was affected by almost everyone who visited Paris in those days. This 'amorous Paris' was, in reality, only one phase along the road of Ady's maturing. In Paris he quickly became a genuine intellectual radical.

His hero was Jaurès,[72] the humanist and socialist leader. And through Jaurès we can better understand that, in spite of his early, shallow resemblances to Baudelaire and Verlaine, Ady's real kinsman among French writers was the great revolutionary Romantic, the novelist Victor Hugo, who, like the Delacroix painting mentioned above, also 'wrestled with the angel' in his insular exile on Guernsey. The role of the Romantic spokesman for democratic causes thus passed in a direct line from Vörösmarty to Ady through the mediation of Paris, although not through the Paris of the early 20th century, but that of the 19th.

The truly unique, and indeed the most valuable, phase of Ady's work is found in his later years, when he developed a two-fold relationship to God, on the one hand, and, on the other hand, to death through self-destruction. What makes Ady's body of work unique is that these tendencies do not contradict his poetry, but form along with it an organic whole, moulded into the figure of a Judaeo-Christian existentialist—perhaps the first true existentialist in European literature. His God, neither Jewish nor Christian, was a 'terrible God' with whom Ady, once embodied in an earthly incarnation, tested his ability to fight. Ady sensed that World War I would end in a disaster for Hungary comparable only to the catastrophe of Mohács in 1526. He was quite correct. In the peace treaties of Versailles in 1920—after Ady's untimely death at the age of 42—and in the wake of the destruction of the Austro-Hungarian Monarchy, Hungary lost two-

---

[72] Jean Jaurès (1859–1914), French politician of the radical left. He founded the newspaper *L'Humanité*, which later became France's Communist daily newspaper. A pacifist, Jaurès bitterly opposed World War I and, as it began, was shot by an assassin who believed him to be insufficiently patriotic.

thirds of its former territory and some five million of its people, who became minorities within Romania, Czechoslovakia, Yugoslavia, and even Austria. One of his poems is entitled 'People Before the Scattering'; it was written before the Treaty of Versailles became a reality.

Ady is perhaps best remembered as a major innovator in the Hungarian language. His verbs, adjectives, nominal compounds, and rhyme schemes were all so new and so characteristic that parodists like Frigyes Karinthy (q.v.) have had a field day imitating him. His vocabulary came from the Old Testament, from the *kuruc* songs of the 17th century, from folk ballads, and from 16th-century Calvinist psalms, giving his voice an almost untranslatably archaic clamor. Toward the end of his life, Ady composed in long breaths, not in lines. He became the possessor of a language truly worthy of a struggle with the Angel.

Ady's best friend was a novelist named Gyula Krúdy (q.v.) who is included in this anthology because of the special poetic status of his prose style. Only moderately interested in foreign literature, he knew little of foreign countries; in order to make up for it, he knew about older Hungary to a frightening extent—especially about its social, rainbow-hued backwaters.

Although his contemporaries did not appreciate him so highly, there is general agreement today among Hungarian literati that Krúdy is, if not in the exact nature of his prose, then in his general attitude to life and his significance on the Hungarian literary scene, roughly equivalent to Marcel Proust and Thomas Wolfe. Not really a story teller, Krúdy wrote the finest prose-poems of surrealist day-dreaming; he produced haze-covered pictures with recurrent rhythms of an enclosed Hell with its own laws in which his phantom figures constantly experience polyphonic time. He was the Hungarian forerunner of *écriture automatique* and a good deal of 'stream of consciousness' writing, in this resembling Proust rather than Joyce. But he was not consciously aware of how revolutionary his style was. And if he had been aware of it, he would not have been interested, because he trusted mainly to his own intuition about the affairs of the dead, adventurers, funeral directors, and abandoned women—both real and invented figures with romantic names. Through these, Krúdy created a unifying, hypnotically effective tone and mood replete with people's alter-egos, ghosts, and haunting memories.

In a happier vein, Krúdy could write about food, wine, and cooking with a gusto that makes the most colorful cookbook of Hungary's deservedly famous cuisine pale into prosaic insignificance. He also showed great interest in folk customs and superstitions—his book about dreams and how to interpret them has been popular throughout the century. In the United States, the Hungarian-born Pennsylvania historian John Lukacs devoted some memorable pages to Krúdy's style and personality on the pages of *The New Yorker*, comparing his voice to that of a bass cello.

Just as Ady and Krúdy were in some way a pair, so were the two great Western-orientated geniuses of the *Nyugat* generation, Árpád Tóth and Mihály Babits (qq.v.). With them there begins an activity for which Hungarians are justly famous—the systematic, ongoing, and poetically highly inspired translation of world literature into Hungarian. János Arany (q.v.) had, of course, set the staggering standard with his renditions of Shakespeare's *Hamlet* and *A Midsummer Night's Dream*. But Tóth and Babits—later joined by Kosztolányi, Lőrinc Szabó, Sándor Weöres, Ágnes Nemes Nagy (qq.v.) and many more—became the founders and initiating masters of a major intellectual industry: the formal, artistic translation of world poetry. Babits, for instance, took Dante's *Divine Comedy* and created from it a three-part Hungarian classic of *Inferno, Purgatorio,* and *Paradiso* that people still recite by heart in Dante's original meter and rhyme scheme as though it were original Hungarian poetry.

One of the early masters of the Western European orientation of the *Nyugat* generation was Árpád Tóth (q.v.). He was intimately familiar with the French, English, and German literature of the post-Renaissance period and produced memorable translations of Goethe, Verlaine, Baudelaire, Milton, Shelley, Keats, and many others. His own poems are in no way imitations of these poets; they show his almost psychic sensitivity as he describes objects in the dark and addresses the stars in the heavens. Tóth yearned for peace and considered human beings to be trouble makers. One of his best remembered poems, the famous 'Elegy to a Broom-Bush Gorse' yearns for 'post-human peace' on the planet Earth. His style as a translator created a school of translation. In his outlook, Western orientation, and exquisite literary erudition, he is closely linked with Dezső Kosztolányi and Mihály Babits (qq.v.).

At one time, it was customary in Hungarian literary criticism to consider the Tóth–Kosztolányi–Babits triumvirate as the 'Urbanites,' as opposed to the 'Populists.' Mihály Babits was in many ways Ady's balancing opposite. Besides being an 'Urbanite,' he is sometimes seen as a 'learned poet' or *poeta doctus,* while Ady is seen as an untutored, instinctive genius, a *poeta natus.* This is an exaggeration, however, since the real differences between them are found on a deeper level, in their respective relationships to God. Ady wrestled with the protean Lord of Zion, but he was doomed to surrender in advance, because he was a Calvinist thrown upon the mercy of Grace without any sort of dogmatic faith. Babits was a Catholic believer who bore God's yoke with humility, even as he lay dying of throat cancer. He was able to clarify his obedience to himself as an act of his own free will.

From 1914 onward, Ady and Babits both knew that Hungary could only emerge from World War I badly beaten and dismembered, and both gave sharp expression to this tormented vision. There is a view on the surface: if any Hungarian writer and poet could be credited with having read 'all of world literature,' it was Babits. In Hungary, it is customary to compare him to T.S. Eliot. His masters were Swinburne and Tennyson, but in his brilliant formal exploits he also shows the influence of the orchestration of the late Victorians, and particularly of the American Edgar Allan Poe. It was through them that he found his way back to Shelley and Keats. Because of the enduring influence of Babits, there was a renaissance during the 1920s and 1930s of Hungarian interest in these two Romantic English poets at a time when, in England, Shelley's stock was particularly low.

On his sick bed—which would be his death bed—Babits wrote a poem entitled *The Book of Jonah* [Jónás könyve], which is arguably the greatest Hungarian poem written in the 20th century. Reacting to the approaching horrors of the Nazis and World War II, he wrote, in somewhat the same way as Thomas Mann, whom he knew personally, about Christian patience, suggesting that the reserves of faith in God would survive aggression and violence. In the poem, Jonah is sent by God to Nineveh to preach against the sins of the city, but no one listens to him. He begs to be released from his unwanted job as prophet, but God wants him to finish the job, since a prophet's task is to persevere in his prophecy, even if his reward is sarcasm and derision. How could 'Nineveh' possibly deserve mercy for the sake of only one just man? Babits answered his own question and wrote, "for amidst sinners, 'mute' means 'accomplice.'" At that time, Hitler's death-squads were already loading their weapons and the blueprints were already finished for the gas ovens.

Dezső Kosztolányi (q.v.) also died of cancer—that of the tongue.

Next to Ady and Babits, he appears a fun-loving, merry-making, flirtatious troubadour, a 'man about town.' He and Babits were very close friends during their student days—their correspondence is an important source of literary materials. But while Babits froze when faced with the *vulgus,* Kosztolányi, like a born gambler, moved with great ease through different cultures and life-styles. Besides writing superior poetry, Kosztolányi also excelled as a novelist. His historical novel *Nero, the Bloody Poet* shows deep psychoanalytical insight into the nature of a vain and untalented terrorist. In some of his other novels, he showed himself to be a connoisseur of the feminine psyche. His essays on language reveal him to be a sophisticated and insightful linguist. He was also an outspoken critic. He took exception to Ady's early mannerisms and emerged in posterity's estimation as a truer 'Latin spirit' than Ady, despite all Ady's trips to Paris. Kosztolányi was an inveterate punster who played passionately with words. Even on his death-bed, unable to speak, he jotted down puns in a notebook.

As mentioned above, Both Kosztolányi and Babits were dazzling translators. The translations which they wrote, although faithful to their originals in form, bear their individual styles so unmistakably that later generations of translators still imitate them. Modern Russians feel the same way about Boris Pasternak's translations[73]—they say that they are excellent Pasternak poems *à propos* of someone else's work. In the West, on the other hand, this has been an unfamiliar phenomenon, since literary translation there has been done there more literally. The French, for example, refuse to translate according to form—even Shakespeare is rendered in precise, accurate prose. English and American poets have usually been translated into other languages; they themselves have seldom become artistic translators who place their personal imprints on a foreign author's work. But other art forms have fared differently. Consider, for instance, English painting: By 'freely translating' the brush strokes of Flemish, Dutch, French, and Italian painters, the golden century that extends between Gainsborough and

---

[73] Boris Leonidovitch Pasternak (1890–1960), one of the most important Russian poets and novelists of all times; author of *Dr. Zhivago.* Pasternak systematically translated from most European languages, including Hungarian. He translated Sándor Petőfi's *Sir John the Hero* and the work of many other 20th-century poets; from English he translated Shakespeare's *Hamlet* and the poetry of Shelley and Keats; from French he translated Verlaine; from German he translated Goethe's *Faust* and the poetry of Rilke.

Turner produced splendid paraphrases. It seems remarkable to students of art history that the great-grandfathers of these English canvasses vary among Rubens, Van Dyck, Ruysdael, Claude Lorraine, and Veronese, yet these paraphrases are all quite clearly the first English paintings that rise to artistic greatness by any international standard. Perhaps this analogy can shed some light on what has happened in Hungarian poetry since the work of Babits, Tóth, and Kosztolányi.

We have spoken above about the classical education of the old Hungarians. In England, too, under the old order a bishop, a member of parliament, or a cabinet minister always carried with him his pocket edition of Horace in the original Latin, paying less attention to Dryden's brilliant translation. In Hungarian literature during the past two hundred years, the classical Greek and Latin authors have been periodically retranslated. The Homeric epics and the Homeric hymns were translated by the late Gábor Devecseri, a personal friend of Robert Graves,[74] and there exists the complete Virgil in sonorous versification, faithful even in its alliterations, by István Lakatos.[75]

We now turn to Gyula Juhász (q.v.), who was an attractive and characteristic East European poet. He suffered from an incurable nervous disease, and he retired to a town on the Great Hungarian Plain where he met his death. His concept of the world resembled that of Leo Tolstoy grafted onto the psyche of a Franciscan friar. One can visualize him as a volunteer, joining the rebellious serfs in the peasant wars of the 16th century, carrying a crucifix but no arms. Like Ady, Juhász began to write in the Secessionist manner of the early 20th century, but his style matured into an original voice that was all his own as he continued to witness the struggles of a poor, downtrodden peasantry that was half-Catholic, half-heathen in its beliefs and practices. He was at his very best when he forgot that there was such a thing as 'The West.' It was Gyula Juhász, the poet, and Gyula Krúdy, the novelist, similar in temperament, who were able to discover the erstwhile brave Eastern nomads in the midst of today's miserable

---

[74] Robert Ranke Graves (1895–1985), English poet and writer. He made three visits to Hungary, where he established the Robert Graves Literary Prize in 1968. He is the author of *I, Claudius; Goliath and David;* and many other well-known works.

[75] István Lakatos (b. 1926), winner of the Kossuth Prize, lives and works in Budapest; he has also translated portions of the Mahabhārata from Sanskrit, as well as Latin, Italian, and German classics.

village peasants.

At long last the battle around the periodical *Nyugat* died down, and both its critics and its readers had a little better view toward the horizon. Today we are in a better position to see that some things which this generation saw so enthusiastically as precious discoveries from the West were only perishable fashions. Not everything in the West was gold—the British themselves knew that very well, as can be told from Gilbert and Sullivan's devastating comic opera *Patience,* in which Oscar Wilde is wickedly parodied.

Hungary's answer to Gilbert, however, came from the very inner circle of *Nyugat*'s sharpest minds. He was Frigyes Karinthy (q.v.), who wrote the immortal collection of Hungarian literary parodies entitled *That's How you Write!* Although this book is more than seventy years old, it has remained devilishly entertaining, and it also manages to be a penetrating critical study; indeed, it is the best stylistic analysis of the entire *Nyugat* generation. Instead of making its points in pompous academic jargon, it reflects the rich folklore of the city of Budapest, replete with puns, nonsense words, and all the associations that can only come from truly knowing a field from within. Countless anecdotes are still being told today, recounting the verbal wit that was fired across the marble tables of the famous Café New York in Budapest where Karinthy and Kosztolányi used to meet, regularly surrounded by colleagues and younger admirers. In his serious poetry, Karinthy, the great humorist, confessed the torments of a Rigoletto-like clown, in total nakedness and with no self-pity.

In the midst of this turbulent generation, Milán Füst (q.v.) was the first practitioner of free verse in Hungarian. He reached great heights of perfection in this genre. A rarity in Hungarian literature, he was a ruthless critic of everything that he had written. He regularly and systematically discarded a great deal of what he had already written—because of this his total output barely increased over the decades. His concise, nobly-cast rhetoric reached back all the way to the style of Berzsenyi (q.v.), but his elevated tone clashed ironically with his sometimes malicious and sometimes terrified, but always minutely exact, vision. In his nightmarish world, he would spin Pirandello-like[76] phantom figures in the imaginary landscape that

---

[76] Luigi Pirandello (1867–1936), Italian playwright, philosopher and critic. He won the Nobel Prize for Literature in 1934. His play *Six Characters in*

surrounded his alchemist's workshop, but the effect was always a realistic one, because his poetry is the dense distillation of stubborn passions, not of meaningless, empty fancies. He was capable of being in equal measure a great enthusiast and an embittered hater—he was a poet who stored his emotions in an underground hothouse of his pent-up, furious passions. There is something of Jeremiah's lamentations in his poetry. It is perhaps not coincidental that both Karinthy and Füst came from Jewish backgrounds. They both had particular ways with words—Karinthy's was that of the unstoppable, witty iconoclast; Füst's was that of a prophet right out of the Old Testament. Füst created a whole school of modern poetry. A mesmerising teacher and university professor, he attracted numerous young, independent, highly talented future poets of considerable significance.

The Waves of the Parisian Avant-Garde
Reach the Shores of the Danube

Around 1910, the triumphant young dictators of the avant-garde's artistic and literary movements invaded the scene everywhere in Europe. The best known of the leaders were Apollinaire,[77] Marinetti,[78] Wyndham Lewis,[79] Kandinsky,[80] and Tatlin.[81] The multiplicity of their explosive manifestos rivalled the number of their actual works—sometimes it was nothing but the manifesto itself that

---

Search of an Author premiered in 1921 and became a landmark in the new theatrical wave of the grotesque double vision of seeing tragedy in humor, and humor in tragedy.

[77] Guillaume Apollinaire (1880–1918), born a Pole named Wilhelm Apollinaris Kostrowitzky, became one of France's leading literary figures; he also exerted a major influence on Hungarian poetry between the two World Wars.

[78] Filippo Tomasso Marinetti (1876–1944), an Italian Futurist poet.

[79] Percy Wyndham Lewis (1884–1957), English writer and painter, established the Center of the Protesting Arts against academic painting in 1913. A year later, he and Ezra Pound founded the periodical *Blast,* which functioned as the organ of Vorticism, an ally of Futurism.

[80] Vasily Vasilevich Kandinsky (1866–1944) was one of the main founders of modern abstract painting.

[81] Vladimir Evgrafovich Tatlin (1885–1953), Russian painter, sculptor, and architect, was one of the main founders of Constructivism.

was the main work. Most of these movements came to an abrupt halt with the romantically optimistic outbreak of World War I, only to have their explosive force even more sharpened and elevated by the ferocious nausea and revolutionary fermentation when the bouquets finally wilted on the decorated rifle-barrels.

In Hungary, the leadership of the avant-garde was seized by Lajos Kassák (q.v.) who was every bit as much a painter as he was a poet. A former foundry worker, he was a companion-in-arms of László Moholy-Nagy.[82] Kassák stayed independent of the *Nyugat* group as well as of every other tradition, recognizing Walt Whitman as his only intellectual ancestor.

There was a famous Budapest joke which claimed that Kassák had a secret, private telegraph line that told him what was happening in Berlin and in Moscow on any given day and also told him who was behind the latest contorted, experimental '*ism*' in any major city on any continent. Somewhat like Trotsky, with his idea of the 'permanent revolution,' Kassák believed in an unceasing, eternal avant-garde, of which he was to be the leader in Hungary. He behaved rather dictatorially and tolerated only followers, not real companions.

To this day, many Hungarian critics and readers consider Károly Tamkó-Sirató, another Paris-based avant-garde poet with a Manifesto of his own (entitled *Manifeste dimensioniste,* 1936), to be more talented than Kassák. Yet Kassák's mystique endures, despite the fiasco of Hungary's experiment with Communism in 1919 after World War I, and despite the four decades of Communism after World War II.

But the descendants of Kassák lack the force of the earlier movement. The belief in world revolution and in poetry-by-proclamation and art-by-proclamation has died down and now is usually met with only a polite yawn. Ultimately, as we know only too well, it was petty terrorists and kidnappers, not the 'workers of the world,' who united to form the glorious Workers' Soviets.

---

[82] (1895–1946). Originally a painter and photographer, he is remembered today as one of the main exponents of Bauhaus architecture. He died in Chicago, Illinois.

Between East and West

The major figures of the Hungarian *Nyugat* generation resemble the world's great Romanticists in their individual human fates as well as in their literary effect. They directed literature into deeper channels, and they all perished relatively young, almost all of them shortly before age fifty, most of them dying in slow, hard torment. Yet in the 1920s and 1930s their figures still towered above the rising younger generation in a dismembered country and in a self-destructive Europe.

Nous autres, civilisations, nous savons maintenant, que nous sommes mortelles. ('We modern civilizations have now come to realize that we are mortal.') This slogan by Paul Valéry fitted Central Europe even more closely than the West, as the effects of World War I tore into the very fiber of a dozen European nations, all seething with hatred for one another. This is perhaps why the artists and the literati of the years following World War I clung so desperately to the dissolving foundations of the model civilization far away in France. For whatever seemed to be mortal and spoiled to Valéry in the shadows of the wooden crosses of Verdun seemed quite solid and powerful from afar. Ady had been dead for some time and his surviving companions were now getting cleansed by the acid horror of all that was decorative, fashionable, and perishable. The poetry of *Nyugat*'s second generation was more objective than that of its first, as these poets were turning toward our denuded century.

Partly under the influence of his disciples, the young essayists around Babits eventually surpassed even his culture. From their outpost in Paris they crossed more often than Babits did to England—and not just intellectually, but physically as well. T.S. Eliot and James Joyce were their new sources of inspiration.

The standard was set by Eliot's magazine, *Criterion,* and Bloomsbury became an important place to visit. At the cost of a slight exaggeration, it might be said that in educated Budapest circles Virginia Woolf was now the new 'Artemis of Ephesus,' with Aldous Huxley the omniscient 'oldest son' of the family, whose younger brothers in Budapest were enthusiastically imitating him.

The main essayists of this period were László Németh,[83] Antal

---

[83] (1901–1975). Physician turned major national essayist, novelist, and philosopher of education. He was also an early pioneer of ecological thinking.

Szerb,[84] and Gábor Halász,[85] the latter two of whom would later be murdered by the Nazis in 1944–1945 because of their Jewish ancestry. They were both disciples of Babits who was, among his many other accomplishments, an extraordinary master of the history of world literature. Antal Szerb, who wrote what is arguably the best history of Hungarian literature, was also an extraordinarily talented novelist. His novel *The Pendragon Legend* showed his leaning towards England, but he was equally at home in the history of France, as shown by his enduring classic, *The Queen's Necklace,* which deals with the age of Marie Antoinette. Gábor Halász is best remembered today as a critic with the highest standards that have been reached in Hungarian literature.

László Németh had trained as a physician, but after a brief time spent as a high school doctor, he decided not to practice medicine. Instead he decided to throw himself into writing. Hungarian literature owes this exceptionally erudite essayist and prose writer some of the best insights into the 'Urbane' and 'Populist' traditions in Hungarian literature, although Németh's views were echoed by many who did not understand what he really meant. Németh, who was not unlike the Russian Anton Chekhov in his psychological sensitivities regarding the female sex, wrote with astonishing psychological realism about a frail woman who eventually murdered her oppressive bully of a husband. The novel, entitled *Revulsion,* was a major success in its German translation, entitled *Wie der Stein fällt.* In his essays Németh, uniting the neurological insights of a trained physician with the literary insights of a sophisticated critic, explained why and how metric versification forces the unconscious to reveal its deepest secrets. He thus shed new light on the significance of the work of Berzsenyi (q.v.).

This second generation of the *Nyugat* circle included Lőrinc Szabó, Miklós Radnóti, György Sárközi, and Sándor Weöres (qq.v.), all of them highly educated, and also the more instinct-driven poets István Sinka and József Erdélyi (qq.v.). Those who were fluent in the

---

[84] (1901–1945). Author of a history of world literature, he was an expert on William Blake (1757–1827) and on Stefan George, the great German poet (1868–1933).

[85] (1901–1945). Outstanding essayist of the second *Nyugat* generation. He contrasted 20th-century literary trends with those of the 19th century. He wrote about Balzac, Proust, Joyce, and Virginia Woolf; among Hungarians he treated Kazinczy, Batsányi, Bessenyei, and Madách (qq.v.).

Western languages formed an amazingly knowledgeable group, who, barricading themselves behind a 'Maginot line' of culture, resisted the onslaught of barbarism with the help of Spengler, Huizinga, Ortega y Gasset, and Maurras. Their collective trust in Ortega was increased by the fact that his review, *Revista del Occidente,* made by its very title the same kind of proclamation that their common spiritual nurse, *Nyugat,* had made by its title, 'The West,' back in 1908.

Lőrinc Szabó (q.v.) was the bridge between the first and second *Nyugat* generations. For a while he came under the influence of German Expressionism, especially because of his fluency in the German language and the huge number of his superior translations of Goethe, Hölderlin, Schiller, and Rilke.

It is significant that he was born in the year 1900; he was the son of a locomotive driver who fought against the bourgeoisie with fierce determination and anger. During his 'rebellious decade,' as he came to call the 1930s, Szabó wrote:

> *... and I shall throw the howling bomb of my cut-off head through the window of the first contented man.*

Szabó was, at first, a cultural pessimist whose intellectual poetry turned the Christian faith inside out—the spirit was sad while the matter was merry and robust. In this poetry only the lustful and eternally curious scenes were able to brighten up the probing reason of brotherless metropolitan man. Szabó was a stubborn materialist and yet disappointed in social ideas. As a result, Death figured prominantly in his writings. This led him to a sort of neo-hedonism which seemed to say, 'Let us defend ourselves as long as we can do so not by metaphysics, but by means of pleasure, which is more innocent.' Szabó never went as far as Goethe's Faust in signing a pact with the Devil; he settled for the role of a pagan faun escaping from the noisy city into the woods. (This may the reason why his translations of Horace read like some of his own very best poetry.)

This angry young man turned back, just after World War II, to Mihály Csokonai Vitéz (q.v.), as did his close friend and colleague, the important genius Sándor Weöres (q.v.). Csokonai, in fact, could have been—and still could be even today—the well-spring of rejuvenation for Hungarian poetry.

In the ripe fulfilment of his poetry, he twice revived the tradition of the cyclic poem, which the British have not touched for a while (with the exception of Ted Hughes and a few others). This is understandable, of course, because the last masterpiece of this genre was Words-worth's *The Prelude,* written one hundred fifty years ago.

Szabó first cycle, written just as World War II drew to a close, consists of 307 sixteen-line stanzas written in rhyming couplets. It is a beautiful autobiography in the *parlando* mode and bears the appro-priate title of *The Music of a Cricket.* Szabó's rhyming technique is characterized by nonchalant rhymes and brilliant enjambments which he probably learned from the mature Shakespeare whose sonnets, as well as several plays, he translated with phenomenal success. Shakespeare's sonnet 50, in Szabó's translation, has become a Hungarian classic; many people can recite it by heart to this day—some even write parodies of it.

His second cycle is a sequence of 120 strictly regular sonnets which amount to a long dirge in memory of his dead mistress. In this dark garland of poetry, balancing the quieter glow of his earlier autobiography, a plundered human being is helplessly protesting his own oncoming death, fuelled by a love that stretches even beyond the grave. What else could this great anti-Manichean, for whom the 'flesh was happy' and the 'spirit sad,' have done?

It is a major testimonial to Babits's inclusive, comprehensive, Christian humanism that the so-called 'Populist' or peasant poets (the Hungarian term for them is *népi,* for which 'folk' is the nearest English equivalent) could grow up under his wing at the very side of the 'Urbane' intellectuals, although the 'Populists' seemed to be so far from the master's style and taste.

The two pioneers of this stylistic revolution who occasioned a re-orchestration of Petőfi's style were József Erdélyi and István Sinka (qq.v.). While Erdélyi used folk songs to shape his own poetry, Sinka used the ballad form. A fairy-tale brightness shines through Erdélyi's poetry, even when he is making grimaces.

István Sinka was like a shaman—an intermediary between the living and the dead, a true 'mystic' in the ancient Greek sense of the word. Because of the richness of his language, most Hungarians think of him as János Arany (q.v.) come back from the 19th century.

Erdélyi shines and glitters; Sinka whirls and intoxicates like the smoke of the shepherds who work and sleep under the starry sky every day of the year, huddled around a campfire in the sub-zero weather of January. In terms of lexical depth, imagery, and the use of dozens upon dozens of personal names, Sinka's great book *The Book of the Islands* [Szigetek könyve], published posthumously in 1972, reads somewhat like the *Spoon River Anthology* of that great American lyric chronicler, Edgar Lee Masters.

'Populism' has been generally equated with Illyés. The reason has been that politically—and particularly as a prose writer and dramatist— Illyés aligned himself from an early age on with the socialist cause. Illyés had, of course, nothing to do with later unhappy developments perpetrated in the name of 'Socialism'; he was merely enthusiastic about its ideals, hoping that they would bring an end to the exploitation of the downtrodden peasantry, of which he was an educated and outspoken member. His sociographical work *The People of the Puszta* [Puszták népe] is an enduring classic of its genre.

He was an emigré in Paris for several years after 1919 and became good friends with Aragon, Éluard, and other left-leaning French intellectuals. He even wrote a few poems in French. After his return from France, he made his uneasy peace with the Horthy régime[86] and eventually inherited the editorship of *Nyugat* from Babits. After 1945, Illyés remained the country's best-selling author.

Then came a miracle. The Hungarian *Literary Gazette* [Irodalmi Újság], right in the middle of the 1956 Uprising, published one of the most important poems of this century. It is called *One Sentence on Tyranny*. Its author: Gyula Illyés!

This poem is the most outspoken and most scathing indictment of any totalitarian régime written by a European poet in any language. It is, of course, featured in this anthology. It was not available to Hungarian audiences until the pre-1989 changes. Now that Erdélyi, Sinka, and Illyés are dead, they have arrived at the most important common characteristic that any Hungarian poet can achieve: the passionate defense of the survival of the nation. Whatever motivated Erdélyi and Sinka before the end of World War II, one thing is certain: They were out to defend and uplift the poor and the downtrodden. Accordingly, shortly before 1956 and continuously afterwards, Illyés started to speak up for Hungarian minorities in the neighboring countries. He saw that 'Socialism' was incapable of solving the problems of nationalism and the oppression of one nationality by another. Protected by his impeccable credentials as a left-wing Socialist, Illyés succeeded in raising his voice against the genocidal

---

[86] Admiral Miklós Horthy de Nagybánya (1868–1957), a naval officer and conservative political leader, was Regent of Hungary from 1920 to 1944.

chauvinism of Romanian dictator Nicolae Ceauşescu.[87] Anyone else would have been jailed or silenced immediately. But, approaching eighty, Illyés was the undisputed heir of the title 'The Greatest Hungarian' ('A Legnagyobb Magyar'), whose bearers before him were Count István Széchenyi in the 19th century and Zoltán Kodály, the composer, in the 20th. As such, he became the conscience of the nation. Whether he was in France speaking to André Malraux or in Ireland speaking at the International PEN Congress in Dun Loaghaire in 1971, Illyés spoke out about the fate of over two million Transylvanian Hungarians who were treated like the Jews of Germany under Goebbels. (Except that they were not being deported and gassed. However, by orders of Ceauşescu, many villages were bulldozed, the Hungarian language was banned from the schools, the Hungarian University of Kolozsvár [Cluj-Napoca in Romanian] was Romanianized, and many Hungarian intellectuals were killed or pushed into suicide.)

When President Mitterrand visited Budapest in the summer of 1981, the Government hastened to produce Illyés with his fluent French to head up the reception committee. The octogenarian Poet Laureate wasted no time—he called on Mitterrand to put an end to cultural genocide in Romania. That the United Nations' Geneva Branch did so label Ceauşescu's activities is the direct result of Illyés's private diplomacy, which he began to pursue in 1961 and continued until his death.

Side by side with the tragically successful life of Illyés, we must set the brief, tragically unsuccessful life of Attila József (q.v.). When the newspapers reported that he had committed suicide by throwing himself under the wheels of a freight train at Balatonszárszó in 1937, his works became immediate best-sellers. For although it is true that the poets are the only genuine legislators of the Hungarians—as we remarked at the beginning of this essay—we must sadly add that the Hungarians do not always recognize those who are the truly great ones. Today—as throughout the years between 1949 and 1989—József has become an officially acknowledged classic, a truly great poet who is a part of every school curriculum. He ranks as the equal of Ady and Babits and, seen strictly as a poet, he is considered by many as greater even than Illyés at his best. Many epigones have exploited his poetic formulas.

---

[87] Nicolae Ceauşescu, the Romanian dictator, was born in 1918 and executed, together with his wife Elena, by rebels on Christmas Day, 1989.

Every twitch of pain within Attila József turned into song—into the kind of song which was sometimes as evanescent as a breath of air, sometimes terse and weighty. Poetic discipline had seldom hidden such frightening inner chaos—his formal perfection which appeared effortless and natural was, in fact, a painful acrobatic exploit above a schizophrenic whirlpool which eventually swallowed him. As a patient of psychological disorders, he decided to study Freud thoroughly, which only resulted in the exacerbation of his condition. Instead of following a prescribed cure, he started to lecture to his analysts. At the same time he misbehaved during the most rigid era of the underground Communist Party's activity—he daringly coupled Marx and Freud as the St. Peter and St. Paul of materialist liberation. Enraged, blinkered denouncers ganged up on him, and the orphan, who was already suffering from a deep-seated Oedipus complex, was repelled by his second mother, the Communist Party. During the Communist régime (1949–1989) he was usually depicted as a persecuted sacrificial lamb. In reality, he was a strong and aggressive individual, powerfully possessed by dialectics. He had the kind of mind that could have argued a dozen Church Doctors under the table during the Middle Ages on any point of theology or otherwise. Arthur Koestler,[88] in the second volume of his autobiography, painted a memorable portrait of him.

It is difficult for poets to speak either about the troubles they see around themselves or about the 'ideal community.' Although their profession anchors them in a given tradition, they are constantly challenged by change within the tradition from which they come. Poets, after all, are greatly concerned with form. Ever since Sappho in ancient Greece, poets have sung of love and death with great conviction and spontaneity. But if poets turn to the desires of the community and thus to social ideas, they become easily intoxicated by great, sublime ideas which, in turn, turn them into 'ineffectual angels'—precisely what happened to Shelley.

Attila József fought a double struggle. He had to balance himself over the whirlpool, striving both to keep his song from being smothered by its socialist content and to save his mind from being

---

[88] (1905–1983). Hungarian novelist and journalist who joined and then left the Communist Party, and whose work discussed questions of moral and political responsibility. His most widely read novel is *Darkness at Noon* (1940).

wrecked by madness. He waged a two-front war for the Beauty of the Word and for the Beauty of Reason while he himself was staggering at the very edge of lunacy—a situation which made his poetry both great and shattering. Psychologists are well aware that many victims of madness who resist receiving help while they are choking are the very people who, before the complete darkness sets in, achieve great clarity in their formulations. Their style can be translucent and crystalline, as though they bear a weightier responsibility for their words than their fellow humans who are, or appear to be, better balanced. Attila József is always exact and concrete, while his poems glitter like dew-drops and float weightlessly, like the floss of the birch tree. One feels that one is sinning against his poetry by using such similes for image and object, since in his poetry images and objects shine through each other and become identical without any mediating comparisons. József's poems are, like the poems of Rimbaud, 'illuminations.'

It is not surprising that the Hungarians, with Attila József in their midst, are not overly impressed by the left-wing poetry of Auden's generation of the 1930s. Socialist poetry, Hungarians think, ought to be like József's, whether one feels like being a socialist or not. Many Hungarian writers, however, were tormented by the Spanish Civil War. They felt that Hungary was the twin of Spain. It is no coincidence that the political alliance of the folk-poets which was called the *Márciusi front* [March Front] was founded in the same year that Picasso painted his *Guernica*. Several Hungarian writers and poets saw the painting in 1937 at the Paris World Exhibition—among them Miklós Radnóti (q.v.), who read his approaching destiny depicted in it.

Lőrinc Szabó was born with the century, Sándor Weöres (q.v.) ten years later. He was one of the last disciples who emerged from the circle of Babits—or 'from his stable,' as the writers jokingly told one another. There, every racehorse could feel that it was the first among equals.

The protean, chameleon-like Weöres has become a legendary figure. One way to characterize him is to visualize the Englishman Keats, transported in time into the 20th century, speaking Hungarian, and endowed with the talent of changing personalities—indeed of changing sexes! Weöres wrote effortlessly in every genre, form, and rhythm, from single-liners to long romances, from children's verse and nonsense verse for adults to the small epic. There is no verse form in Hungarian that Weöres did not practice and master better than everyone else.

In his youth, Weöres had travelled to the Far East, and he knew about transcendental meditation. He knew that much can be achieved with modes of consciousness that are beyond the dubious logic of spoken language. He trusted the ritual effects of rhyming intonations and used them successfully to create bridges between human beings from all walks of life. Indeed, whether the consumers of poetry are Stone Age islanders or metropolitan hippies, poetry of a certain kind can reach them all, because the archaic time, although submerged, still lives on under the threshold of wakeful consciousness. Accordingly, Weöres could write about religious myths in poetic form, and he could imagine that he was a woman poet in the nineteenth century. His book *Psyche* has become the envy of many female poets in Hungary, some of whom have admitted in writing that the best poetry by a woman in Hungarian was written by that verbal magician, Weöres. His ability to stretch his skin extended to historical, exotic, and modern styles—he could change himself into a Hindu or an Egyptian, a Mesopotamian or a Maori, or a baroque, rococo, or surrealist poet.

Weöres's self-revelations and his adaptations from the Asian past were, to a certain extent, misunderstood in Hungary. It went unnoticed that there were significant Western precedents for this kind of writing, particularly in the later, 'orphic' works of Rainer Maria Rilke and, of course, in the works of William Blake, who invented myths freely and played with gods and anti-gods. All of this was largely beyond the comprehension of the Marxist critics who, in general and for a long time, did not know what to do with Weöres. Before 1956 he supported himself as a translator, somewhat like Lőrinc Szabó. (Their names often figure side by side in anthologies of translated materials.) His collection for children, *Bóbita* (which can be translated either as 'Topknot' or 'Bob of Ribbons' because it can be applied to either birds or children), which was passed by the censorship and appeared before the 1956 Uprising, became a best-seller and was recited not only by thousands of youngsters all over the country, but by adults as well. We feature in this collection his poem 'Brambleberry' because it holds a very special place in the history of Hungarian poetry. This poem can be said to be almost meaningless. However, the images and rhythms which it conjures up put a Hungarian who recites it into a trance. The reader is asked to understand that being apolitical under the Communist editorial policies of the 1950s was in itself an act of great political courage. Here was a poet who did not sing about the production of corn or the output of the coal mines—he entertained the children of his country with the enchanting rhymes and rhythms of 'Topknot.'

As a literary historian, Weöres distinguished himself by unearthing numerous pearls of old Hungarian poetry that sound like archaic variations of his own writings. But, however familiar he was with China, ancient Babylon, the founders of the World Religions, or Gauguin's Oceanic Paradise, his genius was that of a poet of instinct, the antithesis of the type of Eliot's or Babits's genius. He could circle the earth on the wings of a bird or an angel, and he could descend into hells with an intuitive flair, coming out unscathed. If he had been blindfolded, he could have found his way about the landscapes of the millennia just as easily, with a smile upon a mask of an infant's face, but not unsuspecting—certainly never unsuspecting.

Other than Attila József, it was Weöres who had the greatest influence on the young poets, due both to Weöres's ingenious handling of form and to their own political disillusionment. Weöres is like velvet only on the surface—inside he has a dark, pessimistic core, because he never believed in 'progress.' He was too much under the influence of tragic myths from all over the world to be able to feel optimistic about mankind's future. His symbolic heroes keep struggling, but they all stay vanquished until Doomsday. His Jesus is not a saviour of souls but a spiritual initiator into the secrets of a God who remains indifferent to the very world he created—a gnostic Jesus.

But a genuine poet of Weöres's talent cannot remain indifferent. Amidst the high-tension chaos of the present moment, even the pessimist wants to erect new woof and weave new warp to produce new fabric out of a world that has dissolved into a million loose threads. As one of the heirs of the Curse of Babel, he has to remain, in the meantime, a user of a language which has replaced its ancient meaning—assuming it ever had one—by a watered-down imitation, something that happens more often at the higher levels of civilization than among savages. This dilemma is not a new one—an early warning of it came in Mallarmé's and Rimbaud's poetry, but the Betrayal of the Words really hit home hard and consciously in the literature and philosophy of the 20th century. This is what motivates writers such as James Joyce and Sándor Weöres to create a new language. Weöres never went as far as Joyce went in *Finnegans Wake,* but the outer limits of the Hungarian language have certainly been reached in Weöres's poetry.

Weöres's companions of the vintages before and after him felt like a sacrificial generation. Their youth was deprived of the journeys to the West and the Orient that had shaped the consciousness of their immediate predecessors. Only belatedly did they find out about the great wide world out there, but they found out far too soon about its horrors. Certain key words—such as 'forbidden,' 'looted,' 'steep,' and 'subterranean'—betray their general emotions even in the titles of their volumes of poetry.

At first they called themselves, rather affectedly, 'The Sons of the Silver Age'—alluding to the 'Golden Age' of Ady and Babits. In reality, they were eventually dumped into an 'Age of Iron.' From the deceptively peaceful pastoral landscape from which they started, they soon arrived in a land of devastation. Some of them perished physically in it.

Miklós Radnóti (q.v.) shared this fate among those in the forefront of the élite. In a more protected and gentler age, he would have persisted for a long time with his sophisticated song, orchestrated somewhat like Virgil's bucolics and similar to the writings of the English Georgian[89] poets; but amid the apocalypse of Central Europe, his transformation became bitterly accelerated. He became the most outstanding singer of the death camps, for he depicted their humanly inconceivable horror with almost superhuman discipline, in strict and noble forms. He kept his sense of proportion unflaggingly—or rather he kept his perspective as the Classical poets had demanded. And, as a result, rarely in the history of European literature has the art of poetry merged so closely with moral power. Where we would not expect even an inarticulate stammer, but only a blood-curdling scream, he spoke of his own death like a Roman hero in a Shakespearean drama. But the blood which flowed from his mouth at the unspoken cues was his own blood, not theatrical catsup.

Destiny granted Radnóti's close friend István Vas (q.v.) a fuller career. Perhaps the most accomplished Hungarian translator of this century, he happened to be the lucky survivor, with the same sort of troubled conscience that János Arany felt after the death of Sándor Petőfi. He wrapped his deeply moving self-characterization into a poem that recalled his murdered friend. He was a most complex poet. His

---

[89] A group of English poets, many of them minor poets writing Romantic lyric poetry, whose work was published in certain anthologies between 1912 and 1922; so called because they wrote during the reign of King George V.

aggressively rhetorical defense of pure reason was constantly tinged with wry irony directed toward himself, reminding his reader that the opposite might also be true.

For Radnóti, Virgil was the guide who led him on his way. István Vas's faithful travelling companion was Horace, who linked him, along with Lőrinc Szabó, to the 18th century. Vas was also tied to the 'elegant century of reason' by satire, although not of the mild, Horatian variety. Vas was a son of the 20th century, a modern Juvenal,[90] 'tremblingly brave,' resurrected in a new Byzantium. In a dogmatic age, he chose to defend the sceptics, and this was an act of immense courage during the forty-two years of Communist rule in Hungary, which Radnóti escaped only because he was murdered by his captors near Bor in November of 1944. Vas lived until 1991 and even witnessed the dissolution of the Soviet Union. It was his credo that the guarantee of our dignity lies in our being a self-searching node of contradictions.

Hard Times

A devastating tank battle between the German Wehrmacht and the Soviet Red Army took place in 1944 on the Great Hungarian Plain. In a panicky miscalculation of the direction of the inevitable Russian attack on the Hungarian capital, the Germans blew up all of the seven bridges that tied Buda to Pest, some of them of extreme beauty and historical value, such as the Lánchíd, the 'Chain Bridge' which had been built by the British Adam Clark in the middle of the 19th century. The Germans expected the Red Army to come from the east, through Pest, but the Russians crossed the Danube far to the north and stormed southward along both sides of the river. The German plea of 'self-defense' as the reason for destroying the bridges of Budapest therefore made no sense.

The Royal Palace in Buda, where the Germans dug themselves in and held out the longest, was almost totally destroyed. Among Europe's capitals, only Berlin and Warsaw sustained more damage than

---

[90] Decimus Junius Juvenalis (about A.D. 85–after A.D. 127), the most powerful of all Roman satiric poets, who, in his writings, attacked the follies and corruption of those whom he saw around him. Many of his phrases, such as "Who will guard the guards themselves?" have become proverbial.

Budapest. Its inhabitants had, of course, no say in the matter. 'German self-defense' and 'inevitable Russian liberation' were beyond the Hungarians' power to decide. 'I dreamt that the Russians left and no one came in their place' was a typical Budapest joke after the repeated, insane, back-and-forth battles between the Wehrmacht and the Red Army. And the Red Army did not leave. In 1956 Khrushchev's tanks crushed the workers' and students' councils. Twelve years later, in 1968, these same tanks, manned by lackeys from the countries of the Warsaw Pact, rolled into a reformist Prague. And two years later, in Gdańsk, Poland, local troops sufficed to deal with rioting workers. Hungarian, Polish, and Czech literature are well accustomed to such backdrops.

On a global scale, the intellectual scene was not much different. The generation born around 1900 still believed in the possibility of a War to End All Wars; later generations, who lived during the Cold War, feared a war that would finish off Planet Earth. In the meantime, minor massacres could always be organized—the modern technical know-how of Old Europe had instilled a poison into the awakening continents of the Third World. Brown against Brown, Yellow against Yellow, Black against Black—even people of the same color could now turn against one another in nakedly genocidal fights for power. Some recent productions of Shakespearean historical plays such as Richard III offer a similar sight—one can visualize packs of wolves feasting on each other's flesh. This was certainly the version seen by the Polish emigré author Jan Kott,[91] who became deservedly world famous for his modernizations of Shakespeare which showed that human nature has not changed.

The new generation of Hungarian writers and poets who became visible during World War II inherited the unfortunate 'Urbanist'– 'Populist' dichotomy (discussed above) from their predecessors. Their debates often became overheated, bordering on the hysterical. At issue was the question of land reform, which the 'Populist' writers embraced with great ideological zeal. In so doing they had drifted to the right, since this Hungarian variety of Russia's *narodnik* movement picked up

---

[91] Born in Warsaw in 1914, Jan Kott left for the West in 1967 after a career as literary critic, essayist, and professor of world literature. In 1961 he wrote his famous *Szkice o Szekspirze* [Shakespeare Our Contemporary], which was eventually translated into nearly every language and was even produced on stage in London and elsewhere through the efforts of Peter Brook.

a romantically colored, racist overtone. (Both Erdélyi and Sinka found themselves in this situation.) It would be wrong to accuse these writers *en bloc* of having become pioneers of Fascism—the overwhelming majority of them were chiefly interested in raising public consciousness regarding the sociological facts about rural Hungary. The writers of this group were only partly of peasant origin, but they all took the trouble to penetrate deep, often on foot or on bicycle, into the festering, largely unknown misery of the poor villages which had no electricity or running water, hidden behind the garish folk costumes that the general public thought of as 'folk art.' Their review was edited by György Sárközi (q.v.), a Catholic poet of Jewish origin who refused suggestions as to how to escape military labor and was killed by the Nazis.

As World War II ended, Hungary had a brief spell of democracy which lasted only until 1949, the year of the Communist coup d'état that was ordered and assisted by the Kremlin. In 1945–1946 it had seemed that the new, post-war order would finally solve the land reform problem. All major estates were broken up, and formerly landless peasants could sign up for 25 or 30 or 50 acres of land. At the time they could not yet foresee that within three years they would be forced at gunpoint onto collective farms.

It is understandable that, under these circumstances, young peasant writers, still euphoric from the unfolding of the long-awaited land-reform, should have flocked to the banner of Socialism. The best-known ones of them were László Nagy and Ferenc Juhász (qq.v.). But as time passed, they all became bitterly disenchanted with Socialism. Nagy, who died young, turned into a Hungarian Federico García Lorca, replete with a mystical spiritualism and ardent love of his fatherland.

Juhász, who was the influential editor of *Új Írás* [New Writing] for several decades until it ceased publication in 1990, reaped early recognition, even in the West, as a sort of Hungarian Walt Whitman. It is characteristic of his kind of Populism that Ferenc Juhász learned more from Weöres than he did from Illyés or Sinka, both of whom, despite their individual differences, belong in the 'demotic' or 'folk' group. Without knowing any Hungarian, but purely by virtue of excellent intuition, it was David Wevill, the Canadian poet, who identified the wellsprings of Juhász's inspiration underlying the poem 'The Boy Turned Into a Stag Clamours at the Gate of Secrets' in

modern Hungarian music, in Béla Bartók's *Cantata Profana*.[92] Both
W. H. Auden and George Steiner, as well as other literary critics, have
called this the 'best long poem written in our age.'

In the same way that Bartók and Kodály did research into genuine
Hungarian folk music, as contrasted with popular compositions and
Gypsy music, these young writers and poets drilled down to the pre-
Christian layers of folk tradition, all the way to shamanism. What
ancient Iceland did for Auden, the Uralo-Altaic lands did for Ferenc
Juhász and László Nagy, except that their views were amplified in their
effects by Weöres's internationally oriented approach to myths. It be-
came desirable to add local knowledge to the general knowledge
already available, and Hungarian folklorists and poets therefore started
to visit Asia.

Ferenc Juhász first felt responsibility for his poverty-stricken
village, a feeling which prompted him to embrace Communism. But as
a mature poet, he has dazzlingly ensconced himself in a teeming
biological network whose every knot, from the infusoria to the
galaxies, promotes his neuroses. He is an uneven poet. When he is in
good form, he can write about the metropolitan night, or the cemetery
around a poet's grave, or outer space itself, much like Hieronymus
Bosch. In temperament and rhetoric Dylan Thomas seems to resemble
him most closely. How often was this great Welsh poet torn to pieces
by the critics in England! Hungarian poets as well as practitioners of
the other arts would consider such treatment to be lèse majesté.

However complex the thought of the deceased László Nagy and of
the still living, but essentially completed, Juhász may be, their
language is as colorful as a piece of embroidery, referring back to the
Oriental origins of the Hungarian language—a language which, once
upon a time, used to weave imaginative words about grasses, bushes,
bonfires, tulips and roses, reindeer, slow rivers, rare water-holes, and
nightingales, and which definitely did not speak about theology,
mysticism, ideologies, emperors, tsars, or commissars.

---

[92] See *Sándor Weöres and Ferenc Juhász*, Penguin Modern European
Poets, London, 1970. The legend of the 'Boy Turned Into an Stag' has
inspired both József Erdélyi and László Nagy. It is not only a symbolic
rejection of the big city and a return to the country where folk traditions are
alive, but it also alludes to the Hungarians' Asiatic origins, as related in the
'Legend of the Miracle Stag' at the beginning of this volume. Juhász's poem
is featured as the closing piece of the present Volume.

János Pilinszky and Ágnes Nemes Nagy (qq.v.), now both dead and considered classics, were sparing to the point of terseness in their use of words. They used to be referred to as 'Urbane' during the Kádár régime,[93] in contrast to László Nagy and Juhász, although this dichotomy has been long outdated and certainly makes no sense after 1989.

Stretching between 'morality and terror,' as she says in one of her poems, the work of Ágnes Nemes Nagy offers a refreshingly different, dry glow within the steamy, humid atmosphere of Hungarian poetry. By the time of her untimely death in 1991, she had undoubtedly become Hungary's foremost poetess of all time. Her condensed passions are projected from a rationalist mind, while her acute, immensely economically worded poems are brought to white heat by an emotional puritanism which, paradoxically, approaches the mysticism of 'Pascal's Wager.'[94] Just as the devoted, stubborn pedagogue in Truffaut's[95] L'enfant sauvage wants to teach the savage forest-dwelling child to speak, Ágnes Nemes Nagy strives to instruct a fearful world not with human speech, but with the timeless language of the trees. Heightened mental passion is only credible in prose when it is linked to some tenet of a faith to be transmitted—whether this is Christian metaphysics, socialism, humanism, or some type of moral maximalism. In poetry, however, especially if that poetry has to balance a surrounding atmosphere of Romanticism, a high-temperature, condensed, enigmatic terseness may suffice.

However, Ágnes Nemes Nagy gives much more. She never indulges

---

[93] János Kádár (1912–1989) was First Secretary of the Hungarian Communist Party from 1956 to 1988.

[94] Blaise Pascal (1623–1662), French mathematician, physicist, and religious philosopher; inventor of the adding machine and possibly of calculus. After his sister became a nun, Pascal became converted to the Jansenist version of Catholicism in 1654. He wanted to write an 'Apology for the Christian Religion' but was stopped by his death. His notes were published later as his Pensées ('Thoughts'). One of these contains his famous Wager: 'If God does not exist, but you pretend that He does, there is nothing to lose, because you will not be responsible to anyone after death. But if God does exist, and you ignore Him, you will be in big trouble after death. Therefore it is reasonable to wager that God does exist.'

[95] François Truffaut (b. 1932), one of the most important French screen playwrights and directors, who created The Four-Hundred Blows (1961), The Savage Child (1969), and The Last Metro (1980).

in overt sermonizing. She is an uncompromising moral maximalist who communicates her demand for the almost irretrievably lost virtue of heroism in mysterious images and cryptic references, which often give the effect of belonging not to the 20th century but to the Stone Age. Although their styles are different, her inner kinship with Emily Brontë, the savage virgin who froze into stoicism, is strikingly obvious.

The international reputation and domestic authority of János Pilinszky is based on a few slim volumes which took him three decades to write. He is justifiably ranked with the Christian existentialists and, more generally, with the mystics. According to his own confessions, both in writing and in radio interviews, such as those conducted in London by the BBC, what he was doing was an "independent reshaping of Simone Weil's diary."[96] If by this he meant that he was dipping into the Fount of Mercy, he was entirely correct.

Pilinszky's determining experience was the feeling of being at someone else's mercy, which explains that in his view 'heroism' equals 'self-defense.' His political statements are not expressly pointed at any one particular kind of oppression, but Pilinszky was equally opposed to Fascism and to Communism, and there was no need for him to name the enemy. He developed instead his own inner thoughts about how life went on around him, and to this inner vision and conviction he clung unto death, indeed at the level of heroism in his fierce determination.

'Mysticism' is an expression that is used widely and much too loosely. The general, superficial view of it identifies it with a kind of incense-laden ecstasy, but the tormented, mystical eye-witnesses of the Thirty Years' War[97] during the 17th century were ruthlessly true to reality—they precisely delineated hell on earth in their poetry. It is in

---

[96] (1909–1943). French philosopher and mystic, deeply interested in social justice. Her best known work is *La pesanteur et la grâce* [Gravity and Grace], which appeared in Paris in 1947 after her death.

[97] (1618–1648). The Thirty Years' War, which originated as an ideological conflict between Catholic and Protestant powers, eventually engulfed all of Europe in a war in which the political advantages of nations were as important as their religions; it resulted in the Habsburg Dynasty's loss of power in Germany, the rise of the modern nation-state system, the final division Europe between Catholicism and Protestantism, and the movement of the center of commerce from Central Europe to the Atlantic Coast.

this sense that Pilinszky was a 'mystical poet.' He, too, registered, in a morally anchored, theocentric fashion, a huge quantity of facts about a disjointed world that was about to spin off its axis. Some of his poems are as concise as an ancient epitaph or as blank as a gravestone. He wanders through a gray, drought-ridden landscape covered with granite dust, which has been contaminated forever by the death-camps. This infernal landscape is both exterior and interior—it is there in the soul, in everyone's soul if one is a Christian—it is there in Europe and everywhere else that has been rolled over by the plague. Although it is a bleak and frightening landscape, the lonely wanderer through it—the poet himself—somehow manages to make it hauntingly attractive. One is tempted to compare the general atmosphere of Pilinszky's poetry to the paintings of Salvador Dalí,[98] on whose canvasses a similar magic transformation takes place: the barren and the desolate become dignified and beautiful.

It is well known that the French Jansenists were the prisoners of their own guilt and that Dostoevsky's foolish saints were possessed by their acceptance of the sufferings of others. In a similar way, Pilinszky's poetry is stretched between the charged poles of these two self-chosen kinds of Christian captivity. And what a risky condition it is for a poet to perceive the world through Jansenist–Dostoevskian eyes! Pilinszky was doomed to long stretches of silence between poems, yet any inner resolution of his basic conflict could have made his poetic inspiration perish. As his body of work stands after his premature death at the age of sixty, it carries the marks of true greatness—unspoken, of course. Nor could the Sermon on the Mount have been preached more than once, although it has been sermonized about ever since. Pilinszky chose terseness and silence because he knew that preaching is not poetry, or else it makes for very poor poetry.

In the early poetry of Illyés and in the work of Attila József, Sándor Weöres, Ágnes Nemes Nagy, and János Pilinszky, the ambition of Endre Ady's generation—the generation of *Nyugat*—was at last fulfilled. The timetables of Western and Hungarian poetry were finally reunited, at approximately the same level as they had stood when the English Sir Philip Sydney and the Hungarian Bálint Balassi were equal

---

[98] Salvador Dalí (1904–1989), Spanish surrealist painter, the undisputed master of 'beauty within death and desolation.'

contemporaries in the 16th century. The poetry of this generation is not unlike the music of Béla Bartók—typically Hungarian and also truly international.

A large number of talented poets have been at work who may be considered the third and fourth wave after the *Nyugat* generation. Most of these will be featured in the second volume of *The Poetry of Hungary*. Amy Károlyi (Weöres's wife), Magda Szabó, Magda Székely, Ágnes Gergely, Judith Tóth, Éva Tóth, and Ida Solymos are an incomplete list of the female poets; Pál Toldalagi, István Pákolitz, Gyula Takács, József Tornai, Sándor Csoóri, Győző Csorba, Márton Kalász, István Simon, István Lakatos, Gábor Garai, Mihály Váci, István Kormos, György Rába, Sándor Rákos, Imre Csanádi, György Somlyó, László Benjámin, Dezső Tandori, Ottó Orbán, Imre Oravecz, József Utassy, and Szabolcs Váradi are an incomplete list of the men.

In Foreign Parts

Following the two World Wars, revolutions, counter-revolutions, and territorial dismemberment, every third Hungarian today lives outside the current geographical borders of his country. Just like the Jews, the Greeks, and the Poles, Hungarians have created a diaspora that covers five continents. Hungarians have been whirled around so much by history that eventually the whole world has started to spin around them. Anyone who wants to define what 'Hungarianness' means under these circumstances—whether in terms of state, country, nation, nationality, citizenship, people, or race—must be a semantic genius; it is a commonplace, however, that the Hungarian language has remained inaccessibly unique. Nothing is more natural today than for a writer of Transylvanian origin who spent decades in Budapest and who, after the 1919 changes of the frontiers, could have been just as easily a Romanian as a Hungarian, to have moved to London and, while holding a British passport, to be considered a 'Hungarian writer' in the eyes of his readers back in Hungary, in Romania, or in any other place in the West.[99] His readers, scattered all over the globe,

---

[99] László Cs. Szabó is describing his own personal situation in this paragraph. To be of 'Transylvanian origin' could, additionally, be fairly complex: there are the unmixed pockets of the *Székely* or 'Székler' population that go back to the 9th-century Magyar invasion from the East; there are Hungarian

are not his compatriots from a legal point of view, but they really do belong to his fatherland. Whatever looks 'schizophrenic' if we consider it on the basis of 'nationality' has now become natural. It will, most likely, be accepted by everyone as natural in the 21st century—but for that we will need a greater fatherland: The United States of Europe.

The position, importance, and freedom of minority literatures in different places differed greatly after World Wars I and II. Hungarian literature in Romanian Transylvania between 1920 and 1940 still had national proportions. It was able to spread into Hungary with an invigorating and innovating effect. But Hungarian literature in Transylvania after 1945 entered an almost cataleptic period, from which it began to recover after 1960.

Hungarian literature in Yugoslavia, on the other hand, was rather provincial between the two World Wars, but during the 1960s and 1970s it managed to become truly modern. Not only did it give a home to the new avant-garde, but it also provided a haven for literature which was being silenced in Hungary itself by the Kádár régime. In Novi Sad [Újvidék in Hungarian] almost everything was above-ground that was totally or partly underground in Budapest, a mere 300 kilometers to the north. This was also true of the other arts—painting, sculpture, and surrealist Polish cinematography.

Some of the more visible Hungarian poets in Yugoslavia include Ferenc Fehér (1928-1989), Károly Ács (b. 1928), and József Pap (b. 1926).

Hungarian poetry even survived in the northeastern part of Hungary (known as the Carpatho-Ukraine) which was taken by the U.S.S.R. Its outstanding practitioner was Vilmos Kovács (1927–1977).

Back in historical Hungary, the hotbed of poetry was Transdanubia, but the home of prose was Transylvania. The first significant Hungarian prose writer, Kelemen Mikes, had been a Transylvanian who followed Prince Ferenc Rákóczi II into exile in Turkey after the

---

or 'Magyar' groups that moved to Transylvania starting in the 16th century; there once were significant Saxon settlements speaking 17th-century *Plattdeutsch* (most of which have now been repatriated to a reunified Germany); and there still are significant numbers of Armenian, Jewish, Gypsy, and even Turkish settlements, in addition to a growing Romanian majority. Farther to the east, Hungarian-speaking groups in well over a hundred settlements are known as the *Csángó* people. Cs. Szabó was of Hungarian-Saxon ancestry.

failure of Rákóczi's Freedom War of 1703–1711.

Among the Transylvanian poets of the generation of Babits and the *Nyugat,* a puritan Calvinist, Lajos Áprily (q.v.), stood out. He wrote with the same craftsman-like care as the tradition of his partly Saxon goldsmith ancestors obliged him to. His was a finely chiselled style, mixed with a virginal modesty which made him conceal his great love for his native land, replete with the memory of wars and of wild mountain ranges whose valleys were the homes to vagrant balladeers. Áprily's earlier, somewhat old-fashioned, Classicist tone began to sprout wings and to take off toward the middle of his life. This metamorphosis produced almost the effect of a Chinese still-life, in contrast to his former, dark-hued landscapes. Áprily was a master of striking rhymes placed at the end of dactylic scanned lines. His poems were often used for training actors and at recital contests.

The flirtatious, poetic art of Jenő Dsida (q.v.) was more independent of landscape and situation; with his effortless technique he could have played ornamental scales even on the alpenhorn. Before his premature death, his mawkish, rococo Catholicism was authenticated in harder poems by the anxiety of an ailing heart.

The voice of the ancient land of Transylvania could be heard more clearly in the work of the son of Lajos Áprily, Zoltán Jékely[100] (q.v.), who moved from Transylvania to Hungary. His basic experience is that of nostalgia for his native country—for something that is not quite real but is rather imaginary and imbued with the eerie mood of history. This nostalgia joins the shadow of the novelist Gyula Krúdy (discussed above), that of the doomed amorous lover of the *fin de siècle*. Jékely would sometimes poke fun at himself at the end of a poem as if making a grotesque grimace in the midst of an eroticism mixed with death-wish. It was much more than a mannerism—we can rest assured today that he unconsciously anticipated the horrors that were in the offing. He was influenced by the Italian *crepuscolari*[101]

---

[100] The original family name was Jékely; 'Áprily' was an assumed pen-name. The son, in order to distinguish himself from his famous father, returned to the name Jékely.

[101] The Italian 'poets of the twilight,' a term coined by the Italian critic, G.A. Borgese (1882–1952). They reacted against the content-poetry and the rhetorical style of Giosué Carducci (1835–1907) and Gabriele D'Annunzio (1863–1938), favoring instead the unadorned language and homely themes of Giovanni Pascoli (1855–1912). They had an affinity with the French

poets and by the French Laforgue,[102] and he translated their works.

Jékely, who was, after all, a 20th-century figure, would have been satisfied with a lesser dosage of cynical melancholy as fuel for his own poetic fires—not unlike those who lived in the *belle époque*—but his poetry reveals more of this ugly world because he saw so much death and destruction around him, as he was himself a stone in the general landslide.

By the mid-1960s, Transylvanian poetry had begun to recover rapidly, and showed increasing promise. For the middle generation, the popular front provided a local variation of the voice of Gyula Illyés, discussed above. The younger poets, however, had already begun to move over to the risky experimental meadows of the avant-garde, where their Hungarian counterparts in Yugoslavia had already gained a firm footing.

The literature of Hungarian Transylvania in general, and its poetry in particular, is really too valuable to be dealt with so briefly; the best that we can do here is to enumerate some of the more important names. Károly Koós (1883–1977) was a novelist and a poet as well as an architect, a painter, and a sculptor. He deserves an anthology all by himself. Károly Molter (1890–1981) excelled as a critic. Sándor Reményik (1980–1941) wrote eloquent poems about the importance of preserving the Hungarian language as the mother tongue of a minority. László Szabédi (1907–1959) (q.v.), a professor at the Bolyai University of Kolozsvár, threw himself in front of a train when his university was taken away and Romanianized. János Bartalis (1893–1967) is one name in the tradition of Dsida, Áprily, and Jékely, whom we must not omit. His poems will appear in Volume II.

The undisputed dean of Hungarian poetry in Transylvania today is Sándor Kányádi (b. 1929). Although relatively young and still alive, he is already a classic, ranking with János Pilinszky, Ágnes Nemes Nagy, and others in Hungary. In 1992 the Hungarian government awarded him the Kossuth Prize—a 'first' in Hungarian–Romanian

---

Symbolists Paul Valéry, Arthur Rimbaud, and Stéphane Mallarmé. Guido Gozzano (1883–1916) was the most talented exponent of the movement.

[102] Jules Laforgue (1860–1887), who died of tuberculosis at the age of 27, was a Decadent French pessimist much influenced by the philosophy of Schopenhauer in Germany. He was discovered by Verlaine. Most of his works appeared only after his untimely death. His English wife, who was also tubercular, survived him by only a few months.

relations since the end of World War II; in 1995 he won Austria's prestigious Herder Prize. Kányádi writes free verse, creatively mixed with rhyming couplets, while his semantic drift takes the reader from the poet's personal life history to the fate of the nation and to the painful coexistence with the Romanian majority that is now in a land which has always been an integral part of Hungarian culture.

Kányádi's great poem 'All Souls' Day in Vienna,' which deserves special discussion, presents the poet's stream-of-consciousness narrative of his own past, mixed with reminiscences of World War II and with the universality of Mozart's music. The poem's speaker is listening to the composer's Requiem Mass while leaning against the wall in a small church in Vienna. In it, Kányádi himself acts as a high priest performing a funeral oration for the past and offers several prayers both for the nation and for the future of humankind. Not since Attila József has any Hungarian poet produced a poem as powerful and memorable as this one. Kányádi's work will be featured in Volume II of *The Poetry of Hungary*.

There were a number of extremely talented younger poets, such as Domokos Szilágyi (1938–1976) and his first wife, Gizella Hervay (1934–1982), who have committed suicide. Ferenc Szemlér (1906–1978) and his contemporary István Horváth (1909–1977) both deserve to be anthologized in a more broadly based volume than this one; all four will be featured in Volume II.

The best-known poet of the Hungarian minority in Czechoslovakia was László Mécs (q.v.), a Premontransian canon and a village priest. Mécs fell victim to the notorious occupational disease of clerical poets —that of confusing a poem with a sermon. Yet in his finest pieces his poetry is redeemed by a clamorous joy of life and a naive love of humanity. After having read only a few translations of his work, Paul Valéry overestimated him, while the younger members of the *Nyugat* circle, enraged by Valéry's opinion, underestimated him; on both sides of the issue thousands listened, moved to tears by his highly effective recitals of his own poetry. Mécs was declared by the Marxist critics to be a reactionary and an amateur, which was wrong. After several years in hiding, Mécs, who is now dead, lived the last few years of his life like a hermit in Pannonhalma, a famous Catholic Benedictine shrine near the Austrian border. This shrine deserves special mention because it dates back to the earliest days of the Hungarian nation; it was founded in the year 996, and it will therefore see its one-thousandth birthday in 1996, when this book is scheduled to appear.

Pannonhalma had such high renown that the Communists did not dare to close down its excellent high school, even between 1949 and 1989.

The younger generation of Hungarian poets now working in the former Czechoslovakia include György Dénes, Tibor Bábi, Árpád Ozsvald, János Veres, István Gyurcsó, Vilmos Csontos, Olga L. Gály, Árpád Tőzsér, László Cselényi, Lajos Zs. Nagy, Sándor Gál, Imre Varga, and László Tóth. Several of them will appear in Volume II.

Between the two World Wars, Mécs's fellow priest, the older Sándor Sík (q.v.), produced beautiful translations of many Latin hymns. Such translation is a tradition that goes back to Mihály Babits who, while translating the *Divine Comedy,* also translated hymns from the Latin.

The first diaspora toward the West, during the 1930s, was composed of uprooted refugees from Fascism. It was followed by hundreds of thousands more in 1945 and 1946. The displaced persons of this generation (or 'DPs,' as they were called) never became assimilated into their various western habitats, but they could not help losing much of their Hungarianness—much faster in Europe than in America.

Two figures of this group stand out as classics—Győző Határ and György Faludy. Both Határ and Faludy were awarded the Kossuth Prize in the wake of the events of 1989–1990. Faludy has returned permanently to Hungary; Határ maintains a museum-like household in Wimbledon, near London, which he calls *Hongriuscule* ('miniature Hungary').

Both Faludy and Határ opposed Fascism and Nazi Germany. Faludy left Hungary and joined the American armed forces during World War II. Back in Hungary, Határ wrote poems in jail in 1943–1944, thinking that the U.S.S.R. would bring real liberation; but in 1945, he bought up all the copies of his book which contained those poems and burned them. He soon became the leader of the intellectual resistance against Communism and found himself behind barbed wire at the infamous Communist concentration camp at Recsk.

Faludy, who took off his American uniform and returned to Hungary, had a similar fate; he was also imprisoned for several years. He wrote up his experiences in Communist prison in a best-selling novel entitled *My Happy Days in Hell.* In 1956, both of them escaped to the West. Határ settled in England, where he became a member of the Hungarian Section of the BBC; Faludy, after short stays in London and in Paris, moved to Toronto, Canada. An extremely learned cultural historian, Faludy has written a major book on Erasmus, and the

University of Toronto has awarded him an honorary doctorate.

As Hungarian poets, Faludy and Határ are as different as two poets can be. Faludy writes in traditional form—his love sonnets follow the tradition of Shakespeare that was so successfully transplanted to Hungarian soil through the labors of Lőrinc Szabó. Faludy is a master of rhyme and rhythm. Many of his readers can recite his 'Ode to the Hungarian Language' from memory. His early fame was due to his extremely successful renditions of Villon's ballads into Hungarian. If they were not entirely precise from a philological point of view, they made up for it in originality and the use of modern Hungarian vocabulary.

Határ, who is also a prodigious novelist and dramatist, writes the way Bartók composed and the way Picasso painted. He mixes a Rabelaisian lust for life with a dark, peculiar 'gallows humor' and cries 'A plague on both your houses!' to both the East and the West. A great deal of linguistic inventiveness characterizes Határ's writings.

Since both Faludy and Határ, although in their eighties, are vigorously active, their oeuvres are definitely uncompleted, and they will therefore be presented in Volume II.

Advantage, mission, service—none of these are lacking among the Hungarian literati now living in foreign parts. The deformations which politics places on literature tied to a country can be seen more clearly from a distance. In 1981, as the Kádár régime began to relax the ideological orthodoxy of its earlier period, Miklós Béládi succeeded in publishing a volume of poetry written by poets living in the West. And in 1980, shortly before its appearance, László Kemenes Géfin had published an anthology of Hungarian poetry at the Hungarian Protestant Free University in Bern, Switzerland, featuring mostly the same poets but with a few additions of his own. The Budapest volume, which had been delayed for many years, was hurriedly published after the Kemenes Géfin anthology appeared in order not to seem to lag behind.

Áron Kibédi Varga in Holland, György Gömöri in Great Britain, László Kemenes Géfin in Canada, and Sándor András in the United States are university professors; Alajos Kannás in California and György Vitéz in Canada have doctorates in psychology. József Bakucz, prematurely deceased, is considered to have been an avant-garde leader of the group in the United States. He supported himself as an industrial draughtsman.

Once considered 'the boys,' some of these poets have died and the rest are now grown people in their fifties and sixties. They are a ruggedly individualistic, often quite quarrelsome bunch. 'We came to be free, not to make money'—seems to have been adopted as their common slogan. András, Vitéz, Kemenes Géfin, and the prematurely deceased Bakucz published a journal named *Arkánum* [Arcanum], while their more accessible writings appeared in *Szivárvány* [The Rainbow], published by Ferenc Mózsi in Chicago and in Budapest.[103]

Living in their small country, the Hungarians yearn for Western appreciation, while those living abroad yearn for domestic recognition. At long last communication has increased in both directions. There is now private publishing in Hungary, whereas before 1989 there was only state publishing with very few, minor exceptions. The price for this freedom is, alas, a ruined economy in which publishers can undertake to issue a book, no matter how excellent, only if its author can obtain a grant to subsidize its publication.

Real liberation for Hungarian poets would mean that their works could be read in the original. This may be wishful thinking. Who will learn Hungarian for the sake of reading Hungary's poets? In China there are more than 1.2 billion people, but foreign students do not flock to classes in elementary Mandarin. Hungary is a country smaller than the State of Indiana, with ten million people inside it and five million more scattered around the globe. Why do we not speak in a world language or two or three like the Swiss? Why do we bottle ourselves up like the Basques, the Armenians, and our northern kinsmen, the Finns?

The answer is Hungarian poetry. It is so rich and strange that the language is worth learning for the sake of its poetry alone. The late Edmund Wilson[104] considered learning it worthwhile.

Translated by †*Paul Tabori, Adam Makkai,*
and *Earl M. Herrick*

---

[103] A complete list of Hungarian poets who have lived abroad will appear in Volume II of *The Poetry of Hungary*.

[104] (1895-1972), American poet, novelist and critic of the *New Yorker*. He specialized in European and Slavic literatures; his essays appeared in Hungarian translation.

X. APPENDIX

THE MUSIC OF THE 'HIMNUSZ',
HUNGARY'S NATIONAL ANTHEM

Composition of
FERENC ERKEL *(1810-1893)*

ség - gel; Bal - sors a - kit ré - gen tép,

Hozz re - á víg esz - ten - dőt, Meg - bűn - hőd - te

már e nép A múl - tat s jö - ven - dőt.

A SHORT HISTORY OF HUNGARIAN VERSE

Comparative studies of musicology by Zoltán Kodály and his followers reveal two layers of musical and poetic traditions. On the one hand, the musical feature of Hungarian laments *(siratók)* conserve some traces of Vogul and Ostyak melodies showing close affinities with the other Finno-Ugric peoples; on the other hand, there are many common features in Hungarian folklore and in the musical material of different Finno-Ugric and Turkic peoples of the Volga region. The first stratum seems to argue in favor of the existence of an old nonsyllabic verse form; the second stratum points to the development of syllabic meters. At any rate, Old Hungarian versification was not exclusively syllabic. The main aim of the anonymous poets and singers was to elaborate on the so-called "segmented verse" *(tagoló vers)*, where only the number of the segments was more or less fixed while, at the same time, the number of syllables could vary from 1 to 4 within each segment, with a musical 'ritardando' at the ending line. According to László Vargyas, the best example of rhythmic freedom in old Hungarian verse is to be found in the famous dance song of the Hungarian swineherds:

Megismerni / a kanászt / cifra-járá-/ -sáról	4,3,4,2
Tűzött-fűzött / bocskoráról, / tarisznyaszí- / -járól	4,4,4,2
Huccs ki, disznó, / a berektűl / csak a füle / látszik	4,4,4,2
Kanászbojtár / bokor alatt / menyecskével / játszik.	4,4,4,2

(You can tell the / swineherd boy / by his fancy / walking
By his rugged- / -leather boots and / satchel-straps he's /
    / wearing.
Shoo, you pigs there / from the marshes / one can see but
    / pigs' ears,
In the bushes / the good swinherd's / gaming with a / damsel. /

In many cases, syllabic variations may be more evident. Among the folksongs collected by Béla Bartók, we find the following text:

Erre / arra, / a boronya / élén	2,2,4,2
Kinyílott a / tulipán / a kalapom / szélén	4,3,4,2
Egy-két / szál, / három / szál,	2,1,2,1
Álnok voltál, / babám, / megcsal- / tál.	4,2,2,1

(This way / that way / the harrow's blade's / turning
The tulip has / blossomed out / on my good hat's / broad rim.
Few its / stems, / three its / stems,
You turned untrue / sweetheart / cheated me.)

Traces of syllabic freedom can be found in the *Lament of Mary* (q.v.) from roughly 1300; the text is a free paraphrase of a Latin *sequentia of Geoffroi de Breteuil*. Its basic principles of composition are the parallelism and the symmetry of the two segments in each line:

Volék sirolm / tudotlon	4,3
Sirolmol / sepedek,	3,3
Buol oszuk, / epedek.	4,3

Világ / világa	2,3
Virágnak / virága!	3,3
Keserüen / kinzatul	4,3
Vas szegekkel / veretül	4,3

(Ignorant of grief / was I
But now I / faint with grief,
Sorrow makes me / dry and wan...

...Bright light / of the world
Flowers a- / -flowering!
Thou art tortured / cruelly,
Thou art pierced with / iron nails.)

In these lines we can also observe a series of other poetical figures such as alliteration, assonance, and rhyme. At the same time, the word stress certainly forms a dynamic nucleus in each segment. In all probability, rhythm was more important than rhyme and assonance in the Middle Ages—some popular ballads which may go back to the fourteenth or fifteenth century have remained unrhymed to this day:

Elindula / Molnár Anna	4,4
Mentek ők a / császárúton,	4,4
S megtalálták / nagy magos fát,	4,4
Leültek az / árnyékába.	4,4

(Anna Molnár / set out going,
They were walking / the King's highway,
Then they found a / tall and wide tree
And they sat down / in its shadow.)

In many cases these old ballads present a kind of partial repetition, called "terrace" by the American Finno-Ugric scholar, Robert Austerlitz; one of the variants of the ballad concerning the construction of the fortress of Déva (q.v.) starts with these lines:

Tizenkét kőmíves / összetanakodék	6,6
Magas Déva várát / hogy fölépítenék,	6,6

Hogy fölépítenék / fél véka ezüstér,   6,6
Fél véka ezüstér, fél véka aranyér...   6,6

(When that master masons / twelve held secret council
That they would construct the / high castle of Déva,
That they would construct it / for a bowl of silver,
That they would construct it / for bowls with gold laden...)

These lines represent the Hungarian *alexandrine* created by the normalization of the segments in the old long meter. Nowadays the obligatory length of this meter is set at 12 syllables with a caesura after the 6th syllable. The normalization of the caesura, however, admitted some exceptions: In the prosody of Miklós Zrínyi (q.v.), the best epic poet of the seventeenth century, there is a fluctuation among different divisions of the Hungarian *alexandrine* (6,6; 7,5; 5,7):

Én az ki / azelőtt / iffiu / elmével   3,3,3,3
Játszottam / szerelemnek / édes ver- / -sével   3,4,3,2
Küszködtem / Viola / kegyetlensé- / -gével   3,3,4,2
Mastan immár / Marsnak / hangasabb / versével   4,2,3,3
Fegyvert s vitézt / éneklek, / török ha- / -talmát   4,3,3,2

(I who did / in the past / with a young / lover's mind
Tinker with / love-melodies' / sweet-sounding / verses,
Struggling with / Viola's / cruelty, un- / -fairness
Now I sing with / Mars's / mightier / melodies
Of heros and / armaments / of the Turks' / great might.)

At the same time when this type of line, which also characterizes nineteenth century epics, such as Petőfi's *Sir John the Hero,* and Arany's *Toldi* (qq.v.), crystallized, the sixteenth century enriched Hungarian poetry with the introduction of new lyric forms. While the octosyllabic meter may yet prove to be of ultimately popular origin, the co-called *Balassi stanza* (q.v.), which would dominate the evolution of lyric forms until the period of the Rákóczi War of Independence, cannot be explained without the influence of Latin, Romance, and German poetry. Up to this time, rhymes had always formed uninterrupted sequences (aa, aaa, aaaa). The Balassi strophe would be unimaginable without regularly alternating rhyme types as such *(aabcb)* as in the *Stabat Mater* of Jacopone da Todi, and of two syllabic meters, as in the majority of cases (6,6,7; 6,6,7; 6,6,7). The European background of this stanza can be illustrated by the French:

CLÉMENT MAROT:

O Seigneur, que de gens
A nuire diligens
Qui me troublent et grèvent,

Mon Dieu, que d'ennemis
Qui aux champs se sont mis
Et contre moi s'eslèvent.

BÁLINT BALASSI:

Vitézek mi lehet
ez széles föld felett
szebb dolog az végeknél?

Holott kikeletkor
az sok szép madár szól,
kivel ember ugyan él;
mező jó illatot,
az ég szép harmatot,
ád ki kedves minennél.

(Soldiers, what finer worth
is there upon this earth
than the borderlands can show?
Where in the time of Spring
beautiful birds all sing
setting our hearts all aglow —
the fields have a fresh smell
were dew from heav'n fell
delighting us through and through.)

Neither Balassi nor other poets of the sixteenth and seventeenth centuries, could recreate in Hungarian the iambic rhythm of some western models; before the eighteenth century, the rhythmical units of Hungarian meters always had a 'falling' feature. The introduction of syllabic and quantitative (or durational) meters must be considered the result of innovations in the eighteenth century.

Theoretically, this new quantitative versification had to be based on the phonological length of vowels (and on the structure of open and closed syllables), but the difficulties created by the normal word accent—which is always initial—and the quantitative alternations were often discussed from the days of Kazinczy and Csokonai (qq.v.) to the end of Hungarian Romanticism. At any rate, even in Vörösmarty's (q.v.) poetry, the role of the word and phrase accent cannot be completely neglected. That is why we shall try to transcribe simultaneously the syllabic quantity and the accents:

Hazádnak rendületlenűl   ∪ — — ⌣́ ∪ — ∪ —   8x
Légy híve, óh magyar,   — ⌣́ ∪ — ⌣̆́ —   6a
Bölcsőd az, s majdan sírod is,   ⌣́ — — — ⌣́ — ⌣́ ∪ —   8x
Mely ápol s eltakar.   ∪ ⌣́ — — ⌣́ ∪ —   6a

(Oh Magyar, keep immovable
Your native country's trust,
For it has borne you, and at death
Will consecrate your dust!)

   In this example the nature of Hungarian iambic meters is well illustrated. The
last measure, or foot, must be a pure iamb, but it is always possible to
substitute a long syllable for a short one in the other measures. After all, it is
a quantitative or syllabic-prosodic meter, as John Lotz once stated it, but in
the words of Kazinczy (q.v.), it can be called a *liberrimus iambus*.
   As we see, the adaptation of West-European iambic, trochaic, anapaestic,
and other forms was not accomplished in Hungary with the help of accented
and unaccented syllables, but was done on the basis of phonological quantity.
The clear opposition of long and short vowels (*kar* = 'arm'; *kár* = 'damage')
determined also the quantitative adaptation of Greek and Latin meters. Let us
quote a very expressive Alcaic strophe by Dániel Berzsenyi (q.v.). In our
transcription accented syllables are indicated too, whereas the metric feature
is not determined by them:

Romlásnak indult, hajdan erős magyar!
⌣́ — ∪ ⌣́ — | ⌣́ ∪ ⌣̆́ — ⌣̆́ —
Nem látod, Árpád vére miként fajul?
⌣́ — ∪ ⌣́ — | ⌣́ ∪ ⌣̆́ — ⌣̆́ —
Nem látod a bosszús egeknek
⌣́ — ∪ — ⌣́ — ⌣̆́ — ∪
Ostorait nyomorúlt hazádon?
⌣́ ∪ ∪ — ⌣̆́ ∪ — ⌣̆́ — —

(Oh you, once mighty Hungary, gone to seed,
can you not see the blood of Árpád go foul,
can you not see the mighty lashes
heaven has slapped on your dreary country?)

   In Petőfi's (q.v.) case, the Graeco-Latin meters play a secondary role, but
the importance of the pure popular models is remarkable. Petőfi also uses an
archaic variant of repeated rhymes in many songs:

Az erdőnek madara van,   8
Ezen kertnek virága van,   8
És az égnek csillaga van,   8
S a legénynek kedvese van.   8

(In the woods are birds a-plenty, (8)
In this yard there's blooms a-plenty, (8)
In the sky there's stars a-plenty, (8)
Many lads have girls a-plenty.) (8)

In Petőfi's iambic meters, we feel the energy of the scansion, based on the strong influence of word and phrase accents:

Fázunk és éhezünk   ´ — — ´ ∪ —
S átlőve oldalunk,   ´ — ∪ ´ ∪ —
Részünk minden nyomor...   ´ — ´ ∪ ´ —
De szabadok vagyunk.   ∪ ´ ∪ — ´ —

(We freeze and we do starve
Our side's peppered with shot —
Our fate is misery
But Freedom is our lot!)

A skillful mixing of Western European anapaests with iambs can be perceived in Petőfi's poem "At the End of September" (q.v.). Petőfi translated Shakespeare's *Coriolan* in perfect blank verse at the time he wrote this poem. This translation thus became the forerunner of different kinds of free verse. His epic poem *Az apostol* [The Apostle] dealing with the fate of a radical revolutionary, shows an impressive mixture of different iambic meters. Here one must, of course, accept a heterometric variant of the customary dramatic diction.

Petőfi's best friend, the epic poet János Arany (q.v.), excelled in the artistic use of such meters as the Hungarian alexandrine. In Arany's versification, each hemistich of the alexandrine was frequently submitted to a kind of quantitative scansion. Whenever this happened, a foot called CHORIAMB occurred in Arany's poetry. In the epic poem *Buda halála* (The Death of King Buda) Attila's monolog contains this beautiful line: *Csillag esik, föld reng, jött éva csudáknak,* which can be scanned as alexandrine (2x 6), or Western European-metric following the scheme ´ ∪ ∪ ´ — ´ | ∪ ´ ∪ ∪ ´ —, meaning 'stars are falling, earth shakes; year of miracles came' or 'stars to the ground, earth shook, came miracle-ages.'We hope that the English-speaking reader will be able to appreciate the subtle difference.

The same complexities can be perceived in a poem such as "The Bards of Wales" (q.v.) which is rendered in this book in Peter Zollman's translation.

The most striking feature of Hungarian versification is what the composer Zoltán Kodály called RHYTHMICAL DUALITY. A Hungarian poem written in ANY WESTERN EUROPEAN METRIC SCANSION can be read out loud with the traditional word-initial stress of natural, spoken Hungarian.

Naturally, many poets of the twentieth century have tried to create a new synthesis of traditional forms and free verse. Simultaneously with Endre Ady's (q.v.) poetical activity, there was a compromise proposed by Mihály Babits (q.v.). Later on a second kind of synthesis was achieved by Attila József (q.v.), whose work had a decisive influence on the whole evolution of Hungarian verse. Attila József's prosody is distinguished by an exceptional sensitivity to several literary tendencies of our century.

Although he first appeared as a disciple of Ady, he later adopted the expressionist free verse of Whitmanesque inspiration. (See his poems "Ode" and "By the Danube" featured in this book both of which successfully mirror much of József's versification.)

Finally, we ought to mention the versification of contemporary poets, emphasizing the serial fluidity of the hexameters written by Miklós Radnóti (q.v.), as well as the virtuosity of Sándor Weöres (q.v.), or the gravity of each line in a lyric or dramatic text by Gyula Illyés (q.v.). We would like to conclude by pointing out two interesting trends in contemporary poetry. The first is the new possibility of using ANY FORM of metric or free verse in ANY COMBINATION; the second is the predominance of the word and of the poetical image over any formal expediency.

† *László Gáldi* and *Adam Makkai*

Notes on the Illustrations
by † George Buday, R.E.

It is not customary that an artist should add written notes to his illustrations for a volume of poetry. But my situation and the illustrations for this particular anthology are unusual. I believe that a few explanatory notes may be helpful in bringing the reader nearer to the poets and to their poetry.

As the verses of this volume try to introduce the poety of Hungary to a wider audience, I—in my illustrations—have tried to introduce these twenty-five prominent and specially selected Hungarian poets graphically. Since, however, the anthology is aimed at an English-speaking public, the great majority of whom have no previous acquaintance with Hungarian poetry, it seems justified for me to add something more than conventional likenesses. In my portraits for this anthology, I have ventured to do so.

In the case of the older poets I have naturally done thorough research to find authentic, contemporary paintings and engravings to use as my sources. I have based my engravings on likenesses which were thought in the poet's own time to be the most characteristic, developing them further with meaningful symbols which echo the meaning that the poet's creative work has in the history of literature—as seen today. Hungarian literature was one of the great experiences of my youth, and to contribute to its presentation to the English-speaking world—my home for many years—has been a pleasure and satisfaction for which I felt no effort should be spared.

A number of the more recent poets have been my personal acquaintances—some, indeed, have been close friends—and in these cases my engravings are based not only on numerous photographs, but also on my personal recollections and sketches.

In some cases when the poet lived long enough to have had youthful, mature, and old-age periods of his poetry, or—when though tragically short-lived like Sándor Petőfi and Attila József—his life and work had a significance and character too versatile to be condensed into a single image, I have not hesitated to depict those various aspects in my compositions, thereby creating multiple or montage portraits in order to express the complexity of these poets and their oeuvres.

It is surprising that some kind of multiple portraiture has not been introduced before now. When Picasso and, after him, some of his contemportaries achieved the freedom for a portrait to depict the full-face *and* the profile of the model in a single painting of the head or bust, they opened the way towards multiple portraiture.

I have always thought that the great innovation of the combination of full-face and profile in portraiture was, to some extent, the logical and rationally justified, though incredibly belated, follow-up of the two-faced image of Janus of classical times. Such representations amount to double profiles or double faces of a single head in the visual arts, even though the practice then was thought applicable only to representations of single personalities. It needed the rise of Cubism and other novel styles to make full-face-*cum*-profile combinations viable in the arts.

This was indeed a great step forward: Images taken from contrasting angles can capture a fuller, more complete visual expression of the features and identity, the full personality of the sitter.

For historical accuracy, we should recall that between the Janus-head of antiquity and Picasso there were rare occasions—two examples come to mind—when artists such as Sir Anthony Van Dyck and Philippe de Champaigne painted, for practical and aesthetic purposes, portraits of King Charles I and Cardinal Richelieu which were multiple portraits. Each of these portraits showed the full-face head of the sitter in the middle between two profiles, one on each side, looking at each other. The heights of the heads were the same, and the whole effect resembled modern police photographs of criminals. Of course, such great masters as the painters of these rare triple portraits could not help using their brushes and paint in their usual masterly way, even though the pictures were not intended principally for hanging on the walls of dining halls.

But, to return to my defense of multiple portraiture: Our eyes, as I mentioned elsewhere, are no longer unprepared to appreciate free and heterogeneous symbols in a single composition. The Surrealists taught us to enjoy unreservedly the "collection of concepts co-existing in the mind of the artist" who wishes to represent them in marble, in wood- or copper-plate engraving, or on canvas.

In recent decades, however, it is no longer only the eyes of the minority who appreciate the language of modern art and who have been trained to accept multiple and simultaneous views of people, taken from different angles. There is no longer anything terribly new in multiple images when millions of television screens all over the world bring the faces and figures of pop-singers—and of course, other people—into our homes, showing them full-face, then in profile, then three-quarter, then from behind; in split-screen images, in sizes varying from small to huge blow-ups more than life size; in wide views or in close-ups, occasionally picking out and enlarging details of singing lips or hands on musical instruments, or instant replays of scenes of a sport event, or dozens of other features practically simultaneously.

Just as ordinary still photography contributed greatly to the development of impressionism in painting, television is bound to have its effects on other media of the visual arts by training people's eyes to new ways of seeing—to new panoramas of people and things. I believe that the multiple portrait may be one result of the habitual viewing of televised images: People expect to see features, figures, and likenesses from various angles and in various contexts, in order to approach them more fully than was formerly possible by means of single representations.

The next step, the crossing of the barrier of the fourth dimension, naturally follows from multiple portraiture: The artist can record in the portrait likenesses of his model at various times of his or her life, as well as background data and associations. Such new potentials in portraiture are giving a great impetus to art, which during the cult of abstraction temporarily lost its public appeal. Because of my long-standing interest in illustrations containing authentic or imaginary portraits, it is perhaps not entirely inappropriate that it should have been my privilege to be the first to try out multiple portaiture. When, in 1940, I illustrated *Timon of Athens* for the famous 37-volume edition of Shakespeare for the Limited Editions Club of New York, I was suddenly inspired to illustrate the tragedy with a sequence of imagined portraits of the principal character, Timon, showing him as the jovial idealist turned into the anti-social, disillusioned man-hater, as the Bard created him. The successive engravings depicted Timon's busts carrying the marks which would have appeared on his face during the bitter events that follow the happy opening scene of the play. As far as I know, this was the first time that a story was illustrated by a number of portraits of its hero. From this, it was only a short step to the creation of multiple portraits for an anthology which aims to introduce formerly unknown poets to a new audience.

In my "graven images" of twenty-five Hungarian poets who have lived from the age of Shakespeare to the present day, I felt the urge to create images of them that would be as real, as expressive, and as pictorially informative as possible, and I tried to follow up the various liberating influences of recent contemporary portraiture without imitating their formalities. So I introduced multiple portraiture when greater realism in interpreting the poets warranted it, showing the poets as young men and at later stages of their development, and occasionally showing their death masks which—for example, in the case of Mihály Babits and Endre Ady—expressed their characters better than late photographs of them.

In order to make the visualization and understanding of these poets easier, I tried to include, by way of montage, background motifs from their lives and their periods. Occasionally, when it seemed particularly relevant (for example, in the case of Endre Ady), I showed the women in their lives who inspired many of their writings. In the background I showed, whenever it helped, some indication of the poet's part in life or poetry, the cottage or castle where he was born or his home in later life, and finally the grave or statue with which posterity in his native land has perpetuated his memory. In the background of each picture, decorative elements allude to the period when the poet lived and to its style. For example, in the Csokonai portrait the cupids besides his fickle Lilla, the subject of so many of his beautiful love poems, and the colt-skin wine flask which he celebrated with a special poem, reflect the Rococo; while in the principal portrait of Ady, his necktie alludes to the *Art Nouveau* period which left its marks on his youth, his life, and poetry. (In fact one photograph of Ady does show him wearing a somewhat similar kind of necktie.)

In each of my montage-engravings I also have recorded some events in the life of the poet illustrated, or of his country. For example, Zrínyi was killed by a wild boar during a hunt, and I based my portrait of him on a wood cut from an old, contemporary broadside. And speaking of Zrínyi, I should mention that in my engraving of him I included another contemporary motif: the frontispiece of one of his principal works, *The Siren of the Adriatic*. My Balassi portrait includes an echo of the tail-piece of his first book of poems, and my Ady engraving includes the small circular emblem with a very Hungarian-looking scribe (which decorated the cover of the most important modern literary periodical, *Nyugat,* 'The West'), as well as Notre Dame Cathedral of his beloved Paris.

But even more than all these historical references, I have quoted from my own illustrations made in former years, usually for volumes of representative works of most of these poets. Naturally, these quotes could not be as extensive in a single block as they were in a whole book. To exemplify this, I refer to my portrait of Madách. When his principal work, *The Tragedy of Man,* was first published in Swedish translation in 1936, I did 25 small and large wood-engraving illustrations for it (soon afterwards these were used for the German translation, too), showing the history of mankind and the reincarnations of Adam and Eve in various periods, as the author of the great dramatic poem presented them. I felt that the poet's complete panorama of history from the Egypt of the pharaohs to the Eskimos, miserably existing on a rapidly freezing planet in the distant future, should somehow be expressed when I engraved his likeness. But in the limited space of this montage, I could only quote an episode here and a detail there, working clockwise from the bottom left-hand corner, until the sequence ends (below the author's head), where Adam intends to jump to his death, trying to prevent the bitter experiences of mankind from taking place. It is then, just in time, that Eve shyly follows him from their cave and tells him that she is pregnant—the first step to human history had already been taken, and Adam's suicide could no longer prevent it. And so, the tragedy of Adam became the tragedy of man.

Another example where I quoted one of my former illustrations in some detail is in my portrait of János Arany. As long ago as 1932, the Transylvanian Art Workers' Publishing Guild commissioned me to illustrate Arany's great ballads. I did twenty full-page wood-engravings, and the volume was first published in Kolozsvár in 1933 in both hard-bound and paper-back editions. Naturally, around the central portraits of Arany, I could quote only bits and pieces from my original illustrations.

Finally, I should like to mention that in one of the engravings, the one portraying Lajos Kassák, in addition to small quotes from my illustration of his writings, I have incorporated one of the poet's own abstract designs in acknowledgment of the fact that he was equally distinguished as a writer and as a painter.

Translated by
Paul Tabori and *Earl M. Herrick*